AMIR SJARIFOEDDIN

A VOLUME IN THE SERIES

Cornell Modern Indonesia Project
Edited by Eric Tagliacozzo and Thomas B. Pepinsky

A list of titles in this series is available at cornellpress.cornell.edu.

AMIR SJARIFOEDDIN

POLITICS AND TRUTH IN INDONESIA, 1907–1948

RUDOLF MRÁZEK

SOUTHEAST ASIA PROGRAM PUBLICATIONS
AN IMPRINT OF CORNELL UNIVERSITY PRESS
Ithaca and London

Southeast Asia Program Publications Editorial Board

Mahinder Kingra (ex officio)
Thak Chaloemtiarana
Chiara Formichi
Tamara Loos
Andrew Willford

Copyright © 2024 by Cornell University

All rights reserved. Except for brief quotations in a review, this book, or parts thereof, must not be reproduced in any form without permission in writing from the publisher. For information, address Cornell University Press, Sage House, 512 East State Street, Ithaca, New York 14850. Visit our website at cornellpress.cornell.edu.

First published 2024 by Cornell University Press

Library of Congress Cataloging-in-Publication Data

Names: Mrázek, Rudolf, author.
Title: Amir Sjarifoeddin : politics and truth in Indonesia, 1907–1948 / Rudolf Mrázek.
Other titles: Politics and truth in Indonesia, 1907–1948
Description: Ithaca : Southeast Asia Program Publications, an imprint of Cornell University Press, 2024. | Includes bibliographical references and index.
Identifiers: LCCN 2023055082 (print) | LCCN 2023055083 (ebook) | ISBN 9781501777455 (hardcover) | ISBN 9781501777462 (paperback) | ISBN 9781501777479 (epub) | ISBN 9781501777486 (pdf)
Subjects: LCSH: Amir Sjarifoeddin. | Communism—Indonesia—History. | Indonesia—Politics and government—20th century.
Classification: LCC DS643.22.A45 M73 2024 (print) | LCC DS643.22.A45 (ebook) | DDC 320.53/209598—dc23/eng/20240318
LC record available at https://lccn.loc.gov/2023055082
LC ebook record available at https://lccn.loc.gov/2023055083

Where there are heroes the world is still soft and glowing, and the web of creation unbroken.
 —Robert Musil, *Man without Qualities*

Contents

Preface ix

Part One. Vastness 1

1. Sumatra 3
2. Holland 15
3. The Batavia Law School 25
4. Kramat 106 32
5. Soekarno 41

Part Two. Saying 53

6. Sleep, Baby, Sleep I 55
7. Sleep, Baby, Sleep II 65
8. Julius Martin Johannes Schepper 76
9. Charles O. van der Plas 95
10. Ships on the Wall 114

Part Three. *Le passage à l'acte* 137

11. Sjahrir 139
12. Musso 179
13. The Long March 222

Part Four. Traces 257

14. The Victors 259
15. The Defeated 284
16. The Observers 303

Conclusion 325

Notes 331
Bibliography 381
Index 397

Preface

Revolution is an attempt at a radical change in a big step: Bertolt Brecht wrote, "To achieve a great goal, great changes are required, / Little changes are the enemies of great changes."[1] Revolution is also an image, memory, and inspiration, as it appears to be done and done with. In the dominant ideologies of today, revolutionaries are bogey people, terrorists at worst and nuisance at best. In the revisionist academia of today, a study of revolution has become an exercise in the "aesthetics of disappearance."[2]

It appears that the world revolution of the twentieth century never had a chance of winning. Walter Benjamin, at the beginning of the century, remarked on the heroes of Shakespeare and Calderon who "enter fleeing."[3] Revolutionaries to Benjamin, and in this book, are *possible* heroes; they inevitably fail. But they aim at a concrete utopia. Ernst Bloch, Walter Benjamin's friend, thought that the concrete utopia was a space *possibly* never to be reached. Through aiming, however, revolutionaries gather the sense of themselves and the sense of the world.

I met some of those revolutionaries, the possible heroes, first in Prague as I was growing up, and then in Jakarta as I became an "expert." In both these places revolution miserably failed. The very idea of radical social change in a big step had been tragically compromised. Some of the revolutionaries I was able to meet were still alive only because an executioner missed them by some accident. Most of the survivors were resigned, often bitter, and, in quite a few cases, they dissipated into the scum. I found them all absorbing. Were it not for their aiming for concrete utopia, even for their failure and humiliation, and defeat, in Prague, in Jakarta, and in other places, our world, I think, would now become completely what it has already almost become—a space without a promise.

Amir Sjarifoeddin failed miserably. But the history of modern Indonesia since his violent death in 1948—modern Indonesia's ideology, memory, and ethics, Soekarno, the army, constitutional and guided democracy, *reformasi*, and the post-*reformasi* era, too—has been built to a large extent as an exercise in the aesthetics of Amir Sjarifoeddin's disappearance.

I never met Amir Sjarifoeddin, and throughout the writing of this book this was a source of frustration. I could still meet some people who had known him, but being what I was at that time, in the late 1970s and in the 1980s, and given what I was then running after, I did not think it important to push them about Amir and I asked them about other things. As a punishment, only words on paper, documents, letters, newspapers, and some photographs, were left to me, and to my desperate attempts to make the paper speak. This will stay with me: the reading room in the National Archives in The Hague, the heavy breathing of me and other scholars as they were opening a box or a folder, and an occasional suppressed giggle as we found something.

Amir Sjarifoeddin was born in 1907 in North Sumatra, Dutch East Indies, at the edge of a modern empire and a modern world made of empires. He passed through—the Batak *marga*, "clan," the ethical and neo-ethical Dutch colonial culture, the Dutch and European, metropolitan, and imperial culture, Christianity, democracy, anti-fascism, Marxism—he *lingered*, stopped at each station, took it in, looking back, looking forth, adding a layer to a layer, letting each blend into the previous ones—at least so I see him. In this way, straight and circular, his journey resembles Walter Benjamin's carousel: "The platform bearing the docile animals moves close to the ground. It is at the height which in dreams is best for flying."[4]

This is a book about revolution of our time, and thus very much and sometimes most of all about language. Eight languages are repeatedly mentioned, and listed, when people talk about Amir's brilliance—Batak, Dutch, Malay-Indonesian, German, English, French, Latin, Greek—all of which, at all accounts, were spoken or written with an accent. Amir lingered on words like he lingered on the stations of his travels. Like Roland Barthes, Amir "struggled through" and "pleasured through" his eight languages.[5] More than Barthes, because Amir Sjarifoeddin as he went, intensely willed himself to be more than an intellectual. With the lingering, stubbornly, he tested the powers of his ways and his language(s), as well. His speaking and writing were aiming at what Jacques Lacan called (referring to it sometimes as something close to madness), *le passage à l'act*, "the passage to action."[6]

At midnight on December 19, 1948, in the middle of a possible revolution, as far as his travels reached, Amir was executed under circumstances that have never been made completely clear but certainly with the connivance of an increasingly right-wing Indonesian government that had its own ideas of revolution. Of the last two months of his life—as he and his columns were being hunted through the mountains and villages of East Java by the army of the republic—no statement of any extent by him had been recorded. A silence with an accent? Before he was shot, some say, he asked for a time to pray. According to others, he sang the "Internationale."

I wrote this book thinking of George Kahin and Ben Anderson, and to continue the debates we had been having since 1969 back at Cornell, in Jakarta, and in Prague about Indonesia, about revolution, about the sense of the world. They did not wait for me to finish the book.

Both Kahin and Anderson led me irresistibly to Amir Sjarifoeddin through the most inspiring and most roundabout ways. Kahin lured me to write a biography of the socialist *and democrat* Soetan Sjahrir: Sjahrir never crossed the line, never brought the house down. Anderson enticed me into a stillborn study of Tan Malaka, a fighter for a utopia without an adjective, *for "100% Freedom."* Topics certainly utmost relevant, but not Amir. Kahin and Anderson made Amir Sjarifoeddin into the fairy-tale thirteenth room for me. Perhaps they worried that if I entered, I would be lost. Certainly, they knew.

I carry an additional heavy debt of gratitude to two men who have written about Amir Sjarifoeddin before me.

Jacques Leclerc was a scholar and a member of the French Communist Party. He dedicated his whole academic career to studying Amir Sjarifoeddin. Through the 1980s until the mid-1990s, he gathered information, traced down and interviewed Amir's contemporaries, and wrote letters, many of which remained unanswered; often because Leclerc was a known Communist and because he wanted to hear about Amir as another Communist. Jacques died prematurely in 1995, with the book on Amir unwritten. In 2014, Harry Poeze managed to acquire Leclerc's archive and bring it in an SUV to the Royal Netherlands Institute of Southeast Asian and Caribbean Studies in Leiden. These are the Leclerc Papers I quote again and again in this book.

Gerry van Klinken has studied Amir Sjarifoeddin as much as Jacques Leclerc. Since the 1980s, he has gathered as many documents and as much knowledge on Amir Sjarifoeddin as Leclerc. His background and perspective were different: he is deeply of the Dutch culture, his work is guided by moral philosophy. His Amir has a Kantian accent. Gerry, fortunately did not die. Even better, the climate crisis threatening Earth made him reconsider what is right for a scholar in our times. As he told me, what might he answer to his grandchildren, if they ask? Recalling his other training as a scientist, he began a book on typhoons. He is, like Leclerc, a possible revolutionary, too, entering in flight. He packed the boxes of his notes on Amir and stored them in his garage in Brisbane. To make my sense of debt still heavier, he gave me access to the garage and the notes.

Goenawan Mohamad inspired me by being skeptical about Amir Sjarifoeddin and the likes of him. Toenggoel Siagian taught me (or tried) to think Batak. Mona Lohanda was my guiding spirit in the Indonesian National Archives in Jakarta, as were all the people at the National Archives in the Hague. The Netherlands Institute for Advanced Study in the Humanities and Social Sciences in Amsterdam gave me shelter and encouragement during the last pre-COVID year; the Royal Netherlands Institute of Southeast Asian and Caribbean Studies in Leiden gave me four post-COVID months to read, in the archives and libraries of the Netherlands.

I hope the book will be read by people who feel that this world of ours is wounded, that its misery increases, and that great change is needed but failing. I hope that I will convince the reader that Jean-Luc Nancy, Emmanuel Levinas, or Søren Kierkegaard, not to mention Benjamin, belong to Indonesian history and the history of revolution as much as Sjahrir, Soekarno, Tan Malaka, and Amir Sjarifoeddin. Or, as much as we do.

There is one serious and authentic biography of Amir Sjarifoeddin written, in fact, and *almost* published. Frederiek Djara Wellem's MA thesis was defended at the Theological Seminar in Jakarta in 1982 and was all but ready to be published in 1984 by Sinar Harapan in Jakarta. The book, however, was banned before it reached bookstores and libraries, and virtually the whole stock was destroyed. I was lucky again: Nico Scholte-Nordholt, who was Wellem's adviser, kept the thesis manuscript, and graciously let me have it. There are several articles on Amir Sjarifoeddin by Jacques Leclerc and van Klinken. Otherwise, Amir remains the only one among the major figures of twentieth-century Indonesia who has received no book-length biography.

To use the spelling correctly in its historical context is impossible, and this book is merely another imperfect way of trying. Colonial *oe* became *u* in the middle of 1947, and it was changed in the names of places: Madioen into Madiun, etc. Many individuals, however, kept the old spelling of their names or, better to say, kept it depending on circumstances: Soebadio but also Subadio, etc. Soeharto's orthographic reform of 1972 made *tj* into *c* (like Tjikini into Cikini), *dj* into *j* (like Djakarta into Jakarta), *j* into *y* (like *rakjat* into *rakyat*). At the risk of confusing the reader, I have attempted to reflect the historical moment through the way of spelling, too.

Part One

Vastness

Chapter 1

Sumatra

> It seems to me, Joshua, that there are always wondrous signs that herald the birth of extraordinary men; it is as if nature went through a kind of crisis, and the celestial powers could engender only with great effort.
>
> —Montesquieu, *Persian Letters*

Amir Sjarifoeddin Harahap bin Baginda Soripada gelar Soetan Goenoeng Soaloan (the chain of names and titles might be longer if another member of the family or *marga*, "clan," is asked) was born on April 27, 1907—that is, if someone did not change the date for official records, which happened often for one reason or another.

Socrates compared names to sketches.[1] A name given at birth is bigger than the baby, and there is a hope that the baby will grow into the name. The baby is also supposed to grow into a mother tongue and carry it through life, either as a gift or as a burden. Then, "in like manner," as Marx believed, "the beginner who has learned a new language always translates it back into his mother tongue, but he assimilates the spirit of the new language and expresses himself freely in it only when he moves in it without recalling the old and when he forgets his native tongue."[2]

I am not entirely sure what Amir's mother tongue was or even if he had one. One would presume that it was Batak, as he was born to a proud Batak family and to a Batak mother. "Among the peoples of the Netherlands Indies," the missionary Dr. Hendrik Kraemer wrote in 1930, "the Bataks are a special people. They are difficult, self-asserting and stubborn people, coarse and lacking refinement of being a culture. They are, however, a highly intelligent people, and, comparatively speaking, spirited and energetic. . . . Someone gave me an apt description of the Bataks, comparing them to the *durian*: on the outside they are prickly and they smell, but inside they are sweet.... Many missionaries declare with a sigh that they here never met a Batak with a true sense of sin."[3]

I am not certain whether Amir's mother, Basoenoe boru Siregar, talked and sang to her son in Batak.[4] What I am sure of is that even if she did so, the Batak was muted and controlled, as Amir was learning to speak properly. Just as the date of birth might have been corrected, so was the language and often for the same reason.

Among the Bataks of Sumatra, Amir's family was among the most ancient and the most exposed to being corrected. Amir's paternal grandfather, Ephraim *gelar* Soetan Goenoeng Toea, was born about 1840 and, according to family lore, was in 1861 the first Batak who became Christian.[5] He was absorbed by the Dutch colonial system into the foreign in a still unsettled region of the Dutch colony. During his brilliant career, he became a *djaksa*, "prosecuting attorney," and then *hoofddjaksa*, "chief prosecuting attorney," the highest rank a native could reach at the time.

Soetan Goenoeng Toea was required by his rank to travel through the Batak lands to map the new colony. He served in Sipirok between 1875 and 1885, in Padang Sidempuan between 1885 and 1907, in Sibolga between 1907 and 1910, and finally after 1910 in Padang Sidempuan, where he retired and, in 1916, died and was buried. In the 1980s, the house there still stood and belonged to the family.[6]

Soetan Goenoeng Toea was, if I can use Heidegger's words, "in the throw," rooted, as the philosopher might say, "in projecting."[7] One of Soetan Goenoeng Toea's sons, Djamin *gelar* Baginda Soripada, who was Amir's father, also served as a *djaksa* and then *hoofddjaksa* in equally different places over all North Sumatra. On his assignments, he arrived at the city of Medan on the eastern coast of Sumatra. In Medan he married Basoenoe boru Siregar, a Sipirok woman whose family had recently converted to Islam and moved there. Amir was born, the first child of the family; three boys and three girls would follow.[8]

At each stop, the family remained on the go. The world never ceased to move under their feet and, in that velocity, they were standing. They had to be eagerly serious about each place they stopped at, and in this way they belonged.

The Batak people came from "paganism," "animalism," or "savagery," as put by the Europeans in the late nineteenth century. Islam and Christianity were equally new and sketchy and Amir's family projected it clearly. Amir's mother and her family were devotedly Muslim, while Amir's father was a Christian, "in the throw" that is, when Baginda Soripada expressed his intention to marry Basoenoe, "to accommodate her family" and "as proper to customary law" he converted to Islam.[9]

The family lore has it that Amir's father, even after his conversion, "did not teach his children Islam." Indeed, the stories go, he "never really knew what Islamic religion was." Basoenoe, it is said, guided their children sternly. They had to pray five times a day and do all the other things devout Muslims were expected to do.[10] Amir, it is said, was his mother's favorite. It was she, the story goes, who gave her firstborn son the name Amir Sjarifoeddin, the sketch, the formula of the future into which he would grow. She wished that one day he would indeed become an *amir*, "a prince of faith," of Islam of course; "the commander of the believers," in the name of one of the nine Islamic apostles he carried,[11] *Sjarif,* or *Sharif* meaning "a descendant from the Prophet Mohammad through his daughter Fatima"; a "religious leader" certainly. The suffix *-uddin* added to *Sjarif* means "the Light" or "the light of the religion."

Medan was the most modern place one might imagine in the Dutch Indies of the early twentieth century, in the whole Asia of the time, and anywhere, in fact, outside the superdeveloped North Atlantic world. A small town around 1900, Medan was a sketch into which the modern, the colonial modern, was to grow. "Medan's age was roughly the same as the age of Amir's father," Jacques Leclerc writes.[12] It was a *Lichtung,* "a clearing," to use Heidegger again, at the edge of the not-yet colonized dark.

Medan was a center of an immense Deli tobacco and rubber plantation zone, with owners, bankers, speculators, and adventurers coming from the Netherlands, as well as from the other countries of Europe and from the United States. The half-enslaved "coolie" labor was being imported from other parts of Sumatra, the neighboring island of Dutch Java, British Malaya, as well as China and India. The "Wild East," it could be called. Every payday, *hari raja,* "the big day," there was general drunkenness of the exploiters and exploited, with firecrackers and real guns. The world in motion was displayed. I do not think *djaksa* or anyone from the family joined in, but certainly Amir saw some of it.

At the northern edge of Medan there was the Deli Maatschappij, "Deli Company" territories, clubs, laboratories, residences of the directorship, a Javanese kampong, "village," for the indigenous labor, as well as the residences for the European personnel. The *Proefstation,* "testing station," and other laboratories had the most modern equipment found anywhere in the world. There were expansive warehouses. Rubber and coffee made most of the money. Cocoa, quinine, cotton, tea, and teak were experimented with. Drilling was going on for some time, looking for other possibilities under the surface of the earth.[13]

There were 575 telephone numbers in Medan by December 1916. The bus service was opened on March 18, 1914, "to be used by Europeans as well as the natives."[14] Trains and trams of the Deli Railway Company with its hub in Medan, by 1916, consisted of six salon carriages, thirty-four first- and second-class carriages, and forty-eight third-class carriages, including "two third-class carriages with women's compartments, with a restroom and electric light."[15]

Just as one should not assume that Batak was the dominant language in Amir's family, one should not assume that Dutch was the dominant language of Medan, a city in the Dutch colony. If only because British Singapore was much closer to Medan than Dutch Batavia (after 1942 Djakarta, after 1972 Jakarta), or rather because Medan looked so far into the future, English was spoken and used as a language of business as much if not more than Dutch, mixed with German and French, even Hungarian and Slavic languages. Chinese, Malay, Javanese, Batak, and Minangkabau were also common.

Basoenoe boru Siregar read the Koran to Amir in Arabic when he was little and it might be presumed, only in part wrongly, that Arabic was Amir's mother tongue. "Child," Maurice Blanchot wrote, "is repeating the last word spoken, when in fact he belongs to the rustling, murmur which is not language, but enchantment."[16]

Families like Amir's, of the clearing, "projected" their children. As soon as a child began to really speak, to speak properly, so to say, the family began to prepare the child for school. For a family like Amir's, the project was a modern school, which meant colonial school, brushing against the linguistic Babel of Medan and cutting through the language Babel of Medan. Amir's father was a *Dutch* colonial official—*Dutch* colonial school.

At the moment when a mother tongue might be received by a child, when the child might begin to talk back, at the moment of a dialogue emerging, of grammar and of an organized knowledge expressed by language, at the age of about three, sometimes four, when language matures into a formula, for a child of a family like Amir's, it became a rite of passage, for the family as much as for the child, if Dutch was not spoken every day and correctly in the family including the mother's lullabies, the child had to go away. The child had to be sent to a family where Dutch was spoken every day and correctly—either to a Dutch family in the neighborhood or to an indigenous family that had already been sufficiently Dutchified.

At the age of seven (the date of birth the family declared), the child was taken to school, as good—that is, as modern and as Dutch a school—as possible. In the school headmaster's office, with the parent standing behind, the child was asked, in Dutch: "What language do you speak at home?" If the answer was "Dutch," in Dutch, and if also the family was otherwise in good standing, the child was admitted.

It was a breaking moment. "It seems to her," a heroine of David Grossman's novel, *To the End of the Land*, states, looking at her son, "that shortly after he mastered speech, speech mastered him."[17] Marcel Proust recalls the same moment "I had lost the privilege," and it was French to French, "just after one's first years one loses the ability that baby must break up the milk which he ingests into digestible fragments, so that the prudent adult will drink milk only in small quantities whereas babies can continue to suck it in indefinitely without pausing for breath."[18]

In the 1980s, in Jogjakarta, Central Java, I interviewed an elderly prince of the court, a brother of the sultan. He told me how his brother and he, at the age of four, had been "borrowed," in his words. They were sent to stay with Mrs. Resink, a well-known local Dutch family.

> PRINCE PUGER: It seemed no problem—as if without knowing it . . . customary. . . . When we reached the age of four, we were supposed to move to a Dutch place. It was conceived as a sort of a bridge to the West. . . .
>
> RM: Not difficult?
>
> PRINCE PUGER: Oh, because it happened so early, it did not seem unusual . . . also with my brother, who were sent there, too. We had to speak Dutch. If we slipped into Javanese, Mrs. Resink got angry. Because we were there to learn. . . .
>
> RM: Did not you whisper in Javanese at least, with your brother?
>
> PRINCE PUGER: At the beginning.
>
> RM: Aha, so later when you whispered among yourselves, you whispered in Dutch?
>
> PRINCE PUGER: Yes.[19]

As the school year of 1915 in Medan began, the seven-year-old Amir answered the question correctly and was admitted.[20] The school could not be more modern even by Medan's standards, where the choice was of the best in the colony. The Europese Lagere School (ELS), "European Lower School," was the pride of the Dutch empire—a projection of what was and what was still to come. By its statutes, it was equal to the best elementary schools in the metropolis, the Netherlands itself.

ELS was primarily designed for the children of the Dutch families in the colony. In Medan this meant planters, bankers, people in the shipping business, officials. The school was to familiarize the students with what otherwise would be and remain an exotic, strange, and threatening, dark edge of enlightened North Atlantic West. In 1915, when Amir was in the second grade, there were 26,817 European students in the ELS schools in the whole colony of sixty million. But there were also 4,631 natives, students like Amir.[21] The Dutch colonial policy emerging at the early century, partly a Christian-charity drive, partly ethical "to pay a debt to the colony," mostly pragmatic, to produce an educated local labor force, made the schools for natives possible.[22]

Not all colonial clichés were true. Amir did not have to feel uncomfortable in the school. The image is rather of him arriving, like the other students, in a cart with a coachman, the cart pulled by one horse or even two. The coachman let the boy out at the gate and took the horses home or waited for Amir, smoking and talking to the other students' coachmen until the classes were over. Amir wore either the ELS uniform or his own, modern, that is colonial, that is Western dress, shorts and shirt, possibly a tie, complete with shoes and knee-high socks.[23]

It does not seem inevitable or even likely that Amir was embarrassed in school by his clothes—or his language. The "Dutch-ness" of the Dutch students of the school was self-evident, a matter of race, of blood indeed. The question "what language does the child speak at home" was not asked. Many of Amir's Dutch schoolmates might come from white families living in the Indies for years and sometimes generations, *blijvers*, "those who remain." The families and the children might mix with the indigenous strata, and sometimes more than Amir, a son of *djaksa* and aristocrat. They and their children, Amir's classmates, might carry into the school strong street accents and their Dutch was often questionable. According to the official statistics, at the beginning of the twentieth century, 4 percent of the European students in the Indies elementary schools knew "on the whole no Dutch," 29.3 percent "knew only a little Dutch," and only 29.2 percent of the European students in the elementary schools understood and spoke Dutch "well enough to be able to follow the instruction."[24] Not all European students, of course, went to the elite ELS. Still, it is easily possible to imagine Amir helping a Dutch classmate with his or her Dutch.

The teachers at the ELS schools in Amir's time were exclusively Dutch, recruited for the job in the Netherlands. "Salaries were very decent," a Dutch historian writes, "and it was not difficult to attract a good working pedagogue in the motherland. . . . In general, the teachers in the Indies came from better parts of the Dutch society at home."[25]

Fresh, young, and mostly enthusiastic, the teachers, men as well as women, familiarized their students with the exotic and potentially threatening periphery of the empire at the same time as they familiarized themselves. Most of them returned home after six years, as contracted.

Being more challenged, and often lost in the foreign, they differed from teachers in the Netherlands. They might have been more exposed for the students to see. "To be dedicated to their students and to take their profession seriously," wrote a pedagogic authority in the Indies, "demands ethical stance: A teacher cannot be an official who happens to teach. He must be capable to help a student to stand on his own feet, he has to be someone, too. . . . Teaching means giving a child a pleasure to know, a good knowing, to convince the child. . . . The teacher has to stand between the blackboard and the child; not to place a book between himself or herself and the child."[26]

Most of the ELS primers, textbooks, storybooks, and songbooks were printed in the Netherlands, published by the J. B. Wolters company in Groningen and The Hague and imported to the Indies. They were material for the Dutch schools, "adjusted" for the colony.[27]

They were, to be sure, on the whole, in correct and proper Dutch, with snippets of words and phrases in Malay—the lingua franca of the colony, spoken in certain parts of the archipelago but mainly a street and market language, used by the Dutch to communicate with the indigenous population beyond the well educated. The books were optimistic. Elementary-school textbooks are optimistic everywhere but, in the Indies, anxiously, it meant modern, colonial, Western, and familiarizing oneself. They "projected" the students.

In a 2018 study, a curator of the Dordrecht National Museum of Education, along with a colleague, described the schoolbooks of the Indies of the time as modeled in part on adventure stories and in part on missionary tales. They were to make the students "see, hear, and touch."[28] They were called *door-ren-boekjes*, "run-through little books," to make the students read as if they were on a journey.[29]

The students were to run along a well-defined and safely-staked road. In a schoolbook titled *Hoofdpersonen uit de algemeen geschiedenis*, "The Main Characters in the General History," heroes (heroes who accomplished what they had set out to do) were numbered: "1. Columbus; 2. Cortez; 3. Charles V; 5. Calvin; 6. Ignatius de Loyola; 7. Willem of Orange; 8. P.P. Coen [founder of the Dutch empire in the East]."[30] The textbooks were "written in a lively, graphic style akin to that of tour guides."

The textbooks were to be written "face-to-face," as "dialogues rather than enumeration of facts."[31] "In one of Andersen's tales," Walter Benjamin wrote, "there is a picture book that cost: 'half a kingdom.' In it everything was alive. 'The birds sang, and people came out of the book and spoke.' But when the princess turned the page, 'they leaped back in again so that there should be no disorder.'"[32]

Indigenous students, too, entered the book as they turned the pages. They, too, became the book and the story and the picture heroes. They got into danger, but they familiarized themselves and if they read on, they were saved. They reached the clearing. Often, as a rule in fact, they were saved by being borrowed. Many stories ended by a hero being adopted by a family of the clearing, of light skin and Christian faith, as it happened. Projected, the indigenous students were getting lighter as they read. Sometimes, the story went all the way. The heroes brought the light as far as back to a dark place from which they had originally departed, were projected. They returned to their biological family or community, the space of twilight and murmur, as agents of light. "We need to plait a braid of sympathy connecting the Netherlands and its overseas dominions."[33]

Let's just read a little:

A Trip to Haarlem

"So, Kees, tomorrow, at sunrise we go. Don't be late. Train does not wait." . . .

It's a splendid spring morning in Amsterdam! . . . The bakers hurry with their carts and smell of fresh bread is in the air. The milkmen and the vegetables people are also already on the streets. . . .

Train is puffing on. The boys yield to joy and they start a cheerful song.[34]

There was a timetable in the Indies. Some points of departure were marked grander than the other on the calendar. Some were the ultimate.

It's Wednesday morning.

Tandjong Priok [Tanjung Priok, Batavia harbor] is unusually busy. No wonder: in an hour, the steamer '*Sindoro*' departs for the Netherlands![35]

From the book the world was expanding.

In the Wilderness

Our travel party consisted of gentlemen, ladies, and six children. There were also several native bearers, males and females . . .

We have walked through the nature, got tired and then drank to our fill the crystal-clear cold water in a little stream . . .[36]

"Children's books," says Walter Benjamin, "do not seem to introduce their readers directly to the world of objects, animals, and people, in so-called life. Rather, if anything remotely like the Platonic anamnesis actually exists, it would take place in the lives of children, for whom picture books are paradise."[37]

The Grateful Javanese

(A story by Uncle Karel)

"Once," so the Uncle began, "I became seriously ill.... Early in the morning, doctor had to be called from town. He arrived and ordered that I do not remain on the plantation. The same day, I had to go to the hospital.

When the people in the kampong had learned about it, they became worried and wished to do something.... They insisted and I became a little impatient and told them that all I needed was just eight men to carry my palanquin.

But they kept on repeating: "Master! You have done so much good for us. How could we not carry you, all of us? Please, let us to do this little for you."

There is an illustration in the schoolbook showing the whole kampong carrying the palanquin with Uncle Karel. "Was not it wonderful," Uncle Karel ends his story, "of these good people?"[38]

There were natives in the schoolbooks: often of Amir's age but still in the twilight. "Good people" were taking care of them.

An Accident

Poor Amat!

Mama required a couple of young coconuts to make a glass of sirup for us, so Amat climbed up a palm tree....

What a shock! Poor Amat fell from the tree ...

Doctor examined him and found out that the arm was broken. But, he said, Amat would be fine. A couple of weeks, and he would be climbing trees again.[39]

I can only guess what the student Amir saw when he happened to look away from the teacher, the blackboard, or the textbook, out of his classroom window. Possibly trees, perhaps a bed of flowers; most of the schools at the time had only the ground floor.

From the map of Medan of the time I may guess a little. If Amir's classroom windows faced east, he saw the Spoorwegmaatschappij, the "Deli Railway Company," the railway tracks, and, closer to the school, the horse-race stadium. If the windows faced north, there was a Roman Catholic church that hid most of the view and a Protestant church farther on in the distance. To the south there was the *koeliehospitaal*, the government hospital for the natives: to the west, there were the gardens of the North Sumatra Province governor's residence, the prison, and, too far to be seen clearly, the Deli sultan's palace and the European cemetery.[40]

The immensity, however, of the world to be seen one day and perhaps conquered, was elsewhere. The walls of the colonial classrooms in the colony at that time were hung with, broken in, by *wandplaten*, "wall charts." Through the charts rather than through the windows, the world faced the student. I have asked Jacques Dane, a curator of the Netherlands National Museum of Education, how many wall charts from the era were kept in their storage. About fourteen thousand, he said, a large part of them from the Indies.

Jacques Dane and Evelien Walhout wrote an essay on the wall charts in the colony. "Wall charts," they wrote, "were discussed in class," one or another had been picked up at a time and "the teacher showcased it in front of the blackboard."[41] They made for a "picture essay":[42] "Great Dayak House in Borneo," "*Pasar* [market] in the island of Java," "Weaving hats for European women in West Java," "Natives playing cards," "Martin Luther at the Reichstag in Worms," "Cultivation of tobacco in Deli," "The conquest of Tjakranegara in Lombok, 1874."[43]

Amir, as he looked away from his textbooks, teacher, or blackboard, was supposed to see the world opening to him, in the wall charts: "Canadian geese in flight," "Forum with philosophers in discussion," "Dutch cow in the meadow." "This wall opens up for children," wrote Walter Benjamin who is best when he writes about children, "and more brightly colored wall can be glimpsed behind it."[44] "The blue distance . . . is the painted distance of a backdrop."[45]

On December 4, 1917, Amir's father, Baginda Saripada, the assistant *djaksa* in Medan, was appointed to succeed his father, Soetan Goenoeng Toea, and become a *hoofddjaksa* in Sibolga, a town across Sumatra, on the island's west coast, much smaller and substantially more provincial than Medan, but also with an ELS. Amir finished the third grade in Medan.

"'A charming Bay of Tapanoeli,' a Dutch official report on Sibolga wrote in 1918, "is strewn with greater and smaller islands and to the north and to the south it is framed by two peninsulas projected into the sea and sheltering the bay from the swelling of the Indian Ocean . . . Behind the town of Sibolga, hills are raising sharply from the sea. They offer a beautiful panorama, deeper and broader every moment as one climbs the hills."[46] There are photographs accompanying the report. On one of them, "a section of the new European quarter can be seen, *Si Mare Mare*, which was till recently rice fields and marshes. Now, new residential buildings, a park, and paved streets give the place a completely different appearance."[47]

The moment Amir arrived at Sibolga the town was still recovering from a major malaria epidemic two years before. So, wrote Dr. Vogel in his report of 1913: "Already at the first encounter, Sibolga inhabitants gave an impression that their energy is sucked by the illness to the limits. All Europeans take quinine against the fever that in town struck all and made them unfit not just for work but for normal life. Officials, Europeans as well as native, without exception, they all long for nothing but for a speedy assignment somewhere else." As Amir's family settled in town, however, there was an improvement: "the works of drainage are finished in a great part . . . and a comparison even is sometimes made with what the Americans had achieved in Panama and Colón. . . . One only wonders why the Americans built a public water-distribution system, and the Dutch in Sibolga had not."⁴⁸

Sibolga, also, hosted one of the only three ELSs in the whole vast area of North Sumatra, besides Medan to the east and Padang Sidempoean to the south. In 1918, probably in summer, so that he would not lose a year, the nine-year-old Amir, who had just finished fourth grade in the Medan ELS, with family and, of course, servants, followed his father and traveled to Sibolga.

I guess they went in a car, either rented or their own. Medan was already that kind of place, and they were already that kind of people. Their itinerary also almost certainly was the newly standard route, and quasi-prescribed for that kind of a trip. One started from Medan to the east, up the hills of Prapat, a famous resort favored by the Deli planters. "[Twenty-five] years ago," a Dutch Dr. Kraemer wrote in 1930, which meant he spoke of 1905, "Parapat [Prapat], at present an ideally situated center of modern hotels and tourism, was a dangerous mission station surrounded by hostile Bataks who did not yet care about Dutch colonial power." "The highway from Medan to Padang," Dr Kraemer wrote, "has forever broken the isolation of the Batak lands." "Toba, the region situated on the south and west shores of lake Toba, was considered the heart of the Batak lands. . . . The lake was [sic] considered the national shrine and its waves wash the foot of the holy tribal mountain of the Bataks."⁴⁹ The whole trip could be made in three days at the time, but only when the travelers were in a hurry.

It was a picturesque and exotic journey, certainly its first part. Recommended to white tourists and to planters on vacation, it passed the landscape offering sights—the wall charts, in sequence and in motion, cinematic, just when cinema became a thing to do—"Geese in Flight," "Natives in kampongs," even a possibility of the "Dutch cows in the meadows." "Only the movement of the fleeting images," wrote Marc Augé, "enables the observer to hypothesize the existence of a past and glimpse the possibility of a future."⁵⁰

Given the way Amir's family already was, it is not far-fetched to imagine them bringing a travel guide and Amir leafing through it as they traveled:

> The Bataks are scarcely yet emerged from animalism, yet the tombs and monuments that are to be met occasionally in the villages exhibit a style

of art curiously reminiscent of the temples of Chichén Itzá in Yucatan or these of the Incas of Peru, or, at times, of the art of early Egypt or of the Minoan civilization. . . .

Lake Toba . . . is one of Nature's most beautiful sights. It is situated at the height of about 8,000 feet (2,438 meters) above sea-level and is surrounded by mountains, many of them active volcanoes. . . . Prapat is ideally placed on a peninsula jotting out into the lake and offers facilities for tennis, boating and swimming as well as wonderful views of the scenery. . . . Lake Toba . . . is not merely a repetition of a Swiss mountain lake with added splendor of tropical forests and colors; it is an enormous fire-opal in a setting of malachite.[51]

"The adventures," says Robert Musil, another boy of this story, "are instances of standing still in the grander perspective. . . . Who among us does not spend the greater part of his life in the shadow of an event that has not yet taken place?"[52] Toenggoel Siagian, my Batak friend, is a writer, educator, and publisher. I do not necessarily trust each of his stories, but I love them and have learned much from them. Once, he told me how he decided to make a film about ancient Batak tombs. He put together a crew, they flew to North Sumatra and found a spot—a splendid stone, he said, centuries old and wonderfully carved. They placed a camera on a tripod and got ready to shoot. "At this very moment," Toenggoel said, "at the word 'shoot,' the tomb quivered a little, and then crumbled down into a heap of a rubble."

The trip to Sibolga might feel to Amir like a country feast. "Countless layers of ideas, images, feelings have fallen successively on your brain as softly as light. It seems that each buries the preceding, but none has really perished."[53] The boy Amir traveling across Sumatra to another school might feel like the boy Baudelaire, or boy Benjamin on a carousel. Recall: "The platform bearing the docile animals moves close to the ground. It is at the height which, in dream is best for flying."[54] "It may be," says Benjamin, "that in childhood we wander through the world of things like the stations of a journey of whose existence we can form no conception. Couldn't it be the case that childhood makes a start with the most remote things?"[55] "In childhood," writes Marcel Proust, one starts with "the inaccessibly remote tracks of which one never knows anything on this earth except the direction, except the way."[56]

CHAPTER 2

Holland

> No one who has never seen himself surrounded on all sides by nothing but the sea can have a true conception of the world and of his own relation to it.
>
> —Goethe, on the way from Rome to Napoli, *Italian Journey*, 228

In the summer of 1921, with the Europese Lagere School (ELS) behind him, just fourteen years old, possibly from the Medan harbor of Belawan Deli or perhaps from the island of Sabang off Sumatra's west coast, closer to Sibolga, Amir Sjarifoeddin boarded a big ship sailing from Batavia to Amsterdam.[1] In François Rabelais's *Gargantua and Pantagruel*, Gargantua's letter to his son Pantagruel, Gargantua says:

> I intend and will that you acquire a perfect command of languages—first Greek (as Quintilian wishes), secondly Latin, and then Hebrew for the Holy Scriptures, as well as Chaldean and Arabic likewise—and that for your Greek, you mold your style by imitating Plato, and for your Latin Cicero. / Let there be no history which you do not hold ready in your memory; . . . / And as for the knowledge of natural phenomena, I want you to apply yourself to it with curiosity; let there be no sea, river or stream the fishes of which you do not know, know all the birds of the air.[2]

It was reported that another Batak boy of Amir's age, Ferdinand Tambubolon, traveled with Amir, and that Dr. W. G. Harrenstein, a thirty-five-year-old pastor of the Protestant Reformed Church Congregation in Medan, was entrusted as a chaperone for the boys on the way.[3]

Neither Ferdinand Tambubolon nor Dr. Harrenstein, however, can be found on the ship's passenger list. It is impossible to ascertain if Amir had any companion on the ship. Amir's name, moreover, is the only native looking name on the list except that of R. M. Djoemadi who traveled from Batavia. All other passengers, according to the names at least, were European, and one was Chinese.

The ship was the *Jan Pieterszoon Coen*. It left Batavia in the middle of July and was expected in Amsterdam on the morning of August 13. It stopped at Belawan and Sabang. Amir is listed among the *nagekomen passagiers*, "those passengers who joined later," who joined the ship at one of those two places. The ship then continued via Colombo, Suez, and Genoa to Amsterdam, where it arrived as planned in the second week of August.[4]

The *Jan Pieterszoon Coen* was new and modern. It made its maiden voyage on November 11, 1915, in the middle of the First World War, when it sailed from Amsterdam to Batavia. It was equipped with "wireless, submarine signals (bells) and 14 [life]boats, two of them powered, sufficient for all persons aboard." Of the ship's seven decks, three were continuous through the full length of the ship, which was 153 meters long. The ship could take 202 passengers in first class with 107 cabins and 4 suites, 128 passengers in second class with 49 cabins, 46 passengers in third class with 16 cabins, and 42 passengers in fourth class. The first-class passengers had access to a deck saloon, a verandah café, smoking room, nursery, gymnasium, photographic dark room, and a 138 seat dining salon. In all probability, as it was proper for his family's standing, Amir traveled in second class.

Amir arrived in Europe just in time for school. His older cousin Datoek Moelia, who had studied in Holland and lived there for several years, waited for Amir at the harbor and took him to Oegstgeest, a place at the outskirts of Leiden. Then Ferdinand Tambubolon appears, from however and whenever he got to Holland. For the first few weeks, the two boys stayed together, in the house of Mrs. A. P. van de Loosdrecht-Sizoo, a missionary widow.[5]

The Indies followed Amir as a higher-grade school storybook adventure. The late husband of Van de Loosdrecht-Sizoo was a missionary of the Dutch Reformed Mission Congregation, and he served among the Toradjas on the island of Celebes (Sulawesi). In August 1917, he was murdered by the natives at a place called Rantepao. "It was night, two o'clock in the morning, and there was a knock on the door," Van de Loosdrecht-Sizoo wrote in a letter to the Dutch paper in the Indies, *Java Bode*, a few weeks later. She did not understand, she wrote, what the *opstand*, "revolt," was about. Possibly her husband was mistaken for a government official.[6]

Ferdinand stayed in the house of the missionary widow, but Amir moved on, most probably before the school started in September. He became a lodger in Leiden, closer to the Leiden City Gymnasium where he enrolled. Amir now lived with the Dutch family of Dirk Smink where his cousin Moelia had lived before him. Todoeng gelar Soetan Goenoeng Moelia, eleven years Amir's senior, lived with the Sminks when he studied at Leiden, at the Protestant Christelijke Kweekschool, "Protestant Christian Teachers' College." He left back to the Indies in 1921, possibly soon after Amir arrived.[7]

It is still a quiet middle-class suburban street, small family villas in a row, identical except details: the chimney, the color of the doors, different flowers in the little front gardens. The house at the address where Amir moved from Oegstgeest is not there anymore. It is, in fact, the only villa missing in the row, but I could easily envision it given the still standing neighboring houses—or imagine it, nice to cozy—from one of the illustrations in Amir's ELS primer about exotic-yet-familiar Holland. The last time I was there, in the fall of 2019, two boys played ball on the street in front of where the house used to be. Indeed, one was white and the other rather dark. Neither was Amir.

The son of Amir's landlord, a boy of Amir's age, Smink Jr., recalled to Jacques Leclerc that Amir had been received as a member of the family. In other words, Amir was "borrowed." Smink Jr. saved a few photographs from that time and gave them to the Leiden University Library. In one of the photographs, Amir sits at the garden table, likely at the back of the Sminks' house. The other people at the table are Mr. Smink Sr., Mrs. Smink, and Smink junior. On the verso side of the photograph is written, evidently by Smink Sr.'s hand: "The little brown is a Batak from Sumatra, Amir Sjarifoeddin. He stays with us."[8]

The photograph had to have been taken during the first weeks of Amir's life in the Netherlands. In another photograph, probably also from the villa's garden or from the street in front of it, there is Amir, Smink Jr., and another Dutch boy (or girl?), looking at the camera. It appears to be raining, the light rain as is so usual in Holland. All three wear identical raincoats, all have the hoods up, and all are grinning.

On Sundays and holidays, the burghers of Leiden packed their picnic baskets, took the *Blauwe Tram,* "Blue Tram," and in thirty minutes they were in Katwijk, then still largely a fishermen's and painters' village but already on the way to becoming a fashionable North Sea beach resort. There is another photograph, this one taken in Katwijk: Amir sits on the beach in a lounge chair. According to Smink Jr., the two of them entered the Katwijk sandcastle-building competition and won second prize. Their entry, Smink Jr. says, was "the Lioness of Nineveh." "It was Amir's idea," Mr. Smink says.[9]

Smink Sr. was a professor at the Leiden Protestant Christian Teachers' College, a school which Datoek Moelia, Amir's cousin, had attended before Amir arrived. Smink Sr was also a member of the Dutch Reformed Church, a denomination reputed for having a very severe idea of religion. And Mr. Smink was a devoted member of the church. As one of the family, the "borrowed one," Amir was expected to do the chores, and, despite being Muslim, he was to visit the church with the family every Sunday and on Holy Days, at least.

"We had the same rights and the same responsibilities," Smink Jr. says. "My father was 'reformed' to the deepest of his soul, and he demanded of his family to obey the rules, 'to live in the church'; it seemed completely natural to him." "This clearly," Smink Jr. added, "was the cause of Amir's departure to Haarlem."[10]

It was still like in the primers. The "dark one" was "borrowed," "taken care of" and "sheltered," "helped to the light." However, now, as Amir was turning a page, the good Uncle Karel, unlike in that picture book, did not leap "back in again so that there should be no disorder."[11]

For one thing, Mr. Smink's family lived on limited means: a teacher's salary was good enough to keep their little villa and do their Sunday trips to the beach, but one would hear complaints that teachers' salaries were in fact pitiful. The family might feel in need of the extra money brought in by housing a student from the Indies.

Amir came from a family that could afford to send a child to Europe. The money with which Amir came was for sure more than welcomed by Mr. Smink. The money, if there was nothing else, could make the fifteen-year-old Amir feel still projected, in the throw, and toward the light, except now no longer in the entirely primer-like way.

Through the first year after his arrival, Amir attended the City Gymnasium in Leiden. On September 25, 1922, however, he left the Sminks' little villa and moved with his baggage to Haarlem. Haarlem was a city twice the size of Leiden. It was twenty minutes by train from Leiden, on the main line to Amsterdam, which was only another half an hour or so further on. I do not know which adult, if any, gave Amir permission to leave the Sminks. Amir, it appears, without difficulty, got himself admitted to the City Gymnasium of Haarlem. Again, without losing a school term.[12] "A man . . . is continually becoming a new person. . . . What we call *coming* implies that our knowledge is departing since forgetfulness is an egress of knowledge, while *coming* substitutes a fresh one in place of that which departs. . . . Every mortal thing is preserved in this way; . . . by replacing what goes off or is antiquated by something fresh, in the semblance of the original. Through this device . . . a mortal thing partakes of immortality."[13]

The Stedelijk Gymnasium Haarlem, "City Gymnasium of Haarlem," is still there, an impressive and indeed elite institution of learning in the city and the whole country. Its building still stands at the same place where the Latin school, the Gymnasium's predecessor, had been founded in 1389, in the center of Haarlem, at Prinsenhof, "Prince's Court," a quiet enclosure that still retains a medieval air about it, a few steps from the city's magnificent cathedral. The main building of the Gymnasium dates from 1648.

In the memorial book published in 1990 on the Gymnasium's six-hundred-year anniversary, *Tempel van Hovaardij*, "Temple of Haughtiness," there is a photograph of the students skating in the Hortus, the school flower garden, during the harsh winter of 1940.[14] The memorial book mentions that in 1900 the school's classrooms and halls were adorned "with 100 photographs of Athens, 40 photographs of Rome, several wall charts. In 1916, several plaster replicas 'of various value' from the Rijksmuseum in Leiden were added."[15]

On July 4, 1924, in Amir's second year in the school, a new natural-science wing of the Gymnasium was opened. The main entrance was now through the new wing. The architect of the addition, van Buys, belonged to the Nieuwe Bouwen, "New Style," of architecture. An imposing *traphal*, "monumental staircase," as well as the halls and classrooms of the new wing had windows of colored glass; the *Haarlemsche Courant* clarified that "the green [was] for calm, the blue for thought, the yellow of uplifting power, and the red giving the whole a triumphant accent."[16]

Dominating squares and right angles imposed on the ancient interiors suggested the "deliberately elementary and democratic ideas." The American Frank Lloyd Wright was mentioned, and the windows were said to resemble Wassily Kandinsky.[17]

The institution of Gymnasiums, throughout Europe since the nineteenth century, was a standard and highly competitive preparatory school for students to advance to universities.

The Real Gymnasium placed more emphasis on science. The Classical Gymnasium, which Amir attended in Haarlem, focused almost exclusively on classical languages and cultures—one might say imperial—like ancient Latin and Greek, classical French, German, and English, that is Racine or Voltaire, Goethe or Schiller, Shakespeare, or Chaucer. Dutch, of course, had been presumed in Haarlem without asking; it was a matter of the natural everyday.

Even Western languages were not necessarily thought to be "sublime" enough. Miss Land, who was still teaching English at Haarlem when Amir was there, complained in 1920, "It is shame how a world language like English is handled." During Amir's time in Haarlem, there was one lesson of English (fifty minutes) a week in the curriculum compared to nine lessons a week of Latin.[18]

The Classical Gymnasium was designed to teach the students translation of classical texts into good Dutch. Greek and Latin were the most important.

Some time, also, was given to German philosophy.[19] "We learn to speak as children," wrote Ernst Bloch, "but only as youth do we try it, namely totally. Then comes the drive to let up rise into the word, the remarkable drive to say our life, so momentary and full."[20]

Occasionally, the Haarlem Gymnasium organized trips to other places in the Netherlands. In Amir's time, once they went to Arnhem, a town a hundred kilometers southeast of Haarlem, close to the German border. The students of the Arnhem Gymnasium were giving a performance of Sophocles's *Oedipus Rex*, in classical Greek, of course, and they invited their sister schools. The visiting students were to be put with local families for the night, and each student was asked to fill in a questionnaire so that a good match could be found. A classmate of Amir, Loes Spruit, recalled decades later in a letter to Jacques Leclerc:

> Amir showed me his questionnaire. You had to tell if you were a boy or a girl, and so on, and what was your religion. Under "the religion" Amir wrote "a liberal Mohammedan," and he told me with one of his slightly sarcastic grins: "I wonder what they'll make of that." As it turned out, in the end, they found a nice family of a Deli planter for him, and he told me that he had a good time. "I am afraid that we were not much interested in religion," Loes said, "despite the fact that our *rector* [principal] always tried to hold us in the line, pointing to the medieval Latin School, the Gymnasium had evolved from. The only time when religion surfaced were the situations like that in Arnhem."[21]

For the six years when he was a student in Haarlem, Amir lived in a rented room in Vredenhof 6, in Heemstede, a little town one stop by train or ten minutes by city bus from Haarlem. But most often, we might be certain, Amir rode a bicycle like all the Dutch do. The house on the Vredenhof still stands, more prosperous than the Sminks' little villa in Leiden. There is a large garden at the back of the building, with big trees, some of them may remember Amir's time.

According to the Gymnasium's records, Amir's landlady was Mrs. B. van Lengering.[22] It was still a kind of "borrowing," but very much a looser one. Van Lengering and her husband were still referred by Amir's friends and probably by Amir himself as *pleegouders*, "foster parents." But they were said repeatedly by Amir's schoolmates, as they heard it from Amir, to be "more kind," evidently "more kind" than the Sminks.[23]

Loes Spruit answered Jacques Leclerc's inquiries in greater detail than did his other friends. How she wrote to Jacques about what had happened half a century ago, had so much warmth, that one is made to feel there was love between the two people. "Romance flowered briefly with a Dutch girl," one hears from at least one other source.[24]

Loes writes with pride how, among all of Amir's Haarlem classmates, only she could remember and wrap her tongue around Amir's "long string of names": "I was the only one who could say all the names and as they followed one other without stumbling once."[25]

"The democratization of the Netherlands education system," the Gymnasium memorial book wrote in 1990, "was far behind the public systems of the neighboring European countries which were [since the beginning of the twentieth century] experiencing a larger influx of students from 'lower classes.'"[26] "The social milieu from which the students of the Haarlem City Gymnasium came had something 'posh' about it.... Even as late as 1989 only 8 percent of the students came from the workers' families."[27] "Gymnasium was a sheltered world of learning. The manner in which it was sheltered gave the school its raison d'être and its prestige."[28]

Students published their own newspaper, *Mirabele Lectu*, "Amazing Read," and they met at the school's *crème* debate society Amicitia Iuncti, "Friends United." In the school year 1926–1927, his last year, together with two male and two female students, Amir was elected to the board of the Amicitia Iuncti. There is a photograph of him, sitting at a low table with four colleagues, two men and two women, debating. The members of the board look very thoughtful and certainly self-confident.[29] "There was a liberal climate in the school," one former student recalled, "a fertile ground to learn critical thinking."[30]

"Amir," Loes Spruit wrote to Leclerc, was "brilliant" and was "one of us." "He belonged to the superior group in the class, however, to say the truth, there had been not much difference between 'the number 1' and 'the number 18.' Because ranking did not matter much to us."[31]

Some days, Loes came to Heemstede to the house of Van Lengering to visit Amir: "I still remember those long evenings under the lamp in his room, as we were doing our homework. We were working hard, and were focused, until suddenly Amir jumped up and began one of the fantastic solo dances of his— which lasted perhaps a minute. Then, as suddenly as that, with a perfectly solemn face he sat down again, and the work went on." The room is described:

> There was nothing much of really his own in his room, only a very beautiful *kain* [Indonesian for cloth] on the wall opposite where I usually sat. This *kain* he had brought when he came to say good-bye to my parents, on an afternoon carefully chosen so that I will be away. We both dreaded the moment when we would have to say good-bye, but we never spoke about it. I was not with the class when they went to see him off to the

dock, and only when the ship left, my mother, as instructed by Amir, gave me the *kain*.[32]

According to Loes and other Haarlem schoolmates, Amir was artistic. He played violin, and well. He sang and showed "a great appreciation for world literature, Shakespeare most of all."[33] He drew and painted. One classmate recalled Amir's drawing: "Once he made me a present, a magnificent sketch (in black and white) of a Dutch ship with sails. Too bad, it got lost."[34] In yet another recollection, "Amir was talented; often we hiked or biked around in the country and when we stopped, he sketched nature."[35]

There were sights around Haarlem, the windmills, the tulips, gladioli, lilies, and caladium fields, the sea—the beach resort of Zandvoort was as close to Haarlem as Katwijk was to Leiden—Dutch villages like on the wall charts, with the spires of churches, most of them Protestant, clean white and pure light inside, the Dutch cows in the meadow.

I can be sure that Amir visited Amsterdam many times; the city was just a short trip away and there was a train several times a day. I can be almost sure that he went to Paris, which could be made over a weekend. From Loes we know about Amir dancing. "The week before the *bal* [Dutch for 'prom'] was to be held, we spent hours rehearsing together: the most sophisticated steps of the tango, which was *de rigueur* then. All the girls at the *bal* wanted to do tango with Amir. But with them it just did not work. And we never told them about our rehearsals." "As far as I know," recalled Loes, "and I think I knew him rather well, Amir never searched for Indonesian fellows."[36]

As far as Loes knew, at least, there was only one exception. Even after Amir left Leiden, he did not break contact with Ferdinand Tambubolon, the Batak friend with whom he shared a room during his first weeks in the Netherlands. Ferdinand stayed in Oegstgeest. He was a Christian and seemed to deepen his Christian faith in Holland. He still lived in the house of the missionary widow and he and Amir continued to see each other. Together, and it seems through Loes Spruit, they came to know Marie van Zeggelen, a well-known Dutch author at the time of exotic and inspirational stories and travelogues about the Indies.

Marie van Zeggelen (1870–1957) spent a quarter of a century in the East, as the wife of an officer of the KNIL, the Royal Dutch Indies Army. In 1916 she came back to the Netherlands. Her books were aimed at adults and young readers, and at times are undistinguishable in spirit, style, their heroes, and their pedagogy, from the stories Amir read in ELS in Medan and Sibolga. Indeed, several of Marie van Zeggelen's short stories became suggested reading in Indies' schools.

Marie van Zeggelen lived alternatively in the Hague and Haarlem at the time and, Loes says, she became fond of Amir and Ferdinand. They and Loes sometimes came to see her, in her house. These were afternoons when, Loes recalls, Marie van Zeggelen dressed Amir and Ferdinand in "traditional Batak costumes," which she probably brought from the Indies among many other things. I try to imagine Amir, on one of those afternoons, perhaps taking it seriously, perhaps "with one of his slightly sarcastic grins."

"She had the loveliest things in her home brought back from the tropics," Loes wrote. "She was already elderly then, but she liked me to bring Amir, and during the holidays Tambu [Tambubolon], and they loved to dress up as Batak princes. I remember a photo of her and Amir which I took, kept for years, but unfortunately destroyed along with a lot of other souvenirs."[37]

In summer 1927, the final examinations of Amir's class at the Haarlem City Gymnasium were taking place: the *matura*, "maturity test." Amir shocked his class, Loes says. He failed the exams; as Homer (the Homer of the City Gymnasium) might put it, "he fell, hand clawing the earth."[38]

Dutch history 3+
General history 3–
Algebra 4–
Geometry 3+

Not bad on a scale of "1" the worst and "5" the best, but not good enough. But there was a second chance. Amir could re-sit the exam and it seems (the records are incomplete) this time the tests were more focused on what the Gymnasium was really about, the classics. Amir spent the summer cramming and, on the second attempt, in July 1927, he made it:

Old languages
1:15–1:35 Herodotus
2:35–3:15 Homer
History 2:30–3:00
Science 3:00–3:30.[39]

It was an assumption of most of Amir's classmates that he, of course, would go on with his studies in the Netherlands, at a university. When they learned that Amir was packing, they were looking for reasons. Some thought that the money had run out. "His father paid for everything," Loes seemed to know.[40] And there was a rumor of serious trouble in which Amir's father found himself.

Indeed, on May 25, 1926, a year before Amir's *matura*, "for assaulting a prisoner in Sibolga jail" (the severity of his subsequent sentence suggests a very serious matter)," Amir's father was condemned to three and a half years in prison to be followed by five years of prohibition of employment in government service.[41] That seemed to explain it. In September 1927, Amir boarded a ship to the Indies. All his classmates—except Loes, who could not bear it—accompanied him to the dock.

It was a few weeks' journey again, but the sea this time had to be different. If nothing else, Amir knew his Homer, and so, when he looked around, he saw the waters and the horizons "wine-dark," and "many voiced," and "spinning."[42] Or it might be, as he was going back, like the wall charts in his ELS classrooms—a wall opening into another wall, still almost but already not quite, the colonial immensity.

At the first port the ship from Amsterdam to Batavia called on, Port Said, he might have seen what most travelers of the time through that place recall, a big neon sign glowing at the entrance to the Suez Canal:

EAST IS EAST AND WEST IS WEST
VAN HOUTEN COCOA IS THE BEST[43]

"Sure," Loes Spruit wrote to Jacques Leclerc, "he must have had moments of homesickness. Now and then he pinched my sketchbook and covered a page with a drawing. . . . I remember extremely funny illustrations of the story of Doctor Faust. . . . But I still have a sketch of a shore. It is a view of Lake Toba where his family lived." Also, Loes remembered, "Amir had at least one sister who he was very fond of. I remember some lovely pieces of Batak bead-work made by her."[44]

Chapter 3

The Batavia Law School

> Chimneys and spires, these masts of the city . . .
>
> —Baudelaire, *Tableau Parisiens*, quoted in Augé, *Non-Places*, 92

The Law School in Batavia (Rechtshoogeschool), opened three years before Amir Sjarifoeddin passed his final exam at the City Gymnasium in Haarlem. This, as much as the family troubles, might have been the reason why Amir did not remain in the Netherlands.

The very sight of the new Law School was something that a poet might call the masts of the city. In the very center of the colonial space, on the western side of the colony capital's main square, Koningsplein, "King's Square," with the white eighteenth-century palace of the governor general just across the corner, at the square south side, the building of the Law School was an exemplary piece of the modern. Designed by Johan Frederik van Hoytema, the chief engineer of the colony's Department of Public Works, it was built of reinforced concrete, in an angular style. The Frank Lloyd Wright-like structure resembled the science wing of the Haarlem City Gymnasium. The large windows of colored glass resembled the Haarlem school and, sort of, Wassily Kandinsky.

In July 1928, Amir passed the entry candidate examination to the school.[1] In 1928, Amir's first year at the school, there were 138 students, of which 40 were Europeans, 75 natives, and 23 Chinese, meaning Indonesians of Chinese origin. The course of study took five years, with a doctoral candidate taking exams after the first two years, with a doctoral examination at the end. Graduates were awarded a tile of *meester in de rechten*, "Master of Law," with the right to use *mr.* in front of their names and to practice law in the colony.

CHAPTER 3

The Batavia Law School, rather than a crashing, seemed a continuation of Amir's journey toward the light.

There was no suggestion of the disheartened Odysseus as Amir's ship docked at Tandjong Priok, the harbor in Batavia:

> . . . So up he got,
> And stood there, gazing round at his own native land.
> After a moment he groaned and struck both thighs
> with the flat of his hands, and sorrowfully exclaimed:
> ". . . Where am I supposed to be taking all this wealth?
> Where indeed am I wandering to myself? . . ."[2]

The men who became Amir Sjarifoeddin's professors at the Law School, with one single exception, were Dutch, and all without an exception with a doctorate from a Dutch university: actually, all of them from the University of Leiden. The single non-Dutch exception was Professor Hussein Djajadiningrat, also with a Leiden degree, but of the most-elevated aristocratic Javanese family, a proof that it could be done. There were two lecturers, both Dutch: Dr. E. Bessem taught Latin, and J. Kats taught Javanese. I asked one of Kats's students whether it was not strange for a Dutchman to teach Javanese when there were some Javanese among his students. "No," I was told, "Kats was a good man."[3]

There is a well-known official portrait of the faculty taken on the Law School's opening day on October 28, 1924. Professor Scholten, the man credited with inventing the idea of the school, sits in the middle of the group, in a jacket. Seven professors surround him, Professors Schrieke, ter Haar, Baron van Asbeck, Kollewijn, Boeke, Djajadiningrat, and Logemann, all in black togas. Dr. Bessem and Mr. Kats are in a light *colbert* and in an *echt* (colonial all-white suit) respectively.[4] The portrait was conferred to the Dutch Indies governor general as a souvenir.

This seemed a step forward for Amir. Compared to the Amir's teachers at the Europese Lagere School (ELS), and then at the Haarlem Gymnasium, this group is a step more interesting—and a step more vulnerable, too. All the professors in the Law School portrait, the Dutch, and the Javanese too, traveled ways, lingered, were "in the throw." However long they might stay in the Indies—and some did for the most of their lives and one was born there—they were all, in the portrait and in the memories of the people who knew them, as if they had recently arrived.

Batavia and the Law School with them resembled a ship, the masts and all, and they, despite the jackets, togas, and the *colbert*, resembled sailors.

They could hardly envisage decolonization otherwise than the end of the world as they knew it and as they had helped to build it up. But they were, more than Amir's ELS primary school teachers, a frayed edge of the empire. At their best moments, they were exiles:

Don't knock any nails in the wall
Just throw your coat on the chair[5]

Much later, in 1949, after the independent Indonesia replaced the colonial Indies, a former student at the Law School, Amir's friend, with a help from another classmate, published a memorial book of the school.[6] Short biographies of the professors made up a substantial part of the volume.

Professor Jacob van Gelderen is not in the 1924 portrait, but he is remembered in the book. Van Gelderen was born in 1891 in Amsterdam, a son of a Jewish middle-class family. During his youth he moved in Amsterdam's intellectual socialist circles "in which Marxism in those days," as the book commented, "was only a little less than the Doctrine of the Holy." "From Marx," the book says, "his ways led to Hegel." Van Gelderen, the Festschrift says, did not belong among "the exuberant" professors, and neither was he one of "the adored Masters." Still, "Till his late years, when he spoke about Hegel, and also about Marx, we could hear a reverential and at times a little hurt quivering in his voice."[7]

Professor Bernard J. O. Schrieke was acknowledged as "the first Netherlands sociology scholar of some name."[8] He taught sociology and ethnology at the school. His voice did not appear to quiver. But he was remembered as a pioneer—of "an American type." He "made his students read current books of American anthropology, which he asked his colleagues to translate."[9] He was also remembered as encouraging his students in what became known as an "indocentric tendency."[10] In 1928, when Amir was in his first year, Schrieke's report, commissioned by the government, appeared on "the course of the Communist movement on the West Coast of Sumatra."[11] In 1929, Amir's second year in the school, Schrieke edited and published a book—in English!—*The Effect of Western Influence on Native Civilizations In the Malay Archipelago.*

Five professors, Logemann, van Asbeck, Ter Haar, Kollewijn, and Schepper, were especially recalled in the memorial books. The five men, the authors wrote, were the spiritual center of the school. All of them, in the years to come, also played a role in Amir's life.

Professor A. H. M. J. van Kan taught commercial and civil law of the Indies. Between 1924 and 1929, he was the Law School chair (dean was not used). Van Kan is recalled as making efforts to put the new school "on the European level." He helped to expand the length of the course of study from the initial four years to five years. He also introduced Malay and Javanese as obligatory subjects at the school, reducing, at the same time, the time devoted to Latin; he even made Latin a facultative subject only. The language of instruction, of course, remained Dutch. "As a scholar," says the memorial book, "van Kan had written only a few reviews." However, memorably, "he wrote an essay about the role of property in the comedies of Plautus."[12]

Van Kan had to have a sailor's heart, a heart of an exile, or both. He taught "history of law in the Indies, France, and the Netherlands, legal history of the Dutch East Company, and history of the peace movement."[13] However, the memorial book notes, "increasingly apparent was his preference for the life of Jeanne d'Arc." About her he gathered "more than 1,000 volumes in his library." "I still cannot forget," a memorial book contributor wrote, "the enthralling talk he gave in 1928 on the role of law in her personal tragedy." On this occasion, it is recalled, van Kan "used *Jeanne d'Arc au bûcher* by Paul Claudel, put famously to music by Arthur Honegger."[14] Does it mean that van Kan—in toga?—played Honegger's revolutionary oratorio in the school auditorium on a gramophone? Amir, I imagine—and timing points to it—was present.

Professor J. H. A. Logemann came to the Law School from the government service, and he taught Indies administrative law at the school. Professors Bernard Ter Haar and R. D. Kollewijn previously had a law practice in the Indies. Ter Haar taught *adat*, Indies "customary law," while Kollewijn taught Indies commercial law and social aspects of law. Professor F. M. Baron van Asbeck also used to serve in the Indies, at the General Secretariat of the Governor General. At the Law School he taught international law and colonial law outside the Dutch Indies.[15] Van Asbeck was called "the red baron," both by the students and the faculty, with affection rather than dread.

Professor H. Boeke, another of the men in the togas on the portrait conferred to the governor general, introduced in his lectures on law and economy terms like "auto-activity" among "arising indigenous bourgeoisie."[16] Boeke's ideas of a dual economy would dominate thinking about the colonial question long after the Second World War.

Professor Julius Martin Johannes Schepper (1887–1967) was for Amir, beyond a doubt, the most important. He was appointed with the first group of Law School professors to teach state law, criminology, and philosophy of law.[17] He is not on the group portrait only because he arrived in Batavia a few weeks later.

Schepper was born in Amsterdam in 1887, and so was forty years old when Amir met him at the school for the first time. Schepper came from a strict, "indeed sectarian," community of Dutch Protestant Darbyites, known as Vergadering der Gelovigen, "Community of Believers." The Darbyites, like other fundamentalist groups, understood and tried to live their whole lives strictly and exclusively according to the words of the Bible. The foundations of Schepper's beliefs, in this sense, could not be firmer. At the same time, a contemporary of his remarked later, "it is indeed remarkable, that a sect like the Darbyites, with typically narrow sectarian views, could produce someone like Schepper."[18] Without losing the religious zeal. Schepper's biography reads like a log of a ship on an open sea, or like a travelogue, or a missionary story, or an adventure story, almost but not quite like one of those stories Amir read at the ELS.[19]

Like virtually all his colleagues at the Batavia Law School, Julius Schepper received a doctorate from Leiden University. In 1917, under the supervision of the Dutch Kantian philosopher W. van de Vlugt, he defended a doctoral thesis on "Nieuw-Kantiaansche rechtsbeschouwing," "Neo-Kantian Consideration of Law." Dr. van den End, a historian of Dutch Protestantism with a deep interest in Julius Schepper (and Amir Sjarifoeddin), wrote to me that, "as Immanuel Kant was important to van de Vlugt, and as van de Vlugt was important to Schepper, so Schepper became important to Amir."[20]

In 1918, after he defended his dissertation in Leiden, Schepper became a missionary and boarded a ship to the Indies. Except for a few short trips afterward back to Europe, he remained in the Indies for the next thirty years.

Like his most memorable colleagues at the Batavia Law School, Schepper was a scholar of a particular kind. He produced "forty articles, no magnum opus."[21] In April 1924, when Amir Sjarifoeddin was a student at Haarlem, Schepper was still a missionary. He traveled to Europe on one of his short visits and spoke in the Hague at the Colonial Education Congress. He explained his mission as a Christian and, soon to come, as an educator: "Our aim should be to form, among the grown-up portion of the population, a community of self-standing workers and leaders. . . . Thousands are calling to us to guide them so that they can accomplish their enormous task—to help them, the grown-up peoples of the Indies, to establish their own, autonomous social order and in not-so-distant a future."[22] Schepper explained to the congress that this was a mission in the spirit of "Kant's critical idealism and Hegel's dialectics." He talked about the Batavia Law School already and he called it, long before its time, a "university." He also called the "Indies grown-up population" "the Indonesian peoples." "The Indonesian peoples," he said, of course, "have to pass through the school of Western humanism," however, "not to lose themselves in it, but to find themselves in it."[23] Schepper was critical in a Kantian sense. "There is something in [Kant's] critique," wrote Foucault, "which is akin to virtue."[24]

Like the ELS teachers in Medan or Sibolga, the professors at the Batavia Law School familiarized themselves and their students with a strange, exotic, and potentially threatening land. Like the teachers at the elementary schools, the professors of the Law School found themselves in a between-the-students-and-the-blackboard moment.

Among the most memorable professors at the Batavia Law School connections emerged between teachers and students that often resembled friendship and lasted on both sides for years, and sometimes for life. It tells much about the sailor-like, "in the throw" character of the professors, and the students too. It still was the Indies, of course: the students so attached to the teachers were usually called sons or, as it was a coeducational college, daughters.

Professor Logemann, G. J. Resink recalls, "was generally hiding behind books and writing." But still, "he had many 'children.' They came to his house to debate, to play music and afterwards they stayed to eat." Professor van Asbeck, Resink says, "also received many Indonesian students in his house."[25]

Amir Sjarifoeddin, as he settled in the school, also visited professors at home; Van Asbeck and Kollewijn are named.[26] Already in his first year at the Law School, however, he became known as Schepper's *anak mas*, in Malay literally "golden child," a favorite son. "Amir," writes Resink, "was *anak mas* of Schepper. Another student close to Schepper was Muljanto, later a leader of Masjumi [Islamic party in Indonesia after 1943]. . . . Also Ani Abbas-Manoppo, a female student, who later became a professor at the University of North Sumatra, used to visit the childless Schepper at his home. She was a *putri* [Malay for 'daughter'] visiting her *bapak* [Malay for 'father']."[27]

"I do not believe," a nephew of Schepper later recalled, "that uncle ever spoke good Malay or any Malay except the few words to his house personnel."[28] Still, *anak*, *putri*, or *bapak*, this was what the favored students called Schepper and what Schepper called them back, in a communication; otherwise, of course, purely Dutch. Not exactly "good Uncle Karel" anymore and not really "poor Amats," either. But still the words were borrowed, and still, both Schepper and his students, were borrowed people.

Amir Sjarifoeddin became a visitor, and soon a prominent member, of the circle of Law School students who gathered around Professor Schepper. This was an extension of the school. Selected students were invited to Schepper's house. They read and debated texts Schepper suggested. "Syncretism—nationalism, Christian prophetism/socialism/humanism." "Schepper lived grandly," Resink, one of the participants, recalled, "students sat on Persian carpets, he had a car driven by a private chauffeur, when other lecturers used bicycles."[29]

"The regime was not light," Gerry van Klinken gathered the information from Resink among others: "All were asked to read Rudolf Otto's *The Idea of the Holy* (1923). Like Schepper, Otto began with Immanuel Kant and progressed to Friedrich Schleiermacher's feeling of 'absolute dependency.' They explored Quaker-like silent worship, the 'numinous,' the 'Wholly Other,' the *mysterium tremendum*, the feeling of ultimacy in present history. They debated the German Lutheran theologian Hanns Lilje, and of course the neo-orthodox yet socialist-leaning Karl Barth."[30]

Kant especially, Schepper's hero, was the meetings' star. His maxims were moral, which meant they could become "universally established." They were "a priori," which did not mean "innate," "inherited like the instincts of animals"; they searched for "universal application" and therefore "necessary truth." In the Schepper's house they all recognized "demands of the moral 'ought', the Kant's 'categorical imperative,' moral sense, 'stern and unalloyed with sentimentality', 'I shall, therefore I can.'"[31]

Hanns Lilje was read too. Born in 1899, he was in his youth a general secretary of the German student Christian movement. He "was also a Barthian" (meaning Karl Barth). Lilje's "writings were mostly concerned with the post-Christian secularization process in Europe, to which he attributed the looming apocalypse of war. Lilje was [later] a well-known as a member of Germany's anti-Nazi 'Confessing Church.'"[32]

In Schepper's house, Amir with the others also read Rabindranath Tagore, Mahatma Gandhi, and the Japanese Christian social philosopher and activist Toyohiko Kagawa. "A book almost certainly circulating in the group described him as a prophet, who translates [moral principles] into heroic living."[33] An illegitimate son of a samurai, Kagawa as a young man visited the United States "where the Social Gospel influenced him." Returning to Japan he lived for thirteen years with the poor of Kobe's disease-ridden slums. Kagawa was a pacifist and Saint-Simonian socialist and he helped to found Japan's Labor Party. "He believes in communism," wrote Kagawa's biographer, "but it is the communism of the early Christian church and of Tolstoy, rather than of Karl Marx." Kagawa "rejected institutionalized religion."[34] One can see Amir's philosophy emerging.

Chapter 4

Kramat 106

> Thinking of his adventure, he goes along: doubts fill his heart, he knows not what to believe, dazzled he can't believe that it's the truth.
>
> —Marie de France, quoted in Agamben, *Adventure*, 25

"People's last possibility of experiencing themselves has been cut off by organized culture," wrote Theodore Adorno.[1] "It is the task of the school to educate youth to aspire to the educational ideal," as Robert Musil put it another way.[2]

It was the modern in Europe, progressive, forward looking, as much as in Asia: Amir Sjarifoeddin had to be told innumerable times: "Be good, be diligent—after all you have talent and the right diplomas."[3] Parents especially, wrote Franz Kafka about his Jewish family in Prague, "are afflicted by particular spirit from which children cannot be shielded, this small dirty, lukewarm, squinting spirit."[4]

As far as I know, Amir did not stop over in Sumatra to visit his parents' house on his way from Europe. This felt clearly against the norm, so much so that at least one later author, writing after Amir had become famous, probably invented the visit: "The village in Sipirok on the coast of the island of Sumatra is festooned. Villagers gather to welcome a son of an esteemed family who is coming home from the studies overseas. The house stands up among the others in size as well as in appearance. Since morning, guests come to welcome the young man."[5] The festivities are described and then Amir, after the last guests have gone and he remains alone with his parents (the fact that his father was in prison at the time is unmentioned): "'Mir,' mother now tells her son. 'You distinguished yourself in your studies and you made all the people happy.' 'Alhamdulillah, all praise be to God,' says Amir, and he bows to his mother deeply."[6]

This is how in all probability it did not happen. A letter that Amir possibly wrote to his father after his arrival from Holland and while in Batavia tells another story. His father's sentence had been reduced and he was already out of prison. (In 1929, it seems, he was permitted to work for the government again, but merely in a lowly position of an ordinary clerk.[7]) It seems from the letter that Amir, after arriving back in the Indies, was invited by his father to come home, perhaps to marry a local girl according to custom. "Keep the girl you chose for me," wrote Amir, "and if you really insist to see me in Sumatra, send me a ticket, the first class."[8] The ticket, as far as we know, was never sent, and Amir, as far as we know, did not go.

Probably already in Haarlem, Amir learned that he had been awarded a Dutch Indies government scholarship to study at the Batavia Law School. The scholarship was generous enough that Amir would not have to worry about the cost of living in Batavia or, for that matter, about family support. His cousin Moelia, who helped him in Leiden with the Smink family, had since become a prosperous and respected native in Batavia. He even became a member of the Volksraad, People's Council, a partly elected, partly nominated, quasi-parliament body advising the governor general. In fact, Moelia was the youngest member of the body.

Moelia was also the director of a Batavia teachers' college. He was an influential member of the congregation of the Reformed Church of the Bataks who had migrated from Sumatra to Batavia.[9] Moelia offered Amir to stay in his house in a wealthy, partly European, partly Indonesian neighborhood of Batavia, Meester Cornelis (now Jatinegara). Amir stayed with Moelia for a few weeks but then he chose to live without his family support, sort of, on his own.[10]

He moved to the complex of buildings at Kramat 106, just southeast of the Koningsplein, "King's Square." The Law School was a fifteen-minute bicycle ride away. The complex at Kramat 106 was owned by an Indonesian Chinese, Sia Kong Liong, a dealer in cotton. Sia Kong Liong established a dormitory in the property, primarily for the male indigenous students of the Law School and then for the indigenous students of Batavia's Genees-kundige School, "Medical School," which opened in August 1927, three years after the Law School and a year before Amir arrived from Holland.

The complex at Kramat 106 consisted of a main building and fourteen pavilions.[11] The fee for room and board was between 12½ and 20 guilders, with three meals a day and laundry included.[12] It was not cheap. As Amir himself recalled later, a worker in the kampong, the native quarters of Batavia, might earn 2½ cents on a good day, and 1 cent on a not-so-good one. The students at the dormitory, however, belonged to an Indies world already closer to the light. Amir could easily afford to live at Kramat 106 on his government scholarship: he was guaranteed 1,000 guilders a year, beginning when he arrived on August 1, 1927.[13]

No diary of Amir's survives, and Amir was not an autobiographical writer. A typewritten Indonesian text, with handwritten corrections, less than two pages long, written by Amir sometime shortly after the Second World War (probably in 1945, as this is where its chronology ends), perhaps as talking points for an interview, a document that somehow found its way to Dutch archives, is Amir's only known autobiography. Quite a large amount of space, a whole paragraph on the three-quarter-full second, and last, page, describes Amir leaving Holland and around the time he lived in Kramat: "Already in Holland I learned to appreciate literature and philosophy.... *kunstliteratuur* [Dutch for 'literature on art'], and also sports, like swimming (for one year, I was a junior swimming champion), tennis and soccer. Music, also, I like very much, and I myself play violin. I enjoy drawing. I never liked movies, but for the theater I had a great *sympathie* [Dutch for 'sympathy']."[14]

The students spent nights and much of the days at Kramat 106, whenever they were not in school or did not go "missing on the town." They read newspapers in the dormitory, studied, played billiards, table tennis, chess, or bridge. They debated, made music, sang, and played theater. They might have thought with young Nietzsche: "I cannot sleep on straw and drink common gin [say tea or lemonade rather; it was the Indies] . . . if I am to accomplish the cruelly difficult task of creating in my mind a non-existent world."[15]

Abu Hanifah, one year Amir's senior, was a student at the new Batavia Medical School, one of the Kramat 106 boarders, and soon one of Amir's closest friends. His recollections of Kramat 106 and Amir are lively and often warm. It is difficult to sense in them what would happen between the two men later, when Abu Hanifah became Amir's political opponent and then enemy. "We had the same tastes," Abu Hanifah wrote, "and we both loved music, art and all the good things in life such as fine food and good company."[16] "When we got too tired," Abu Hanifah wrote, meaning tired from studying for school, "about one at night, we collected some money among us to buy coffee plus *sate* [pieces of roasted meat on a skewer] or *sotong* [cuttlefish] at the Senen market. Amir Sjarifoeddin relieved fatigue by taking his violin and playing Schubert or some sentimental serenade. . . . I took my violin, too, and played the same thing."[17]

"Amir Sjarifoeddin," Abu Hanifah wrote, was "one of the brilliant minds of the group."[18] "He was full of emotions, sentimental, he got angry easily but became good again, liked to fight but he was happier when playing violin exuding sadness or joy . . . he resembled a Bohemian, artist, sometimes he behaved like a gypsy."[19]

However much Abu Hanifah might be making light of their lives, they clearly had a dandy time, being young and growing up, privileged and standing on uncertain ground, a swaying deck, so to speak.

Speaking about revolution, and this being about Amir, the future revolutionary, they lived at the edge of it. The dandy, Jean-Paul Sartre wrote in his *Baudelaire*, likes "putting on an act" but, in fact, he smashes "nothing at all."[20] "The ruling class," Sartre wrote, "always preferred a dandy to a revolutionary," believing it "a childish game which adults [watch] indulgently . . . the dandy is déclassé."[21] "What spectacle," Faust might say in the same tone of arrogance, "But alas! the merest show!"[22]

They, indeed, *played* history at Kramat 106, and they *played* revolution. The students divided roles among themselves, and they identified with revolutionary heroes of the past. Often, they called themselves by the heroes' names even "outside of play." They organized theaters and evenings of declamations. Abu Hanifah recalls that Amir identified with Robespierre; Muhammad Yamin, another student, and a politician to be, with Jean-Paul Marat; Asaat as Danton; while he himself, Abu Hanifah, favored Count de Mirabeau.[23]

Robespierre, then. What could Amir declaim? Robespierre, "the long-winded incorruptible man . . . fifteen hundred human creatures, not bound to it, sat quietly under the oratory of Robespierre, nay, listened nightly, hour after hour, applausive, and gasped as for the word of life."[24] Robespierre, "on the extreme left."[25] "That anxious, slight man, under thirty, in spectacles. . . . The son of an Advocate . . . the first-born . . . thoroughly educated . . . in the College of Louis de Grand, at Paris . . . a strict, painful mind."[26]

There is a famous quote from Marx's *Eighteenth Brumaire* that makes one think of Kramat 106 and its students: "they anxiously conjure up the spirits of the past to their service and borrow from them names, battle cries and costumes to present the new scene of world history in this time-honored disguise and this borrowed language."[27]

I would give much to know which of Robespierre's speeches Amir declaimed. Perhaps this, Robespierre's "On the Condition of Free Men of Color" from May 13, 1791: "Faught! Perish your colonies if you are keeping them at that price. Yes, if you, had either to lose your colonies, or to lose your happiness, your glory, your liberty, I would repeat perish your colonies."[28]

Or perhaps "On the Right of Societies and Clubs" from September 29, of the same year: "If I must applaud the ruin of my country, give me any orders you want, and let me perish before the loss of liberty! (Applause, murmur)."[29]

Or the speech to the National Convention, "On the Principles of the Political Morality That Should Guide the National Convention in the Domestic Administration of the Republic," February 5, 1794: "Now, what is the fundamental principle of democratic, or popular government, the essential mainspring that supports it and makes it power? It is virtue. I am talking about the public virtue that worked such prodigies in Greece and Rome, and that should produce far more astonishing ones in republican France; the virtue that is not other than love of the homeland and its laws."[30]

Perhaps Amir declaimed different Robespierre speeches. But I am almost certain that some of them, at least, he learned at the Haarlem Gymnasium. And that, at least sometimes, for the pleasure of the audience and himself, he declaimed them in French.

The Kramat 106 dormitory, writes Gerry van Klinken, "was frequently visited by European missionaries": "The main Catholic visitor was the Jesuit Jan van Rijckevorsel, while the main Protestant was Kees Van Doorn. Amir's contact with the Christen Studenten Vereeniging in Java (CSV, Christian Student Movement) came through Van Doorn as well as through . . . Moelia, who had been a member of the related NCSV in the Netherlands."[31]

Professor Julius Schepper had been a frequent visitor to Kramat 106, too. "Both Van Doorn and Schepper," writes Van Klinken, "were pietistic, highly educated men drawn to the Indies by a mixture of Protestant missionary 'zeal' and ethical sentiment." Relations between Amir and Schepper became even deeper through their meetings at Kramat 106. "Schepper grew quite fond of Amir, perhaps for the intellect they shared, and for the spontaneity Schepper lacked. He saw in Amir the kind of strong personality, the Kierkegaardian 'knight of faith' that he admired more than any political movement."[32]

According to Abu Hanifah, "We several times had as our guest speakers priests of the Catholic church and Protestant ministers—some of us were invited to their homes or clubs for dinner and a talk."[33] "It was strange," Abu Hanifah added, "but Muslim ulamas, religious scholars," in spite of the fact that most of the Kramat 106 students, including Amir, were Muslims, "never came close to us."[34]

Augustine Leonore Fransz, called "Tine," was Amir Sjarifoeddin's colleague at the Law School, one year beneath Amir. She came from a Dutch *blijver* family, which means they had been settled in the Indies for several generations. "Because my parents lived in Semarang [Central Java]," she wrote in her memoirs, "I lived in a dormitory, on Mataram Street, and I biked to my classes at the Law School. Later I moved to Dr. and Mrs. Van Doorn's in the *clubhuis* [clubhouse] of the CSV at Kebon Sirih Street 44." "This was," Tine adds, "where Amir visited often, however he was still a Muslim."[35] Tine also recalled

Professor Schepper: "Among other teachers I well remember Prof. Kollewijn but especially Prof. Schepper who taught criminal law. Once he told us that a colonial state which did not accept a moral responsibility for defending a nation did not have a right to govern the nation. And he said this before the Japanese attacked the Indies and Holland capitulated! . . . If anybody, he had to be considered the true 'Professor-cum-Christian.'" "Every week," Tine Fransz recalled, "in his house, which was not far from Kebon Sirih Street, Professor Schepper hosted a Bible Reading group. Amir Sjarifoeddin with some friends, students whom I also came to know well . . . frequently appeared at the Bible Reading. We dug quite deep in our debates during these sessions. Amir and I became good friends mainly because of these meeting[s] at Prof. Schepper's house. But Amir had been active in other places, too. He was often leading discussions. His mind was very sharp."[36]

Different dates are given in different sources, but it must have been very soon after Amir arrived from Holland that Ferdinand Tambubolon died. Mrs. van de Loosdrecht-Sizoo, Ferdinand's landlady in Oegstgeest, saved two letters that Amir had sent her after they let him know about his friend's death. The first letter is dated June 27, 1928, was sent from Kramat 106, and it appears to be Amir's immediate reaction to the news. The second letter, half a year later, still from the address at Kramat 106, reports to the widow that Amir was very busy with his school exams.[37]

Ferdinand Tambubolon was sick for some time, and he eventually succumbed to viral pneumonia, still a deadly disease at the pre-penicillin time. He was buried at the Oegstgeest cemetery and before he died, as it appears from the letters, he had asked the landlady to send his prayer book to Amir.[38]

As the Indies had followed Amir to Holland before, now Holland followed him to the Indies. The prayer book Ferdinand passed on to Amir, according to some, was by Hanns Lilje, the same German Lutheran priest and missionary whose thoughts had also been discussed at Professor Schepper's house. The walls still opened to other walls, and the carousel height at which Amir traveled, still appeared best for flying.

Abu Hanifah remembers that at the time of Kramat 106 he began to attend lectures, and a whole-semester course at the Batavian branch of the Theosophical Society. Since early in the twentieth century, the Theosophical Society in the Dutch Indies focused especially on the Javanese aristocracy and, through it, on the Javanese cultural movement. "Javanese nobles were considered by Theosophy to be of Aryan kin or descent."[39] Nevertheless, there were not many other choices in Batavia and Abu Hanifah, a Sumatran, and his fellow Sumatran, Amir, joined the group. Abu Hanifah recalls that there was a time when Amir and he went to the Theosophical Society several times a week. "Amir and I," Abu Hanifah adds, "were the most fanatic students."[40]

In his less-than-two-page-long autobiography, Amir Sjarifoeddin writes still about his Kramat 106 years, that "At the second year of study at the Law School, I discovered politics. In 1928, I became a member of Perhimpoenan Peladjar-Peladjar Indonesia [PPPI, "Indonesian Students' Association"] and the editor of the PPPI's magazine '*Indonesia Raja*' ['Great Indonesia']. At the same time, I taught at 'Pergoeroean Rakjat' ['People's University'] which was founded by the PNI [Partai Nasional Indonesia, 'Indonesian National Party']. At that time, I came to know the PNI leadership."[41]

In October 1928, the twenty-one-year-old Amir, as a representative of another youth organization, Jong Batak Bond, "Young Bataks' Union,"[42] was present at the Second Congress of Pemoeda Indonesia, "Indonesian Youth." The first congress of the organization, two years earlier, "was a flop";[43] it did not quite work and had been largely forgotten. The Second Congress, however, to the emerging politics of Indonesia—the still largely imagined land of freedom that would one day replace the colony—was the iconic beginning. And Amir Sjarifoeddin stood out. "The first session (Saturday, October 27, 1928) took place in Gedoeng Pemoeda Katolik (Katholieke Jongelingen Bond) ['House of the Young Catholics' Union'] on the Waterloo Square, next to the Cathedral [and next to the Koningsplein]. The second session (Sunday morning, October 28) met in the movie house 'Oost Java' ['East Java'] in Koningsplein Noord, ["King's Square North"]. The third session convened at Kramat 106."[44]

Reportedly, seven hundred delegates and guests took part. The Gedoeng Pemoeda Katolik and the Oost Java movie house proved to be too small, and for its final, crucial session the congress moved to the main hall of the dormitory at Kramat 106.

> At the third session, the agents of PID [Politiek Inlichten Dienst, colonial political police], became increasingly unable to restrain themselves [sic] and they began to interrupt speakers with an increasing frequency.... Then, something quite unexpected happened. Wage Rudolf Soepratman, a young journalist from *Sin Po* [Batavia Chinese-Malay newspaper], stood up and started to play a song he had composed especially for the occasion. The police who had to see the lyrics in advance, forbade that word *"Merdeka"* ["Freedom"] be sung. Soegondo Djojopoespito, however, who presided over the session, suggested that the song be played without words. So Rudolf Wage played the song on guitar [other sources have "ukulele"] and on violin, while Dolly Salim accompanied him on piano.[45]

In the Special Collections at Leiden University Library, among the papers of Han Resink, two years Amir's junior at the school, there is a sheet of paper with what is clearly Han Resink's handwriting. This had to be written on the spur of the moment, and it looks like an attempt at the translation of the song, for some reason—a dandy-an gesture, too, perhaps—into English. Resink's now-forgotten attempt to transcribe the song that became the anthem of the movement, and, after 1945 of the independent Indonesian state, is, in part, as follows:

Indonesia Raja
Indonesia, our dearest Fatherland,
. . .
Where we all live, where we all stand,
Watching Her with all our love.
Indonesia of our Nationality,
. . .
For Thy Freedom and greatness, we sing.

Refrain:
Indonesia—Indonesia
Beulah and Beulah Land.[46]

First, I thought that I had misread Resink's writing. "Beulah"? But then it dawned on me, it was the Biblical Beulah, Isaiah 62:4, Hebrews, from a prayer to Zion: "Beulah, Lord's Country, My Delight!"

Amir Sjarifoeddin had been elected the treasurer of the Organizing Committee of the congress and, with the rest of the presidium, he had been seated on the podium during the final session, in the *aula* of Kramat 106: "On the concluding day of the Congress, mr. Soenarjo had the word. While he was speaking, Mohammad Yamin, at the presidium table, pushed a small piece of paper to the chair. A few lines to be read at the conclusion of the congress were scribbled on it. Soegondo, the chair, glanced at the paper, he paraphed it and with a smile pushed it back to Yamin. Yamin made his own paraph and moved the paper to Amir. Amir did the same and after him the other members of the presidium."[47]

The few lines, wrote a Dutch historian half a century later, became "the collective mantra of the Indonesian movement making it a reality."[48] "Soempah Pemoeda," "The Oath of the Youth," it came to be known:

We the sons and daughters of Indonesia, acknowledge one motherland, Indonesia.
We the sons and daughters of Indonesia, acknowledge to be of one nation, the nation of Indonesia.

We the sons and daughters of Indonesia, uphold the language of unity, Indonesian.

It was Robespierre declaimed. It was dandy-near to the real.

The sessions of the Indonesian Youth Congress were open to the public. It is hard to imagine that Professor Julius Schepper, or Professor F. M. Baron van Asbeck, or Professor J. H. A. Logemann, perhaps in their morning coats, had not been sitting among the guests; perhaps close to the political police agents whose presence at such meetings was required by law, and who had reserved seats in the front row. The professors might even have stood up with the rest, except the police agents of course, when Wage Rudolf Soepratman and Dolly Salim played their song. They might have experienced the scene, perhaps with some apprehension, as an extension, sort of, of the Law School classroom and the debates in the professors' houses. Han Resink recalled: "It should not be overlooked that the law students played an important if not crucial role in the congress. If nothing else, Soegondo Djojopoespito, a law student, was the chairman of the congress and Amir Sjarifoeddin, Soegondo's schoolmate, was the congress treasurer. Muhammad Yamin, a student at the Law School, too, was the congress secretary. Also, not in the least, on October 28 [the second of the three days of the congress], it was exactly four years since the Law School had been ceremoniously opened."[49]

Chapter 5

Soekarno

> I have been loath to use the word "language." . . .
> A more fitting word? . . . The word "saying."
>
> —Heidegger, *On the Way to Language*, 47

In December 1928, in Jogjakarta, an ancient city in Central Java, a day's train ride from Batavia, the National Conference of the Indonesian Youth was convened as a sequel to the Second Youth Congress. Abu Hanifah went to Jogjakarta as a delegate, but Amir Sjarifoeddin, perhaps because of Law School examinations, remained home.

"It was not so easy," Abu Hanifah wrote in his memoirs, "to have contact with intellectual Indonesian girls of good families." In Jogjakarta, however, there "were more girls attending the conference than boys."[1] At the conference, Abu Hanifah added, gathered "the flowers of the Indonesian youth." When Abu came back to Kramat 106, Amir "could not stop complaining that he could not go to Jogja. I stopped him taking my violin and playing the melody of the German students' song: 'I have lost my heart at Heidelberg.'"[2]

In 1929, the Great Depression hit the modern world and in its exotic periphery, like the Dutch Indies, it hit with a particular severity.

Amir and his friends still lived in a space where only echoes of the new and brutal misery of the world and colony could be heard. They still had ways largely to bypass the native kampongs of Batavia where the strain of life was flagrant and inescapable. On August 1, 1931, Amir's scholarship was reduced from 1,000 to 700 guilders a year.[3]

Migration to big centers, 1930

	ORIGINALLY OF THE PLACE	COMING FROM ELSEWHERE
Batavia	15.95%	84.05%
Bandoeng	31.82%	68.18%
Djokjakarta	55.09%	44.91%
Soerakarta	68.18%	31.82%
Soerabaja	15.92%	84.08%[1]

[1] *De sociale en geographische herkomst*, 16.

Batavia and other Indies cities swelled with people escaping villages, and escaping plantations especially, where the products for export—coffee, tea, or sugar—became worthless and where all the possibilities to make even the barest living disappeared.

Amir continued to teach at the Pergoeroean Rakjat, "People's University," and in 1931 he became the school director. The People's University had been housed in an old warehouse in a side alley, Kenari II / 15. Adjacent to the People's University was the Gedoeng Permoefakatan, "House of Deliberation," where many Indonesian public meetings took place.[4] The People's University was actually a series of evening courses at a high school level. To the teachers' great satisfaction, people from the kampongs also came. One of Amir's co-teachers at the school recalled, "Amir Sjarifoeddin stood out among us by excellent knowledge of eight languages [sic] and as he produced two plays. One was called 'No News from the Western Front' and it attracted large crowds by its realistic stage effects. The other play was written by Armijn Pane and it took place in Sunda [Western Java]."[5] A recollection also mentions Amir at the school teaching French.[6] It was a moment dandy-near to the national awakening of the Amats, "the darker ones" of the Dutch-Indies primary school books, "the borrowed ones." The Kramat 106 people, the Second Congress of Indonesian Youth, Amir, and Abu Hanifah, all were a part of a wave and "Soekarno" was the name that by many the wave was to be called.

In 1927, a new Partai Nasional Indonesia (PNI), "Indonesian National Party," had been founded by twenty-seven-year-old Javanese intellectual and orator Soekarno. In a few weeks, the party and Soekarno rose and rode high on an unexpectedly high tide of popularity and mass excitement, on what to many appeared as power.

"Proud and all-knowing," wrote Soekarno's biographer Bernhard Dahm, "this was Sukarno toward the end of 1928."[7] In his autobiography Amir mentions that also the People's University "was founded by PNI."[8]

In May 1928, a reporter for the Indonesian newspaper *Pemberita Kemadjoean*, "News of Progress," wrote that at the PNI meetings, "he had been so carried away by Sukarno's imagery that he believed he himself was already *merdeka*, 'free.'"[9] There were indeed prophecies heard of an impending end of the "three hundred years" of Dutch colonial rule. The end would come, the prophecies had it, on the last day of the decade, on December 31, 1929. The Indonesian people, under Soekarno, would take over and be *merdeka*.

On December 29, 1929, Soekarno and handful of his principal associates were arrested and, as Bernhard Dahm writes, "the entire [Soekarno's and PNI's] power structure was shown to be an illusion."[10] Soekarno and three of his top associates were imprisoned and put on trial on August 18, 1930. The colonial court proceeding's aim was indeed, "to indicate that Partai Nasional Indonesia had actually planned an uprising." In December 1930, Soekarno was sentenced to four years in prison, and his three codefendants to a shorter prison term.[11]

Abu Hanifah recalled in his memoirs a chance encounter he and Amir had with Soekarno before the arrests, sometime in 1928 or 1929, on a train between Bandoeng and Batavia. Soekarno happened to travel in the same carriage, he saw Amir and Abu Hanifah, two promising young men of the movement, and he invited them to his compartment. Inggit, Soekarno's wife, traveled with her husband. "She wore a very dark red rose in her blue-black hair," Abu Hanifah recalls (his Indonesian was translated by an Australian editor of the memoirs, and it shows): "and she really looked smashing. . . . She did not seem too much impressed with us, and compared with Soekarno, we were just badly dressed youngsters. He was dressed in the shantung silk and snow-white shirt and dark blue tie. His black shoes shone, and he wore his *pitji* [rimless black velvet cap, a symbol of the movement] rakishly on his head. Indeed, our clothes were a little wrinkled, we had no ties, only sports shirts and our hair was ruffled."[12]

Soekarno was only six years older than Amir and five years older than Abu Hanifah. But he seemed to offer a very different possibility of a hero. "When I was born," Soekarno told a US journalist toward the end of his life, "Mount Kelud, the nearby volcano, erupted. Superstitious folk prophesied, 'This is a welcome greeting to baby Sukarno.'"[13]

Soekarno's father was a *kweekschool*, "teachers' college," teacher, of a position and an ambition strong enough to send his son to the best school there was, the ELS in the Javanese port city of Soerabaja, the Medan of Java of sorts, the same type of school Amir attended just a few years later: the same language, the same primers, textbooks, and songbooks, the same poor Amats and the same good Uncles Karels. The same wall charts.

Soekarno proved to be brilliant and lucky enough to be accepted at the age of fifteen to the Soerabaja Hoogeburgerschool (HBS), "Higher Burgher School," an elite Dutch-language secondary school in the Indies; not in the Netherlands, and not a Gymnasium, yet still elite and prestigious. According to official statistics, in 1920 only seventy-eight Indonesian students graduated from HBS schools in the whole colony.[14]

In July 1921, Soekarno graduated from the HBS and became again one of the first of the Indies natives to be admitted to the new Technische Hoogeschool (THS), "Technological Institute," opened in 1920 in Bandoeng, under a motto since often repeated, "In Harmonia Progressio." Soekarno enrolled at the THS in the school's second school year as one of the six indigenous students in the class of thirty-seven. He graduated in 1926 with a civil engineering degree, and therefore since then there has always been *ir.* in front of his name.[15]

The complex of the Technological Institute in Bandoeng, like that of Amir's Law School in Batavia, was the modern embodied. It was built "in the Indies style" by a Dutch architect—in a "traditional-Sumatran style" on the island of Java!—to say it in another way, in a sailor's style. Like Amir's Law School, Soekarno's Technological Institute had been conceived as a pivot from which "harmony and progress" would radiate through the colony.

Soekarno was a brilliant student and several of his student technical drawings—of bridges—were exhibited on the walls of the school as models of good engineering for other students, Dutch as well as Indonesian. The drawings, I was told, remained hanging in the halls, even after Soekarno went to prison in 1931.[16] Wall charts, sort of.

Soekarno's mother tongue is as difficult to be sure about as Amir's. Soekarno's mother was Balinese, of royal blood (Soekarno insisted) yet she lived her whole life in Java and at home with her family she had no choice but to speak either Dutch or Javanese. Soekarno's father was Javanese but most likely, with his education, he spoke Dutch to his son or tried to speak as much Dutch as he could. A situation not much different from Amir's, it seems. Unlike Amir, however, Soekarno never got a chance to study abroad, to sail across the winedark sea, to hear an echo of Sophocles in Utrecht. In fact, until the Second World War, Soekarno never left the Indies; as far as I know, he never spent any significant time away from Java.

Until Soekarno, at the age of twenty-one years, moved to Bandoeng, West Java, where Sundanese was spoken rather than Javanese, he spent all his time in the east and central provincial towns of the island, in Sidoardjo, Blitar, and Modjokerto, following his father, and then in Soerabaja. In these cities were Javanese and Javanese-speaking common people, the population. One did not buy a cigarette, a train ticket, or a snack at the stall on the street without asking for it in Javanese. Among his educated consociates, too, whenever he happened to struggle with Dutch, in contrast to Amir Sjarifoeddin, Soekarno had Javanese to fall upon.

Soekarno's Dutch never got the harsh bruising and gentle stroking that Amir's Dutch did—that struggling through and pleasuring through, with not much to fall upon, certainly in Leiden, Haarlem, Amsterdam, and Arnhem, among the educated as well at the shops and the railway stations. Soekarno never got Amir's speaking and listening against and with the multiple Dutch accents, dialects, and jargons, the lazy Dutch, the intimate, the bad, the angry, the sensual, and the literary Dutch, in drawing room, movie house, and classroom, when teacher was in, and when teacher was not, the Dutch rubbing against and making love to French, German, English, and also Latin and Greek. Soekarno's Dutch, to use Abu Hanifah's term (or perhaps of his Australian editor's?) was not "ruffled."

Among acts of "political courage," Michel Foucault emphasized "the mastery of oneself and of one's language." He has this in his essay fittingly called "For an Ethics of Discomfort."[17]

Soekarno's Dutch was more "nationalist"—anxious, acutely self-conscious of being conceived in and by the foreign, among native Dutch speakers listening for a native accent as an unforced error. Han Resink once tried to explain to me the language space given to "an educated native" in the modern colony. Looking for the right word, he said it was "Dutch-Dutch."[18]

Mohammad Bondan, a young man who would become an ally of Soekarno later in his life, recalled that as he was passing through the Javanese city of Tjirebon in the 1920s, he saw a leaflet lying on the street. Thinking it was an advertisement for the local cinema he picked it and read: "It was not at all what he had thought. It was not an advertisement for the cinema at all, but a notice about a public meeting. Bondan said it struck him immediately as rather odd and 'Dutchy.' Dutch words converted to Indonesian were scattered here and there when the writer had been unable to find an Indonesian word to suit his meaning."[19] This was what Bondan found funny then and later, and what Soekarno tried to avoid at all costs. He spoke Indonesian-Indonesian.

Soekarno, in fact, might have been more borrowed than Amir Sjarifoeddin. He avoided ruffled language, and the more well-tailored his language became, the more, to use Jean-Luc Nancy's phrasing, it became "enclosed within a homogeneity."[20] Such language, wrote Yuri Tynianov about Russian of the same time, finds refuge in "smothered-over words," like "revolution," for instance. Tynianov wrote: "the words used as the 'name of a name,' the words spelled with a capital letter: Motherland, Revolution, Insurrection. . . . It is the absence of specific meaning that leaves room for the emotional shading that surrounds the words beyond concrete meaning."[21]

CHAPTER 5

The more the deck might have been uncertain under Soekarno, the more he clung to what he believed was an anchor. And, as he had been taught in the Dutch schools, he clung to tradition.

Soekarno spoke in "names of the names"; his were images on a classroom wall: "Golden Java" like "The Conquest of Tjakranegara in Lombok, 1874." "Gamelan of Indonesia," Soekarno said in 1928 about traditional Javanese gong orchestra, "sounds and talks to you in all the homes of the land. It sings the unity, during the holy days, under the full moon with the air full of the intoxicating scent of flowers in full bloom."[22] This is, he wrote at the same time, "the deepest inner harmony [*harmoni sedalam-dalamnja*]!"[23] Soekarno, when he spoke, took care that a moment never happens like that when Toenggoel, my Batak friend, set up a camera on the tripod, and the ancient monument crumbled.

Already the first steps Soekarno made into the limelight of the Indonesian movement signaled the kind of character he would like to play. At the Young Java conference of 1921, when he was twenty, "Sukarno acquired the name of Bima,"[24] a wayang hero, one of the five Pandawa brothers of the Indian *Mahabharata* epics adopted into the Javanese traditional shadow-puppet theater. Already at that early moment, Soekarno proclaimed, as an imperative for himself, for the movement, and for the nation, "Javanese maxim: 'all things are one.'"[25]

This was to be a kind of rebellion. Bima was the one among the Pandawa brothers who dared to address even gods in *ngoko*, the lower register of the hierarchical Javanese language. "Sukarno addressed a meeting of *Jong Java* in *ngoko*, low Javanese, causing uproar."[26] The line was not to be doubted. Pure Java, expanded into a pure Indonesia, *sini*, "us," in "deepest harmony," against *sana*, "them"—the Dutch. Black and white, we the dark, they the white. "The Europeans," Soekarno declared in 1926, "came here only to fill their rumbling bellies."[27] In a speech in December 1927, Soekarno called on the Indonesian movement to unite as a "Brown Front'" against the "White Front."[28]

Soekarno became famous by naming names: Gandhi, Jefferson, Marx (their enumeration supported his argument); Ernst Renan, the "desire d'être ensemble"; Otto Bauer, "it is the very first duty of the working class in Asia to work for national autonomy."[29] The man who told me how Soekarno's technical drawings were exhibited in the Institute of Technology in Bandoeng even after Soekarno went to prison, told me also about the textbooks in the institute library in which he discovered Soekarno's markings. He found words and phrases underlined in the texts on civil engineering, like "bridges," "torsion," "mass," which were then used in his speeches on movement and unity.[30]

Soekarno's world was held compact, dense, thick, close packed, slurred over, by a mythical sense of nation, much of it based on the Dutch modern,

Western, and colonial schools' curriculum. Indonesian nationalism, Soekarno was saying, "is not a copy or imitation of Western nationalism, but nationalists receive their nationalist feeling as a divine inspiration (*wahju*) and express it as an act of devotion (*bhakti*)."[31]

Soekarno was modern, meaning colonial and meaning "indigenous." Java, and by extension Indonesia, was to him what Marc Augé calls an anthropological place.[32]

"Ethnological linkage," says Maurice Blanchot, "appears to promise us the security of a native habitat. It is the hiding place of . . . homelessness."[33]

It was often noted that Soekarno built his "wholesome oratory"[34] in the likeness of the *dalang*, the wayang (shadow-theater) puppeteer. In the wayang performance the *dalang* speaks all the voices: the servants, the knights, the heroes, as well as the demons, and the gods. The *dalang*, with his voice and how he moves the puppets, gives all the actors in the drama their characters and, at the same time, he conducts the gamelan orchestra. Sitting in front of the screen with the orchestra behind him, he sets the rhythm, and signals changes in mood and pauses, by tapping toes and a heel of his foot or beating a little bronze mallet against the box where the puppets momentarily not at play are stored.

Soekarno became one with "his deep baritone." He was said to be able to bring his listeners into the midst of the world of heroes. A victory in battle and eventually freedom, in wayang and at the public meetings where Soekarno spoke, tasted, to use the words of Jean-Luc Nancy again, of "ontological dolorousness."[35]

In the weeks after its four top leaders, including Soekarno, were sent to prison, the Indonesian National Party "voluntarily" dissolved itself. Like the Batak tomb to be filmed, suddenly, wondrously, unbelievably, it crumbled down. In haste, on April 29, 1931, a new party had been established, Partai Indonesia, or Partindo, the "Indonesian Party." It declared itself to be the heir to Soekarno and his PNI but, without Soekarno, it was a new entity, looking for a new way.

In 1930, the same year that Soekarno went to prison, Amir Sjarifoeddin, suddenly, wondrously, became a vice-president of the most influential Batavia branch of the new party. As he wrote in his autobiography, "I became a propagandist and traveled around the whole island of Java."[36]

He was still a student at the Law School yet was already mentioned as one of the "two young men" who were Partindo's "young flames." The other was Mohammad Yamin, also still a student at the Law School and Amir's friend and co-resident at the Kramat 106 dormitory. It might be a new stage of dandyism. "The idealism of these young activists," writes Gerry van Klinken about Amir and Yamin, "strikes the observer as almost religious."[37] Perhaps "religious" does not express the new aspect completely. Another contemporary describes Amir and Yamin attending meetings of Indonesian groups they deemed not radical enough, "for the single purpose of heckling the speakers."[38]

Two men of the Soekarno generation, *mr.* Sartono and *mr.* Ali Sastroamidjojo, both lawyers, were still formally listed at the head of Partindo. But "young leaders such as Amir Sjarifoeddin and Mohammad Yamin rapidly appeared in influential positions."[39] On November 7 and 8, 1931, Partindo held a conference in the Central Javanese city of Jogjakarta, and the local police reported "The central committee . . . consists of *mr.* Sartono as chairman, *mr.* Ali Sastroamidjojo as vice-chairman . . . the newly established commission for education elected Amir Sjarifoeddin as . . . chairman."[40] A young activist of Partindo in Sumatra, Adam Malik, later recalled: "In 1932, two members of the central leadership in Batavia visited East Sumatra on a speech tour. They were Mohammad Yamin and Amir Sjarifoeddin. They explained to us that after the PNI of Soekarno had been dissolved, we had a duty to carry on the national struggle through Partindo."[41]

With Soekarno in prison, much of the mysticism of the "smothered-over words," like "freedom" or "revolution," of the "anthropological place," of "the deepest inner harmony," of "us against them," was gone.[42] Yet Partindo was still able to attract large numbers of people, including those from the kampongs, ricksha drivers, unemployed and day workers, and even peasants, as well as students and clerks. And they appeared to be coming to the public party meetings for different nutrients.

At one such Partindo public meeting in Batavia, in March 1932, an Indonesian journalist reported, "after reading messages from the party branches to the central committee, Amir Sjarifoeddin of Batavia spoke about democracy and the right of self-determination."[43] Partindo, the government's adviser for Indigenous affairs reported in the same year, "held several well-attended public meetings in Batavia. . . . At a meeting which took place on April 24, 1932, a decision of the U.S. Congress was discussed that would grant the Philippines self-determination in 1940. It had been praised as an act of application of democratic and non-racist principles in US education and government policies. A contrast had been pointed out with the situation in Indonesia."[44] About another Partindo meeting of the time, a government observer reported that "the chairman (Amir Sjarifoeddin) ended the meeting with words '*Tot weerzien in Indonesia Merdeka*' ['See you in free Indonesia']." "Literally he said," the agent added, seeming a little confused, "*Auf Wiedersehen* in Indonesia Merdeka."[45]

The first Partindo congress took place in Batavia, between Saturday, May 14, and Tuesday, May 17, 1932. It was attended by some 2,500 people. "Fervor and irreconcilable attitude," a government agent reported, "permeated the sessions."⁴⁶ Mohammad Yamin was put in charge of the whole party's propaganda and Amir in charge of the whole party's education policy. Education in a broad sense. According to the agent,

> Amir Sjarifoeddin, a student at the Law School and one of the leaders of the Indonesian Students Association, spoke about the "shady character of imperialism." He said that "the expansive imperialist policies of the Western powers are rooted in the capitalist system," that "imperialism is a parasitism, which means living at the expense of the others. It works against the freedoms of the peoples. It brings the Eastern peoples down with all kinds of nice phrases, masking its deeds as spreading of religious teaching and helping the population through blessings of education and civilization. All what the peoples are getting, however, are only leftovers from the table."⁴⁷

In September 1932, Amir spoke to another public meeting of Partindo, and the government agent observed: "The last speaker deserves attention, Amir Sjarifoeddin, a Batak student who expects to pass soon his doctoral examinations. This young man is a talented speaker. He formulates his ideas well and he clearly studies his subject before he speaks of it. He grasps the public by the power of his revolutionary temperament, and he can bring his listeners into a state of excitement."⁴⁸

Soekarno was released from prison on December 31, 1931. The governor general, whose term of power was ending, wanted to show some leniency, and Soekarno reportedly behaved well in prison.⁴⁹ The prisoner's sentence was cut in half.

Soekarno was warmly welcomed by the leaders of the new party, and Amir was present. One of the other Partindo leaders, *mr.* Ali Sastroamidjojo, recalled: "I arrived in Bandung at the end of December 1931, on the day before Sukarno was released. Party friends such as Sartono, Anwari, Mohammad Yamin and Amir Sjarifoeddin were already in Bandung. Mohammad Husni Thamrin also was there. At about 8 a.m. we went in procession by cars to Soekamiskin prison. Thamrin's car, in which Sartono and *Ibu* [Mrs.] Inggit were passengers, led the procession."⁵⁰

Soekarno, however, was clearly weakened, physically, but even more by rumors, which soon proved to be true. It was whispered that his conduct in prison was less than courageous. The whispers had it that he made a deal with the government.

Still, from the moment he stepped out of prison the welcome he got was that of a hero who accomplished something. The Indonesia Raja, "Great Indonesia," congress in Surabaya, at the beginning of 1932, was the first event in which Soekarno took part after his release. He spoke at the congress in his old style. He compared himself to Kokrosono, the mythical wayang knight, "legitimate heir to the land of Mandura, ruled by the demon Kongso." As the wayang story goes, Kokrosono "reappears out of the life of hermit," and with the help of "the miraculous weapon Nanggala," wins back the kingdom.[51]

This was Soekarno's reappearance. "The most rousing speech at the congress, however," the government observer reported, "was delivered by Amir Sjarifoeddin. . . . He had to be stopped midway through his speech and led from the platform by the local police because he described radicalism as an audacity to uproot a tree, root and branch. The speech was provocative by being suggestive, although the speaker also openly and sharply attacked the harshness with which land is grabbed from the peasants, and how taxes since the outbreak of the depression affects the masses. This only added to arousing the police reaction."[52] "In the fire of his speech," the agent reported, "Amir Sjarifoeddin even let it to be known that during the closed session of the congress they had talked about 'a parliament of the future *Republik Indonesia.*'" (The last two words in the Dutch report are emphasized and in Indonesian.) "After Amir's speech," the agent added, the congress listened to "an academically delivered lecture by *ir.* Soekarno."[53]

The new party's permanent committee was elected at the congress. Soekarno was welcomed to the new party and became its new president.[54] Sartono, Soekarno's colleague from PNI times, was the first vice-president. Amir Sjarifoeddin was elected the party's second vice-president, with a special responsibility for national schools.[55] "Overall," writes historian John Ingleson, the new leadership of Partindo, centered around the Batavia section, and "continued more or less to restrict Sukarno's influence to the confines of Bandung."[56]

Late in 1933, Indonesian paper *Bintang Timoer*, "Eastern Star," reported that Soekarno might be thinking about leaving the party. A respected Indonesian writer and activist, Sanoesi Pane, wrote to the paper that he saw Soekarno during their meeting "in a moral state which might lead him to become a cooperator with the government. He seems to be just a step from it." Sanoesi Pane met Soekarno at Malabar, a hill resort south of Bandung. "[Soekarno] expressed doubts about the inner strength of the Indonesian people." They talked as they walked in a garden of a local mystic: "What great works did we accomplish?" asked Soekarno: "Where are our grand images of Buddha? Our Angkor Wats? . . . Our Homers? Our Dantes? . . . It will take a long time before we may ever be able to build up a national movement of some meaning; before we may be worthy of freedom."[57] On November 24, 1933, the Partindo executive committee announced: "Soekarno's resignation from Partindo . . .

is a saddening event. We are disappointed and cannot but to express our disappointment as strongly as possible."[58]

It was not a good time for Soekarno. The new governor general of the Indies evidently concluded that his predecessor was too soft on Soekarno. "On the night of August 1. 1933, after having been free for exactly nineteen months, Soekarno was again arrested. From the beginning there was no doubt that this time exile was in store for him."[59]

It was not the terrifying Boven Digoel camp, far in the jungles of New Guinea, where the Communists attempting a rebellion in 1926–1927 were being held, "the hell of Digoel," "the phantom of Digoel."[60] Soekarno, academically educated, of other stuff, was early in 1934 put on board a steamship and sent to Endeh, a little town on the south coast of Flores, one of the Lesser Sunda Islands midway, in fact, between Batavia and New Guinea. Inggit, Soekarno's wife, her mother, and Ratna Djoeami, her niece, were allowed to accompany Soekarno.[61] While in Endeh, Soekarno was to be free to move around the area and to participate in local life, whatever life there was: a local theater company, several Dutch missionaries, several mosque officials.

On November 20, 1933, four months after Soekarno was gone, a new central committee of Partindo was elected. Soekarno's name was missing; mr. Sartono was now the chairman and Amir the first vice-chairmen.[62] In January 1934, *Bintang Timoer* wrote, "Now, mr. Sartono tries his luck by placing the movement in the hands of youngsters, people of ebullience, smart, and talented but without experience. In the central committee of Partindo, students are ascending and about to play a significant role. We mean Mohammad Yamin and Amir Sjarifoeddin."[63]

Part Two

Saying

Chapter 6

Sleep, Baby, Sleep I

> Sleep, baby, sleep—
> Outside there walks a sheep.
> A sheep with white feet,
>
> —Dutch lullaby

It seems that the first newspaper article by Amir Sjarifoeddin was published in January 1928. He had to have written it in the first months after he arrived in Batavia from the Netherlands. The article appeared in the student magazine of the Haarlem City Gymnasium, *Mirabele Lectu*, "Amazing Read."

The Race-Problem in the Netherlands Indies

The question of race is no question. . . . Especially in a country like the Indies where so many races live together, . . . the Eurasian for whom the Indies is the *patria*, or the Chinese who feel Chinese first. . . . It is for the present generation to face it.

And God forbid that someone from the Haarlem City Gymnasium arrives to the Indies with a feeling that he or she belongs to a "superior race." . . . Down with the Kipling's "East is East, and West is West, and never the twain shall meet."

Weltevreden [Batavia], January 1928, Amir Sjarifoeddin.

The editors of the *Mirabele Lectu* placed Amir's article on the title page and they added a comment: "*Ed*: Our heartfelt thanks to Amir. It appears that he has not forgotten the school."[1]

CHAPTER 6

Amir discovered politics or politics discovered him, first of all, as a gifted orator. In "saying," to follow Heidegger, there emerged Amir's "publicness of being." In "saying" he moved, "from a contemplative to an active life."[2] He tested a "possibility of saying."[3]

Like Soekarno's speeches at the height of his fame, virtually all Amir's public speeches after he came from the Netherlands were in Indonesian. Unlike Soekarno, however, if only because he was Sumatran and the crucial events, and thus speeches of the movement were happening in Java, Amir did not have much of a possibility of falling back on a language of origin to evoke anthropological place, as did Soekarno. Amir could not fall on Batak when Indonesian failed him or when his speech reached a certain emotional height. Soekarno could and did fall back on Javanese, easily, effectively, and often.

Both Amir and Soekarno were acutely aware as they spoke to the people that their audience's capacity to understand Dutch and even Indonesian varied. Some did not understand Dutch at all and most understood Indonesian in the untamed and uncorrected Malay form of market language or as a purely utilitarian lingua franca. It would be politically unwise, suicidal even, to fall upon Dutch when Indonesian failed them, though both Soekarno and Amir spoke Dutch in their everyday life, with friends, almost always when not on the podium or in public.

Dutch was a part of the two men, and of most of the schooled people of the colony and of the movement, a crucial part of their being modern. In public and on the podium, Dutch remained unspoken, a murmur, an accent, basso continuo. Still, there was a difference. For Soekarno, there was a glass wall. Dutch was *sana*, "they," and in public speaking it was to be avoided as saying most carefully and on principle. All echoes of it had to be kept under control.

Amir's, in language like in other things, was a journey along and through the sites, with moments of lingering when every moment could be a new beginning or a question about the past. Amir spoke in "saying," "languages . . . their passages from land to land, landscapes, worlds that are the world, worlds that are a world."[4]

Both men translated. Soekarno used foreign quotations profusely and his speeches were full of authoritative names. He "took them home." They had to fit, and if they did not, they were made to. Amir's translation rather was of the kind that "finds itself not in the center of the language forest but on the outside facing the wooded ridge; it calls into it without entering, aiming at that single spot where the echo is able to give, in its own language, the reverberation of the work in the alien one."[5]

There is always, in modern times, a sense of something frivolous about newspapers. Nietzsche wrote with contempt about newspapers: "this viscous stratum of communication which cements the seams between all forms of life, all classes, all arts and all sciences and which is as firm and reliable as the newspaper is, as a rule."[6] Goethe would leave a newspaper as it came, lying around for a few days before he read it. He let it lie in hope that it might mature and settle into something more respectable and less vibrating with the everyday.[7]

The newspapers of the Indonesian movement of the 1920s and early 1930s were more modern than most contemporary newspapers. They strongly resembled the Russian revolutionary newspapers of their time, in writing as saying, to use Bertolt Brecht's term, in their "gestic language."[8] Benjamin, who visited Moscow in 1927, recorded his impression: "In today's Russia, reading is more important than writing, reading newspapers is more important than reading books, and laboriously spelling out the words is more important than reading newspapers. . . . If Russian literature is what it ought to be, its best products can only be *the colored illustrations in the primer* from which peasants learn to read in the shadow of Lenin."[9]

The newspapers of the Indonesian movement in the Indies of the 1920s and 1930s were short lived and transient like a spoken word. They appeared as one might rise on a podium and give a speech at a public meeting. Most of them came out in a burst of enthusiasm, or as money somewhere somehow unexpectedly became available. Then, as a speaker might finish a speech and step down to applause or booing, or as the police might cut a speaker off in the middle of a speech, after money ran out or enthusiasm dwindled, after a few issues and often just after one issue, a newspaper closed.

Therefore, the newspapers were lively. They happened at a very particular place and at a very particular moment, out of a very particular situation only. They might have a few readers or unexplainably many, but they always remained close to their readers, intimate. The newspapers, the magazines, and the single-page sheets spoke with an accent, they stammered, and they echoed their readers. They were their readers in translation. Like in Russia in the early years of the revolution, so in the Indies, they were often read aloud to those not schooled enough to read them themselves. Sometimes even a newspaper's typesetter was not able to read correctly what he was typesetting. They, too, were "laboriously spelling out the words." For many of the writers themselves the written Malay-Indonesian language was new and most of them, too, learned it as they wrote—and they fell back on whatever language of home they could.

After Soekarno disappeared, for all intents and purposes into exile in Endeh, the few relatively professional and established newspapers and magazines he had managed to bring to life in his glorious years, closed or lost their shine. Instead, small, ephemeral, and amateurish newspapers, often student ones, entered—bawled into—a space that would otherwise stay hushed. This was the moment when Amir Sjarifoeddin's star as a journalist rose.

Already in 1928, still in his second year at the Law School and as a resident at the Kramat 106 student dormitory, at the height of Soekarno's era, Amir became the chief editor of *Indonesia Raja*, "Great Indonesia," a bulletin as it described itself, an organ of the Perhimpeonan Peladjar-Peladjar Indonesia (PPPI), "Indonesian Students Union."[10] Still three years later, in the volume of 1930–1931, Amir was listed as the chief editor, and, in the following few issues, as a "collaborator." A large part of the bulletin was filled by Amir's articles, some of them signed, others by what was clearly his chiffre, and still some unsigned but easily identified as his by his increasingly distinct style or, better, "accent."

Indonesia Raja was very much a student paper, still with a strong feel of the dormitory and the school about it. There were clear dandy echoes, too, but virtually nothing of Soekarno's golden and glorious rootedness, or his anxious elegance.

There was, in *Indonesia Raja*, no Soekarno's "Indonesian-Indonesian." There was rather struggling and pleasuring through languages—Indonesian mostly, but there was also unashamedly, nonchalantly, quite a lot of Dutch, and even occasional "falling back on" Latin, Italian, German, or Russian. It gave the bulletin much of its flavor. The articles, feuilletons, letters to the editors, causeries, and poems were published, so it seemed, as they flowed by, caught by ear. Some were in Dutch, as the author might feel more comfortable in that language, even just at the moment. Some contributions were more schooled, and some less. Completely unschooled Malay, like Latin, was often left in.

Indonesia Raja, no. 3–4, 2nd year, January–April 1930

This in Indonesian:

> Our administration is now located at Kembang Alley, Weltevreden [Batavia].
> *News from the redaction*:
> Brothers and sisters, members of the PPPI. Gently but urgently: please, use the upcoming vacations and do write. An article, a poem, whatever. Don't let the July issue of our bulletin be late!

Indonesia Raja, no. 5–5, 2nd year, June–August 1930

This in Dutch:

> Are we *"onverzoenlijken"*?

(The Dutch word *onverzoenlijken* means "irreconcilable." It was a term notorious at the time, used by the government to describe the Indonesian Communists who had attempted a rebellion three years before. Many of them had been "isolated" in the Boven Digoel camp in New Guinea.)

Indonesia Raja, no. 8–9, 2nd year, October–November 1930

This in Indonesian:

> Our administration moved to Oengaran street no. 17, pavilion (back in the garden). Weltevreden [Batavia]

This in Dutch:

> The PPPI members gathering will take place on November 9.

This in Indonesian and emphasized:

> *The illegal pawnshops bring suffering to the common people.*

This in Indonesian:

> PEOPLE'S UNIVERSITY, Volksuniversiteit, Kenari alley no. 15, tel. 1076, Weltevreden [Batavia]
> Do become a student of the People's University! Everything that might be wished for, you will learn: languages, general knowledge—
> Each Tuesday and Thursday special lectures.
> For more information visit our administration.
> Open every day:
> > Morning from 8 to 1 p.m.
> > Afternoon from 5 to 8 p.m.

Indonesia Raja, no. 10, 2nd year, December 1930

This in Dutch:

> Dodo, telephone 500, Senen market 167, Weltevreden [Batavia]
> WE SUPPLY ALL TENNIS ARTICLES

This in Dutch, too, signed "S," meaning Sjarifoeddin

> *The Indies Milieu and Its Impact on European Youth*
> Not entirely correctly, as it is typical for, the [Dutch magazine in the Indies] Rijkseenheid ["Empire Union"], it decided to engage in comparing races. . . . It is peddling again the infantile argument that

in the Indonesian youth, sexuality dominates all the other impulses. It is an idea worthy of a cheap florist.... I [wrote Amir] spent several years in a high school in the Netherlands, and can attest that one meets excesses over there like here.... To build up an argument the way the *Rijkseenheid* does is an example of a policy tricks to keep the masses dumb.... These are quasi-Western theories,... arrogant and self-deceiving.[11]

Indonesia Raja, no. 4–5, 3rd year, July–August 1931

This in uncorrected street Malay:

> COIFFEUR DANIE. *Tengah Alley no. 43 Weltevreden* [Batavia]
> Informing: I do not exaggerate!
> The most esteemed gentlemen! This is a sensational chance.
> In my establishment you can buy a coupon for the price of only 1.20 guilders—and get three haircuts!... Peace be with you.... DANIE

Indonesia Raja, no. 7, 3rd year, October 1931

This in Dutch, signed "S":

> *Colonial Exposition in Paris.*
> With a military display, fanfares, pomp and grandeur, the cosmopolitan Paris in full force paraded as the Colonial Exhibition opened.... Champagne bubbled; girls showed bare shoulders ... all dernier cri.... Men in proper attire, some saber-rattling, even spur-clanking.... *Mission civilisatrice* ... exotic ... lyrical ... pharisaical ... *shocking!*

(The word *"shocking"* is emphasized and in English.)

> Native costumes, imported villages, dances, the folklore of primitive peoples.... Say *emancipation*! ... Say *rising tide*! ... *The underwear of the properly clothed begs for a good washing?*

Indonesia Raja, no. 1–2, 4th year, January–February 1932

This in Dutch, signed "XYX":

> *On Inevitability*
> In every battle, of course, there is a possibility of victory and a possibility of defeat, of making a step forward or a step back. This is what

Karl Marx pointed out in his analysis of the social processes and his insights into a society in change.

Amir had possibly read something by Marx already in Haarlem, either in Dutch or, easily, in the German original. I imagine that now in the Indies, to Amir, listening to Soekarno's Indonesian-Indonesian, the voice of Marx had to sound attractively frayed. Like to Jacques Derrida, I dare say. Derrida wrote in his *Specters of Marx*:

> Marx's voice is at once tacit and violent, political, and scholarly, direct indirect, total, and fragmentary, lengthy, and almost instantaneous. Marx does not live comfortably with the plurality of languages that are always colliding and disjoining with each other in him. Even if these languages seem to converge toward the same end, they could not be translated into each other, and their heterogeneity, the divergence or gap, the distance that decenters them, renders them non-contemporaneous. In producing an effect of irreducible distortion, they oblige those who must withstand the reading (the practice) of them to submit themselves to a ceaseless reassessing.[12]

The voice of Marx, to Amir like to Derrida, I imagine, might sound like a voice of adventure, in a "trajectory that is necessarily without heading and without assurance,"[13] "rupture . . . revolution not as a final necessity but as *imminence*."[14] The voice of Marx had to sound to Amir like a voice of ethical daring.

It is almost certain that Marx had been debated in Julius Schepper's Batavia house, on the Persian carpet. There is a little doubt, too, that in the circle of Julius Schepper, professor and missionary, Marx had been appreciated. "The imprecation of the just," wrote Derrida on Marx's saying, can be found even "in the most analytic text of Marx." Marx's *German Ideology*, for instance, writes Derrida, "does not theorize, it is not content to say how things are, it cries out the truth it promises, it provokes. As its name indicates *it is nothing other than a prayer*."[15]

Marx's perspectives, too, appear already in Amir's early newspaper writing. An article published in *Indonesia Raja* in April 1933, was signed "A.S.," which for sure was Amir Sjarifoeddin. The article was written in Dutch, and it dealt with a just-issued government ordinance about Indies schools. The schools that did not comply with the new standards were not to be allowed to function. In fact, the edict was aimed at the national schools, schools that were under the influence of the Indonesian movement, the "wild schools," as they now proudly began to call themselves. Marx's voice, or its echoes at least, could be heard in the article distinctly.

CHAPTER 6

Indonesia Raja, no. 3–4, 5th year, March–April 1933

This in Dutch, signed "A.S.":

> *The Wild School Ordinance.*
> Why has no protest against the ordinance been heard in the Dutch press? But how could it be? . . . The education of the people was conceived as factory systems to produce cheap labor, intellectual labor in this case. Inevitably, when there is an overproduction of the cheap intellectual labor, the production has to be reduced or for a time stopped.

The saying, in public or on the page of a newspaper, tasted of adventure. The saying tested itself from the moment it was emitted. It tested its limits, itself as a mere saying.

On February 4, 1933, a mutiny broke out on board HNLMS *De Zeven Provinciën*, "Seven Provinces," a class cruiser of the Dutch Navy, off Kota Radja, Atjeh (today Banda Aceh) at the north tip of Sumatra. There were native crew members and machinists as well as Europeans among the mutineers. The mutiny was quickly crushed, with a brutality widely reported in the newspapers. The ship was bombed by an airplane, the bomb allegedly designed as a warning shot, hit the ship. Twenty-two sailors were killed. As the *New York Times* reported, "Air Bomb Killed 22 on Dutch Warship; Three Hollanders among Dead."[16]

Amir's *Indonesia Raja* responded to the event in its March–April issue of 1933 with an article in Dutch. It began with a report on the actions organized by the Dutch socialists in the Netherlands. The article quoted from Dutch papers on the speeches at the protests, calling the sailors on the *Zeven Provinciën* "the workers," and the ship itself "a new *Potemkin*."

Potemkin was, of course, the legendary Russian cruiser whose crew mutinied in support of the "first" Russian revolution of 1905. *Indonesia Raja*'s commentary, signed "Sn", in Dutch, accompanied the report:

> The cruiser *Zeven Provinciën* has written an indelible page in the Dutch-Indies Marine book of history. But it will also remain forever branded in the memory of every Indonesian. This is why the colonial *blandas* [street Malay for *Belanda*, "Dutch"] now whip up still more of their campaigns of hate. This is how they dig even deeper the trench between the Browns and the Whites.[17]

Digging the trench, wrote Amir, whipping the hate between the *sini*, "us," and *sana*, "them." Did Amir realize at that moment how different his and Soekarno's perspective was? Did he mean it?

I did not find any next issue of the *Indonesia Raja* bulletin. But, at the moment of *Indonesia Raja*'s evident closing down, in February 1933, a new magazine, *Banteng*, "Buffalo," appeared. In a survey of the "native and Malay-Chinese press" published regularly by the Indies government, the new magazine was described as "affiliated with the Partindo," and "under the redaction of Sjarifoeddin."[18]

Even fewer *Banteng* issues survive. From those that are available, all of the contributions, in contrast to *Indonesia Raja*, are in Indonesian: the articles, the advertisements, the letters from the readers. Almost all, that is.

Banteng, no. 5 and 6, 1st year, March 15 and 30, 1933

> In Russland gibt er keine Arbeitslosigkeit.

(This is in German, for once: "In Russia there is no unemployment.")

> The five-year plan and the ten-year plan and the fifteen-year plan, these are the stations on a journey towards the world revolution. . . .
> The five-year plan is the experiment opening the way to the overthrow of the capitalist system and the victory of the peoples of the world, unified, all the workers of the world![19]

"[A]lmost magical fervor," Gerry van Klinken wrote about the young people around Amir at the time, was "made more delicious by the possibility of police intervention."[20] The people around Amir were outrageous and déclassé. Whispers were being heard that the Politioneel Inlichtingen Dienst, "Political Intelligence Service"—the political police—had their eyes on Amir.

In the *Banteng* magazine issue at the end of February 1933, an announcement appeared. "*Banteng Dibeslag Polisi* [*Banteng* confiscated by the police]."

> From our office in Kenari Alley, about 1700 copies of the no. 3, February 16 issue of the paper were seized and carried by the police agents to their headquarters on the Gambir Square [east section of the Koningsplein]. We redactors were summoned to the police headquarters and interrogated. The reason given to us for the confiscation was an article published in the February 16 issue of *Banteng* about the school ordinance.
> This event will not make *Banteng* retreat. On the contrary, it pours gas on our fire.[21]

There was a pause and, on July 15, 1933, in issue number 9 of *Banteng*, a change in redaction had been announced:

> *Brother Amir Sjarifoeddin*
>
> In connection with the amount of work Amir faces, beginning with no. 9, the redaction of *Banteng* will be led by brother Deva.
>
> Our heartfelt thanks go to brother Amir for his service to *Banteng*. It brought him an annoying accusation of a *pers delikt* [Dutch for "press delict"]. Let us hope that this is just a speed bump in the road and not a booby trap laid by colonial law. What Amir has done, should not be considered illegal in any society. Again, let us believe that this is merely a hurdle to be stepped over on Amir's road through a dark forest into the open.

The announcement ended:

> As for the *Banteng* paper, it will carry on and continue to serve the readers—to cleanse the air of capitalism and imperialism.[22]

The editors of *Banteng* and Amir might still be thinking of oppression as the well-schooled Marquis de Sade, a dandy-daddy, did in his cell in the Bastille prison—as of stupidity. "Censorship," the marquis wrote, "is abhorrent on two levels, because it is repressive, because it is stupid; so that we always have the contradictory urge to combat it and to teach it a lesson."[23]

Chapter 7

Sleep, Baby, Sleep II

> Who drinks his milk so sweet?
> Sleep, baby, sleep,
> Outside there walks a sheep.
>
> —Dutch lullaby

In 1931, Amir converted to Christianity. He was baptized in Batavia in the Huria Kristen Batak Protestan, "Batak Christian Protestant Church" a just-built edifice in the center of Batavia, in fact not far from Kramat. "I still recall," the pastor at the church, Reverend Peter Tamboenan told a Dutch friend seventeen years later, "that I christened Musulman Amir."[1]

In a dark, dramatic, but apparently not-far-from-true story told by Amir's cousin F. K. N. Harahap and suggested by others, Amir is said to have written about his decision to leave Islam and become a Christian to his mother Basoenoe in Sumatra.[2] It was Amir's mother who gave Amir his name in the hope that he might grow into it, "the prince of faith"—the Islamic faith Basoenoe presumed, of course.

Mother answered: "If you become Christian, you have to know, I will not be able to accept such a thing and I will hang myself!" On receiving the letter, Amir's reaction was: "Dear mother. I am sorry, but it already happened. I am truly sad about how you feel, but I hold fast to my new religion." The mother indeed carried out her intention and she hanged herself as it became clear that Amir had really changed religion.[3]

Jacques Leclerc heard the same story: "June 16, mother hanged herself in the kitchen of the family house."[4] In his autobiography Amir does not mention his conversion nor his mother's suicide. Amir's schoolmate and friend,

65

Tine Franzs, wrote: "Amir Sjarifoeddin became Christian. Perhaps it happened under the influence of Professor Schepper."[5]

In the same year, in 1931, when Amir became Christian, Julius Schepper caused a scandal. The professor published a pamphlet in which, with all his moral and professional force, as a teacher, a missionary, and a sailor, he attacked the just-announced verdict against Soekarno and his three coleaders of the Partai Nasional Indonesia (PNI).[6]

The Verdict in the PNI-Case
by *mr.* J.M.J. Schepper. Professor in Batavia
De Unie, Batavia-Centrum
Per copy 0,30 guilders.

Better to say, Schepper tried to publish the pamphlet, and he pushed until one publisher relented. In a long introduction to his brochure, Schepper described the troubles: "The text on the PNI-case that now can see the light of the day had originally been offered to the *Indisch Tijdschrift van het Recht* ['Indies Journal of the Law'], the flagship journal of *Nederlandsch-Indische Juristenvereeniging* ['Netherlands-Indies Lawyers Association']. The redaction of the journal rejected the offer by the vote of most of its members."[7] "I consider it my sacred duty to speak out," Schepper wrote. The verdict, he went on, is in "conflict with . . . modern constitutional law."[8]

Two extensive quotes from Kant introduced the argument. Kant's categorical imperative was Schepper's principal motivation, and it made the brochure and the scandal an extension of what Amir and the others had been hearing, debating, and learning in Schepper's house.

The text of the brochure itself appeared so radical, and so youthful, that some of the contemporaries who knew both Schepper and Amir felt that Amir might have been behind at least some of Schepper's choice of words as well as behind the overall style and ethos. "The style," said Pastor Johannes Verkuyl, one of the contemporaries and later a friend of Amir, was "peppered with colorful expressions . . . much livelier than was Schepper's wont. The brochure came close to declaring the Indies a police state."[9]

In Schepper's view, as he expressed it in the brochure, the charges against Soekarno and his codefendants revealed the government's moral weakness and twisted reason. The charges, the trial, and the verdict compromised the culture and morals, of which Schepper—as a professor, as a Christian, and as a missionary—felt to be a part. "Those of us, who always cherished and trusted the traditions of our fatherland," he wrote, "after April 17, 1931" (the day of the verdict) "have all reasons to remain silent."[10]

Schepper, as a jurist, had been "offended." "All evidence," he wrote, "was based on witnesses' statements, the content of which had never been made public."

What Schepper articulated in his moral and lawyer's outrage, however, was the futility of "sayings." He argued against punishing Soekarno for what he said while, in fact, doing nothing. These were merely "phrases," Schepper argued. "Let us destroy imperialism," "freedom will come in 1930," "we will force the government to run."[11]

All these "expressions," Schepper wrote, and he could have written "sayings," "must be understood as 'stirring up public opinion' and 'rousing popular mood' [*stemming maken*, literally 'making mood']." And yet, the government reacted as if this was real. "Article 153 had been applied in these cases," as against "real rebels," the people of "real action." "The declaration of the first defendant [Soekarno] that, in the party courses and elsewhere, he had warned against revolution in a sense of 'insurrection' was never considered [by the judges]."[12]

Schepper focused on, and remained in, language and logic. He wrote about the court's "jungle of assumptions, syllogisms and suggestions" that "gave the statements of the Bandoeng court the character of a political exercise." He wrote how "the barren soil was overworked with the lush flora of reasonings." The Bandoeng court, Schepper wrote, produced "parallels," "ideas," "methods," and "plans" to prove "ties between Soekarno's PNI and the outlawed PKI ['Communist Party of Indonesia']." In this false way, the court constructed Soekarno's conspiracy "with the aim of an armed uprising."[13]

Soekarno's slogan "to destroy imperialism" through "organized mass action," Schepper wrote, "was just that—an expression and an image." Still, the court interpreted them as being "the means to a violent action against the legal authority." "In order to overthrow an authority," wrote Schepper, "more is needed than words. The condemned, however unruly and even sometimes inflammatory, produced declarations and tendencies, . . . rebellion on paper."[14]

Schepper concluded his brochure by referring to "newspaper reports" that, as the PNI dissolved, a new party had been formed "with the same aim (freedom of Indonesia) and based on the same principle (of self-help)." This, of course, was Partindo, Amir's party. "Let us hope," wrote Schepper, "that the new party will be led in a more sensible way . . . that it will avoid the actions based on the unreal. . . . Let us hope, too, that the government will turn out to behave in the same way. Deep truth resounds in the words of a Jewish prophet of more than twenty centuries ago, 'righteousness exalts a nation.'"[15]

The new and tougher governor general of the Dutch Indies, Bonifácius Cornelis de Jonge, sent Soekarno to Endeh and he did not take Schepper's brochure lightly. "Prof. Schepper!" he wrote in his memoirs with an exclamation point: "Schepper has written not a very nice brochure about the guilty verdict of Soekarno; not a legal discourse in a scholarly journal, but a political pamphlet."

Schepper was just returning at that time, the end of June 1933, from an overseas vacation and expected to resume his teaching at the Law School. Not so. "I have already signed the re-appointment," Governor General de Jonge wrote, "but that night in my feverish head [he happened to be sick that day] it struck me that it would be too crazy [*te gek*] in this case to consider the reassignment as a mere formality. . . . And so, I let him come to see me." Schepper came. "He said something to the effect that he thought his right to express his views as a scholar should be respected, etc. I told him that this right made no sense given the manner in which he had written the thing, and that I only wished to know whether he planned to continue this way. I threw him a rope, which he promptly took. Therefore, then, I felt no need for a further objection to his re-appointment. He was being read his lesson [*Het lesje had hij gehad*]."[16]

After some time, the governor general still returned to the matter. "It worked," he wrote in his diary, and he quoted a widely read Dutch daily published in the Indies, the *Nieuws van de Dag*, "News of the Day." There had to be a leak. On the very day of the governor general meeting with Schepper, June 27, as De Jonge quoted, the paper wrote that Schepper "fell on his knees [*een knieval gedaan*]" and promised, in order to be reappointed, that he "will behave better in the future." Schepper's anxious denial was published in *de Bonie*, a much less widely read paper, and *Nieuws van de Dag* simply answered, "we know with certainty that the promise was given."[17]

Schepper, now, coming out of his crash against the governor general, might feel like Soekarno might have felt coming out of his crash against the Bandoeng court—to use Emmanuel Levinas's words, in a state of an "anxiety of solitude." The anxiety of solitude, Levinas writes, "points to a weakness of him who literally is himself no longer able but needs a hand to support his forehead so that he may vomit."[18]

On October 29, 1930, a letter arrived, stamped "Secret," from the office of the Dutch Indies attorney general to *mr.* F. M. Baron van Asbeck, Amir's teacher at the Law School and Schepper's friend. It was addressed to Van Asbeck's domestic address, at Pegangsaan 56, Batavia. The letter was semiprivate and was signed by the attorney general himself.

In the letter, the attorney general referred to "a discussion" he had with Van Asbeck "a short time ago," "about several students who had shown little desirable political tendencies." "Now," the attorney general wrote, "the concern has been raised again by the last issue of the bulletin *Pedoman*

['Compass']." "I share the opinion of the Resident," wrote the attorney general, referring to the Dutch top official in Buitenzorg, today Bogor, a town a little over an hour from Batavia, the center of many schools and government offices, "that, in this particular case, a criminal proceeding against the author of an article in *Pedoman*, 'Slaap, kindje, slaap—' ['sleep, baby, sleep'] *still* should not be opened."[19]

The letter was clearly so important for Van Asbeck that it was kept in his files for years and, indeed, till his retirement. In the following weeks and months several such letters arrived and Van Asbeck kept them as well. Now, they are in one folder in the Dutch National Archives in The Hague.

The letter by the resident of West Java mentioned by the attorney general, perhaps through the attorney general, got to Van Asbeck and into the folder as well.

To: Attorney-General
From: The Resident of Buitenzorg
Via: The Governor of West Java in Batavia
October 17, 1930

Subject: The first number of the magazine *Pedoman*, published in Buitenzorg, the organ of the *Indonesia Moeda* ["Young Indonesia"] . . .

(Again, "saying," was the matter.)

> The language of number of articles [in *Pedoman*] leaves very little *not* to be complained about. Some phrases are so fierce, that they are not fit anymore for the eyes of the indigenous youth, like for the Scouts, to read them, however eager to read them they might be.
>
> The article "Slaap, kindje, slaap—," namely, has made the indigenous officials and the members of nobility here to feel "maloe" [embarrassed], namely the *regent* [*boepati*, the top official of the *regency*, the province, as a rule a member of the high indigenous aristocracy].
>
> Nonetheless, hurtful the *Pedoman* magazine as it shows itself to be, I still do not consider its content to require as yet a prosecution on the grounds of article 315 of the criminal law. . . .
>   [signed] The Resident.[20]

I was not able to locate the relevant, in fact any, issue of *Pedoman*, and so I do not know why the "Slaap, kindje, slaap—" article was as hurtful as the resident wrote it was. Except, of course, that "Slaap, kindje, slaap" is the title of a well-known Dutch lullaby. *Pedoman*, however, it was mentioned, belonged to *Pemoeda Indonesia*, and so Amir could not be far from it. So, also, possibly, "one of his slightly sarcastic grins" was not far from the mood of the lullaby piece.

70 CHAPTER 7

Maloe is the only Malay word in a letter otherwise written in official and very proper Dutch. To make the local indigenous nobles embarrassed and fall back upon a native word, was a victory for the writer of the "Slaap, kindje, slaap—." A small victory but a victory. But a small victory.

For a few months, the matter seemed to be put aside. The next year, however, another letter arrived, this time at the official address of the Law School. On October 16, 1931, the letter had been put on the agenda of a regular faculty meeting as "item no. 5." The minutes of the meeting were also saved by Baron van Asbeck, who was present.

> *Minutes of the 62nd faculty meeting held on Friday, October 16, 1931, in the building of the Law School.*
> *Agenda*
> . . .
> *Item no 5.*
> *Letter by the Director of the Education and Industry regarding an article in the magazine 'Indonesia Raja'*
> In *Indonesia Raja*, the organ of PPPI [Perhimpoenan Peladjar-Peladjar Indonesia, "Indonesian Students Union"], an article has been published dealing, as it says, with the problem of the inviolability of home. However, the article, according to the attorney-general, has crossed the line set by the Indies law. . . . This is a student newspaper. . . . The chair of the Law School requests the faculty to consider the director's letter addressed to the school.
> The author of the article is not known. . . . It may be added that, besides the students of the Law School, also medical students are listed on the redaction of the journal.

"The students of the Law School," of course, were Amir Sjarifoeddin and Mohammad Yamin. Amir, in fact, was the chief editor of the magazine. The Law School faculty was called to action.

> *The chair* [*mr.* Kollewijn] . . . The faculty is asked to take a decision based on the school principles . . .
> *Mr. van Asbeck* notes that the Department [of Education and Industry] reflects the position of the attorney-general. The last year, the attorney general met with the speaker [Van Asbeck] and *mr.* Schepper and asked them, through their personal influence, to guide their students along the better ways. This, however, [Van Asbeck added] is something beyond the authority of the faculty as specified by the Disciplinary Code of the school . . .

All: Agree that the faculty should keep out of the matter.
Thus concluded.[21]

Whatever the professors might have thought, at the next faculty meeting, the matter appeared on their meeting agenda again. This time it was the main and only item on the program. Baron van Asbeck again, saved the transcript of the minutes:

Minutes of the 63rd Faculty meeting held on Saturday, October 25, 1931, in the building of the Law School.
Agenda
Discussion about the Disciplinary Code . . .
Mr. van Asbeck noted that in the past the students' lives took place fully inside academia. This is not so anymore. . . .
Dr. Logemann . . . We can approach a student "as a student" and "as a person." . . . But we can supervise only the part of his or her life of a student, a member of the student community. . . . How can we be even aware in what direction an indigenous political student association might take our students and what they are talking about in their *Gedong Permoefakatan* ["House of Deliberations"]?[22]

The professors resisted, arguing as strongly as they could with the "saying" they had, with the principles of the modern, education, academic freedom, or, in the case of Van Asbeck and Schepper certainly, of moral imperative and dignity of man. They might think with De Sade again: "Censorship is abhorrent on two levels, because it is repressive, because it is stupid; so that we always have the contradictory urge to combat it and to teach it a lesson."[23]

Still the matter did not stop there, naturally. The names of the Law School students to be disciplined, possibly suspended, and possibly criminally prosecuted, had been conveyed to the faculty "for the professors' comment." In Baron van Asbeck's folder, there is a piece of paper, one page covered by a scribble, without a date and address but, from the context clearly, a concept of a personal letter by Van Asbeck to Julius Schepper. Ideas and suggestions are dotted, talking points, how to react and save the students, how the faculty should respond to the increasing pressure, what to say to the real:

Dear friend,
Here are some notes . . . as we have spoken . . .
We, as faculty, stand on principles and keep our obligations as teachers. Our first obligation is work against our students to slacken or being led astray. . . . Our students have to trust that we keep off their politics and their political activities as far as those are pursued outside the school.

They have to trust that, in the process of education we treat all students equally, notwithstanding their belonging to any student group outside the school. . . .

In our treatment of each student, we must be trusted that we consider only whether a student's work is on the level of the school standards, and whether he or she respects, and contributes to, the academic community of the school. . . . At the school we prevent a political action. . . . The faculty, however, does not feel to be called upon to set norms or to censor a behavior as far as it does not disrupt the academic order and the working of the school.[24]

To the letter, Van Asbeck attached a list of students, those mentioned in the authorities' inquiry. Two professors, deliberating, standing upright, but already now being aware of the futility of their efforts, increasingly anxious, it seems at moments desperate, tried to keep some humor in it, perhaps trading innocent jokes at the expense of the strong, with slightly sarcastic grins, perhaps. This was the list Van Asbeck produced and sent to Schepper:

Moh. Yamin, popular; average student.

Amir Sjarifoeddin, examinations done on time and with good results; never gave a reason to withdraw his scholarship.

Soewardi Tirtosoepono, such a person was never a student here; neither "Soewardi" nor "Tirtosoepono".

Miss Manoppo, examinations done on time and with good results; never gave a reason to withdraw her scholarship.

Reksodipoetro, bad student; scholarship withdrawn; lacks required diligence, etc.

Jahja Nasoetion, the person is unknown to the faculty; one "Jahja" is at our school, and one "Nasoetion," also; both average students.

Koentjoro, examinations done on time. . . .

Soegondo, an average student.

Soenarto, . . . examinations done on time and with good results.

Hindromartono, examinations done on time and mostly with good results.[25]

They were good Uncles Karels in trouble. Their stance, their principles, academic, ethical, judicial, crumbled as they touched on the real. The government authorities were deciding what would happen in the Indies. The professors' was the saying, and the government's was the action.

"You will certainly recognize the names of the students who are most often heard at the various meetings," the attorney general wrote to the governor general on June 28, 1932. "Foremost among them are those of Moh. Yamin, Amir Sjarifoeddin and Soewardi Tirtosoepono, all three from the Law School. And I do not understand how the faculty expects to face these students with purely theoretic, passive attitudes, or even with an outright defending them."[26]

The next letter was kept in the Van Asbeck folder and can be found in the National Archives.

To: *The Governor of West Java, Batavia*
Batavia-Centrum, October 10, 1933

VERY SECRET
Case: Exile of the Partindo leader, Amir Sjarifoeddin, son of Baginda Soripada. . . .

Request by the police to exile Amir Sjarifoeddin, a student at the Law School. With 8 appendices. . . .

Amir Sjarifoeddin is a radical leader of the PI [Partai Indonesia, Partindo] popular among the extremist circles . . . an intelligent and bold speaker. His speeches at public meetings appeal especially by their humor and their use of sarcasm.

In *Banteng* of March 30 of this year, an article appeared entitled "Massa Actie" ["Mass Action"] which we consider inacceptable. Amir Sjarifoeddin, who is the chief editor of *Banteng*, declined to disclose the name of the author.[27]

The action had been prepared since the previous year. According to a letter by the attorney general to the governor general dated September 14, 1933 (this is a letter not in Van Asbeck's file): "The well-known student Amir Sjarifoeddin, the editor of the PI [Partindo] magazine *Banteng* is legally responsible for the article 'Massa Actie' in *Banteng* no. 6 of March 30 and should be prosecuted according to the art. 153bis of the criminal law."[28]

Almost everybody even a little concerned knew at the time that the author of the *Banteng* article "Massa Actie" was Mohammad Yamin. The police probably knew it, too. Amir, however, on principle, did not tell. Therefore, "Based on the aforementioned, prosecution has been launched on the ground of the art. 153bis sub155 of the criminal law."

The government saw good reason for it beyond the "Massa Actie" article:

Amir Sjarifoeddin exerts great influence on the youth movement, Indonesia Moeda ["Young Indonesia"], and especially Perhimpoenan

Peladjar-Peladjar Indonesia. The last-named Association has been completely politicized by now and shows an extremist disposition.

From the attachments to this letter, it is evident that in person Amir Sjarifoeddin is an extremely dangerous element. Multiple police reports attest to his constantly stirring his audiences against the authority.

Merely a criminal prosecution and imprisonment would have a little effect, and there is even a chance that it might increase the man's popularity even more. In the interest of public order and quiet, therefore, his sending to internment camp without a trial is called for. . . .

[Signed] The Resident of Batavia, van der Hoek.[29]

The resident of Batavia pushed the matter. On November 10, 1933, the governor of West Java, where Batavia belonged, in a letter to the attorney general agreed with the resident. Amir must go as far away and with as little ado as possible—meaning to New Guinea, to Boven Digoel, the place that Soekarno had been spared and where the Communist rebels of 1926 and 1927 were locked, also without a trial. In a letter to the attorney general, the governor of West Java, as an additional argument for the exile and internment, added "a brief description of Sjarifoeddin's personality."[30] He compared Amir with his friend, Mohammad Yamin:

Amir Sjarifoeddin is completely different from Mohammad Yamin. Yamin is an extremist who is, first of all and above all, after his own popularity and his own triumphing at public meetings.

. . . In contrast, Amir Sjarifoeddin, is an extremist in body and soul [*in hart en nieren*, "hart and kidneys" actually], of powerful inner conviction and strong will to serve. He disseminates extremist propaganda methodically. He is strong of character [*karaktervast*] and will stand for his principles to the end.

Amir Sjarifoeddin is honest in his convictions. He is subtle and as such he compels respect. Without a doubt, he is a person who has to be taken very seriously. . . . He is a born leader and he might rise in a short time to the top . . . to become the head of the extremist action.

Only exile and internment might bring to an end his increasing influence.

[signed] The Governor of West-Java Schnitzler.[31]

"If it were not for Schepper," Jacques Leclerc wrote a note on one of his papers, "Amir will be deported to Digoel."[32] "It was a close thing," wrote Gerry van Klinken, "but pleas by Goenoeng [Datoek] Moelia and Schepper on Amir's behalf probably meant that instead of being sent extrajudicially to . . . Boven

Digoel . . . a judicial process was instituted that led [merely] to his conviction on a press offense."³³

Perhaps thanks to Schepper, too, Amir had been even given time, at the Law School, to take his final examination first.³⁴ On December 5, 1933, he passed and became a *Meester in de Rechten*, "Master of Law," with *"mr."* now properly before his name.³⁵ Two days after he passed the examinations, on December 7, 1933, Amir went to prison—for eighteen months, "six months in Struiswijk [now Salemba]" in Batavia, and a consecutive one year in the new Soekamiskin prison in Bandoeng. But the verdict of the internal exile and internment to Boven Digoel was not erased from his file. The threat was merely suspended. It was made clear to Amir as well as to Schepper and Datoek Moelia evidently, that what would happen after his prison term is over, depended on Amir's "good behavior" during the time of his imprisonment.³⁶ He was read his lesson.

CHAPTER 8

Julius Martin Johannes Schepper

> [B]etween December 1933 and June 1935 . . . Schepper came to see him with a Bible nearly every day.
>
> —Klinken, *Minorities*, 127

"Nearly every day," could only be during the time Amir was in the Struiswijk prison in the center of Batavia, a few minutes' drive from Julius Schepper's house. The Soekamiskin prison, where Amir was moved after the first six months in Struiswijk, and where he spent the remaining time of his sentence, was in Bandoeng, several hours by car or train from Batavia. A visit to the Soekamiskin prison would take Schepper a very long day at best.

Nevertheless, according to many memories, even in Soekamiskin Schepper visited Amir as often as he could, on many weekends and holidays. That he brought a Bible with him seems natural, except that the prison library almost certainly would have several copies of the Bible of its own. It would not be like Amir and like Schepper too, when they met, not to be reading or discussing a book together, whether the Bible or some other. It was the next station of both their journeys. They would go on in their debates that began at the Law School and at Schepper's house.

There is a good description of Soekamiskin from just a few years after Amir was there, by Willem Walraven, a Dutch author who had lived in the Indies since the First World War, when he came to the colony as a soldier. A few years after Amir, he was put in Soekamiskin for a year, for talking on the train so much that he became suspected of subversive intentions, a delict not too different from that of Amir's, and not too different even from Schepper's, when

Schepper had been "read a lesson" by the governor general. For all three of them, Amir and Walraven and Schepper, despite the bars and absence of the wall-charts, the prison must still have had a feeling of a classroom.

Walraven wrote a little book about Soekamiskin when he was let out, just before the beginning of the Second World War.

> On Friday, one can order books from the library. I took the catalogue into my cell and wrote down the titles: enough for the whole time here. The library is not modern . . . far from it—Het Joodje ["The Little Jew"] Corry van Bruggen. [Corry van Bruggen was a contemporary of Mary van Zeggelen by the way. She, too, spent much of her life in the Indies and her novel Walraven mentioned, from 1914, would fit the Indies school reading as well.] I have also borrowed and read *Majoor Frans, De Delftsche Wonderdokter* ["The Delft Wonder Doctor"]; I borrowed and reread *De Negerhut* ["Uncle Tom's Cabin"] . . . There were not many German books, neither French nor English. . . . But there were bound volumes of *De Gids*—[the oldest and most prestigious Dutch literary magazine published since 1837]—and Carlyle's *French Revolution*. Enough to keep a reader busy for months. I also noticed a large amount of literature of a lighter genre, but very little of a tickling [*prikkelende*] kind—which might be advisable for a prison.[1]

Amir was put in the section of the prison for "Europeans and developed [*ontwikkelde*] natives." "The former director," wrote Walraven about the chief of the prison who would be the director of Amir's time as well, "allowed visits quite easily. The prisoners may also sign up for several training courses and attend lectures. There are language lessons offered, but then one has to attend the lesson on a regular basis. Writing material is allowed in the cells. 'Do you go to the chapel?' I asked a friend . . . 'If there is a good preacher on program today,' he answered."[2]

Soekamiskin was the most modern prison in the Indies and one of the most modern in the East. It was built in "the American way." All is concrete, wrote Walraven: "Everything is built for our ideal-less time." "The buildings are nothing but amplifications of stone. Who stays longer in this surrounding has very little left to hope for."[3]

> One passes through the prison's narrow side alleys enclosed on both sides by white walls with doors to the individual cells. The sun pounds on the ground of the cemented alleys mercilessly. Now and there, mats from the cells are spread on the cement to dry. Pillows and towels hang on the ropes.[4]

There is a padlock on the door of each cell. The wood of the doors is smeared with a thick layer of a substance which releases a smell which stays with you all the time.[5]

In many ways, discipline is not very much enforced. On command "Forward!" a party of prisoners gets on the move, but they do not march in step. They pass through the prison as a troop of oxen. . . . Some salute the higher personnel, others do not. I never heard anybody complain about discipline. It exists only so far that the prison may keep on existing, and everybody seems to understand that.[6]

With the absence of the wall charts and the presence of the bars on the windows, the prison for Amir might signal a moment of freedom. Books were purely for reading and they offered themselves *shamelessly*, at random. Discipline became *nakedly* a means to keep the machine of the prison going. It is not by accident that revolutionaries are made as prison recidivists of sorts.

The possibility remained that Amir would be sent to New Guinea after his prison term was served. The verdict was only suspended, and Amir was made very much aware of it. The wheels of the real were turning while Amir sat in prison, and the portfolio on him was growing. The documents involved, as a rule, were stamped "secret" or "very secret," but the whole thing was leaking; just enough for Amir to know.

The Indies' was a modern regime based on equivalence: what would happen to Amir depended as much on the regime as on him. On February 13, 1935, with Amir in the second half of his sentence, the attorney general, through the governor of West Java, sent a letter of inquiry about Amir to the director of the Soekamiskin prison:

SECRET
Subject: The prison term of Amir Sjarifoeddin expires on June 5, 1935.

I request a report from you concerning this political convict and his behavior up to the present time. I also wish to have your report on the above-mentioned person's frame of mind.

[signed] Attorney-General.[7]

The answer by the Soekamiskin prison director to the attorney general arrived in two weeks.

To your inquiry of February 13, 1935, . . .
On August 6, 1934, political prisoners, en masse, including the convicted *mr.* Amir Sjarifoeddin, were punished for an unauthorized gathering in the recreation hall. Time for recreation had been restricted to between 6.30 p.m. and 8.30 p.m., for the duration of three months.

As for the frame of mind of the convicted *mr.* Amir Sjarifoeddin, I can report the following: It is difficult for me to make a judgment. He carries himself well, he works, and he gives no reason for any further punishment.

As for what the convict's feeling about the government is, I cannot say.

[signed] Director of Prison Soekamiskin Bandoeng[8]

There was something akin, in the director's letter, to the letters by the Law School faculty a year before. Amir was still graded, on a scale from good to passing and unsatisfactory. Still there was the space of classroom and still the space was given to him with walls opening into other walls. But this was a prison, and the illusions of classroom were more closely tested. The debates in Schepper's house, in one way or another, were replayed by Amir in prison. Hegel's was the colonial regime of reason: "philosophy becomes a headmaster or indiscriminate lawyer for the Being that hired him, and the night of the world retreats into the merely ignorant subject. Here spreads the beautiful warmth of the classroom." The Kantian sense of the world "was a solitary light meant to burn up the night of this world."[9]

The resident of Batavia, evidently not a softie among the Indies bureaucrats, was still convinced that Amir deserved exile.

To: Governor of West Java
From: Resident of Batavia

VERY SECRET. FOR YOUR EYES ONLY
February 20, 1935

... It is my firm conviction that a person like this [meaning Amir] has to be ranked among the irreconcilables [*onverzoenlijken*] and that it would be irresponsible to let such a person out into society.... Agitators like this convict, from our society, have to be made to disappear.[10]

The governor of West Java again let the higher authorities decide.

From: Governor of West Java
To: His Excellency Governor-General of the Netherlands Indies

SECRET
March 14, 1935

... He [Amir Sjarifoeddin] was convicted on November 10, 1933 and jailed on December 7, 1933. His prison term expires on June 5 of this year. Now some decision must be made.[11]

It was just weeks before Amir was to be released, and perhaps sent to Boven Digoel, that his case reached the highest body of deliberation in the colony, the Raad van Nederlandsch Indië, "Council of the Netherlands Indies." The council debated Amir early in May and it conveyed its advice in a letter to the governor general:

> *The opinion of the Council of the Netherlands Indies agreed upon during its meeting on May 3, 1935*
> ... Mr. Vonk [the attorney-general], asked by the Council, expressed a view that an internment of the man would bring no political-tactical advantage. ... It seems to him better to allow some time to see how this Partindo leader would behave. Several persons have been consulted (*among them Prof. Schepper and Dr. Moelia*) and they expressed expectations that Amir Sjarifoeddin might tone his political agitation down. ...
> ... The attorney-general ... is of the opinion that the suspended verdict [of exile] is not to be cancelled but should rather be kept on file for further consideration with the possibility to decide later. For now, a chance might be given to *mr.* Amir Sjarifoeddin to begin a new life.

Therefore:

> The Council of the Netherlands Indies advises that the attorney-general convey to *mr.* Amir Sjarifoeddin a warning on the line of the above.
> Council of the Netherlands Indies
> [signed] J. W. Meyer Ranneft. The Vice-President[12]

On May 25, 1935, the secretariat of the governor general instructed the attorney general: "There is no reason at this moment for exile. But a stern warning should be given. His Excellency the Governor-General suggests that you keep the internment order in readiness, so that it could be applied in future if needed."[13] On June 5, 1935, Amir left prison a free man "for the moment" and "under a condition." As he later recalled he "was summoned to the house of the Priangan's [West-Java] Resident for the warning."[14]

Boven Digoel was still across the line for Amir. It was implied that he was still of the classroom space. Not "of the act" enough to be sent to the jungle, but still of "the space of saying." The government adviser for indigenous affairs, in a letter to the governor general on June 29, explained the kind of freedom in which Amir found himself now: "Boven Digoel," the adviser wrote, "is little suitable for intellectuals."[15]

Two other letters can be found in Baron van Asbeck's folder. Both were written at the time when Amir was in prison, both were written by Julius Schepper and addressed to Van Asbeck, who had already left Batavia Law School and was now retired in Leiden. Both concerned Amir Sjarifoeddin very much.

Batavia (Centrum.), September 4, 1934

Dear v. Asbeck

... About Amir Sjarifoeddin. I have several important news to convey.... With the help of a special commission (missionary Kraemer,[16] myself, and few others), I have managed for Amir [after his release] to be offered a job. A possibility is economic-research work for the Mission. He, however, does not appear to be willing. Instead, he still plans to remain on his path in the movement.

I hope I still will have an opportunity to visit Amir in the Bandoeng prison and to speak to him more. You may want to know, also, that the courts and now the Council of the Indies are still deliberating whether to send Amir to exile, even when Vonk [the attorney general] has assured me that a positive decision is foregone.

[signed] JSch[17]

The second letter by Schepper to Van Asbeck is dated eight months later, May 7, 1935. It was written during the critical days when the decision was just about to be made. Unlike in the first letter, Amir appears already in the opening paragraph and, in fact, most of the letter is about him.

Batavia, May 7, 1935

Dear van Asbeck,

Your letter of February 24 still lays on the pile "to be answered." ...

I have visited Amir in Soekamiskin over Easter (we have made a trip to Bandoeng, in fact, in order to see him). I forwarded your greetings. The talk with him, however, was still not easy. First of all, he looks on the offer of a job at the Theological Seminar in Buitenzorg [Bogor] with suspicion. I was quite disappointed. Still, we talked for an hour and half between four eyes and some misunderstandings were cleared.

The main difficulty is that he cannot expect any financial help from his father, who categorically refuses to give him anything because of, as Amir put it, his son's "immoral behavior." We must do everything to have the father change his mind. (I have already written a long letter trying to reason with the man.) It's too bad, too, that Amir himself is so egocentric and so hypersensitive. It certainly does not make things easier.

Besides, Amir does not seem to really appreciate how critical his situation is. Many in the government still insist that the Governor-General send him to Boven Digoel. I fear that it might still happen, even when the attorney-general (Vonk) assures me that matters are not so bad. It is now in the hands of the Council of the Indies. . . .

. . . Greeting to Bep [Van Asbeck's wife] and the children.

[signed] Sch[18]

The professors cared, and so did Amir's cousin Datoek Moelia. They vouched that Amir would behave, they pleaded for him to be given an opportunity to prove himself. He was taken care of, and all was attempted to make him good.

Late in May 1935, Amir Sjarifoeddin stepped out from the Soekamiskin prison with the Boven Digoel sentence still suspended above his head. On October 16, 1935, Amir married. It was a Christian wedding, and it took place in the same Batak Krenolong church in Batavia, where four years earlier Amir was baptized—by the same pastor, Peter Tamboenan. Friends from the time before Amir went to prison were present and Julius Schepper was also there. No doubt, at least one police agent was there, too. There was a memorable reception after the wedding. "On Saturday evening a reception was given by Mrs. and Mr. Amir Sjarifoeddin, a well-known leader in the indigenous movement, after their recent marriage, in the building of the Pergoeroean Ra'jat ["People's University"] in Kramat. It attracted great interest of the indigenous leading lights. There were many flowers. Among the guests we have noticed Mrs. and Prof. Schepper and Dr. van Doorn."[19]

Tine Fransz, Amir's friend from the Law School and beyond, who also knew him from the Kebon Sirih 44 Christen Studenten Vereeniging meetings, and who also was present at the wedding, recalled: "Amir had an open personality, he was liked by the common people and he liked to be with them, as well. Too bad that he had to spend such a long time in prison. After he was released, he lived in a little house in Menteng Pulo [a lower-class quarter of Batavia at the time, with many artists and Bohemians living there]. The reception at his wedding took place at an aula at Kramat, in front of where the cinema Rivoli is today." It was the Kramat 106 dormitory. "It was after sunset and I recall some people arriving on foot and carrying flashlights. Some arrived by bus from as far as Buitenzorg."[20] "To his wedding reception," Tine Fransz recalled after years, "a very simple affair, all kind of people came, the highest and the lowest in the land."[21]

The bride, Manii Inang Djaenah Zainab Harahap, was four years younger than Amir. In an interview with Jacques Leclerc in Jakarta in 1982, she described her background: "My father Soetan Sajoer was a *demang* [customary law expert], very close to the authorities. Before he retired in the 1920s, he had served as a *demang* at the Department of Religion in Batavia. He died at the age of sixty-five. Father was a relatively open man. He was active in Muhammadiyah [a Muslim reformist association], but one of his sisters was a Protestant."[22]

Djaenah and Amir met in the movement. Djaenah graduated from Batavia Teachers' College and became a teacher in a Batavia kindergarten. Her whole education as well as her language of the everyday, like Amir's, was Dutch. She "learned Indonesian 'much later,'" she told Jacques Leclerc. However, "already in her teens she became a member of the 'Indonesian Girl Scouts.'"[23]

Djaenah's parents still lived at the time, in Kemajoran, a quarter of Batavia with a mixed Dutch and Indigenous population, a middle class. Djaenah met Amir, she recalled, in a group of young Bataks at the Christen Studenten Vereeniging, "Christian Students Union" in Kebon Sirih 44, the part of Batavia where Kramat 106 also was. She became an instructress at Amir's People's University, and she recalled Amir talking to her at the time about Haarlem and Holland. He was lending her books. The marriage had been planned for sometime in 1933 but it had to be postponed because Amir went to prison.[24]

It was another lingering and breaking away in Amir's life. The marriage could not be more unconcerned with tradition. On his father's side, Amir belonged to the Batak *marga*, "clan," of Harahap, and Djaenah was of the same clan. Thus, their marriage was a violation of Batak custom. "Yes," Helena Lucia, Djaenah and Amir's daughter recalled half a century later, *"mami* was from Losungbatung, *papi* from Pasar Matanggu (Padang Lawas) . . . both descendants of Sutan Sirok."[25]

Djaenah did not receive *restu*, "blessing," from her parents,[26] and Amir, whose mother was already dead at the time, probably did not even ask his father for it. The newlyweds were embarking on a journey. "With the family," wrote Theodor Adorno, "there passes away . . . the most effective agency of the bourgeois past . . . the Utopia that once drew sustenance from motherly love."[27] Djaenah, moreover, like Amir four years before, left Islam, the religion to which both of her parents belonged. She was baptized during the wedding ceremony.[28] Weeks before the wedding, another source says, "she was getting ready studying Christian religion with Prof. Schepper."[29]

It might just reflect Jacques Leclerc's impressions from what Djaenah was telling him that, on a margin of his notes from the interview, he scribbled: "Marriage sans romantisme."[30] It might be, for Djaenah or for Jacques, a way of saying "modern" or a way of saying (possibly) "revolutionary."

Amir was a lawyer now, with *mr.* in front of his name, and he had to think of supporting family, especially after Djaenah soon became pregnant. He did not take any of the jobs Professor Schepper tried to get for him. One thing seemed clear. Like Goethe, he abhorred the prospect of a career fitting the system, "to float around in the end," to say with Goethe, "in a gondola and go hunting spiders and frogs with great affability."[31]

In July 1935, Amir began to work in the law firm owned by him and Mohammad Yamin, an old friend from the Law School and Kramat 106, the author of the "Massa Actie" article in *Banteng* that, among other things, got Amir sent to prison. Yamin and Amir's office was in Sawah Besar, a largely Sumatran, mainly Batak, neighborhood of Batavia.[32] Another lawyer and friend of Amir and Yamin, Soetan Mohammad Sjah, worked in the same office, and in a letter to Jacques Leclerc, he later remembered: "Amir as a lawyer was a freethinker and a radical [*libre et radical*], . . . He did not own a car and he moved around the city on a little D.K.W. motorcycle. He lived in Menteng Pulo, in what today is the Gunung street, in one of the back alleys." "Mohammad Yamin," Mohammad Sjah also recalled, "was a bad lawyer . . . while Amir was serious. A Dutch colleague once told me that in his opinion, Amir's briefs were written in a classical style—they were rigorous, that was what he meant. Amir was like Stendhal who had *Le Code Napoléon* at his bedside and read it every evening to keep his language in shape. . . . His Dutch was exquisite, and so was his Indonesian."[33]

According to Van Klinken, Amir joining Mohammad Yamin in one law firm was a "bad decision" and, in two years the two friends from school and politics had a "falling out."[34] Late in 1937, Amir and Djaenah (their child died soon after birth), moved to Soekaboemi, a provincial town about a hundred kilometers south of Batavia. "Soekaboemi," according to the tourist guide of the time, "the favorite hill-station, 750 m above sea-level, has a population of 23,413, including 1,451 Europeans. It is the seat of a Resident and is much frequented by the inhabitants of West Java. 'Soekaboemi' means 'paradise.'"[35]

On December 3, 1937, Amir registered with the Soekaboemi court of cassation (Hooggerechtshof) as an advocate and attorney. "There are stories," Amir's youngest daughter told a journalist years later, "*mami* told me about *papi*, of the time when he was a lawyer. . . . *Papi* when he was hired by a client, did not think about money. People might have brought a chicken or a bag of rice, he did not mind. When there was no money, *mami* said, he did not care. According to *mami*, all the time when he was a free-lance lawyer, there was no money."[36]

Another lawyer, *mr*. Wikoto, knew Amir at the time. He also practiced law in Soekaboemi and remembered Amir: "Brother Amir Sjarifoeddin lived in the section of Soekaboemi called Kota Paris, the "City of Paris." . . . We met frequently, and we often had a drink. Sometimes, I ate at his home and I knew both, husband and wife, well. . . . His life in Soekaboemi was ordinary, but simple is not the word. He was focused and severe in his work, and he kept very much to himself." As in an afterthought, *mr.* Wikoto added that he had known Amir before, "since we worked together," he said, "in the Batavia branch of Partindo."³⁷

Still another lawyer, Indonesian Chinese, *mr.* P. C. Tjiam Djoe Khiam remembered Amir in Soekaboemi: "Soekaboemi was a small town, . . . plantations and unsignificant legal cases. . . . Once Amir asked me to fill in for him. I sat in his office, alone with the *oppas* [warden], from the morning till the afternoon, and not a single person came. So, we locked the office and went home. This is also what I recall about Amir: He was fluent in French, Dutch, English, and German. And, I came to respect him as someone courteous even to colleagues, even to those with political ideas other than his."³⁸

In August 1938, Amir and Djaenah, still just the two of them making a family, returned to Batavia.³⁹ Politics might be the reason. Amir began to work with a law firm of another Indonesian Chinese *mr.* Lie Tjiong Tie. Tjiam Djoe Khiam, Amir's Soekaboemi colleague and friend, happened to move to *mr.* Lie's office as well: "The office," *mr.* Tjiam Djoe Khiam remembered, "was in Voorin Zuid Straat ("In-Front South Street") no. 41, above the Overseas Chinese Banking Corporation."⁴⁰

Amir and Djaenah now lived at Tjideng, very near the Koningsplein, "King's Square," and the center of Batavia (and Kramat), behind the Vliegveldlaan, "Airport Avenue," in the house of Amir's brother. Then they moved, still in the family, with one of Amir's sisters and finally to their own house, at the corner of Malabar and Oengaran street, still very much in the center. There they lived till 1942.⁴¹

In the middle of 1935, just about the time Amir was released from prison, Musso arrived in Java.

Musso, born 1897, was one of the leaders of the failed Communist attempt at a revolution in the fall of 1926 and the early months of 1927. When the rebellion failed, Musso managed to escape. From 1927 until 1935, when he suddenly reappeared, he was rumored to live largely in Moscow when not travelling through Europe in the service of Communist International. Nothing certain, however, had been known. Neither was it known whether he even was still alive.

In mid-1935, Musso landed on Java undetected, and he spent most of the following year in Java, mostly in and around the East Javanese port city of Surabaya. He left again, in mid-1936, unarrested; however, the police seemed now to be on his tracks and, after he left, made several arrests of people who had allegedly met him while he was there.

There is no direct evidence of Musso meeting Amir at the time. But there is much circumstantial evidence. "Between mid-1935 and mid-1936," Jacques Leclerc wrote, "Musso, in Soerabaja, made contact with the leaders of the local branch of Partindo."[42] On May 11, 1936, "Musso left Soerabaja for Shanghai," so a police report said, "accompanied to the ship by Achmad Soemadi, known as an editor of a Partindo journal on which editorial board also Amir Sjarifoeddin had been listed."[43] "When Musso arrived at Java, in May 1935," writes Harry Poeze, "the PKI [Communist Party of Indonesia] had been re-established . . . Roeskak became the chairman, Soemadi became the secretary, Djokosoejono was charged with cadres' formation and Siti Larang [thus known because she was said to sell forbidden (*larang*) drinks] worked in an unspecified role."[44]

Anton Lucas, an Australian historian, talked after the war to some of the left-wing people in and around Soerabaja, who told him that they had contact with Musso: "Musso lived in Kedoeroes hamlet, Goenoengsari village on the Sepandang-Wonokromo *keboepaten* [regency] border." they said. "Siti Larang . . . accompanied Musso on two trips outside Surabaya, one to Malang, and one to visit relatives in Pagu subdistrict in Kediri."[45]

According to Van Klinken, Partindo, Amir's party, had been "reduced to a shadow" after Amir went to prison.[46] "Shadow" might be a good word to describe Partindo at the time, as it might be a good word to describe Musso. In fact, as Musso left Java, Partindo formally ceased its activity, but shadows remained and sometimes they seemed to be one shadow.

On the ruins, or from the shadow, of the disbanded Partindo, after a period of preparation, on May 24, 1937, the establishment of a new party was announced, Gerindo, Gerakan Rakjat Indonesia, the "Movement of the Indonesian People."

Despite all the warnings and the only suspended verdict of Boven Digoel, Amir's name began again to appear in politics. In a police report on the first *Gerindo* public meeting, in August 1937, in Batavia, in what for him was the usual place, Amir reappeared:

> *Report on the first public meeting of the Gerakan Rakjat Indonesia (Gerindo), Sunday, August 8, 1937, in Batavia in Gedoeng Permoefakatan Indonesia.*
>
> At 9 p.m. the chair, a Minangkabau student of medicine, Adnan Gani, opened the meeting as the hall was still only half full. But the people kept coming until about 800 persons filled the hall.

Adnan Gani opened the meeting by an announcement that all persons under the age of 18 were required to leave. (This was the law, the age limit required to attend a political meeting.)

The police report went on that "It should be noted that, while there were, according to the rules, seats reserved in the hall for the police and the press, none was made available for *wakil pemerintah* [Malay for 'a representative of the government']."⁴⁷

On September 17, 1937, five weeks after the meeting, the government adviser for indigenous affairs wrote to the governor general: "Persons with much political experience as *mr.* Sartono and *mr.* Amir Sjarifoeddin were not included in the Gerindo Board. According to some, however, the reason is simply that these people wish first to wait and see how much freedom Gerindo would be allowed."⁴⁸

The first Gerindo congress opened in July 1938 again in Batavia and Amir was already visible. Well noticed in fact. The reporter for the Indonesian newspaper *Pemandangan*, "Outlook," present at the congress, wrote: "The first Gerindo congress was attended by about 2,500, among whom the ordinary people were strongly represented. Also, there was a great number of advanced women. [The Dutch official translation of the report had 'ontwikkelde' (developed) women.]"⁴⁹

The meeting was late beginning, and Adnan Gani, in chair again, when he finally opened it, apologized that people were left waiting. Last night, he said, a closed meeting of the Gerindo was held by the party leadership, and it lasted till six o'clock in the morning. "After this," wrote *Pemandangan*, "the Gerindo youth sang 'Indonesia Raja' and the whole hall joined in."⁵⁰

It had been announced at the congress that Gerindo had already established branches in East, Central and West Java, North and South Sumatra, South Borneo, and South and North Celebes. The Gerindo Youth branches had also been already active in most of these places. "The student A.K. [Adnan] Gani remains the chairman of the central committee," wrote the government observer, "but the well-known lawyer from Soekaboemi, *mr.* Amir Sjarifoeddin, becomes the vice-chairman." "It was decided that the Gerindo Second Congress would take place in Palembang, South Sumatra, July 24 of the next year."⁵¹

In the words of Amir's autobiography, "[i]n 1936, as new restrictive laws had been issued, Partindo dissolved." "However, with several friends we did not stop and in May 1937 Gerakan Rakjat Indonesia ('Movement of the Indonesian People') was founded. At first, I could not take a direct part in the leadership, because I moved to Soekaboemi in between, where I spent a whole year. In 1939, however, after the Party Congress in Palembang, I was appointed (*ditoendjoek*) the General Chairman of the Gerakan Rakjat Indonesia."⁵²

Palembang, the site of Gerindo's second congress, was a place of oilfields and refineries and one of the largest concentrations of industrial labor in the colony. The Palembang congress of Gerindo marked the high point of Amir's reappearance, both to the public and to the police. He was elected the chairman.[53] "Photo shows Amir to be a little overweight, self-assured, looking serious with his dark-rimmed glasses."[54] Each time his speech was "eagerly awaited and often interrupted by applause."[55] "Fascism has its influence also here. It is the opposite of democracy. Fighting in Ethiopia, Austria, Czechoslovakia, China, is a struggle between democracy and dictatorship. The Indonesian people, too, have to choose, and now, not later—choose democracy, which is all powers of the state to the people."[56]

The Palembang congress met just weeks before the outbreak of the Second World War in Europe. The German army invaded Poland on September 2. "This is no longer a struggle between East and West," Amir declared in his opening speech at the congress, "'dictatorship' is now found equally in Europe (Austria and Czechoslovakia) like in the East (China under Japanese overlordship)."[57]

Becoming more of the world, Amir was becoming more of himself. Almost exactly, almost verbatim, like in his student article for the Haarlem City Gymnasium *Mirabele Lectu*, now, at the moment when Hitler's *Blut-und-Boden*, "blood-and-soil," ideology was overwhelming Europe, Amir talked to the Gerindo congress about race. "The Chinese, the Arabs and the Indo-Europeans of the Indies, the *peranakan* [locally born Chinese]," he said, "are all Indonesians." Even "the whites," he added, against much of what the feeling in the Indies had been, "are Indonesians, too."[58]

This was "ethical," of course, in the way of saying, and Julius Schepper and Baron van Asbeck would applaud. But it was revolutionary, too, and in its calling to action. No more "natives," "Orientals," "Chinese," "Arabs" or "Whites," but: the people of the colony, unite!

This was a little like Amir on his way from Holland not stopping at his paternal house. It was shocking for many among Amir's co-fighters in the Indonesian movement. For the Indies, Amir said in his speech in Palembang, "Switzerland and the U.S.A." should be "held up as examples."[59] Chinese, Arabs, and Eurasians "are brothers."[60] Amir, reappearing from the world stood against the accepted wisdom of the Indonesian movement. "Nationalism," he said, "is not determined by the criteria of blood or color of skin."[61] Amir's speech created a sensation especially among the Indonesian Chinese, some called them "the Jews of the Indies," and now, when the real Jews in Europe were already escaping the Nazis or put in camps, it gained a double-new meaning.[62]

At the moment, and for the moment, Amir carried the day. The congress voted to open Gerindo to all the inhabitants of the Indies.[63] "Amir Sjarifoeddin's idea of Gerindo," wrote Adam Malik, at that time one of Amir's young followers but later his passionate political opponent, and one can hear a bit of distance already in this pronouncement written much later, "had been to build up a version of the League against Fascism."⁶⁴

At one moment in his "minorities" speech at the Palembang congress, and I think a crucial moment of it, without revealing its biblical origin, Amir quoted the New Testament parable of the Samaritan. He told it as a fable, of a student who learned by experience "that his 'true brother'" "was not the rich trader of his own people, but the 'poor' and despised person of an unknown race." "*Kaoem soesah*, the miserables," Amir called it, in a moral opposition to *kaoem senang*, "the happy ones." "*Kaoem soesah*, the miserables," Amir said, "should be welcomed as guests, when they knock on the door."⁶⁵

In the moment of need, those whom we had respected might pass us, and the most despised might help. Then one of them might come to our courtyard and ask for friendship. The word *Indo*, "[Indonesian Eurasian]," Amir said, "has an unpleasant association about it in Indonesia" and we as an avant-garde party [*pelopor*] have to do something about it. In fact, he said, it was nothing new to accept these groups, Eurasians, Chinese, Arabs, among us, for the common fight. In the early 1920s it used to be done. But then the idea "faded and disappeared." Did Amir suggest Soekarno's era?

Someone from the audience objected. Eurasians, Chinese, and Arabs, it was argued, did not belong to in the movement. They have frequently stood on the Dutch side. Amir answered:

> When a guest knocks on our door and asks for help, we will give him a soy-bean cake and chili sauce [*tempe* and *sambal*, something comparable to "bread" in the European context]. There are poor and needy [*kaoem soesah*, "the miserables"] among the *Indos* and those we will accept [*Indos*, and Chinese and Arabs, too, by implication]. There is, however, *kaoem senang* ["the happy ones"] among the Europeans, Chinese and Arabs, those in the habit of eating dishes in palm oil and with dates [*minjak samin* and *korma*, luxuries]. In the face of those, our doors will be shut. We will check everybody before letting him in.⁶⁶

A government observer at the congress did not seem to notice the Bible as a source of Amir's story. But he pointed out that Amir's and Gerindo's "idea of national freedom" began now to be based "on the principle of class struggle."⁶⁷ The Gerindo Palembang congress had been a moment of Amir's reappearance, a *revenant*, as Jacques Derrida might put it, which in French, he explains, "is also a term for a 'ghost' or a 'specter,' which comes back,"⁶⁸ "repetition, resurgence, revival, or haunting."⁶⁹ Amir was becoming more of himself, repeating what he was writing and thinking since Haarlem. For the defenders of the existing order, however, it was a ghost reappearing: the specter of Communism haunted the Indies.

It was at the Palembang congress, according to some memories, that rumors began to circulate of Amir clandestinely attaching himself to the extreme left, the people known, or rumored, to be trained by Musso and left behind by Musso to continue his work. "It has been an oral tradition also among the PKI [Indonesian Communist Party] followers," Jacques Leclerc heard from several Indonesians in the 1980s, "that Amir 'adhered' himself to Communism at the time of the Palembang congress in 1939."[70]

In 1936, about a year after Amir left the Soekamiskin prison, a new Indonesian daily, *Kebangoenan*, "Awakening," appeared. The editorial board was made of Sanoesi Pane as the chief editor, with Liem Koen Hian and, for the first year at least, Amir Sjarifoeddin as advisers. Between April 9 and 13, 1936, also, the congress of the Pergoeroean Rakjat, "People's University," took place in Batavia. Amir was still listed as the university's vice-president.[71]

In September of the same year the first issue of Indonesian monthly *Ilmoe dan Masjarakat*, "Science and Society," came out. In the first issue, Amir's signed article appeared, "The Rebellion in Spain and the International Law."[72] In following issues of the magazine, Amir published articles on "abuse of freedom," and on "freedom of association,"[73] two longer essays, one on "the threat of fascism" and the other on the "Pacific War," a conflict still far away from the Indies, or so it seemed to many, but not to Amir.

Poedjangga Baroe, "New Writer," a new Indonesian magazine for culture and politics appeared already in the early 1930s, under the initiative, among others, of Amir's friend Sanoesi Pane. In December 1938, in the magazine regular rubric *Tjatatan*, " Notes," Amir wrote on "Pogroms against Jews in Nazi Germany." "This is the culture of Europe of 1938," Amir wrote in this article: "Jews are being chased and put in concentration camps . . . *ohne Ende* [German for "without end"]. . . . It is considered 'normal' by the German nation . . . nation of '*Dichter und Denker*' [German for "Poet and Thinker"]. . . . The mass becomes anonymous, . . . homogeneous, . . . a crowd." The hope, Amir wrote, is in a "heterogenous mass." "A heterogenous mass comes together at a public meeting where a speaker might still inspire a heroic stance. Heterogenous mass might even become superior to an individual."[74] In another Indonesian paper of the same time, *Indonesia Berdjoeang*, "Fighting Indonesia", Amir wrote "a number of articles about socialism."[75] *Indonesia Berdjoeang* was published in Soerabaja and it was edited by Pamoedji, a man known as close to Musso when Musso was there.

Increasingly, Amir wrote articles and glosses about Marxism, socialism, and the USSR. He published a feuilleton about the October Revolution.[76] He wrote essays like "Marx and Marxism," or "Alexander Ulyanov Hanged," a story of the older brother of Lenin who attempted to assassinate Tsar Alexander II.[77] In the first May issue of *Kebangoenan* in 1939, Amir wrote an opinion piece: "The Perspectives of the Trade Unions in Indonesia."[78]

Ever more Amir appeared, wrote, and spoke as an individual to whose level the heterogenous mass can arise. He was still propelled by thinking critically, individually, and morally, as demanded by the categorical imperative. He was still more Kantian than Hegelian. His stance was predominantly ethical, but ever more it resembled what Roland Barthes called "Neutral": "Neutral is the dialectic of the getting beyond. . . . Neutral outplays the paradigm or rather . . . [is] everything that baffles the paradigm . . . an ardent, burning activity. . . . The thought of the Neutral is in fact a borderline thought. . . . The Neutral is difficult, provocative, scandalous: because it implies a thought of the indistinct, the temptation of the ultimate paradigm."[79]

In the July–August 1940 issue of *Poedjangga Baroe*, again as a *Tjatatan*, " Note," Amir wrote: "There is just one and single crisis . . . of Europe . . . of East Asia . . . of Ethiopia . . . of Spain. . . . Because there is a war, a military conflict, many people forget that this is also a social crisis, crisis and a change that developed gradually, through history, and not just somewhere outside, beyond the borders of one nation and one country."[80]

In some ways, as if Amir was still in the Netherlands, inside of the inside of Europe, and thus, in this Eurocentric era of the world. As he wrote, his case was losing. In Spain the pro-Franco "homogeneous crowds" were celebrating the end of the republic and the victory of fascism with *Han passado!* "They have passed!"[81] "We have learned to look at the world like if we were merely an audience," Amir wrote in May 1940—like at the classroom wall charts, he might have said:

> now, there is a chance, at least, that we might see the spectacle as it is. . . . A typhoon that has been tearing through the world, blows at us. . . .
>
> After the war . . . the leaders of Europe and America will get together to build a new world . . . We must make our voice to be heard. Indeed, we must make our voice to be born.
>
> These days, an airplane flies from Batavia to Singapore no longer than a train goes from Batavia to Tjimahi, a town 150 km away from the capital! Distances collapse. We buy American books in Batavia. In Batavia, we buy English and Japanese stuff and without even thinking about it

anymore. The Indies' oil burns in Turkish ships. . . . Time is changing and, after the crisis in Europe would be over, and after they will get together to build a new world, where will we be?[82]

In January 1937, in *Poedjangga Baroe*, again as a "Critique," Amir published a long essay on Niccolo Machiavelli.

"Often these days, we hear about 'de sterke man' [Dutch for 'the strong man']," Amir wrote. "Is it him who does not look left or right to achieve his aims? . . . Is it courage, to get rid of moral and religious considerations when they happen to stand in our way?" The present times, wrote Amir, were very much like those of Machiavelli's Italy:

> In Italy of the fifteenth and sixteenth centuries everything was on the edge. The Renaissance already begun to force away the old ideology and to exchange it for its very opposite. . . . It might seem that all the moral and ethical norms were about to disappear in the commotion. . . . It was a high-risk time . . . but strangely, exactly during this time, *cultuur* [Dutch for "culture"] developed gloriously.
>
> Machiavelli is to be seen as a true Renaissance man. . . . His *methode* [Dutch for "method"] was no more based on the codex of either the *moraal of ethiek* [Dutch for "moral or ethical"] or of religion. . . . It was based on vigor . . . on the courage to face the concrete situation and actual reality. . . . Machiavelli wrote that among bad people, a gentle man is often destroyed. Therefore, the prince [man] must learn to become a person who is not gentle in principle.

Amir quoted Machiavelli on cruelty: "Cruelty, as long as it brings good results, is not to be rejected."

The importance of Machiavelli, wrote Amir, rested in his being "the first one who completely liberated himself from a medieval ideology and understood '*staat*' [Dutch for 'state'] not anymore as 'civitas dei' [Latin for 'City of God'] but as 'civitas' [Latin for 'body of people constituting a politically organized community']." To achieve "civitas," Amir wrote, "Machiavelli conceived a personality of a prince [man] as 'homo politicus' [Latin for 'political man']!"[83]

In June 1937, number 7 of *Poedjangga Baroe*, Amir published a gloss on Thomas Mann: "Thomas Mann no longer lives in Germany. The giant of the German letters was forced out of the land of Hitler. . . . It was not enough. Thomas Mann was now informed that his degree of doctor honoris causa that had been awarded to him some years ago (it does not make sense to name the school) has now been revoked. . . . Thomas Mann answered with an open letter—a writer raised his voice. In Germany today, however, almost certainly, nobody hears it." In the same note, Amir mentioned Thomas Mann's open letter, to the *Nation* magazine, in support of the Spanish republic against the generals.[84]

Nothing was marginal to Amir, increasingly so. In fact, the glosses, the edges, of politics, religion, morals, increasingly appeared to be what mattered. The edges increasingly defined Amir—at the edges of saying with an increasing awareness, evidently, that it was not enough.

Some suggested that Amir read Molière seriously when he was imprisoned in Soekamiskin, as his friend at the time Soetan Mohammad Sjah, believed "Poerbo [another friend of Amir at the time] was an *orientalist*. Amir and I were rather inclined towards the European culture. For his article, 'Molière as a social critique,' Amir probably used the complete works of the great author from the Soekamiskin prison library."[85] (Amir might, indeed, have read the complete works of Molière in prison, or he might have read it in the Haarlem Gymnasium library; in effect, the same thing.)

"These were treacherous times," Amir wrote on Molière in the essay published four months after he was let out from prison. "Strangely" (again, as he wrote about Machiavelli and his times), "*cultuur* [Dutch for 'culture'] during these times had developed greatly." The motto to the article is from the Molière preface to *Le Tartuffe*, left by Amir in French: "On souffre aisément des répréhensions; mais on ne souffre point la raillerie. On veut bien être méchant, mais on ne veut point être ridicule ['People can put up with rebukes, but they cannot bear being laughed at; they are prepared to be wicked, but they dislike appearing ridiculous']."[86]

While Amir's Machiavelli article dealt more with politics, and a strong man at the edge of the ethical, Amir's Molière was squarely about faith and religion. Amir focused on Tartuffe, the epitome of religious hypocrisy. "During the third performance of his comedy *Le Malade Imaginaire* ['The Imaginary Invalid']," Amir wrote, "Molière vomited blood and he died the same day. . . . When his friends wanted to give him a burial [the archbishop] Harlay de Champvallon stepped in and forbade a church ceremony."[87]

Molière, like Robespierre, the hero of Kramat 106, and like Amir, was, but was not really destined to become, a lawyer. "The profession," Amir wrote,

> his father chose for him was the law. . . . Initially, it appeared that Molière agreed. But how easily had he moved away from it! Since he was little, he loved theater and—*die erste Liebe sei die einzige* [German for "The first love is the only one"] as Goethe says. . . . Molière's studies of the law, however, were not wholly in vain. . . . He learned philosophy, especially

the Epicurean system. . . . Molière's aim became to present "tableau de la vie humaine," a canvas of human lives.

There are . . . both aristocrats and rich bourgeois in Molière's plays. . . . But *djongos* and *baboe* are never missing. They subvert the plot, to their plain language nothing is safe, nothing that is going on among their masters and mistresses.

In an Indonesian text and writing about seventeenth-century France, Amir used two Malay and colonial terms for servants—*djongos* for a male and *baboe* for a female. Molière lived in the Indies.

Molière was a man of a genuine and uneasy faith. *"Le Tartuffe* presents a hypocrite who waves the flag of religion. . . . Here," Amir wrote, "the *comédie* becomes tragic." In quoting Misanthrope, Molière's failed hero, who had lost his faith, Amir again quotes in French: "Je ne trouve, partout que lâche flatterie, / Qu'injustice, intérêt, trahison, fourberie ['I find everywhere nothing but cowardly flattery / But injustice, interest, betrayal, deceit']."[88]

Between June 25 and 28, 1938, in Soerakarta, Amir took an active part in organizing the Kongres Bahasa Pertama, "First Congress of Language." He served as the vice-president of the program committee, and he also gave a talk on "Indonesian Adaptation of Foreign Languages." In the talk, Amir proposed ten points of "adaptation." In the first and main point, he said: "Every revolutionary language faces a problem of dealing with foreign words and concepts." "Exact language," he said, "the language of a philosopher," must point out the way. *Vocabularium*, a depository of Greek and Latin terms, should became the conduit through which the foreign, into each revolutionary language, is to be adapted.[89]

CHAPTER 9

Charles O. van der Plas

Tine Fransz, a schoolmate, and a friend, recalled a remark by Amir, though she did not say whether he said it when they were still at the Law School or later: "In our struggle for freedom, we do not really face the Dutch, but the whole discriminatory and oppressive system of social relations. Everything that stands behind the system has to be opposed, whether it is of ours, or of another nation."[1]

According to G. J. (Han) Resink, someone asked Schepper if he, already in the 1930s, wanted independence for the Indies and "Schepper answered 'yes.'" "Schepper was regarded as an 'extremist,'" Resink added, "and that was what attracted Amir."[2]

The years after Amir was released from prison were the last years of the Dutch Indies. There was an increasing unease during the 1930s among the Dutch of the Indies, a tiny minority of the population. People like Schepper or Van Asbeck worried no less, as they saw an increasing decline of morals and democracy in the colonial regime and attitudes—expressed most immediately as an increasing stiffness.

On the other hand, the Nationaal-Socialistische Beweging, "National-Socialist Movement," a political organization of extremely nationalist Dutch and Eurasians in both the Netherlands and in the Indies, growing ever more openly pro-Nazi with the passing years, was well on its way by the late 1930s to become a dominant political force in the colony.

The Spanish Civil War was the test, and fascism was winning. Thomas Mann had been exiled, and his doctor honoris causa decree was taken away. Molière, of time long ago, stood up—anxiously—for the humanity today. Machiavelli stood up as a warning. The specter of Communism haunted the bourgeois world, yet many, and an increasing force in the world too, looked to the specter as signaling something still possible. Amir Sjarifoeddin's release from prison, noted Arnold Brackman, a journalist turned historian, "coincided with the enunciation of the popular front line, a new political line of Communist International offering a cooperation of democracy against fascism."[3]

In September 1936, Edgar Snow, a US journalist and adventurer, wrote about his visit with Mao Tse-tung in northern China. At the time, news of the Seventh Congress of Communist International, held just a year previously, had already reached the guerilla base, a "fully developed thesis of the international anti-Fascist united front tactic."[4]

Musso was in the Indies that same year, in 1936. Seemingly far away, in Vienna, Austria, Robert Musil, one of the finest European authors and thinkers of the time, wrote that "People expect that now someone, a hero perhaps, will do something. People know what's to be done. How to do it, I won't give the German Communist Party, etc., any tips." Yet, what was "clearly needed," Robert Musil wrote, was "active spirit and spirit of action."[5]

"The conflict between Indonesians and Dutch," wrote Brackman, was now being "overshadowed and depreciated" by the global threat of fascism.[6] Certainly for the Indies this was an overstatement. Only few among the Dutch and even fewer among the Indonesians had seen the contradiction of colonizer-versus-the-colonized being overshadowed by anything. To the opposite: increasingly many on both sides saw the moment as an opportunity to push harder for nationalist aims. Increasingly, too, the aims were expressed through arguments, slogans, and clichés of race and blood. To think otherwise in the Indies of the time, be it Schepper's way or Amir's way, was to find oneself in a state, increasingly, of anxious solitude.

Gerindo, for a while, became Amir's party, speaking his way. Especially at the time of the Palembang congress, it regarded "colonial independence for the time being as a secondary goal."[7] "In Gerindo analysis," wrote a historian who knew the period best, John Legge, "the European dictatorships were linked with military fanaticism in Japan and together they represented a material outcome of the evolution of capitalism. As such they posed a world threat to democracy and in this situation of global crisis, resistance to fascism was more important than resistance to the evils of colonial rule. Indeed, the outcome of the independence struggle in Indonesia and elsewhere would, in the end, depend on the defeat of fascism."[8] "Gerindo," John Legge concluded quite categorically, referring to Communist International's new program, "was certainly a popular front with a difference."[9]

In July 1936, at the same moment, a member of the Volksraad, "People's Council," Soetardjo Kartohadikoesoemo, of the high Javanese aristocracy, in a conservative wing of the Volksraad—formally a co-legislative body but in fact a body with power only to voice an opinion and to offer advice to the governor-general—suggested a petition to be sent to the Dutch queen to inquire about a possibility to convene in the future an "imperial conference" at which a self-government of the Indies in the framework of the existing constitution and kingdom could be discussed. Certainly, an act both careful and polite.

Except for the conservative segment of the indigenous political forces, and of course for the conservative Dutch majority inside and outside the Volksraad, the reaction to Soetardjo's petition had been negative, and overwhelmingly passionate in its negativity. Now, at the moment of the Western world's crisis, all suggestion of petitioning for a gift should be rejected. Yet, with its argument for a united front against fascism and in defense of democracy, radical Gerindo supported the petition!

The Indonesian newspaper *Pemandangan*, on November 29, 1936, in the heat of the Soetardjo-petition discussion, reported on a public meeting the previous day of a broad coalition of the Indonesian parties in Batavia. The single topic of the meeting was the petition. The meeting took place in the Gedoeng Permoefakatan, "House of Deliberation," in Kenari Alley, where so much had happened in the Indonesian movement and in Amir's public life in the past.

"Messrs. Adnan Gani and mr. Sjarifoeddin of the Gerindo central committee," *Pemandangan* reported, "read a declaration proposing that the meeting approve the aim to convene the imperial conference and, in this sense, the petition. Mr. Sjarifoeddin pointed out the fact that the petition was the first ever event when a proposal in the name of the people was coming from the Volksraad."[10]

Most of the participants at the meeting in Kenari Alley, however, in the end declared themselves fiercely against the stance of Amir, Gani, and Gerindo. On the contrary, as another Indonesian magazine, *Perasaan Kita*, "Our Sense," wrote on the same day as the *Pemandangan* report was published, the meeting "decided to stay off any action which might support the petition. Some parties explicitly forbade their followers to take any part in such actions." The *Perasaan Kita* reporter added that the atmosphere at the meeting was "good and the spirit excellent, only one thing grieved the writer, namely the position of Gerindo as expressed by Messrs. Gani and Amir Sjarifoeddin."[11]

For anyone who thought of the radical Indonesian movement in terms of *sini–sana*, "we–they," and strict noncooperation, as Soekarno had done in the

1920s, and as most, on the Dutch as well as Indonesian side still did, Amir's, Gani's, and Gerindo's stance was confusing: the radicals approaching the Dutch! In an extensive report on the state of the Indonesian movement, the governor of East Java, Charles O. van der Plas, a man well known for his penetrating expertise, wrote (and one can still sense how baffled the brilliant official was): "Gerindo is now to take part in the municipal and Volksraad elections."

It seemed awkward to say in the least. The parties who opposed the Soetardjo petition were socially moderate, even conservative. They worked in the comfort zone of the leaders of the nation, inside of a secure political zone of "anthropological space"—"our home, our nation, our language, our leaders." Gerindo, willing to join in defense of democracy including, for the moment, the colonial one, against fascism, was, as Van der Plas expressed the dilemma in his report, "destructive," "extremely radical," and "widely suspected of being tied with the Communists."[12]

On April 2, 1939, in the spirit of participation in the colonial democracy, Gerindo indeed nominated Amir as its candidate in the Batavia municipal elections for Volksraad to take place on April 26. Eventually, Amir obtained 240 votes (out of 1,430), and was not elected.[13] But still, the moment was historical. According to *Kebangoenan*, on the day of the elections, April 26, 1939, the presidium of Gerindo's Batavia branch at its meeting heard Amir's report on "the right to vote as a tactic of struggle."[14]

Three weeks after his unsuccessful candidacy for Volksraad, under Gerindo and clearly very much on Amir's initiative, Gaboengan Politik Indonesia (GAPI), "Indonesian Political Federation," was put together, a capacious and loose association in which Amir and Gerindo, against all odds, attempted to push for the program of supporting democracy—including colonial democracy—against fascism. The permanent committee of the GAPI was led by Abikoesno Tjokrosoejoso, for the Muslims, the general secretary was Mohammad Husni Thamrin, for the nationalists. Amir Sjarifoeddin was a commissar.[15]

In late December 1939, Amir, as a secretary of the Kongres Rakjat Indonesia, "Congress of the Indonesian People,"[16] which met between December 23 and 25, 1939, in Batavia, announced that by December 17 of that year, meetings of GAPI had taken place in ninety-nine places all over the Indies and that they were attended by about eighty-one thousand people.[17] Amir himself had to know the sheer vacuousness of these numbers.

It was the best of times and the worst of times, a moment in which the contours of the landscape, political, ethical, and personal, for Amir and for the Indies, cleared.

Mohammad Yamin, perhaps his best friend from the time of Kramat 106, the Law School, politics, and journalism, left Amir. According to *Kebangoenan* of April 26, 1939, Gerindo's Batavia branch, at its recent meeting suspended the membership of Mohammad Yamin. At the Palembang congress in July of 1939, Yamin was expelled.[18] The main reason seems to be that, while Amir was putting democracy first, including colonial democracy, Yamin increasingly talked about the identity of nation and the need for a patriotic upheaval in the face of the upcoming war. In the Dutch Indies being threatened, he saw a chance for the nation. On July 21, 1939, Yamin founded the Parpindo, Partai Persatoean Indonesia, "Party of the Indonesian Unity."[19]

The air around Amir was clearing up. Amir had rejected Schepper's offer of a job with the Protestant mission. In Soekamiskin prison, Amir seemed to Schepper "egocentric and oversensitive." It might not have occurred to Schepper that Amir was becoming more himself, more Schepper than Schepper, so to speak, less borrowed.

It did not mean that Amir distanced himself from Christianity. His faith only appeared more a part of his constitution, including his politics, his conviction that democracy had to be defended against fascism at all costs, and that the fate of morality—that is Christian morality—depended on the outcome of the struggle.

Despite Amir declining Schepper's offer, he remained close, and grew even closer, to Protestant circles in the Indies. In December 1940, after the Netherlands had already been occupied by German armies, a new weekly, *Semangat Baroe*, "New Spirit," came out in Batavia. It was Protestant, Indonesian, and Dutch. The magazine redaction was made up of Amir's cousin Datoek Moelia, who had introduced him to the Sminks in Leiden, of Kees van Doorn, a Protestant pastor who used to visit Kramat 106 when Amir was a resident there, and of another priest, Dr. Johannes Verkuyl, a man of Amir's age, who studied at Haarlem at the same time as Amir but at a different school. Amir was also a member of the board. *Semangat Baroe*, in a sense, was a sequel to another Malay-language Protestant weekly, *Zaman Baroe*, "New Era," published between 1927 and 1929, and edited by Datoek Moella.[20]

The articles Amir wrote in *Semangat Baroe* were no less political than those he wrote for the other Indonesian papers. In *Semangat Baroe* he wrote with enthusiasm about "Roosevelt's four freedoms": "It is our duty to support values such as those enshrined in the Atlantic Charter: the equality of political rights, economic opportunity, and social justice. These give an opportunity to all groups to create a new society, without distinctions based on race or *religion*."[21]

Amir wrote in support of another proposal emerging in the Volksraad, for a popular militia, that is for weapons and military training to be given to

Indonesians and not only, as was still the case then, to the professional colonial army. "Only a nation of citizens can ask its members for the supreme sacrifice," he wrote—quoting Machiavelli, indeed, almost verbatim.[22] "Total war like this requires a *total* mobilization."[23] The basic issue, Amir wrote, was that of political change: if the Dutch were serious, Indonesians had to enter the militia "with a pure heart . . . as a way to political change. If we do not do it, we resign ourselves to defeat."[24]

Amir pointed to armies with and without militias. The French army in 1793 and 1794 sang "La Marseillaise." "The power of this army," he wrote, was in its "desire and inspiration," the "spiritual power of the people," which is its *"faith"* in "fraternity, liberty, equality." "The foundation of modern life, modern society, and the modern state" is based on this, "in other words, on democracy." "A state has the right to its citizens' lives. But only if these citizens have equal rights"—"no representation without taxation," Amir writes, "no taxation without representation."[25]

In late May 1941, with the war already close to the Indies, with everything at stake, in *Semangat Baroe*, Amir's article appeared, which, as Van Klinken notes, became "the most theological piece he ever wrote."[26].

"Do everything," Amir wrote, to be worth of "a Kierkegaardian individual morality under conditions of modernity." Young people in this moment between tradition and modernity, Amir wrote, "are confused," and he listed what might help them to make a stance: feminism, democracy in struggle with fascism, Kant, Hegel, modern music, and labor unions. It is up the Indonesian churches, he concluded, "to give the youth the leadership."[27]

A Dutch Protestant missionary and a member of the *Semangat Baroe* redaction, who possibly knew Amir back from Haarlem, Dr. Johannes Verkuyl, invited Amir to a conference he was helping to organize for October s0–24, 1941 (just weeks before the Pearl Harbor attack and the outbreak of the Pacific War).[28] The conference of the Nederlandsch Indische Zending Bond (NIZB), "Netherlands Indies Mission Union," which Amir attended, took place in Karangpandan, a small resort near Soerakarta, Central Java.

Datoek Moelia and Van Doorn of the *Semangat Baroe* attended Karangpandan, too, besides about 280 missionaries, theologians, and individual guests. Thirty-three Indonesians, members of the NIZB were also present.[29] Amir appealed to the missionaries, recalled Dr. Verkuyl, because they needed someone who "thought laterally."[30]

Amir took part in the third section of the conference dealing with the calling of churches on political terrain. "Discussion was opened by *mr.* Amir Sjarifoeddin, who, in an animated way, explained how in the clash between the

East and the West, the East is not being ruined, but it comes to itself and with ever stronger urge moves towards the fulfilment of the needs of the Eastern people, in the Eastern people's own manner, its own mentality, cognizance, culture, and ideals. . . . It is up to Christians to stand next to the Islamists and other nationalists." "In formulating the problem," Amir said, "a Christian vision is needed."[31]

In conclusion of his speech Amir questioned whether it was needed for the Christians to form a separate political party or whether they should exercise their faith and pursue their aims inside the existing structure of the national movement. This is a dilemma, he said, and he did not know "a way out," but he declared himself to be "ready to stand on the side of a Christian party if he becomes convinced about its necessity."[32]

The reaction was immediate. The most influential figures of the Indonesian movement, and many of them Amir's allies and friends till then, now said and wrote they felt threatened to the core of their political lives. The Dutch press added to the furor. "According to a press report," the widely read Dutch *Java Bode* wrote on October 28, 1941, "Amir Sjarifoeddin told a conference at Karampangan: 'We, as Christians, must have our own ground to stand on: not to be drowned through the Islamists and nationalists.'" "If the report is incorrect," the paper added with clearly a tongue in cheek, "Amir must let it be rectified! It might be a cause for misunderstanding." "The cat was set among the pigeons," wrote Abikoesno Tjokrosoejoso, Amir's partner at the GAPI leadership, representing, at the GAPI executive, the Partai Sarekat Islam Indonesia (PSII), "Party of Islamic Union."[33] Mohammad Natsir, a man of Amir's generation and till then close to Amir in many actions of the movement, now publicly warned that Amir (and he mentioned Datoek Moelia with him) "can take over the essentially Islamic Indonesian national movement because," as Natsir put it, "they are clever."[34] Amir, wrote Natsir, was "a danger to the community of Islam."[35]

Even Amir's own Gerindo reacted "with surprise." According to rumors "the leaders of Gerindo were indignant about Amir expressing himself as a Christian so openly."[36]

"Amir himself was surprised," recalled Pastor Verkuyl who had invited Amir to Karangpandan in the first place. Pastor Verkuyl says that he got a letter from Amir at the time: "Now I have learned," Amir wrote, "how it was when the people had chosen Barabbas over Christ, the Man of Nazareth—what a delicious feeling it had to be in the middle of all the ecstasies."[37] These formulations look to me much like Pastor Verkuyl's rather than Amir's. Ecstatic! Except, perhaps, for the "delicious feeling." Here Amir, if he ever wrote it, resembles Roland Barthes struggling and pleasuring through the "Neutral":

"The Neutral is difficult, provocative, scandalous: because it implies a thought of the indistinct, the temptation of the ultimate paradigm."[38]

Fascism expanded, from Italy and Germany to Spain, throughout Europe, to China, and to Japan. An increasing number of people in the countries affected—intellectuals, reformers, revolutionaries, Jews but not just them—tried to flee. Democracy as a system and as a faith was in a state of anxious solitude.

From the Netherlands, across the wine-deep sea now full of German submarines, people were fleeing, very much along old imperial routes, as far as they possibly could—to the antipodes if possible, to Australia, where the surge would reach them last or perhaps never. Many of those who hesitated a little longer were stopped at the outset or on the way, at the end of 1941, by the outbreak of the Pacific War; some were stuck in the Indies.

Many of those on the run embodied qualities of missionaries and sailors, with the ground swelling under them like the deck of a ship, with having, suddenly and for who knew for how long, to familiarize themselves with the exotic and often threatening land of the Indies. There was many of those now on the run, like Schepper and Amir had been for a long time. Except that now, the Indies and the world appeared sinking.

Kritiek en Opbouw, "Critique and Development," was a Bandoeng-based political-literary magazine founded in 1938 by D. M. G. Koch, a self-declared socialist, who had lived in the Indies for most of his life. He was one of those people as troubled with the growth of fascism as with the state of the Indies.[39] *Kritiek en Opbouw* was an example of saying, a presence never outside the narrow margin of the colony, never read by more than a few hundred readers.

One of the authors of *Kritiek en Opbouw* and member of the journal's circle was Willem Walraven, the author of the description of the Soekamiskin prison where Amir, perhaps, read his Molière. Walraven was with *Kritiek en Opbouw* from July 1, 1939, until the magazine's last number, in February 1942. Amir's name is listed among *Kritiek en Opbouw*'s collaborators. No doubt he wrote for the magazine, but in the manner of the time only a few articles in *Kritiek en Opbouw* in general were signed. Only the letters beneath the article help; other times the style or topic makes it (almost) evident that the author was Amir. All the articles in *Kritiek en Opbouw* were in Dutch.

The article "Twee Werelden," "Two Worlds," is signed "A" and, guessing from its slightly sarcastic grin, is almost certainly by Amir. It is a report on a brochure published in 1938 by Hamilton F. Armstrong, the editor of the US journal *Foreign Affairs*. Armstrong, Amir (almost certainly Amir) writes, is "very American," and his opus is "a hymn on democracy as a system in which majority rules and minority has a right to offer criticism and to oppose the majority." Amir's grin become more visible as the reader reads: "The book praises democracy as a system that gives everyone the right to be a democrat and to which anti-democrats have no right to belong. A Nazi, in other words, does not have the right to be a Nazi and a Communist does not have the right to be a Communist."[40]

Yet another *Kritiek en Opbouw* article signed "A.S." is dated a day before the outbreak of the Second World War in Europe and it is "about Asia":

The Pan-Asiatic Movement

Under the slogan "Asia for the Asians" Japan declared . . . a kind of Monroe Doctrine for the continent. . . . Let us not fall for the charm of this cliché, which is not new at all. Indonesians were always vulnerable to the spiritual currents, specifically those coming from Asia. . . . Against the clouds of the Pan-Asiatic propaganda . . . a policy is needed which is constructed of ideals to which the Indonesian people might adhere in the fullness and spirituality of their own.[41]

Charles Edgar du Perron was a major Dutch writer of the 1930s and an important man of the European letters. In 1933, André Malraux dedicated to him his *Condition Humaine*, a novel about the (failed) revolution in Shanghai. Du Perron was an intellectual on the run, too. He was a son of a Dutch family who had lived in the Indies for generations, and he described himself as *een Indische jongen*, "an Indies lad." He became best known for his 1935 novel *Land van Herkomst*, "Country of Origin," meaning the Indies.

Du Perron left the Indies for Europe in 1921 (the same year as Amir but he was older than Amir), when he was twenty-two. Du Perron settled in the Netherlands (or was trying to) but, as fascism expanded and began to reach Europe's every corner, despairing of the West, Du Perron "returned" to the Indies in 1936. In 1938, as *Kritiek en Opbouw* was launched, he became a major figure of the journal.

Du Perron did not resemble Julius Schepper in many ways. But he had the same passionate way of gathering around himself young, educated Indonesians. He built a circle, too, where they debated books Du Perron pointed out. The outside reaches of the circle touched upon Amir.

Soewarsih Djojopoespito was perhaps the circle's most remarkable member. She was the wife of Soegondo Djojopoespito, one of Amir's schoolmates at the Law School and, in 1928, the chair of the historical session of the Second Youth Congress at Kramat 106, as Amir also sat in the presidium. Soewarsih, with Du Perron's help, encouragement, and under his mentorship, published, in Dutch, what is sometimes described as the first modern novel written in the Indies by an indigenous writer, published only after the war,

Buiten het Gareel, "Out of Line." ("Out of the Harness" may be a more literal translation.)

Ali Boediardjo, another Indonesian of the Du Perron circle, was a former student at the Law School like Soewarsih's husband Soegondo. As Amir was the *anak emas*, "favorite child," of Professor Schepper, Ali Bocdiardjo was the *anak emas* of Schepper's colleague, Professor Logemann.[42] Soejitno Mangoenkoesoemo was the third member of the group and, of the three, he was probably closest to Amir.

Du Perron was instrumental in getting these young Indonesians accepted by *Kritiek en Opbouw*: he cleared a way for their contributions to be published and he read and very probably corrected their manuscripts. All of them knew Amir, some very well and some more loosely. From August 1938, for instance, there is a note found in Du Perron's correspondence. Du Perron wrote from Bandoeng to Soejitno who then lived in Buitenzorg about a meeting they planned: "I have something still to talk about on Saturday with *mr*. Amir Sjarifoeddin. But do come in the evening, about eight, then we will be less hurried and can ramble as long as we wish."[43]

In March 1939, Du Perron noticed what to him seemed an interesting article in *Poedjangga Baroe*. He asked Soejitno about the author who was unknown to him: "Could you tell me something," Du Perron wrote, "about that piece where so many authors are cited including me (by Soetan Sjahrir—or Sjahrar). Please!"[44] Soejitno got the copy, sent it to Du Perron, and, ten days later, Du Perron wrote to Soejitno again: "Sjahrir is 'subtle' [*subtiel*]. No fun. To him Takdir [Soetan Takdir Alisjahbana, the editor of *Poedjangga Baroe* at that time and a writer, too] seems as wonderful as Ehrenburg."[45]

The sarcasm notwithstanding, Du Perron felt he was on a mission—not unlike Schepper did and was. It helped, sort of, that Sjahrir for the last few years was in exile in Banda Neira, in the remote eastern Indonesian Banda Archipelago—the same place where, as it happened, Soejitno's older brother Tjipto Mangoenkoesoemo had been held, too.

Letters had been exchanged between Du Perron and Sjahrir. Sjahrir was interesting. He had been to the Netherland for a year, 1929–1931, moving quite loosely, in a Bohemian manner, through Dutch independent-socialist circles. Together with an older Indonesian colleague, Mohammad Hatta, a student at the Netherlands School of Commerce in Rotterdam, he stood up, not unlike Amir Sjarifoeddin, against Soekarno and his grand-orator methods. He and Hatta, however, also got into conflict with Perhimpoenan Indonesia, the Indonesian students' association in the Netherlands, as Perhimpoenan moved to the left and toward the Communists. Both Sjahrir and Hatta had been expelled from the association in 1931.

Sjahrir returned to the Indies first, and Hatta followed him in a few months, after he finished his Rotterdam economic studies. In the Indies, Sjahrir's and Hatta's tactics of anti-colonial struggle, with its emphasis on educating and preparing cadres for a battle in the future, appeared to the government as more dangerous than Soekarno's vacuous eloquence. In 1934, Sjahrir and Hatta had been exiled, no mercy shown, to Boven Digoel. After a year, as the camp was in the end anyway deemed "not suitable" for them, Sjahrir and Hatta were moved to a softer place of exile, more Endeh-like, Soekarno-like, Banda Neira. Out there, through a couple of letters and a budding sense of respect and affection by the group, Sjahrir became part of the Du Perron and *Kritiek en Opbouw* circle, at a social distance, so to speak.

Amir is listed as a member of the *Kritiek en Opbouw* redaction until the journal's very last issue, February 2, 1942, until the final days of the Dutch Indies as everyone knew it, at a time when the Japanese armies were already in Singapore.[46]

In the last weeks of the journal, and of the Indies, *Kritiek en Opbouw* was one of the last voices still speaking. A sense of anxious solitude thickened around the journal. An increasing purity might be noticed in the journal. *Kritiek en Opbouw*, exclusive anyway, had increasingly been closing on itself, clinging to values that suddenly appeared to the leading members of the editorial board as still remaining.

At the same time, the leading role of the Dutch members of the board, always there, became most evident. In distress, with disaster closer to them every day, the Dutch members of the *Kritiek en Opbouw* board realized that they were Dutch—"Dutch-Dutch," G. J. Resink might say. As one reads through the last issues of *Kritiek en Opbouw*, the Indonesian authors and Indonesian themes progressively become less frequent and important. Instead, articles, essays, and poetry concerning the tragedy of Europe filled the journal's pages—it is Europe-Europe now. As if the Dutch members of the journal circle, including those who had run, literally in fact to escape fascism in the West, were now, in fantasy, retracing their path, back to Europe, which, of course, was not there anymore.

The books now discussed in the journal were almost exclusively of a European provenance, by European (or North Atlantic) authors and on European (or North Atlantic) problems, without much reference to whether they might or might not have some relevance for the East or for the Indies, for the Indonesian movement, the colonial democracy, the Indies as a part of the world: *Derde Rijk*, "Third Reich," Goethe's *Faust*, Gladkov's *Cement*, Ilya Ehrenburg, Louis Couperus, Arthur van Schendel.

Eddy du Perron embodied the progression. Increasingly depressed with fascism gaining ground also in the Indies, with the pro-Nazi National Socialist Movement coming close to becoming a major and possibly dominant force in his land of origin, Du Perron, left the Indies again. In August 1939, he boarded a ship to Europe. Over the wine-deep sea. He arrived, began to settle down, and died of a heart attack in the Dutch village of Bergen on the evening of May 14, 1940, the day when Dutch radio announced the capitulation of the Dutch forces to Hitler's Germany.

Amir was losing friends. But out of the desolation of people leaving, new ones appeared around him. They were attracted by Amir, seemingly standing still and thus, among the others, appearing increasingly radical, at the edge, baffling, a neutral. The new people were overall ten or fifteen years younger than him, almost none of them had been abroad. They did not live through the economic depression and they had not experienced Soekarno. Like Amir, however, like Schepper, or like the people of the *Kritiek en Opbouw*, Indonesian or Dutch, in the late colony, they sailed, so to say, dragging anchors behind their ships. They were intense and uncertain.

They moved around Amir, as the French anthropologist Marc Augé might say, like trains are moving past each other in the Paris Metro. The newly emerging network around Amir was not really a group, nor was it a cluster of groups. It was not compact and it was not really connected by links. It held together by the people passing each other. The moments of their staying together, like the trains at stations, were defined by what the French, says Marc Augé, call *correspondences* and the Italians call *coincidences*.[47]

"Perhaps in part because the core of the illegal PKI [Communist Party of Indonesia] lay in Surabaja," wrote Benedict Anderson in his history of the revolution on Java, "the main strength of Amir's group seems to have been concentrated in that city and generally in East Java."[48] When Anton Lucas, during the 1980s, did an oral history in the Soerabaja area, he heard from his elderly informants most often about "a group of four confidants, to whom Musso on his departure entrusted the revival of the party [meaning the Communist Party], namely Siti Larang Sosrokardono, Achmad Soemadhi, Djokosoejono, and Mas Roeskak."[49]

Amir's name, however, was almost never missing. "Amir had spent a lot of time in Surabaya in the 1930s and worked closely with *peranakan* [Indonesian-Chinese] leaders," wrote Siauw Giok Tjhan, one of the new young people around Amir at the time. Siauw described Amir as "an emotional leader who often acted without consulting his associates." "Though a part of Amir's group," Siauw writes about himself, he "was also able to work closely with . . . Djohan Sjahroezah," a cousin of Sjahrir.[50] "There was a newspaper reflecting the looseness and the energy, *Menara Merah* ['Red Tower,' could also be translated as 'Red Minaret']. Anton Lucas writes what he was told: "*Menara Merah* began irregular publication in 1938 and became the basis for recruiting new cadres. . . . It was . . . pocket size and had different covers advertising the contents as a sewing course, cookies recipes or a novel." It was intended, Anton Lucas was told, "only for members or candidate members, . . . printed on a hand press, type was taken from Kolff and Faningen, two Dutch printers in Surabaya. . . . The press was located in the progressive Islamiah School at Kramat Gantung 81 [in Soerabaja], an old hotel which had been made available by progressive *santri* [strict Muslim] H. Zainoeddin, [where] Pamoedji [one of the people close to Musso when he was in Java] lived."[51]

Pamoedji, after Musso left Java in 1936, is said to have led "a small clandestine organization. Among them were Wikana from Gerindo and Siauw Giok Tjhan from the Indonesian Chinese Party [Partai Tionghoa Indonesia]." According to this oral tradition, Amir "joined this illegal PKI through the young East Javanese activist Widarta, Pamoedji's follower, at the second Gerindo Congress in July 1939 in Palembang."[52]

It was also rumored that *Menara Merah* in fact was a paper "under secret redaction of Amir Sjarifoeddin."[53] As significant as that, no copy of *Menara Merah* was ever found and, according to some contemporary commentaries not friendly to the group, *Menara Merah* either never existed, or, worse, it was produced in the Netherlands and smuggled into the Indies as one of the colonial intrigues against the movement.[54] In other words, *Menara Merah*, like the activity around it, was spectral. In its being spectral was much, if not most, of its energy, its appeal, and to its enemies, its menace.

In 1938, "several individuals suspected of connections with Musso," two years after Musso left Java, were sent to Boven Digoel.[55] It might have broken many links in any political structure. But it appeared, rather, to strengthen the spectral power and to "pour more gas on our fire." Besides, heroic escapes from Boven Digoel, however in reality almost nonexistent, were whispered about. There were rumors to linger, wander around, organize, and haunt. "Virtualization" inspires "hauntology," as Jacques Derrida convincingly manifested, and like Barthes's neutral, it leaves paradigms baffled. It baffles a historian as well, of course. As Marcellus, Hamlet's friend, knew, too, "a classical scholar would not be able to speak to the ghost."[56] So the police would not. One should never underestimate the staying power of the swirl.

Names popped up and some disappeared like into thin air. Others remained with Amir for the rest of his life.

Soemarsono was born in 1921, in Kutoardjo, Central Java. He was educated in the local Schakel-School Kristen, "Connecting Christian School."[57] Soemarsono's father was a devoted Muslim, but he let his children attend Christian schools.[58] Soemarsono, as historian William Frederick writes, "had no introduction to political thought until 1938, when he was invited by an artist neighbor of his in Jakarta to attend a meeting. The well-known Amir Sjarifoeddin was present, and there was much talk of working for the Allies for the cause of democracy, fighting fascism, and the like. Sumarsono became interested and soon took an active role in the Gerindo."[59] "With Amir Sjarifoeddin," Soemarsono himself recalled later in his memoirs,

> we became very close to each other. He was a Christian and I was on the way to becoming one. The first time we met was at a Gerindo meeting in the Kenari Alley but then we saw each other often in the Kernolong church in Kwitang near Kramat and Pasar Senen. Amir Sjarifoeddin often preached in the Kernolong church. Except the Christian faith, which we had in common, I told him I wished to learn from his experience in the movement.... He said: "It's fine that you wish to become a good Christian. But the foundation of Christianity is humanism, and to practice humanism, you have to join the political movement."[60]

In 1989, in Hotel Wisata International, Jakarta, a large group of elderly people, students during the last years of the prewar Indies, held their reunion.[61] They were laughing, in the hotel *aula* now, as if they were still young, and they were singing dandy songs. The most hilarious song was sung in Dutch and its lyrics were printed in the memorial brochure of the reunion. In part it roughly translates as:

> *Those women*
> Among Papuans in Fak Fak
> I saw a woman of great charm
> With hairdo as a roof
> She sat on a buffalo!
> Through its nose was a bamboo stick[62]

The list of the invitees at the Hotel Wisata International reads like a rollcall of the other group, of people, of a swirl, of Amir's space: "Hamid Algadri . . . Zainal Abidin . . . Soedarpo Sastrosatomo . . . Soedjatmoko . . . Ali Boediardjo . . . L. Sitoroes . . . Soebadio Sastrosatomo . . . Hazil Tanzil . . . Soedarsono . . ."[63]

John Legge of Monash University wrote a book in the 1980s mostly about these people, about the time when they were young, in the last years of the Indies: "Amir Sjarifoeddin," he wrote, "formed a study club of students and ex-students . . . Soedarpo, Andi Zainal Abidin, Soedjatmoko, Amir Hamzah and others."[64] Did Amir resemble Schepper, or even Socrates, "standing around, standing still, on every *stoa*, on every street corner, on every walk, tugging the Athenian youth by the mantle and keeping asking questions," "corrupting the youth, not acknowledging the gods that the city acknowledges, but introducing new divinities"?[65]

Soedjatmoko, Soebadio, Soedarpo, and the others from this group were clearly urban, indeed, metropolitan. Virtually all of them were graduates of the best, that is, modern Dutch and colonial, Indies high schools. The more assertive among them were already college students, either at the Law School or the Medical School. Looking at Amir and them, at the brink of the colonial disaster, they appeared like a classroom bursting with energy.

The star of these youths was Soedjatmoko, called "Koko" by his friends, son of an aristocratic Javanese family, and a Medical School student. Many years later, Soedjatmoko recalled:

> I had three political mentors at the start of the Pacific War. I had three political mentors who in various degrees and in various ways, have influenced my political perspectives. The first of these three was Amir Sjarifoeddin . . .
>
> I had many searching discussions with Amir Sjarifoeddin, a man of great erudition, immense personal warmth, and charm. . . . In particular, our discussion often centered on how he had reconciled his deeply felt Christianity with his equally deeply felt views of Marxism. From my conversations with him, there emerged insights that helped to shape many of my own personal considerations that have guided me in later life.[66]

Soedjatmoko's other two mentors were Soekarno and Sjahrir, but it would come later.

Two weeks after Pearl Harbor, on December 22, 1941, Amir introduced a new series of lectures to his old academy, the Batavia Volksuniversiteit, "People's University."

Amir's opening talk was on "The World after This War." The next lecture in the series, the following month, was given by a Dutch writer and member of the *Kritiek en Opbouw* circle, Dirk de Vries. He spoke on "Du Perron's Generation." Jacques de Kadt, another *Kritiek en Opbouw* figure, and a recent émigré from Europe, was scheduled to talk next. But, by that time, the Japanese had already arrived.[67]

During the last months of the Dutch Indies, the government and the police were increasingly suspicious of Amir, baffled, indeed, by Amir's "contacts with," "links to," his *correspondences* and *coincidences*, with people known as, suspected to be, "the Communists,"[68] or unknown but the more so causing one to wonder. After May 10, 1940, as the Netherlands was attacked and occupied by Nazi Germany and as the Dutch queen ran, as had so many before her, and settled with an exile government in London, the government in the Indies panicked.

Waves of arrest of a potential and often largely imagined "fifth column," hidden allies of Germany or Japan, followed. On June 10, 1940, Amir Sjarifoeddin was detained for several hours, not for fascist sympathies as might have been expected, but "as part of an investigation into the distribution of the illegal communist bulletin."[69] As historian Harry Poeze writes: "PKI paper *Menara Merah* produced in Batavia [sic] was found in Amir's home. . . . The police suspected PKI . . . but lacked sufficient evidence to prosecute."[70] Amir was released, but on June 20, 1940, he was detained again and this time held until June 27. At least one of the two detentions, he spent in Soekamiskin, the Bandoeng prison where, ten years previously, Professor Schepper used to visit him, as it was said, to read the Bible together.

According to Amir himself, as he wrote in his autobiography, "[i]n 1940, after the war with Germany broke out, I was arrested again" (he means after the arrest in 1933) "and I was accused of clandestine activity [*actie rahasia*] in cohort with the Communist Party of Indonesia and against the Dutch. After being kept in prison for about a week, I was released." At this place in his autobiography, without a pause, and without even a beginning of a new paragraph, Amir continues: "In October of that year, I was placed [*ditempatkan*] in the Department of Economic Affairs, section Research, subsection Export, and I worked there until Japan arrived, in 1942."[71]

The verdict of Boven Digoel was still hanging over Amir and, the war notwithstanding, the sea route from Java to New Guinea was still open. A. M. Sipahoetar, another of Amir's friends of the past, and a cofounder of the Indonesian national press agency *Antara* in 1937, in a series of articles in *Kebangoenan*, launched on November 7, 1941, wrote that Amir "has gone weak."[72] Sipahoetar, till then an admirer of Amir, wrote in the Protestant, and Amir's, *Semangat Baroe* a week later: " But something has changed in his soul. He is not anymore strong enough to face the consequences of his duties as a leader of a movement like Gerindo. He looks how to run away from it all, and he leaves behind great sadness. I have lost a friend of whom I was proud above the others. . . . He does not accept that becoming a victim might be one of the consequences a leader has to expect. Instead, he had chosen a steady life and career."[73]

This expressed a suspicion that Amir, in fear of being exiled, finally decided to cooperate with the Dutch fully and, what the articles suggested, beyond the limits of decency.

There was an uproar also elsewhere and there was disappointment. Even G. J. Resink, gentle and loyal, told Gerry van Klinken many years later that "he was surprised and didn't agree with it." Few if any had seen Amir as going his way, since Medan and Sibolga, with the ELS classroom wall chart picturing "Martin Luther at the Reichstag in Worms": "I can't do otherwise," through Haarlem, Batavia, Soekamiskin prison, and Palembang Gerindo congress, of course with the anxious and increasing solitude, and with deepening awareness of the world being one, and Indonesia being part of it. Datoek Moelia, a kind of a solid base, or memory, to Amir of Batak-ness and Christianity and of what had remained of the family, in the words of Resink, "in the late 1940s was cynical."[74]

The offer to Amir to join the government had to come it appears through Dr. Hubertus J. M. van Mook, the chief of the economic department at the time. Van Mook was a rising star in the Indies government and, in fact, not so different in his ambition, frustration, and moral compass from men like Schepper or Van Asbeck or Logemann. Indeed, Van Mook, used to be an active member of the Stuw, "Stimulus," in the early 1930s, an exclusive group, collegium might be the word, of intellectuals and officials who believed that the existing system of government might be reformed with the help of the "advanced" indigenous.[75]

Indeed, when Professor Logemann was leaving his post at the Batavia Law School, he suggested to the governor general that Van Mook be appointed in his place as a worthy colleague of Schepper, Van Asbeck, and others. The suggestion was quickly rejected. Van Mook did not seem to the governor general to be solid enough.[76]

Still, Van Mook was rising in the government as a dynamic force and when he was appointed to lead the economics department in August 1937, the move was warmly welcomed, for instance, by Amir's friend Sanoesi Pane and in *Kebangoenan*, a paper with which Amir was also affiliated. Sanoesi Pane even described Van Mook as "a Red."[77] There were other *correspondences* and *coincidences* at work in the increasingly hazy, foggy, cloudy—and potentially revolutionary—space. Amir's cousin Datoek Moelia, who so often had staked, or tried to stake, a way for Amir, used to be for a time affiliated with the same department.[78]

Amir was appointed to a middle-level position of the Directorate of Research in the department's Office of Exports. He wrote several reports for the office. In "Nieuwe aspecten in de rijstsituatie van Azië," "New Aspects of the Rice Situation in Asia," for instance, he focused on the rice policy of Japan.[79] "Under the supervision of the economist J.C.W. Cramer," Van Klinken writes, "Amir wrote studies on staple and cash crop markets mainly for the Department's economic journal." An evaluation of Amir by his chief survived: "I do not see a great organizer in him," wrote ir. Cramer. "His extremely intellectual attitude puts a brake on his ability to act.... This is a default of his qualities, a result of his desire to look at everything from all sides."[80]

In July 1941, half a year before the Indies fell, Charles O. van der Plas, after being five years the governor of East Java, was moved to Batavia "and announced he was commencing a big anti-fascist 'educational' campaign among the Indonesian population." Van der Plas was aware, he said in a testimony after the war, that "we can only achieve things if the people are enthusiastic," and he was aware how "very anti-propagandistic [sic]" the situation was. We had to "encourage people," he recalled, "not to feel abandoned." The situation, Van der Plas added, looking back in 1950, was "chaotic."[81] Amir Sjarifoeddin ended one of his articles in *Kebangoenan* on August 14, 1941, with "We wish van der Plas well."[82]

"The frequency with which Amir appeared on a variety of speaking platforms," writes Van Klinken, "suggests that he was working with van der Plas already in August 1941." In September 1941, Amir spoke on the government radio: "a society with moral unity was a strong society in time of war," he said. China, he added, was an example—the government and the "Reds" together. The Indies, Amir said, "could work together in facing common external threat and hence lay the basis for a moral democratic future" like in China. "This is our war," Amir wrote again, in *Kebangoenan* two weeks after Pearl Harbor. His message was, "Fight on!"[83]

December 7, 1941, the Japanese attacked Pearl Harbor and the Japanese army rapidly moved south. On December 17, 1941, Amir's article appeared in *Semangat Baroe*:

> This is our war, on this moment depends the life or death of our ideals, of our nation, and also the life or death of our culture. If we lose, will we ever be able to carry through our ideas of just society? of parliament? For the answer look at China, Formosa, Manchuria, Korea—they are now getting ready to die. The Japanese do not bring an opportunity for democracy. If we win, the chance is there that we will reach democracy. Our culture is such that it can grow into full democracy. We do not have to be just optimistic. There is a way to go: "Keep fighting!"

The Japanese invasion and, as might be expected, the occupation of the Indies, became a matter of weeks and then days. The space grew foggy in the extreme, and rumors abounded. Mohammad Sjah, Amir's friend and colleague from the time at the People's University, told Jacques Leclerc in 1980, and he might have believed it: "Amir was imprisoned but, at the last moment, he became *ambtenaar* [Dutch for 'official']. He even departed from Batavia for Australia, but did not make it further than Tjilatjap [a port southeast of Batavia]."⁸⁴

This is one of several wild stories. At least, there is no sign anywhere that Amir was about to pack his bags or be packed away by the escaping Dutch to be taken with them to a safe place, which was Australia. What really happened in these chaotic days and hours was not known except by very few people at the time.

Besides "to do propaganda," the governor general asked Van der Plas "to lay a basis for underground action by the Indonesians for the time of the coming occupation." The idea was Dr. P. J. A. Idenburg's, of the governor general's staff, "who had talked to some Indonesians already." Now, Van der Plas added some "independent people of strong character I knew." One of them was Amir, "very well known figure in the Netherlands circles."⁸⁵

Probably in December 1941, Amir received 25,000 guilders from the Indies government to put together an underground resistance during the time the Indies would be occupied by Japan.

Van der Plas was an Indies official of renown in government circles for both brilliance and deep interest in Indigenous affairs. Van der Plas, however, at the same time, had been widely known, or rumored, as an official increasingly disillusioned by the stiffness of the colonial regime. Indeed, at the same time as Van Mook and together with him, when he served in Batavia in the early 1930s as an active member of the dissident Stuw; one of the men whom G. J. Resink, Amir's friend, called a "Young Stuwer, one of the Stuw younger and more dynamic groups."⁸⁶

There is another story about Van der Plas's money and Amir. According to a later recollection by Resink: "In 1940 van Mook started his efforts to buttress the state system with anti-Japanese Indonesians and he asked *Schepper* to give him names. (It was Schepper who had been charged with convincing Amir, so that Amir became ready to invest in the system and to build cadres on a higher level in belief that thus he was preparing for independence.)"⁸⁷

The Dutch forces command, including the Allied forces, capitulated to the Japanese forces, with the area of surrender including the whole of the Indies, on March 9, 1942. The governor general of the Indies, Alidius Tjarda van Starkenborgh Stachouwer, was detained and spent the rest of the war in Japanese internment. Van Mook, since late December 1941 the lieutenant-governor general, became the highest Dutch official in the Indies, which were no more. Van Mook managed to escape with his staff to Australia, and in Brisbane he established the Indies administration in exile. Van der Plas became his principal coworker.

CHAPTER 10

Ships on the Wall

Historian Anton Lucas spoke in the 1980s to people in East Java who said that they had been close to Musso in 1935 and 1936, and then close to Amir: "According to oral tradition some of the money [from Van der Plas] was given to Pamoedji by Atmadji, a Surabaya Gerindo leader and a close associate of Amir Sjarifoeddin. With part of the money the underground PKI is said to have purchased a printing press and stenciling machine with which to continue producing *Menara Merah*. A manifest printed on the same press urged the population to resist the Japanese [as they were close to arriving], with power if necessary. However, just as it was off the press, the Japanese began bombing Surabaya." Lucas adds that "Another oral source claims that Atmadji received a sum of money from the Dutch independently of Amir Sjarifoeddin. Pamoedji is also said to have received money from Sudjarwo who was a Gerindo representative responsible for labor relations on the Surabaya Municipal Council."[1]

Masses of the population, homogeneous masses, crowds, on the islands close to the battle lines, on Sumatra and then on Java, welcomed the Japanese as liberators from the Western white colonialism. In the conquered Indies, red-and-white flags of the Indonesian movement were allowed to fly, and "Indonesia Raja," the anthem of the movement, was allowed to be publicly sung.

Still, the Japanese were looking for people who could help them to spread the message of the new era and the war being about to be won.

There was no shortage of the willing among the politicians and activists of the Indonesian movement, as well as among the Indonesian officials serving the Dutch in various capacities before the war.

Soekarno was one candidate. He was martyred by the Dutch. He was also on the record as an extraordinary orator capable of moving masses. In February 1938, as his biographer Bernhard Dahm put it, Soekarno's "banishment was mitigated" and Soekarno with his family was moved from Endeh, Flores, to Bencoolen (Bengkulu), South Sumatra, a place much closer to Java. But still, the reality of the politics in the Indies was that Soekarno appeared to be "out."[2]

Abu Hanifah, Amir's friend from Kramat 106, remembers how in the 1930s he and Amir—Abu Hanifah was now practicing medicine in Central Sumatra and Amir was living in Java—occasionally exchanged letters and sometimes mentioned Soekarno. Abu Hanifah quotes from one of the letters he got at the time from Amir:

> I very often hear news about Soekarno from Endeh in Flores. Not from him personally of course, but I have a friend there, a relative so to say, who is a doctor. He visits Endeh quite regularly once a month as part of his job. He has met Soekarno and his family there and he heard stories from the other islanders.
>
> It seems Soekarno is not very happy there. . . . You know he liked sunshine and glitter and he liked nice and beautiful company. He misses all that in Endeh. . . .
>
> His books consist mainly of religious Islamic books. It seems that he is trying to find some solace in religion. Imagine, Abu, Soekarno becoming a saint!
>
> They have not forgotten him here in Jakarta. His name is still good. But you see, because he is absent, he has no influence anymore doing things. . . . You remember of course, Abu, that in fact, we of the old PPPI [Indonesian Students Association], were never very nice to him. . . . I believe he knew it too. . . . However, I still believe that he is still one of our top leaders. I personally don't think he liked us too much. Do you remember the time when he gave a speech about Socialism to our circle in Jakarta in Kenari. . . . Only his vanity made him blind to our sneers because they were cast in questions with a tongue in cheek.[3]

Soekarno still had a good name. When he arrived to Bencoolen, in 1938, a group of local activists, Gerindo people among them, welcomed Soekarno with elaborate care—Gerindo people, namely, one source says, "considering themselves as the true and active heirs to Soekarno's Partindo." Because Soekarno was known to be a movie fan, and suspecting that he was not able to see movies in Endeh for years, "they took him to Bencoolen Royal Cinema."[4]

Whatever the Dutch might have planned for Soekarno, it did not happen. When the Dutch capitulated in March 1942, Soekarno was left behind.

It took the Japanese some time. Four months after they established themselves on Java, a ship was made available to take Soekarno to Batavia—now officially renamed Djakarta. "On July 9, 1942, after a stormy voyage in a small motor launch that took four days and four nights, he arrived in Java with members of his immediate family."[5]

Soekarno was willing. In the following three years he became the principal figure of the Indonesian movement cooperating with the occupying regime. His saying did not change fundamentally. The powers fighting Japan, whatever their democratic credentials might be—the Netherlands, United States, Great Britain, Soviet Union—were the *sana*, "them" against the *sini*, "us."

Soetan Sjahrir and Mohammad Hatta, also made their appearance on Java. In their case, the idea might have been to evacuate them with the Dutch. Just ahead of the advancing Japanese army, in February 1942, in a military plane, the two men with three children they adopted in Banda Neira, were flown from their place of exile to Java. In Java they were lodged in a police dormitory in Soekaboemi. They were free to receive visitors, and they waited there for what would come next.

According to Mohammad Hatta's memoirs, in their first days in Soekaboemi, days before the Japanese actually arrived in town, Soejitno Mangoenkoesoemo, Amir's friend, visited them. Soejitno arrived, Hatta wrote in his memoirs, to inquire whether they, Hatta and Sjahrir, might be inclined to engage in an anti-fascist underground as the Japanese arrive and whether they would be willing to accept some Dutch help. Soejitno's visit, Hatta wrote, "was followed by a visit from Amir Sjarifoeddin." According to Hatta, and also by what Sjahrir wrote later, another possibility Amir suggested was that both Hatta and Sjahrir evacuate and again intimated that the Indies government might help. Both of them, Hatta and Sjahrir later wrote, rejected the ideas.[6]

It looked from the picture both men later painted that Amir was peddling resistance and being not much more than a Dutch messenger, to use a gentle word. Amir, so Sjahrir wrote in his recollections published in 1949, had been known at the time as "a gifted orator and was particularly popular among the educated youth." "But from what I knew of his political past," Sjahrir added, "I had the impression that stability was not one of his outstanding characteristics." Sjahrir, in other words, suggests that he was little impressed. Amir, he wrote, "had let his beard grow but was still easy to recognize." Sjahrir says he even warned others not to have anything to do with Amir, and that it would be dangerous to embark on underground activity with an unstable man. Amir, wrote Sjahrir, appeared "overexcited, and besides, evidently he did not have much interest in me." "Probably," Sjahrir adds, "because I had remained so silent."[7]

According to a Sjahrir's interview with George Kahin, in 1961: "Sjarifoeddin tried very hard on the eve of the Japanese occupation to convince Sjahrir group [sic] to collaborate [sic] with [the] Dutch whom he claimed willing to collaborate with the Communists. But [Sjahrir] does not know whether he had actually joined [the] Communists."[8] In Hatta's account, at some point during his visit with the two men, Amir suggested that he, Hatta, issue a public statement about the Indies facing fascism. Hatta's biographer writes that Hatta told him he "had made his decision. He was not going to cooperate with the colonial government or encourage his people to die defending the Dutch."[9]

In the end, Amir was let go, and Hatta joined Soekarno. During the next three years of the Japanese occupation, he became the second most prominent Indonesian figure cooperating with the Japanese occupational power, the second most visible, and much used in Japanese propaganda of war and mass mobilization, second only to Soekarno. Like Soekarno, Hatta "collaborated tactically," that is, as they both repeatedly said then and after, in the interest of the Indonesian movement, using one outside power, Japan, against another outside power, the Netherlands, *sana* versus *sana*, for the ultimate goal of Indonesian independence and freedom. Sjahrir, for himself, decided not to join Soekarno and Hatta, at least not openly.

The Japanese arrived and the scenes in the towns and villages of Sumatra and Java, staged or not, of homogeneous masses or not, were those of jubilation. The cooperation of the Indonesian movement, united behind Soekarno and Hatta, with the Japanese was massive, overwhelming, and joined by virtually all of the nationalists and indigenous-officialdom elite. Soekarno's golden voice exhorted the glory of home. Amir's anxious solitude appeared to be at its apogee.

There are few recollections of Amir Sjarifoeddin during the first eleven months after the Japanese invaded. There were sightings and memories of him moving around. In the beginning, he was seen in Batavia, now Djakarta, lecturing—and, on one occasion, in the same series of lectures as Soekarno and Hatta—in one account "on psychology and oriental philosophy," according to another, on "politics and general topics." The audience on these occasions was a group of young Indonesians, gathered under the name Angkatan Baroe, "New Generation," meeting at Menteng no. 31, formerly Dutch Hotel Schomper and now a student dormitory and the Angkatan Baroe headquarters.[10]

For nine months, in a space of rumors and whispers, of *correspondence*s and *coincidence*s, Amir lived underground and aboveground at the same time.

In December 1942, Soekarno and Hatta petitioned the Japanese administration to allow the establishment of a mass Organisasi Rakjat, "People's Organization," to help, as they argued, to spread the propaganda of the new regime more broadly. On December 12, 1942, the Badan Persiapan Organisasi Rakjat, "Preparatory Committee," referred as Panitia Sebelas, "Board of Eleven," was announced, located in Hatta's office. Mr. Amir Sjarifoeddin was among the eleven. By the end of the month, however, the Japanese changed their minds. The People's Organization came to nothing and the Board of Eleven was disbanded.[11]

According to Sjahrir's memoirs, Hatta had been helping Sjahrir to organize an underground of his own.[12] As for Amir's underground, Hatta, talking later to his biographer, looking back, was dismissive. "Amir Sjarifoeddin's underground group, which had been amply funded by the colonial government before it surrendered to the Japanese, operated in the sensitive naval port of Surabaya." Soon, however, "sensing that the *kenpeitai* was closing in on him, Amir sought Hatta's assistance. Hatta responded by requesting that Amir join his staff, offering to be responsible for him, a risky proposition as Sjahrir had already criticized Amir for lacking discretion in his modus vivendi."[13]

Contrary to a feeling one might get from Hatta's and Sjahrir's descriptions of Amir, the Japanese did not seem to take Amir lightly. Two extensive entries on him appeared in the Japanese official handbook on "The Foremost Indonesians in Java" which had been compiled in the initial period of the occupation, or perhaps as a preparation for it, and published in 1944:

> *Mr. Amir Sjarifoeddin gelar Soetan Goenoeng Soaloan, marga Harahap*
> formerly an official at the Department of Commerce [Syogyo Tyuo Dyimasyo]. Born . . .

All dates which follow are correct.

> *Education*: ELS, Gymnasium Leiden and Haarlem, Law School, teacher at Pergoeroean Rakjat, Volksuniversiteit Djakarta, Evening Section . . . Attorney in Djakarta and Soekaboemi . . . *Handelsconsulaat* official of the second class, section of Research, section of Export matters . . . editor: *Weekblad*; from June 2602 [1942] up to today . . .

What follows still is detailed and correct.

> *Articles* . . .

There are many data and, as far as I am able to ascertain, all are correct.

Political functions: Vice President Partindo, Secretary of Gerindo.[14]

On the Board of Eleven, which came to nothing, according to Jacques Leclerc, "Amir represented the Protestants."[15] At the same time, under watchful Japanese eyes, Amir's Protestant friend, Dr. Johannes Leimena, was attempting to establish another preparatory organization, the Persiapan Persatoean Kaoem Kristen, "Preparatory Committee of the Christian Unity," with headquarters at Kramat 65. Amir became the vice-chairman of the committee.[16]

Structures, organizations, committees, and unions, as fitted the space, were preparatory, temporary, brittle, and ephemeral. The Japanese occupational authority was ultimate, that kind of the real.

There is a "Short record of the general meeting" of the GPKK, Gerakan Persatoean Kaoem Kristen, "Movement of the Protestant Christians," another group that emerged in the span of the occupation's first months, ephemeral, and, like Augé's trains, passing the other groups without touching. The meeting of the GPKK took place on June 26, 2602 (1942). Among those present, again, *mr.* Amir Sjarifoeddin is listed, as an adviser. According to the minutes, "*mr.* Sjarifoeddin," "in a language of an attorney, talked about the position which the GPKK should take." He finished, the minutes say, "with quoting an African people wisdom [*sic*]: 'Do all you want, only do it in the purity of your heart.'"[17]

In the archives of the GPKK, which survived, contrary to the GPKK itself, there is a short memorandum of another meeting, one month later, on July 20. A representative of the Japanese was present, Shimizu Hitoshi, and also Dr. *mr.* Moelia, as a delegate and chair of the Indische Kerk, Dutch for "Indies Church," a group established days before the Japanese invasion, on January 3, 1942, and evidently still surviving. Mr. Amir Sjarifoeddin is listed as his assistant.[18]

On September 1, 1942, Amir appears as presiding at another meeting of the "Protestant Christians' formation committee."[19] On November 14, at Kramat 65, a preparatory (again, preparatory!) meeting of the committee took place. Among the members of the "Committee for the Preparation of the Christian Union," which also met in November, *mr.* Amir Sjarifoeddin is listed as the general chairman.[20]

As Amir's wife later recalled, through the first months of the Japanese occupation, in 1942, her husband "still could move through Djakarta." In December 1942, at the Djakarta Zoo, a popular place for public meetings, a gathering of Christians took place themed Menoedjoe ke Djoemaat Indonesia Asli, "Toward the Genuine Indonesian Congregation." "Amir," his wife recalls the occasion, "spoke to a large audience."[21] He called on his listeners "not to hide in their homes despite the difficulties of the present day but to come forth for the truth and spread light on which just and harmonious society can only be built." He brought up the example of Moses "who left behind a life of luxury to lead a leaderless people out of Egypt."[22]

On December 25, of that year, Amir celebrated ecumenical Christmas. "They did not have *pohon cemara* [casuaris tree] as was usual, but *pohon beringin* [banyan tree], a tree with a special meaning for Indonesia."[23] *Pohon beringin* or waringin (*ficus benjamina*), originally from India, is the Indonesian national tree, as well as an ancient symbol of life and unity. It usually grows in the middle of a village or town, its huge aerial roots resembling a forest. It embodies the oneness of man and nature. But ghosts and spirits are also believed to live in it, good ones and bad ones, guarding and haunting the place.

Amir kept visiting and is remembered as preaching in the Kernolong church in Djakarta, the same place where he had been baptized and married.[24] Tine Francz, Amir's friend since Law School, recalled Amir at the time: "As a woman of Dutch origin, by the regulations issued by the Japanese, I was required to pay for my KTP [residency card] 80 guilders, and I had no money.... Amir came and said that he brought me 80 guilders. He said, 'I recalled that I had borrowed a book from you. I lost it somewhere.' It was not true. The book he talked about was a gift to him from me. It was the last time, that we saw each other."[25]

Amir, at the center of several networks—if the networks had any center, if they were networks at all—was a network in himself. He himself had been kept together by *correspondences* and *coincidences*. They were his moral compass, pointing the way, decreeing the speed and the moments of lingering. Amir kept steadying himself by moving, through Batavia, the metropolis's street corners, corrupting the youth, traveling through Java, trying to plant Van der Plas's money, peddling resistance with all the talent he had for that kind of work—or which he did not have. "Before Japan arrived," Amir wrote, "I had been involved in *actie rahasia* [clandestine activity] to make sure that the movement of the Indonesian people does not stop when the Japanese arrive in 1942."[26]

Marc Augé wrote in his *Metro* book that "Each city has an underground." Soerabaja certainly did.

Darmawan, another Mangoenkoesoemo brother of Tjipto and Soejitno, built a foundation in Soerabaja in the last months before the Japanese conquest, with a chain of cooperatives in "small rural industries: metal works, furniture making, brick making, leather work, ceramics, etc." Darmawan's foundation had been originally helped by the Dutch government, "but it carried on under the Japanese." Wide and loose, Darmawan's group was in touch with similar groups and with individuals in Soerabaja and about, with other "networks," many of them not necessarily of an underground kind. Amir Sjarifoeddin, often through Djohan Sjahroezah, Sjahrir's cousin, maintained contact with Darmawan's group.[27]

It was the energy of the networks, their élan, and Amir's, that was what many of the participants pointed out as the real. Sometimes, even without ever meeting physically, the sense of the spectral built up a belonging in adventure—and in fear; the Japanese were not the Dutch.

Mr. Ali Sastroamidjojo, a man of Soekarno's generation and his ally in the prewar Indonesian movement, lived in Soerabaja at the time:

> [S]everal months into the Japanese occupation, one morning I traveled to Jogjakarta on family business. As I returned to Soerabaja and came home, I was surprised to hear from my child, Kemal Mahisa, that *brother* Amir Sjarifoeddin, about whom I knew from others that he was being active in the anti-Japanese underground, came to our house at Kedungsari Street no. 72 and that he brought a packet which, my child said, looked like it contained books. Amir, however, in the end did not leave the packet in my house and he only wrote a note with a greeting. I was afraid he would be caught in the net of the Japanese secret police, even though according to my son he was almost not recognizable because he had grown a very bushy beard and moustache.[28]

"The meaning of life in the underground," recalled Sitha, one of the young women of Amir's network, talking to Anton Lucas many years later, "was survival—survival in the face of suppression and illegality—and to maintain the continuity of the movement, 'to keep the movement going' . . . resisting destruction or trying to do so."[29]

There were also funny stories. Another young woman of Amir's East Java underground, Miss Lo, told Lucas how, one day in the first year of the occupation, she was asked to hide "someone important who will be coming incognito." The man arrived and, in her haste to find a place, as she was inexperienced in these matters, she pushed the man into the shack in the house where coal was stored. So, they sat there, hidden, and they were talking: "In my stupidity," the woman told Lucas, "I reacted to that person whose life was at stake by asking him really dumb questions, like 'Have you ever been to see the summit of Mount Bromo?' or 'Have you ever visited Bali?' It was truly bizarre." Only weeks later, after the man left, Miss Lo was told that the man whom she hid in the shack was *"mr.* Amir Sjarifoeddin." "He was risking his life," Miss Lo said, *"mr.* Amir did not dare to protest, and kept quiet."[30] Perhaps with one of his slightly sarcastic grins.

On January 30, 1943, as part of a sweeping operation by the Japanese military police, Amir Sjarifoeddin was arrested. "Amir," wrote Benedict Anderson in the vein of Hatta and Sjahrir, "was no match for the *kenpeitai* army of informants and spies." Amir's underground was, Anderson adds, a "complete failure," even a "disaster."[31] However, Abu Hanifah, who at the time of writing was no friend of Amir anymore, took Amir's underground and Amir as a resistance fighter more seriously: "At the beginning of the Japanese occupation . . . Amir had a formidable underground body with branches in several big cities in East Java. . . . One night they caught Amir during a meeting. . . . But his underground organization stayed nearly intact."[32] Sjahrir wrote laconically: "We daily heard of arrests, particularly of [Amir's] group, and of those of our people who had come in touch with him."[33]

The Japanese, on their arrival at Java, according to many sources, were able to capture the archives of the Dutch colonial police, including the lists of Indonesian activists and Indonesian informants. Besides, the Japanese were readily able to trace the money the Dutch had given to Amir Sjarifoeddin and others because it was in the form of a cheque or money order rather than cash. "I made drafts available to them, but they had to be countersigned," Van der Plas admitted later that the signatures fell into the Japanese hands at the moment "when no structure, not radio, could yet be organized . . . only courage and energy."[34]

"There were two series of arrests," writes William Frederick, a historian of Soerabaja of the time. "One occurred in September 1942, the other in January of the following year. The well-known arrest of Amir Sjarifoeddin took place on the later date according to his own account which says that fifty-four persons, all members of the PNI, PKI, and Partindo [meaning Gerindo?] were detained."[35]

Years later, after Amir was dead, a Soviet story of his underground and arrest had been published in Moscow, dramatic, made of bronze, if I could only write like this: "When the Japanese army occupied Indonesia, the Japanese intelligence service began to search for Sjarifoeddin. Where was he? Even people who had known him well failed to recognize him in the disguise of a street vendor which he adopted to evade the police. In this disguise he continued to organize resistance to the invaders, traveling up and down the country. . . . But in 1943, the Japanese sleuths picked up his scent."[36]

According to Djaenah, Amir's wife, Amir was arrested on January 4, 1943, between 3 and 5 a.m., in their house in Malabar Street in Djakarta. They had moved to this house six months before.[37] Pastor Verkuyl thought, it appears wrongly, that the arrest took place in Surabaya: "arrested by *kenpeitai* in

Soerabaja . . . jailed in Kalisosok in Soerabaja . . . then Salemba [Struiswijk] in Jakarta, then Tjipinang [at the outskirts of Jakarta] . . . then Soekamiskin. . . . When they were taking him away, he told his wife to be brave."[38] After a year of being moved from prison to prison, Amir was put on trial by a military tribunal. On February 29, 1944, he was sentenced to death. The family was officially informed.[39]

Amir was not executed this time. His sentence was commuted to life. But it appears that Amir was not informed. He remained in prison, so to say, alive until further notice. On October 17, 1944, he was moved to Lowokwaru prison in Malang, a city ninety kilometers south of Soerabaja, where he remained until the end of the war, awaiting execution.[40]

The Soviet story, again, had a bronze-hero ring to it, but it does not seem that it swerves too much from what actually happened. After the arrest, the story goes, "For ten whole days they subjected him to the most sadistic torture. . . . His face was covered with a handkerchief and a constant stream of water was poured on him until he choked and lost consciousness. The Japanese sadists cynically called that method of torture 'the water cure.' When they saw that they would not make him talk, the Japanese sentenced him to death. The news leaked out, and the wave of indignation was so overwhelming that the hangmen took fright and commuted the sentence to life imprisonment."[41]

Except for "the wave of indignation," Arnold Brackman, a journalist who was in Java in 1947 and 1948 and had many occasions to talk to the people around Amir and with Amir himself, tells the same story. "Amir," writes Brackman, "was given the water treatment but denied a communist affiliation."[42] In the words of Amir's autobiography, "In January 1943 I was arrested by Japan and taken to Soerabaja, where I remained until February 1944, when the sentence was announced. I was sentenced to death, but because the pressure of my friends [teman-teman saja], the death sentence was changed into that of life in prison."[43]

Five men of Amir's network, however—some sources say four—arrested in the two *kenpeitai* sweeps together with Amir were executed.[44] Amir mentions that it was thanks to his friends that his death sentence was commuted, and it became generally accepted, and Amir never challenged it, that Hatta, and perhaps Soekarno, were the friends. Some mention also Amir's cousin Datoek Moelia, who was then also one of those collaborating with the Japanese. He is said to have appealed to Soekarno on Amir's behalf and convinced him to act.[45]

I know nothing about Amir's three years minus a few months spent in Japanese prisons, waiting for death. Nothing except what Amir said when he was freed after the war, or what he was said to say.

Pastor Verkuyl met Amir in the first days after he got out of prison in October 1945. Amir then told him, Pastor Verkuyl says, about him reading the Bible, not just the New Testament, the gentle Christ, but the prophets—the prophets especially. Verkuyl wrote that Amir told him of "several people repenting [sic] and becoming Christians. . . . Amir preached to the detainees in prison."[46]

"It was only in 1945," Ali Sastroamidjojo, the man scared by Amir's visit at his home in Soerabaja at the beginning of the Japanese occupation, wrote in his memoirs, "I was told by Amir Sjarifoeddin that Sukajat, one of the people arrested with Amir, had been held in detention with him in Malang. Amir told me how Sukajat had been tortured by the *kenpeitai* and finally hanged."[47]

One of the young people who knew Amir since before the war, Tahi Bonar Simatoepang, a fellow Batak and Christian and, after 1945, one of the top officers in the Indonesian army, was told by Amir a story of his time in prison and of a Bugis sailor. Amir shared a cell, he said, with this Bugis sailor. Bugis are people known as sailors. They live most of their lives on the sea, which is their home, between the islands off South Sulawesi; at least, they are known to live this way. The Bugis sailor, Amir told Simatoepang, longed for home badly and he kept drawing Bugis ships on the wall of their cell. After months in prison, Amir said, the man resigned to his fate and stopped drawing.[48] I strongly believe, whether the story is true or not, that these ships on the wall were the ultimate wall charts for Amir, making the walls of the cell open finally not into another wall, the real windows.

Behind the walls, the windows, rumors, whispers, and élan especially, the energy of the network making the network, were filling the space, and Amir, spectrally, was present.

Mrs. Pri, another female member of Amir's East Java resistance also talked to Anton Lucas many years later. She told Lucas how she and her husband Soekarno (not "the big one") were both in Amir's network, and how they *almost* physically touched Amir in prison and how Amir *almost* physically touched them—how they passed each other memorably. At one moment, Mrs. Pri said, she and her husband *almost* helped Amir to escape from prison. When he was in jail in Malang, the brother-in-law of Mrs. Pri indeed managed to get a job in the prison. The mission failed, Mrs. Pri told Lucas, "Because their party mandate, the only means to prove their identity to the local party leaders, had been stolen along with their other belongings." Still, Mrs. Pri said, she and her friends were "able to persuade the prison deputy ward to move Amir Sjarifoeddin to a more secure [sic!] cell."[49]

Logic was powerfully absent. Despite the failure, and possibly other failures to help Amir break free, they kept close to Amir, through the wall, no more wall charts or false windows. Mrs. Pri told Anton Lucas: "Included in the food for Amir Sjarifoeddin were messages written on the shell of duck eggs which had been boiled, causing the message to disappear from the shell. However, it could be read on the outside of the cooked egg after the shell was removed."[50] (I tried it, and it did not work. Maybe because I used chicken eggs. It made me think as I tried, however, what kind of messages might be put on an egg? "Freedom"? "Courage"? "Fuck them"?)

The Dutch police after the war tried, hopelessly like me, to detect, outline, connect the dots, make sense of the links, structures, and duck-egg messages. "A Sajoeti group of the arrested," a Dutch intelligence report suggests, "decided to cooperate with the Japanese, while the Sjarifoeddin group kept contact with Moscow."[51]

Soeryana was one of Amir's contacts in East Java who talked to Anton Lucas after the war. Soeryana was caught, spent time in Japanese prison, and survived. He had been arrested, taken to prison in Blitar, a provincial town southwest of Malang, and released after some months by the Japanese before the others and, unlike the others, "because," as he said, "I was underage. In two years' time I would be 18."[52]

We know about Blitar prison, thanks to Soeryana and, of course, thanks to Lucas. Soeryana's prison, not unlike Amir's most probably, was a space whereto the networks extended, and where the *correspondences* and the *coincidences*, the echoes, and shadows got packed tightly. "In Blitar prison," Soeryana recalled, then sixteen years old, using the words of the party:

> the arts nights were organized by the Party Committees. They posted someone at every window to keep watch for guards. The programs varied. Sometimes there would be a "makeshift" *wayang* [shadow puppet theater]. This was a *wayang* story recited by the *dalang* [puppeteer] in the usual fashion but without the [gamelan] orchestra or puppets. Voices were used in place of an orchestra. Each person imitated an instrument . . . one was a *kendang* [drum], another a *bonang* [kettle], another a gong and so on. Actually, *Bapak* [Father] Harjosoedarmo from the village of Tangkil in Wlingi district really was a *dalang* and a well-respected one!

This was a real *dalang*, and real *bonang* and drum, and gong, real-real.

There was a prisoner in cell seven called Tchordi from Garum district who had a good voice. At some celebrations he was asked to sing as loud as he could in order that the whole prison could enjoy his songs. He usually sang songs by the composer Gesang from Surakarta, like *Dibawah Sinar Bulan Purnama* [In the Light of the Full Moon], *Bengawan Solo* [Solo

River], *Telaga Biroe* [Blue Lake] or *Jembatan Merah* [Red Bridge] and some of Darmakawi's songs *O Nasib Tulungagung* [O, Tulungagung] which was popular at the time [it was a song about recent deadly floods].[53]

The old prophesy of King Djojobojo (the twelfth-century Javanese king), Soeryana recalled, circulated in the prison: "The dwarfs will only rule for the lifespan of a corn plant." It meant the Japanese, and their lasting for only two or three years. Then, the dwarfs will be gone, and freedom will arrive.

There was the real modern or a real attempt at it. The modern of the prison, like of the network, had been made of élan and of not much else. All links might be cut, but the prisoners owned the echoes. Soeryana said "ramoe," short for **radio moeloet**, "mouth-radio." Soeryana said, the prisoners were "informed." "I have forgotten," he said, "the exact date we were brought to court, because paper and writing materials were strictly forbidden in the prison cells. I only know that it happened at about the time of the Normandy landings, when General D. Eisenhower established the second front in Western Europe. So, it must have been about 6 June 1944."[54]

The news coming to the prison from the outside, had a resonating quality. "We heard reports," says Soeryana, "from the agitation propaganda section of the cell nine. This cell was near the Blitar prison officers' room. . . . Two people . . . were assigned the task of listening each night to the broadcast of the communiques by Sendenbu [Department of Propaganda] and the Dai Honei [Imperial General Headquarters]. The prisoners gave up the beds by the window for this purpose. Every morning after drill, the cell representative whose job it was to empty the latrine buckets, gathered by the well and the area where the latrine buckets were kept, to listen to the *ramoe* reports."[55]

Soeryana and the other prisoners in Blitar were linkless to Amir, but they were of one space, of resonance, shadows, prophecies, and the breaking news; also of schooling.

Soeryana was talking to Anton Lucas as if still in awe of the "Blitar prison political courses." They were chaotic, free, baffling, and they should make Roland Barthes happy: "Most of the [agitation-propaganda] committee men were also 'kursus kiper.' Each of those 'kursus-kiper[s]' had in their pockets a wrinkled 'Kôa' [Japanese-brand] cigarette-paper covered in notes which they called 'nota-bellen.' I discovered all of that from *Pak* [*Bapak*] Marjuni. Being his nephew . . . and the youngest prisoner, he trusted me. . . . When I asked where the material which was written in these 'nota-bellen' had come from, he answered, 'We got all of it from Soekamiskin [prison] and when we were in Tjipinang prison.'" Soeryana wondered, "I pondered for a long time the meanings of 'kursus kiper' and 'nota-bellen.' . . . I asked and found out that both terms had come from Dutch. 'Kursus-kiper' was from the Dutch 'kursus gever' [teacher], 'nota bellen' was from the Dutch 'nood tabellen' or emergency notes. Many of the prisoners who prepared the notes had been to Dutch schools."

So, it was a classroom. Not of the Hegelian warmth of the classroom kind. Rather, it was, as Kant might say, sublime. The *nota-bellen* and the *kursus*(es) based on them, Soeryana remembered, dealt with themes that could be clustered in four subjects.

1. Origins of mankind.
2. Beginnings of society.
3. Age of slavery and rise of overlord—*voorman* [Dutch for foreman].
4. Overlords and birth and growth of despotism until the time of the October Revolution.[56]

Also, this, "I recall," Soeryana said, "was in Dutch."

The network could be called the Soerabaja underground or Blitar prison or Amir's group or Boven Digoel space. "There were Boven Digoel people among us," Soeryana recalled, "prisoners, especially those from the Generation of '26 [1926], tough people despite their ideological and theoretical weakness [*sic*] . . . From the time they had joined the Party, they had been prepared for 'tiga B': 'three B's'—'bui, buang, bunuh,' ['jailed, exiled, killed']. . . . Their fundamental strategy was 'above all else the Party must always be kept alive!'"[57]

There were no Boven-Digoel people, as far as I know, in the Blitar prison or, in fact, anywhere in East Java, at least physically. There were hardly any successful escapes from the New Guinea camp during the colonial era—yet the three Bs people wandered around, indestructible, like specters.

In the three and a half years of the occupation, the euphoria of the homogeneous masses and of the Indonesian elite that had decided to cooperate with Japan faded. Liberation from the Dutch increasingly appeared to be nothing more than a change of rulers. The misery of the country was much deeper than anything experienced during the Dutch period.

Still, it was a new situation. The structure of calm and order and resistance in the framework of the state, the system of colonial democracy, had been broken. Says Soeryana: "The Dutch had never seen the need to operate the special PID [political police] at the district level. The work of monitoring people's movement was only carried out by the Pangreh Praja [Indigenous civil service], the *wedana* [district chief], or the local police superintendent. None of the national movement in fact had legal branches below the district level: Parindra, PNI, Partindo and Gerindo operated only at the regency level."[58]

CHAPTER 10

In the new situation, as contrasted to Dutch times, wrote Jacques Leclerc, "[n]either PNI, not Partindo or Gerindo appeared fit to survive in illegality.... They were used to being authorized by the state." Under the Japanese, wrote Leclerc, "they might hide ... but being secret had stripped them of a way to exist inside the order of invisibility."[59] Japanese rule opened space for people like Soeryana and the others in Blitar prison, and those still at large, for networks consisting entirely of élan, with leaders, in this case Amir, most properly and powerfully spectral.

This was a space in which Soeryana found it easy, natural, and only possible to operate. Such was the Soerabaja underground and the Amir group in East Java, with their mouths, radios, messages on duck eggs, news as prophecies, with and in prison, and, as the ultimate value, with and in death.

For the other youth, however, the Socratic, mostly students, and mostly in Batavia, all from upper-class Indigenous families, Amir's disappearance in prison in January 1943 was simply that, the disappearance of a leader—and an impulse to look for another one. Zainal Abidin, one of the group, told John Legge about the moment and Legge recorded what Zainal Abidin had said: "The closing of the Law School by the Japanese interrupted his legal studies.... Together with Soedjatmoko, Soedarpo and Amir Hamzah, he was for a time a member of a study group organized by Amir Sjarifoeddin. This group met twice weekly to inform its members of the progress of the war and to discuss future political action, but with the arrest of Amir by the Japanese in 1943 the group disbanded."[60] According to Soedjatmoko, the star of the group, for whom Amir had been influence number one, he and others "formed a study club of students and ex-students ... but with Amir's arrest it collapsed."[61]

In Batavia, now called Djakarta, during the first months of the occupation, a white man or woman, however rarely, could still be spotted on the street. The Dutch and Allied soldiers who surrendered or were captured were sent to the prisoner of war camps, but Dutch civilians were being interned only gradually. Some survived outside the camps for a very long time, bribing their way, finding proof of at least some Indigenous blood in their veins, coloring their hair. The Indonesians were walking around, whatever they thought about the recent invaders, with a new sense of dignity: they were only expected to bow to any Japanese soldier they happened to meet.

Virtually all the leaders of the prewar Indonesian movement, and virtually all the Indigenous officials who served in the Dutch Indies government, collaborated with the Japanese. Unprecedented poverty in the countryside was coming closer to the city with each month. It overwhelmed the city as the villagers flooded in, looking to survive. Batavia/Djakarta remained metropolitan but in a brutally new way.

The metropolitan youth, Amir's followers before Amir was arrested, with their schools, colleges, and dormitories largely closed by the Japanese, began to meet in private homes—they mostly had private houses at their disposal—at picnics and sometimes in cafés, sort of European-style cafés as they survived, some of them, into the Japanese era. They had their poets. This is by Chairil Anwar, twenty-one years old at the time, a nephew of Sjahrir:

Ordinary Song
Djakarta, May 1943

On the terrace we face each other
. . .
When orchestra begins "Carmen"?
. . . She laughs
The dry grass is ablaze
. . .
When orchestra begins "Ave Maria"
I drag her over to the corner.[62]

Soetan Sjahrir, back from Banda Neira and out of the police dormitory in Soekaboemi, lived both above- and underground, very much like Amir before Amir was arrested. In contrast to Amir, he did not know much about the Indonesia of the ten years before the Japanese arrived. He knew what he had read in newspapers and in the letters friends sent him to exile. He had been physically involved in the movement for only a very short time before he was exiled, and he was largely forgotten in the movement when he and Hatta suddenly reappeared in the last days of the Indies.

However, for these reasons, and very much like Amir, he exuded an anxious solitude. Most significantly, he became known, and through whispers and rumors, too, as not serving the Japanese. Like Amir, he was well read. Like Amir, he was brilliant. Now, when schools were closed, he appealed to the youth forced from their classrooms.

According to John Coast, an Englishman who learned about Indonesia firsthand after the war, "Sjahrir [became] the chief resistance leader, since the Japanese had imprisoned and tortured Sjarifoeddin."[63] In John Legge's words, "Hatta and Soekarno were . . . caught up in formal positions within the Occupation regime, and it was left to Sjahrir to recruit a younger generation of followers and to prepare them in the *pendidikan* [cadres' education] tradition for a later political role." "Amir's 'study club,'" Legge adds, "was to become part of the Sjahrir circle in due course."[64] According to Hamid Algadri, of the metropolitan youth, "Two times a week we got together in the house of Amir Sjarifoeddin on Tangkoeban Prahoe Street in Menteng Pulo to listen to his lectures about the politics of Japan. After he was captured, we dispersed to avoid arrest."[65]

In the 1980s and 1990s I talked to some of the youth who were still alive. All of them—Soedjatmoko, Soebadio, Soedarpo, Sitoroes, Aboe Bakar Loebis—sooner or later in our conversations, unprompted, began to talk about Amir. More than three decades after Amir's death, surprisingly—shockingly even, given the turn their and Amir's lives took after 1945—they all in various ways suggested: were Amir not arrested in January of 1943, they said, they would not have "switched to Sjahrir."[66]

They not only switched, but the contrast between them and the Soerabaja youth grew sharper. Something was happening to the swirl and the élan. Those who did not switch, Benedict Anderson wrote in his *Java in a Time of Revolution*, "were dominated by members of the Soerabaja underground, many of whom had suffered severely under Japanese repression. . . . In the main its members had humbler origins and less Western education than the [new] followers of Sjahrir." As for "Amir's group," Anderson writes, those who did not switch, "its [worldview] was less sophisticated . . . less academic, and at the same time more populist and tinged with apocalyptic romanticism. Its radicalism was more experienced than read about. . . . Just below the surface Sjahrir's men [and women] were inclined to view Amir's associates as somewhat provincial, romantic, and intellectually confused, while among the Amir group there was often a feeling that Sjahrir's followers were intellectually snobbish and unwilling to undertake the risks and hardships of working among the masses."[67] John Legge, again, says essentially the same by calling "Sjahrir's youth" "well-educated and essentially upper-class."[68]

Sjahrir lived most of the time in Djakarta and around the city, in West Java, much of the time in Bandoeng. His sister lived in Bandoeng and she had a second house in the nearby hills. There, mainly in the second home's garden pavilion, she told me when I wrote my biography of Sjahrir, how he listened to shortwave radio with earphones on and a ski cap. Sjahrir then moved through Djakarta and around Java, gathered his young people, lectured, and spread the news. Clusters of study clubs changing every time, or individuals meeting him in their houses—or cafés perhaps—made this network, this swirl.

Sjahrir was in touch certainly with Hatta and perhaps Soekarno throughout the occupation. Living under- as well as aboveground. As far as I know, he was never really harassed by the Japanese. There were some arrests among his youthful followers, but they were soon released. As far as I was told by those involved (and still alive), his network, his underground, his "Metro," also never ceased to exist.

Through his cousin, Djohan Sjahroezah, who lived in Soerabaja and had also been close to Amir since the 1930s and until Amir was arrested, Sjahrir was introduced to some of the Soerabaja youth in resistance. Soemarsono, who never switched, and who belonged to the Soerabaja youth, recalled: "The people around Djohan Sjahroezah avoided too big a risk. . . . But they existed. Sometimes I stayed in Soerabaja in the same house with Djohan. Soetan Sjahrir came at least once a month, he convened people and spoke. He brought education. I took part on these occasions, too. Sjahrir in fact stayed in the same house as Djohan Sjahroezah."[69] This is an unfinished chapter, a prologue like the others. Except feelings, suggestions of difference, and moods, no clear lines between Amir's and Sjahrir's Metro networks appeared to be drawn. No crushing—yet.

Charles O. van der Plas gave Amir Sjarifoeddin money and relocated to Australia. He became the second in importance in the Dutch Indies government in exile, next to Lieutenant-Governor General Hubertus van Mook. Theirs was a government without a country to govern, except for the few other secretaries. It governed in an anxious solitude and space, in all the differences, not so very other compared to that of Amir—at least, before he was caught.

The edges of the empire were frayed in the extreme. All the sailors and dissidents, unhappy ethical professors, the ultimate others, the detainees of the Boven Digoel, were now made to belong. Not to be left behind, as the Japanese armies advanced toward the Dutch New Guinea, not to let them be used by the Japanese propaganda of the liberation, like Soekarno and Hatta were, just before the expected Japanese entry to Boven Digoel (which ultimately never happened), in early 1943 the Boven Digoel internees with their families were evacuated to Australia, where Van Mook's and Van der Plas's government-in-exile was.

In a sense, at this moment, the ex-internees of Boven Digoel became closer to the Dutch Indies government than most of the rest of the colony. A significant group among the ex-internees, and the most radical, were still the Communists. After the Soviet Union was attacked by Nazi Germany in June 1942, a year before the Boven Digoel evacuation, acting in the intentions of Communist International and its policy of a united front, the Communists of Boven Digoel were not averse to, and indeed joined, the colonial and anti-fascist government of Van Mook and Van der Plas. They were welcomed.

Several of the most prominent Communist leaders out of Boven Digoel took an active part in a propaganda campaign aimed at the occupied Indies—led mainly by Van der Plas. The Communists from Boven Digoel accepted positions offered them, by Van der Plas, in the Indonesian-English bulletin *Penjoeloeh-Torch*. Some spoke on Van der Plas's broadcast to Indonesia, not knowing really, of course, who, if anyone, listened. They fought in their own way for a victory, a postwar, reformed, and democratic Indies/Indonesia. They joined Van der Plas, so to say, in sending messages on duck eggs.

Van der Plas's, Van Mook's and the Boven Digoel Communists made for the same shadowy space: not much seemed real but many things seemed possible. In the way of prophecies and, easily so, in the manner of the prewar police reports on the Indonesian movement, Van der Plas during the three years of Australian exile produced huge number of pages, summaries, and memoranda, detailed, brilliant, with swarms of numbers, maps, and graphs, all based largely on memory and imagination. Groups and subgroups were listed, individuals back in the Indies/Indonesia, imagined to be doing their jobs as they were supposed to, at the time of the temporary absence of the Dutch, waiting for victory, resisting the Japanese. Undergrounds, routes and timetables, names (for security reasons, of course) withdrawn.

Some of the reports were sent to General Douglas MacArthur's Allied command, and still others to the Dutch queen's government in exile in London. In the collapsing space of the bourgeois and the colonial, they were driven by Van der Plas's and colleagues' neo-ethical conviction that, after the war, Indonesia might be reformed. One can hear, if one listens closely, echoes of Julius Schepper, Van Asbeck, *Kritiek en Opbouw*, and even the ex-Boven Digoel Communists, of Sjahrir and of Amir. The reports and memoranda and the pieces of propaganda made sense as something that consists entirely of élan, of oneness based on not knowing.

This is an example of a document sent to MacArthur's office, and so the original is in English.

> Most secret memorandum
> *Additional Report on Conditions in the Netherlands Indies especially in Java*
> . . .
> *para 7: Underground movement*
> . . . disappearance of a certain Javanese high official connected with this movement . . . has been reported by a source.[70]

Often, professionally drawn graphs were attached to the reports, of schemes of the groups and subgroups, with names and often locales withdrawn. These are in essence wall charts of the new generation surrounding Van der Plas and his government. A special space is now needed to store them in the National Archives in the Hague, where they were taken after the war, so huge are they.

Most of Van der Plas's reports were most probably composed or at least corrected by him personally, and they are written in the excellent Dutch by which he was widely known. The reports in English are correct and fluent, as far as I may judge. Van der Plas cared about language. He struggled and pleasured through languages. I was told by Mrs. Widajasih, who was a nine-year-old girl, the daughter of an internee in Boven Digoel when Van der Plas came to the camp early in 1943 to make the camp ready for evacuation, that he sat her on his knees and asked her in what language she would like to talk to him, Dutch, Javanese, or Sundanese. This was the Indies culture at its gentlest, the warmth of the classroom, belief in the power of saying, which makes still Van der Plas's reports, and himself, when we think of Amir, so alive and disturbing.

Situation in the Netherlands Indies

[This report is in English].
Recent Data, up to January 4th, 1944, for Java, and of January for some islands in the East
Melbourne February 19, 1944
. . .

2. Attitude of the population towards the Japanese

The masses feel the deepest hatred for the Japanese. . . . In Java, the training of boys is considered by the people as the only danger for the allied cause. Well-dressed, taught to exert power, having Japanese ideas drilled into them daily, these children in the end must feel superior to everybody else and become Japanese pawns. However, at present such is not yet the case. . . .

[signed] Ch. O. Van der Plas[71]

Another report was sent already from Hollandia, on the north coast of New Guinea, where Van der Plas moved with US troops in the closing months of the war, already advancing toward Japan. This document is in English, too.

Secret

Anti-Japanese Activities in Java

Hollandia, April 30, 1945
III. Subversive and underground (intelligence) . . . activities in Java . . .

. . .

f. communist activities
By January 1944 . . . 1,468 members of subversive underground (spying) groups were arrested in 42 incidents, and 378 communists in 3 incidents . . .

> In Soerabaja . . . The gathering of ordnance or military information in addition to the aggressive enlisting of group members whose activities were prevalent in 1942, seem to have decidedly fallen off.

This particular report appears to almost touch on Amir (name withdrawn): "The nature of the Javanese Communist Party organizations as ascertained from the arrests and investigations since 1942 are shown in separate Chart No. 5." The chart is one of these especially large charts in The Hague's archival storage.

In the same folder, with another huge chart attached, Van der Plas expanded, in English again, on his view of the character of the Communist underground and its potentialities for the future:

> All of them [the Communists] are anti-imperialist (Japan is synonymous with imperialism). . . . They intend to cooperate with the Allied forces and establish an Indonesian Communist State with Anglo-American assistance.
> N.B., they believe that, following the occupation, the United States will set up a democratic form of government and that by cooperating with them at the time of the counter invasion . . . they will be able . . . to establish an Indonesian Communist State.

"The utmost precaution is required," Van der Plas concluded. "Conditions are such that police supervising is always required."[72]

In the Van der Plas collection in the National Archives in the Hague, there is also a draft of an article that Van der Plas planned to send while in Australia to *Vrij Nederland*, "Free Netherlands," the Dutch paper published by Dutch exiles in London. It deals with the language question, most seriously. The text is in Dutch. "As if our task to liberate the Indies was not difficult enough," wrote Van der Plas, "it will physically be accomplished by troops speaking English. The army of liberation will understand no Malay or any of the local language, and the troops of liberation will not be inclined to learn Dutch. The country faces a vast invasion of English, what I mean is a crippled [*kreupel*] kind of English. Nevertheless, even in this crooked form the language will awake in the Indonesians a new ambition to install English as a global language."

Van der Plas's draft is dated August 1, 1944, and carries an apocalyptic title (kind of a prophesy, too): "Dutch in the future as the second language."[73]

There is another folder in the Van der Plas collection in the National Archives, a few loose sheets of paper covered by Van der Plas's handwriting, hurried and in places illegible. These appear to be ideas hurled on the paper for what might be imagined as short propaganda films or perhaps sketches to be performed, by theater teams, possibly underground, behind the enemy lines. The notes are in English, as if Van der Plas, nolens volens, wrote already for the Indies with Dutch as a second language.

Data for 3 K.Z. [?]

A.

Place
Island Natuna (invented name), northernmost of Netherlands Indies, far flung into the South China Sea. . . .
Cast
Neth. civil officer ("controller"): Jansen.
Wireless operator: Karno.
Sergeant, commanding soldiers: Kromo.
Police sergeant: Mohammad.

Here, on the margin, there is scribbled by Van der Plas as a second thought: "Perhaps better not name 'Natuna.' Just say: 'farthest flung island etc.'"

On still another thought Van der Plas seems to suggest another possibility or a second version.

B.

Place
Island somewhere in the Eastern archipelago
Story
Willems, Netherlands government official caught, hung by his hands for 36 hours, a bayonet fixed against his forehead, so that if he fell asleep or nodded, he hurt himself. His wife interned. Later they are together in the camp. Starving. At night their native servants (call them Andreas and Minah—pronounced Meenah) crawl into the camp and bring them fruit and eggs.

After six weeks, Japanese sentries relax. Andreas with villagers arrange their escape, tunnels under the fence. They are weak. Natives [sic] carry them up the mountains to their fastnesses [sic]; feed them; help them (who possess nothing!) to escape one month later on a sailing vessel.

Might Van der Plas be thinking here of Amir and of the money he gave him? Might Amir, if he ever had an opportunity to read this, think of good Uncle Karel?

On yet another sheet of paper in the folder in the Van der Plas collection, there is a third thought or version, again in Van der Plas's handwriting and in English.

C.

Story

The native clerk of the Dutch Resident, as instructed, hid the secret papers relating to the underground movement as planned before. The Japs arrived and captured the Resident and his other officials. Nevertheless, the clerk hid the money.

The Japanese suspect him. They know he hid something. They arrest the clerk, Theodore Laftään (not his real name for obvious reasons).

They torture him. He refuses information. Then his wife is arrested, questioned, and threatened in a cell next to him. He hears that he would be executed in her presence the next morning. She manages to send word to friends through her child (Japs are kind to children, strangely enough!) and the natives free her husband who joins the guerilla and goes on fighting against the Japs. He does not know what happened to his family.

There is still the fourth, shortest sketch, in English, too, marked "D" in the folder:

D.

Perhaps something can be made of a nightly airplane trip from and back to Bandoeng (Java) to an aerodrome in the heart of Borneo (about 1,000 miles each way) to bring supplies to the small unit defending the airfield. Marooned plane. Radio silence. Nothing but a small petrol lamp on the aerodrome in the heart of Borneo's jungle, the stars to guide them.

N.B., here might be something in depicting the people looking out for the plane.[74]

Part Three

Le passage à l'acte

CHAPTER 11

Sjahrir

On August 6, 1945, the United States dropped the first atomic bomb on Hiroshima. On August 8, the Soviet Union declared war on Japan and on August 15 Japan surrendered. It was expected by many resisting fascism in the West as well as the East that this was the moment of radical change, following Marx, when the matters of mankind would be dealt with "by an abbreviated revolutionary method," that the world reached "the conditions under which alone modern revolution becomes serious."[1]

On August 17, in front of his residence at Pegangsaan Timoer 56, formerly Pegangsaan Oost 56 (and before the war, Professor van Asbeck's house), with Hatta at his side, Soekarno declared Indonesian independence.

In the name of the people of Indonesia.
Soekarno/Hatta

Proclamation

We, the people of Indonesia hereby declare the independence of Indonesia. Matters which concern the transfer of power etc., will be executed by careful means in the shortest possible time.

Djakarta, 17 August 05 [45][2]

The date on the proclamation was still Japanese. No Allied force was anywhere near Indonesia, except on Morotai, a narrow strip of New Guinea, as the Allied, mainly US forces moved toward Japan. Allied forces, and the Dutch units

CHAPTER 11

who were a part of them, were not expected to reach the crucial Indonesian islands for another few weeks. Depending on who was speaking, the weeks began to be called either "lost weeks," by the Dutch especially who hastened back to "their" Indies/Indonesia, or "gained weeks," by those Indonesians who decided to use the vacuum of power, the window of opportunity, to act on their own.

It had been agreed by the Allied powers at several wartime conferences, and finally at the inaugural conference of the United Nations in San Francisco in the spring of 1945, that the sovereignty over the Indies/Indonesia remained with the Netherlands, one of the Allies and, thus, the victors. Japanese forces in the archipelago were to stay where they stood on August 15, keep public order, and wait for the Allies, the Dutch included, to come.

Thousands of prisoners in Japanese camps, civilian as well as military, Dutch as well as other Europeans, and many Eurasians, were to stay in the camps, too, until the Allies, including the Dutch, arrived and released them safely.[3] The new republic proclaimed by Soekarno and Hatta was unexpected and not included in the victors' plans. The victors might have resembled King Louis XVI as the crowds converged under his windows in the Versailles: "The Duke the Liancourt . . . gained access to the Royal Apartments . . . Louis: . . . 'Why, that is a revolt!' . . . 'Sir,' commented Liancourt, 'it is not a revolt—it is a revolution.'"[4] It remained to be seen what kind of revolution this one would be.

The new republic proclaimed by Soekarno and Hatta was hastily assembled from all available forces. The new republican police, weeks after the proclamation, still wore Japanese uniforms, used Japanese ranks, and issued orders in Japanese fashion. The task given to them by Soekarno and Hatta, now the president and vice-president, was to keep order, and not much beyond that was clear. Some of the new Indonesian police communications in Jogjakarta, Central Java, were intercepted and translated by British intelligence:

August 24

Shotjo and Pakem Sotyo at 22:00 sent in Dutch flags [red, white, and blue]. Asking permission to use material to make Indonesian flags [red and white].

25 August. Soetlawono Keibu [Keibu is Japanese for "police inspector"] reported Daroe heard from many sources that on 28 August P.O.W. and Internees be released.

31 August to honor Wilhelmina [the official Dutch queen's birthday] all sirens must be sounded . . .

Verhey [?] asked what to do if internees from other districts passing Jogja [Jogjakarta] wore orange roses [the Dutch royal color] or red, white, and blue [the Dutch tricolor].[5]

The first few days appeared chaotic but quiet. Soon, however, began what Van der Plas back in Australia feared as a catastrophic scenario. The children, the boys—and there were many "girls," too—trained and indoctrinated by the Japanese, with sharpened bamboo spears or wooden rifles, and increasingly with bayonets attached, began to take over the streets, squares, crossroads, buildings, and private homes. The Indonesian units of Peta, Pembela Tanah Air, "Defenders of the Motherland," trained by the Japanese in Java—there was a similar force in Sumatra—disbanded and disarmed by the Japanese in the wake of the surrender to obey the Allied orders, now began to reassemble. They were composed of local men who, during the Japanese occupation, had been stationed in the villages and towns of their origin. They were at home, and now they began to get back their weapons from the demoralized Japanese, either by bribes or by force. They joined the children, in Van der Plas's apocalyptic terms, in a wave of euphoria, chaos, frenzy, and élan. They called it *merdeka*, "freedom."

"By vehemence of character," Thomas Carlyle wrote about the French Revolution, "terror grows transcendental."[6] "Revolutions," Isaac Deutscher wrote in his biography of Trotsky, are engendered by "the conviction that what they have begun is mankind's 'leap from the realm of necessity to the realm of freedom.'"[7]

The Dutch, European, and Eurasian prisoners first trickled and then poured out of the camps despite (lukewarm) Japanese efforts to stop them. Sometimes more than three years of confinement did not prepare them for what they now saw. In a sense of frenzy, euphoria, dizziness, and chaos, comparable to those of the Peta and of the children, they called the state in which they found themselves *vrijheid*, "freedom."

The senses of freedom clashed. The people coming from the camps did not find the Indies they left three years before, and the Indonesians would not return to the prewar times. Clashes and killing began. The weeks, gained or lost, passed. The Allied troops landed on Java, first British—mostly British Indian troops—and then the Dutch. Clashes multiplied, and the Allies, Dutch prominently, became involved and joined in the killing.

There are several versions, and myths, of how Amir Sjarifoeddin got out of Japanese prison. According to what Amir's wife later told Jacques Leclerc, "The Japanese did not dare to release him except to the Allies. On September 29, other prisoners were being released but there was still no news of Amir. . . . In the morning next day came a postcard, 'I am in Malang. Please, inform UN people as soon as possible.'"[8] Djaenah said she contacted a secretary in the office of Soekarno.

Later, when they were reunited, Amir told his wife that he did not know about the proclamation of independence when it happened or days later. Only, at a certain moment, the Japanese guards became a little more friendly. Thus, he concluded that his execution was imminent.[9] On the outside, however, in the meantime, "a group of young people began to negotiate with the Japanese." He was released. "All the time accompanied by Japanese guards, he was driven to Soerabaja and put on the train for Djakarta."[10] So Amir told Djaenah and Djaenah told Leclerc.

Rudjito, one of the group of young people, sort of Amir's underground in Malang, later wrote about the time: "couriers arrived from Jakarta to Malang . . . and brought a new order. The Japanese fascists had surrendered on August 14." The order was to attack Lowokwaru (prison) from the outside and call upon the prisoners to rise up from the inside.

> People's movement with sharpened bamboo spears led by the youth attacked the Lowokwaru prison. Without us asking, [the prisoners] took heart [*djagoan*, "to behave like champion fighting cocks"], disarmed the enemy and exterminated 21 fascist Japanese soldiers. In this manner, the prisoners gained their freedom by their own hands.
>
> Bg. [*baginda*, Malay, Indonesian, meaning "father,"] Amir Sjarifoeddin was brought to the youth headquarters from the Lowokwaru prison. I was selected to watch over the safety of Baginda Amir until he was in his carriage on the express train to Jakarta.[11]

According to Arnold Brackman, who might have heard the report when he was reporting from Java in 1947 and 1948, "Amir was freed from a Malang jail by an armed band of *pemoeda* ['youth']."[12]

W. F. Wertheim was a Dutch lawyer and the successor to Professor Kollewijn at the Law School.[13] He had been interned in a Japanese camp throughout the war. Now liberated from the camp he worked for the Red Cross. He recalled in his memoirs how he learned about Amir still in prison. He knew Amir from the prewar times, and he informed the UN's RAPWI (perhaps the "UN" Djaenah meant?), or Rescue of Allied Prisoners of War and Internees. "In October," Wertheim recalled, "Sjarifoeddin was indeed released." There is nothing in Wertheim's recollection of Amir being liberated by an "armed band of *pemoeda*." "If the step by the Red Cross hastened the release," Wertheim writes, "I do not know."[14]

Soekarno, "The Proclamator," as he began to be called after August, offered a version which, as was his style, so to speak, did not limp on human legs. "Since the time of the struggle against the Dutch and the Japanese Bung [Indonesian for "elder brother"] Karno [Soekarno], was very sympathetic to *mr.* Amir Sjarifoeddin." Now, Soekarno as president, was putting his first cabinet together: "'Who should the candidates for the Minister of Information be?'

asked one of the advisers. Bung Karno answered: 'There is only one candidate, *mr.* Amir Sjarifoeddin.' 'Is he not still in prison in Malang?' asked another one present. With a smile, Bung Karno answered, and without a moment of hesitation: 'You speak as if we were still in the Japanese times. But we are now free, and I myself will get Amir out.'"[15]

Twenty years later, in his *Autobiography as Told to Cindy Adams*, Soekarno told the US journalist a more elaborate version of this story, with timing conflated and dramatic effect enhanced: "Reports reached me that for weeks the *kenpeitai* had Amir Sjarifoeddin, one of our captured underground leaders, hanging upside down by his feet. He was drinking his own urine. He couldn't last much longer. I negotiated his release by ordering the officials in charge. 'Free him or you no longer have my cooperation.' It took iron guts to make such a statement. But it took even more guts to look at him when they let him out. He was thin as a finger. It is unbelievable that a person can suffer like that and still live."[16]

One fact is certain. On September 4, 1945, while still in prison, Amir Sjarifoeddin was appointed the new republic's minister of information. *Mr.* Ali Sastroamidjojo (the man who was so disturbed by Amir's visit to his house in Soerabaja in 1942) was asked "temporarily to take over Amir Sjarifoeddin's functions until the latter returned from prison in East Java."[17] Amir learned about his appointment, Djaenah told Jacques Leclerc, "from newspapers which 'clandestinely' got to him."[18]

On the last day of September or the first day of October 1945, Amir was on his way to Djakarta. "On that occasion a team from the Department of Information made a documentary film," wrote Rudjito (I am still looking for the film). Rudjito writes that he was with Amir all the way: "At each stop between Malang and Soerabaja, there were crowds of people, mainly youth, who wanted to get close to Baginda Amir Sjarifoeddin; but he, every time, merely cried out 'Onward Indonesian revolution,' 'Onward youth, the hope of the nation,' and 'Freedom or death,' 'Thank you,'" and put his head back inside the window." Along the way, writes Rudjito, Amir "did not give a speech once, because his health was still weak."[19]

One of Amir's youths who switched to Sjahrir after Amir was arrested, Soedarpo Sastrosatomo, by chance—so he later told his biographer—traveled on the same train:

On October 1, 1945, on the Surabaya–Jakarta train, Soedarpo by accident met Amir Sjarifoeddin, who had just been released from the Malang prison. At the start of the conversation Amir did not recollect ever meeting Soedarpo before, although he had led a discussion group in which

Soedarpo and Soedjatmoko had participated, and it was obvious that Amir had been tortured in prison. He was tired and emaciated. His memory was faltering. On arrival at Jatinegara [Jakarta] Station, Suwirjo, the Mayor of Jakarta, met Amir. There was also a reporter from *Merdeka*, the daily that had just come out with its first edition that day, but Amir was not able to give any statements. He went directly to his house on Malabar Street.[20]

According to what Amir himself wrote in his autobiography, "[i]n October 1945, I was released from prison and after about three years of separation I again met with my wife and two children. But my third child, who was born while I was in prison, had already died."[21]

Pastor Verkuyl, who had recruited Amir, the reader may recall, to take part at the missionary conference in Karangpandan in 1941, and who, at least since then, had become Amir's friend, was present at Djakarta main station among the crowd waiting for Amir:

> When the train with the prisoner arrived in Djakarta, I was at the station. There gathered a huge mass of people to welcome him. . . .
> A couple of days later I visited Amir in the house of his brother. . . . One of the first things Amir told me was: "In the Malang prison I read the Old Testament, the Prophets, Amos, Jeremiah, Isaiah and so on. I had known virtually nothing of how deeply these Prophets had been engaged politically. You all in the colonial time talked to us and taught us so little about this. The Book of Prophets used to be a closed book for me. But now, it was opened, and for good."

"And he told me," Pastor Verkuyl continued, "how he lived in prison with the Bible and with his beloved *Gebetbuch* [prayer book] by Hanns Lilje of the Christian student movement."[22]

Several decades later, Professor Nico Scholte-Nordholt of Enschede told me about Pastor Verkuyl's lectures in the Kraemer Institute in Oegstgeest. In the lectures, Pastor Verkuyl still recalled what Amir told him that day, pointing out to him that during the colonial time the Dutch missionaries failed to explain the crucial parts of the Holy Script, "in particular the strong verses of the Prophets like Amos and Micha against oppression and injustice." Amir "reproached" Verkuyl, Verkuyl said: "why didn't you ever tell us about the Prophets!" And Amir's conclusion was: "You kept us ignorant about our rights and justice!"[23]

In the Leiden University Library Special Collection, there is a photograph someone took of Amir as he stepped out of Djakarta train station. He is on the building's stairs, facing the crowd, surrounded by a small group of young people. I believe I can recognize several of them, the metropolitan youth, who used to be followers of Amir in the last months of the prewar Indies and the first months of the Japanese occupation and then, after Amir was arrested, switched to Sjahrir.[24]

I only knew these men (they are all men on the photograph) thirty to forty years later, but I think I can still safely recognize handsome Soedarpo and his brother Soebadio next to him. The tall young man in glasses almost certainly is "Koko" Soedjatmoko, and next to him it may be L. M. Sitoroes, Amir's fellow Batak Christian.

Sitoroes and the others were now all Sjahrir's followers, of Sjahrir's group. And it might have been there that Sitoroes approached Amir, "directly after his arrival," as he told Leclerc, with a message: "Do not accept the appointment to the Soekarno cabinet." The message, according to Sitoroes, was from Sjahrir.[25]

Amir entered politics. Ali Sastroamidjojo, who had overseen the Ministry of Information in Amir's absence, was also among the people greeting the released prisoner and minister-elect of the cabinet:

> I, among others, was to meet him at Gambir Station. He was very thin . . . his hair was very short and had only just started to grow again, his wrists still showed the marks of the ropes by which his body had been made to hang when he was tortured. I accompanied him from the station to his family's house and after he had rested, we had a serious discussion. . . . I was startled to hear him say that he very much doubted whether Sukarno and the members of the cabinet would accept him wholeheartedly. The reason, he told me quite frankly, was that he received twenty-five thousand guilders from the Dutch for his underground activity against Japan.[26]

There is another story, by Soemarsono, Amir's follower throughout, close to the Soerabaja group, who did not switch to Sjahrir. This is a story not repeated by others. It may express the chaos, or the élan, or politics already at work.

The leaders of the various youth organizations, Soemarsono says, gathered on August 14, when news of the imminent Japanese capitulation was heard on the shortwave radio. At a former student dormitory at Kramat 106—Kramat 106 again!—not used as a dormitory during the war.[27] Three days before Soekarno's and Hatta's proclamation, the group of activists met, says Soemarsono, all of them young and virtually all of them ex-students, with the schools closed. At the meeting they debated who should be the "proclamator" and thus the person to lead Indonesia to independence. On August 14, 1945, at Kramat 106, Soemarsono says, "First it was debated what moment to choose for the proclamation. Then the debate moved into who was to enact the proclamation and who subsequently was to become the President of the Indonesian Republic. A name that had been raised first was that of Bung Amir Sjarifoeddin. And all the youth agreed."[28]

Amir, however, writes Soemarsono, was still in prison, and for all that was known, he might be dead. Then Soebadio of the Soedjatmoko and Sitoroes circle, of those who had switched, "suggested that perhaps Sjahrir might become the President." "They all knew that Sjahrir [like Amir] did not work for the Japanese. . . . So, the second choice was Sjahrir. A delegation had been sent to Sjahrir from the meeting. It was early morning and Sjahrir was out, playing tennis. They waited, Sjahrir came back from tennis and . . . refused straight on. They thought: 'Is he afraid to take the risk, or what?' But he said he preferred a safe way." Sjahrir suggested Soekarno and Hatta, for the sake, he told the young people, of stability and continuity. "I was not there," writes Soemarsono, "but I heard about the talk between Sjahrir and the youth from others, Wikana and Aidit." "Amir Sjarifoeddin," Soemarsono adds, "did not know about it. He did not know that he almost had been nominated the proclamator."[29] Whether he had known about it or not, or whether he had been later informed about it or not, Amir does not mention it in his autobiography.

Adam Malik, one of Amir's ardent prewar followers, and soon to be Amir's adversary, one of the young activists in August 1945 wrote that Amir was appointed a minister while he was still in prison, under the pressure of the youths.[30] According to Soemarsono, from the station, after his arrival from prison, Amir's first steps did not lead to his family house, but to Menteng 31, the other youth headquarters of the moment. In any case, whether or not Amir got Sjahrir's message not to accept the Soekarno appointment, Amir went very soon, if not the first day, to see Soekarno and accepted the job.[31]

This was another moment of crossing the line. Perhaps *the* one. The mere saying had been passing to action. It was a moment of possibility. The possibility had been, that the saying, in passing, tested, will be found to have power.

During a press conference with foreign journalists in Djakarta on October 4, where Amir for the first time appeared as a minister, he "wore shorts and long knee socks just like Marshall Wavell."[32] He talked about work to be done. Indeed, he began to organize a new network of republican radio stations in as many cities and towns of Java as possible. He hired Soedjatmoko and Soedarpo, now Sjahrir followers, to help him with the job.[33]

Soekarno and Hatta had known Amir Sjarifoeddin as a charismatic figure of the Indonesian movement during the time of the prewar Indies, but also as a man skeptical of their own policies. But both Soekarno and Hatta needed Amir badly.

The first Soekarno and Hatta cabinet was called "cabinet *Buchó*," *Buchó* being a rank in the Japanese occupation administration, the highest an Indonesian might ever be granted. This was now a derogatory name and the Allies, who would reject collaborators and collaborationism, were coming. In other parts of the world, collaborators with the fascist powers were dealt with as war criminals. Virtually all the ministers of the first Soekarno and Hatta government were taken over from the war-time Japanese power structure in Indonesia. Amir, meanwhile, was a proven anti-fascist and proven democrat.

Sjahrir was reportedly also offered a ministerial position in the government, but he declined.[34] He chose not to cross the line yet. He remained with the saying, meeting various people, keeping in touch, traveling the network.

Soetan Sjahrir was born in the Minangkabau region of West Sumatra, bordering on Batak lands. He was born in Minangkabau but his father, a *hoofddjaksa* like Amir's, was transferred to Medan, where Sjahrir spent his childhood. In Medan he attended a Europese Lagere School (elementary school)—the same, in fact as Amir, only one grade below.[35] It is not recorded whether the two boys met in school.[36] Certainly, they looked from the same windows and at the same wall charts. They had the same teachers. The families, at least at some distance, probably knew each other.

On October 4, during his first press conference, "Amir Sjarifoeddin talked to the correspondents of the Indonesian and foreign press accredited in Djakarta and said that Indonesian freedom is not made-in-Japan and that, if it were, he would never agree to serve as the Minister of Information."[37] Anti-fascism was what now seemed to matter most to Amir, but also to Sjahrir.

At the end of October, Soetan Sjahrir, still traveling the network, circulated a statement through Djakarta and beyond, called "Perdjoeangan Kita," "Our Struggle." It was a most strongly worded manifesto of anti-fascism and democracy, designed as a compass for the emerging Indonesian republic and the upcoming phase of the Indonesian revolution. In places its language was close to cursing. It was the saying at its crudest, and on the brink of action. On November 10, 1945, "Perdjoeangan Kita" was published.[38]

When, in the early 1970s, Frank Weinstein, a US student of government, interviewed people who had been Sjahrir's friends in 1945, several of them told him that "Sjahrir's way of thinking" late in 1945 was "so close to Mao Zedong's that some people thought that the two must have met." Sjahrir's "Our Struggle," they said, "was often compared with Mao's 'On New Democracy,'" "and even 'people in the communist world' [?] accepted 'Our Struggle' as 'a contribution on the same level as Mao's.'"[39]

Sjahrir's "Our Struggle" attacked collaborators with fascism. Those ready-to-help and ready to be enslaved had to be eliminated from the leadership of the Indonesian republic. None was named in "Our Struggle," but everyone knew that the whole *Buchō* cabinet could easily be placed under the rubric, including Soekarno, if not Hatta.

Amir Sjarifoeddin crossed the line. He already moved inside the machine of the government, between different parts, gadgets, switches, of the machine. Amir's biography was closer than ever to becoming, using Jacques Derrida's words, a "history of apparatuses."[40] Like Franz Kafka's apparatus in *In the Penal Colony*. Showing it to the traveler, the officer says: "well it's not primary school calligraphy, that's for sure."[41]

"While the formalists believe that at the beginning was the word," said Leon Trotsky, at the outset of the Bolshevik revolution, "the Marxist thinks that at the beginning was the deed—the word follows the deed as its sound shadow."[42] Or, as Trotsky would agree and I think Amir, too, at that moment, "Formula" must be "substantiated" so "that Society might become *methodic*."[43] And so the revolution.

On October 7, 1945, a letter was sent to President Soekarno, signed by forty members of the 135-member KNIP, "Central Indonesian National Council," according to the new Indonesian Constitution, *pembantoe*, "helper" to the president: a body of selected influential personalities of the land. The KNIP, the letter demanded, should become "true legislative." Cabinet ministers should become responsible to the KNIP and not, as now, to the president.

The republic was to become a parliamentary democracy. On October 16, with Soekarno unavailable, Hatta as the vice-president answered in his name. This became known as *Maklumat X*, "Declaration X," and in it Hatta accepted the demands of the letter of October 7. The next day, a fifteen-member Working Committee of the National Council was created. Sjahrir was behind the maneuver and his "Our Struggle" was the formula behind it: democracy against a system that smelled of fascism. Sometime in October 1945, Amir shifted to Sjahrir.[44]

Sjahrir became the chairman of the new Working Committee of the KNIP, and Amir became the deputy chairman. Now, Soekarno had to be found. "Sjahrir did not know when Soekarno would return," Soedarpo told his biographer later. It was at a Working Committee meeting. "Amir Sjarifoeddin then said in Dutch, 'ik heb twee cowboys' (I have two cowboys'). Soekarno knows them well. Let them contact Soekarno and bring him back to Jakarta.' Soedarpo and Soedjatmoko departed."[45] Amir was in action, and light footed at it.

Soekarno was found and made to agree. On November 11, Sjahrir, as the chairman of the Working Committee, had been named a formator of the new cabinet, the second cabinet of the republic, and on November 14 he became the prime minister. Amir, in the new Sjahrir cabinet, kept a portfolio of information from the first *Buchō* cabinet, and in addition became the minister of defense.

The line between saying and acting was tested. The composition of the cabinet was a result of political maneuvering and manipulation, machine working, with the Allies coming close, saying "anti-fascism" and saying "democracy." The composition of the cabinet was to manifest that the new republic was worthy of becoming a member of the new world, the free world, so to speak. This was where saying "freedom" was now getting its echo and resonance.

"Four of the eleven ministers," historian Anthony Reid commented, "were (Protestant) Christians, and the non-representation of Muslim interests brought immediate complaints."[46] Dr. Sukiman, the chairman of Masyumi, a Japanese-established Islamic party, "voiced a strong protest to the President, accusing him of violating the Constitution by permitting such a cabinet to be formed."[47]

This cabinet certainly was not a *Buchō* one, but still, as Benedict Anderson commented, "it contained not a single person, aside from its two leaders [Sjahrir and Amir] who had played a prominent role in the proclamation crisis, or in the dramatic developments since that period." Sjahrir's—and now Amir's too—formula worked but lacked substance. "The narrow composition of the cabinet," wrote Anderson, "offered further evidence of how little [Sjahrir] trusted the forces which had brought him to power. Sjahrir and Amir between them monopolized all the five key political posts (Sjahrir taking internal and foreign affairs as well as the premiership). The remaining nine posts appear to have been filled with an eye to technical competence or acceptability to the Dutch."[48]

What was to happen to élan, to the Augé-like, Metro-like swirls, to the semi-crazy people of three Bs? And what was to happen to the revolution?

Amir again traveled, between Batavia, now Djakarta, and Central and East Java especially. On October 24, still before the new cabinet was formed, still as a deputy chair of the Working Committee, in a speech on republican radio, he issued a call to the Indonesian youth to gather the following month in the Central-Javanese city of Jogjakarta

The Congress of the Youth opened on the morning of November 10 in the city Gedoeng Merdeka, "House of Freedom."[49] As Indonesian papers reported, 580 delegates and 700 observers attended in the presence of Soekarno, Hatta, and six other cabinet ministers (these were the last days of the *Buchō* cabinet).[50]

Amir, who was widely understood to have been the main promotor of the assembly, gave a fiery address, culminating in the following appeal: *"Pemuda* ['Youth']! If you hold a rifle in your right hand, you must hold a hammer in your left!"[51]

Francisca Fanggidaej, a woman of twenty-one years old, half-Dutch but from a family who had lived in the Indies for generations,[52] participant in the Soerabaja youth anti-Japanese movement during the war, was present at the congress as a Soerabaja delegate. "I do not recall anymore what points Bung Amir was making in that speech," Francisca wrote forty years later:

> I do not remember, even recall clearly what the main theme of the congress had been. I did not really pay much attention. I was busy as a committee member, and I was so young . . . so green. I remember, however, the enthrallment at the moment Bung Amir stepped up on the podium. His hair was ruffled, he wore glasses, his look was compassioned and still full of confidence. For a long moment he merely looked into the audience. Then he raised his right hand in fist. His voice was hard and clear. He repeated one word three times: "Freedom! Freedom! Freedom!"
>
> We roared back the same word. . . . I was in trance. As if grasped by a wave, a tide, frightful yet gentle. . . . "Freedom!" as if I had always been listening for this particular word and now I felt like "at home." It was a *"rediscovery"* [this word is in English] . . . "Freedom." "Freedom," "Freedom or Death."[53]

"This huge insurrectionary Movement," wrote Thomas Carlyle about a similar moment in the French Revolution, "how will it be henceforth shape itself? Settle down into a reign of law and liberty, ascending as the habits, persuasions and endeavors of the educated, moneyed, respectable class prescribe?"[54] "Freedom! Freedom or Death," Carlyle wrote, was the "consummation of sansculottism."[55] But Amir came to Jogjakarta ex officio, as a minister of the government. To better the machine. To endow it with what, as he had to see, had increasingly been lacking. To contain chaos, channel the flood, structure, apportion, manage, rank the fire.

At the congress, Amir Sjarifoeddin attempted to fuse the armed militia as it had emerged during the last phase of the Japanese occupation and in the first days and weeks after the proclamation; to fuse the multiple groups of widely different characters into an organized force listening to the government. His success, to use a word increasingly fitting the situation, was measured. On November 11, in Jogjakarta, at the side of the Youth Congress, only "seven of the 28 major [youth] organizations attending, announced that they were fusing into a single organization, to be known as the Pemuda Sosialis Indonesia, or 'Pesindo,' the 'Socialist Youth of Indonesia.'"[56]

As the Youth Congress was about to meet, three-hundred kilometers east, in Soerabaja, clashes began between local youth and Allied forces. The Allied troops, mainly British, were attempting to land in Soerabaja and occupy the city to restore order. The clashes erupted into a full-scale battle and then a brutal total war. "Three [British] armed ships steamed into Surabaya on the 9th [of November]."[57] The youth of Soerabaja, loosely organized, answered by a mode of resistance bordering on suicide. Just as the Youth Congress in Jogjakarta convened, the Battle of Surabaya was "at its fiercest."[58]

"Already in August 21 the workers of the city oil refineries had formed their own organizations, and on August 25 a subsidiary Angkatan Moeda [was created] led by Soemarsono and Roeslan Widjaja." At the Youth Congress at Jogjakarta, Angkatan Moeda became a member of Pesindo.[59]

Just a little over a week before the Youth Congress met in Jogjakarta, "in desperation," writes Anthony Reid, "the British flew Sukarno, Hatta, and Amir Sjarifoeddin to Surabaya as the only Indonesians likely to be able to call a halt to the carnage."[60] William Frederick, a historian of the Battle of Soerabaja quoting a contemporary Indonesian newspaper, wrote: "Sukarno arrived [in Surabaya] in the morning of October 29 with Vice-President Hatta and Amir Sjarifoeddin 'amidst a hail of bullets.'"[61]

Like he would a week later in Jogjakarta, Amir arrived in Soerabaja to channel the flood, rank the chaos, the élan, the revolution, and to remain himself.

A young leader, who would epitomize the battle more than anyone, Soetomo, Bung Tomo, approached Amir as he arrived at the city. Soetomo was the voice of the battle, a sound of élan of the youth. He was a radio voice, too. He spoke regularly on the local Soerabaja station, his voice carried through the streets on a public system. He began each of his programs with "Allahu Akbar!" "God is Great," and he called for holy war.

An idea was brought by Soetomo to Amir: "Would the minister permit him to set up and operate his own radio transmitter?" Amir "could do no such thing, and he found unconvincing Soetomo's warning that the minister simply did not understand the *rakjat* [people]." The most that Amir was willing to do was to allow Soetomo continuing "access to broadcast facilities in government hands."[62] Soetomo's wife later remembered:

During the Battle of Surabaya, Mas Soetomo [*Mas*, an endearing term of address for a man] received a telegram from the Prime Minister [*sic*] Amir Sjarifoeddin, containing a very curt message. Bung Tomo was to decide—either to become "a General" and then he should shut his mouth—or he could stop being a General and go on talking . . . Mas Tomo's face reddened with anger. How offensive! He was insulted. . . . "Who, then, would be in the city to raise the spirit? Who would be the soul of the people? Who would be the voice of Surabaya?" Mas Tomo made the decision: his voice kept ringing.[63]

"At a conference of 30 October," writes Anthony Reid, "the presidential group browbeat the extremely reluctant *pemuda* leaders into accepting a cease-fire agreement."[64]

On the same day, October 30, Sjahrir in Djakarta, from his new position of the chairman of the Working Committee, issued a declaration. By a stroke of a pen a multiparty system had been installed in Indonesia.[65] It appeared as a move in step with Amir's corralling the revolution in Soerabaja. Perfecting democracy, rejecting fascism. Amir, as the deputy chair of the Working Committee, was generally seen as the coauthor of the declaration.

When Soekarno and Hatta proclaimed the Republic of Indonesia on August 17, 1945, it was assumed that the nation in revolt stood behind them, and that, when it came to organizing the nation, there would be one party. The party was vaguely (or gloriously) meant to be the PNI, "Indonesian National Party," pointing back in continuity to the Indonesian National Party as it existed under Soekarno's leadership before 1931, when he first went to prison.[66]

Sjahrir (and Amir, as generally assumed the coauthor), by issuing the declaration of October 30, implied that this concept of national and revolutionary unity, the one-party system, was just another remnant of the Japanese fascism in Indonesia, and that in order for a true and complete democracy to be installed, such a system had to go. Soedjatmoko, now the star of Sjahrir's group, who had switched from Amir after Amir was arrested by the Japanese in 1943, later recalled the moment: "One of the most unique features of the Indonesian revolution was the establishment of a multi-party political system in the midst of a revolution. It is especially striking in comparison with the one-party system with which many other countries emerged from revolution. . . . The single national party Sukarno established almost immediately after the proclamation of independence was to be the expression of and the sole vehicle for the Indonesian revolution." But to Sjahrir, Soedjatmoko wrote, "the release of tremendous social forces had both great creative but also destructive potential. It was the task of the revolutionary leader . . . to harness these forces and to direct them to democratic and humanistic goals."

Soedjatmoko wondered. He did not mention whether he went to talk about it with Amir, his "mentor number 1." But he went to Soekarno, his "mentor number 2." "We are in a revolution," Soekarno told Soedjatmoko and then he explained what he meant by "being a revolutionary leader." "It is too early to be concerned with democracy and human rights. . . . A revolution is like a run-away horse. It goes its own way; the task of a revolutionary leader is simply to stay in the saddle until the horse run[s] its course. Only then can he steer him in the desired direction." "When I asked him," Soedjatmoko recalls, "about the danger of being thrown off the horse, he replied: 'That is a risk a leader should take in a revolution.'"[67]

Instantly, as in a click by Sjahrir's (and Amir's) declaration, parties came into being—Muslim, Christian, socialist, parties around individuals, parties based on territorial, ethnic, and tribal loyalties. Communist parties, too—several of them.

On November 13, 1945, at a two-day conference in Jogjakarta, the Partai Sosialis Indonesia (Parsi), "Indonesian Socialist Party," was founded, and Amir Sjarifoeddin became its chairman. According to Anderson, the new party "urged the formation of [a] Popular Front to defend and strengthen the republic, to work toward the socialization of key enterprises, forests, and land, and to promote industrialization, transportation, a cooperative economy . . . and the formation of unions. The Popular Front was to be the means of linking up workers, peasants, the army, and the *pemuda* [youth]." Amir Sjarifoeddin's party chairmanship, writes Anderson, as well as the list of the "other leading figures indicated that the nucleus of the new party was to be formed by loose associate[s] of Amir Sjarifoeddin in the prewar Gerindo and the labor groups associated with it."[68]

A week later, November 19, 1945, at a conference in Tjirebon, a port city two-hundred kilometers from Djakarta, Paras, the Partai Sosialis, "Socialist Party," was formed, in Anderson's words again, a "ghost of the prewar Pendidikan Nasional Indonesia [of Sjahrir]." Its principles were "to oppose capitalistic, *ningrat* [feudal] mentalities, to eliminate autocracy and bureaucratism, to struggle toward a society of egalitarian collectivism (*sama rata sama rasa* ['the same level, the same sense']) to enrich the spirit of the Indonesian people with a democratic outlook and to urge the government to cooperate with all organizations at home and abroad to overthrow capitalism."[69]

The next month, in December, in Tjirebon again, Parsi under Amir's leadership and Paras led by Sjahrir were consolidated. On December 17, the composition of the new party's executive committees was announced with Sjahrir and Amir at the top. "The fusion," writes Anderson, "was never fully achieved in practice, and insofar as it was effective depended heavily on the trust between Sjahrir and Amir themselves."[70]

On January 4, 1946, a special train stopped off Djakarta station, behind the house where the republic had been proclaimed four months ago, the former house of Van Asbeck before it, at Pegangsaan Timoer 56, the residence of Soekarno. The president, the vice-president, and other figures of the state leadership boarded the train. Djakarta, now Batavia-Djakarta, or even just Batavia again, was becoming a city under Dutch occupation and the Indonesian government decided to move to Jogjakarta, in the island's interior. The Sultan of Jogjakarta, who according to the ancient treaties with the Dutch was an autonomous ruler of the city and region, offered Jogjakarta as the republican capital for the duration of the crisis.

"The center of national politics," wrote Anthony Reid, "moved to the free air of Central Java, where the revolution was intoxicating reality."[71] "Sjarifoeddin," Dutch intelligence reported, "moved to Jogjakarta, where he had many connections with the communists and intellectual extremists."[72]

Sjahrir remained in Batavia/Djakarta. As the prime minister and minister of foreign affairs, he took it on himself to lead the negotiations with the Allies and the Dutch. George Kahin, a historian of the revolution, who may have heard it directly from Sjahrir, wrote: "Sjahrir in particular strongly urged Soekarno and Hatta to go to Jogjakarta not only because of the danger of arrest by the British or assassination by the Dutch troops but also because he felt there was a danger of their being assassinated by [an Indonesian extremist] group."[73]

There was indeed a real danger. Hatta later described the atmosphere in the city to his biographer: "Dutch troops, the majority of them Ambonese, cruised around Djakarta in jeeps or trucks, shooting at random, in particular at the cars of Indonesian dignitaries which they identified by the red and white flags flying at the front." On December 26, less than a week before the government moved away, "Sjahrir narrowly escaped death. . . . Two days later an assassination attempt was made on Amir Sjarifoeddin."[74] Wertheim, of the Red Cross, wrote in his diary: "*January 2, 1946*, . . . visit to ministers Sjahrir and Sjarifoeddin. Sjahrir, just a few days ago, was stopped with his car by the Dutch military on the street and assaulted. It is not clear whether they knew who he was. In any case there is a breakdown in security in Batavia-Djakarta, and for everyone. Sjahrir still has a blue eye from the incident."[75] "December 28, 1945," Jacques Leclerc wrote, "Amir's automobile is fired on outside Soekarno's residence."[76] During the same month, wrote a British journalist in Indonesia, "Sjarifoeddin's car was fired upon twice in one week."[77] "In the first days of January 1946, Mohammad Natsir took over Amir's functions as the minister of information."[78] Natsir was now one of the cochairmen of the Islamic Masjumi. In 1941, he had been enraged by Amir's attendance at the missionary conference at Karangpandan. He was clearly not a friend of Amir. But the multiparty system of government demanded a tweak in the apparatus.

As far as I know, Amir Sjarifoeddin's article on Machiavelli in *Poedjangga Baroe* in January 1937, its section namely on Machiavelli's *The Art of War*, and the series of articles in the late summer and fall of 1941 on the Indonesian popular militia, were the only signs of Amir's interest in military matters before November 1945. Then, Amir became the minister of defense. Amir, as Sjahrir's deputy, embarked upon channeling the élan, or desire and inspiration (*tjita-tjita*) as he called it in 1941, and, of course, chaos, in what was to become the armed forces of the revolution.

Pesindo, created at the Youth Congress in Jogjakarta in November 1945, might have been a way to begin. "The power of the Pesindo," Anderson wrote, "had two bases. The first was . . . appealing to the prevalent hostility to the Japanese by making use of the underground association. . . . The second was its association with Amir Sjarifoeddin. . . . While there was no direct evidence to prove it, the widely held belief that he as the Minister of Defense was instrumental in providing the organization with a considerable variety of facilities, including money and guns, seems hard not to accept."[79] On December 15, days after its formation, "the Pesindo leadership issued a program and demanded an army with a 'people's ideology' and the elimination of military 'methods' that might separate the army from the people."[80]

According to Arnold Brackman, who reported for the United Press from Java during the revolution, "Amir's idea" upon becoming the minister of defense, was that of "a people's army" and it presumed the creation of "coordinating committees at a village level in which leaders of political parties, the irregular fighting organizations, and the regular army would have authority."[81]

Machiavelli wrote, whether now Amir remembered this passage from *The Art of War* advising the young prince or not, that "Many, Lorenzo, have held the opinion and still do, that nothing in the world is more unlike civilian life than military life, this is the way of thinking in our times. But if one considers ancient institutions, one will not find anything more united, more harmonious, and of necessity with greatest affinity for each other than civilian and military institutions."[82]

Amir Sjarifoeddin, wrote Jacques Leclerc, drew on the experience of the French Revolution, "when an 'amalgam' of the enthusiasm of youth and the military skills of the former members of the King's Army was formed in the '*levée en masse*' plus the Red Army."[83]

"The army was to become permeated with the spirit of civilian citizenship," wrote Leon Trotsky, the founder of the Bolshevik Red Army. "Its detachments," he wrote, "were to be organized on the basis of productive units." "Trotsky insisted," wrote Trotsky's biographer, that "a barracks must be made to resemble a military and general school, not a mere drilling place, a 'well-arranged school, especially one which combines education with physical labor . . . broad and purposeful sporting activities.'"[84]

There were dandy ways to attempt to structure the élan and there was much that resembled the ways of Kramat 106. Tahi Bonar Simatoepang, Amir's fellow Batak and Christian, who had known and admired Amir since before the war, was one of the cadets, whose courses at the academy Koninklijke Nederlandsch-Indië Leger (KNIL), "Royal Netherlands Indies Army," in Bandoeng, were interrupted by the Japanese invasion, and he now joined the revolution. "I met with Bung Amir," Simatoepang wrote in his memoirs, "several times before the Japanese time in Clubhuis [Dutch for "Club House"] of the Christian youth in Kebon Sirih 44 in Jakarta [Batavia]. I was a high-school student, and I was amazed at his speeches at the time presented in eloquent and beautiful Dutch. At the congress of GAPI at the Gang Kenari, I listened to his speech in fiery Indonesian."[85]

It was a kind of beauty, fire, and ethics of saying, which attracted Simatoepang to Amir:

"What I have read of Marx and Engels often captivates me for one can often feel echoing in their words the fears and lamentation of workers who functioned as modern slaves during the early days of the large-scale industrial development of Western Europe. The works of Stalin and Lenin often astonished me by their penetrating and daring analysis. However (Simatoepang wrote this in hindsight), does this mean that we must introduce into our nation the endless mutual recriminations, so characteristic of Western (including Russian) thought, between Marxism and non-Marxism, between revisionism and non-revisionism . . . and so on? Must that lead us to hating and even killing one another?"[86]

"Following the proclamation," Simatoepang wrote, Amir, not yet the minister of defense, still the minister of information in the *Buchô* cabinet, "contacted former officers of the KNIL, with Didi Kartasasmita acting as the liaison officer. At one point these former KNIL officers issued a statement over the radio . . . declaring their allegiance to the republic."

These were the KNIL cadets, who might be Amir's hope. They were young, they were educated and professional, struggling and pleasuring through Dutch military culture and lingering on the way. Their élan was close to Amir's, when he lived at Kramat 106 and studied at the Law School. They were as dandy-close to the real as he had been back then.

"In the second half of the Japanese occupation," Simatoepang wrote, "I too came to live in Bandung. Askari, Kartakusuma, Nasution [other KNIL cadets] and I, together with Sasra and Badjuri (who had both been reserve officers before the Japanese attack) often used to practice fencing on the flat roof of the Bumi Putra building where Nas [Nasution] lived. In those days we worked to widen and intensify our military studies, interrupted by the arrival of the Japanese. Reading Clausewitz gave me the impression that the textbooks at the [KNIL] military academy gave only superficial quotations and adaptations from the work of the German writer who was a real *Denker und Dichter* [German for 'thinker and poet']. The works of Liddell Hart and de Gaulle, which were not covered in the lessons of the Military Academy (the textbooks there were simply copies of those used at the Breda Military Academy in Holland, the most important was a text on strategy by Captain Spoor) introduced me to the new ideas developed in Western Europe between the world wars."[87]

It was a time, more significantly, of a sense that a new world might be created: "A book by Tom Wintringham [who fought in the Spanish Civil War and later taught guerilla tactics in Britain], written when Britain was threatened by German invasion, and particularly a number of books dealing with the people's war in China, opened my eyes and mind to a type of warfare based on a politically conscious population."[88]

"Well, it's not primary school calligraphy, that's for sure," says the officer to the traveler, pointing to the blueprint of the wonderful apparatus. On May 30, 1946, 55 members of the newly created corps of political officers were sent to the Indonesian army units. A number of the units' commanders protested, some of them, like Major-General Gatot Subroto, outright refused to receive them. Each division, also, had been assigned five political officers who were to hold an autonomous position in the division leadership."[89] Abdul Haris Nasoetion, a cadet who used to fence with Simatoepang on the roof in Bandoeng, now one of the Indonesian army's senior officers, also "categorically refused to accept political commissars in his units."[90]

Amir pushed toward a people's army as some helped, some resisted, and some observed. Lieutenant Colonel Laurens van der Post of the Allies, was a figure of some renown as a writer, socialite, and adventurer.[91] In the early months of 1946, Van der Post traveled on an assignment, possibly for the British mission in Batavia/Djakarta, with Amir on one of Amir's rare official trips outside Java. On April 24, Van der Post sent back a secret report from Fort de Kock, Bukitinggi, in West Sumatra:

> At Fort de Kock itself, I saw a parade of about 10,000 *pemoedas* and *pemoedis* [youth, male and female]. The parade was held in honor of Amir Sjarifoeddin and it is reasonable to assume that the Indonesians put forward their best military effort. The parade started with a procession of the Indonesian mechanized division.
> This division consisted of what looked like two Japanese Bren carriers and a truck equipped with light armored plating. I counted in all about 7,000 boys [*sic*] and 3,000 women. They were all very young and

the boys carried about 120 rifles with the inevitable *bamboe roentjings* [sharpened bamboo spears] and wooden rifles, sometimes fixed with homemade bayonets at the end.[92]

"Pikemen and Pikewomen," wrote Carlyle about the *pemoeda* and *pemoedi* of the French Revolution, and without Van der Post's kind of sneer, "the twenty-five million . . . rose with pikes in their hands."[93] Carlyle considered them the soul of the revolution.

Van der Post reported from the trip, too, that "Amir Sjarifoeddin made various speeches to the people of Sumatra." "He did a lot of talking but as far as I know he only repeated what Sjahrir has been saying in Java. Sjahrir's secretary was with him all the time and I saw for myself that he carried different copies of Sjahrir's recent speeches and used these as talking points for all he said." Dutch intelligence, who clearly knew, reported on the mission and Van der Post's comments in a telegram sent on May 13: "first impression republican mission according vanderpost . . . —stop—sjarifoeddin finds this land does not follow directives from java—stop."[94]

Against the odds, on May 25, 1946, back from Sumatra, Amir Sjarifoeddin announced the establishment of the Biro Perdjoeangan, "Office of Struggle,"[95] to direct the policies of the military. Soemarsono became the Office of Struggle's deputy commander. The head of his staff was Simatoepang. Djokosoejono, a man, like Soemarsono, one of Amir's long-standing supporters, a man also connected with Musso when Musso was in Java in 1935 and 1936, became the Office of Struggle's head. "Djokosoejono," recalled Simatoepang, "came from Madiun and he had been imprisoned by the Dutch in Djombang or Modjokerto for a considerable time." During the Japanese period, "The lessons he had received in politics, history, sociology, organization, socialism, and Marxism have taken deep root and assumed the character of dogma for him. The mental and emotional traits common to members of a movement who believe themselves persecuted had become second nature to him, he had a deep sense of solidarity with fellow victims and comrades-in-arms with whom he shared frequent suffering and occasional joy, and he had a deep hatred for the enemy (the Dutch) and for the 'aristocracy,' the 'bourgeoisie,' and the *prijaji* ['officialdom']." "To a certain extent," concludes Simatoepang, "I had come to understand this way of thinking and feeling when we lived and worked together in Jogjakarta."[96]

Soon after the Jogjakarta Youth Congress at the end of 1945, and after the Battle of Soerabaja where the young fighters were pushed out of the city and the city had been occupied by the British, Pesindo moved its headquarters from Soerabaja where they were till then to Madiun, a city between British-occupied

Surabaya and Jogjakarta, the center of the Indonesian government. A cultural center, dormitory for young fighters, training center and school—Marx House—was moved at the same time.[97]

The model for the Marx House, according to contemporaries, was the Sekolah Pepolit, "School of Political Officers," the school for the political commissars in the army. The course in the Pepolit school took three to five months and student-trainees graduated with the rank of lieutenant colonel. A Dutch spy at the time gained access to a notebook of one of the school's frequenters. Some lines in the document are highlighted by a Dutch official.

NEFIS doc. 3358
Excerpt from a notebook of TNI [Indonesian National Army] Lt. Col. La Mannoeki.
Lessons taken.
. . .
7. Leninism December 16, 1946
. . .
9. Leninism December 18, 1946
10. International I, II and III December 20, 1946
—*Lenin, Stalin, Alimin, Musso, Semaoen*[98]

Alimin and Semaoen were the leaders of the Communist Party in the Indies: Alimin was now back in Indonesia, Semaoen was still in Europe where he had been sent in exile by the Dutch.

This curriculum of the Marx House according to a contemporary, "almost did not differ from the one at the Pepolit school."[99] If anything, it might be more on the side of élan, as the weeks of the revolution were passing by, structures emerged, and big change was not coming—of élan and impatience.

The young people of the anti-Japanese resistance were very visible among the school, dormitory, and garrison students. The "old cracks," people of the generation of 1926, ex internees of Boven Digoel, the revenant, the three Bs people—*bui, buang, bunuh* (let us be) "imprisoned, exiled, shot"—were now teaching some of the Marx House courses, some of them maybe transcribed from *notabellen,* "emergency notes," or, perhaps, duck eggs.

Francisca Fanggidaej, the young woman who was so excited during Amir's speech at the Youth Congress in Jogjakarta in November 1945, was now one of the Marx House student-trainees. "Bapak Djaetan," she wrote in her memoirs about one of the Boven Digoel former internees, "was in fact the leader in 'Marx House,' never mind that his Indonesian was hesitant, and that often he had to help himself with breaking away into Javanese words and phrases."

One day Francisca asked Bapak Djaetan to explain to her a term often used in courses, "Sama rata sama rasa," Indonesian and Javanese for "the same level, the same sense."

She vaguely knew it signified egalitarian collectivism or democracy. She approached Bapak Djaetan, "in hope that he would explain to me a phrase that sounded so melodic." However," she writes, "I got no explanation, except that he merely said: 'It's up to you.'"[100]

Francisca was from a good family, meaning modern, Westernized, Indies, and colonial. She was well schooled, well behaved, and she was shocked by Bapak Djaetan's response. Not just by the abruptness with which Bapak Djaetan answered her, a young woman (from a good family), but by the language he used. "I was really offended. We barely knew each other, and he talked so, yes, coarsely, to nearly a stranger. And the way he said 'kamu' [Indonesian for 'thou']! Why did not he say, 'jij' [Dutch for 'you'] or 'zus' [Dutch address for 'sister' or 'younger woman']." "He came, I thought," wrote Francisca, "from Digoel and through Australia, so his Indonesian was confused. Even more," she added, "than was my Indonesian, the language of a 'black-Dutch' lady."[101]

They were all in the Marx House wearing "khaki uniforms distributed to the trainee-students and instructors alike." Only Bapak Djaetan "wore sarong." The Marx-House was like the army garrison of Leon Trotsky's liking, and not much different from the Kramat 106 student dormitory of Amir's time either, except "closer to the people." "In the Marx House," Francisca Fanggidaej wrote, "we had to sleep on the floor on a mat, but without a mosquito net. We all also had to tidy up our rooms ourselves! They said, it was a 'dormitory.'"[102]

"Everybody knew, of course, why it was called 'Marx House'" Francisca wrote. "But who had come up with the name, I did not know. And the name was always used in English, 'House,' not Indonesian 'Rumah' or Dutch 'Huis.'" "Perhaps," Francisca wondered, "because the teacher-trainers came through Australia as the Boven Digoel people, and because many of them had studied abroad."[103]

The Marx House was like a garrison, a dormitory, like the Blitar prison of the Japanese occupation, and like a modern classroom, it was all of that and thus it was new. Francisca Fanggidaej explained that "In Madiun, the activists of Pesindo and Pepolit lived together. There was a dormitory for men and another dormitory for women. . . . There also lived the comrades who already had a family. Mbakyu Soedisman [*Mbakyu*, Javanese address for 'woman'] was a 'mother of our household.' Comrade Soedisman, her husband, was the first secretary of *Pesindo*. Nobody was paid a salary. . . . We received food every day and on certain days uniforms were distributed, of the color of young coconut." "During the time between lessons and training," still Francisca, "we read poetry together."

> We played music and sang, solo and in choir. A great part of our repertoire were fighting songs, as far as we knew some. Sometimes, there was a dance performance, mostly Javanese dance. Mas Sukarno [not the president] was the chair of Pesindo and of the Pepolit section of information. He was to become my husband. He was good at dancing *bambangan Arjuna*, *gagahan Bima*, or *Gatotkaca* [Javanese dances based on the Mahabharata stories, the first two gentle and amorous, the other two martial]. . . . Bapak Soedisman would sometimes also perform a dance, and he liked to recite poetry, including some poems of his own.[104]

"Why are so often the Dutch times [of the Indies] called 'normal times?'" Francisca asked at this point in her memoirs. "As if the time of struggle for the liberation was not 'normal'?"[105]

The main enemies of every revolution, of course, are the forces of the established order. Equally strong enemies, however, are the competing forces in the revolution itself, of equal or sometimes greater intensity, élan, and purity of conviction.

Mohammad Yamin, Amir's friend at the Kramat 106 student dormitory, the Law School, the Youth Congress, and a political ally during the early times of Gerindo, moving his own way, published a pamphlet early in 1946 called *Tan Malaka: Bapak Republic Indonesia*, "Tan Malaka: Father of the Indonesian Republic."[106]

"Tan Malaka," wrote Anthony Reid, "was badly out of touch with Indonesian realities," "having lived an underground existence for twenty years, an inveterate political loner, enjoying the freedom as well as the inconvenience of the prophet."[107] A Sumatran like Amir, Tan Malaka was also one of those very few Indonesians who early in the twentieth century acquired a complete Dutch secondary education in the metropolis, a teacher's college, and indeed like Amir, in Haarlem, though a decade earlier.

He was ten years older than Amir. Like Amir he did not stay in Europe and returned to the Indies, to Medan, and worked in the Deli plantation complex as a teacher. Like Amir, he discovered politics and experienced a meteoric rise. In a matter of a few years after returning from Europe, in Java he became the chairman of the Communist Party of the Indies. He was exiled back to Europe only three years after his return to the Indies. In contrast to Musso, he disagreed with launching the rebellion in 1926, split from Communist International, had been accused of Trotskyism, and for the years that followed conspired, ran, and evaded the colonial police; became *patjar merah*, "red darling," of a series of semi-fictitious thrillers widely read in the Indies through the 1930s.

In 1942, in the chaos of the Japanese conquest of the Indies, Tan Malaka returned. Incognito, he lived in Banten, West Java, as a clerk at the local coal mines. As Soekarno and Hatta proclaimed independence, Tan Malaka appeared in Djakarta. Reportedly, Soekarno and Hatta welcomed him as a mythical figure of past battles and, according to some sources, offered him, like Amir and Sjahrir, reputed as an anti-fascist, a seat in the government. Like Sjahrir and unlike Amir, Tan Malaka rejected this offer. Instead, he began his own movement, struggle, revolution, to attain *100% Merdeka*, "100% Freedom," pure and undiluted.

During the late months of 1945 and early in 1946, Tan Malaka attracted followers, many of them young and enthusiastic, and potentially even formerly in Sjahrir's and Amir's now-emerging camp. He gathered them in a movement, without much structure and contour, expanding everywhere, the Persatoean Perdjoeangan, "Fighting Front," growing day by day.

Amir, still with Sjahrir, still channeling the revolution, might appear manipulative or even counterrevolutionary compared to Tan Malaka. Amir's saying might increasingly sound as rhetoric, however much Kierkegaard, Kant, Marx, Schepper, Jeremiah, Isaiah, and Lenin might still appear to be nodding.

Tan Malaka called on his followers to meet on March 17, 1946, in Jogjakarta for a congress under the banner of 100% Freedom. According to Soebadio, now of Sjahrir's group but still also close to Amir, "Sjahrir relayed a secret letter to Yogyakarta that the *Dwitunggal* ['two-in-one],' Soekarno and Hatta] and Amir detain the Persatoean Perdjoeangan leadership temporarily."[108] "On the charges," writes Hatta's biographer, "that inflammatory, antigovernment sentiments had been expressed at the Persatoean Perdjoeangan congress, Tan Malaka, Amin, Sukarni, Chaerul Saleh, and Abikusno Tjokroaminoto [the Persatoean Perdjoeangan leaders], were arrested."[109]

An article appeared in *Rakjat*, "The People," an Indonesian newspaper, ten days after Tan Malaka's arrest, signed 'Am,' which, as everybody seemed to know, was Adam Malik, another of Amir's followers at the time of Gerindo and another politician going the other way. Now, Malik, like Mohammad Yamin, was on Tan Malaka's side. The article pointed out that Tan Malaka had been arrested by "people who had previously accepted money and jobs from Van der Plas."[110]

Now Amir Sjarifoeddin by his former friends was exposed. And Sjahrir and him put other revolutionaries in prison! As politics was being discovered, as the machine worked, and its wheels screeched, trains in the network were coming too close together, there soon appeared other revolutionaries' blood on Amir's hands! This was the so-called Widarta Affair.

According to convoluted and foggy history, Musso, when he sneaked out of Java in 1936, left behind a small clandestine organization led by Pamoedji. Among its members were Wikana from Gerindo and Siauw Giok Tjhan from the Indonesian Chinese Party (Partai Tionghoa Indonesia). According to oral tradition, Amir joined what a source describes as the "illegal PKI [Partai Komunis Indonesia, "Indonesian Communist Party"]." Next to Pamoedji, the leader of the group was Widarta, Pamoedji's protégé since the second Gerindo Palembang Congress in July 1939.[111]

During the Japanese occupation, Widarta became a mythical figure of the order of Musso or Tan Malaka. In evading the *kenpeitai*, for instance, wrote Soemarsono in a personal recollection,

> Widarta sent a message that he would get a weapon to me through a go-between. I was scared, how he will make it. Then he let me know it was done and where in my house I will find it. Under the table under the large table cloth, you know. The risk was great.
>
> Widarta's influence was everywhere. He had the people of his even among the Japanese and he was even in touch with the Japanese underground. Wow! There existed Japanese communists who stood up against their own government. There was even a company commander [in East Java] who was a communist.[112]

Pamoedji was arrested by the Japanese in late 1942, a few weeks before Amir, and in early 1943, wrote a participant in the movement who became its historian, "the secretariat moved to Widarta."[113]

There is a photo of Widarta in Anton Lucas's book. A young Javanese leaning relaxed against a waist-high wall, at a garden perhaps. He looks straight into the camera and has a very sympathetic face. To Sintha Melati, a young woman in the East Java underground during the occupation, Widarta was "stern, relentless, always serious-minded." Others said that he was "a man of integrity, quiet, fair, hospitable, thrifty with Party funds, giving accurate, precise instructions."[114] He was known to gather around himself people of his kind: "'Bung Kecil' ['The Little One'] liked to regard himself as Widarta's closest companion, . . . a daring character, riding a bicycle all over East Java to deliver underground party messages under the nose of the Japanese . . . himself quasi-mythological."[115]

Widarta was sometimes called *patjar merah*, "red darling," a sobriquet under which Tan Malaka became best known in popular thrillers, a man never caught. Of Bung Kecil, Widarta's associate, "the police thought he must possess a white eel amulet which enabled him to vanish, because although his place was raided seven times, he always managed to escape."[116]

Widarta's life, and Amir's, both possible heroes, was the story of Augé's trains coming closer together, and eventually crashing. Or, of the wonderful apparatus working. "Enter the Party," wrote Soemarsono, an ally of both for some time, at the moment of the proclamation of independence. "[T]here was a central committee, provincial committees, and section committees, but about how it was organized we knew only a little. There were connections and ways how one was to identify oneself when representing the party? He carried a mandate, right? This mandate was a piece of paper, like the paper one uses to roll a cigarette. When it was put above a cup with steaming water, the words appeared. The central committee mandate. Terrific, *wow*! Not just anyone could have got hold of it."[117] Whichever leader might be arrested, Soemarsono recalled, the party was still there. "Tidak kosong," "not empty." "There had always been somebody whom one could contact. We existed as the party. . . . . I was a member of the party led by Widarta."[118]

As the Japanese capitulated, the republic was proclaimed, and the revolution broke out, Widarta emerged as a leader in the Peristiwa Tiga Daerah, "Three-Region Affair," a permanent revolution, kind of, a continuity, in the three districts on the north coast of Central Java, a largely spontaneous uprising as much against the invading Allies as against the local elites and forces of status quo. Anton Lucas, who studied it most closely, too, calls it a "revolution inside revolution."[119]

Sjahrir was still not in the government, but Amir seemed to be involved. It was him, it is almost certain, who, still as the minister of information in the *Buchō* cabinet, sent Widarta to the area as the government representative. It is impossible to measure whether it was Sjahrir's cabinet coming to power in mid-November 1945, and his becoming a minister in it, that changed the situation. The upheaval in the three districts and Widarta's doing was suddenly described by the government as "an affair," "a moment of fury," an "excess," an act of discipline lost.[120] Anthony Reid writes that "The determination to avoid bloodshed and anarchy threw its weight against the social revolution. Sjahrir and Amir had insufficient trusted cadres of their own to restructure the government, they distrusted the process engaged in pulling down the old order. . . . [It was] the government's dilemma . . . bringing the leading social revolutionaries in the region to trial and making the hairline distinction between righteous revolutionaries and criminality."[121]

The republican army, now Amir's army, sort of, he was the minister of defense, intervened and the leaders of "the affair," including Widarta were arrested. In the mean logic of the moment, if there is such a thing, or as the apparatus wanted it, Widarta and his associates had been put in the same prison in Jogjakarta where Tan Malaka's people were locked up. A revolutionary space inside another revolutionary space? Widarta's people and Widarta himself, and Tan Malaka's people, whatever their differences—and there were differences, bitter ones—are remembered as organizing for their coprisoners a "political course on Marxism."[122]

Amir, the minister of defense and the second man in the government, urged that Widarta be dealt with "legally rather than extra-parliamentary." But here was an apparatus working. The Communist Party, now emerging as one of many in the multiparty system, took over the Widarta case. He was released from prison where he was put by the military, but captured again. Before an Emergency Central Committee of the Communist party, Widarta still tried to argue that he was the one holding the mandate as it was passed from Musso. He was put on a party trial, was convicted, and taken first, of all places, to the Pesindo headquarters in Madiun, perhaps even to the Marx House, And then, sometime in 1947, to Parangtritis, a village on the southern coast of Java, and there, on the beach, shot.[123]

"Amir didn't help Widarta when Widarta was jailed," wrote Jacques Leclerc expressing a general mood among Widarta's supporters when Leclerc spoke to them years later. "[H]e didn't help him when he was brought to court, not when the Communist Party took over the case; he may even have given the green light to his execution."[124]

I do not know whether Widarta, a *patjar merah*, was on Amir's conscience. But certainly, increasingly he appeared to speak "to convince impatient revolutionaries." For example in a speech from April 4, 1946: "as a Marxist . . . I want an egalitarian society with fair distribution. . . . But every theoretician of revolution must accept that that aspiration must be attained in stages. . . . Mao Tse-Tung once said, 'Our struggle now must be directed to the first phase, with the second phase delayed for the time being.'"[125] Increasingly, to use Victor Hugo's image from the French Revolution, between two kinds of barricades, Amir appeared to stand and try to fight on the geometer's side. "The barricade Saint Antoine was monstrous. . . . Ruin. You might say who built that? You may also say, who destroyed that? . . . A mile from there, at the corner of the Rue du Temple—rose this obstruction, which made of the street a cul-de-sac; an immense and quiet wall; nobody could be seen, nothing could be heard; not a cry, not a sound, not a breath . . . the chief of that barricade was a geometer."[126]

When the composition of the first Sjahrir–Amir cabinet was announced, in November 1945, Van der Plas, back on Java and writing memoranda again, sent a secret report to Van Mook. It expressed a measured satisfaction and clearly a hope:

> To: His Excellency Lt.-Governor General
> From: van der Plas
> In composing his cabinet . . . Sjahrir kept to principles he expressed in his "Our Struggle." The list of the cabinet members does not include a single collaborator with the Japanese.

(Which was a hyperbolic statement to say in the least.)

> Many [sic] of the ministers had been during the Japanese occupation active in the underground. . . . Sjarifoeddin, Moelia, Putuhena and Abdul Karim are Christians; Moelia, moreover, is well known among the missionaries. . . . Clearly, the cabinet is soundly democratic-socialist. . . . It consists of . . . intellectuals, state administrators, and a number of students

"Students" in the Van der Plas report is a slip Freud would love. While writing the secret report, Van der Plas might still be thinking as if the Indies were still there and as if the figures in the new cabinet he knew from before the war, like Amir, were still in school. It was the carousel, he was riding. "The new cabinet," Van der Plas concluded his report in a more factual way, "paradoxically perhaps, needs support of the Allies to function and to survive."[127]

If the world, during these first months, saw any difference between Sjahrir and Amir, it was a difference in temperament and style. In a reportage from the early time of the Sjahrir–Amir cabinet, a British journalist John Thompson, wrote: "Minister of Information . . . Dr. Sjarifoeddin, who was also [like Sjahrir] born in Sumatra, is more impulsive and less given to yearning. He is a man who personally follows things through and see[s] that they are done. . . . Sjarifoeddin is two years older than Sjahrir. Short, lively, he uses yellow-rimmed glasses, caries a briefcase, and often wears a light coat over his white shirt. . . . He is a family man and a Christian, plays the violin—Handel and Beethoven [sic]—and reads for preference philosophical and political works."[128] John Thompson saw Amir as of apparatus; Sjahrir was "subtle": "Sjahrir's mind is wide and subtle, Sjarifoeddin seems an honest fellow. There is burning devotion in the neat young men who publish newspapers or sit around in the government offices, but where is the firm guidance, where are the commanding personalities to pull things together and prevent them from falling apart? Sjahrir smokes cigarettes, but otherwise his hands invariably seem to be empty. Sjarifoeddin is quietly busy, but the rest of the cabinet are neither heard nor seen. Hatta had gone away, to get married, carrying Sukarno with him."[129]

Thompson tells a story how, with a group of foreign journalists, he was taken on a tour to Malang, where there was a Japanese internment camp located near the city, with Dutch internees still inside and still waiting to be released. There had been rumors of atrocities happening in the camp. "Then there was obstruction. 'Very sorry [they were told,] but the TKR [the Indonesian army] will not permit foreign correspondents to visit the Dutch internees. . . . The TKR fears that such a visit might have an unsettling effect on the local population.'" Thompson says, the journalists persisted.

> Eventually two of us got into a car and went to find Sjarifoeddin [who happened to be in Malang, too, at a conference]. . . . Sjarifoeddin showed annoyance when we told him what was wrong. He immediately accosted a tall, handsome leader of the TKR, but this officer shook his head and continued to shake his head and would not relent. The Minister of Information [Amir] buttoned another officer. . . . [Then] Sjarifoeddin said that he would accompany us to the camp himself, but he added gruffly: "You'll have to look in at the gate; they won't let you go inside." We replied that apparently the TKR had no faith in the common sense of the Indonesian people, and Sjarifoeddin nodded in an impatient manner but said no more.
>
> Sjarifoeddin rode in the leading car with the TKR officer, and he must have gotten his own way, for he greeted us at the camp gate with a broad smile. "It's all right," he said. "You can go in the camp and go wherever you like. Talk to anybody, take pictures, ask any questions you want to."
>
> It took a little time for the gate to be opened, and a crowd of Indonesians began forming behind us, while within the gates a multitude of white people, men, women, and children quickly assembled. When we walked into their midst, they thought we were to liberate them, and we were surrounded by rejoicing.

A Dutch woman gave Thompson a letter for her husband who hopefully had got out of the camp already. "I ask Sjarifoeddin if he would like the letter to be passed over for censorship, but he rejected the suggestion almost brusquely, saying, 'Certainly not! I censor nothing.'"[130]

On the very first day their cabinet took office, Sjahrir opened negotiations with the Allies and the Dutch.[131] Like how the composition of the Sjahrir–Amir cabinet gave rise to some hope in Van der Plas, the composition of the Dutch delegation sent to the negotiations certainly raised hope in Sjahrir, and especially Amir.

Hubertus van Mook, now the lieutenant-governor general of the Indies/Indonesia with the governor general still absent, became the dominant figure in the negotiations—a former neo-ethical Stuw member, a man some wished to become a professor at the prewar Law School, a man reportedly instrumental in giving Amir the money for the anti-Japanese underground. Possibly next in importance in the Dutch delegation was Dr. Johann-Heinrich Adolf Logemann, in the old times professor at the Law School and one of the faculty who in 1931 tried, in vain, to defend Amir and Yamin against the government's allegations, the newly retired Dutch postwar government's minister of overseas territories.

Willem Schermerhorn, another man on the delegation, used to be a professor of land surveying and geodesy at the Delft University of Technology, a school to train experts and administrators before the war for the Indies. Schermerhorn, a free-thinking democrat in his early years, turned to socialism and became a founder of the Dutch Labor Party, PvdA, Partij van de Arbeid. During the Nazi occupation of the Netherlands, Schermerhorn organized a resistance movement. In June 1945, as the leader of the Labor Party, and on his wartime record, he became the Dutch prime minister, witness to the Netherlands' postwar move to the left. "It should not be forgotten," Anderson wrote about the postwar years, "that at this period the prestige and power of the Dutch left was at its height."[132]

Schermerhorn held office until early July 1946. Then, as the ex-prime minister he was sent to Batavia/Djakarta as a the chair of the delegation.

There was still more to the history of Schermerhorn that made him interesting to Indonesians. After the Netherlands was occupied in 1940, and after Hitler attacked the Soviet Union in 1941, Communist-leaning members of the Perhimpoenan Indonesia, "Indonesian Association," Indonesian students stuck in the occupied Netherlands, joined the Dutch resistance. Several wound up in German concentration camps and some paid for their actions with their lives.[133] Amir had to know this. An Indische Commissie, "Indies Commission," had been organized in the occupied Netherlands, with Perhimpoenan Indonesia as its members and Willem Schermerhorn as the commission chairman.[134] The Indies Commission held secret meetings where debates were held over reforms of the Dutch colonial policy for the hopefully newly democratic postwar era.[135]

The members of the Dutch delegation, and Schermerhorn in particular, were getting ready for a historical encounter. Clearly with encouragement and perhaps some help from Schermerhorn and his party, several Indonesians, members of the Perhimpoenan Indonesia, and its more radical members among them, set out, after years in the Netherlands, to travel home. They became the group from Holland.

Abdoelmadjid, Moelwalladi, and Tamzil appeared to be the first. They left the Netherlands in September 1945 and probably arrived in the first week of October.[136] They were soon joined by others.

Drs. Maroeto Daroesman (*drs.* is a Dutch academic title, Hatta held one, too; it meant that one finished everything required by doctoral study except defending the dissertation) was described as a "cultural centrist" and "a devotee of Javanese culture." *Ir.* Soeripno (*ir.* means a college trained civil engineer, Soekarno held the same title from Bandoeng) was "brilliant, dashing, well-mannered and compassionate . . . socialist coming from an aristocratic family. In Holland he was influenced by Setiadjit."[137] Soeripno was an accomplished dancer too. He arrived in Indonesia through London where, between Javanese dance performances, he worked on the first translation of Sjahrir's "Our Struggle" into English.[138] According to some, in the later 1930s Soeripno studied for some time in Moscow.[139] Mr. Abdoelmadjid Djajadiningrat was "of the highest Javanese aristocracy, a lawyer educated in the Netherlands." Abdoelmadjid was a member of the executive of the Dutch Communist Party in the Netherlands before the war.[140]

Drs. Setiadjit was the oldest of the group and probably the most respected. He was also close to people close to Amir since the second half of the 1930s. He published regularly in Sanoesi Pane's and Amir's daily *Kebangoenan*, from the Netherlands, on the European policy and especially growth of fascism.[141] On October 18, 1946, Schermerhorn, already in the Indies/Indonesia, like Setiadjit, wrote in his diary: "on Wednesday had a further and superb talk with Setiadjit. I have no regret that we have sent this man and some others in April to the republic."[142] "It was natural," wrote Anderson, that these people now, after 1945, "should generally urge a cooperative line in dealing with the Dutch." And as for the Dutch–Indonesian negotiations, "for the Indonesians who had fought underground against the Nazis, there had been a real sense of camaraderie with the Dutch at the conference."[143]

It took some remembering in the time of élan, chaos, and euphoria at the end of 1945 and early in 1946, and in the ebbing of wartime fervor, the time of commonsensical anti-fascism and of a new world coming, to recall that the most influential among the group from Holland were the same people who back in 1931 were behind turning the Perhimpoenan Indonesia in the Netherlands toward not merely the world socialist but communist movement and who, consequently, were behind Hatta's and also Sjahrir's expulsion from the organization.

Early 1946 was still the time of a united front against fascism, however the fervor was beginning to pass. Amir's activity in the anti-Japanese underground and his suffering in prison was still a memory alive among both the Dutch and the Indonesian delegations. On February 22, 1946, the chief liaison officer to the commandant of the Dutch military forces in the Indies wrote to Schermerhorn about his own years of surviving in Djakarta during the Japanese occupation, under the fear of an internment: "I had many contacts with Amir Sjarifoeddin in that time. . . . After the war I talked to him again. . . . When I asked him how he felt about the Dutch rule [as compared to the Japanese occupation], he answered, 'it is like this: when you have to be bitten by a dog you better choose the small against the big one.' His hate against the Japanese is terrifying." When Amir was arrested by the Japanese, the officer wrote to Schermerhorn, "he did not forget to send me a warning not to come to his neighborhood, to his house or office, as the *kenpeitai* was busily searching for eventual European accomplices."[144]

The united front against fascism, however, was fading. Fascism was believed to be defeated and now new, or old-new, specters began to lurk. Some in the Indies/Indonesia were more sensitive to the specters than others, while still others were in a state of high alert. This is a report which originated already at the end of 1945 in the office of Van der Plas:

Soerabaja AMACAB 112
October 9, 1945

Moeso [the Dutch used the colonial spelling of the name] was seen in Soerabaja last week

Baars is said to have died on the way to Java and Sneevliet is reported to be on his way. Insiders try not to build myths around this intelligence and to keep cool minds.[145]

Musso, in fact, was still far away, in Moscow probably. Adolf Baars, a Jewish-Dutch Communist who had helped to build the socialist and communist movement in the Indies in the late 1910s and early 1920s, was dead. He died in Auschwitz in 1944. Henk Sneevliet, a Dutch Communist turned Trotskyist, had left the Indies also long before the war, and he also died, in a Nazi concentration camp, in Amersfoort, the Netherlands, in 1942. The real ghosts.

With the specters around, Indonesian socialists and democrats, reasonable people hopefully, became precious. To the Dutch socialists, democrats, and reasonable people especially. Willem Wertheim, formerly of the Law School and now of the Red Cross in Batavia/Djakarta, wrote on October 10, 1945 to his brother in the Netherlands: "Soetan Sjahrir, and Amir Sjarifoeddin are to the core pure and competent figures."[146] "Amir Sjarifoeddin used to be a very appreciated official at the Department of the Office of Commerce," wrote a deputy chief of the Dutch information service on September 16, 1945, as if he were writing Amir's recommendation for another civil service job.[147] On November 18, 1945, in a note to the higher places, Van der Plas himself wrote: "Soekarno gave up his dictatorial powers under pressure by the 'Working Committee' led by these two [Sjahrir and Amir]. The 'Working Committee' will function as a proto parliament." And Van der Plas went on to note that "Sjahrir and Sjarifoeddin are both convinced socialists."[148]

Sjahrir had to be aware of the rumors about Amir and Musso in 1935 and 1936, and he had to see that many of Amir's followers, both in resistance and in postproclamation politics—Soemarsono, Soedisman, or Widarta, before he was shot—were at least said to be either very close to, or completely of, the Communist ideology and Communist idea of action. Sjahrir probably watched rather than inspired Amir's policies, especially as the minister of defense, which were increasingly compared with those of Bolshevik Russia.

But Sjahrir also could see how Amir, despite the Communist shimmering of the air around him, remained an ally, and was especially useful in the negotiations with the Allies and the Dutch. "The most astute man of the [Indonesian] delegation is Sjarifoeddin," wrote Willem Schermerhorn in his diary on November 8, 1946.[149] "Sjarifoeddin," he wrote five days later, as a case in point of Amir's importance, "at one moment sat himself between Soekarno and Hatta and pointed to them in Malay, what is today called Indonesian, which points were still open."[150]

Dr. P. J. A. Idenburg, who, according to his own account was also involved in Amir's being chosen as a grantee of Van der Plas money in 1942, was now a high official in the Dutch administration in the Indies/Indonesia, and a close associate of Schermerhorn at the Dutch–Indonesian negotiations. Early in 1946, Idenburg visited Jogjakarta and sent a secret memorandum to Batavia/Djakarta describing his impressions: "I had a talk with mr. Sjarifoeddin . . . a most pleasant character [*een zeer aangenaam karakter*]. . . . Mr. Sjarifoeddin is an old acquaintance of mine, and I consider him a competent and thoroughly honest man. Next to Dr. Hatta he is perhaps the most competent figure in the republic."[151]

Such pronouncements could not be a secret to Amir, and he might have thought (with one of those slightly sarcastic grins of his) that the sweetness was just another way for the Dutch to sneak back into the lost Indies. But he might also think that there was a possibility of the world opening, the trust in the modern and the democratic spreading after fascism had been defeated, the world coming to itself in a way he hoped in and wrote about since the time of the Haarlem Gymnasium *Mirabele Lectu*.

In the spring of 1946, Baron van Asbeck, long retired from the Batavia Law School, arrived back in the Indies. There were even rumors that he might become the new governor general. On May 12, 1946, from Batavia/Djakarta, he sent a letter to his wife in Leiden; later, he placed the letter among his papers in the National Archives in the Hague, in the same folder with the documents about the Law School professors, in 1931, trying to save Amir and Yamin from criminal prosecution. In the letter, Van Asbeck wrote,

> This morning to Verkuyl, to the reformed church where he preached about the second coming of Christ. . . . The church was packed . . . all doors were open, chairs were on the sidewalk. After this, to the hotel Der Nederlanden on the Rijswijk near the [governor general] Palace. Marie Cohen [a friend of Van Asbecks from prewar times] lies there sick. They did not operate on her gallstones but perhaps they would be able to fly her to Holland. There is something timeless in the bond you keep with the people whom you had come across in that past. She had in her eyes the same gentle but otherworldly look which I had earlier seen in Schepper's, and, through the last week, in the eyes of those who came out from the camps—kind of a detachment from all earthly possessions, giving up or escaping the submersion of oneself in the world.[152]

Julius Schepper was in Batavia/Djakarta, too, and Van Asbeck visited him as well. When the Japanese invaded in 1942, Schepper did not escape and possibly did not want to. With other Europeans caught in the war, he was put in a camp. Schepper's nephew later wrote to Professor van den End, what Schepper had told him after the war. "The 'Great' camp in Tjimahi [West Java, west of Bandoeng] had been set up in a former KNIL-garrison and held 10,000 civilian internees. . . . Schepper was sent there after being first held in Soekamiskin prison in Bandoeng and then in the Struiswijk prison in Batavia."[153] The same prisons, again, where Amir had been held in 1934 and 1935, and where Schepper used to visit him, "with the Bible."

When Schepper was moved from the prisons to the camp, Schepper's nephew wrote to Van den End, "uncle held readings for small groups of internees . . . and they would also hold church services regularly": "Uncle also told me that he was being helped by his former student Amir Sjarifoeddin. I do not know in what form, but I think money and clothes, when Schepper was in the Soekamiskin prison." Schepper's library, according to Van den End, remained in his house where the debating circle used to meet. After the war, the source says, a large part of it was moved to the old Batavia Law School library, now Faculty of Law of the University of Indonesia.[154]

Sjahrir conducted the Indonesian negotiations with the Allies and the Dutch in Batavia/Djakarta. Amir came from Jogjakarta when needed, when a serious problem arose.

Blood trickled and was running in places where the Allied military forces and the armed Indonesians came close to each other, and fighting became the expression of the élan, chaos, and euphoria. Negotiations, little changes, incremental, step by step, increasingly, among the youth especially, became identified with "a pessimistic view of the world balance of power and of the strength of Indonesia's revolutionary forces."[155] In the view of the fighting Indonesians, increasingly, negotiations became a hindrance to the revolution.

There was growing impatience with the step-by-step movement on the Allied and especially on the Dutch side, as well. The Dutch officials and those in the Dutch delegation still believing in a future based on ethics, trust, and on Indonesians coming to meet them halfway, were losing ground. Van Mook, Idenburg, Logemann, Schermerhorn, or Van der Plas were increasingly often seen by the others as radicals in their willingness to negotiate in good faith.

The people leading the negotiations, delegations on both sides, resembled dancers on a tightrope—a loose rope, to push the metaphor further. "Last evening," Schermerhorn wrote in his diary on October 22, 1946, "a member of the Dutch delegation was approached by two people from the other side, Soebandrio and Tamzil." They came, Schermerhorn was told, "in the highest state of emotion" to protest news that appeared in the *Nieuwsgier*, the Dutch paper in Batavia/Djakarta, that the official language of the conference was Dutch. "Why these donkeys are leaking what is true," Schermerhorn wrote in despair.[156]

After months of negotiations and fighting, as a compromise and in small steps, on November 15, 1946, in Linggadjati, a hill resort near Tjirebon, east of Batavia/Djakarta, a preliminary agreement between the Dutch and Indonesians was signed. The Linggadjati Agreement acknowledged the existence of the republic, but only de facto and only on Java, Sumatra, and Madura, not on the eastern islands, the huge remainder of the archipelago of the former Indies.

It was a channeling, or rather damming, of the revolution and Amir, the able orator, a man close to the people, close to the élan, euphoria, and chaos, and the minister of defense moreover, rather than anybody else in the government, rather than Soekarno or Hatta, and rather than Sjahrir, was to explain the compromise to the people.

The text of one of Amir's speeches explaining the Linggadjati Agreement to the people can be found in the archives. It seemed to be taken down by a Dutch agent in the old Dutch Indies style of police reporting on a public meeting of the Indonesian movement. Amir talked in Indonesian, of course, and the speech was translated into Dutch in the report for the higher-ups, with the agent's occasional comments added to explain some of Amir's expressions.

The public meeting took place in Taman Merdeka, "Freedom Garden," in the town of Pematang Siantar, in North Sumatra, south of Medan, on December 6, 1946, three weeks after the Linggadjati Agreement was signed. There were a few thousand people present. Amir was the main speaker and after the speech he answered questions. The meeting lasted till the early morning of the next day.

Among the phrases Amir used in the speech and which the Dutch agent thought needed to be explained was "aksi-aksi." It is literally the plural of "action," but the Dutch agent, probably an Indigenous, knew better. He translated the phrase into Dutch as *comedie*, "comedy." Amir spoke about *aksi-aksi* of "our delegation at the negotiations" in Linggadjati, and, once again, later in the speech, about the *aksi-aksi* in the spring 1945, when Dutch and Allied representatives talked about the Indonesian future at the inaugural conference of the United Nations in San Francisco. "Our present struggle," Amir said, according to the Dutch agent, "is to be performed a *comedie*, whose production [*regie*] had been prepared in San Francisco and whose stage and all its theater props were then moved to Batavia."[157]

This is the *aksi-aksi* they want, Amir said, but ours is to be the real "action." Whatever "script had been written for us in San Francisco, we have to stand on our own."

> It is we who understand the necessity of revolution. It is we who make ourselves the masters of this country, we are the organs of power, the infrastructure, the arms warehouses. We are a new state without asking anybody. [*Applause*]

"Brothers!" (Amir is here noted to interrupt the applause angrily), "it is easy for you to clap your hands, but do you have any idea of the difficulties your government has to face?" "When we first arrived to the talks," said Amir,

> they led us to our seats and said. "Take a seat, leaders of the Indonesian movement." They did not call us "Ministers," they did not call us "President." This changed. History has moved on. Now, some even call us "Excellencies." But still they are telling us, "Look! We have our script, our own *comedie* to play."

Here, Amir switched to English.

> "*What should we tell our people?*" they say. We answered: "We do not care about your people. We care only about the sovereignty of our state and about our people." [*Applause*]

At this place in the transcript, the agent who made the report, wrote on the margin, "the speaker used coarse personal pronouns for 'you': 'loe' and 'goea'" ("penis" for the masculine, "womb" for feminine).

"Never in this world," Amir continued, "have two states been able to come to an agreement without mediation by a third power. In this present disagreement between Indonesia and the Netherlands, it is important to involve a third party," and Amir listed, "the English, the Soviets, and the Americans." The sequence, "Soviets" in second place, was significant and the audience, like the Dutch agent, as it appears from his transcript, understood it well.

Progress had been made, Amir said, thanks to the fighting. "Read article 15 of the Linggadjati Agreement," he quoted: "After January 1, 1949, the republic will be recognized."

> As soon as this agreement is ratified, our ships will sail under our flag, our diplomatic representatives will be sent abroad, our planes will fly. There are some who laugh at this agreement, and there are some who cry. Indeed, there is a good reason to cry when one looks at the agreement as the whole result of our fighting. But let's take it as a project, as a plan, for more fighting, fighting until our aims are reached.

Amir speech ended on the Old Testament—or Koran—prophecy (as far as his own life was concerned, to be fulfilled):

> Together, we will enter the paradise and together we will pass through the desert unscathed. . . .
> Before I left for here, I was with our President observing the *10 Moeharram, Asjoerah*. . . . On that day . . . the prophet Moses led the Israelites out of Egypt, across the sea. . . . We too journey to another land. Forty years the Israelites struggled through the desert to the promised land. . . . There were among them many who were so permeated with the colonial spirit that they wished the journey to stop and them to turn back to Egypt. . . . In dread, the Israelites journeyed, forty years in the desert, but they reached the Land of Canaan—

here, Amir paused:

> —albeit without their leaders.
> We will be healed, cleansed of the plague, the capitalist and imperialist bacteria. . . . Think of it! The people of Israel reached the Land of Canaan, but Moses did not.
> So it is, and good night.[158]

At the ceremonial signing of the Linggadjati Agreement, on November 15, 1946, in Batavia/Djakarta, Amir was not present. According to Simatoepang, now a colonel in the Indonesian army, Amir traveled to Modjokerto, a provincial town in East Java, to protest, Simatoepang wrote, against a recent assault by the Dutch military against the Indonesian positions in the area.[159] Dutch intelligence recorded Amir's words as he arrived at Modjokerto: "The basis of the agreement must be considered a temporary and transitional compromise signed in efforts to drive imperialism and capitalism out of Indonesia.'"[160]

Amir was still generally seen as part of "Sjahrir–Amir," one force and one mind in the government, apparatus and efforts to channel and rank the revolution.

Toward the end of November 1945, soon after the Soekarno and Hatta proclamation, Soedjatmoko, a former follower of Amir, and presently one of Sjahrir, recalled,

> an American war correspondent from *Newsweek*, Harold Isaacs, arrived in Jakarta from Indochina, bringing with him a letter from Ho Chi Minh to Vice-President Hatta, whom the Vietnamese leader had met in Europe many years earlier at a meeting of the Anti-Imperialist League. In his letter Ho suggested that the two revolutions be coordinated. Hatta transmitted the letter to Sjahrir. When I subsequently asked Sjahrir how he would respond, he said—to my immense surprise and disappointment—that he was not going to respond to the letter. He intended to simply ignore it. I asked him, "Why? Wasn't it a betrayal of the Asian revolution?" Sjahrir then said the following: *"Our national movement is led by nationalists—theirs by communists.* They are bound, therefore, to have more enemies than we do. This means that we will gain our independence more quickly than the Vietnamese. And once we are an independent nation, we could help them more effectively than anything we could do now."

"I remember," wrote Soedjatmoko, and it was many years later, "how disappointed I was. I felt a deep sense of betrayal. But, of course, Sjahrir proved to be right in the end."[161]

Alain Badiou formulated the Communist truth: "Communism is not consistent with 'democracy,' equality is not consistent with 'freedom,' any positive use of identity terms such as 'national' or 'international community' or 'Islamist' or 'Europe' should be banned, as should psychological terms such as 'desire,' 'life,' 'passion,' as well as any term related to established state constructions such as 'citizen,' 'voter,' and so on."[162] Soedjatmoko wrote about Sjahrir, his "mentor number .3": "He taught me that there need not be a contradition between a totally committed revolutionary and democrat as well as a socialist and humanist."¹⁶³

With the arrival of the group from Holland, memories of the Indonesian ex-students in the Netherlands—Setiadjit, Abdoelmadjid, Maroeto Daroesman, Soeripno, and others—were coming back, a *revenant* and haunting, a specter; the memory of Hatta and Sjahrir being expelled from Perhimpoenan Indonesia in 1931, as it was turning to Communist International. There "always remained," wrote Anthony Reid, "some muted suspicion between Sjahrir and the communists who returned from Holland in 1946, which became more obvious as the 'anti-fascist' cause failed."¹⁶⁴

When Sjahrir spoke in 1946 and in 1947, he sounded increasingly subtle, didactic, priestly, as if absorbed in the world of ideas. In his radio speech on the first anniversary of the Soekarno and Hatta proclamation, on August 17, 1946, for instance, Sjahrir asked the listeners to: "aspire to perfect humanity. . . . Let us liberate our souls through liberating our nation. . . . Become MATURE HUMAN BEINGS . . . Of humanity of the future . . . Not of national egoism. . . . Let us be honest in our hearts, and we will succeed. Let us be honest in our hearts and minds . . . Not believe in cunning. . . . Let us believe as a nation in more perfect human relations. . . . There let our spirit go to find it shelter."¹⁶⁵ In the conclusion of another radio speech in the same month Sjahrir said: "Like the *satria* [noble knights of the wayang epics] . . . we will fight the narrow nationalism, egoism and *nafsoe* [low passion]. . . . OUR NATIONHOOD MUST BE A BRIDGE TO PERFECT HUMANITY. . . . FREEDOM!!!"¹⁶⁶

Trotsky might say about Sjahrir now what he said about US socialist Morris Hillquit, as brutally as that, that he was an "ideal socialist spokesman for successful dentist."¹⁶⁷ Even as these were merely words, Sjahrir, in the midst of revolution, sounded tired and retreating. Or, perhaps, taking another path.

Amir had to be tired. But when he spoke, at the same time and on the same government radio station, compared to Sjahrir, he sounded muscular, his saying was of the Old rather than the New Testament, or like that of Trotsky, or Lenin, at the height of the revolution, long before its failure:

> For us, 1945 was the year of revolution. 1946 must be the year when the revolution is consummated. . . .
>
> Through our strength we dig trenches on the outside and buttress our ranks on the inside. We are under attack. Under attack, every day. . . .
>
> Our Constitution demands that each citizen be made free, free from hunger, from poverty, and from ignominy [*kehinaan*]. . . .

> To gain the freedom, freedom from hunger, poverty, and ignominy, we will fight with all the passion [*tjita-tjita*] that is given to us. . . . FREEDOM![168]

In October 1946, a coalition of the Indonesian Left, Sjahrir's and Amir's party, militias, with Pesindo as its most important collective member, and left-wing trade unions, came together in the Sajap Kiri, "Left Wing," still in support of the Sjahrir–Amir government, but reflecting a rapidly growing restlessness in its ranks as well as among its leaders—a body driven now as much by revolution as by politics and manipulation.[169]

The Linggadjati Agreement was to be ratified by the Indonesian government; only some details were still to be worked out. A few new minor concessions had been agreed to by Sjahrir. On June 21, 1947, Amir arrived in Batavia/Djakarta and, as the coleader of the Sjahrir–Amir cabinet, expressed his support for the concessions. As he returned to Jogjakarta, however, the republic capital, he found out that the top leaders of the Sajap Kiri condemned Sjahrir's last, and now also his, concessions.[170]

On June 26, Sjahrir, too, arrived at Jogjakarta. It had not been known at the time, but he had already quietly submitted his resignation to the president.[171] The next day, June 27, Sjahrir resigned formally as prime minister and Soekarno accepted the resignation. "Indeed," John Legge wrote, "it has been suggested that Sjahrir welcomed his departure from government—if had not actually helped to bring it about."[172]

CHAPTER 12

Musso

It was the highest point. And it was the lowest point. On June 27, 1947, the Sjahrir–Amir cabinet resigned. On June 30, Soekarno designated four formateurs of a new cabinet: Amir Sjarifoeddin; A. K. Gani, Amir's former colleague in Gerindo, now of the nationalist Partai Nasional Indonesia (PNI), "Indonesian National Party," and close to Soekarno; Setiadjit the oldest and most respected of the group from Holland; and Soekiman Wirjosandjojo of the Islamic Masjumi. On July 3, the new cabinet was announced. Amir Sjarifoeddin became the prime minister and kept his post of the minister of defense. Gani and Setiadjit became the vice-premiers.[1]

Amir's new government inspired a name for itself, the "Ali-Baba cabinet" "because of so many of its ministers, forty [indeed] including the holders of lower cabinet seats."[2] In April 1947 Amir declared a ten-year plan of economic recovery and development and a three year "more urgent" plan. The government declared as its aims: 1. industrialization; 2. transmigration; 3 cooperation. Nationalization, however, of either indigenous or foreign properties, was not mentioned.[3]

After a few months, Dutch Minister van Boetzelaar wrote in a memorandum composed at the Netherlands Ministry of Foreign Affairs in The Hague and sent to the Dutch representatives in Batavia/Djakarta: "Sjarifoeddin is an enigmatic figure. Without doubt, he is one of the most capable Indonesians, but, so it appears, blind ambitions make him unappealing to our eyes as well as to the eyes of those among his compatriots who have, so to say, eyes to see. He will always follow his impulses, put himself first and has few scruples in the choice of his means and allies."[4]

Arnold Brackman wrote later what Sjahrir might have told him at the time, namely, why he did not enter Amir's cabinet. "Sjahrir realized," Brackman wrote, "that he [Amir] had become a pawn in the communist game and rejected their invitation." Islamic Masjumi initially did not join Amir's cabinet, either. In Brackman's words, it "had thrown its support behind Sjahrir." Sjahrir, after his resignation, was appointed a special adviser of the president, until July 22, 1947, when under a completely new situation, he departed from Indonesia for New York to advise the delegation of the republic in the United Nations, where the Indonesian question had been placed on the program.

"On paper," Arnold Brackman wrote, Amir's cabinet "was ostensibly a Sajap Kiri–PNI coalition, however—this was known only to the Communists—it was a cabinet of the PKI [Communist Party of Indonesia]. It was dominated by assorted Nenni-type fellow travelers."[5] (Pietro Nenni was an Italian Socialist Party leader cooperating with the Communist Party of Italy in the first postwar years.)

The Sajap Kiri, "Left Wing," originally a coalition supporting the Sjahrir–Amir government, through the months following Amir's becoming the prime minister, crystallized, "showed its face," as many would say, became a more unified body of Amir's own Socialist Party, the Communist Party, Labor Party, SOBSI trade-union federation [Serikat Organisasi Buruh Seluruh Indonesia, "All-Indonesian Federation of Workers' Organizations"], and Pesindo.[6] According to later recollections of Abu Hanifah, Amir's former friend, who now became an important figure in Masjumi and in the anti-Amir opposition, now "Soekarno . . . was surrounded by Communist leaders in the government. In fact, he was isolated from the other leaders of the republic. The man who was always in his whereabouts was Setiadjit. . . . If one wanted to talk to [Soekarno] one had to ask for an appointment through Setiadjit."[7]

A Soviet history of Indonesia published in 1956 saw the matters already in 1947 as baked and done: "After the fall of the Sjahrir cabinet a coalition cabinet had been formed at the head with the communist premier, a member of the political bureau of the central committee of PKI, Sjarifoeddin."[8] Anthony Reid, in a book published in 1980, was more careful, yet he appeared to agree with the general view of how things were moving: "Amir Sjarifoeddin's communist allies controlled only about ten of the thirty-four places in the cabinet and only Amir's defense ministry was a key one. Nonetheless, this cabinet marked the highest point in the movement of the revolution towards orthodox communism."[9]

It was about this time that a Soviet journalist on assignment in Indonesia wrote about being "invited by the Prime Minister Amir Sjarifoeddin to his house in Jogjakarta":

> I arrive at Amir Sjarifoeddin's house on the dot.... It appears that the security was informed about my visit. Soldiers greet me *Merdeka! Merdeka!* ... Amir Sjarifoeddin comes to the gate, he smiles.... He invites me into the house. Premier's study looks more like a student's den ... Books, books, books everywhere. I notice the works of Marx and Lenin. Amir warns me, laughingly, that he would not let me go until I tell him all about Soviet life, all! ... "Tell me what Moscow looks like. What sort of city is it?" he wants to know. I describe Moscow, the Red Square, Lenin's Mausoleum, manifestations of the people rejoicing in their freedom.

Then the talk turns to Indonesia:

> His face darkens
> —Our situation is very complicated and serious.
> —Damn, all these glib politicians![10]

On July 20, 1947, three weeks after Amir's cabinet came to power, the Dutch broke negotiations and the Dutch military forces launched an attack against the republic. The Dutch called it police action, suggesting it was an internal affair of empire: policing the unruly.

The action had been expected for a long time. But, in a significant measure, it was the Dutch authorities' reaction to what they had perceived as a sharp left turn in the republic. A possible continuation in negotiations, as some in the Dutch delegation still evidently pushed for—Schermerhorn, Logemann, even Van Mook and perhaps Van der Plas—began to be generally seen in Dutch circles as procrastination, weakness, or as treason. General S. H. Spoor, in charge of the police action, was the same soldier who as a captain authored the Dutch Military Academy textbook on strategy, which Simatoepang, Nasoetion, and the other cadets had studied in their Koninklijke Nederlandsch-Indië Leger (KNIL), "Royal Netherlands Indies Army," academy in Bandoeng in the last months of the prewar Dutch Indies.

On August 8, 1947, little more than a fortnight after the police action started, under pressure from the United Nations where Dutch policy now was found too radical, and as the Indonesians defending the republic resisted more than expected, a ceasefire was agreed upon. A United Nations Commission of Good Offices, also called the Three State Commission, arrived at Batavia/Djakarta on October 27 to mediate.

At the first meeting of Amir's cabinet after the ceasefire, Amir decided that the Indonesian representative to negotiate with Van Mook and the Dutch would be Setiadjit, the most respected of the group from Holland. Some of Amir's ministers were skeptical—why negotiate with the Dutch at all?[11] At the first meeting with the UN Commission, Amir suggested that he would prefer Singapore as a "neutral place" to hold negotiations.[12]

The suggestion was rejected. The new superpower was becoming increasingly involved. On December 8, 1947, negotiations opened between the Indonesian and Dutch delegations, with the UN Commission mediating, on board the US attack transport ship USS *Renville*, at anchor just off the Batavia/Djakarta harbor—"the harbor of Tandjong Priok is unusually busy." On January 17, after a month and a few days of negotiations, the Renville Agreement—another compromise—was signed.[13]

The signing was done under a canvas awning on the forward deck of the ship.[14] Amir sat at the table with the representatives of the Three State Commission, Richard Clarence Kirby for Australia, Paul Van Zeeland for Belgium, and Frank Graham for the United States. Ali Sastroamidjojo, who sat next to Amir as a member of the Indonesian delegation for the flamboyant Indonesian National Party, wrote in his memoirs that "as a representative of PNI, I refused to sign."[15]

The Renville negotiations in the Batavia/Djakarta harbor might have still given a glimmer of hope to Amir that Indonesia was opening to the world of the modern, of all he considered as modern, and that the world of the modern might still be opening to Indonesia. There certainly were flashbacks on the deck of the USS *Renville*. Certainly they struggled through language.

"At Renville," Ali Sastroamidjojo recalled, "English was the official language." But there were problems: Frank Graham had a "southern drawl," Judge Kirby spoke with an "Australian accent," and there was the "French-accented English of the Belgian." Ali Sastroamidjojo might add to the world of tongues coming together the Dutch-accented Indonesian of the Indonesians and the Indonesian-accented Dutch of some of the Dutch who spent their lives in the Indies. "In the end," says Ali Sastroamidjojo (with tongue in cheek?), "all ended fine, went smoothly."[16]

The main change from the Linggadjati Agreement was Indonesians agreeing to the Van Mook line of the ceasefire, a line cutting Java into three parts and leaving the republic de facto only a shrunken area of the extreme west and the middle part of the island. That was not all. "Under heavy pressure," wrote a Dutch historian, "Sjarifoeddin could not react otherwise than how Sjahrir had reacted before him. He gave up on all points, except regarding the constabulary. Yet, also here the Netherlands and the republic reached a compromise. . . . And even this caused a great anger of the armed forces commander S.H. Spoor and fleet commander A.S. Pinke. They argued that it compromised the position of the Netherlands military."[17] A Soviet reporter, perhaps the same who visited Amir in his house weeks before, was present at the signing of the agreement on the deck of the ship and he provided, again, a dramatic account. "The Dutch and other delegations signed. Then Amir Sjarifoeddin stood up. He adjusted glasses on his nose and began to speak in Indonesian. Many were taken aback. Until that moment, the working languages of the conference were only two—English and Dutch. Here was a challenge . . . 'Freedom! Freedom Forever!' he repeated several times the sacred words."[18]

Colonel Simatoepang was also present at the ceremony and later recalled his feeling: "I thought that Bung Amir had understood from the military as well as from the economic point of view, the Renville Agreement was disastrous for us. Yet he had believed that, by yielding to the pressure of the Three State Commission, in particular the urging of Dr. Graham, he could 'buy' a political guarantee, especially from the United States, against another Dutch attack. . . . Our mistake was that we had overestimated the effect of the Three State Commission. Probably Bung Amir himself had also overestimated Dr. Graham's personal statements."[19]

There was struggling through language at the USS *Renville* and perhaps pleasuring through it, too. And there were certainly flashbacks. Frank Graham, the US delegate whose personal statements Amir, in Simatoepang's view, trusted too much, came to Indonesia on a mission and struggled and pleasured not only through language. "Arriving in Batavia," Graham's biographer writes, "the committee members and staff were given comfortable rooms in the Hotel des Indes, and they set down to work. Simply learning the names of the chairmen of the delegations—Amir Sjarifoeddin for the republic, Raden Abdulkadir Widjojoatmodjo for the Netherlands—was a major task for the committee members."[20]

There might have been some possibility, against the odds, that both Amir and Graham felt that they could build something together. There is a story; Dr. Graham fell sick and stayed for a few days off the negotiations, in the hotel: "Weakened by a tropical stomach disorder, he was under the care of a physician. During a previous sick spell of Graham, a conservative member of the American consulate in Batavia, fearful of Graham's democratic sympathies, had communicated with the State Department, trying to have him returned home, and now, at the most critical juncture in the negotiations, Graham was apparently immobilized."[21]

On December 31, 1947, the Dutch prime minister Louis Beel wrote to his deputy: "Via the American Consulate General I got a note this morning that

Sjarifoeddin had a breakdown and Dr. Setiadjit, the vice-premier, will be deputized in his place to continue in talks."[22] "I remember the belief then prevailing among us," Colonel Simatoepang recalled later, "that if we accepted the agreement . . . the Three State Commission would ensure that the struggle would shift from the 'bullet to the ballot,' and we were convinced that through the ballot we would be able to drive the Dutch out! Today [1949] one may consider this belief rather naive."[23]

At another place in the memoirs, Simatoepang returned to it: "I heard from Bung Amir himself, that he had accepted the Renville Agreement in the belief that a basic *political solution* could be reached within a few months, possibly even a few weeks."[24]

And there was a Christian story. Frank Graham told it later to Amir's longtime friend, Tine Fransz, and Pastor Verkuyl wrote, too, that he heard this from Amir. "Amir told me," wrote Pastor Verkuyl, "that he had the leader of the American delegation visiting him in his cabin on the ship. Graham was an exceptionally devoted Christian and just in this they found each other. In the evenings they read the Bible together getting ready for the days of the conference."[25]

On January 9, nine days before the signing of the Renville Agreement, Amir and the minister of foreign affairs, Hadji Agoes Salim, flew to Singapore to meet Sjahrir, who was returning to Indonesia after six months abroad, mostly in New York with the United Nations. Amir might have hoped to convince Sjahrir to support the Renville Agreement. Sjahrir, however, "on the grounds that international sympathy was now with the young republic, and this was no moment to give to the Dutch," refused to give his support.[26]

Still, Amir signed the Renville Agreement (speaking Indonesian). There was not much hope anymore. After the signing, Amir took the document back to the capital, Jogjakarta, and submitted it to his cabinet for approval. The ministers of the PNI declined, as did the ministers of the Islamic Masjumi who in between had entered the cabinet. Demonstrators gathered in Jogjakarta and some other towns and cities of the republic, and especially the Islamic Masjumi followers were activated. "Three hundred people" from Islamic militia Hizbullah entered the courtyard of the presidential compound in the Sultan's Palace on January 21, "behaving noisily." They shouted slogans and carried signs like "Reject Renville, Amir is a traitor!"[27] and "Allahu Akbar, Kabinet Amir bubar!" "God is great, dissolve Amir's cabinet!"[28]

Ministers of the nationalist PNI and of the Islamic parties resigned. According to what Soemarsono heard, perhaps from Amir, "Amir was called to the President. Bung Karno said: 'It would be the best if you surrender to me your mandate.' Amir said: 'Aduh [Ouch]—this is a complot!'" "Amir," writes Soemarsono, was "emotional." "Take it!" according to Soemarsono Amir told Soekarno referring to the mandate of the prime minister, "in the coarse way like that." Soemarsono wrote Amir said: "eat it! [*makanlah*]."[29]

"Amir felt scammed," wrote Siauw Giok Tjhan, one of the Soerabaja youth and still close to Amir. Soekarno wanted Amir to form a new cabinet, but Amir refused, "without consulting the others," Siauw writes.[30] Amir resigned as prime minister on January 23. Soekarno appointed Vice-President Hatta as a formateur of the cabinet. Sometime between January 23 and 29, Hatta offered Amir to choose among three (not crucial) positions in the new cabinet, one of them the minister of youth. Amir rejected again.[31] Whispers spread that Amir was definitely moving to the Communist side, was unstable, or both. "We were stabbed from behind," wrote Soemarsono. "Hatta had already been involved in the complot and Soekarno in this instance stood on Hatta's side."[32]

On February 2, 1948, the first meeting of the new Hatta cabinet took place. The big headline in the papers in the Indies/Indonesia as well as in the Netherlands was "Hatta Cabinet without Left-Wingers."[33] "The Masjumi action," wrote Arnold Brackman, and he might equally have said, "the anti-Amir action," "was endorsed by Sjahrir, who, as in the days of the Japanese, was working behind a screen." Brackman at the time worked in Indonesia as a reporter for the United Press and it would be rare for him to quote a Soviet colleague, but in this case he did: "Georgi Afrin, a TASS correspondent who had arrived the previous October to cover the U.N. negotiations, wrote in *Pravda* that Amir fell as the result of an intrigue between the Masjumi and the United States."[34]

The new cabinet of the prime minister and Vice-President Hatta was labeled in newspapers as a "cabinet sharp as a knife."[35] Abu Hanifah, a former Kramat 106 friend of Amir and now with Islamic Masjumi, commented with satisfaction: "There was not one Communist in the cabinet, not even a fellow traveler."[36]

The Renville Agreement came into effect notwithstanding the turmoil and the government change. According to the agreement, the armed forces on both sides had to move behind the Van Mook line of the ceasefire. For the republic, whose territory had shrunk, it meant a retreat in most cases. Most significantly, Siliwangi, the powerful republican division based in Western Java, also where most of the former KNIL officers and cadets served, had to leave its home base, now under Dutch control, and move east.[37]

The *Panglima Besar*, "great commander," of the Indonesian armed forces, General Soedirman, used a charged word for the Siliwangi retreat and the word had quickly been accepted as official—or sacred, *hidjrah*, like the *Hidjrah* of the Prophet Mohammad, his retreat from Mecca to Medina in 622. A total of

35,000 Siliwangi troops, many with their families, had been evacuated to the republican territory.[38]

The Siliwangi division was led by the former cadet Nasoetion. "Nas," who used to fence with Simatoepang on the roof of the Bumi Putra building in Bandoeng in the final months of the Japanese occupation, marched the Siliwangi across the Van Mook line into Central and East Java, areas foreign to them in custom, history, and language. While Sundanese is the local language in West Java, in Central and East Java people speak Javanese; the two languages are mutually unintelligible. The forced march east, according to Indonesian paper *Nasional* of February 1948, "hurt the hearts of young soldiers, especially those in the Siliwangi division. *Hidjrah* . . . made them sick in body and soul . . . wounded. . . . A feeling arose that the division ought by now to be called 'a division of honor.' The *hidjrah* army was being forced from its home into the territories where other peoples lived."[39]

By being torn from home, freed from its home, and asked to operate in an area foreign to it, Siliwangi became an elite unit. "Amir Sjarifoeddin's idea of the People's army embodied in the Office of Struggle [Biro Perdjoeangan] had to be abandoned."[40] To the Siliwangi leadership, namely to Nasoetion, the idea and policy of political commissars had been a grave danger even before this. Now, the command had to be unified, tough, and professional.

Besides the system of commissars, proposed during Amir's time as the minister of defense and then prime minister, in the process of channeling and ranking the revolution, an extra-military militia emerged. In August 1947, less than two months after Amir became the premier, around the Biro Perdjoeangan, "Office of Struggle," under some control at least of the Ministry of Defense, the TNI-Masjarakat, "People's Army," somehow armed 350,000 troops. It included 100,000 fighters from Pesindo. "Recall the Paris Commune of 1871," Jacques Leclerc wrote in his essay on Amir. "In many aspects Hatta reminds one of Thiers,"[41]

After February 1948, the new Hatta government, "sharp as a knife," decided to fix the apparatus against the chaos, to make its parts to fit one another, and click. Not what Ludwig Wittgenstein once described as a machine made of butter. Hard. "Rationalization," which became the motto of the new government, was to bring about an efficiency in the revolution: "Military ranks were lowered. A major general was reduced to the rank of colonel, a colonel to lieutenant colonel, and a lieutenant colonel to major. Even General Soedirman was reduced to the rank of lieutenant general and Lieutenant General Oerip Soemohardjo to major general."[42]

As the immediate effect of the rationalization in the military, by June 1948, 40,000 men and women were demobilized and 60,000 were earmarked to go soon.⁴³ Colonel Nasoetion became the main proponent and executor, if not the initiator, of the new government's rationalization. He asked rhetorically: "Is inefficiency particularly revolutionary?"⁴⁴ Colonel Simatoepang, close to Amir, but a professional soldier in his soul and close to Nasoetion, agreed with at least some aims of the rationalization: "There rose a widespread feeling that all ranks in the Indonesian National Army should be reduced; at one point no less than sixty generals wandered about in Jogja [Jogjakarta] every day, each with a yellow flag on his car, just like the Japanese generals during the occupation."⁴⁵

Revolution was in danger and there was something rotten in the state of the republic. But it was also becoming very clear that Hatta and Nasoetion targeted the People's Army, especially the people whom Amir Sjarifoeddin brought into the military with the élan without which the revolution, most probably, would have rotted completely. As Amir and many around him might have seen it, élan was as much in danger now as was the revolution.

Atmadji was one of the Soerabaja youth reported in the last months before the Japanese invasion in connection with the Van der Plas money as it was received and distributed among the resistance. He was a Gerindo leader during the last years of the Indies and a "close associate of Amir."⁴⁶ "In 1945, Atmadji formed the Naval Marine Security (*Marine Keamanan Laut*) of the new republic and was later the head of the People's Security Naval Force [*TKR Laut*] in Surabaya. Still later he worked in the naval section of the Ministry of Defense, representing the East Java wing of the navy. Despite continuing accusations of corruption and an attempt by Hatta to arrest him, he survived in this position because of Pesindo protection."⁴⁷ Now, Atmadji was almost at the top of the list of those recommended either for outright dismissal or at least demotion in the framework of the rationalization.

Djokosoejono had also been suspected by the Dutch police before the war as being close to Musso when Musso visited Java in 1935 and 1936. During the Japanese occupation, Djokosoejono became a member of Peta, Pembela Tanah Air, "Defenders of the Motherland," the Japanese-trained Indonesian voluntary corps. During the early months of the revolution, during Amir's tenure as the minister of defense, Djokosoejono served as Simatoepang's boss in the Organization Section of the Central Command. As a part of the Hatta program, Djokosoejono was demoted down from the rank of general-major to colonel and more was expected.⁴⁸

Pesindo, in the new vocabulary of rationalization, became "the Red-oriented guerilla band."⁴⁹ The situation in the republic after the Renville Agreement, with the territory shrunk and revolution rationalized, was getting tense. The space began to resemble the Blitar prison:

On some days, the Pesindo units came to Madiun from all over East Java. They gathered on the main square of the city, armed, with tanks and combat vehicles. Sometimes, comrade commandant Roeslan Widjasastra carrying a[n] FN pistol gave a speech, short and simple, as simple was his life.

Comrade Soemarsono spoke often to the gathering, too, and he rarely wore a Major-General uniform and insignia of his rank. He also never used a Major-General flag on his car. Comrade Amir came often to Madiun, too. . . . He chatted with the youth in the dormitory in which Comrade Soemarsono and others lived.[50]

As for them, Hatta and Nasoetion announced a plan, as part of the rationalization, "to make Madiun the new military capital of East Java."[51]

The shrunken area of the republic became a place where also tens of thousands civilian refugees moved. This new influx aggravated the already desperate situation caused by the years of Japanese occupation and, still earlier, of the Great Depression of the 1930s. In this sense, too, the Indies/Indonesia and especially Central and East Java became a revolutionary space. In addition to the soldiers on *hidjrah*, the shrunken area of the republic had to receive about a million civilian refugees. This increased demand for available land and exacerbated tensions between large and small landholders, and between the landowners and the landless peasants.[52] The republic remained surrounded.

> The commercial life of the republic had been brought to virtual standstill by the disruption of the internal marketing system, the loss of all deepwater ports, and the continued Dutch maritime blockade. . . . [It all] compounded long standing shortage of essential commodities and caused a catastrophic inflation in republican areas. . . . Many observers feared that any delaying tactics by the Dutch in the political discussions . . . would precipitate the collapse of the republic from within.[53]

Prices shot up beyond the reach of most of the Indonesians:

	August '47	April '48	June '48	August '48
Rice	1.66	6.76	7.44	17.50
Sugar	1.58			7.30
Salt	3.48			14.30
Coconut oil	5.09			36.20[54]

"Hatta was aware," wrote Mavis Rose, based on her interviews with Hatta, "that Amir commanded considerable popular support and that therefore the PKI threat must be taken seriously."[55] "Hatta's 'rationalization'," wrote George

Kahin, who was in Jogjakarta at the time, tried "to eliminate redundancy and inefficiency even if alternative jobs were not available for the displaced workers." "During the spring of 1948," Kahin wrote, "there had already been stirrings of discontent among corn-field workers and processors in the Delanggu area of Central Java, and it was believed that oil-field workers at Tjepu and the railroad repair workers at the major repair yards in Madiun were apprehensive and restive. Indeed, by mid-September, rationalization of the 6,000-man force of railroad workers living in [Madiun], the republic's third-most popular and largest industrial city (with certainly the largest concentration of skilled labor in the republic) had been slated to get under way."[56]

The group from Holland, now with virtually all its members on Amir's side, became particularly active among labor unions, "*Drs.* Setiadadjit among the sugar-mill workers, *Drs.* Maroeto Daroesman among the plantation workers, Gondopartomo and Zainoeddin among the railway workers."[57]

The other revolutionaries did not resign, at least not all of them. Tensions inside the Left increased as the Dutch kept their blockade and Hatta with Nasoetion proceeded with their rationalization. "There were tensions increasing between PKI-oriented and Tan Malaka-oriented sugar unions."[58] Tan Malaka was still in prison, but newspapers associated with him wrote about the unions sympathetic to the PKI: "Recently the Sarbupri [Sarekat Buruh Perkebunan Republik Indonesia, the 'Plantation Workers Union'] went on strike in Delanggu. They do not realize that they are duped by Amir–Setiadjit into attempts to overthrow the government."[59]

Sjahrir formally resigned from the Sjahrir–Amir fused socialist party and, on February 13, 1948, announced the formation of his own, Partai Sosialis Indonesia (PSI), "Indonesian Socialist Party, "with emphasis," Arnold Brackman comments, "on 'moral Indonesia.'"[60] An eyewitness described a meeting during which Sjahrir's and Amir's followers parted ways. He recalls Amir standing quietly in a corner of the room. He was overheard as saying what could be a motto for the third part of this book: "It is so hard to establish a state."[61]

"Only the intellectuals joined Sjahrir," Amir told Brackman sometime around the moment of the split, "I have the masses."[62] John Coast—a young Brit, a rare case, a volunteer for the republic, who happened to be in Jogjakarta at the time and who got especially close to Sjahrir's circle—wrote memoirs of these months: "Sjahrir, nominally the Special Advisor of the President, retired to his private eyrie, where only the independently minded and a few faithful adherents followed him; while Sjarifoeddin . . . with his greater sense of popular appeal and with his emotional and more tractable character, rapidly accelerated his leftward movement, taking the bulk of the Socialists with him."[63]

Sjahrir himself wrote a special memorandum in 1948 for members of his new party, and he later let George Kahin, an American in Jogjakarta, see it. In Kahin's translation the memorandum is entitled "Political Conditions in Indonesia." Amir's "turn to Communism" is the memorandum's main theme. "There is hardly," Sjahrir wrote about Amir's way, "any connection with Marxism or Leninism which is based on the interpretation of political realities, on an analysis through a dialectic materialistic approach." Amir, Sjahrir wrote, "has not a high level of political understanding, particularly as regards socialism and true Marxism."[64]

To John Coast and his informants, as well as in a wider court of opinion, Indonesian as well as Dutch and Allied, Sjahrir was rapidly acquiring the aura of a thinker, while Amir sank into politics. Sjahrir's people sank in thinking, if I may say so.

> *Written by Soedjatmoko early in 1948.*
> *Translated* [from Dutch to Indonesian?] *by Chairil Anwar* [Sjahrir's nephew and the poet quoted above], *published in* [cultural magazine] *Gema* ["Echo"]
> *On the true and the untrue articulation of a cultural problem.*
> The existence of the Indonesian revolution equals in its essence the faith
> ... an awareness of the cultural self-determination as a nation.

Soedjatmoko wrote in this essay, in this spirit, that he expands on the ideas of "existentialism and personalism."[65]

Sjahrir argued that Amir was at a crossroads and would have to make a choice. Already in December 1947, Kahin heard of this interpretation, probably from Sjahrir himself or from one of his close associates. Sjahrir said, Kahin wrote later in his *Nationalism and Revolution in Indonesia*, "that Sjarifoeddin would have to decide whether he was first a nationalist or first a Communist. Sjahrir and most of his group felt ... that application of the Marxist doctrine of class warfare was absurd in the Indonesian community since there was practically no Indonesian bourgeoisie, that class in Indonesia being almost exclusively made up of Dutch and Chinese. Secondly, [Sjahrir and Sjahrir's people] were strongly opposed to a policy of alignment with either Russia or the United States, [they favored] 'positive neutrality.'"[66] Dutch intelligence reported, what it also might hear from Sjahrir or someone of his circle: "Soetan Sjahrir is of the opinion that Amir Sjarifoeddin is now under complete influence of Setiadjit."[67]

Amir Sjarifoeddin, so it seems, was now almost completely embroiled in politics—but the élan and euphoria followed him. Recalling all that he had written and said since the 1920s, *Mirabele Lectu* and the discussions in Schepper's house, the ships on the wall, and the prophets, he stood, or lingered, where he had to, not to lose oneself.

In Soerakarta on February 26, Sajap Kiri, "Left Wing," underwent a reorganization. Amir's Socialist Party with the other collective Sajap Kiri members—PKI, Labor Party, Pesindo, SOBSI trade-union federation—came together in a hopefully more compact, disciplined, and yet fervent, Front Demokrasi Rakjat (FDR), "People's Democratic Front." Amir Sjarifoeddin became the FDR chairman. The program of the FDR was announced by Amir at a public meeting in the city. In Kahin's description, the program "put more emphasis upon the interests of labor and the peasantry, but otherwise was almost identical with the Sajap Kiri. . . . During the course of the next two weeks, however, the program of the FDR underwent a basic change . . . called for repudiation of the Renville Agreement . . . [and for] nationalization of Dutch and other foreign enterprise[s] without compensation."[68]

On April 1, 1948, an alleged FDR secret directive was published in the Indonesian daily *Merdeka*, known to be close to Tan Malaka. The methods that the document directed the FDR sympathizers to use, included "disturbances, kidnapping, and thieving to break the people's confidence." The authenticity of the document, at least of its most compromising parts, was immediately denied by the FDR, and the republic's attorney general was asked to investigate.[69]

The more the revolutionary forces gathered, articulated their élan, the more they structured themselves, the more they were becoming fragile and prone to breaking apart.

Still, it was not clear who the Communists were. Dutch intelligence did its best to understand, and in mid-1948 put it this way:

> FDR now has a governing body made of six persons:
> Alimin—communist
> *drs*. Maroeto Daroesman—communist
> *mr*. Tan Ling Djie—communist
> Setyadjit—SOBSI [trade-union] leader
> Abdul Madjid—(left) socialist
> Amir Sjarifoeddin—Idem.[70]

There was an apparatus at work in a larger revolutionary space. The apparatus and the revolutionary space in which the apparatus clicked, as its mechanics put it, had been in place since the Second World War ended at least, and in fact long before, since the Great Depression, indeed, since the first echoes of Lenin's and Trotsky's revolution reached the Indies.

In the first weeks after the Soekarno and Hatta proclamation, before the end of 1945, Dutch intelligence reported the publication, in Madioen, of "a pocket-sized handbook in Indonesian, *Riwajat Perhoeboengan Inggris-Russia dan Perang Doenia ke-III*, 'Story of the English–Russian Relations and the Third World War.' A certain Soebianto was signed as author, and the brochure was thirty-four pages long."[71] The brochure was not attached to the report, nothing more was said about the content, and I could not find the book anywhere.

In Indonesia, as everywhere, the Cold War meant a gradual but inevitable breaking up of the united front against fascism. The widening distance between Soetan Sjahrir and Amir Sjarifoeddin, and their final separation, was also a manifestation of the Cold War's increasing presence in Indonesia.

For some time, the increasing distance could be passed over by the sheer willpower of those involved. After the fall of Sjahrir's cabinet, Willem Schermerhorn of the Dutch delegation in the negotiations had been disturbed that many pro-Amir members of the Socialist Party turned against Sjahrir and that Sjahrir's people responded the same way. But soon, on the same day that Sjahrir resigned in fact, Schermerhorn had an "extremely pleasant talk with Setiadjit," who was, as he happily wrote in his diary that day, "a man who knows Holland splendidly, and who knows the world and looks at things in an utmost rational manner."[72]

But the Dutch police action against the republic in June 1947 was a blow. It broke Schermerhorn's, Logemann's, and other sympathetic Dutchmen's will. "Yesterday," Willem Schermerhorn wrote in his diary on July 19, 1947, "I became too depressed to put my thoughts on the paper,"[73] "Yesterday afternoon at four o'clock," Schermerhorn wrote, "a telegram came that forthright authorized military action. . . . At five o'clock met the commander with his advisers and the precise hour was set."[74] "Justly, he [Kees Vervink, Schermerhorn's adviser] noted that for the Partij van de Arbeid [Dutch 'Labor Party'] it will mean a greater blow than for anybody else and that with one strike all will be destroyed what has been built during the past two years."[75]

Saying shifted and overnight it became a Cold War language which, in the Indies/Indonesia, equaled an old-colonial language precisely: "Our principal aim," wrote Schermerhorn in his diary on September 13, 1947, "remains putting the republic in order [*de saneering van de republiek*]." He pauses and writes, "Remarkable, how quickly terms take over: today the word 'put in order' [*saneering*] became generally all right."[76]

"The war in Vietnam," recalled John Coast, the British volunteer and adventurer, looking at the world from Jogjakarta, "was assuming very critical and costly character for the French."[77] It was still months before Mao Tse-tung's People's Liberation Army entered Peking. Nevertheless, the specter haunting the world, haunting Asia, and haunting Indonesia grew larger, and it became articulated and structured, too. The domino effect, unsaid yet, was in fact already a guiding principle of the new policies of the Western powers: the Reds in China and Ho Chi Minh in Vietnam had to be stopped before they joined with the power of the Soviet Union, and before the Communist armies advanced east and south, into Europe, into Asia, Czechoslovakia, Poland, Malaya, Burma, Philippines, Indonesia.

Another publication was reported by Dutch intelligence in Java, in Solo, Surakarta—the spelling changed in 1947, with *u* replacing the Dutch-styled *oe*—again with no date but, according to all the markings, from early 1948. Like in the previous Madioen brochure on the "Third World War," the Surakarta booklet was in Indonesian, but, as it was stated on the cover, it was a translation:

International situation

(Marxist Analysis)
  by A. Zhdanov

Introduction: Alimin
  Printed by *Makmur*, Solo [Surakarta], [no date], 38 pp.[78]

The booklet was the text of the "famous Zhdanov doctrine," a pronouncement, a saying, most clearly articulated, the language of the apparatus fully and without compromise, on the world divided in two parts, two camps, one capitalist against the other, socialist, in a death struggle on all fronts, by all methods, except, for a while and if possible, "hot" war. Two wonderful apparatuses, East and West, and many smaller apparatuses, were expected to fit into one another and fix against each other. The world was in misery, big changes were needed, and this is how Zhdanov and the new Communist Information Bureau, successor of Communist International that dissolved in 1943, proposed the process should go.

In the middle of 1947, when Amir Sjarifoeddin was still the prime minister, ir. Soeripno, one of the group from Holland, had been sent on a diplomatic mission. "Soeripno," the Dutch consulate in Singapore—kind of an intelligence hub for the Dutch in the Indies/Indonesia—reported, "left for Prague as the official delegation of the Indonesian republican government to the International Youth Festival. He was accompanied by Miss Francisca Fanggidaej."[79]

"We left from Maguwo [Jogjakarta airport]," Francisca recalled, "on July 20, 1947, a day before Holland launched its first colonial aggression.... The plane was private property.... At the airport... I saw Bung Hatta... Bung Amir and Bung Sjahrir. . . . The name of the pilot was Patnaik."[80] They first flew to Padang, West Sumatra, and that far Vice-President Hatta flew with them. Then to New Delhi, India, where they changed planes. "Only two of us," wrote Francisca, "I and Soeripno, would go on to Europe. . . . All the costs of the trip," she added, "were covered by the Indian government of Nehru."[81]

The World Festival of Youth and Students, the first of what was to become a regular event in the following years and decades, had been organized by the World Federation of Democratic Youth, in 1947, in Prague.

In 1947, two years after the defeat of Nazism, the delegates, who came from many countries, were still full of élan, and indeed of euphoria. To many, and to the young participants at the festival especially, the world seemed still on the verge of becoming radically new. The delegates of the festival were called *pemuda* by Francisca Fanggidaej, the same charged Indonesian word she used for the youth of Soerabaja, the youth of the Youth Congress in Jogjakarta in 1945 where Amir spoke, and the youth of the Marx House in Madiun.

The festival in Prague took place many months before the first show trials in Eastern Europe took place (and many months before the—only much less bloody—McCarthy hearings about Un-American activity began in Washington). Some of the Czechoslovak Communist Party leaders who were to be hanged in the trials appeared on the tribunes and among the young people at the festival.

"For the first time," Francisca Fanggidaej wrote, "at a large mass meeting in the city of Prague, Soeripno raised a cry 'Stop the war in Indonesia!'" "A roaring cheer," she writes, "answered the speaker." "Several *pemuda*, representing different countries raised Soeripno on their shoulders and carried him around the hall. This was what was happening in Prague to me, as well. . . . The name 'Surabaya' became known all over the city. . . . To experience scenes like that warmed my heart."[82]

The Dutch embassies and missions kept an eye on the Soeripno–Fanggidaej mission while they were in Prague and as they were on the way there. "Soeripno stays in Prague," wrote the deputy director of Dutch intelligence to the attorney general in Batavia/Djakarta, "in the house of the well-known communist Jerina [Jiřina] Tardyová, Cukrovarnická 34, Praha XVIII. Abovementioned Tardyová is considered a liaison man [*verbindingsman* (*sic*)] between the Indonesian republic and Moscow."[83] The Dutch ambassador in Prague, in a "very secret" communication on May 3, 1948, reported: "Mr. Soeripno, maybe to make some additional money, gives lessons in Malay at the Oriental School here in Prague. He is being assisted by unprofessional Indonesian helpers. In the fall semester of 1947, they had seventeen students. The address of Soeripno's office is Třída Krále Jiřího ["King George's Avenue"] 1072, Prague."[84]

In another Dutch report, a Soeripno office with the same address is described as "The Indonesian Information Service."[85]

I was six years old, Prague was my city, and I might have crossed paths with Soeripno as I went for a walk with my mother. Among Soeripno's seventeen students, moreover, were Ms. Horáčková and Mr. Oplt, who, fifteen years later, became my first teachers of Indonesian. I may still have a Soeripno accent.

After the Prague Festival was over, there was a visiting troupe of Balinese dancers among other attractions, Francisca embarked on safari, as she called it, to other East and Southeast European countries potentially friendly to the republic, to Yugoslavia, and Bulgaria.[86] (It was still the Tito era, of the heroic Yugoslav guerilla leader and his fight against Nazism. He was now the country's prime minister. Amir called his son, born on April 8, 1948, Tito Batara, *Tito* for Josif Brosz Tito, and *Batara* for "god" or "divine." It was still many months before Tito became a "bloody murderer" in the saying of the Communist Information Bureau.)

Soeripno remained in Prague, after the weeks of élan and teaching Indonesian, his true mission only beginning. On December 25, 1947, Amir Sjarifoeddin was still the prime minister, Soeripno received an official letter from Jogjakarta, signed by President Soekarno:

> Know ye that . . . Soeripno / Special Envoy and Minister Plenipotentiary of the Republic of Indonesia, I have invested . . . to meet and confer with any person or persons duly authorized by the governments in EAST EUROPE and CENTRAL EUROPE and of the USSR . . . and . . . to negotiate about the establishment of friendly relations between the governments and the government of the Republic of Indonesia, conclude and sign any agreement or another nota adopted by the said negotiations, the same to be transmitted to the President and the government of the Republic of Indonesia for his [sic] ratification.
> Done at the city of Jogjakarta, December 25, 1947
>
> Soekarno,
> President of the Republic of Indonesia.[87]

In January 1948, Amir Sjarifoeddin's cabinet resigned and, in mid-February, the new prime minister, Hatta, recalled Soeripno from Prague.[88]

Soeripno did not obey. On May 22, 1948, at the Soviet Embassy in Prague notes had been exchanged between the Soviet ambassador to Czechoslovakia, Mikhail Silin, and Special Envoy and Minister Plenipotentiary of the Republic of Indonesia Soeripno on the opening of consular relations and the exchange of consular offices between the two countries. "Soeripno was accompanied by a secretary. According to the ambassador Silin, the name of the secretary was Musin Makar Ivanovich. Musin Makar Ivanovich presented himself as a Soviet citizen currently at the office of the military mission in Germany and visiting Prague."[89]

The same day, a draft of the note in Russian was translated by Musin Makar Ivanovich into Indonesian. The documents, in Russian and Indonesian, then had been signed. "Soeripno made a statement that the note was the first official document of diplomacy written in Indonesian, a formerly oppressed colonial language. He also said that the Soviet consul as he arrives will be the first consul of a foreign country stationed not in Batavia-Djakarta, but in Jogjakarta, the capital of the republic."[90] On May 26, 1948, four days later, the Soviet Communist Party daily *Pravda* and the Soviet trade-unions' *Izvestia*, reported the signing of the Soviet–Indonesian agreement.[91]

Of course, Musin Makar Ivanovich was one of many revolutionary aliases of Musso. Five months after Soeripno and Musso met with Ambassador Silin, when Musso's visit to Prague already became known and as a historical event indeed, the Dutch ambassador to Prague had a flashback. He cabled to his minister of foreign affairs in The Hague:

> *Prague, October 11, 1948*
> *Re: Moeso*
>
> . . . the former Czechoslovak Prime Minister Gottwald [now the president of the republic], when I visited him on August 17, 1946, talked about Dutch friends he had during the war in Moscow. In this connection, next to [Louis de] Visser and [Paul] de Groot [Dutch Communist leaders] he mentioned an Indonesian, he said "Moeser." I have noted it in my letter of August 21, 1946, No. 310.03-4167/569. At the time, however, the name did not mean anything to me.

"Gottwald," the ambassador added, "had spent the years of the war in Russia and during these years of 'training,' evidently, he met Moeso."[92]

On February 25, 1948, when Soeripno was in Prague and Musso had not yet arrived, Gottwald, then the prime minister, and the chairman of the Czechoslovak Communist Party, at the main Wenceslaus Square in Prague, announced to the masses that President Beneš gave in to the pressure of the people, and accepted the resignation of the right-wing ministers. A new government had been appointed, fully dominated by the Communists. Soeripno, it can hardly be doubted, stood among the masses on Wenceslaus Square and in four days on the Old Town Square, witnessed Gottwald speak and what became known as the February Victory of the Czechoslovak Working Class.

Musso arrived in Prague a few weeks later and he certainly heard from Soeripno about the victorious February. At the same time, he did not seem to fully appreciate that Amir Sjarifoeddin's cabinet in Indonesia fell, and that Hatta had become the prime minister. Or, if he did, he might take it as a nudge that he should hurry. Musso was fifty-one years old and this might have been his last chance.

In October 1946, with the Sjahrir–Amir cabinet recently in power, Musso wrote a highly optimistic, euphoric, article in the Soviet Communist Party Central Committee bulletin:

On [the] situation in Indonesia

Marxist literature is widely circulated in the republic. Books like *"On the Problems of Leninism," "The Communist Manifesto,"* or *"The Biography of Josef Stalin,"* for example, have been translated into Indonesian and can be found everywhere. The texts by Mao Tse-tung, also, are very popular.[93]

In January 1948, by pure coincidence the same day that Amir Sjarifoeddin emotionally returned his mandate to Soekarno, "Eat it!" he said, Musso published another opinion piece about the tide of the Indonesian revolution still rising. In the "Notes on the situation in Indonesia," of January 23, 1948, Musso explained what he saw as the current policy of the PKI and, rather impatiently, he offered ways yet to improve it. In Indonesia, he wrote,

> the communists do not realize their real strength and they hesitate to assume the decisive role in the government. Leaders of the Socialist and Labor parties (for instance Sjarifoeddin, Tamzil, Setiadjit and others, in fact communists, but known officially as socialists) should have more courage to step forward. The cabinet of Amir Sjarifoeddin [this Musso wrote when the Amir's cabinet was to all effect gone], is a clear proof that the communists may attain a position of power. . . . Now, it is important to draw the armed organizations of various Indonesian parties under one command of the Indonesian national army which stands under the leadership of Amir Sjarifoeddin [sic!].[94]

Musso presented and evidently believed in Indonesia as a country on the brink of a Communist revolution. "In Indonesia," he wrote, "not merely the Communists sympathize with the socialist states (Soviet Union, etc.), but people of many layers of the Indonesian society do as well."[95] Musso badly wanted to go, it was the time of a big change in Europe and in Asia, and Moscow clearly stood behind him. It was the Zhdanov era. On June 21, 1948, with Soeripno, Musso departed from Prague.

Certificate
Mr. Soeripno, Prague I, Hotel Centrála ["Central"], was vaccinated against typhus, typhoid fever, small-pox, cholera, yellow fever, and plague, in our institute on June 16, 1949.
[signed] Dr. Jiří Sedlák, Department of Public Health, IV Microbiological Diagnosis, Praha XII, Šrobárova 11.[96]

A photocopy of the passports of Soeripno and Musso, six months later, when both were dead, fell in the hands of Dutch military intelligence and now they are filed in the National Archives in The Hague. In pencil on the top of the first page of Soeripno's passport, there is written in Czech longhand: "The owner of this passport Mr. Soeripno, on July 13, 1947, has been issued food stamps for three days." Visas of both men are stamped in the passports on the same dates, as they traveled home together via Egypt, Pakistan, Siam, India, and Burma. They arrived in Burma on July 26, 1948.[97] Musso's passport was issued in the name Soeparto, another assumed revolutionary name:

Name: Soeparto Raden [*raden* is a title for a lower nobility; it is uncertain whether Musso was entitled to it]
Born: Blitar (Java) [wrong]
On: August 12, 1912 [wrong]
Issued Prague April 1, 1948, by the Special Envoy and Minister Plenipotentiary Republik Indonesia [which was Soeripno], Prague.[98]

Musso's vaccination certificate was issued in Prague, for Soeparto, on the same day. "This health certificate," it says, "is valid for a visit to Indonesia and expires on 1 April 1949."[99]

Dutch intelligence on the way did their best to follow Musso's reappearance. They sent secret and highly secret reports on the specter becoming flesh. Musso and Soeripno traveled so fast that the spies were not always on target.

Korte levensbeschrijving van Moeso Boedisoetjitro, "Short Description of the Life of Moeso Boedisoetjitro," one of the most exhaustive of such reports, reflected this. Moeso is Musso all right. Boedisoetjitro was a name that seemed to ring right, too, to the ears of the Dutch spy, as he or she recalled the specters of the Indies. It was not Musso's, however. It was the name of another Communist leader, perhaps the most famous one among the internees in Boven Digoel since the Communist rebellion of 1926 and 1927.

According to the "Short Description," too, Musso in Prague was "known under the name of Musinov." Not Musin Makar Ivanovich. Moesinov might have sounded right to the author, too, and suggesting "Moscow connections." In fact, it was a name that Matu Mona, author of the thriller series about Tan Malaka, *Patjar Merah*, gave in the 1930s to one of his fictional heroes.[100]

On July 27, 1948, still on his way to Indonesia with Soeripno, Musso wrote a letter to the Foreign Department of the Central Committee of the Communist Party of the Soviet Union. He spoke of the coming time as "crucial and interesting."[101]

Another letter, allegedly written by Musso on his way from Prague, and found in the house of Amir Sjarifoeddin after Musso's death, is postmarked from Bukittinggi, West Sumatra, August 2, 1948, evidently the first stop of Musso's and Soeripno's plane on Indonesian soil. The letter was addressed to a certain Faninco, most probably in Moscow. Musso signed himself again as Soeparto. The letter is in English:

Dear Faninco,

Here on the spot, I have got information that I am coming just in time. Several people whom I have seen here have assured me that the chance is great that I will lead the new cabinet. I hope that it would be so. . . .

Yours Soeparto

P.S. Be kind to write to my wife [Musso was married in Moscow and had a daughter Sunar; or Sinar?] that I am already in Indonesia and at the same time send her the stamps.[102]

After perhaps one more stopover, Musso and Soeripno landed in East Java, on the swamps of Tjampur Darat, a district in Tulangagung, three-hundred kilometers east of Jogjakarta. Soerjono writes:

There was no airfield in that area, just a huge swamp. The only correct conclusion is that Musso came in from Bukittinggi on a Catalina amphibious plane. His landing did not particularly attract the attention of the local inhabitants, for . . . during the Pacific War the Dutch had used the swamp as an amphibious airbase. And during the Japanese occupation, the same swamp was often used by planes to bring in high Japanese officers to inspect the New-Yama Project [which] involved a tunnel under the mountains to drain the swamp into the Popoh Bay in order to prevent floods in Tulungagung.[103]

(*O Nasib Tulungagung* [O, the Tulungagung] was a song about recent deadly floods in Tulungagung, which prisoners used to sing in the Blitar Japanese prison.)

"Musso returned to Indonesia, after an absence of thirteen years, and for the umptieth time eluding the Dutch colonial government secret police."[104] Like a ghost, a "revenant,"[105] as "repetition, resurgence, revival, or haunting."[106] Dutch intelligence got some information about Musso's arrival later, and there was one intriguing detail in it: "From the VH-BDP plane as it taxied in over the waterway," it says, "among other passengers, *Col. Simatoepang stepped out.*"[107]

On August 11, 1948, Soeripno, Musso, and perhaps Simatoepang, were flown to Jogjakarta "where Musso stayed overnight in Amir's house."[108]

Two days later, on August 13, Musso and Soeripno met Soekarno. A single Indonesian journalist was invited to witness the meeting, a reporter for the Jogjakarta daily *Revolusioner*, "Revolutionary," H. B. Jassin.[109] A week later, *Revolusioner* published Jassin's report: "Musso met President Soekarno. . . . They knew each other from the time when Soekarno [as a high-school student] was a boarder in the house of Hadji Tjokroaminoto in Soerabaja. . . . Musso was a 'teacher' of Soekarno. . . . Boeng Karno kissed Musso and Musso kissed Soekarno. There were tears in their eyes. Happiness did not let them speak for a moment. They just smiled. . . . Then, they chatted about the old times. Soekarno gave Musso a book, *Sarinah*." ("Sarinah," was a book Soekarno just published, named after his nanny when he was a little boy.) Fatmawati, the third wife of Soekarno, now also came into the room. "The first lady asked Musso: 'Is Pak Musso married? If yes, where is his wife now?'" A photograph was taken on the occasion, and it appeared in the *Revolusioner* issue with a caption: "Soeripno and Musso meet President Soekarno. All three are smiling."[110]

Jassin, the only journalist present at the meeting, was already on his way to become the most influential literary critic of independent Indonesia, a mentor of several generations of Indonesian poets, writers, and intellectuals. His sense of language already showed in this newspaper piece: "Soekarno is to talk first: 'Hou je?' [Dutch for 'How are you?']. Their eyes and expressions of their faces express delight. . . . [Soe]Karno says 'Lho, kok masih awet muda?' [mixed Javanese and Indonesian, or rather street Malay, 'Wow! How you did it! Still young?'] Pak Musso answers: 'O, ja. Tentu saja. Ini memang semangat Moskow, semangat Moskow selamanya muda!' [the same mixed style, *gado-gado*, 'salad,' as Indonesians might say, 'Oh yah, the Moscow spirit, spirit of Moscow, young forever!'].

Jassin goes on reporting that Soekarno "proudly told *Saudara* [Brother-Comrade, Citizen] Soeripno about Pak Musso in 'the old times'": "This Musso in the old times was a *djago* [Javanese for 'rooster,' 'gamecock,' 'champion,' 'hero']. He liked to fight! He was also a *pentjak* expert [Javanese martial art]. He also liked to play music. And when he gave a speech, he always rolled up his sleeves first." Before they parted Bung Karno asked "whether Pak Musso might be willing to help make the republic stronger and to put the revolution on the move again [sic]. Pak Musso answered: 'It is my duty. *Ik kom hier om orde te scheppen*' [Dutch for 'I came here to create order']."[111]

In a letter written to Jacques Leclerc thirty-five years later, Jassin, now the most distinguished man of Indonesian letters and with a record of an outspoken non-Communist, recalled the meeting: "At that moment," Jassin wrote, "I believed that Musso was the only leader who could set the revolution back on its track. That Musso had a clear idea how to do it."[112]

An informant for Dutch intelligence, who was listening to people in the republican capital Jogjakarta who were, or said they were, in the know, reported a special detail: "From a particular person, I learned that Moeso had been offered a beautiful villa in Kaliurang [a hill resort near Jogjakarta often used also by the Sultan and Jogjakarta elite], an offer which Moeso declined."[113]

Musso's return was presented as "an unexpected development to Amir Sjarifoeddin."[114] In Anthony Reid's view, Musso came with "reputation and authority as an interpreter of current Soviet thinking." "It is difficult to believe," wrote Reid, that Musso "would have been allowed to guide the FDR on what proved a disastrous course, but for the demoralization of existing leaders, particularly Amir." "Musso arrived," Reid wrote, "as if from the clouds, untainted . . . bearing a confident blueprint for a new and certain path to history."[115]

"In short," wrote Roeslan Abdoelgani, at the time in the republican Ministry of Information and later Indonesia's foremost official ideologue, upon Musso's arrival, "the Cold War influence reached Indonesia. Musso, a communist leader, brought communism on to the political scene."[116] "In Prague," wrote Harry Poeze, "Musso worked on a document that drew a new course for the PKI . . . a *'sharp turn.'*"[117]

It cannot be denied, however, that the Indonesian people at the moment of Musso's return were in a state of misery, that the country became a state of discontent, and that Musso had been pulled into Indonesia from the inside as much as he was pushed from the outside, out of what he certainly saw as a revolutionary space in the world.

Late in 1947, when Amir Sjarifoeddin was still prime minister, a Soviet journalist in Jogjakarta, Olga Chechetkina (it might be the same one who had visited Amir in his house and sent a report on it, and the same one on board the *Renville* when the agreement was signed), met several Indonesian Communist leaders. "In her secret communication to the central committee of the Soviet Union [sic]," a Russian historian who got access to the relevant archives wrote recently, Olga Chechetkina "reported that a secretary of the central committee of the PKI Alimin asked her 'urgently' for help to establish contacts with other Communist Parties." Alimin was a veteran of the Indonesian Communist Party, one of its oldest leaders now, and he had been a close associate of Musso back in 1926. According to Chechetkina's report, Alimin conveyed through her "a special appeal to check the possibility of Musso . . . to be as soon as possible dispatched to Indonesia."[118]

"'Well, my friend,' says a clever student in Petrograd in winter of 1917," as John Reed reported on the Bolshevik revolution, "do you know that Lenin was sent through Germany in a closed car? Do you know that Lenin took money from the Germans?"[119] Musso might have been awaited, and there might have been a desperate need among the Indonesian revolutionaries, blended with an urgent sense that victory was possible. In a flash, in a matter of hours, Musso's presence, as he arrived, was felt everywhere.

Djalan Baroe, "New Road," was a program, a radically new course for the Indonesian revolution that Musso supposedly refined in Prague and brought to Indonesia. In a session of the Central Committee of the Indonesian Communist Party on August 26 and 27, two weeks after Musso's return, the thirty-four-page document was accepted: "after World War II PKI went astray—it overestimated the strength of the capitalist world. . . . It dissolved the army in three parts. It made too many concessions to the imperialists, and it placed not enough emphasis on either labor or the farmers." Now, the Indonesian Communist Party "must gain HEGEMONY (the largest strength). . . . A National Front must be set up from below and PKI must hold its leadership. Plans for deep social reform must be immediately declared. Diplomatic relations with the Soviet Union must be established."[120]

There was a criticism of Amir as a prominent and actually decisive figure in the revolution, for the course it had taken till then. In the words of the New Road, it was a particularly grave mistake that in January 1948 he had resigned as prime minister "without any resistance whatsoever."

On August 27, in the hours after the New Road was proclaimed, Setiadjit fused his Labor Party with the PKI. Four days later, on August 31, Amir Sjarifoeddin issued a statement on "past errors." "The postwar policy of cooperation with the imperialists against fascism," he admitted, "should have been replaced by an anti-imperialist policy under the leadership of the communists immediately after fascism was beaten."[121]

On August 31, Amir announced what the mainstream of the revolution took as shocking news. Musso, Amir declared, in fact, had recruited him into the "Illegal PKI" as early as 1935 and Gerindo, in fact, had been presented in such a way that it "concealed its communist aspirations."[122] As for taking Van der Plas's money, which thanks to Tan Malaka's followers was widely known, Amir now said that he took it, "because the Communist International had proposed to cooperate with the colonial powers in the struggle against fascism."[123]

"To be illegal used to mean to be invisible," Soemarsono recalled the moment. "Now, we decided to come forward, to show ourselves." "People used not to know whether I was a communist or not. In 1948 Amir had been directed to speak out: 'I am communist.' I had also been directed to disclose myself: 'I have been a communist since the time of Soerabaja!' . . . It was Musso's correction. . . . All who used to be illegal were directed to emerge."[124] "I suspected it back then," wrote Van der Plas about his suspicion then, in 1941, and about the aha moment now. Now, "it was proven."[125]

"Reports of fusion of Socialist Party led by Sjarifoeddin with Communists," the US ambassador in the Netherlands cabled to the secretary of state, on August 31, 1948, "is extremely disturbing." Some people clearly feared that the Communists in Indonesia might be at the brink of victory. The US ambassador cabled to the secretary of state again on September 3: "Reason why Dutch have not acted more energetically against Communism, was fear such action might precipitate fall of Hatta government. . . . Dutch entertain same fears as Department that successor likely to be Communist controlled. Developing situation in the republic, Boon [an official in the Dutch government] thought, was somewhat analogous to that in Burma."[126]

On September 1, 1948, the Politburo of the new PKI was announced in *Suara Ibu Kota*, "Voice of the Capital" (i.e., Jogjakarta):

DEFENSE: Amir Sjarifoeddin
LABOR: A. Tjokronegoro, Aidit, Sutrisno
PROPAGANDA AGITATION: Lukman, Alimin, Sardjono
ORGANIZATION: Soedirman [not related to *Panglima Besar* Soedirman]
REPRESENTATION: Njoto.[127]
GENERAL SECRETARIAT: Musso, Maroeto Daroesman, Tan Ling Djie, Ngadiman
YOUTH MOVEMENT: Wikana, Suwirjo
FOREIGN AFFAIRS: Soeripno
FINANCES: Roeskak[128]

"Enthusiastically and by acclamation" Musso was voted the party's general secretary. The party congress, it was announced, was to take place between October 1 and 3, 1948.[129]

Musso gave a lecture at the University of Gadjah Mada in Jogjakarta and the press was present. "There was a student who asked a question in what Musso may have felt was a rather 'skeptical' tone. The student asked, 'In the present situation are we capable of resisting the Dutch?' Musso rolled up his sleeves [*sic*] and answered, 'Why not? Here is Musso, my friend, who once joined the International Brigade to fight against fascism in Madrid.'"[130] There is no suggestion anywhere else that Musso was indeed in Spain, fighting against fascism, but it was *possible*.

His was a "short, dumpy figure,"[131] and there were such figures in wayang, too, wise and rebellious characters who were immensely popular among the common folk and the schooled ones alike. He might have appeared to be a hero to many. Some sources later implied that in his many years of exile in Moscow Musso might not have been just a radio announcer.[132] Some mentioned missions for Communist International to Western Europe, his special task being, they say, to gather information on Indonesian students in the Netherlands.

In 1939, on the eve of the war, reportedly, Musso was arrested in Belgium and spent some time in a French detention camp. He was said to have got out somehow before the Nazis reached him, possibly during the time window of the Molotov–Ribbentrop Pact between August 23, 1939, and June 22, 1941. He returned to Moscow, where he stayed through the war years with his Russian wife and their daughter.[133]

"What has brought to the red flag those who did not, in a sense, need it?" asked Ernst Bloch, the author of *The Spirit of Utopia* .[134] If there were to be a possibility in the world, Ernst Bloch seemed to answer, there had to be people with a mission, "to emancipate the weary and the heavy-laden."[135] Musso might be that man, like Bloch, a Kantian up to a point. As Marx wrote, "the categorical imperative [is] to overthrow all conditions in which man is a degraded, enslaved, abandoned, and wretched creature."[136] Musso was, perhaps, in the words of Marc Augé, "a shimmering figure of absolute evil . . . something resembling freedom."[137]

While other leaders around Musso were being addressed as *Bung*, *Saudara*, or *Kawan*, "Brother," "Citizen," or "Comrade," Musso was always, as far as records go, *Pak* or *Bapak*, "Father." He might also occasionally be addressed "Ouwe Heer," Dutch for "Old Man"; however, the records do not dwell on this too much.

Even Musso's closest followers were not always sure where his strength and appeal were coming from. Soerjono, one of Musso's younger admirers at the time, still asked years later:

> Did he return simply to meet old resistance comrades, or to see his family, or because he was homesick for his country? I think such a conclusion is too simple or *letterlijk* [Dutch for "literally"] Musso only once, and for a very brief time, met his woman relative from Pagu (East Java) and only once met his son Margono [from his Javanese marriage] from

Magetan. All of this took place in the Party office at Bintaran Wetan Street, Yogyakarta. After the meeting, Pirngadi, a member of *Bintang Merah*'s ["Red Star"] redaction, told me about it. He said that, at the end of the meeting, Musso gave his watch to his son as a souvenir and said to him: "Here is keepsake from me. When you go home, you must have the courage to fight for the revolution." In these matters, Musso was a puritan. And this was the first and last meeting with his son.[138]

Soemarsono recalled that he did not have necessarily a great personal respect for some other PKI leaders of the older generation:

> But as far as Pak Musso was concerned it was completely another matter. He was "the number one" and I could not have esteemed him more. When he did speak, it was never *ik* [Dutch for "I"], it was never himself. Devotion, to him, meant sacrifice, ideology meant to live as an example. He was a man of strong principles. . . . Some may say "Pak Musso was *kampungan*" ["boorish," from *kampung*, "village"]. I say, "if you say that Pak Musso was *kampungan*, excuse me, you did not know him. . . . It must be you who is *kampungan*." Pak Musso was an intellectual. He went to the HBS, Hogere Burger School. He got to study at the HBS because he became a foster child of a Dutch man, this is why. He was abroad, and his battles in the field of theory and science were many. His art to analyze the problems of the people's struggle in Indonesia was sublime and profound. So how could he be called "boorish"?[139]

Musso came back to Indonesia after thirteen years, from Moscow, and perhaps through Brussels and Amsterdam, and perhaps through Madrid. On the way to Indonesia and immediately before he went, he had been in Prague in the weeks after Gottwald's February Victory of the Czechoslovak Working Class had happened. Soeripno was there at the crucial moments and in crucial places, and he certainly told Musso.

The Gottwald coup was a momentous event in a possible world revolution and certainly it appeared as such to Soeripno and Musso. As it happened, the coup, the act of revolution, had been achieved through a parliamentary maneuver. Gottwald had provoked the right-wing ministers to resign in the expectation that it would cause a government crisis in which the right-wing parties would lose their power. The bluff worked. The president of the republic, Edward Beneš, Masaryk's closest ally before the war and no-nonsense democrat, accepted the resignation and asked Gottwald, the chairman of the largest party at the moment, to form a new government. The Gottwald cabinet of the "National Front," was dominated by the Communists and only parties could join that agreed to the Communists' leading role. No blood was spilled, except that of a few of the defeated politicians, in a wave of suicides that followed.[140]

Musso's first public statement after he reappeared in Indonesia was an open letter to *Suara Ibu Kota* and the *Revolusioner*. The main point of the open letter was a "National Front." The idea was that the political parties and affiliated organizations, as well as influential individuals from public life, come together, "from below," in unity built on a common "revolutionary platform."[141] The "National Front," recalled Soemarsono, "was to be a union of different classes. Not merely workers and peasants but also nationalist and religionist representatives of different classes."[142] Musso called it his "Gottwald plan."[143]

To build a National Front, Musso believed, required a disciplined Communist Party. Purity had to be an important part of it. Soemarsono recalled that "Pak Musso was very angry, he thought that it was a great mistake by the PKI to execute Widarta. Pak Musso said: 'This was Trotskyist thinking! The ultimate punishment for a party member is expulsion and it has to be confirmed by the Party Congress. And the accused has to be provided with all means to defend himself.'"[144] In foreign policy, Musso's New Road rejected both the Linggadjati and Renville Agreements, even as tactical moves.[145] They were spineless acts.

"Musso's new line," wrote Anthony Reid, "showed immediately in the readiness of the PKI and its allies to foment action by workers and peasants as part of the party's role of revolutionary leadership." "Strikes became endemic in the oil-refining center of Cepu [Tjepu], a PKI stronghold, by early September, principally on political rather than directly economic grounds. . . . In Madiun, a strike of municipal clerical workers began on September 13, on the grounds of repeated rudeness towards workers by members of the military."[146] Already in late August, there were reports of action by peasants to distribute some land and some forests to landless and poor peasants. On 4 September, addressing the Congress of Barisan Tani Indonesia, "Peasants' Front of Indonesia," Musso declared that "land must be returned to the peasants."[147]

Soerjono wrote years later: "In my view, things might have developed differently in Indonesia if Musso had come earlier, if he had come before the Amir Sjarifoeddin cabinet resigned. . . . The general feeling was that the climax of all the mistakes was Amir Sjarifoeddin's resignation as Prime Minister simply because of a demonstration by [a] few hundred Masjumi people. . . . To this day, I still think that Musso would have more easily corrected the errors of the FDR if he had returned when Amir Sjarifoeddin was still in power."[148]

At this crucial moment in history, Amir stood exposed. According to *Locomotief*, the most widely read Dutch daily in Java, published in Semarang, East Java, now under Dutch authority, "Amir took off his mask as Moeso forced him to."¹⁴⁹ Indonesian papers, in the republican as well as the Dutch areas, increasingly wrote in the same tone. On a caricature published in several Indonesian papers, Amir appeared with Stalin with several *topeng*, Javanese dance masks, in front of them on a coffee table. The Soviet boss points out which one of the masks Amir should choose.¹⁵⁰

Amir now had been pictured perhaps most often as clumsy and indecisive. "It may be," wrote a historian, "that Amir, while considering himself a Communist, had never been forced to submit to party discipline, and had never held any formal place in the party hierarchy." Never, that was, till now.¹⁵¹

It might, however, have been otherwise: a moment of Amir's final and decisive *passage à l'acte*. "The authority of Amir Sjarifoeddin," recalls Soerjono, now also a self-declared Communist, "was still so great"; mistakes were made, but "we did not lay the blame on Bung Amir."¹⁵² And, in the late summer of 1948, Soerjono says, there was still not "any question of a loss of hope." "What Bung Amir was saying, was 'The arrival of our *ouwe heer* [Dutch for 'old man'] Musso means a *versnelling* [Dutch for 'acceleration'] of a process which was already developing among us."¹⁵³

When Prime Minister Mohammad Hatta recalled Soeripno from Prague, he was in his rights, and he acted in the spirit of the Renville Agreement. The agreement, among other restrictions, forbade the republic, until the final transfer of sovereignty, to open any official links with a foreign power.¹⁵⁴ Amir Sjarifoeddin, on his side, now out of the government, declared his opposition to Soeripno's recall.¹⁵⁵

The Hatta government and its allies presented this as major proof of the masks falling. According to Abu Hanifah, now fully on Hatta's side, still before Musso's arrival, "The FDR tried to make the most out of the fact [of a Soviet willingness to send a consul to Indonesia] and let it be widely known that Russia would shortly send arms, ammunition, and other material to the republic, by breaking through the Dutch blockade with Russian ships and planes."¹⁵⁶

On August 17, 1948, on the third anniversary of the proclamation of Indonesian independence and a week after Musso's arrival, Musso, Soekarno, and Amir attended a large public meeting in Jogjakarta. Arnold Brackman for the United Press, evidently, was there too: "Musso, Amir and Soekarno engaged publicly in a strained dialogue. Musso criticized . . . Hatta's cabinet, denounced Renville, and called for a creation of a strong national front. . . . Amir, in a spirit of self-indictment, said the republic had wavered in the struggle for independence. During the Japanese occupation Indonesia not only failed to build a national front, but 'cooperated' with the Japanese. . . . Since 1945, the republic had pursued the policy of 'cooperation' with the Dutch. . . . 'From now on,' Amir concluded, 'the revolution must be placed in the hands of revolutionary elements.'" Soekarno replied to both: "Let us together defend this republic as our common property," he said.[157]

To Musso, and perhaps to Amir, Soekarno might still have appeared as a possible Indonesian Beneš. A witness recalled Soekarno's visit to Madiun at this time, the center of the labor unrest, headquarters of Pesindo, and site of the Marx House. At a mass demonstration at the city central square, Soekarno stepped on the podium with Musso and Amir. Soemarsono was in charge of the Madiun administration, and he presided over the meeting.

"President Soekarno began his speech," a witness says, "and he addressed Soemarsono as 'Adinda,' Javanese endearing for a 'younger brother.' He also called him 'Kokrosono of Madiun.'"[158] Which brings back the memories of years ago when at one moment of his own political career Soekarno invoked Kokrosono as himself, a wayang figure, hero, hermit reappearing out of the wilderness with a miraculous weapon to reconquer an empire.

At that meeting, Musso stood on the podium next to Amir Sjarifoeddin and Soekarno. According to a Dutch agent also present, Musso began his speech: "I am Musso. Exiled in 1926. I returned [in 1935] to rebuild the Party with Sjarifoeddin and his friends. In the Japanese time they put them in jail, but the party lived on. . . . *Broeders* [Dutch for 'Brothers']! I thought I would speak to you in Javanese, but in the twenty years that I was away, I have forgotten much of it. Still, allow me to try and to say a Javanese word here and there [*Cheers*]." Musso ended his speech: "*Kameraden* [Dutch for 'Comrades']! I am tired now, and other speakers are waiting. Freedom!"[159]

After he came back to Indonesia, in several speeches Musso "savagely attacked Tan Malaka."[160] The split between the two, in 1926, had not been forgotten, when Musso supported the rebellion and Tan Malaka opposed it. And the animosity only grew more bitter through the twenty years when Musso was in Moscow and Tan Malaka parted ways with Communist International and eventually built his own Partai Repoeblic Indonesia, "Party of the Indonesian Republic." According to each man, the other betrayed the revolution.

The followers of Tan Malaka who had been caught and interned in the camp at Boven Digoel, alleged that Musso's followers, caught and in the camp as well, spread rumors of Tan Malaka's death and that they were even showing around the camp a faked photograph of Tan Malaka's grave.[161] When the news spread in the camp and outside it of Musso's reappearance on Java in 1935, and his actions to reestablish the Communist Party, Tan Malaka's people expressed doubts about Musso's very being in the Indies. *Menara Merah*, the illegal paper of Musso's followers at the time and later, was said to be either published in the Netherlands, and smuggled to Indonesia, by Dutch agents it was implied, or not existing at all, a phantom, an invention.[162]

After May 1948, as the tensions between Amir's FDR and the Hatta government were increasing and nearing boiling point, Tan Malaka's associates, and then Tan Malaka himself, were released from prison. The official explanation was that "no charges were brought against them."[163] The followers of Amir, and then Muss, and many others, were convinced that Hatta needed allies.

This might be the most calamitous development during the Indonesian revolution.

Roestam Effendi was an Indonesian who lived in the Netherlands between 1928 and 1947. Between 1933 and 1946 he was a member of the Communist Party of the Netherlands and a deputy for the party in the House of Representatives of the Netherlands. After the Soekarno and Hatta proclamation he returned to Indonesia like the others of the group from Holland, but he joined Tan Malaka. He was most efficient among the revolutionists, through his position and talent, in stirring up tensions. "At a public meeting in Jogjakarta on September 5, 1948, Roestam Effendi mentioned a secret, that Setiadjit and Maroeto Daroesman agreed behind the screen to conspire for a Dutch–Indonesian Union . . . together with a group of Dutch socialists [Schermerhorn, Logemann and others] . . . to work against the radicals [the Tan Malaka movement] in Indonesia."[164] At the same time, Roestam Effendi spoke about revelations about Amir's acceptance of Van der Plas's money. He "provided new ammunition," Brackman writes, to the Tan Malaka group in talking about the money "as proof that the PKI had collaborated with the Dutch; that it was a foreign agent."[165]

On September 9, 1948, in Jogjakarta, at the congress of the sugar labor union, a union leaning toward Tan Malaka, Amir reacted to Roestam and the atmosphere that was arising. "People say I have to hang. I am not afraid. In the difficult times, now behind me, I have trained myself well enough to be ready."[166]

There might have still been revolutionaries lingering on both sides. Very late in the story, on September 3, 1948, S. K. Trimurti, minister of labor in Amir's former cabinet in 1947, but also wife of Sajoeti Malik, a prominent follower of Tan Malaka, wrote an open letter to Setiadjit, now considered the most important figure on Musso and Amir's side:

Jogjakarta, September 3, 1948.
To Comrade Satyajit

Freedom!

Brother,
You know me for a long time, me and my soul, and this is why I am writing this letter to you. . . . I will be happy if also Comrade Musso, the

communist *djago* [champion, fighter, hero, fighting cock], whom I have also known for a long time, agreed to read the letter.

... Since 1935, I held the communist movement and its ideals in the highest esteem.... In 1936 I heard the name "Musso" for the first time.... Let me put it like that, I have become a communist-illegal.... Now, the return of Comrade Musso made me happy in my heart.

Trimurti went on and recalled a recent public meeting in Jogjakarta where she was present and where also Musso spoke. From the floor, Trimurti asked Musso a question: Was it possible to be a communist and not to be materialist at the same time? Musso, Trimurti wrote, "answered brusquely." In the Soviet Union, he only said, there was a freedom of religion. She insisted, and told Musso that it was not her question; what she meant was whether someone, for instance, who appreciated Kant or Hegel, might still be a communist. This time, he "answered sharply" [*dengan tegas*]. Who is with Kant or Hegel, Musso said, cannot be but "tentang," "against us." Musso added, losing patience with the woman it seems, "the stupid ones" should "just be ignored."[167]

Trimurti still wrote to Setiadjit,

There is a technical problem besides what I have written. I am a wife of Sajoeti Malik, a man who is looked at as a suspicious man by some PKI members, and I have some other ties with the people around Tan Malaka.... Those are, dear Comrade, the difficulties, technical and philosophical. They make me to hesitate. Should I become a member of the PKI or shouldn't I?

Yours comradely,
S.K. Trimurti.[168]

The hearts, to fall upon a cliché, were in flames. There is no sign of an answer to Trimurti by Setiadjit, by Musso, or by Amir. Instead, there were increasing signs of the amazing apparatuses being perfected, parts hardening, structures and formulas coming together and masks falling. Saying was passing *à l'acte*, and in the way the language was becoming barbaric and slaughter was coming with an increasing inevitability.

Abu Hanifah, Amir's former friend from Kramat 106, now an important figure in the Islamic Masjumi and very much "on the other side" still, in the critical days of August 1948, or it might even been in early September, visited Amir at his house in Jogjakarta. They had not seen each other for years. Abu Hanifah might still be thinking of saving Amir, separating him from Musso. Musso, however, as Abu Hanifah later recalled, was present when Abu Hanifah arrived: "Musso and Amir drank together [a] half bottle of whiskey during the meeting," Abu Hanifah wrote. He also wrote that he found Amir nervous. His inner equilibrium, wrote Abu Hanifah, appeared disturbed. The mission, in other words, failed.[169]

The stories from the other side multiplied: of Amir losing his inner balance, going down the slope or, at least, becoming nervous. Ali Sastroamidjojo recalled that:

> Amir Sjarifoeddin's attitude, which had been such a friendly one to me from the time of the PNI, Partindo and Gerindo, changed completely. He became hostile and did not want to talk to me. His wife, who was a very close friend of my wife, often came to our house in Jogjakarta, complaining about the complete change in her husband's behavior. He was often angry with her and had even threatened to beat her. This was very strange, because all the time my wife and I had known him, Amir had always given us the impression of being a loving family man.[170]

According to Ali Boediardjo, formerly of the Law School, then of Amir's circle, and still later, and now, solidly behind Sjahrir, in the summer of 1948 Amir, "fretted and was anxious, restless [*gelisah*] and got easily angry, so much that he often was not pleasant anymore to his wife and family, he drank too much alcohol, shouted when he was drunk, and was prone to make wrong decisions."[171] Talking to Frances Gouda in the mid-1980s, Soedarpo Sastrosatomo, another formerly of Amir's and now of Sjahrir's circle, described Amir at the time, adding another layer to all that, as "alternatively praying and drinking."[172]

To many, Amir was seen as a mystery. *Sin Po*, a Chinese-Indonesian paper published in Batavia/Djakarta, wrote in mid-September 1948:

> Although much came to be known about Bung Amir, he still remains a *mysterie* [the Dutch word is used in the otherwise Indonesian text for "mystery"]. His views are still not clear. He is still a contradiction. He is a Christian—but he admitted that he was a Communist. He signed [the] Renville Agreement—but he resists the Hatta cabinet which tries to implement the agreement. If it were not for the help by Soekarno and Hatta, he would have been executed by Japan—but now he makes it difficult for those two friends to go on working. He says he opposes Holland—and admits that he had accepted from Holland 25,000.[173]

He was seen carrying a little Bible, everywhere he went or, in other versions, carrying a prayer book. This must have been the prayer book written by the German Lutheran priest and missionary Hanns Lilje, which Ferdinand Tambubolon bequeathed to Amir when Ferdinand was dying in Oegstgeest, the Netherlands, in the house of the missionary widow Mrs. A. A. van de Loosdrecht-Sizoo.

Hanns Lilje was one of the writers Amir Sjarifoeddin had read in Schepper's house in Batavia during his student years, and perhaps, too, read and discussed with Schepper when he came to visit at the Soekamiskin prison. Now, it was a revolutionary space, Jogjakarta, Indonesia, Asia, Europe, and the world. Hanns Lilje, in the 1930s, became a prominent preacher of the anti-Nazi Confessional Church. His sermons in Berlin, and all over Germany, attracted thousands.[174]

In 1944, suspected by the Nazis of involvement, as a priest and confessor, with conspirators planning an assassination of Hitler, Pastor Lilje was arrested and spent the rest of the war in Berlin's Moabit prison—at the same time as Amir sat in prison in Java, by the way, and also under the constant threat of being executed. Hanns Lilje also survived and the little book in which he, after the war described his thoughts from prison, had been published in 1947. I have no doubt that Amir managed to get it and read it in these crucial, and final, months of his life.

"How grateful I am," Lilje wrote in the book, "to all my teachers who had made me learn by heart hymns and poems, Greek lyrics, Latin odes, Hebrew psalms."[175] He describes what courage he took in whistling "antiphonally" Lutheran chorales with a coprisoner in the next cell: "Oh for a thousand tongues to sing."[176]

Hanns Lilje's book might have been read by Amir as, kind of, his own autobiography. A life resting, as Lilje wrote, on "ethical will,"[177] on a trust in saying that does not lose its power as it passes to the act. Hanns Lilje wrote that "Lutheran Reformation leaders did admit that man has a right to resist authority.... It is very wrong to say that the Lutheran statement, 'The Christian's weapon against a godless government is the Word alone,' means that a good Lutheran can take no part in ordinary life. People who say such things say them because they have lost faith in the Word, that is the Word of God.... What mightier weapon can there be than this 'Word that breaketh the rock in pieces'!"[178]

What Hanns Lilje believed, as Amir might have read it, had to sound to Amir as Christian *and* Marxist, no contradiction and almost no *and*. "The political prisoners ... of *petit bourgeois* class have been all right," Lilje wrote about the Nazi era, the "shopkeepers," those who "dared to listen to the BBC," and who might even speak against Hitler "when they were a little tipsy." But there were "the genuine *political* prisoners—the Communists ... or the Trade Unions and those who had shared in the plot of the 20th July." And it was not "after all so very 'arrogant'" that they "insisted that they did not want to be included with such [petit bourgeois] companions."[179] Close to the end of his book Hanns Lilje wrote: "Many considerations led me to this conclusion. It is all very well to talk about righteousness, justice, and expiation; but if such ideas are to have any effect, they presuppose a social order which is still sound and is governed by such aims. But does such an order exist—now in 1945?"

Amir continued to preach. In Jogjakarta, during the spring and summer of 1948, in and then out of the government, he went on preaching.[180] One sermon in the largest Protestant church of the city, the HKBP (Huria Kristen Batak Protestan), is remembered in which he talked about Toyohiko Kagawa, a Japanese pacifist and Saint-Simonian socialist with whom he had reportedly at the time actually begun to correspond. Like Hann Lilje's, Toyohiko Kagawa's writings were debated in Schepper's house.

Professor Nico Schulte-Nordholt told me once about a talk he had with the Indonesian poet Sitor Situmorang. Sitor was in Jogjakarta in 1947 and 1948. All the churches, of course, he said, in the revolutionary capital were half empty if they were still open at all. It was, first, a revolutionary and, second, a Muslim place. But when Amir gave a sermon, Sitor said, the largest Protestant church in the city was packed. And after I told Nico Schulte-Nordholt about the story of Amir reading the Old Testament and Prophets in Japanese prison, he wrote me a letter, "Sitor fully seconded this: 'Yes,' he said, 'Amir used to refer to the Prophets when he gave his sermons.'" "In my opinion," Schulte-Nordholt added in the letter, "Amir was led by a deeply felt connection to follow the command of Micha 6:8 'Do right!'"[181] Ali Sastroamidjojo, not a great admirer of Amir any longer, wrote: "I myself heard him one Sunday delivering a sermon.... He explained the verses of the Holy Bible so beautifully that many of the congregation were moved to tears."[182]

Two months before Musso reappeared, Julius Schepper came to Jogjakarta. Out of the Japanese camp, he stayed in Indonesia for a while. In February 1948, on assignment for the Mission Council of the Netherlands, he left on a tour through the prewar mission stations in the Dutch-controlled as well as the republican areas of Indonesia. The mission published a report of the trip. "The chairman of the Netherlands Mission Council, Prof. Dr. J.M.J. Schepper traveled through Indonesia between February and May of this year. In Batavia he began by giving a reception to seventy persons . . . among them various Indonesians belonging to the republic."[183]

Schepper traveled to Makassar, Ambon, and Toradja, where the activity of the mission before the war had been strongest, to Timor and Borneo.[184] In May 1948, at the moment of impending crisis, Schepper visited republican territory. "In Jogjakarta," Amir's cousin, F. K. N. Harahap recalls, "Schepper stayed in the house of Amir Sjarifoeddin, who displayed a great respect for his former teacher."[185] According to the mission report, "In Jogjakarta, Professor Schepper visited [the] theological seminary and talked to students. There are five Javanese at present in the seminary from Central and South Java, one Javanese from

Poerwodadi [Central Java], twenty Sundanese [from West Java] and ten Chinese [Chinese Indonesians]." Then Schepper visited the "Sekolah Menengah Kristen ['Christian Secondary School'] which has [a] three-year curriculum, and now about 700 students. In the Petronella [former mission] hospital . . . he was shown around . . . by Pastor Tamboenan."[186] (Pastor Tamboenan baptized Amir in 1931, at the Kernolong church in Batavia and, in 1936, at the same church, he married Amir and Djaenah. Now, Tamboenan resided in Jogjakarta as the chairman of the Partai Kristen Indonesia, Parkindo, "Christian Party of Indonesia.")

The report on the trip continues:

> On the last evening of his stay in Jogjakarta, Prof. Schepper spoke to a group of about forty persons, all of them Islamists, about the problem of religious freedom. In the audience there also were several former students of the professor, a number of other lawyers, students of the republican university [in Jogjakarta] and some others. . . . Despite Prof. Schepper being quite outspoken about the great danger that, as he put it, the orthodox Islamic traditional churches [sic] pose in Indonesia, [a] calm and sympathetic atmosphere prevailed during the meeting, and this was in no way affected by the way questions had been asked and answered.[187]

Amir might have been present at the meeting, and he hosted Schepper in his house.[188] But not everything evidently went well. Henk van Randwijk, a well-respected Dutch journalist, close to the *Kritiek en Opbouw* circle before the war, who had known both Schepper and Amir well, met Schepper at that time and recalled: "Schepper appreciated Amir for his character and talents. But [as far] as politics was concerned, he thought Amir 'has a devil in himself.'" "These," Van Randwijk added, "are the words which Schepper used."[189] Devil indeed, it might be. Or, Schepper, perhaps, might have used the Kantian concept of radical evil.

Amir was still in office, in late 1947, when he arranged the formalities for Pastor Verkuyl to travel to the republican territory and visit Jogjakarta. "He himself," Verkuyl recalled, "took care of collecting all the documents we needed, and he put *drs*. Gransberg and me on the train."[190] In Jogjakarta, Verkuyl and Amir probably met for the last time. Pastor Verkuyl later wrote about his impressions of Amir at the time: "He was a deeply disappointed man. He had staked everything on 'Renville' . . . and he told me when we met, 'Now, . . . Soviet Russia is the only world power which still offers us friendship.' . . . I told him: 'Amir, you are like a man who stands close to an airplane. Each moment the propeller can catch your coat and pull you to your undoing.'" Amir answered, wrote Verkuyl, "He said that even Karl Barth [a Swiss Protestant theologian] warns against too severe a censure of communism." Verkuyl's impression was, he says, that "Musso played upon the feelings of this brilliant man."[191] Still later, Verkuyl wrote in a personal letter to Jacques Leclerc: "My impression is that you overestimate Amir's influence on the Christian community in Indonesia. He certainly did not enjoy confidence. He was regarded as a newcomer and his leadership was considered as being too whimsical, too much fixed upon ambitions and too little directed to vocation."[192]

Catholics might appear more perceptive than Amir's Protestant friends—to Amir's dilemma, and to Indonesian chaos, élan, revolution, and misery. It is doubtful, however, whether Amir even knew about it. In mid-1948, the Vatican sent its own observer, Monsignor de Jonghe d'Ardoy, to the Indies/Indonesia, and he also visited the republican territory. A summary of his report was published in the *Osservatore Romano*, the article found its way to Lieutenant-Governor General van Mook in Batavia/Djakarta and from there to the archives. "Communism in Indonesia makes progress," the monsignor reported.

> It is well organized, and it receives money from Moscow as well as from some of the Indonesian neighbors [?]. The disciples of Marx sow on receptive soil.
>
> The [Dutch] military occupation, so called "police action," ruined the country. In the intimate proximity of . . . great wealth, the people of Java suffer a gaping poverty. Workers in the factories and on the plantations are paid starvation wages.
>
> Social work is nonexistent. One should not be surprised that, according to the statistics, as of October of the last year, 850,000 plantation workers and 192,000 textile, transport, and sugar-industries workers, became members of the Communist Party.[193]

In May 1948, Sjafroeddin Prawiranegara (the author of the dandy-student song about "Those Women"), now a leader of Islamic Masjumi, approached Amir's cousin Harahap with a question "Is your cousin really a communist?" The question prompted cousin Harahap, wondering himself, as he says, to see Amir about it. Amir, Harahap later recalled, had reacted. "Read this book," he said. "It is by a bishop from Canterbury [*sic*], about church and state, and about the bishop's recent visit to the Soviet Union." "Simply put," Harahap wrote, "the way Amir talked has proved to me that in those last months his mind was wounded, and that the wound did not heal."[194]

Amir still found time to teach. "Officially, in 1948, Amir Sjarifoeddin had been promoted to professor at the Law Faculty of the Gadjah Mada University in Jogjakarta."[195] Amir in all probability knew about the martyrdom of Hanns Lilje in the Berlin Moabit prison. He certainly heard of the martyrdom of one of his former professors at the Law School—Van Asbeck's, Schepper's, and Logemann's colleague—Professor B. ter Haar, who died in Buchenwald.[196] P. J. Koets, who now served in Van Mook's administration, had known Amir since before the war, and now he had several intimate talks with him. In one of their meetings, Koets later recalled, Amir told him: "You Dutch held us on the leash in the most commendable manner. But you held us on the leash."[197]

Kritiek en Opbouw reappeared in Bandoeng. In a review in the magazine of the Indonesian young writer Idroes's *Soerabaja*, a short story that became an iconic representation of the early months of the revolution and the Battle of Soerabaja, Ida Nasoetion, at one time a lover of the poet Chairil Anwar, and the muse of his 1943 poem "An Ordinary Song," wrote: "a story of the people's resistance against the British, contains some excellent segments. As a whole, however, it is less successful because of its lack of style [*stijlloosheid*]. Episodes do not hold together in the narrative."[198]

After the Linggadjati Agreement of November 1946, and even more so after the Renville Agreement of January 1948, what had remained of the Indonesian republic was a multiple amputee. Life in Jogjakarta, the republic's capital, was like the beating of a heart of a gravely wounded body.

In daily news in Jogjakarta papers, "A doctor refused to visit a patient because the sick man was not rich."[199] In the Presidential Palace, Abu Hanifah recalls, "Every week Soekarno was giving lectures to the ladies of Jogjakarta in the palace. He very much enjoyed his weekly gathering of Jogjakarta intellectual families, mostly young and pretty. These lectures were afterwards published in his first book, *Sarinah*." This was the book Soekarno gave Musso when they met after the years. "There was a revolution going on as the country was in trouble, yet still most of the leaders appeared well groomed and at their best."[200]

On the gallery of the Constitutional Convention in Paris in 1792, Thomas Carlyle writes, as Robespierre spoke, "high-dizened women of conditions were rustling with laces and tricolor."[201] Soerjono, of Amir's youth, and still with him, wrote of life in Jogjakarta:

> In those days, there was a *warung* [stall] by the Gondolayu Bridge, right in front of the FDR secretariat, a bit off to the right. I still remember the girl who served the food there, though none of us knew her name. All we knew that we called her Ju Tien. The *warung*'s name wasn't at all wishy-washy. On the roofing above the door was attached in big letters: Warung Revolusi (Revolutionary Stall). Almost every day, around noon, the young people would gather there for lunch and even in the evenings they'd quite often take dinner at the Warung Revolusi.[202]

There is a large oil painting from the time by Soebijakto. A group of young men (there are only men), some in fatigues, most of them with heroic faces and ruffled hair, this could easily be in front of Ju Tien's Warung Revolusi. There is one face in the group, a face not so young anymore, a little in the background but, as if the painter did not respect the law of perspective, in a pre-Renaissance way, a little larger than the rest. It is the only one with glasses. It could be Amir's. (Only on a second look at the painting one can see that some of the men's hands are shackled. What was to come is suggested.)

"At Gololayu 13," Soerjono recalled, next to the Warung Revolusi, "the FDR secretariat occupied the front part of the premises. . . . At the rear was the headquarters of the Yogyakarta municipal branch of Pesindo, which also stored a 500 kg long-fuse bomb."

At that time, the élan increasingly manifested itself in street-wolf ways of life. Soerjono continued: "As one squatted there at the Warung Revolusi, among the things one gossiped about there was the armed clash that developed out of the football match between PSIM (Mataram Football Club) and Persidja (Jakarta Football Club). In what nota bene, the players consisted of boys from the Krawang Lasjkar Rakjat ['Krawang Militia'] and former players from Jong Ambon Betawi ['Young Ambon-Batavia'] who were now refugees in the Klaten area [northeast of Jogjakarta]; the secret 'Golden Chain' organization said to be a Dutch-organized spying utilizing beautiful girls; and the plantation workers at Delanggu; and the Hatta cabinet."[203]

Amir lived in Jogjakarta most of the time, with his wife and three small children. There were rumors that his wife was getting tired of the ways they lived. "A man who could be only described as the most extreme," wrote Amir's cousin Harahap again, "and who was with Amir day and night, month after month, was mr. Tan Ling Djie. . . . Zus [sister] Amir [Amir's wife], it increasingly appeared, felt 'less nice' about it, and whenever I came to Jogjakarta (which was about once a month) she asked me to stay a little longer."[204]

There were rumors that family might have been exerting pressure on Amir to retire from politics and, perhaps, even, to leave Indonesia. "The *Nieuwe Courant* of the nineteenth reported: 'Indonesian representatives are expected to attend the meeting of the World Council of Churches to be held this coming August in Amsterdam. The H.K.B.P. [the Protestant Batak Church] in Jogjakarta is going to propose two or three of its representatives from Java be sent to Amsterdam, namely mr. Amir Sjarifoeddin, drs. Harahap and mr. Tamboenan. The date of their departure was not yet announced."[205]

There might have been angels tempting Amir to go. At the First Assembly of the World Council of Churches to take place in August 1948 in Amsterdam as announced, Hanns Lilje, now Bishop Lilje, was to be present and preside as the chairman of Section I at the congress: "The Universal Church in God's Design"![206]

Amir's wife, Djaenah, told Jacques Leclerc in 1982 that in those months in the early summer of 1948 Amir became "very bitter" (*trés amer*) about being "abandoned by his most precious friends." She herself, she told Leclerc, pushed Amir to leave for Holland and she even asked, she said, "for help from Schepper" to convince Amir "to become a pastor."[207]

Helena Lucia, Amir's daughter, born in March 1949, after Amir's death, recalled later what she had been told as a child: "Mami said that papi talked about friends leaving him. Perhaps papi was *hopeless* [Helena Lucia says "hopeless" in English]. Papi was thinking about leaving government [*sic*] and going to Holland to study theology. But, mami said, there were people like Musso, and they often came to our house." "Our *ompung*," Helena Lucia used a Batak title of respect for a man, and almost certainly she meant Datoek Moelia, Amir's older cousin, who had helped Amir since his first visit to the Netherlands at least, a conservative Indonesian and a man of a solid position in postwar Indonesia as well. "Our *ompung*," said Helena Lucia, "suggested we go to Sidempuan [Padang Sidempuan, North Sumatra, where Amir's ancestral house was still standing]. Another plan was to go to Jakarta and then directly to Holland. The foster father of papi [did Helena Lucia mean Schepper?] was to wait there for us. We wished to go, but papi didn't. Papi was stubborn. *Ompung* was upset."[208]

Perhaps if Helena Lucia had been a bit older at the time, she might have seen her father differently. Like Odysseus, for instance, saw his father Laertes: "My father, / It must be that one of the gods who are forever / Has improved your looks, made you taller, and more handsome."[209]

Andrea, the elder sister of Helena Lucia, about eight years old at the time, came a little closer to Odysseus, and her Amir to Laertes, as she described her father at the time. In the same interview, she recalled how her father bought her a piano at the time and how he played a violin with her. "He liked very much to play violin," she said.[210]

Every Sunday they went to church and Andrea attended Sunday School. At home, the family read the Bible together every morning, and every evening after dinner. They had begun, Andrea said, with the Gospel according to St. Matthew and went, throughout, day by day, to the Revelation to John.[211]

"Papi liked to play violin," Andrea came back to this, "and piano, too. When I was little, I was already taught to play piano. And he liked to sing. His favorite song was 'Ise Do Ale-Ale Ta.'" "Ise Do Ale-Ale Ta" is a Batak version of Joseph Medicott Scriven's mid-nineteenth century Irish song "Pray without Ceasing."

"As for Christmas," Andrea said, and she had to be talking about their last Christmas together, in Jogjakarta, in 1947, "we celebrated it at home. Christian colleagues and friends of papi and mami were there and we sang together."²¹² "Of course we prayed."

> Each morning mami read to us from the Bible. In Dutch. She said that in Dutch it sinks in more. Also, at home, we spoke Dutch with mami. We were brought up the Dutch way. That is, we had to eat together; even when papi was busy, when he had some meeting, we had to eat together. We were taught by our parents the stern way.
>
> Papi was stern: "A" meant "A." It could not be made into "B," neither by us nor by mami. Uncle Ari [Harahap] said, "When papi becomes angry, do not say anything. Become invisible." But they liked to have fun with mami. In the past, mami said, he used to be very good with children and with young people in general.

Still Andrea:

> I was the first child born to them after seven years. Before me a baby was born but it died soon. I was, too, born prematurely, in the seventh month, and I was very little and often sick. Papi was frightened whenever I was sick. When he had to travel, he telephoned home, "How is Andrea, mama?" I was often angry and sometimes I almost hit papi. I cut my long hair, for instance. When he saw it, he wanted to hit me. He liked my long hair. I still remember, papi could become angry like that.

"As a husband, how was Amir Sjarifoeddin?" a journalist asked Helena Lucia who, of course, could only have heard about it from her mother.

> Mami said little about it. Not very close, because he was busy. He came and went. He just asked: "Have the children already eaten?" He talked with us for a little while, no longer than an hour, and he had to go. Sometimes he did not come home for two or three days. Sometimes for a week. They did not see each other often. But mami did not complain. It was the risk she had taken, remember. . . .
>
> However, when he was at home, in the morning and at night they prayed. Mami, when she was alone, prayed too. Sometimes I could not sleep, and I saw her through the open door as she prayed and sang.²¹³

Exactly two weeks after Musso and Soeripno arrived at Jogjakarta, two representatives of the Communist Party of the Netherlands, Paul de Groot and Gerber Wagenaar, arrived in Moscow. "On August 25, they asked for a meeting with the secretary of the Central Committee of the Communist Party of the Soviet Union, Suslov. During the meeting they gave Suslov a letter from the

Dutch Communist Party, suggesting that the Indonesian Republic should be helped in acquiring weapons in Czechoslovakia. There were illegal channels of [Czechoslovak] weapons sale to Israel and the channels should better be shifted to Indonesia. Or there is a possibility to buy arms officially in Sweden."[214]

During the same weeks, Dutch intelligence in the Indies/Indonesia was describing politics in the republic in increasingly dramatic, now-or-never terms: "Mass meetings are organized by Amir Sjarifoeddin, Maroeto Daroesman and Alimin, who all know how to whip the crowds into a frenzy, a talent with which even Dr. Soekarno cannot compete. Setiadjit can be heard in close circles saying that now it is up to them to make the Indonesian situation analogous to what has been happening in Greece and Czechoslovakia. His only worries are about 'the aggression' from the outside, against the national struggle of the republic. . . . According to the informant, Setiadjit is the *auctor intellectualis* of the FDR [sic]."[215]

At a meeting with representatives of the press, on August 22, 1948, in Jogjakarta, "for invited only," a Dutch spy managed to get in and sent a report of a meeting on fire: "Is there a possibility of a civil war?" Musso was asked. "It depends," he answered, "I hope it would not happen," and the spy added, in brackets, "(he said it with a sneer)." "Of course," Musso added, the agent reported, "it may come to a situation when the troops of the Soviet Union might be asked to come here on a short notice." "When Musso said this," the informant wrote, "I noticed that several automatic weapons were being displayed in the auditorium and in such a manner that I did not even feel at ease to go to the W.C."[216]

On September 7, 1948, *Sin Po* newspaper in Batavia/Djakarta reported another Musso speech under a doomsday headline: "In Three Weeks Russia Will 'Liberate' Indonesia." According to a Dutch intelligence report from the same days, time was up: "Third World War in Six Weeks, Says Musso."[217] On September 2, 1948, the *Nieuwsgier*, possibly the most widely read Dutch paper in Batavia/Djakarta wondered: "Is Amir sincere? He appears confused." "Perhaps," wrote the *Nieuwsgier*, "Moscow has not yet finish[ed] composing the song he is to sing."[218]

On September 4, 1948, the Dutch commissioner in the Indies/Indonesia wrote to the Dutch prime minister in the Hague: "It is quite possible that the republic, which is the Hatta group, may ask for our help." However, the Dutch official added, "I do not believe very much in such a possibility given the indecisiveness of the group."[219] On September 10, the Dutch ambassador to Washington cabled to the Dutch minister of foreign affairs in the Hague, that in the case of "a possible American–Russian conflict," "the importance of the countries of Southeast Asia would increase," while the "worries about stability of Indonesian nationalism are deepening after Sjarifoeddin took his mask off."[220]

Sjahrir, mostly invisible through these weeks, and mostly speaking through his followers, suggested that the republic rely on the United States as the solution. "Sjahrir's presence at Lake Success," wrote John Legge, "enabled him to make direct contact with representatives of other countries . . . and to observe the sharpening of tensions between the Soviet Union and the U.S. that he had already foreseen."[221] On September 7, 1948, the premier and Vice-President Hatta talked to the US consul-general in Batavia/Djakarta and, according to the consul's cable to Washington, he told him that in Indonesia "lines now were clearly drawn and are generally non-communist versus communist."[222]

The US secretary of state George C. Marshall answered the consul's cable two days later. "You may [at your] discretion communicate to Hatta following: the U.S. is ready to assist democratic non-communist moderate republican government in every practical way [to] successfully resist the Communist tyranny." However, the secretary of state added, the help should not get in the way of the US agreements with the Dutch. Nothing much more than financial help might be expected.[223] On the same day, Secretary Marshall wrote to the US embassy in the Hague that the Dutch government should be encouraged to support Hatta, "stressing the importance which U.S. attaches to bolstering the Hatta government at this juncture."[224]

The Dutch were aware that this, indeed, was a crucial moment, historically, for their empire, and that the initiative might be taken from their hands. "Hatta knew," wrote *Merdeka*, an Indonesian paper in Jogjakarta, in mid-September, "Dutch Foreign Minister Stikker was to arrive in the U.S. on September 16 for talks, which are aimed at convincing the U.S. officials that the republic was a hotbed of Communism and that the Dutch government would be doing the U.S. a favor if it decides to launch a new police action to put this problem to rest once and for all."[225]

"The man in revolt is ultimately inexplicable," philosopher Slavoj Žižek quotes Michel Foucault in a book on Maximilien Robespierre.[226] "One should be aware of the Kantian connotation of these propositions," Žižek adds, "a revolt is an act of freedom which momentarily suspends the nexus of historical causality."[227] This is, Žižek writes in another place, "What Lacan called a *passage a l'acte*."[228]

Like the groom-to-be in Nikolai Gogol's *Marriage*, who, at the very last moment, when the wedding ceremony is to be consummated, saves himself by jumping out of the window, or like Jesus on the Mount of Olives, at the last moment, too, and perhaps past it, asked his Father to reconsider, if possible,[229] Amir, perhaps, might still have had time to decide otherwise. "Of course, I understand it," wrote Kafka. "It's boring to stand for years in front of an ugly wall and it just won't crumble away."[230] "Well," Kafka wrote, too, "I usually solve problems by getting them devour me."[231]

Chapter 13

The Long March

> Do you lose your temper easily? I don't on the whole, but when I do, I really feel closer to God than at other times.
>
> —Kafka, *Letters to Felice*, December 12, 1912, 11

The disappearance of five military officers sympathetic to Musso and Amir in early September 1948 in Surakarta, a city sixty kilometers from Jogjakarta, was the breaking point. Rumors started immediately that the Siliwangi Division, the military unit most loyal to Hatta's government, was behind the kidnapping.[1]

Fighting broke out in Surakarta. The Barisan Banteng, "Buffalo Front," a militia close to Tan Malaka and now supporting Siliwangi, accused the pro-Musso and pro-Amir Pesindo of the kidnappings and then murder of the Barisan Banteng commander, Dr. Moewardi.

On September 13, 1948, the Siliwangi Division took control over the left-leaning city of Blitar and, on September 17, of Surakarta.[2] The troubles, however, came to a head in Madiun.

> In 1948, Madiun, with a population of two hundred thousand, was the third largest city in the [shrunken] republic after Yogyakarta and Solo [Surakarta]. It was situated in a fertile riverine plain bounded by a line of undulating limestone hills in the north. . . . Largely because of its strategic position at the crossroads between Central and East Java, Madiun evolved a sophisticated urban *priyayi* [*prijaji*, officialdom] culture and as a political and administrative city of some significance both before and after the Second World War. . . .

Some of the left's support in the residency came from the trade unions, especially the strong railroad unions, the plantation workers union, the unions of civil administration employees.[3]

Before the war Madiun presented an image of a good solid colonial city, and, sure, a possible tourist destination. According to the Stockum travel guide of 1930:

The town has a population of 32,732 of which 1,517 are Europeans.... The Chinese temple here is well worth visiting, while the large workshops of the State Railways and the Madioen irrigation works are of the utmost interest to engineers....

> *Clubs*: There are two clubs.
> *Banks*: Javaasche Bank.
> *Amusement*: One moving-picture theatre....
> *Excursions*: To Lake Ngebel...
> *Hotels*: Hotel Meerzicht [Lake View]... fl. 10.- per person[4]

Francisca Fanggidaej was back from Prague, Bulgaria, Yugoslavia, and India. She called the next chapter of her memoirs *Madiun Jadi Pusat*, "Madiun Becomes the Center": "I have never thought why Madiun was chosen as the seat of the Office of Struggle, of Pesindo, of the Marx House, and, in general, as the base of the left movement. I could only guess. First, Madiun was far enough from Surabaya, which became the stronghold of the [British and Dutch] occupational forces in East Java. Second, Madiun was not too far from Jogjakarta, the seat of the republican government.... Military consideration played the fundamental role."[5]

On the night of September 17–18, 1948, the day after the Siliwangi took over Surakarta, Soemarsono, acting as the chief administrator of Madiun, "in the interest of public calm," ordered some of the possibly disloyal army units in Madiun to be disarmed. The naval commander Supardi, a member of the Front Demokrasi Rakjat (FDR), "People's Democratic Front," was appointed the new resident of Madiun.[6]

At 7.30 in the evening on September 18, Radio Gelora Pemoeda, "Voice of the Youth," in Madiun, on 51m wavelength broadcast:

> At a mass meeting in Madiun, a resolution has been accepted, read by Soemarsono:
> [he spoke in Javanese]
> 1. dissolve Hatta cabinet [*applause*]; to be replaced by a cabinet working on the principles of the National Front; ...

2. revoke . . . the rights of foreign properties [*applause*] . . . cancel Linggadjati Agreement [*applause*] . . . cancel Linggadjati *and* Renville [*applause*].
3. end all negotiations with the Netherlands [*applause*].
4. introduce just distribution quotas for peasants and workers, enact agrarian reforms.
5. establish consular relation with the Soviet Union [*applause*].

"We are sending this resolution," declared Soemarsono,

1. to the people and the President of the Republic.
2. to the Working Committee of the National Council of the Republic.
3. to the central committee of the PKI in Jogjakarta.
   . . .
6. to the press.

Then, Soemarsono is reported as asking from the tribune: "Do you agree?" "Upon which," the transcript of the broadcast has it, "there was a loud laughter." "The ceremony [*sic*] had been concluded by signing of the *Internationale*."[7]

Musso, Amir, Setiadjit, Wikana, and Harjono, chairman of Serikat Organisasi Buruh Seluruh Indonesia (SOBSI), "All-Indonesian Federation of Workers' Organizations," were at that time on a speaking tour through the towns of East Java. They had departed from Jogjakarta a little more than a week earlier. "On September 7," wrote Amir's cousin Harahap, "Amir left Jogjakarta. It was the last time I saw him alive."[8]

On September 7, Amir Sjarifoeddin and his group were in Surakarta, on the eighth they were in Madiun, the eleventh in Kediri, the thirteenth in Djombang, the fourteenth in Bodjonegoro, the sixteenth in Tjepu, and the seventeenth in Purwodadi. The plan reportedly was to be in Madiun again on September 24.

It was in Purwodadi, 140 kilometers from Madiun, that they heard the Soemarsono broadcast. Instantly, according to the same information, Musso, Amir, and their party left for Madiun, "escorted by a heavily armed truck." George Kahin, a US student who managed to get to Jogjakarta in the previous months, and who was busily interviewing the republican leaders for his PhD thesis, later to become the classic, *Nationalism and Revolution in Indonesia*, wrote that in Purwodadi, Musso and his party "learned that the initiative had been taken from their hands. . . . They were presented with [a] fait accompli. The Communist revolution had begun."[9]

It is about three hours from Purwodadi to Madiun by car. Musso, Amir, and the others arrived at the house of Soemarsono on the outskirts of Madiun the same night. Here they talked to Soemarsono, and to Djokosoejono, another of Amir's admirers since before the war, now in charge of Madiun military affairs. "It is possible," wrote Kahin, "that once they had learned the full facts concerning the development in Surakarta, they would have themselves made the same decision as Soemarsono and Djokosoejono."[10] According to a later account by Soemarsono, "They stayed in my house. When they learned everything and they saw all, Pak Musso embraced me. . . . I was kissed by both," Soemarsono wrote, "Amir and Pak Musso."[11]

The leaders in Madiun, "Setiadjit, Musso and Sjarifoeddin," Dutch historian Henri Alers writes in his *Om een Rode of Groene Merdeka*, "To a Red or Green Freedom," "tried to contact Soekarno and Hatta in Jogjakarta." "It is not probable," he adds, "that they succeeded but it cannot be said with certainty."[12] According to another source, "On September 18, Musso offered to settle the uprising [sic] if Hatta would include PKI [Communist Party of Indonesia] in his government."[13]

Colonel Nasoetion, however, in charge of the Siliwangi Division and present in Jogjakarta at the moment, described the situation without much tiptoeing around it, as an opportunity. The time had come, at last, he wrote later, for decisive action by the army, namely Siliwangi, against the troublemakers. Revolution should be ranked, channeled, and rationalized once for all and fully. Recalled Nasoetion:

> On September 18 in the evening, we received the news about the uprising [sic]. At [that time] the *Panglima Besar* Soedirman was out of town. I got to the palace. . . . Members of the cabinet were arriving for [a] meeting, but it was difficult (it was Saturday night) to get them all together. I asked the President what measures he would take. His answer was that it was to be discussed by the cabinet.
>
> In my view it would be too late because every wasted hour meant increasing danger. . . . I quickly prepared a draft of an order by the President. . . . He agreed but decided to wait till the cabinet met which could happen at best at midnight.
>
> Being certain, however, that the order would be issued, I made concrete preparations.[14]

"A cabinet session had been called," recalled Colonel Simatoepang, who was also present. "In a conversation outside the meeting Bung Karno asked me, 'Wat wil die Amir toch?' [Dutch for: 'What does that Amir want?'] but Bung

Hatta said: 'Now it is a question of life and death,' ['Er op of er onder,' Dutch for, 'Hop or drop']."[15]

Nasoetion and Hatta, clearly, called it a day and Soekarno, perhaps, tried to stay in the saddle of the balking horse of the revolution. After the cabinet meeting, at 10:00 p.m. that night, however, President Soekarno went onto Jogjakarta state radio:

> Brothers,
> ... Yesterday morning the Communist Party of Musso staged a coup in Madiun and formed a Soviet government there under the leadership of Musso.
> ... you and I are experiencing the greatest test, to make a choice between following Musso and his Communist Party, who will obstruct the attainment of an Independent Indonesia, or following Sukarno–Hatta, who, with the Almighty's help, will lead our Republic of Indonesia to become Independent Indonesia which is not subjected to any other country whatsoever. ...
> ... We shall win if the Almighty wills it. Freedom! Freedom Forever![16]

"In spite of its crucial importance," wrote Jacques Leclerc, "it will probably never be known why on 19 September 1948 Sukarno decided to turn the incidents in Madiun into a civil war by denouncing the proclamation there of a Soviet republic. This proclamation, however, had not actually been heard by anyone and nobody bothered to verify the report which had quoted it."[17]

Through these hours, the members of the Politburo of the PKI, Tan Ling Djie and Abdoelmadjid remained in Jogjakarta. Waiting? They had been arrested. The families of the leaders of the uprising remained in Jogjakarta as well, including the family of Amir.[18]

Soekarno's radio speech was heard in Madiun. Whatever Musso, Amir, Setiadjit, and the others might have expected, or planned, they were now not given much choice. Ninety minutes after Soekarno's speech ended, Musso spoke on Madiun radio. With rolled-up sleeves, should we say? It was the decisive moment of the decisive months of his life and, as he certainly saw it, of the revolution, too. *Er op of er onder*. Musso spoke:

> On September 18, 1948, the citizens of Madiun seized the authority of state in their own hands [*sic*]. With that the citizens of Madiun have done their duty in our national revolution, which as a matter of fact must be led by the people and not by any other class.
> Our revolution has continued for three years under the leadership of the national bourgeois class, which has always been uncertain and vague

in its stand in fighting the Imperialists in general and America in particular....

... Soekarno, the ex-Romusha dealer [*Romusha*, the forced-labor program during the Japanese occupation].

"Soekarno," Musso went on, burning other bridges, "released Tan Malaka, a criminal." "The happenings in Madiun and elsewhere are a signal to the whole people to take the power of the state into their own hands.... The people of Indonesia were asked by Soekarno to choose Soekarno or Musso.... We are certain that the people will say: 'Musso always serves the people of Indonesia.'"[19]

The next day, Hatta spoke to the Working Committee of the KNIP, "Central Indonesian National Council," laying out for them what it would mean if the other side had it its way: "Musso becomes the President of the republic and *mr.* Amir Sjarifoeddin the Prime Minister."[20]

On the same day, the Islamic "Masjumi head Soekiman called for a holy war against communism."[21] This had been, of course, Koranic wisdom not to be doubted:

There shall be the people of the right hand.
While they who disbelieve our signs,
Shall be the people of the left.
Around them the fire shall close.[22]

"The thought of Muslims taking independent action," Ann Swift wrote in her history of Madiun, "horrified non-Muslims, and within a few days the PSI [Sjahrir's party] loudly demanded that only official government troops be used against the PKI."[23] Otherwise, however, about Sjahrir's position there was to be no doubt: *"Statement by Sjahrir's Socialist Party, Jogjakarta, September 21, 1948. The Madiun Affair on its surface appears revolutionary but it is reactionary or even counter-revolutionary in its essence."*[24]

The Dutch were watching. On September 22, the representative of the queen in the Indies/Indonesia Lambertus Neher, in a cable to the Dutch prime minister in the Hague wrote: "In connection with the reports on the taking over [of] Madiun by the PKI, I worry that repercussions in the areas of Java controlled by us cannot be excluded. I recommend the highest vigilance."[25] On September 30, commanders of Dutch military forces in the Indies/Indonesia met with their chief, General Spoor:

Minutes of the meeting in the house of the army commander on September 30, 1948:

... The army commander Spoor gave an exposé of the military-political situation in connection with the latest reports on the Madiun events. . . . He pointed out that this was the key point of history. . . . The only correct policy is to push for an action towards Madiun, and also towards Jogjakarta. With the eyes upon the rain season coming in the middle of the next month, it is urgent to act quickly.

Besides, the minutes say, "His Excellency Beel [high commissioner for the Dutch East Indies] is extremely worried about what the Russians might do."[26]

All history in the end is global history and Indonesia had been opened to the modern. As for the United States, hours after Soemarsono's coup, on September 20, H. Merle Cochran. who took over from Frank Graham as the chief of the US delegation at the now moribund negotiations, told Hatta as they met in Jogjakarta, "I cabled [State] Department republican communique on action against Communist uprising. I said while outbreak [is] regretted, crisis gives republican government opportunity [to] show determination [to] suppress communism."[27]

A correspondent of the *Times of India* in Batavia on September 21 reported under the headlines:

> *Premier of "Red" Regime in Java*
> Indonesia's former Socialist Premier, Dr. Amir Sjarifoeddin was today reported to have become Prime Minister of the new "Communist republic" in Java under the presidency of Musso, 50-year-old ex-teacher who returned from Moscow 37 days ago.[28]

According to the *New York Times*, already two days before Soemarsono's coup: "Army Seen Facing Stalinists."[29]

Soekarno's speech on September 19, Soemarsono recalls, was received in Madiun as a bad sign. "When Bung Karno spoke, we were all shocked. It was not a guessing anymore. It was clear that Hatta's government borrowed [*memindjam*] Bung Karno. The President's voice had been known to the people. If Hatta spoke, it would be different. But this was Bung Karno. 'My beloved people,' he said." As Soekarno spoke, says Soemarsono, "it struck Pak Musso in his heart. Yes, he changed."[30]

In *Front Nasional*, the official paper in Madiun, the next day, September 21, the lead article was signed by Musso, in which he, according to Kahin, "took pains to point out that the Madiun coup was not directed to the establishment of a Soviet government. . . . Only at a later date, after completion of the national revolution and the commencement of a socialist revolution would a Soviet government be established." It was Soekarno and Hatta, Musso wrote, who "betrayed" revolution. He expressed a hope, nevertheless, that there still existed "progressive bourgeois elements that might understand and put themselves behind the movement in Madiun."[31]

Djokosoejono, too, the military principal of the events, went on Madiun radio claiming that the events in Madiun were not an uprising against Soekarno and Hatta. The events were only an attempt at a "correction."[32] A speech by Soeripno, "equally mild," says Kahin, was broadcast the same night.[33]

"Between September 22 and 23," wrote Soemarsono, "I received in Madiun Lt. Col. Soeharto, a messenger from *Panglima Besar* Soedirman."[34] Fifty years later, Soeharto, now the Indonesian president, wrote about the moment: "On arrival at Madiun, I was to meet Amir Sjarifoeddin, whom I already knew, but he was asleep. Then someone else came in, and I was aware it was Musso. . . . We began to talk freely, but I didn't mention that Pak Dirman [Soedirman] had sent me there."[35] According to Soemarsono, Amir was woken up. "Bung Amir then wrote a letter to President Soekarno, despite the fact that Soekarno had already given the speech—Amir wrote the letter to calm the situation. . . . He wrote the letter himself. I have not read it. . . . There had still been some hope for peace. This was why the letter was not addressed to Hatta but to Bung Karno." Soemarsono continues: "Later we heard that Soeharto had been detained by Siliwangi in Sregan [a town between Madiun and Jogjakarta]. The letter did not reach President Soekarno. What happened with Soeharto's report to General Soedirman I also do not know, . . . I only heard that Soeharto was detained by Siliwangi. I do not know what happened to Amir's letter."[36]

The day Soeharto left Madiun, September 23, Amir Sjarifoeddin went on Madiun radio. It was, Kahin says, "the last recorded broadcast by a member of the top PKI leadership," and the last broadcast ever by Amir: "The struggle we are carrying on here is no more and no less than a movement to correct the evolution of our revolution. Therefore, the basis remains the same and never changing. The revolution according to our consideration remains one which is national in character, which can be called a revolution of bourgeois democrats. Our constitution remains the same one; our flag is the same red and white; while our national anthem is none other than the *Indonesia Raja*."[37] Nasoetion quoted a different part of the same speech: "We are not afraid of government using force to suppress the people's struggle. The government of the republic, with every passing day, distances itself from the people, from the people's struggle."[38]

George Kahin, in order to get a press pass in Jogjakarta, occasionally reported about day-to-day events in Indonesia as a reporter of the US Overseas News Agency. On September 23, 1948, Dutch intelligence intercepted one of his cables which he was sending through India. Kahin reported: "dutch distortion of news coming out of Indonesia great—stop—all foreign correspondents are in dutch controlled area—stop— . . . threat and potency of communist coup greatly exaggerated by dutch—stop—chief fear of republic is dutch attack—stop—. . . *habis* [end]."³⁹

Van der Plas was still watching. He was still stationed in Surabaja as the Dutch Recomba, Regeringscommissaris voor Bestuursaangelegenheden, "Government Commissar for Administrative Matters," for East Java. He collected reports by various informants in the republican area, including in Madiun:

> **Data from the republican areas**
>
> . . . In Madioen, in fact, there was no fighting. Except for the telegraph office no building was damaged. . . . According to two of my informants, the population in and around Madioen is under a strong communist influence, without having any real understanding of what communism as an ideology means. . . . Terror by the Siliwangi troops is a cause for a great unease among the population.
>
> The communists, in their turn, are reported to be acting especially against the *kijais* [Islamic religious leaders]. . . . In Poerwodadi they stuffed a dead dog in a *bedoeg* [a big drum with which the prayers in mosque are announced]. Equally offensive and disgusting is, however, when the government troops leave behind unburied corpses of their victims.

While there still might be some attempts at "clearing the misunderstanding," the killing began and expanded. There is a handwritten note on the margin of one of the reports to Van der Plas's office from Madiun, a note probably written by Van der Plas himself: "An Indonesian, a Catholic and of a good standing, a self-declared republican and anti-communist, has told me last Thursday with much indignation that he had heard on the republican radio how Sjarifoeddin, Maroeto Daroesman and Soeripno, as they were on a podium on the Madiun central square, were spat upon and called the dirtiest of names. My informant, found such kind of reporting unworthy of the republic, yet fully in the style of what the government is now doing."⁴⁰

On the night from September 28 to September 29, 1948, ten days after the uprising began, as misunderstandings were not cleared, and also as the masses did not rise up in response to Musso's appeal to make a choice between him and Soekarno, and as the Siliwangi advance units approached Madiun, the military and civilian forces of the FDR in Madiun, officials and their families if the families happened to be in the city, and a large number of civilians, in separate columns, led by Musso and Amir, left Madiun. Without firing a shot.

"Musso and his aides fled the city," reported Dutch intelligence monitoring Madiun radio. "The Communist regime in Madiun collapsed."[41]

Already on the third day of the Madiun affair, September 21, the vital services of state infrastructure on republican territory, telephone and telegraph, were taken over by the army, specifically Siliwangi and Nasoetion. Electricity and gas followed on September 27, roads and highways on September 28, all motor transportation on September 30, public works on October 10, enterprises under the Ministry of Finance on October 22, printing businesses on October 23, oil industries on October 30, sugar industries, plantations, textile industry and forestry on November 11.[42]

There is a photograph of seven army commanders who defended the republic against the coup, seven officers, not really smiling, facing the camera with a relaxed self-confidence. The caption says: "Gatot Subroto and his fellow officers; from left, Slamet Rijadi, Soeharto [the one who did not deliver Amir's letter], Soeadi, Sarbini, Gatot Subroto himself, Bachrun, and A. Jani."[43]

Caricatures appeared in the same Indonesian republican newspapers and magazines. Most expressive are those by Ramelan. One of them shows the majestic volcano southeast of Madiun, Mount Wilis. A hairy beast, three-quarters of the size of the mountain, a bear or a boar, hovers and falls hopelessly down the slope of the mountain. The monster, it is painted on it, is "PKI-Musso." A tiny puppet-like figure, a mannikin, in shorts, its matchstick-like arms and legs are flying in the air in all directions. As if it were not clear from the midget's dark horn-rimmed glasses, it is written with white letters on its shorts: "AMIR."

Still, an officer, it is made clear by a military cape, with a shade of moustache, clubs the beast as it falls—with a chair for some reason. "AMIR," clearly, is the next to be dealt with. On the chair, again to make the message clear, in capital letters, is written "MADIUN." On the officer's cap there is "SILIWANGI," the officer's left hand free of chair holds the Indonesian flag, the red and white.[44]

The Communist Party of the Soviet Union might have been deciding what action to take. None, really, was taken in the end. As for the West, the Dutch ambassador in Washington wrote to the Dutch minister of foreign affairs in the first hours of the Madiun Affair, on September 22, that the Americans were watching whether "the republican government proves to be capable to recapture Madiun and prevent further sovietization by its own force."[45]

On September 25, the consul general of the United States in Batavia/Djakarta dispatched one Arthur Campbell to the republican capital "with a message to Hatta." Campbell, working for the CIA (Central Intelligence Agency), departed at 7:00 a.m. by a special plane to Jogjakarta, he met with

Hatta, and he came back on the same plane at 7:00 p.m. of the same day. Hatta's message for the Americans, which Campbell carried back to Batavia/Djakarta, was:

1. Favorable military situation to republic will be achieved in about 10 days in Madiun.
2. Republic has 7 battalions (battalion is about 750 men) attacking and Communists have about 5 battalions defending city; lack of transportation hindering republican troops. . . .
4. About 400 Communists are under arrest at Jogjakarta.
5. Hatta feels situation is in hand.[46]

The Dutch ambassador in Tokyo (because of the US occupation of Japan, it was to Asia a second Washington), as Siliwangi established itself in Madiun, sent a telegram and some Japanese newspaper clippings to the Dutch minister of foreign affairs:

The *Nippon Times* of October 10 (U.P. dispatch)
One U.S. official said that "Madiun" fall constitutes the first time that the Communists sustained a major defeat in Asia or in the world by forces of arms, since the war's end.

"United States circles here," wrote the ambassador in the telegram that went with the clippings, believe the fall of Madiun "strengthens Hatta's position" because:

1. It presents concrete evidence that the republican government is non-Communist
2. It offers proof that the republic is strong enough to put down such a disturbance.[47]

On October 11, another telegram, again coded, was sent by the Dutch embassy in Tokyo, this time to the Dutch office in Batavia/Djakarta:

From: Van Adenaard, Tokyo
To: Stikker and Elink Schuurman, Batavia-Djakarta
Secret.
Yesterday I had a meeting with MacArthur, about Indonesia.

General Douglas MacArthur, who was overseeing the US occupation of Japan, perhaps the most important US figure in the East at the time, was not easily convinced that all was well and over in Indonesia after the fall of Madiun. The ambassador wrote:

In his vision, the recent events in the republic must be still seen as give-and-take squabbles between groups fighting for power and which . . . all of them more or less are communist influenced and infiltered. . . . He believes that Moscow has been significantly involved in the events and suspects that it is content with the successes of Hatta.

There is a danger, he says, that, as for Hatta's successes, the situation in Indonesia may be understood in a wrong way.[48]

The Dutch were still not sure either. "I saw [the] Foreign Minister," reported the US ambassador in the Netherlands to the secretary of state on September 26, 1948. "They feel that Hatta [is] not great impeccable national figure and understand he is already dealing with Musso, Alimin and Sjarifoeddin for compromise and their voice in republican government."[49]

The Dutch authorities in Batavia/Djakarta became nervous that the new situation might affect the position of the Netherlands in the Indies/Indonesia finally and fatally. Elink Schurman, a Dutch delegate in the Indies/Indonesia wrote to the foreign minister in The Hague on October 18: "I receive lately the increasingly strong impression from my contacts with British and American representatives and with the American delegation that these circles are planning to support the Hatta's regime at any cost."[50] The Dutch tried to prove that they were still in play but they saw their position increasingly depended on Great Britain and especially on the United States. On October 19, a confidential and coded telegram was sent by the Dutch to the US delegation on the United Nations Committee of Good Offices in Indonesia:

> As you are no doubt aware the unrest in republican territory was yet by no means satisfactorily subdued by republican authorities. . . . At [the] oil center of Tjepoe new fires are continually breaking out and the fires occur over considerable areas. Netherlands government wishes to draw attention of CGO to existing danger that vital economic interests not only of Indonesia but of [the] world at large might be jeopardized beyond repair. Netherlands government feels as sovereign power it bears ultimate responsibility. . . . If republican government should not be able to cope with it, Netherlands government would, if requested, be prepared to render immediate assistance for the purpose.[51]

"As it was becoming clear," wrote a Dutch observer who was there at the time, "through the month of October, as Hatta was able to keep himself in power, and as the republic bloodily suppressed the communist rebellion with completely unexpected energy, the stocks of the republican government with the Americans went up considerably."⁵² An Indonesian semi-official history of the time, titled *Lahirnja Satu Bangsa*, "The Birth of a Nation," wrote: "Madiun changed the view of the United States as regard[ing] the republic. The republic became the only state in East Asia which had been able to put a stop to the incursions by agents from Moscow."⁵³

Amir, Musso, Soemarsono, Djokosoejono, Soeripno, with the units of Pesindo and the other loyal army units and militia, with civilians and their families, fled Madiun without firing a shot.

Throughout the Indies/Indonesia, through newspapers, radio, through leaflets distributed in towns and villages, through graffiti on the walls, government controlled the narrative. Musso, Amir, and the others were on the run—they were running from justice, from the republic as it had been proclaimed by Soekarno and Hatta, from the nation. And, as it appeared in the republican media, too, Musso, Amir, and the others were on the run to get across the line, into the areas controlled by the enemy, the Dutch.

In his meeting with the new Dutch foreign minister Dirk Stikker, who arrived in the Indies/Indonesia on November 6, 1948, in Jogjakarta, Hatta said: "Now, when he [Amir Sjarifoeddin], with a small group of fanatical followers, is locked in the mountains, he might take his struggle into the Dutch areas."⁵⁴

On November 27, in another meeting with the minister, Hatta informed him that Amir and those with him "move on foot through forests and are followed by the government troops also on foot." The distance between the two was kept about the same. This meant that Sjarifoeddin's group was not soon to be annihilated or even attacked. Hatta asked Stikker and other Dutch officials present what the Dutch side would do if Amir crossed the line. The Dutch assured Hatta that "they would be arrested and held in prison."⁵⁵

One version of this traitors' narrative was that Amir and the others might turn toward Patjitan, the nearest port from Madiun, on the south coast of Java.

"Excursions from Madiun: To Patjitan," one could read in the Stockum tourist guide of 1930:

> Passing through Ponorogo and Slaoeng one reaches Tegalombo in the Duizendgebergte, "Thousand Mountains." . . . From there the road leads through the beautiful valley of the Patjitan river to Patjitan on the South coast, where there is a small provincial hotel.⁵⁶

Through the port of Patjitan, across the sea, a possible escape route might lead to the Dutch area.⁵⁷

There is another caricature by Ramelan that appeared in the pro-government press as Amir, Musso, and the others were on the run. A banteng, Indonesian for "wild buffalo," symbol of the Indonesian nation, is shown in a life-and-death combat with a *leeuw*, Dutch for "lion," which is Holland. The banteng fights valiantly; however, a vicious dog can be seen snapping at his tail. The letters on the mongrel, again, say "Musso."[58] Yet another Ramelan caricature shows a tiny boat on stormy sea. The boat is the republic. There are little figures packed in the boat, all recognizable as the leaders of the republican non-Communist political parties. One figure, a little apart from the others, marked "PKI," does what it can to rock the boat. "HATTA" stands at the rudder and tries to keep the nutshell of the vessel afloat.[59]

Leaflets were being distributed throughout the area. One of them found its way to the Special Collection at the Leiden University Library: "These agents of foreign powers! These gamblers with the fate of the nation! Their disguise, however, is now dispelled!"[60] The newspaper *Merdeka*, "Freedom," wrote in September 25, as Madiun was taken by Siliwangi, to explain what was happening: "Amir Sjarifoeddin is in the employ of the Dutch. He has received 25,000 guilders."[61] Colonel Nasoetion, now the main figure of the military campaign recalled: "Amir and his friends were now like in the proverb: 'Een kat in 't donker maakt rare sprongen' [Dutch for 'In the dark, cat makes strange jumps']."[62]

In mid-October 1948, as Amir, Musso, and the others were on the run for two weeks, there was a debate in the Working Committee of the KNIP in Jogjakarta. "Minister of Justice Susanto Tirtoprodjo . . . was asked what was the proof that PKI Musso–Amir worked with the Dutch. The minister said that until now he was not shown documents concerning the matter, but that pennants and badges of the Dutch Navy, both ordinary sailors and officers, had been found in the PKI Musso–Amir headquarters." "In any case," Minister Susanto added, "all those who are active in this movement or are suspected of assisting the movement, had to be quickly captured."[63]

There might be a design behind the Siliwangi troops merely following, on foot, at a steady pace, as Hatta told the Dutch foreign minister, remaining at a distance and avoiding the final encounter. There is a possibility that Amir's and Musso's columns were to be pushed along the traitors' route, across the line, and to the Dutch.

Or Amir and Musso were not giving Siliwangi a chance; not losing hope. From Madiun, Amir's and Musso's columns moved toward Dungus on the slopes of Mount Wilis—yes, the volcano in Ramelan's caricature—nine kilometers from Madiun, to establish a base in the mountains, to make a stand, and perhaps to launch a counterattack, or to start a guerilla war. Then, the plan might be, to push further, from Dungus to nearby Kandangan where, as the rumors had it, Amir had stored a large amount of weapons in secret depots when he was the minister of defense, to prepare for resistance against the widely expected next Dutch attack.⁶⁴ "Long before the Madiun Affair," Hariandja, one of Amir supporters and associates later recalled, "at the Mount Wilis complex between Madiun and Kediri, we set up a radio station, storehouses of rice and textile etc."⁶⁵

This plan, however far it was a plan, failed. The Siliwangi troops seemed to learn about the plan, and they moved quickly and occupied the Dungus base before Musso's and Amir's people arrived.⁶⁶

What the next move should be, except surrender, became unclear possibly even to the people who led the columns. However, if surrender was rejected, this still would be revolution. "They went," Thomas Carlyle wrote about the other revolution, "amid the infinitudes of doubt and dim-peril; they not doubtful: . . . Dusty of face, . . . they plod onwards, unwearable, not to be turned aside. Such march will become famous."⁶⁷ At least this could be a self-image Amir's people had. "Somebody among those on the run," wrote Francisca Fanggidaej, who joined Amir's column on the first day in Madiun, "began to call the running 'the Long March.'"⁶⁸

Edgar Snow, a young American in China wrote about the original Long March of the Chinese Red Army in 1934–1935 from Kiangsi to the northwest: "They had only 6,000 able-bodied regular troops, and 20,000 wounded, sheltered among the peasants. . . . From the farthermost point in Fukien to the end of the road in far northwest Shensi . . . it was one long battle, from beginning to end."⁶⁹ Mao Tse-tung wrote a poem about the march for Edgar Snow when he reached him at his base:

The Red Army, never fearing the challenging Long March, . . .
Looked lightly on the many peaks and rivers.⁷⁰

Besides Thomas Carlyle and Mao Tse-tung, Niccolò Machiavelli could have been on Amir's mind, if he thought of books as he marched: "As for action," Machiavelli wrote, the prince "must also continuously go out hunting, keeping his body accustomed to hardship, while learning the lay of the lands how the mountains rise and the valleys dip, how the plains lie, and the nature of the rivers and marshes." "A prince who lacks this knowledge, lacks the most essential quality in a general."⁷¹ Amir, as far as I know, was an urban boy.

"Marsdjauh," "Mars Djauh" [literally "Far March," "March to Far"] was what they called the Long March in Indonesian. Soemarsono, who walked with Amir and Musso, recalled: "Orders were issued so that the column would not be surprised while resting. If we were forced to resist, we would, if there were a chance to reconquer some ground, we would. Amir said: 'Why should not we be able to take Madiun back?' . . . It was matter of numbers, how many battalions, how many companies. But first, we had to avoid being destroyed."⁷²

Nasoetion in his published account, reproduced a map that Siliwangi used in its campaign.⁷³ The Stockum tourist guide of 1930, in a different sequence, describes the same route and landscape:

From Surakarta via Madioen and Kertosono to Sourabaja

From Solo [Soerakarta] the main line of the State Railways extends to Sourabaja . . . it does not offer much splendid scenery.

It runs for the greater part through a flat country, chiefly planted with rice, sugarcane, and other crops of the lowlands, near Sragen and Madioen teak forests are to be seen. To the right the country is very mountainous. After leaving Solo and beyond Sragen the principal mountains are the Lawoe (or Emperor's Mountain), (3265 meters), just before coming to Madioen, the Wilis (2556 meters), the Kawi (2868 meters), the Kloet [or Keloed] (1731 meters) and the Ardjoeno ranges (3339 meters), all south of the line.⁷⁴

Giorgio Agamben wrote about *Homo Sacer*, a person excluded from the civic order. "Perhaps the reason why immigrants worry settled people so much (and often so abstractly)," wrote Marc Augé, "is that they expose the relative nature of certainties inscribed in their soul."⁷⁵

The whole landscape around Madiun, and the territory of the republic now centered on Madiun, shuddered. It surged and plunged with its inhabitants becoming slowly, imperceptibly, or suddenly and flagrantly "excluded from the civil order," becoming "immigrants" and "worrying settled people." People with weapons were on the run, or marching. The whole landscape became a landscape on the run, the *paysage*, indeed, the "passage." The moment pushed its way "up inside the landscape."⁷⁶

People were lost, wrote Thomas Carlyle about the French Revolution, "in the confluence of infinitudes."⁷⁷ People with weapons or without found themselves in the revolution. "The present location of mountains and rivers, fields and green steppe, forest and maritime coasts," wrote Leon Trotsky about revolutionary Russia, "should be by no means considered as final."⁷⁸ "Here, at last," writes Isaac Deutscher, "Trotsky unfolds his vision of man in the realm of freedom, and up-to-date Marxist version of it: 'Equal, unclassed, tribeless, and nationless, exempt from awe, worship, degree, the king.'"⁷⁹ Or, thinking of Amir, Marxist, Christian, revolutionary, possible hero in the concrete utopia, in the landscape revolutionary and divine: "For God, history is a landscape of events. For Him, nothing really follows sequentially, everything is co-present."⁸⁰

In the Dutch intelligence archive on Madiun, now in the Hague, there is an eleven-page typescript, by a teacher at the Pondok Modern, "Modern Boarding School," in Ponorogo, a town about thirty kilometers south of Madiun, dated November 3, 1948. It is a diary the teacher wrote, on the run, through the surging and shuddering landscape, "amid the infinitudes," homeless.

Notes on "Modern Boarding School" during CHAOS caused by PKI–Musso and his associates.

Introduction
The week before chaos.

Atmosphere was calm and happy. All 200 students, teachers, and staff were busy getting ready for the beginning of classes.... New furniture was being installed in the kitchen.... During the prayers, the mosque was full.... Still nobody knew about the *Coup*....

September 18. Rumors were heard but nothing was clear. However:

a. trains stopped running
b. police disappeared
c. guards left the prison
d. PKI got on the move....

September 19. Market was empty and panic started.... In the evening people talked about the Red Army coming....

September 21. ... In the name of all students, by Bapak Sahal and Bapak Zarkasji, the teachers' decision had been taken: to *hidjrah* ... On bikes, we reached village Bondrang.... In Bondrang we heard that village of Gontor had already been burned down.... Some books and bikes were left in Bondrang.... We entered forest and walked, uphill and downhill.

Some have eaten in the morning, but some have not.... We passed food-stalls but they were empty, and we stopped looking for food-stalls anymore.... Still ninety students walked with us.... We found a grove of coconut trees and had young coconuts to drink, and we found *ubi sentah* [edible tubers].... In village Trenggalek ... most of the inhabitants were still polite and human.

... We were detained, ... and then let go ... We met groups of young men on the road, armed with spears. In front of the local school building in village Klepu people took away our things, especially clothes and shoes.

... Village Soko.... Money was taken away from us on the way, so many of us had nothing.... We were permitted to keep only shorts and undershirts ... all the rest was taken, also eyeglasses, fountain pens.... They said it was because we were not military, and that the things would be sent after us....

... We were getting ready to go back to Ponorogo, but ... it looked like it would not happen.... A soldier from the former Battalion Ponorogo whom we met with a unit whispered to us that his heart is still red-white [that he is still for the government], even when now he was forced to fight with the Reds.

After a week of traveling, at seven o'clock in the evening, on September 28, teachers, students, and staff, those who remained with the group, arrived back to Ponorogo. The school was not yet ready and we had to wait overnight at the side of the road: "We saw army ... trucks. Siliwangi, ..."

Conclusion: Truly much we had seen.

[Signed] Ahmad Zanoeddin, teacher, November 3, 1948.[81]

Half a century later, Arief Djati, an Indonesian researcher and activist, with Benedict Anderson, interviewed elderly Mr. Bungkus, back then a guerilla fighter in East Java, fighting, as he said, since the time of the Japanese occupation, a paragon of élan, chaos, and euphoria, and chaos of the time, the revolution. A young man then, Bungkus might easily have met the teachers and pupils of the Modern Boarding School on the road near Ponorogo, in the same landscape in surge. During the interview, he was asked about the Madiun affair.

ARIEF DJATI: The Madiun Affair?
BUNGKUS: I don't know about that. I never met any. Nah, while I was there. I was taken aback by news of a Madiun Affair—a disturbance (*pergolakan*). Wah, how could it have come to this?
ARIEF DJATI: Did you hear about it from the radio?
BUNGKUS: Hah?
ARIEF DJATI: From the radio?
BUNGKUS: No. By then it had already begun.... At that moment we were really taken aback. How could it be? So, I asked around why it had happened. Before this, we had never had a problem with the PKI, because we were always side by side at the front. Together ... into Surabaya. So, I always took my hat off to them. There was never any conflict. After that, I heard that the trouble had arisen from a misunderstanding.

Bungkus is pushed by Arief Djati:

> In other words, it wasn't clear to me. Nah, when the shooting started—the fighting between the army and the PKI—Pak Magenda, in command of my battalion [guerillas], the Seadogs, decided that, rather than participating in a civil war, we should abandon our position, and head back to our original "pockets" in the countryside. So, I set off from Kediri. On foot.[82]

Everybody, all of a sudden, was a stranger in the landscape, even if he or she was born in it. It was how the landscape trembled and surged. But some were more strangers than others. Siliwangi troops had recently moved from West Java. They spoke Sundanese, a language incomprehensible in Central and East Java, and they did not understand Javanese.[83]

As he walked, marched, and ran, tried to defend himself and those with him, or looked for an opportunity to attack back, Amir was a stranger several times over. Unlike most of the leaders marching or running with him—Musso, Soeripno, Maroeto Daroesman, Soemarsono, Djokosoejono, or Setiadjit, all of whom were Javanese—Amir, like the Siliwangi, did not understand the language. He had to guess, test, and try, or to have the language, together with the norms and the landscape, translated to him as they marched or ran.

Even many Javanese with Amir, were less strangers, true, but only by a measure. They were not fully of the place. They were modern, educated, and living elsewhere—and very elsewhere—for years, often for most of their lives. Those of the group from Holland and Musso, and those from Boven Digoel, spoke the language of the place, and behaved, with an accent.

It cannot be excluded, too, that now Amir's faith in revolution, Christianity, Kant, Kierkegaard and Luther, and Marx and Lenin and Trotsky, equally foreign and accented, stayed with him and even became stronger than ever.

It was not just an accent. The people around Madiun and throughout the republic on Java did not respond to Musso's call for uprising. "All previous historical movements were movements of minorities. . . . The proletarian movement is the self-conscious independent movement of the immense majority. The proletariat, the lowest stratum of our present society, cannot stir, cannot raise itself up without the whole super incumbent strata of official society being sprung into the air. Though not in substance, yet in form, the struggle of the proletariat with the bourgeoisie is at first a national struggle."[84]

The wonderful apparatus of the party, at the ultimate moment of action, clicked by itself. It became clear now that the debates among the Sajap Kiri, FDR and PKI, about whether the time had arrived for a big change, especially about collective property to become the law of the land, about factories and plantations being nationalized, had been only debates. Between the saying and act, among the revolutionaries, the saying still had it.[85] The effort, to borrow from Kant, "to get out of one's minority" failed.[86]

There was still a hesitancy among Amir, Musso, and the others, in the hours before leaving Madiun, about whether to establish some structure of government. This was partly out of fear that it might be a cause for them being accused of a coup—which, of course, happened anyway.[87] They appeared unable to govern. "In merely two days, after the events in Madiun erupted," Soerjono recalled, "it became clear that the people did not answer by mass uprising."[88]

It was one of Lenin's dictums and Musso had to know it: "The proletariat must win the support of the peasantry—without it cannot hold power. The only way for it to attract the mass of small rural proprietors is to show vigor and determination in the contest for power."[89] Musso's and Amir's column, however, was running. The Jewish heroine of a David Grossman Israeli novel—on the run, too, in "her own land"—asks a Palestinian taxi driver she had hired, to take her "to where the country ends." "'For me it ended a long time ago,' he hissed."[90]

Stories as gruesome as Ramelan's caricatures were spread by both sides of the conflict. "Many Islamic schools," wrote an Islamic source, "were burned down in the area around Madiun, Magetan, Goreng-goreng, Ponorogo.... All praises to Allah, it did not come to the worst."[91] "Many corpses were thrown down the old wells," wrote a history for the younger readers.[92] "Women and girls were raped," wrote Abu Hanifah, "often in front of their helpless parents and husbands, before they were killed."[93]

Abu Hanifah was particularly prone to tell these stories. He relates how Dr. Moewardi, the leader of the pro-Tan Malaka Barisan Banteng, "Buffalo Front," had been allegedly kidnapped in Surakarta by Amir's Pesindo: "The police heard some rumors that he was kidnapped by a guerilla band," Abu Hanifah wrote. They stopped him as he was on the way to see a patient. "The rumors said that they took him to a village in the south and there they cut out his tongue and threw acid into his face so that he could not be recognized again. He became sick and lost his memory. So, he might still be prowling around the southern villages without being recognized. So, the story goes."[94]

"The degree of carnage may only be suggested by random statistics of varying reliability," Anthony Reid wrote. "The Dutch alleged in the UN that 8,000 people were executed by the TNI [the republican army, which was almost certainly Siliwangi] in Madiun. The Tjeepu hospital reported 4,000 deaths in the fighting for that town (*Nasional* of 9 October 1948). [Robert] Jay was informed in 1953 that half of the male population of Ponorogo (population 50,000) were killed by one side or the other, though this appears improbable."[95] In George Kahin's description, observed from Jogjakarta but dependent, of course, largely on government sources, "As Communist forces became harder pressured, many of them, particularly some of the smaller units, became increasingly brutal. Several hundred civil servants and schoolteachers were executed by them, fifty-one out of fifty-six policemen in Magetan alone. In particular, members of the Masjumi appeared to be singled out for cruel enactment, sometimes this being limited to robbery but frequently extended to torture and execution."[96] Like in Homer (the Homer of the Haarlem Gymnasium):

> . . . the shades of corpses and buried:
> brides, still unmarried youth, toil-worn old men,
> tender young girls, their hearts still new to sorrow,
> and many with wounds inflicted by bronze tipped spears.[97]

Still, it could be much worse, Ann Swift wrote, "perhaps because Madiun did, on the whole, remain a confrontation between opposing troops rather than the civilian population."[98]

Machiavelli wrote: "Cruelty can be called well used (if it is even permitted to use the word 'well' in connection with evil) if it is executed at a single stroke out of necessity to secure one's power and is then not continued but converted into the greatest possible benefit for one's subjects. Whoever proceeds otherwise through fear or bad judgement, must always keep a knife at hand."[99]

There are no stories, from the Madiun affair, like the "touching narratives from the First World War," where "to perform bodily functions, the opposing sides grant each other special permission. (Rifle butt raised.)."[100] At the same time, what Walter Benjamin called "divine violence" or also "revolutionary violence," the purity of purpose taken to the extreme, "cruelty well used," was in and around Madiun in the late months of 1948 tragically missing, "a pure immediate violence . . . divine violence . . . law destroying . . . [which] 'expiates' the guilt of mere life . . . for the sake of living . . . revolutionary violence, the highest manifestation of unallowed violence by men. . . . all the eternal forms . . . open to pure divine violence, which myth bastardized with law."[101] Siliwangi pushed the Amir and Musso columns to the enemy.

Like the procession of students, teachers, and staff of the Modern Boarding School, the procession of Musso, Amir, Soeripno, Soemarsono, Djokosoejono, and Francisca Fanggidaej, thinned out as they moved and as they ran. Early in November, a little over a month after they left Madiun, one Abdul Mutalib, who got somehow separated from the main body, was captured by the Siliwangi troops, was interrogated, and before he was shot, disclosed that "Amir Sjarifoeddin still exudes confidence as he speaks to the people. But the confidence of many others who are with him has weakened, some are overcome by fear and some break away from him because they are hungry or sick."[102]

At the time of Abdul Mutalib's capture and execution, in early November, Amir's column marched and ran along the eastern slopes of Mount Lawu, a lofty volcano about sixty kilometers east of Madiun. November 6 was the day when Prime Minister Hatta met the Dutch foreign minister Stikker and told him that Amir was "now, with a small group of fanatical followers locked in the mountains."[103]

Three days later, November 9, Amir's column—"without being harassed," but followed by Siliwangi day and night—crossed railway tracks and the main highway between Surakarta and Madiun near Walikukun. "The inhabitants of the village watched in surprise as hundreds of people suddenly appeared, military, civilians, but also women with children carried on their backs, or babies at their hips, the whole road crowded with people."[104]

From the several thousands of the first days, the column thinned to hundreds and, on November 24, when the major attack by the Siliwangi at last took place, Amir's column consisted of merely 650 fighters and 500 weapons.[105]

In a later comment by Amir's cousin Harahap, Amir had become "a fanatic without a purpose."[106] But the question must be rather asked whether Amir, at that time, as his running was coming to its end, became "a failed person," or, in an exact opposite to it, "a true-strong person," in the categories of Robert Musil's *The Man without Qualities*. In Musil's terminology, "a true-strong person" would mean that Amir was "still aware of a further possibility."[107]

It would mean that Amir now, at the moment of *finita la commedia*, was reaching the state of what Baruch Spinoza called "conatus," of "nothing but inclination to continue to exist and to enhance himself," or what Immanuel Kant called "being of ends."[108] Whether, instead of becoming a fanatic without a purpose, on the run, on the Long March, up and down the hills, across the rice fields and marshlands, hunted by Siliwangi, being a double and multiple stranger in the landscape and among the people, was not this, to use Jean-Luc Nancy's words, Amir's "coming of sense"?[109]

"In Madiun," Francisca Fanggidaej recalled, "I was assigned to the column of Bung Amir Sjarifoeddin. Now, Bung Amir was considered the only one who could be our top leader." At the beginning, says Francisca, the column "was not too large, just a few armed units." "But, along the way, it swelled. Not just single persons but whole families were joining us."[110] Francisca was assigned to lead the *agitprop*, "agitation and propaganda section": "The column did not move in a straight line; its course twisted. Tjepu had to be reached by boats. . . . Where were we going? I did not know. I was moved by a desire but not by a hope. For me, hope would be something I could touch, I could see, somewhere ahead of me. There was something ahead of me, but it only teased me."[111]

The Siliwangi units did not appear to be intent on an imminent major attack. But they were felt behind, constantly, distracting the column, and exhausting those on the run by minor sudden ambushes. Even the tonic of every guerilla, the excitement of the "real" Long March, was being taken from them:

1. When the enemy advances, we retreat!
2. When the enemy halts and encamps, we trouble him!
3. When the enemy seeks to avoid a battle, we attack!
4. When the enemy retreats, we pursue![112]

"It is better to defeat the enemy with hunger than with steel," wrote Machiavelli.[113] But the marchers themselves were becoming the hungry people in migration: "The column of Bung Amir," recalled Francisca, "was getting longer as people were joining us. . . . I think it was in Magetan that a troupe of *ludruk* [street theater of Java] joined us, not merely actors and their families, but musical instruments, costumes, and all the theater stuff."[114]

"Moving during the day was difficult, but at night it was much more so." "I was expecting my first child," Francisca wrote.[115] During one of the small ambushes by Siliwangi, "I ran to take cover under a tree, a rubber or a kapok tree, I did not care!"[116] The joke of the story, of course, is that neither rubber nor kapok tree offers any meaningful cover, just a naked smooth stem and Francisca with her heavy belly. They fell on the ground, Francisca and a friend, who happened to run to the same tree, and they rolled with laughter, she says, silently, so that Siliwangi would not hear them

Hariandja also marched with Amir Sjarifoeddin, almost the whole way, and he also left a record.

> We had a great need of horses. . . . But as the days passed by, we had been not just tired, but hungry, so we killed horses one by one. . . . All the time, there were skirmishes with the enemy. . . . Before Sarangan, close to village Jiblok . . . we noticed that Prawoto, who had been in charge of baggage, including the boxes with gold and silver, . . . was no more among us. Much later we learned that he had bought himself a luxurious home in Jatinegara [an upscale quarter of Djakarta], and, at least so people said, that there he kept a prostitute.[117]

Soemarsono marched, too, leading the column, with Amir almost the whole way. Years later, he would recall: "Until Dungus we still had horses. . . . We also had a doctor, Dr. Djajoed.... We had food and water sometimes, and sometimes not. Sometimes, when the way led through a forest, we ate leaves.... In the end, each of us only had one set of clothes, the one we wore; it stuck to our bodies.... Only the people who were sympathetic to us, gave us help without being forced."[118]

There were breaks in the march, pauses. At one moment, after a few weeks of marching, Amir's column reached Sarangan, a luxury hill resort on the slopes of Mount Lawu. It was a place used by the Jogjakarta elite, including the sultan, and more—a location where the UN Commission of Good Offices stayed when it wished to be close to Jogjakarta. Now, Sarangan was empty. They spent a few days there, says Hariandja, "drinking wine, eating cheese and butter, etc.; beautiful villas and soft beds; vigilance: relaxed."[119]

Soemarsono's story of the Long March ends abruptly. "In Klambu," he says, close to the final stage, "the civilians separated from the military.... I also left and tried to make it to Solo [sic]where my family lived."[120]

Already a few weeks before Soemarsono, quite early in the Long March in fact, Musso went another way. According to one account, at one moment, for whatever reason, he took a few troops with him; perhaps they disagreed with Amir,[121] or Musso went for a reconnaissance. He was of this area, but he had left as a teenager and came back in 1935 and 1936 only for a short time. Now, in 1948, whatever the circumstances, he lost his way.[122]

Hatta's government offered a reward of Rp. 1 million for the capture of Musso, dead or alive.[123] As for what happened to Musso after he separated from Amir we do not know, but about his capture there is a folder in the republican police files, which later got in the hands of Dutch intelligence, and now is in the archives in the Hague:

To: Military Commandant Regency Ponorogo.
Report on the arrest and murder [sic] of Musso.

On October 31, 1948, at 9:45 a.m., I, Soemadi, the Company Commander, with the Police Battalion Commander, Captain Somandar, drove in a police car in the direction of Krebet. Near village Semanding, 2 km south of Samorot, I noticed a dogcart driven by a fat man in short-sleeves and long black trousers. He was hiding something in a sarong.

Two youth in black [this suggests Muslim militia] rode on bicycles behind the dogcart and they signaled to us. We did not understand the meaning of it, but we stopped the car anyway. At that moment the fat man began to shoot. His pistol was a P.N. Luckily, we were not hit.

The police sent a courier for reinforcements, an "emergency section" in Samorot.

The fat man ran to the village on foot and there was a commotion. Then we heard that the individual might be MUSSO and we hastened. For a long time, MUSSO could not be found. In the end, however, by me, the Company Commandant SOEMADI, MUSSO was spotted.

I shouted to him who was he, and he answered that indeed his name was MUSSO. I ordered him to surrender but he answered that he would rather die standing, and he fired his pistol several times. The "emergency section" [which in-between arrived] surrounded him. No farther than thirteen meters from us, he was still refusing to surrender. . . .

He took a cover behind a cement water tank in a bath-house in the garden and from there he cried out "Red-White Forever" . . . He still refused to surrender. Many volleys were fired but no bullet hit him . . .

But finally, Musso was killed.

He had ORI [*Oeang Repoeblik Indonesia*, republican money] and a pistol on himself. The amount of the money is not known, because it was taken to [the police headquarters in] Balong.

Musso did not carry any identification papers. . . .

So much for the MUSSO affair.

[signed] Company Commandant Soemadi[124]

Mrs. Sosrokardono, known also as Siti Larang, who was known to accompany Musso when he stayed in Java in 1935 and 1936, had been found and brought to the police station in Blitar to identify the corpse.[125] Then, according to other documents, Musso's remains were cremated and the ashes scattered in the Brantas River. Two photographs of a dead Musso at the police station are in the file.[126]

"Red Chieftain Reported Slain in Java Clash" was a headline, not a big one and not on the first page, in the *Washington Post* on November 2, 1948. "Red Chief's Death Reported in Java," reported the *New York Times*, on the same day.

But the column, without Musso, was running. "To be in the Long March, in the column of Bung Amir," Francisca Fanggidaej recalled, might be expressed in a few words: "Tugas lari ['The order is to run!']." "I did not know what the destination was. . . . The Long March in China led the troops to a base. . . . Throughout our Long March I never heard people discuss the point."[127]

"In the end," Hariandja wrote, "the column moved only at night. We could not speak, could not smoke, and could not use flashlights. . . . In the rain . . . through a village . . . stop for a while . . . then again up a mountain, down a mountain. . . . If an elderly comrade got too tired and could not go further, he would be permitted to stay. But he was ordered not to move from his hiding place."[128]

"I have never been able fix the concept of freedom of the will at a special point on the horizon as readily as you do," Franz Kafka wrote to Max Brod.[129] Derrida spoke about "awaiting without horizon of the wait."[130] Heidegger spoke about "freezing the horizon,"[131] Kant about "the horizon of common sense."[132] Francisca Fanggidaej, like Kafka, was not able to fix the point on the horizon readily, but she appeared to know what kind of journey it was. And she was convinced that Amir knew. One can take her for a truthful witness because she was absorbed, and she paid the price.

This might be for Amir Sjarifoeddin a *homo viator* moment, of a "'journeying man,' man en route, where journey is not only a passage but constitutes the gait and the progression of revelation."[133] It might be a Kantian moment, too, an echo of the debates in Schepper's house, of Kantian *Trieb*, a journey, a "drive" "towards the 'unconditioned.'"[134] "Sacrifice," says Heidegger, "is free from necessity because it rises from the abyss of freedom."[135]

"I was amazed," Francisca writes. "For instance, we have arrived in a village in which the inhabitants were not really antagonistic to us. There were many coconut trees in the village, and the troops were thirsty.... Several soldiers climbed the trees.... They wanted to bring some of the best nuts also to the leaders. Bung Amir heard about it and became angry. He ran outside the house where they had a meeting. He shot his pistol into the air. Full magazine of bullets: 'Down! Down!' he shouted."[136]

"Objects," Kant claimed, "do not in themselves possess form, but our mind is so constituted that it cannot help attributing form and everything formal to the object of our experience." Keeping to one's principles, one may transcend experience "to the extent of becoming hazy." Even Kant, the Kant of Schepper's house, if it comes to the edge, "fails to be convinced," he becomes "bewildering to the reader," "puzzled," "absurd."[137]

"Wounded were left sheltered among the peasants," Edgar Snow wrote about the real Mao Tse-tung Long March.[138] Levinas writes about "the monstrosity of the neighbor" and Lacan writes about "the inhuman core of the neighbor."[139] But Mao's troops were ordered:

1. Replace all doors when you leave a house! [Doors in Chinese villages were usually unhinged by the villagers for the night and used as beds.]
2. Return and rollup straw matting on which you slept!
3. Be courteous and polite to the people and help them when you can!
4. Return all borrowed articles!
5. Replace all damaged articles!

6. Be honest in all transactions with the peasants!
7. Pay for all articles purchased!
8. Be sanitary, and especially, establish latrines at a safe distance from the people's houses!¹⁴⁰

"On our Long March," a Chinese guerilla told Edgar Snow, "peasants brought us grass shoes made by themselves, and they offered us tea and hot water along the road."¹⁴¹ "They obeyed," Francisca wrote about the soldiers on the coconut trees, "and all climbed down." "Amir ordered that the nuts already on the ground be returned to the villagers. Then, the soldiers of the whole column were called up and Amir spoke to them about discipline." "Loving the people," he said, "is not a matter of good manners. It is not us who defend the people, it is the people who defend us. It is not us who shelter the people, it is the people who shelter us! These nuts are [the] property of the people. These trees grow on the people's land." "Bung Amir did not make it easy to anyone to approach him closely on the march," Francisca recalled. "Not that one would be afraid. It just was not easy."¹⁴²

"A landscape," writes Paul Virilio, "has no fixed meaning, no privileged vantage point. It is oriented only by the itinerary of the passerby."¹⁴³ Franz Kafka wrote to Felice Bauer: "The Bible happens to be lying beside me, and simply to derive some comfort and pass it to you, I opened it three times and eventually found this sentence: 'In His hand are the deep places of the earth; the strength of the hills is His also.' To me, alas, it sounds almost meaningless."¹⁴⁴

For two months, the Siliwangi troops followed behind Amir's now Mussoless column, at a distance, never too far away, never out of sight or hearing or feeling, never so far that at any moment they might not land a final blow. Soemarsono said, before he left the column:

> At times in the lowlands, when the Siliwangi troops came too close, we were ordered to walk faster, seven kilometers an hour if possible, to evade the contact with the enemy. At one of those moments, I saw an elderly man marching with great difficulties, in threadbare pants, with blood on his feet. It was Pak Sardjono, one time the chairman of the central committee of the PKI, and a former internee in Boven Digoel. In addition to everything, he suffered by hemorrhoids. With a little smile, as if *he* [Soemarsono here uses *beliau* for "he," a form reserved for a highly respected person] apologized for being unable to meet the target of seven kilometers an hour, he [*beliau*] looked at me. Then he stopped and pointed at the view that opened at the side of the road skirting the mountain. As if there were no civil war and no Siliwangi, "How pretty it is here!" he said.¹⁴⁵

THE LONG MARCH 249

During the two months on the run, Amir's column thinned and finally almost disappeared. Children, families, elderly, and the weaker slowly stayed behind, and then the soldiers, until Amir remained with a handful. Then, in two blows, Siliwangi finished the chase.

On November 29 in the evening, "a battle took place between the rest of the column and two companies of Siliwangi in the swamps north and west of a small village at the shores of the river Lusi," about 120 kilometers northwest of Madiun. Siliwangi lost two soldiers and a corporal in the battle.[146] Djokosoejono, Sardjono, Francisca Fanggidaej, and some other lesser-known people were taken captives by the commander of a Siliwangi battalion, Kemal Idris. "During the first round of interrogation, Djokosoejono divulged that Amir was still in the swamps."[147]

They, Djokosoejono told the interrogators, were not trying to escape across the line, to the Dutch, but they still hoped "to connect with friendly units led by Sudiarto and Soejoto about whom they heard they might still be active."[148] "Amir's horse was left behind already and his beloved dog Zora, also called Zero, was caught three days ago. On November 29, Amir, Soeripno, and their four bodyguards were captured.... Amir wore a pajamas jacket with sarong and he had no shoes, he had a beard and long hair. His glasses were still intact, but the pipe disappeared. He limped and was emaciated. For the last five days he suffered from dysentery. His weapons consisted of a single pistol."[149] The heroes of Shakespeare and Calderon, Walter Benjamin noted, "enter, fleeing."[150]

The capture of Amir happened near the village of Klambu, the closest town being Purwodadi ("nice waterfalls," says the local tourist guide). On November 30, the day after capture, Amir, Soeripno, Maroeto Daroesman, and Harjono were brought to the local prison of Klambu.[151]

After the first round of interrogations, they were taken to a safer prison in Kudus, a town twenty-five kilometers from Klambu. Amir kept calm. "Soeripno, who remained with him till the last moment, also suffered by dysentery but looked calm as usual," Nasoetion was informed, "and the moment he was captured he actually managed to smile."[152] There is a photograph in Nasoetion's report on the event, of Amir, Soeripno, Maroeto Daroesman, and Harjono, probably in the prison at Kudus, sitting on the floor. Amir is already shaven and his hair is cut. He seems to be holding a book.[153]

Still, in Kudus, it seems, the military let a reporter in, from an Indonesian Catholic paper *Hidup*, "Life," to interview Amir; perhaps in the hope that a Christian paper had a better chance of making Amir talk.

CHAPTER 13

The long retreat through woodlands and through meadows.
What is the sense of the uprising?
Is the published FDR document genuine one or has it been forged?
Amir prefers 'rokok kretek' to ordinary cigarettes.
Amir reads Regina [?] and Shakespeare.

. . .

On December 2 I made it a point to see Bung Amir and his confidant Suripno. . . . When I entered the room where they were confined, Bung Amir stood up from his bed. Suripno also awoke. . . .

Bung Amir remains the same, not so very thin. Only his left leg is swollen. . . .

"What made you start this rebellion which has brought about so much havoc to the country?"

"Hm, I have never started a rebellion."

Amir speaks about a "premature" action and about the FDR documents being "forged." Suripno interrupted: "Has any one of you gentlemen have a cigarette?"

Back to the matter: "Why did not you stop it?"

"I did not stop it. Nothing could stop it anymore; the stone was kept rolling."[154]

From Kudus, by a special train, Amir, Soeripno, Maroeto Daroesman, and Harjono were brought to Jogjakarta. The other group captured earlier, Djokosoejono, Francisca Fanggidaej, and the others, from the place where they had been captured, were taken to the nearest station and then by train to Surakarta. Francisca Fanggidaej recalled: "We were first driven in a jeep to a local narrow-gauge railway probably used in the Dutch time to transport sugar cane." In Delanggu, at the railway station from which they were to go to Surakarta, Francisca wrote, "the crowd pelted us with rotten eggs and banana peels, shouting hysterically and in a threatening manner."[155]

"I was sore and sick," she says, "to see the people giving themselves to such anger and frenzy. I had been wounded not so much by the peel from the orange which cut my lip, but by the art of politics behind the moment."[156]

Djokosoejono, Sardjono, and Francisca Fanggidaej reached Surakarta. "Posters on the walls and fences along the road," Francisca wrote, "contained hateful and insulting messages like 'Dutch spies,' or 'Francisca Fanggidaej a whore of Amir Sjarifoeddin!'" "Such posters," she heard later, "were displayed on the walls of Madiun, Sarangan, Njawi, and in all towns and villages around Mount Lawu."[157]

Amir Sjarifoeddin, Soeripno, Maroeto Daroesman, and Harjono were taken by special train to Jogjakarta. There is another photograph, possibly from the station at the beginning of their journey: "Soldiers of Siliwangi guard a train in which the PKI group, Amir Sjarifoeddin and the others, are taken to Jogjakarta."[158] Captain Soeharto (not the Lieutenant Colonel Soeharto who did not deliver Amir's letter to Soekarno from Madiun, and who would one day become the president) had been put in charge of security and he later talked to Indonesian historian Soe Hok Gie about the trip. Soe recorded the interview: "Amir asked Captain Soeharto to get him some book. The book Captain Soeharto found was *Romeo and Juliet* by William Shakespeare. Amir read the book on the train, all the way to Jogjakarta. He sat by himself [with a guard no doubt] in an empty compartment."[159] Was Shakespeare's *Romeo and Juliet* the only book Captain Soeharto found in Kudus? Was it from the prison library? Was the book in English?

On December 5, Amir, Soeripno, Maroeto Daroesman, and Harjono arrived in Jogjakarta. The arrival of the train had been announced and "thousands" were waiting. A reporter of *Antara*, the republican press agency, was allowed on board to do another interview. "Amir did not speak," he reported, "and continued to read Shakespeare."[160]

"At the Jogjakarta railway station," recalled Captain Soeharto, who traveled all the way, "people walked along the train as it stopped on the platform, and tried to take a peek at the former Prime Minister and Minister of Defense of the republic. Amir Sjarifoeddin kept calm as the people gathered behind his window."[161]

This must be the moment when another photograph of Amir was taken. Camera looks from the inside of a train compartment or from the carriage's corridor, Amir is seen as sitting alone, at the window and holding a book—too thick, in fact, to be just *Romeo and Juliet* (perhaps it is the Bard's *Selected Works* popular edition?). The book seems to be open on the first page, perhaps just the front cover is turned open. Amir does not seem really reading. Behind the window, down on the platform, people can indeed be seen, men and children, some shading their eyes, trying to see the former great man.

From the railway station, Amir, Harjono, Soeripno, and Maroeto Daroesman were led on foot along the main street in Jogjakarta, Malioboro, which led to the sultan's palace, the presidential compound, and the prison. "A large unusually quiet crowd gathered to see the former Premier of the republic," wrote Arnold Brackman who might have been there.[162] A photograph shows them walking through the street, Amir still holding a book.[163] According to Leclerc, Amir "was put on display."[164]

They were led to Fort Vredeburg, the eighteenth-century Dutch fortress next to the palace and Soekarno's residence. There, in the fortress, they were to stay for days. "Noisy demonstrations against the PKI took part daily outside of the fort."[165]

After less than two weeks, in mid-December, the prisoners of Fort Vredeburg were taken to Surakarta. This time they were not paraded through the streets.[166] One story is that it was Colonel Nasoetion and the republic's attorney general who decided to transport the prisoners to Surakarta, the headquarters of the military governor of East and Central Java, and Siliwangi officer, Nasoetion's close ally, Colonel Gatot Subroto.[167] After the outbreak of the Madiun events, Gatot Subroto, as the military governor, acquired extraordinary military and civilian powers

According to Ali Sastroamidjojo, Amir and the others were taken to Surakarta because the town was less vulnerable in case of Dutch "second police action," which was widely expected to take place at any moment, as the Dutch would certainly use the crisis.[168] According to yet another explanation, recorded by Dutch intelligence, Amir and the others were moved from Jogjakarta, "to guard them against the people's anger."[169]

In Surakarta, Amir and his three coprisoners met again with the other group, Francisca Fanggidaej among them: "We were united," Francisca wrote. "With Bung Amir, Pak Sardjono, Soeripno, Maroeto Daroesman, and Djokosoejono we were brought by a narrow-gauge train [Surakarta city tram] to an office where Gatot Subroto was waiting."[170]

Gatot Subroto was from Banyumas, Central Java. Its capital Purwokerto was famous for producing the best officers for the Dutch Indies KNIL, and now for the Indonesian republican army. "It is said," wrote Simatoepang, himself from Sumatra, "that the Banyumas dialect is 'more militant' than the speech of any other part of Java. I often jokingly called these men the Prussians of Java."[171] Jacques Leclerc called Gatot Subroto a *"baron javanais."*[172] Gatot Subroto had also been known, since the early years of the revolution and the time of Amir Sjarifoeddin's tenure as the minister of defense, as the most vocal opponent of Amir's policy of planting political commissars in the army.

In Gatot Subroto's office, wrote Francisca Fanggidaej, "we were received as people who had lost it all. Gatot would talk . . . but no one among us might say anything. . . . I felt like a spectator." "It is long ago," writes Francisca, "I forgot much of what he said." "I only recall his turpentine-colored [*sengir*] face, . . . Even Bung Amir kept his mouth closed, imagine! Amir wore a pajama, we all . . . appeared double rundown in the house of the Military Governor. He wore his military outfit, *complit*, as he sat in a huge armchair."[173]

The Glodok prison in Surakarta, where they were all locked, was "a remnant of the Dutch Indies times."[174] Francisca writes:

> I was put in a cell directly next to the cell of Comrades Maroeto and Soeripno. There was a siphon between the cells serving both our W.C.s. We used it to send "kattebelletjes" [Dutch for small notes, messages] to our friends. We have written a note on a piece of paper, put the paper in a matchbox and sent the matchbox flowing....
>
> There were moments of light. Once, standing before the interrogator's office doors, waiting to be called in, Alimin [contemporary of Musso, the oldest of the detainees] was escorted from his interview. As he passed, he smiled at me.[175]

In Surakarta, Amir's cousin Harahap happened again to be nearby. He had nothing to do with the Madiun affair, was free, and moved around. "During his last days," Harahap wrote later, "Amir got spiritual support by Dr. Walter Tamboenan and Saudara Poerbo." Pastor Tamboenan reappears too. He was the priest who back in 1931 baptized Amir, who married him in 1935, and was also present when Professor Schepper visited Jogjakarta in 1948. "Brother Poerbo," cousin Harahap wrote, "was the prison driver."

Poerbo talked to Harahap after all was over. In prison, Harahap wrote, Brother Poerbo visited Amir often in his cell. From Poerbo, Harahap might have heard the rumor that the prisoners were offered to escape, but that Amir refused. "And how could they escape?" Harahap asked. "With all the enemy on the roads?"[176]

On the night of December 19, 1948, as the radical wing of Dutch politics prevailed, the Dutch military launched the long-expected second police action. The republic was seen as weakened by the internal struggle. Hatta's government, by its victory, was proving its staunch anti-Communism, and there was a danger, if the Dutch hesitated, that the United States might be encouraged to discard any remaining Dutch claims on the Indies.

The news of the imminent Dutch military attack reached the republic on December 18. The acute problem arose: what to do with the prisoners?

Already by December 3, two days before Amir and the others were brought to Jogjakarta, some Indonesian papers wrote that Amir and his associates might be sentenced to death.[177] Djaenah, Amir's wife, she later told Jacques Leclerc that, at this moment, through an ex-secretary of Amir, she attempted to approach Soekarno. But, she told Leclerc, "there was no answer."[178] "A number of high-ranking TNI officers including Colonel Gatot Subroto," wrote Ali Sastroamidjojo in his memoirs, "believed it would be better if the PKI leaders were tried by a military court on the battlefield." But the civilians decided to wait.[179]

On December 18, as the Dutch attack appeared to be in a matter of hours, the Hatta cabinet met. Later, a document surfaced that is believed (but not proven) to be the minutes of the meeting. According to it, the cabinet discussed what should be done with the prisoners in the case of the attack. "Out of the twelve ministers present," the minutes read, "four agreed with execution, four were for release, four did not have an opinion. Then Soekarno announced his veto against the execution."[180]

"Some insisted on a *blitz* execution," the widow of Harjono, one of Amir's fellow communist leaders, told Leclerc." Bung Karno strongly opposed it. But he did not know at the time that Amir had already been secretly surrendered by Mohammad Hatta to Colonel Gatot Subroto." "This proves," Mrs. Harjono told Leclerc, "that Hatta was a ringleader of Amir being killed."[181] David Anderson, a British historian of the military aspects of the Madiun affair, agrees with Mrs. Harjono: "Gatot Subroto," he wrote, "carried out the execution on Hatta's order."[182]

As the Dutch forces entered republican territory, Amir and ten other most prominent prisoners, Soeripno, Maroeto Daroesman, and Sardjono among them, were taken from the Surakarta prison to the nearby village of Ngalihan. "Summary justice *snelrecht* [Dutch for 'summary justice']," says Soerjono.[183] How might Amir feel? "They condemn Him during the night, and in the early morning, almost before Jerusalem is awake, He is already crucified."[184] Or something like Robert Musil's possible hero at another time and in another place: "He was reminded of that special moment just before a plane lands, when the ground raises up again with all its voluptuous contours of the map-like flatness to which it had been reduced for hours on end, and things revert to their familiar earthly meanings, which seem to be growing out of the ground itself."[185]

"We know that a founding figure has to be killed," writes Slavoj Žižek in his book on violence.[186] "Hero," says Ernst Bloch in his book on concrete utopia, "must die before he can truly come to himself."[187] "In the dust he fell hand clawing the earth," says Homer as Amir might hear him in Haarlem, and it might also be one of Amir's thoughts.[188]

"Christianity," wrote Jean-Luc Nancy, "proposed death as the truth of life."[189] According to Plato's *Phaedrus*, death is a "divine release of the soul from the yoke of existence and convention."[190] It is, too, says Levinas, a "possession by a god, enthusiasm, . . . the end of the solitary."[191] It is, Nancy writes, "on the edge of a vacuum of sense. . . . It is precisely there, in the place of our relinquishment, that truth becomes available."[192] Nietzsche offers a darker view: "The goal is too far away . . . when one reaches freedom, one is as exhausted as an ephemeral fly when evening comes."[193]

According to information that reached Amir's family much later, the director of the Surakarta prison had at first refused to surrender the eleven men to the military when the soldiers arrived for the prisoners, and demanded to see a letter from the attorney general. After several hours, the military returned with the letter.[194] Amir, Soeripno, Maroeto Daroesman, Sardjono, Oei Gee Hwat (of SOBSI), Soekarno (not the president, the husband of Francisca Fanggidaej, member of the executive of Pesindo), Djokosoejono, Katawinadi, D. Mangku, Harjono, and Ronomarsono—the last one possibly mistaken for Soemarsono—were taken away to Ngalihan and close to midnight from December 19 to December 20, near the village, shot by a firing squad.[195]

There are a few accounts of the execution, all of them unreliable. According to one, Amir asked for a moment to pray before he was shot. According to another, he led his comrades in signing the "Internationale" and "Indonesia Raja."

Djaenah, Amir's widow, told Jacques Leclerc, that "a friend" told her later that Amir was the last one of the eleven to be executed. He asked the commanding officer to be shot with only one bullet in the forehead. Indeed, Djaenah said, when the dead body of Amir was exhumed in 1950, "there was a single bullet hole in front of his skull."[196]

Part Four

Traces

Chapter 14

The Victors

> Because of Musso, Amir, and Alimin,
> Country is shattered,
> And nation is at war with itself
> Motherland calls for heroes
> For their bravery
> To her defense.
> Madiun and Wonogiri
> Are enraged.
> And so is Purwodadi.
> Hey traitors,
> The defeated
> Leave our country!
>
> —Anonymous song from 1948, in Leclerc Papers no. 229

This is a sheet of music with lyrics from the time of, or shortly after, the Madiun affair, now in the Special Collection of Leiden University Library. There is one more music sheet with words in the same file with "Darah Rakjat," "The Blood of the People," a revolutionary song from the time of the prewar Dutch Indies.

From the first hours after the Dutch paratroopers dropped on Maguwo airport in Jogjakarta, it was clear that the republican military, the victors at Madiun, would be unable to resist the assault. In a few hours, Jogjakarta, the capital of the republic, was taken. The top civilian leadership, including Soekarno, Hatta, and Sjahrir, after brief hesitation over whether the republican military could offer them shelter, decided to wait in the presidential compound in the sultan's palace for the Dutch troops to take them captive.

"In view of the deplorable ongoing performance of the republic's armed forces," wrote George Kahin, who was still in Jogjakarta at the time, a few blocks from the Palace, "it was unreasonable to expect any real protection."[1] "The republican government is very *down* and nervous," reported Captain Gulden of the Dutch military intelligence. "According to Hatta," he wrote, "the army in Jogjakarta offered no resistance, because the [most capable units of] troops were elsewhere on maneuvers."[2]

At Hatta's cabinet emergency meeting in the hours preceding the Dutch attack, where Amir's fate was also being debated, "Soekarno declared that he did not know where the army was." Douwes Dekker, an elder statesman of the republic, a veteran of the Indonesian movement, a fighter for independence since the time of the First World War, said at the meeting "that the hate between the Indonesian communists and non-communists surpassed the hate between the Indonesians and the Dutch. In a frightful way, massacres became the norm. The affliction of the republic was corruption and once more corruption. Of democracy, in the republic, there is no more a word. There is only fighting."[3]

Amir was still alive at the moment. Mohammad Natsir, Hatta cabinet's minister of information, who announced at the meeting that Amir was brought to Surakarta "to remove him from the anger of the people," warned the cabinet that in Jogjakarta "important archives and documents, among them the correspondence with [the US delegate] Cochran and correspondence between Soeripno and Moscow [?], etc. was not secured and is about to fall in the hands of the Dutch."[4]

The Dutch advance unit arrived at the Jogjakarta palace. Soekarno and other civilian leaders were taken to the airport and flown to a place of "internal exile," the old Dutch Indies term used was most fitting the occasion. A Dutch bomber took the leaders of the republic to Pangkal Pinang on the island of Bangka, off the east coast of Sumatra. Later, some of them were transferred to the main island, into a hotel on the shore of Lake Toba.[5]

The Dutch invasion had been watched by foreign observers and described as "a wonderful show." Captain Gulden of Dutch military intelligence reported from Jogjakarta on December 22: "A great admiration of the airborne operation during the taking of the Maguwo airport has been expressed by Cmdr. Matthews (Royal Australian Navy) and Major Montana (U.S. Army) who happened [sic] to be present at the airport. They spoke about a '*wonderful show*' and a tutorial in how military exercise is to be done. They also admired the correct conduct of our military towards the civilian population. They noted the small fact that streetlights in Jogjakarta kept working throughout, as they said, '*this most wonderful military operation.*'" "Equally remarkable," Captain Gulden wrote in this report, "was an apathetic attitude of the population when Soekarno was being taken away in a jeep with a Dutch officer at his side."[6]

Johannes Leimena, Amir's friend since their student years, now a politician, of the mainstream, who rejected Madiun, saw what was happening: "The

Dutch military vehicles were all American or Canadian Fords, Chevrolets, and Jeeps. Some of the American equipment was wartime Lend-lease, some of it brand new products of later-day Lend-lease [and] Marshall-plan aid. The British equipment was largely part of the material left in Java for the Dutch by the British in 1945. Dutch troops riding with the convoy were dressed and equipped American or British style."[7]

Soeripno, were he not dead now, executed with Amir Sjarifoeddin on the night of December 19, might have said, "I told you so." George Kahin met with Soeripno days before Soeripno left Jogjakarta for his last journey. Kahin recalled one part of their discussion: "He seemed confident that in this eventuality [the Dutch attack on the republic] the Communists by virtue of superior organization and training, would soon dominate the guerilla organization on Java. . . ."[8] But there was no Communist superior organization now.

Pesindo had been disarmed and the Communist rebellion was suppressed. T. B. Simatoepang, Colonel, rejecting Madiun, with the army, was now assigned to the headquarters of *Panglima Besar* Soedirman. The memoirs he wrote a few years later are an extraordinary document of the events following the Dutch invasion.

In the early hours of the Dutch attack, on the morning of December 20, Simatoepang was in Jogjakarta. He escaped the city in feverish haste, it seems by car, with only his adjutant. They reached a village a few kilometers from the city, Simatoepang writes poetically or ironically, "in the direction of the Merapi volcano."[9]

In a few days, he managed to connect with the troops of Siliwangi. They were, as it had been planned, on the move after the victory over the rebels. *Hidjrah* was ended, and, mission accomplished, they were heading back home, to West Java. In the chaos of those days, they marched according to the plan and Simatoepang went part of the way with them. The Dutch military now dominated the area. Walking with the Siliwangi, marching, and running—the Dutch were advancing—Simatoepang moved through the same landscape, shaking and in surge, through which Amir had moved and run a few months before. Simatoepang and Siliwangi now repeated the journey.

They were again strangers, double and multiple times over, struggling through the land, and Simatoepang described the mood:

> Many wives and children accompanied the [Siliwangi] troops. Apparently, they had left West Java earlier when their husbands' units had been evacuated. Now, as the troops set off home for West Java after the Dutch attack what else could the wives do but follow? What would be

their fate had they been left behind in the towns occupied by the Dutch, amid a strange [sic] community? During the four days of my journey westward with the Siliwangi troops, I saw wives and children joining the march, setting off into the dark, crossing rivers, and climbing steep, slippery hills. I heard about cases of children who had drowned while crossing flood swollen rivers during pitch-dark nights.[10]

"It was very hard for me to part with the Siliwangi troops," Simatoepang wrote, "not to go with them to West Java. I had to stay."[11] Simatoepang returned and spent the following six months moving, running, fighting as a guerilla leader.

"After writing in my field diary about my experiences and talks I had in the region of Mount Lawu," Simatoepang wrote, "I can see I scribbled seven names without any explanation whatsoever. The names were Amir Sjarifoeddin, Oey Gee Hwat, Djokosoejono, Ronomarsono, Maroeto Daroesman, Soeripno, Sardjono. Around Mount Lawu I heard that they were shot on the first day of the Dutch attack on Surakarta. I did not ask how they appeared in the eye of the storm of anger, fear, disorganization of the first days which I myself witnessed. I might be just pensive as I wrote these names in my diary without adding anything to them."[12] "I knew all of them," Simatoepang writes, "except Ronomarsono [shot probably because mistaken for Soemarsono]. Amir Sjarifoeddin and Djokosoejono I knew well."[13] "How did it happen," Simatoepang asks, "that Bung Amir was swept up in the Madiun rebellion? Many theories have been proposed, but a complete and satisfactory answer to this question will probably never be found. As far as I know, Bung Amir himself left no notes."[14]

After Siliwangi left for West Java, only local troops remained in the republican area around Jogjakarta to face the Dutch—and the landscape in surge. Johannes Leimena wrote in the 1949 brochure that "It had become apparent that this second military action has been a political as well as a military failure for the Dutch. The Dutch thought that the total power of resistance of the republic, military as well as political, could be broken by capturing Jogjakarta, 'the bandit's lair.' . . . It turned out that by carrying off the republican leaders, a colossal spirit of non-cooperation and resistance has been aroused among the population. The Dutch were not prepared for that."[15]

Bungkus, the guerilla leader, interviewed half a century later, whose view of the Madiun affair was confused so that he with his sea dogs simply stayed away, now joined the struggle. He told his interviewer: "If the KNIL [Royal Netherlands Indies Army] people questioned the locals where the 'extremists' were, they'd answer 'up in the mountains.' But actually," Bungkus says proudly, "we were here. That's how it was."[16]

"On December 19, 1948," Simatoepang wrote in his memoirs, "the Dutch considered the time ripe to crush the Republic of Indonesia, since they calculated that its strength had been exhausted by the recent Madiun Rebellion." However, adds Simatoepang, "*Panglima Besar* Soedirman managed to escape . . . together with his troops, and they were warmly welcomed by the people in the villages. It was indeed these villages which became the bases for the people's war waged for several months against the Dutch troops."[17]

The maps of the guerilla movement could easily be superimposed on those of Amir's columns' routes.[18] There very probably was a similar feeling of fear and exhaustion together with that of consummation, freedom or death, and freedom to death. "Personally," wrote Simatoepang, "I felt as if a heavy burden was lifted from my shoulders a few days after the Dutch attack. . . . During a people's war one feels healthier physically and more at ease than during negotiations."[19]

"I am convinced," Simatoepang wrote, "that the ordinary boys, the soldiers and pemuda [youth] who fell on both sides during the Madiun Affair, knew nothing of the issues behind this national tragedy. I was certain that the last prayer of all these boys was for the happiness and greatness of the same Fatherland."[20] These words might signify the ultimate defeat of Musso's and Amir's aspirations, the final demise of their revolution.

At Sitikan, Simatoepang wrote about his unit's stop at a Javanese village in the depths of the island: "Ali Boediardjo [formerly of Amir's circle, then of Sjahrir's, now a member of Simatoepang's staff and soon to be his brother-in-law, a Javanese by birth and culture] explained to me that this year, '1879' of the Javanese calendar, that is to say between November 1948 and November 1949, was a year of calamity, but that in November 1949 i.e., the beginning of the year '1880' of the Javanese calendar, the situation would improve."[21]

"The lurah [village head] of Kalitengah," Simatoepang wrote at another place in his recollections, "received us enthusiastically. He told us he was a descendant of one of the followers of Prince Diponegoro." Diponegoro was a leader of the Java war against the Dutch in 1825–1830, a Jogjakarta prince who was believed to be a rightful heir to the throne. "Clearly," wrote Simatoepang, "the stories about the Diponegoro war remained a living thing for the people in this region. This would obviously be a great advantage in carrying on the people's war."[22] "Surely," Simatoepang wrote as he settled in another base, "it was no accident that Prince Diponegoro, during the last stages of his war against the Dutch, had lived in the same mountainous area, between the Progo River to the east and the Bogowonto River to the west."[23] "Perhaps," the colonel mused at another moment, looking at the landscape, "Prince Diponegoro had also once surveyed the plain of Jogjakarta from the tops of these hills."[24]

"I think it was Sumendro," Simatoepang wrote about another officer on his staff, also a Javanese, "who told me about a peculiar interpretation of Djojobojo predictions." (A twelfth-century Javanese king was prophesying dark times in Java followed by years of harmony and prosperity.) "According to this interpretation," Simatoepang continues, "when the golden age was about to dawn, every 'leader' would have two wives, that is, at least two. Accordingly, as Sumendro told it, the 'leaders' in the area were rushing to take wives under the slogan 'let's follow Djojobojo.'"[25]

In his memoirs, Simatoepang quotes from a diary of Captain Supardjo, who was an adjutant of *Panglima Besar* Soedirman, the supreme commander who was moving and on the run and fighting. Soedirman was now the recognized military leader of the resistance against the Dutch. He was in the final stages of tuberculosis and had often to be carried on litters. On December 22, 1948, three days into their escape to the hills, Captain Supardjo wrote in his diary: "Along the way at Bodojo, the people thought the person on the litters was Sultan Hamengku Buwono IX. Many came to kiss Pak Dirman's [Soedirman's] feet and ask his blessing."[26]

Occasionally still, Simatoepang expressed doubts that are not so far from Musso's, and especially Amir's, doubts and aspirations. He worried that in the present surge of the landscape, energies that may bring about a social revolution are missing. Perhaps, the absence of these energies makes the struggle for freedom impossible. "On January 12, 1949, I went over a number of problems in my diary. First of all, the social developments during the people's war are bringing the townspeople and villagers closer together." However, "Will this trend contain the basis for closer links between village and town in the days to come, when the people's war is over? It would be very regrettable if this closer relationship were to be confined to the period of this people's war."[27]

In the village of Banaran, east of Jogjakarta and on the southeast slopes of Mount Lawu, Simatoepang and his staff established a base where they spent the longest time of the war. About Banaran, Simatoepang noted: "The local youngsters attended the elementary school at Balong, not far from Banaran. Most spoke Indonesian fluently. . . . Some of us tried to teach them. Ali [Boediardjo], for instance, gave English lessons. Whether any of this benefitted them by reducing the backwardness and poverty of life in their village, I do not know."[28] And Simatoepang adds a disturbing note about what one of his officers told him: "Prawoto is a very calm person. I cannot imagine him getting angry, irritated, or impertinent. When we discussed the attitude of the people in the people's war, he said: 'The people accept this war [like] they accept natural disaster, something inevitable, but also, like a natural disaster, something which will run its course in time.' I asked myself: 'Is this also Prawoto's point of view?'[29]

Then, after months of running and fighting, the end of the war arrived. The Dutch could not overrun the republic in a sudden attack, and the great powers—meaning now mostly the United States—became impatient and pushed another compromise. The republic was to be recognized again, *under certain conditions*. Colonel Simatoepang was about to return from his guerilla base in Banaran back to Jogjakarta. "Before entering Jogjakarta, we spent the night in the village where Lieutenant Colonel Suharto had had his headquarters during the last phase of the people's war. When we arrived, an old woman told us that Pak Suharto had already left for the city. 'Being a distinguished *panglima*,' she said, 'he will certainly be rewarded with a beautiful princess.'"[30]

The peasants still did not have land. The workers still earned sub-subsistence wages. Refugees still wandered through the landscape as strangers. Politics still belonged to the rich.

The republican army, the victors over the Communists, now the guerilla force of the republic, became a reservoir, and container, and the only guarantor of élan, euphoria, and revolution. At one moment, on February 14, 1949, still in the middle of the war, Colonel Simatoepang, still at the guerilla base, wrote in his diary: "If the political settlement leaves the Dutch with considerable power and influence in Indonesia, this will give rise to difficulties. If the political settlement leaves us too dependent on the United States, then we may be branded as American puppets."[31]

There was a red line for Simatoepang, however, not to be crossed. "While studying at the Military Academy," he wrote in his memoirs, "I had always heard that a civil war aroused much deeper emotions and hatred than an ordinary war. Now the truth of this lesson has been brought home."[32] Simatoepang and his fighters traveled the landscape where Madiun happened. He saw the consequences of a civil war. And a class war. He learned of Amir's death. Still at the guerilla base, and with the tide of war turning in Indonesia's favor, toward another compromise, Simatoepang visibly was getting somber. *"January 29, 1949*. The resolution submitted by Cuba, the United States, China, and Norway was adopted by the Security Council on January 28, 1949. . . . If we reject the resolution, we have two alternatives. We can work for a new resolution more favorable to us or we can completely ignore the Security Council in our further struggle, basing this struggle solely on the people's war . . . if possible (and that is quite speculative) with material aid from Asian and other countries (Russia)."

But this was again a red line. "The Republic has probably no other alternative than to accept the Security Council resolution even though we know that its implementation will be extremely difficult, perhaps even impossible."[33]

Soekarno, Hatta, and Sjahrir, as the Dutch were increasingly stuck in their attempt to subdue the republic by force, had been allowed to negotiate. "I sent a letter to Mr. Sudjono, the secretary of the Indonesian delegation," Simatoepang wrote. "I asked him to inform our men in . . . Bangka that our position was quite strong and, therefore, they need not concede too much to the Dutch."[34] After some weeks, however, Simatoepang realized: "Although several psychological problems would have to be overcome, there seemed no other alternative than to accept the policy mapped in Bangka."[35]

On July 6, 1949, a United Nations airplane landed at Maguwo airport, Jogjakarta, bringing Soekarno, Hatta, and other civilian leaders back from their place of exile. Another victory. From Maguwo, a motorcade took the leaders to the city. In an open car, Soekarno stood side by side with the Sultan of Jogjakarta, who had remained in his palace through the occupation, both waving to the crowds. Simatoepang was present: "I saw for myself how enthusiastically the people welcomed them all along the road and at the Palace. Who can deny that the *Dwitunggal* [Soekarno–Hatta] was a powerful factor, having an almost 'magic' nature during our revolution? The July 3 Movement [Tan Malaka's attempt at changing the course of the republic in 1947] and the Madiun Rebellion had demonstrated how difficult it was to oppose Sukarno and Hatta."[36] They now, Simatoepang wrote, "would have to establish a New Indonesia which would give real meaning to the blood and tears shed during the war for independence. This New Indonesia would be built within the contemporary world where the ideological and competitive conflict between the forces of capitalism and communism are reaching their climax, 100 years after Karl Marx wrote his work at the Royal Museum Library in London."[37]

On July 10, 1949, the ailing *Panglima Besar* Soedirman, the commander of the republican military, was officially to resume his functions. It was expected he would meet the civilian leaders first, Soekarno and Hatta. Colonel Simatoepang was assigned to accompany Soedirman in his car "from the hills" to the capital: "From our discussion in the car, I got the impression that psychologically, Pak Dirman still could not completely accept recent developments. . . . Still, he intended to advance proposals and suggestions which would prevent future disappointments. . . . Pak Hardjo [Soehardjo, another officer in the car] and I suggested that he should first see the President and Vice-President before he went to inspect the parade at the Alun-Alun Lor. [the square at the main entrance to the Palace]. . . . He did not answer for some moments. Eventually he agreed."[38]

There is a photo of Soedirman meeting Soekarno and Hatta. Soedirman wears a heavy overcoat and looks very ill, indeed he died the next January. Simatoepang describes the parade, before or after the meeting: "The officers and troops just returned from the field did not wear uniform clothing. They had black, yellow, and green outfits. But those watching the parade would not quickly forget the atmosphere of this simple ceremony."[39]

Simatoepang belonged to the victors. He was appointed a military member of the Indonesian delegation led by Hatta, to the Hague, to work out the final points of the new compromise and to sign the document. Simatoepang described the weeks in the Netherlands, and I try to believe that I can still hear Amir's voice a little in his.

"The Report from the Hague," is the title of the last section in Simatoepang's memoirs, perhaps deliberately published as a sequel to his *Report from Banaran*, to his recollections of "the people's war." It was the first time Simatoepang visited Holland, the ships, the cows in the meadows. "Given the bustle of the conference, I did not have much opportunity to see the countryside. Everything looked small, flat, orderly, efficient, safe, tranquil, and prosperous. What enormous difference between this country and the vastness of Indonesia, with its mountains, valleys, and forests, and its society which was turbulently pioneering the way to a new era."[40]

Already at the outset, Simatoepang was "led to believe" that "the most delicate problems" to deal with would be those of keeping or abrogating "the union" between Indonesia and the Dutch Crown, and those "of finance." But "already at the start of the conference," he writes, "the Union became a matter that could no longer be rejected." Likewise, he writes, "the debts which, for the greater part, had been used to finance attacks against the Republic": "The Dutch maintained that we must assume all the assets and liabilities of the Netherlands Indies."[41] The United States with its strongly felt presence at the conference, dominating the conference in many ways, supported the Dutch on both counts.

"Perhaps it would have been better if we had not come to the Hague to negotiate," wrote Simatoepang. "But what else could we have done? While we were in Banaran, the Agreement was reached . . . and had received the blessing of Bung Karno and Bung Hatta. This sealed a situation in which, for all practical purpose, it was no longer possible to reject the agreement without repudiating Sukarno and Hatta. . . . Feeling very upset (many members had tears in their eyes) our delegation decided in the end to accept the UNCI recommendation."[42]

> It doesn't much matter: a corpse is open to all comers.
>
> —Sartre, *Family Idiot*, 1, X

In 1951, Soerjono, a follower of Amir Sjarifoeddin since before the Japanese occupation, and a second-rank PKI (Communist Party of Indonesia) leader, who survived, recalled:

> A year or so after Madiun, . . . I came down into Yogyakarta . . . and found in the reporters' mess a copy of the magazine *Mutiara* ["Pearl"], edited by Mochtar Loebis. There I found the diary of Soeripno entitled "Why We Lost." It seems that this diary was confiscated by the military before Soeripno was liquidated along with Amir Sjarifoeddin.
>
> . . . The notes had been made, if I'm not mistaken, at a meeting in Bantar and in Pulung, after Amir Sjarifoeddin had abandoned Madiun. . . . It's been a long time since I read these notes, and all I remember now is their conclusion, where Soeripno said, quite frankly: "We were not prepared to deal with the situation," meaning that he admitted that the Madiun Affair was not part of his mental preparation.[43]

Other sources also spoke about Soeripno's diary or notes or testimony, or a letter smuggled out of prison, and the authenticity of the document was rarely doubted. "Among other prisoners," Indonesian historian Soe Hok Gie wrote in the 1960s, of the top leaders of Madiun who were captured, "only Soeripno left an account in a form of a memoir." Soe quoted passages from the memoir:

> The most important cause of our defeat was the weak support we had; some in some places, but very little outside the Madiun area. The people in villages were in fact often willing to assist in our capture. But does this mean that our program was not correct? Certainly not. . . . Our error was in not following our program properly.
>
> . . . The Madiun Affair and what came out of it, to say the truth, was not a part of the program. . . . We had been faced with fait accompli, . . . we became desperate. . . . And our excesses then alienated the people.[44]

According to Arnold Brackman, Soeripno's "candid memoirs" were written "in prison after he was captured and his running was over."[45]

According to Soerjono's recollections again, "It seems that the diary of Soeripno was confiscated by the military before Soeripno was liquidated. . . . I heard that the notes were turned over to Mochtar Loebis."[46]

The victors owned the memory. They were the ones who found it and who gave it to the people.

Similarly, statements by Amir, allegedly given at his interrogation in the Klambu prison during the first hours after his capture were recorded and conveyed by the military, as much of it or as little as the army wished. In his notes, Amir allegedly admitted, for instance, that he had "planned, under a disguise of a merchant to escape to Solo [Surakarta] and Jogjakarta."⁴⁷ Memory had been captured, owned, and distributed by the victors. Like the victors themselves, it was memory triumphant and memory anxious in equal measure.

The caches of weapons rumored to be hidden by Amir when he was the minister of defense and the prime minister were never found. Not all Communists were killed, and many were ghosted. As perhaps dead, *revenants,* they were rumored to still haunt Java. The victors, the military, became the vessel of élan, euphoria, chaos, the war for independence, and the new compromise. It was still a time of revolution, and the landscape did not settle down—far from it. The container was bursting, and many, like Simatoepang—now General Simatoepang, second only to Nasoetion in the military hierarchy—were uncertain whether The Hague compromise was worth the tears and blood of the struggle.

While Musso and Amir were still alive and on the run, the army announced that a case (might they say cache?) of documents had been discovered in the house of Amir in Jogjakarta.

> On the second day of the insurrection, Captain Maulana of Siliwangi . . . discovered a number of documents in the cupboard in Amir Sjarifoeddin's house. . . .
>
> From these documents plans of the PKI uprising become clear. From these documents it was learned how, in order to achieve their aims, Amir Sjarifoeddin and his comrades . . . attempted to infiltrate by illegal means the members of the armed forces of the republic . . . using the difficult economic situation. . . . According to the documents, Madiun . . . was to become the principal fortress.⁴⁸

The documents as such were never shown to the public. Whenever it came to it, they were "referred to." On December 6, 1948, a reporter for the republican *Pedoman,* "Compass," "questioned if they really existed."⁴⁹

The triumphant and the anxious, as captured and distributed, the memory of Madiun and of Amir, needed permanent fixing, a base, pillars, and arcs, what Pierre Nora called "places of memory," monuments built up when memory itself becomes uncertain.⁵⁰ The memory of Madiun and Amir by the victors, became structured and hardened, often literary in clay, marble, and bronze.

Nasoetion, one of the fencing mates of Simatoepang during Japanese times on the roof of Bandoeng, the commander of Siliwangi in 1948, became the army chief of staff after The Hague compromise. All the five officers on the photograph from the Madiun time, relaxed on the eve of the victory, had risen to the top positions of the military establishment of the new Indonesia. Lieutenant Colonel Soeharto, second from the left, the one who did not deliver the letter by Amir to Soekarno, the distinguished *panglima* at the end of the war of liberation who would almost certainly be rewarded with a beautiful princess, got well on the way to become the president of the republic in 1968. Colonel Gatot Subroto, another one on the photograph, the man who was most widely considered the man behind Amir's execution, became one of the most celebrated generals of the army and in 1962 was given, by Soekarno, the coveted title of *pahlawan nasional*, "national hero." By the mid-1960s, there could hardly be an Indonesian city, town, or village that would not have a street or a square carrying the name of Gatot Subroto.[51]

Slamet Rijadi, Soeadi, Sarbini, Bachrun, and Ahmad Jani, the remaining ones in the picture, made the Indonesian army, for the next eighteen years, the cream of the corps, the essence of it.

The memory of the victors congealed but, to use Rem Koolhaas's term from the language of architecture, volume matters.[52] "Disinformation," says Paul Virilio, is "actually an excess of information" and "excess of mediation."[53]

"The 'deceased,'" says Heidegger, "is the object of 'being taken care of' in funeral rites, burials, and cult of graves"; memory is born "in lingering together with him in mourning and commemorating."[54] Jacques Derrida says that the memory is rooted "in veiling."[55] "Veiling," again Derrida uses when speaking about a specter, "to make sure that the dead will not come back . . . to keep the cadaver localized."[56]

"Consider, for instance," wrote Kierkegaard, "the invention of the printing press, perfected to a top-speed machine sure to guarantee that no dirt or dreg remains unpublished."[57] The list of books on Madiun, Musso, and Amir got long and longer during the decades after Madiun, as the army joined the compromise, shared power in the state, increased its power, and, eventually, after 1965, after another alleged attempt of a revived Communist Party at another revolution, came to rule the country. The excess of information discovered and leaked, memory captured and veiled, about Madiun, Musso, and Amir, and about their attempt at a big change in Indonesian society, had been recycled, made recyclable and thus, hopefully, assumed a permanent life.

In 1966, eighteen years after the events in Madiun, and at the moment of another specter reappearing, of *revenant*, of anxiety heightened, of another challenge to the established calm and order, and to the memory of the victors, *Menjingkap Tabir Fakta-fakta Pemberontakan PKI dalam Peristiwa Madiun*, "Raising the Screen Over the Facts of the Communist Uprising in the Madiun Affair," had been published. "In connection with the new Communist crimes in 1965," the book introduced itself, referring to the recent events, historian Djamal Marsudi "received an order by the Army Strategic Command to collect and publish documents about the Madiun Affair."[58]

As one opened the book, there were two endorsements first, each under a sign of Garuda, the mount of the god Vishnu, a mythical bird, symbol of the Indonesian state. Next to the *Garuda*, in each case, there were four stars, for the two four-star generals, the best of the victors:

1st endorsement:
Chairman of the Presidium of the Cabinet, General of the Army, Soeharto
  Endorses with pleasure . . .
  Twice, the PKI betrayed the Nation, the Motherland and the Revolution. This gives yet another proof that the teaching of Marxism-Leninism or communism is not in accordance with the identity of the Indonesian Nation. . . .

2nd endorsement:
General of the Army, Dr. A.H. Nasution, Chairman of the M.P.R.S. [Provisional People's Consultative Assembly]
  With happiness,
  I express my appreciation. . . . As we talk about the violent action by the PKI on September 19, 1948, known as "the Madiun Affair," we must not forget the counter-revolution of the "September 30 [1965] Movement."

It is a book to leaf through. There are mostly photographs, with shorter or extended captions. As one turns the pages over, one is supposed to relive the events.

1. Amir Sjarifoeddin [photographed as if deep in thought].
Prime Minister Amir Sjarifoeddin: The only of the communist leaders in the history of the republic who had ever held top executive position. Renville was for him *the greatest debacle.*
2. Mohammad Hatta [smiling].
Vice-President / Prime Minister Mohammad Hatta: He did not hesitate to use "an iron fist" against the Communists.
3. Maoeto Daroesman [looking at the reader from behind bars].
[no caption]
4. Musso [with a grin].
A veteran communist who came to Indonesia in a mysterious manner, injecting insecurity into the republican politics.
5. Maroeto Daroesman [once more; no bars this time]

The second in importance after MUSSO [sic]. In his face, one can read how fanatical he had been in his communist ideology. He died together with Amir Sjarifoeddin and 9 other communist figures executed by the firing squad in Ngalihan Surakarta.

6. [A montage of several photographs on one page.]
   a. Musso [speaking from a tribune to a large crowd]
MUSSO, a political figure and an ace as an orator.
   b. Musso [speaking from another tribune]
Wherever he came, with his simple but interesting speeches, he grasped the attention of the masses
   c. [A large room, perhaps a hall of a mosque or a school; the floor is covered with lines of corpses in white shrouds.]
It's a pity, how many talents were wasted in the interest of this Party and this group. Here are the results of Musso's agitation. Ruins and corpses were everywhere.

7. Amir Sjarifoeddin again [Here Amir is wearing a sarong and jacket and carries a bag on a shoulder strap].
Amir Sjarifoeddin, intellectual and politician, originally from Tapanuli, of a sharp mind and a pious Christian. Everywhere, he carried a pocket Bible with him. . . . People do not believe that he became a Communist—unless he had sold his soul to [the] devil. He fell into the abyss of destruction.[59]

"Fat voice always comes up with directions," wrote Mladen Dolar in his *A Voice and Nothing Else*.[60] "Canned language," wrote Slavoj Žižek, "suggests violence."[61] "Nail down the lid," Kierkegaard quoted an old funeral hymn.[62] There existed a cottage industry of military-endorsed books on Madiun already before 1965. After 1965, after another alleged attempt by the Indonesian Communist Party at a big change, "the second Madiun," and after the army finally coming to power in 1966, the industry grew expeditiously.

Often, it was not even necessary to open the book. The cover said it all. *Bahaja Merah di Indonesia*, "The Red Danger in Indonesia," by *mr*. Isa Anshary, Jusuf Wibisono, and Arif Usman, published by the Penerbit Front Anti Komunis, "Publishers of the Anti-Communist Front," in Bandung in 1955,[63] was dark scarlet on the outside. The other color, faded on my copy, might be white. The whole then would suggest, sort of, *dwiwarna*, red and white, the colors of the republic.

H. A. Notosoetardjo's *Peristiwa Madiun: tragedi nasional*, "The Madiun Affair: The National Tragedy," of 1966, has a scarlet cover, too, suggesting either blood or flames.[64] Marsudi's *Menjingkap Tabir Fakta-fakta*, mentioned above, has a blood-scarlet cover with an image of a monster with more blood (or flames) coming from his jaws. The caricatures by Ramelan from 1948 were clearly the model. Besides flames (or blood) out of the monster's jaws, again, toy-like manikins are seen falling out, but this time already as skeletons. Some more miniskeletons lay scattered on the ground, and some in the process of being crushed under the monster's paw. There is a large yellow sign of hammer and sickle burned in the monster's scales-covered skin.⁶⁵

This should be a scene of victory. The hammer-and-sickle monster is about to be struck down forever. A bare but muscular hand holds a *bambu runtjing*, "sharpened bamboo," the holy symbol of the revolution. There is a tattoo (it must be a tattoo) on the muscular arm, big letters, *PANTJASILA*, "Five Principles," meaning the state principles of the budding Indonesian state as formulated by Soekarno in the last months of the Japanese occupation, in June 1945:

1. Belief in the one and only God
2. Just and civilized humanity
3. The unity of Indonesia
4. Democracy guided by the inner wisdom in the unanimity arising out of deliberation among representatives
5. Social justice for the whole of the people of Indonesia.⁶⁶

Historian of the Madiun affair, David Anderson, argued in 1976, that "the Madiun Affair of September 1948 is best understood as an internal crisis of military politics."⁶⁷ The same has been argued by many influential voices outside Indonesia in the case of "the next Communist coup" in 1965.⁶⁸ The victors were triumphant and anxious. The specter, and the victors themselves certainly felt it, was not merely still there, but wandering *inside the military*.

Film, wrote Paul Virilio, was "the technology of least resistance."⁶⁹ "There is no room [in film] for history," wrote Marc Augé, "unless it has been transformed into an element of spectacle."⁷⁰ Memory of Madiun and of Amir, most triumphant, anxious, and spectacular, was devised as a movie show. The film about Madiun probably had been designed to become a double feature with the existing mega-film on the 1965 PKI affair, a bloody superflick that had been screened on every anniversary of September 30, 1965, in every school, factory, office, and, of course, on television.

The film about Madiun, provisionally called "Madiun '48" was never made. "The script was submitted," writes Harry Poeze, "on December 1, 1981." It was written by Arto Hady who was also to be the film director. "The advisor for the story," according to the script was Pusat Sejarah ABRI, "Center for the History of the Armed Forces." "Madiun '48" was to be "a spectacular action film."⁷¹ The synopsis survived: "Film begins in January 1948, as Amir Sjarifoeddin submits a letter of resignation to Soekarno. On the same day Amir receives a visit from a man representing the Netherlands who brings him thanks for signing the Renville agreement and, as he leaves, gives Amir an envelope."

In the next scene, "Amir is attending a meeting of the leadership of the FDR [People's Democratic Front]." Then the story becomes melodramatic. Wiro appears, a fanatical young Communist, and there is his girlfriend Tini. Wiro loves Tini, but as he tells her in a love scene, his dedication to the Communist Party surpasses his private feelings. All said, there is an attempt at a revolution, defeat of the rebels, and the film comes to its conclusion. Or climax:

And finally.
   Amir is already tied to a pole; his eyes are covered by the black cloth.
   Commander of the execution squad hesitates.

The very last scene of the film shows a battlefield. It is the next morning. The armed forces of the republic are under fire from the Dutch invaders and bombs rains on them from Dutch planes. This ends the film.[72] The audience knew, without more ado, that the armed forces of the republic in the end were victorious.

> [T]he ruling classes capitulate only falsely, abstractly, and undialectically.
> —Bloch, *Traces*, 12

President Soekarno's role in the Madiun affair, was, to say the least, ambivalent. "Ambivalence," wrote Nancy, "is constitutive of sovereignty."[73] "*Herrschaftsbereich des Winkes* is an expression used by Heidegger, "dominion by hints." "Hints" work as "signs of complicity."[74]

According to Guy Pauker, an expert on Indonesia for the RAND Corporation, "Sukarno was hesitant to denounce the Communists and it is, of course, possible that Sukarno and the PNI [Indonesian National Party], and perhaps even [*Panglima Besar*] Soedirman (who seems to have been ill at the time) were attempting to restrain the more right-wing forces in the government in hope that PKI might make some conciliatory move."[75]

"Soekarno," wrote Abu Hanifah bluntly about the events leading to Madiun, "was on Sjarifoeddin's side while Hatta . . . however disgusted and disappointed with the West, still maintained a certain belief in the West."[76] "Of all the senior leaders with whom I discussed Amir," recalled Kahin, "it was Sukarno who seemed to me most empathetic."[77] "President Sukarno and Army commander Soedirman," wrote David Anderson, in contrast to Hatta and Nasoetion, "emerged from the Madiun Affair in a decidedly weaker condition than before."[78]

Soekarno kept in the saddle until the horse stopped balking. Like back in the 1920s, Soekarno increasingly defined himself as just being Soekarno. He defined the nation, as just being a nation, naturally gathered around him—Soekarno. These were words meaning words, increasingly. Soekarno's, increasingly, was a dominion by hints. The president's ambiguity had been vacuous enough to suck in a maximum of diverse forces.

Soekarno embodied ambivalence worthy of the myth of Prince Diponegoro and of the other Javanese heroes, wayang warriors of gamelan harmony. A *Panglima Besar* Soedirman's expression to unite the leaders, army, and nation, was that of a *pajung*, "parasol," the golden parasol really. Golden parasols, at times past, and in the present, too, whenever the Sultan of Jogjakarta appeared, for instance, were carried by the attendants in procession, as a symbol, a sacred mountain, the state, shading the royalty and all the people in all their diversity, lucky to get close. It gave the universe centered on royalty a golden shade.

"If any section of history has been painted gray on gray, it is this," Marx might have said if he witnessed this.[79] Marx wrote it about the Eighteenth Brumaire of Napoleon III as the Bonaparte buried, or rather veiled, the Revolution under bourgeois rule. "The French bourgeoisie," wrote Marx, "had long ago found the solution to Napoleon's dilemma: In fifty years Europe will be republican or Cossack. It solved it in the—*république cosaque*."[80] Marx also quoted Francois Guizot, a conservative constitutional monarchist putting a seal on the moderates' victory: "This is the complete and final triumph of socialism!"[81]

Under the pajung, in the pajung's golden shade, it was the idea, nation would proceed in unity intact. Soedirman said, a general in a speech to the army, when Amir was still alive, "Our state with its apparatus of authority must be held in such a condition that, in its integrity and unbrokenness, it will resemble a parasol [pajung], a shelter, under which we could never be harmed. Indivisible, and united in struggle with enemy, thus, we will live as one."[82]

Only a few weeks after the outbreak of the Madiun affair, Soekarno published a revised edition of his *Sarinah* book—a first edition copy was given to Musso when he met Soekarno in August. Now, the Communists stepped out of the pajung shade. In the second edition of the book, Soekarno wrote that the Madiun affair was a social revolution which began too early, perhaps decades too early. Those in Madiun, he wrote, became "enemies of God, enemies of state, enemies of the motherland, enemies of the nation."[83] Nation as nation, motherland as motherland, enemies as enemies.

On June 22, 1949, still in "internal exile" in Bangka, but already close to his return to Jogjakarta, Soekarno was interviewed by foreign journalists. Indonesian nationalism, he said, proved that its power was in counterweighting Communism. In his speech two months later, August 17, 1949, on the fourth anniversary of the proclamation of independence, already back in Jogjakarta, Soekarno attacked Musso head on, but not Communism, not the PKI, and not Amir by name.[84] As Soemarsono commented, "Bung Karno was silent with a thousand words."[85]

Soekarno's dominion by hints worked for fifteen years. Soekarno remained in the saddle, through the period of parliamentary democracy (1949–1956) and guided democracy (1956–1965), letting the victors' memory dominate, with a hint here and there, the president of the nation and the commander-in-chief of the army, with the army increasingly asserting itself, until, in 1966, when the military, Soeharto and Nasoetion, standing up against Communist danger again, took over.

By the late fifties at least, rumors became making rounds, with a strong echo especially in the United States, of Soekarno getting close to Communism again. In the early 1960s, commissioning a US tabloid journalist, Cindy Adams, who happened to be in Indonesia with her husband on a State Department culture tour, set out to produce *Soekarno, An Autobiography as Told to Cindy Adams*. There, Soekarno, in dire straits, mentioned Madiun, and this time also Musso and Amir by names.

With "visible emotion," Soekarno told Cindy Adams about his "political teachers from Surabaya, Alimin and Musso, and the man whose life I saved during the occupation, Amir Sjarifoeddin." They led, he told Cindy Adams, a rebellion against the nation, and they were stopped. "Let nobody say," Soekarno told her, "Soekarno flinched in crushing the Communist uprising."[86]

Soekarno survived the army takeover in 1965. He was almost accused of being a Communist, which might have led to his being killed with many others. He was allowed to end his years quietly (another internal exile), and he died in 1970, under house arrest in Jakarta.

Mohammad Hatta was the civilian principal among the victors. It was he who, with Nasoetion, had taken the decisive steps throughout 1948. Still, Hatta was wary, too, not to identify himself too closely with the military—still standing for a democrat even a socialist, a Francois Guizot in Marx's description, sort of. And Soekarno's pajung was large enough, for a decade at least, to shade him, as well.

Hatta was much less for hinting than Soekarno, yet, like Soekarno, through the following months and years he remained golden and nation tinted just enough for everyone to guess his true color. In a radio speech on November 17, 1948, with Musso already dead but Amir still at large, Hatta declared: "The Madiun Affair was the greatest national tragedy. Society was divided, citizens turned against each other, harvest was destroyed, workers and peasants were whipped into a frenzy. Democracy demands sportsmanship: majority decides."[87]

Hatta never expressed any doubt about what had happened in Madiun. In his memoirs he still wrote: "Musso's original plan was to proclaim an Indonesian Soviet-state."[88] Still in the 1970s, to all practical purposes out of politics, he repeated: "the communists attempted to build up a People's Army because they failed to infiltrate the army."[89]

But, unlike the army memory, crude, straightforward, and fatigued, Hatta's story of Madiun was nuanced: Musso was the culprit and Amir an enigma. Thus, the Hatta story made it done and complete. It nailed the lid of Amir's possible memory as a hero. Hatta acknowledged that Amir was an enigma. "He was an intellectual who had believed in communism (atheist) and he was a Christian (theist). He questioned the Bible and he was a Christian, he did politics and he was a communist." Hatta admitted: "I do not know how to analyze such a person; that is a job for a psychologist!" Still, Hatta offered an analysis: "Amir Sjarifoeddin and his allies wandered close to the [Van Mook] line; they wanted to cross to the Dutch. But the army finished them off. . . . They were executed because the Dutch attacked the republic. . . . Perhaps Amir Sjarifoeddin did attempt to save himself in the areas controlled by the Dutch. He certainly behaved like that. They were all shot."[90]

To Arnold Brackman, Hatta said that "Amir was vain and influenced by the flatteries of Setiadjit, Abdulmadjid and Tan Ling Djie." "Hatta also felt," Brackman reported, that Amir "was too religious to be a Communist."[91] "In my talks to Hatta," recalled George Kahin, "he insisted that Sjarifoeddin was 'too religious to be a real Communist.'"[92] Quoting this Hatta view, Hatta's biographer expresses a little surprise over this statement: "Many of Hatta's fellow Minangkabau," she notes, "were both communists and practicing Muslims."[93]

For all the years after the Madiun affair Hatta denied categorically that he might have been the one behind the *snelrecht*, the execution of Amir. At the same time, his denials never extended to condemning the execution. He presented himself as not involved and at times he became furious when it was suggested otherwise. According to Kahin, based on Kahin's many talks with Hatta through the years after 1948, "Hatta, who during this period saw Sjarifoeddin as his major political rival, was subsequently bitterly angry at General (then Colonel) A. H. Nasution for which he regarded as his responsibility, along with Colonel Gatot Subroto, in having Sjarifoeddin executed . . . without benefit of a trial."[94]

Soekarno was a pajung, and the pajung's shade was wide enough to give shelter, and cover, golden-tinged comfort, and sense of self-preservation, and also self-aggrandizement, to the army, to Hatta, and in the concentrated circles of the shade beyond to many. The whole nation eventually became tinged, triumphant, and anxious. The new Indonesia learned to live under the shadow.

The golden tinge under the parasol was a man-made light. "The story," wrote Ernst Bloch as if he were talking about Indonesia after 1948, "ends more tenderly than one has ever imagined."[95] History, including the history of the revolution and of Amir, in the words of Jacques Leclerc, turned into "a nostalgic montage of a past that is in fact burst and broken, and a happy diorama of a future which we know to be dead."[96]

Diorama is a fitting word and not only a metaphor—the little mannikin-like figures in dollhouse landscapes, and, behind the glass, tiny guerillas with tiny bamboo spears in postures of attacking. "Forty-eight dioramas . . . constitute the National History Monument in Jakarta."[97] There are many more dioramas in towns, museums, and tourist sites throughout Indonesia, the places of memory, for school tours, attracting students up to the point. They are the wall charts of the Indies of the present.

"Now," wrote Anthony Reid, "social revolution was postponed indefinitely. Although the direction of the revolution was far from settled, it had been jolted sharply to the Right."[98]

Islamic politicians fitted sometimes more and sometimes less comfortably under the Soekarno, Hatta, and army pajung. Indonesia was declared to be a secular state and five officially recognized religions had been permitted (not Judaism). Islam, naturally had been a dominant one and Islamic politics under the Five Principles, respecting the nation's unity, flourished.

The new memory demanded that the past was erased or, to use a better word, waxed. Revolutionary nostalgia, a better word still, was a way to do it. Abu Hanifah, who joined the victors, wrote about the past, and himself, and Amir. "What a great pity," Abu Hanifah wrote, "the compound at Kramat 106 today carries [the] name Gedung Sumpah Pemuda, "The House of the Youth Oath." It is all a little disheartening in there. Where used to be our bedrooms and the common room, it appears dismantled and empty. Chairs, tables, beds, were taken away. The kitchen, the bathrooms are gone. Everything is refurbished. To its ancient inhabitant a building like this offers little."[99]

Kramat 106 has been remade into a museum. A kind of Madame Tussauds representation of the Second Youth Congress of 1928. Wax Rudolf Wage Soepratman plays "Indonesia Raja" for the first time again and again. Unmarked wax figures of the youth leaders, Amir must be one of them, or rather not, sit on the podium behind the presidium table and listen. In another room, other wax leaders, around a card table sit debating. I have it from the museum promotional folder. Through the door in the background, school-tour children could be seen passing.

It might not be all cool and cozy under the parasol. Sometimes, Abu Hanifah's stories look like a warning. "It is remarkable," Abu Hanifah wrote about

Soekarno, "also, not so very strange really that Soekarno never mentioned the 1948 Communist rebellion in his autobiography." This is wrong. Soekarno did!

"Sometimes, people who knew him wondered what he would have done if the '65 rebellion ['"the second Madiun'"] had succeeded. Would he also like Amir Sjarifoeddin, have confessed that he had been a secret member of the PKI since 1935, or much earlier, since 1927?"[100]

Soekarno was warned, and Abu Hanifah was not the only one doing the warning. The message was to keep the parasol steady, if needed with an iron fist.

Soetan Sjahrir fitted under the pajung most uncomfortably. He still professed a belief that socialism and democracy could go together, and that revolution could proceed gradually, in small changes. It gave him some space in the shade. To Arnold Brackman, Sjahrir said that "Amir's admission" that he had been a Communist since the prewar time "stunned" him.[101] He told Brackman that Amir "was a frustrated nationalist." Sjahrir told Brackman, that Amir was *opgegaan*, "wrapped up in, lost in."[102]

Sjahrir had been in Djakarta during the Madiun affair. On September 21, he told reporters that "already for a week he had planned to travel to Jogjakarta, but a plane defect delayed the trip." The leaders of Sjahrir's Socialist Party published a statement in Jogjakarta, no doubt approved by Sjahrir, "regretting that the relation between political parties and between the Indonesian Communist Party and the republican government developed in an injurious way." They expressed a "hope that the government would behave in a democratic manner" and "that the action by government would be exclusively directed against the rebellious and not against a political ideology."[103]

This was a very late expression of anxious solitude. Late in December 1948, according to a Dutch intelligence confidential report based on "a pro-Sjahrir source," the PSI (Partai Sosialis Indonesia), Sjahrir's party, in its attitude to the Madiun affair, "follows a more or less 'balance of power' policy. Sjahrir disapproves of the communist rebellion, yet he laments the reprisals, which the government has now embarked upon, and is especially afraid of too great an influence of the rightist parties as a result of 'the red-baiting drive.'"[104]

Early in October 1948. Sjahrir was quoted in the Batavia/Djakarta press that "a sharply anti-left tide has now arisen also among the moderate parties of the center." It was not just Communists, Sjahrir said, but also "we who are persecuted."[105] "The elimination of the Communist Party," Sjahrir told Kahin in the same month, "does not eliminate the threat of totalitarianism [based on] feudalistic heritage."[106]

Eventually, Sjahrir did not fit under the pajung at all. He was a possible revolutionary hero, too. In the months and years after the Madiun affair, his friendship with Hatta, never absolute, was losing its political substance. Sjahrir's closeness to a few officers of the military, comradeship from the early years of the revolution, had increasingly been seen by the military leadership itself as dissident and, where it lasted, conspiratorial. He was always intensely disliked by Soekarno and suspected of disloyalty. He had no popular base. In 1960, Sjahrir was charged with conspiracy against the state, arrested, got very sick in prison, was permitted to exile himself, not to Holland, as Soekarno decided, but to Switzerland, where he died, during the days of the second Madiun, on April 9, 1966.

In 1984, thirty-six years after Amir Sjarifoeddin's death, the Indonesian Protestant flagship publishing house Sinar Harapan, "Ray of Hope," made a cautious attempt to remember Amir as a religious figure and freedom fighter. They decided to publish a dissertation, "Amir Sjarifoeddin, pergumulan imamnya dalam perjuangan kemerdekaan" (Amir Sjarifoeddin, His Spiritual Struggle during the Fight for Independence), by Frederiek Djara Wellem, defended at the Theological Seminary in Jakarta under the supervision of a Dutch scholar and missionary, Thomas van den End. The book indeed was done, printed, and made ready for distribution, but only a few copies got out. At the last moment, the distribution was stopped by an order from the office of President Soeharto.

According to information which reached Wellem's supervisor, van den End, and what Van den End has told me, the reason why the book was banned was its introduction, by Amir's cousin Harahap, mentioning the emergency session of the Hatta cabinet on December 18, 1948, where the possible execution of Amir and his associates had been discussed—namely the veto by Soekarno, forbidding the execution.[107]

The year Wellem defended his dissertation, in December 1982, *Prisma*, the journal of the Indonesian Academy of Sciences (with its main offices at the Avenue Gatot Subroto), perhaps sensing a little loosening of the Soeharto military regime, published an essay by Jacques Leclerc, on the occasion of Amir Sjarifoeddin's seventy-fifth birthday. *Prisma*, according to rumors circulating then around Jakarta, published the essay despite a warning it had received from the Ministry of Information.[108]

Leclerc's *Prisma* article gave the biodata of Amir, but not much judgment, and no praise, of course. The essay passed. *Prisma* was not banned and there were no repercussions. But neither was there any noticeable reaction beyond; except the whispers. The pajung worked and perhaps now in an upgraded model. Excess of information worked as well as excess of mediation—pajung as a wonderful and postmodern apparatus.

Discomfort might be becoming a distinct feature of the pajung. The new Indonesia of Soeharto, the New Order as it was called, of the victors, settled down and perfected itself. Goenawan Mohamad is a brilliant writer, poet, journalist, and public intellectual, with a deep sense of the ethical, a spokesman for the generation coming of age in the late Soekarno era. He reflected the discomfort under the pajung better than anyone. "Memories die fast and young in this country," he wrote.[109] He certainly was critical of Soekarno, or Hatta, and of the army.

But there was a red line for Goenawan not to be stepped over. It was made of language, perhaps entirely, of saying: "No large-scale totalitarian movement can speak of reconciliation and harmony," he wrote. In 1965, as it came to the second Madiun, he initially applauded the new army victory. "There was such an explosion of joy on that day," Goenawan wrote about the day when the PKI was banned. "And after that," he added, "—silence. I don't know."[110]

Goenawan's father was an internee in Boven Digoel in the 1930s, as Goenawan told me. "You ask me," Goenawan wrote me recently,

> what I think of Amir. Well, I have a very limited reading about him. I have a brother, the one born in Digul who joined the "Reds" during the "Madiun Affair," when he was a member of the Indonesian army (my father sent him to study in Yogya [Jogjakarta], he was a spoiled kid and he dropped out). He once told my older brother and me that when Amir was executed by the TNI [republican army], Amir sang the *Internationale* in front of the firing squad. I guess my brother told us this because he was happy that his kid brother knew the melody and lyrics of the song by heart. I was then nine.
>
> Later I heard somebody told a story of a man who was so moved listening to Amir reading the long text of the Psalms in the next cell when they were both arrested and tortured by the Japanese. The man was so moved hearing Amir reading the Bible when he was hanged with his head down [*sic*]. The man decided to convert to Christianity after he was released.

"I cannot wait to read your book on Amir," Goenawan ended his letter, rather slyly, I thought.[111]

They were killing him again and again, just in case. Like in the Balinese funeral, first a burial, after a time reburial and cremation, after a time ashes taken out in a boat to the sea and thrown in the water.

According to Amir's cousin, Pastor Harahap, based upon what "brother Purba," the Glodok prison driver in Surakarta told him after Amir's death, "until the last moment, Amir was steady in his Christian faith.... When asked for his last wish he answered: 'An hour [sic] to pray.'" According to Purba, who seemed even to suggest that he was present at the execution, "permission was given, and Amir has prayed for an hour." Afterwards, indeed, as Harahap writes, as the corpse was exhumed in 1950, "a Bible was found in Amir's shoulder bag next to his body."[112]

Pastor Verkuyl, Amir's friend since the Dutch Indies times, in recollections published in 1983, wrote that Amir became "a pawn in the game of the world powers." "The leaders of the Madiun uprising, *drs.* Maroeto Daroesman and Setiadjit, *ir.* Soeripno and ... Amir Sjarifoeddin," Pastor Verkuyl wrote, "belonged to the most talented and energetic sons of the Indonesian people. But they became victims of a manipulation by the global communist force." "There still is a scar in my heart, as I think of him," Verkuyl added about Amir, "of his guilt and of how they had played with him."[113] No hero.

Amir's knowledge of Christianity anyway, Pastor Verkuyl wrote as if to comfort himself, was "fragmented," and "fleeting."[114] And, in an interview for Dutch television, Verkuyl even spoke about Amir's "betrayal"! "You must not forget," he said, "that this was year 1948, the year of Gottwald when the communists seized the power in Czechoslovakia and that those students ["the group from Holland"] came from Europe with Musso, and that they all thought along the same line."[115]

No one could be expected, in case of Amir's memory, to be a true Christian witness more than Julius Schepper. Professor Schepper, like Pastor Verkuyl, eventually left the Indies/Indonesia, and spent the remaining years of his life in the Netherlands. In 1948, while Amir and Communism still had to be very much on his mind, Schepper published a book of his thoughts about the freedom of religion. Actually, when I think of it, Schepper might have even been writing it at the time of Madiun, of Amir's running, capture, and execution. Yet, there is no mention of Amir. Schepper's thoughts—the ground appears less swelling or rather the pajung seems to loom above—are church clear and order sharp. "Religion, in the first place," Schepper wrote, "means inner strength of a man and strength of his connection to God.... Traditional Islam, Communism, and (in some countries) Roman Catholic Church, obstruct the working and principles of the religious freedom."[116]

Reverend John Garrett, the general secretary of the Australian Council for the World Council of Churches toured Indonesia between May and June 1950. He visited Java on the trip and met some of Amir's friends, like the reverend *mr.* Probowinoto, Tine Fransz, and Van Doorn. He submitted a report and wrote a diary . On Friday, May 19, 1950, in the diary, Reverend Garrett wrote:

My interpreter was Sri Handoko who was at the Amsterdam *Christus Victor* conference in 1939 and is now an official in the Republic's Ministry of Religious Affairs. . . . Handoko came with me back to the hotel and we talked together off-the-record for a while.

He was a friend of the ill-fated Sjahrifuddin [sic], one-time Minister for Defense, a Christian with very radical social views. A Batak. According to all who knew him Sjahrifuddin was a magnetic person and a man of deep Christian faith. . . . He was deeply influenced by Kagawa, with whom he kept up a correspondence. Following the return of a Communist named Musso from Moscow in August 1948, Sjahrifuddin was somehow induced to announce that he had always been a Communist. Forced into opposition by Hatta and the Moslem Party, the Masjumi, and galled by the delay in the nationalist struggle, Sjahrifuddin led an abortive "coup d'état," was captured and imprisoned and later shot by a frightened prison commandant of the Republican Army at the time of the second military action with the Dutch.

It is reported that Sjahrifuddin, before his execution, asked for a Bible. His name has rapidly become a legend among the Bataks, many of whom claim he is still alive; but he is certainly dead. His widow lives in hiding somewhere on Java with their small son, whose name, it appears, is Tito! Someone with imagination should do intensive research in Sumatra and in Jogjakarta and write a stage-play about the life of this extraordinary man. He is a haunting story.[117]

Reverend Garrett comes in his diary to Amir again. He hears about him from others. "Sjahrifuddin, was [a] name again mentioned, he was one of these brave people who happened to make a tragic mistake—a truly existential figure, great even in an apparently wasteful death."[118]

Chapter 15

The Defeated

> *To My Generation*
>
> Your hands will become hard and stiff
> Your hearts stop beating
> Your bodies harden as rocks
> But we will replace you immediately
> Continue to carve this monument.
>
> —Chairil Anwar, *Complete Poems*, 70

For a Christian like Amir Sjarifoeddin, in the last moments of his life, as he marched, on the run, and as he faced the firing squad, the idea of martyrdom, even of resurrection, had to cross his mind.

In the Gospel of John, as Christ brings Lazar back to life, he says "I am the resurrection."[1] "The resurrection," says Nancy, "is to hold oneself firmly in the assurance of a stance before death. This 'stance' is literally the anastasis or 'resurrection.'"[2] It might have been the thought behind Luther's stance as well, *"Hier stehe ich. Ich kann nicht anders."* Perhaps even more to the point, resurrection," says Nancy, "is the uprising ('surrection', the sudden appearance of the unavailable of the other)."[3]

"The death that is hidden from testimony," Nancy still, "is bitter and cynical."[4] A thought of the twelve who might carry the message on, after the master died, might have crossed Amir's mind, too, in his last moments. Not to die "in bitterness" and "as a cynic," did not have to mean any delusion of grandeur on Amir's side—just a wish to die a good death. In Walter Benjamin's words—a German but of Amir's generation and also his stance—"I believe in 'a messianic power,'" a "weak messianic power" that is, in a *possible* hero. "[O]ur coming," wrote Benjamin, "was expected on earth . . . like every generation that preceded us, we have been endowed with a weak messianic power, a power on which the past has a claim."[5]

In the case of Amir, it turned out, there were to be no apostles(those to be sent off), just as there were none in the case of Benjamin, and even, for sceptics, in the truest biblical case. "The mission of the Twelve is, as an historical occurrence, simply inconceivable." wrote Albert Schweitzer in his *Historical Jesus*.[6]

The victory of the army, of Hatta and Soekarno, scattered Musso's and Amir's followers. "On December 7, 1948," wrote Kahin, "TNI [republican army] headquarters announced the final 'extermination' of the rebellion and stated that approximately 35,000 persons, mostly troops (particularly of the irregular military organizations), had been arrested."[7]

The scattering took various forms. "After the Dutch army already entered Magelang [Central Java]," writes Harry Poeze, "on December 19, at night, forty PKI [Communist Party of Indonesia] people were sentenced to death.... In Kediri [East Java] 130 PKI prisoners were shot by CPM [military police].... According to another report, 2,000 PKI prisoners in Jogjakarta were released one hour before the arrival of the Dutch."[8] "In January," Poeze writes, "35,000 prisoners were released and rearmed to fight against the Dutch."[9]

Those who had been closest to Amir, the possible messengers, if they had not been killed or locked in jails, went into hiding. The handful of those closest to Amir, who lived to emerge again, to bear witness, spoke out or wrote only after years and decades passed, not before the late 1990s, in fact, when Soeharto resigned, his New Order fell, and the postwar history of Indonesia seemed, for a moment, to turn a corner. They were now old and fragile men and women. Whatever they spoke of, they spoke of another time and to another time. It takes a very intense reading to find a weak messianic power in their memories.

Of the group from Holland, "practically all of them," says Soerjono, "fell in the independence struggle against the Dutch or were liquidated by Hatta during the Madiun Affair."[10] Some of the leaders of the Communist Party captured during the weeks of the Madiun affair, making use of the chaos during the first hours of the Dutch attack: in Jogjakarta, Alimin, Abdoelmadjid, and Tan Ling Djie with some others, escaped from jail; in Madiun itself, the city was bombed by Dutch planes and the guards themselves opened the gates of the prison.[11] Some of the escapees were recaptured by the Dutch when the Dutch arrived, and placed in Dutch prisons for change. Those who were not caught lived in hiding.[12]

The landscape of the past battles was to heal without them. Something easily forgotten but steady, laid in wait for the next which might never come.

Some leaders remained silent forever. Others, when they did speak out, still after years spoke in flat bitterness and sometimes against each other. This further enfeebled the message. "Like the story of Soerjono," wrote Soemarsono, "[h]e does not know anything about the Madiun Affair. He was in Jogjakarta at the time. He was never so close that he could understand."[13]

Many and probably most resigned. *Mr.* Soetan Mohammad Sjah, who used to edit the PKI magazine *Bintang Timoer* during the early months of the revolution, and who had known Amir well since before the war, when Jacques Leclerc in 1980 tried to talk to him about Amir, retold him the old story about Van der Plas's money, and then said: "Amir in modern history remains a traitor of the nation. It went *up and down* with him until the dramatic finale."[14] In 1983, Leclerc tried to contact Mohammad Sjah again, and he got a letter from Mohammad Sjah's nephew living in the Netherlands,

Vlissingen, August 3, 1983

Dear Mr. Leclerc,

I have received your letter of July 25, 1983, I am sorry that I can't help you because I want to forget my youth in Indonesia.

I have lost so many families [*sic*] and friends during the revolution! . . .

As for *mr.* Soetan Mohammad Sjah, his daughter told me that her father died this year on July 18, 1983, in Timor, Kupang.

I am sorry . . .

J. E. Moh. Sjah[15]

"The response to the truth that is on the point of disappearing," writes Nancy, "is to leave with it."[16] Soemarsono's closeness to Amir cannot be doubted. He was Amir's admirer and follower since the time of the Dutch Indies, he played a major role in the outburst at Madiun, and he stayed with Amir on the march almost to the end. He was a Christian, too. He might be the one closest to becoming an apostle. His story tells almost all.

After Soemarsono left the column shortly before Amir was captured, he wandered. Half a century later, Soemarsono talked about it to Kusalah Subagyo Toer, brother of Pramoedya, the most celebrated author of the revolution in Indonesia today. Soemarsono told Kusalah that, after leaving the column, he planned to cross into Dutch territory and get to Semarang [*sic*] "where his family lived." "I was arrested on the line of demarcation." Soemarsono was with a group of other fugitives: "We just killed a chicken and were preparing a meal. We were hungry, there were nine of us. We still had weapons, but we were hungry. Preparing to eat, finishing eating, sleeping, like people in trance. . . . When we opened our eyes, Dutch boots stood by our heads, we were arrested and put in the Mlaten prison in Semarang."[17]

Soemarsono managed not to reveal his name. He says that he remained in Dutch captivity for nine months. Then he was released as they did not know who he was. He was on the run again. This time he got as far as to Batavia/Djakarta but there he was put in Dutch jail again. Somehow, he got in touch with Pastor Verkuyl, his and Amir's friend since before Madiun. Verkuyl lived in the city. "Soemarsono asked me," he later recalled, "to help him to escape to a foreign country." "But," Verkuyl wrote, "I could not do anything for him anymore."[18]

On December 12, 1949, as the transfer of power to the new Indonesia of Soekarno, Hatta, and the army took place, Soemarsono escaped from the Dutch prison in the chaos again, but could not feel safe in the new republican Djakarta, either. "I ran to Pematangsiantar, Sumatra, and then to Medan," he recalled.[19] The chronology was compiled by Soemarsono himself:

December 18, 1948, arrested by the Dutch and jailed in the Mlaten prison in Semarang, got away.
August 6, 1949, arrested by the Dutch in Jakarta; ran from the prison on December 13, 1949.
July 1, 1951–August 1, 1958, living in Pematangsiantar, Sumatra.
August 1, 1958—May 1964, living in Medan, Sumatra.
May 1968—arrested in "Operation Bat" [Operasi Kalong, army action against "the second Madiun"]; imprisoned in the Salemba prison, Jakarta, without charge.
1978, released from the Salemba prison.
1987 till now [2008], living in Sydney, Australia.[20]

Another possible apostle, Soerjono, dismissed by Soemarsono as an unreliable witness, likewise survived Madiun but spoke out only forty years later. He said then that he was not silent completely: "While I was on the run, in 1948, I wrote a little book called 'The Solo [Surakarta] and the Madiun Affair' under the pseudonym of Jusuf Bakri." "But I have not heard," Soerjono added, "about anybody who saw the book."[21]

They had been silent for almost half a century and then they came out with stories about running. Francisca Fanggidaej was captured by Siliwangi few hours before Amir, taken to Surakarta, saw the posters along the way describing her as Amir's whore. She had been married to a Pesindo leader, Mas Soekarno (not the president), who was captured with her and who in the end would be shot among the ten others with Amir.

Francisca was pregnant with Mas Soekarno's child. She had been put in the same Surakarta prison where also Amir, Soeripno, the others, and her husband, too, were to spend their last days. Francisca managed to communicate with others, and when she finally spoke out—eighty years old, living in exile in Zeist near Utrecht, the Netherlands, interviewed by two Indonesian journalists and activists—she recalled the last exchange with her husband.

Mas Soekarno had pleaded with her, via secret prison mail, that if he were to die she would continue the struggle and bring up their child in the ideals they both had lived for. "I sent him an answer," Francisca Fanggidaej told her interviewers, "and it certainly would not warm his heart, and it still saddens me whenever I think about it." In this answer "I wrote to him that I did not want to fight anymore. That I am not able to! 'If you ever get out, and if I ever get out,' I wrote to him, 'I only wish to be a good wife to you. I only wish to be with you. I do not want to be a fighter again. I only want to live and to raise our child.'" That night, Francisca added, "I sent the letter through a courier, a non-political prisoner. It turned out to be the last letter between us. At least, I never received an answer."[22] In the hours after the Dutch attack, during the night of the execution of Amir and the others, in the ensuing chaos (a new phase of élan?), Francisca Fanggidaej was let out of the Surakarta prison "by guards and helped by friends from Pesindo."[23]

For the next twenty years Francisca Fanggidaej survived in Indonesia, building a new life, and marrying again. "Then, after twenty years," one of her interviewers writes, "Tante Sisca [*tante* is Dutch for 'aunt,' Sisca is for Francisca] had to move again. She lived in China for the next few years [and then wandered through the world] because of the September 30 Movement [the second Madiun] in which she was not involved but was suspected to be."[24]

Francisca Fanggidaej used the word *tapol* (abbreviation from *tahanan politik*, "political detainee") when she spoke of the people interned in Boven Digoel during Dutch rule, like when she spoke of those interned after Madiun in 1948, and also of those jailed and put in camps after 1965. The word *tapol* did not exist in the Dutch Indies, or at the time of Madiun.[25] Similarly, *basukan* (from Dutch *bezoek*, "visit"), Francisca used in describing visits or, equally so, attempts at visits, by detainees' families, or sending—or at least attempting to send—"packages with food and other basic things."[26] Many other examples could be given of the language of revolution demised, lasting and time imploding.

"I devoted my life," Francisca said, "to a struggle which I thought would be a journey, correct and virtuous." Years later, when she heard about the second Madiun, in which "she was not involved": "When I heard the news I panicked, and I cried, and I felt lost, and I felt nothing but being afraid."[27] There exists a photograph taken of Francisca Fanggidaej and Soemarsono sitting next to each other, in 2002, on the podium, during a conference organized by Dutch historians in Amsterdam. Two elderly people, Soemarsono is talking. Perhaps he is just saying as it is in the conference transcript: "We gather here in 2002 and most of us still hesitate to go back to Indonesia. When we open our mouths, we open our mouths in a foreign country."[28]

It is no good, when the possible Twelve scatter or keep silent. It is even less good when the false Twelve are talking.

The Indonesian Communist Party, the wonderful apparatus, survived Madiun against all odds. Despite what the anti-Communist radicals among the victors demanded, the Communist Party was not banned. The new Indonesia, built on compromise, was to present itself not merely as a force that dealt with the Communist rebellion, but also as a state worthy of international recognition, a democracy, parliamentary democracy, with a multiparty system. The Communist leaders were executed, but the Communist Party remained legal. This was how widely and gloriously Soekarno's, Hatta's, and the army's pajung could be opened, how far its golden shadow could reach.

Some Indonesian Communist leaders—as a rule the younger ones and those quicker and more attuned to the apparatus's needs—did not only survive, they did not even leave the country and, after a few months of chaos and sometimes being on the run and in hiding, they were able to begin politics again.

The most important of these younger and quicker leaders were Amir's followers before the revolution; and they often owed their political careers to Amir. Aidit, Soedisman, Njoto, and Loekman, became after 1948 the big four in the new Indonesian Communist Party. Only Loekman was a newcomer, though only in a sense "being off" when the others entered the movement. Loekman was in Boven Digoel where his father and his grandfather were interned.

Neither Aidit, Soedisman, nor Njoto joined Sjahrir when Amir was arrested by the Japanese in 1943. None of them joined Tan Malaka in the first months of the revolution either, nor did they join Widarta. When Amir was executed, the four—young, brilliant, alert, and eager—promised to be as good as even Jesus could have ever wished for "as doves and as snakes" (Matthew 10:16).

"'The role of the left during the 'second police action,'" Ann Swift writes in her history of Madiun, "made possible the gradual acceptance of 'rehabilitated' party after independence."[29] Many if not most of the ordinary fighters on the side of the defeated Madiun forces joined the national struggle against the Dutch. The Indonesian Communist Party, claiming the ultimate patriotism of its members and followers, was admitted under the pajung.

The party was allowed to publish its own magazine and daily newspaper, hold public meetings, organize branches, and establish affiliated youth's, women's, and peasants' organizations. Its affiliated trade union, federation SOBSI, could renew its activity.

Like the original Twelve, so it might seem, the new Communist Party was permitted to speak in parables: "To His disciples . . . it was given to know the mysteries of the Kingdom of God, but to the people all his teaching must be spoken as parables, that 'seeing they might see and not perceive, and hearing they might hear and not understand.'"[30] "Transparency" can be "supplanted by appearances," writes Virilio.[31] "Nothing is vaster than an empty thing," said Francis Bacon.[32] "Dominant cultures," wrote Paul Virilio again, "exile us from ourselves and others."[33]

Clifford Geertz, sometimes referred to as the founder of US cultural studies, learned his craft in Indonesia. In the mid-1950s, in the pseudonymous Mojokuto (Pare), a provincial town in East Java, fifty kilometers southeast of Surabaya, he did field research for his dissertation, later published as *The Religion of Java*.

National Holidays

With the exception of May First and August Seventeenth [Proclamation of Independence Day], almost all the national holidays are, so far as the mass of the people are concerned, only formalities. Some of them, such as Princess Kartini's Day [National Education Day] or Armed Forces Day, occasion very little celebration of any sort in Modjokuto and are known there mainly from newspaper descriptions of celebrations in the larger cities. . . .

May First is rather more of an occasion. The labor union—by-and-large "Communist dominated," parade around city carrying banners demanding the death of imperialism, the cessation of corruption, the cession of Western New Guinea to Indonesia [Western New Guinea was an area in dispute since the 1949 compromise], and so on. They end up at the town square, where a large rally is held under some huge pictures of Stalin, Lenin, Mao, and national Communist heroes and leaders. . . .

. . . Partly because . . . the Communist Party was supporting the government, partly because the government, afraid of violence, laid down rather strict rules about what could be said and done on May First and enforced them by the presence of a goodly number of well-armed policemen, the rallies and celebrations tended to be rather mild.[34]

"What strength, were it only of Inertia, there is in established Formulas," wrote Thomas Carlyle about the demise of the French Revolution.[35] An "absurd regime," he wrote about the postrevolutionary France, can move "to become less absurd. But then if there be no living enemy, living passivity only?"[36] The wicked professor in Ionesco's *Lesson* worries about what the neighbors might think seeing him and his maid disposing of the multiple bodies of the women he had murdered:

> PROFESSOR: Yes, Maria, yes. (he covers up the body) There's a chance that we'll get pinched—with forty coffins—Don't you think—people will be surprised—Suppose they ask us what's inside them?
> MAID: Don't worry so much. We'll say that they're empty. And besides, people won't ask questions, they're used to it.[37]

"The demand for autonomy," writes Virilio, can be "a symptom of a collective and simultaneous desire for inertia. . . . Alternative or marginal ideologies are not civil resistance to oppression."[38] "There is no longer even a remainder," wrote Alain Badiou, as if writing about the Old Indonesia becoming New, "due to the fact that the remainder is everywhere."[39]

The misery of the country and people lasted. The peasants were still without land and the workers were still without factories. The exploitation was not diminished. If anything, under the pajung the misery grew. "Violence of the state," says Roland Barthes, "does not stand out because [it is] heavily verbalized, surrounded by a vast, uninterrupted ideology."[40] Like Mikhail Bakhtin's tamed carnivals of the Middle Ages in Europe, the parades and public speeches in New Indonesia were to "uphold in the 'normal' functioning of the law as an internal perversion."[41] The trick was to let a significant group of society, its middle class, be "overdetermined by an accumulation of gadgets."[42] One could be allowed to speak publicly, in contrast to speaking openly, and thus listening and participation could be made into "the ruse of the dazzled rabbits."[43]

"A rooster," wrote Kierkegaard, "can no more lay an egg—*höchstens* (at most) a wind-eggs, than a 'real one' can beget or give birth to a conviction, no matter how long their intercourse."[44]

Dipa Nusantara Aidit was the most brilliant, eager, and soon the most visible leader of the new, post-Musso and post-Amir Communist Party. In the early years of the revolution, with Amir still present, Aidit already stood out among the leaders as the most daring youth, most efficiently invoking the élan and euphoria of the revolution. Aidit's radicalism and ideological clarity at the time was not to be doubted. In a typical article of his at the time, on the new bourgeois, he wrote:

> Facing the flames of the revolution, [the new bourgeois] has no courage to even open his mouth. When the republic is in danger and when the youth rise, he prefers to move to safe regions. . . . He had opened his mouth in the past, and as wide as his mouth allowed it, during the colonial

time, and, in fact, these were the Dutch who were opening his mouth for him. . . . Now, the new bourgeois is happy, he lives in comfort, his aim is to attain a higher rank and a higher position, civil or military, in the new setting.[45]

"It is curious," commented historian Soe Hok Gie in the late 1960s, "that this particular article and some others like it from that time, . . . not one of them, appear in the 'Selected Writings of D.N. Aidit' published after 1950, when he became the great leader of the PKI."[46]

Aidit, Njoto, Soedisman, and Loekman picked their enemies selectively. Hatta and the army leadership became their public targets, and this permitted them to leave Soekarno out, indeed, to reserve him for unrestrained praise. Hatta, in particular, was the name to say in order not to say Soekarno. This is from Aidit's speech at the Fifth Congress of the Communist Party, in March 1954: "By means of intrigue and intimidation, the imperialists, with the help of the Hatta clique, succeeded in January 1948 in overthrowing the revolutionary government of the republic and setting up in its place a reactionary government headed by Hatta."[47]

In 1955, Aidit was accused of defaming Hatta. This was an occasion, when Aidit said Madiun and Amir. It was an occasion to formulate the new Communist Party memory under the pajung. In a long and passionate speech in front of the high court in Djakarta, Soekarno was the shield, the shade: "I stand here to defend the honor of my Party. . . . It was a tragic affair. . . . It gives me no pleasure to talk about the Madiun Affair. . . . My comrades became the victims. It brings back a moment when a deep breach had been made into the fortress of our national unity . . . and yet, I am accused of defaming the honor of the Vice-President of the Indonesian Republic, *drs*. Moh. Hatta!"[48]

"What hast thou done," Saint-Just asked in the French Revolution and the question can be turned to Aidit, "not to be hanged if Counter-Revolution should arrive."[49] "Tragic," "victims," and "national unity" were the keywords in Aidit's speech.

Aidit used another keyword in the same speech, developing another thesis, of provocation: "Comrade Musso agreed with sending a report of what happened in Madiun to the central government, with a request for instruction. . . . It would make no sense for the PKI to stage a coup. . . . It was a provocation." They were provoked: "Comrade Musso deserves . . . admiration of the Indonesian nation forever. . . . Musso and his comrades were mountain eagles [*radjawali*] and to them belong the highest peaks."[50] They, the eagles, were "hunted," they became "victims," and they remain "the sons of the nation." "We stand up as accusers, in the name of Amir Sjarifoeddin, a great son of the Indonesian nation from the Batak lands, in the name of Soeripno, Maroeto Daroesman." Here Aidit listed the names of all those executed with Amir, with ethnicity noted, the registry of the nation. He could go on, he said, and list "the names of the thousands of sons and daughters of Indonesia who had become the victims of the violence by the government of the bourgeois Minangkabau [Sumatran] Mohammad Hatta."[51]

Rather than the struggle, or the journey, it was the death, the shooting of Amir Sjarifoeddin and the others, as they were tied to the execution pole. This became the core of Aidit's argument, the high point of his oratory and the *punctum* of the memory. Martyrdom of victims. The crucifixion, the most highly charged moment, true, but the pity for the helpless. This was the blood of Aidit's argument.

"Are you really sure about what you are doing to me and to my comrades?" Aidit said Amir asked the commander of the firing squad as the soldiers were getting ready: the lieutenant answered that he was just following orders. "Comrade Amir spoke again," said Aidit, "would not the Lieutenant think again?"

> The Lieutenant answered that it did make no sense to talk further. . . . .
>
> Comrade Amir then approached the Lieutenant [*sic*], touched the sleeve of his uniform [*sic!!*] and said that what they were asking for was to be given some time to sing.
>
> Lieutenant answered: "Yes, but quickly."
>
> Comrade Soeripno still asked whether he might write a letter to his wife so that she knows.
>
> Lieutenant said: "Yes, no problem."
>
> The comrades wrote letters. Afterwards they submitted them to [the] Lieutenant.
>
> After the letters were submitted to the Lieutenant, the eleven men sang *Indonesia Raja* and *Internationale*.
>
> After they finished with the singing, Bung Amir cried out: "Workers of the world unite! I die for you!"
>
> Then, the eleven men [Aidit concluded], who kept their courage till the last moment, were shot one by one, beginning with Comrade Amir Sjarifoeddin.[52]

"There was darkness over the land, and the earth shook as far as in Rome," says Mark 15:33 about Jesus's execution. Aidit described Amir's end in more quotidian language:

> In the middle of the night, December 19, 1948, on the order of the army, about twenty inhabitants of village Karangmodjo dug a pit to bury Amir

Sjarifoeddin and his ten comrades. According to the order, the pit for the eleven men had to be 170 cm deep.

Comrade Amir Sjarifoeddin wore a white pajama jacket with blue stripes, long brown trousers, and he carried a shoulder bag. Comrade Maroeto Daroesman had hazel-red jacket and white trousers. Comrade Soeripno a tee-shirt and a sarong. Comrade Oey Gee Hwat white trousers, white shirt and white jacket which was dirty. . . .

After the villagers finished digging the pit, they were ordered to leave and only four men were ordered to stay, to cover the pit later.[53]

"We mourn every year on December 19, so that we never forget," Aidit concluded the speech. "We mourn . . . to be vigilant . . . against another provocation. We mourn every year on December 19, so that we never forget that we are the keepers of national unity, this we shelter as the apples of our eyes."[54]

In 1954, Aidit commissioned a white book on the Madiun affair, "to provide arguments against the fear of the public," incited by Hatta, of "momok Madiun," "the specter of Madiun"—"momok jang tidak ada," Aidit's white book asserted, "a specter which does not exist."[55]

"The Indonesian Communist Party," Amir's cousin Harahap wrote, "evidently did not value Amir's 'communism' too high. During the celebrations of its fortieth anniversary in 1965 [sic], on the Senayan Stadium in Djakarta, next to the portraits of the founding fathers and leaders of the Indonesian Communism, as they were paraded around the stadium, there was a portrait of Amir Sjarifoeddin, too, but in a smaller format and carried as if a little diffidently."[56] "Mr. Amir Sjarifoeddin," wrote Francisca Fanggidaej, "was as controversial a figure in the history of the Indonesian national movement as he was for the Christians. People sometimes asked me, who is he?"[57] Jacques Leclerc put it similarly. "Amir Sjarifoeddin," he wrote, "was a *communiste maudit.*"[58]

Pramoedya Ananta Toer, the celebrated author of the Indonesian revolution sometimes described as a conscience of the nation, was twenty-three years old at the time of Madiun, and was thought by many to be a Communist fellow-traveler at least. After the other Madiun in 1965, as a fellow-traveler or suspected Communist, he was sent to an internment camp. In the late 1950s he wrote an eleven-page, single-spaced autobiography for a Leiden professor, Andries Teeuw, who worked on a history of Indonesian literature. There is nothing on Madiun in the autobiography and nothing on Amir.[59] Even in Pramoedya's magisterial literary work, a many-volume sort of history of modern Indonesia, there is only one short story directly concerned with the Madiun affair. Published in 1950, it is significantly called "Dia jang menjerah, "The One Who Surrendered." In 1982, when Pramoedya was asked about Amir Sjarifoeddin specifically, the only thing that seemed to come to his mind after those years was "disappointment" with Amir for accepting the Van der Plas assignment.[60]

> *This is my body . . .*
> —1 Corinthians 11:24

Very few people knew at the time about Amir and his ten comrades being executed. No one knew, in fact, except those directly involved: those who had ordered the execution, the soldiers of the firing squad, the villagers who were ordered to dig the graves, and then to cover the pits. No announcement was made at the time, and not for a long time later. Only rumors circulated in the months following the Dutch attack. Colonel Simatoepang says that he heard something during the war, but nothing about the circumstances.

The families were not told either. There were whispers that Amir, Soeripno, and the others, Musso, too, were still on the run, had even escaped abroad. The rumors were given credence by other rumors, about the caches of weapons Amir reportedly hid in safe places, which were never found and still might be ready somewhere to be used.[61] The specter still walked around.

"Communism in Indonesia is not dead after Madiun Affair," the US consul general in Batavia/Djakarta wrote in a cable to the State Department in Washington.[62] In January 1949, Charles van der Plas, still at his post in Surabaja, reported "accounts" of Musso's survival. Even one "colonel Frank [an US officer]," wrote Van der Plas, was seen "together with Moeso."[63] Still in September 1949, with Soekarno and Hatta already back in Jogjakarta, Van der Plas reported the specter as still very much extant:

> **The latest data on the development of communism in East Java**
>
> . . . Among the educated people as well as the religious leaders, fear of a communist takeover is still noticeable. . . . We are receiving a steady and growing stream of information about expansion of communist activities, in East Java especially, and about growing influence of communism in the Indonesian republican army.
>
> . . . In Blitar . . . the ex-PKI and Tan Malaka groups became coordinated. . . . In the residency Besoeki, some units from the time of Amir Sjarifoeddin still operate.[64]

In late October 1949, Van der Plas included in one of his reports a long interview with Tan Malaka, still defiant and "still at large in the hills."[65] Tan Malaka, increasingly uncomfortable to many, had actually been killed more than half a year earlier, on February 21, 1949. To another report, Van der Plas appended a leaflet, one of many to be found throughout the wide areas around

Surabaja, he wrote. He translated the leaflet into Dutch: "Mijn rode bloed niet meer gekoloniseerd!" "My red blood not colonized anymore!"[66]

It was not just Van der Plas. According to the Indonesian magazine *Pacifik*, of October 2, 1948, "From Russia Whispers: Musso and Amir have run there."[67] The *South China Morning Post*, in late 1948, published an Associated Press report from Batavia about living dead:

> **Sjarifoeddin Slain. Batavia October 18.**
>
> A correspondent of the Indonesian news agency ANTARA reported today that former premier Amir Sjarifoeddin had been slain by his fellow communists.
>
> The report however was not carried on a regular ANTARA dispatch from Jogjakarta. An official spokesman for the government of Indonesian republic expressed a doubt as to the accuracy of the report.[68]

According to *Sin Po*, of October 26, 1948:

> **Rumors circulate.**
>
> A friend of Soeripno reported that he had met Setiadjit, and that Soeripno is still alive and continues fighting around Mount Wilis. There had been an order by Gatot Subroto for an execution, but Soeripno managed to escape.[69]

According to *Sin Po* of December 12, 1948, "The rumors of the death of Amir Sjariffoeddin during the past few days resurfaced again, but the government still refuses to acknowledge any truth in them."[70]

In a cable on October 10, 1948, when Musso had just twenty more days to live, the Dutch delegate in Indonesia, Elink Schurman, wrote to Stikker, the Dutch minister of foreign affairs: "About the arrival of Moeso to Singapore, I have no confirmation. But I want to draw your attention to a report that recently a Catalina plane had made a landing near Singora [southern Thailand] about which the authorities had not been informed. Of some other planes arriving from the republic nothing is known. . . . All outbound flights from the republic have a character of clandestine operations, like smuggling of opium. . . . But they might have also served to transport passengers, like Soeripno or Moeso, from Java to Sumatra."[71]

According to *Nieuwsgier*, a Dutch paper in Batavia/Djakarta, October 12, 1948, "Moeso, Amir Sjarifoeddin, and Setiadjit escaped abroad." According to a Dutch intelligence dispatch of October 16, 1948, "the reports about the flight of Moeso to Bangkok are disseminated as a camouflage. . . . The rebels are in the hills, and it is impossible for a plane to land in the area."⁷² However, the reports persisted: "In the unofficial circles in Batavia, flight by Moeso and the others abroad is being considered a real possibility. Between Madiun, Ponogoro, and Pajitan are several emergency landing opportunities," reported *Sin Po*."⁷³

After Musso was killed, while Amir Sjarifoeddin was still on the run, Hatta's republican government appeared eager to kill Musso's ghost as much as it had been eager to kill him when alive, to make sure that Musso was really dead, dead-dead. "Refusal to be purely and simply integrated into history," says Levinas, "would indicate the continuation of life after death."⁷⁴ "So if someone smashes the lyra," Socrates explained on his last day to his most loyal friends, "or cuts or breaks the strings, atonement must still exist and not be lost. . . . the tuning must itself still exist somewhere."⁷⁵

There is a Process Record of the Indonesian republican authorities, before the Dutch launched their attack, trying to deal with Musso's corpse. In the record, Musso's dead body is described:

  c. On the inside of the left arm between elbow and shoulder, three old scars are visible
  d. Hair is cut short, stubble on chin is about 1 ½ cm, some grey hair.
  e. He had a white shirt on with short sleeves. . . . A certain Mrs. Sosrokardono [this is Siti Larang, who had known Musso since 1935] was called to identify the corpse, and by the scars on the left arm she said it was the body of Musso. . . .

This Process Report written down on October 31, 1948, at 20:00. Madiun [*sic*] October 31, 1948.

[Signature unclear].⁷⁶

On one of the photographs attached to the file, there is dead Musso lying on his back. There is a date, October 31, 1948, too, on the photograph, and someone wrote on the verso what, rather bizarrely (ghastly), supposedly were the last words of Musso: "I am Musso. Red-white forever. I was shot on October 7, 1950."⁷⁷ The date is wrong but what do ghosts care about dates?

Contrary to a previous police report stating that a few hours after his death, Musso's body was cremated and the ashes thrown in a river, new reports on the body—new attempts to prove that there is the dead-dead Musso only—were made, leaking and spreading around: "In republican newspapers around November 25, the death of Moeso was reported. . . . ±5 days later, another report emerged that Moeso's corpse had been placed in alcohol and brought to Jogjakarta. The corpse had been shown in a city hospital to Soekarno and reporters for the Indonesian newspapers *Kedaulatan Rakjat* ['People's Sovereignty'] and *Nasional*. . . . Alimin was also brought from prison to identify the corpse and to make the identification even more certain. When asked if this indeed was the corpse of Moeso, Alimin smiled and denied it."[78]

According to Dutch intelligence, hot on the event, an "informant" "was told that the arms of the corpse were not hairy while it had been generally known that Musso's arms and shoulders were. . . . According to information received earlier," the Dutch intelligence report concluded that "the announcement of Musso's death is being received with some reservation."[79]

It was not until 1950 that the families of the eleven executed men were told officially, sort of, that their men were dead. Until then, only rumors were reaching them like they were reaching everybody. More than seven months after the execution, in summer 1949, foreign papers reported on the deaths, vaguely. According to *Chicago Daily News* of June 26, 1949:

> **Communist Leaders Put to Death in Java.**
>
> Abdoel Gani [Abdoelgani], secretary general of the Ministry of Information said [Tan] Malaka, former premier Amir Sjarifoeddin, former republican envoy in Central Europe Soeripno, and secretary of the Communist Party Harjono have been liquidated. This is the first official word concerning the fate of the four communist leaders.[80]

On August 18, 1949, eight months after the executions, *De Waarheid*, "The Truth," the daily of the Communist Party of the Netherlands, reported: *"Drs. Mohammad Hatta admits: Amir Sjarifoeddin was killed."* In the same issue the paper printed Amir Sjarifoeddin's obituary.[81]

In October 1949, the Communist-affiliated trade-union federation SOBSI, which survived Madiun, demanded confirmation or denial of the reports about the execution. Not waiting, it declared that those "reportedly" killed were "heroes of the working class" and "honorary members of the SOBSI."[82]

In September 1950, the widows of Amir, Harjono, Djokosoejono, and the others received official letters "of some kind" which confirmed that their husbands were executed on December 19, 1948, at 23:40.[83] The letters did not go much further than that. According to Aidit speaking much later, in 1955: "until now . . . nothing has been made known about either process or verdict. . . . The only official letters to the families came from the police of the residency of Surakarta, dated September 20, 1950, signed by a commissar of the police of second class Sempu Muljono."[84]

In September 1950, a Commission for Exhumation was permitted to be established in Surakarta.[85] There might have been some connection here with

Djaenah, Amir's widow, being at last able to approach President Soekarno and ask him for permission to rebury Amir. "If possible," she asked, "in Sumatra."[86]

In November 1950, the bodies were exhumed and then reburied, at the same place. "In the name of the family," wrote Amir's cousin Harahap, "I have received from the government the 'corpse' of the late Amir, his skeleton, and I have buried it again in a Christian ceremony, in the said village of Ngalihan."[87] On a photograph from the event, a row of eleven freshly dug graves can be seen, and a row of family members and friends in a single line facing the graves.[88]

Amir Sjarifoeddin's skeleton, among the eleven exhumed bodies, was identified by the following:

a. large skull,
b. an old wound on the left arm,[89]
c. at a little distance from the skeleton a pipe was found . . . ,
d. next to the skeleton suspected to be Amir Sjarifoeddin's, a shoulder bag was found and, when it was opened by the police, it contained:

1. sarong,
2. fountain pen,
3. broken belt,
4. socks,
5. comb,
6. *notes* [notes? composition book?],
7. towel,
8. toothbrush,
9. soap dispenser,
10. Christian religious book.[90]

> *Ithaca can be just the way this pipe lies there as it does . . .*
> —Bloch, *Spirit of Utopia*, 203

Alimin and Tjugito, two senior and surviving leaders of the Indonesian Communist Party, spoke at the reburial. The red-white flag of the republic was flown at half-mast and the red flag was flown at full-mast.[91]

On the same day, November 19, the government of the republic led at the time not any more by Hatta but by Mohammad Natsir and Sukiman Wirjosandjojo, both men of the Islamic Masjumi, ordered massive raids against the Communists, Communist sympathizers, and pro-Communist unions. Hundreds of people were arrested, according to some, "in connection with the burial in Ngalihan."[92] Soon, however, all of them were released and the situation calmed down—to the normal. It was a warning shot.

Djaenah, Amir's widow, told Jacques Leclerc in 1982: "The grave as it was installed in 1950 was destroyed in 1965, and it had not been restored." "But," Djaenah added talking to Leclerc, "the site is still recognizable."[93]

Helena Lucia, the youngest daughter of Amir, born after his death, on March 7, 1949, told an Indonesian journalist in 2010:

> There was no stone and the earth had been plowed over. Luckily, we remembered the position of the body. We were not permitted to put up a new gravestone. We asked for permission. We wrote to the local authorities, and we were told that we had to try higher, as high as HANKAM ["Ministry of Defense and Security"]. We just wanted to have a stone there, just a sign, for the next generation, when grandchildren will ask us, so that they will know.
>
> When I was still little, there was a grave. There was a guestbook and a little *pendopo* [shelter] where one could rest. Then, the *pendopo* was razed, too.... We have asked Pak Adam Malik for help.

Adam Malik, at the time they asked, was the vice-president to Soeharto; in the 1930s he was one of Amir's ardent admirers, but during the revolution he turned to Tan Malaka and he was possibly the first Indonesian who published the secret of Van der Plas giving money to Amir. "We asked him for the remains [to] be allowed [to] be brought to Sumatra, [where] there are graves of our family. But we got no answer."[94]

As the Madiun affair broke out, Amir's wife and children—Andrea was born in Batavia March 25, 1940, Damaris was born in Jogjakarta in September 30, 1947, and Djaenah was pregnant with Helena Lucia—were brought from their home on Widoro Street in Jogjakarta into the custody of Komando Militer Kota, "City Military Command." In the morning, on December 20, 1948, according to Djaenah's recollection, an Indonesian guard came into the room they were kept and told them "to get quick under the table." The Dutch bombed the city.[95]

"In Jogjakarta," Andrea, who was eight at the time of Madiun, recalled, "I was in the elementary school, I went to school, but not too often, I mostly learned at home.... After papi was shot, we moved back to Jakarta, in 1949, and I began to go to school again."

> QUESTION: *Did your classmates pester you when you were in school in Jakarta?*
> ANDREA: After we were back in Jakarta, no. When we were still in Jogjakarta, yes.... When papi was still the minister, we were friends with the children of Bung Karno, Bung Hatta and Bung Sjahrir. We did often stay in their houses when papi was not at home. There

used to be a photo of us in a swimming pool, but it got lost when
our house was searched. . . . After the events of 1948, there have
been no connections. . . .

QUESTION [TO BOTH]: *When you were young, was it not a strange feeling, to
be daughters of Amir Sjarifoeddin?*

HELENA LUCIA: We did not feel it strange. Of course, we had to watch
ourselves when we were among the people, not to act impulsively,
not to do this or that. But to feel strange? No. . . . People might have
a Parker [fountain pen] and we might have Ero. Okey ["okey" is in
English]. . . . But we had access to the government facilities, too, also
after papi was no more. I still remember, when there was a distribution to the ministers, a car, or a television set, for instance, mami got
it, too. There were papi's pensions, too. Three pensions, in fact, the
Prime Minister's, of the Minister of Information and of the Minister
of Defense. It was usually [Vice Prime Minister] Chairul Saleh who
called us that there would be a distribution. People had cars; we also
had a car. We did not feel strange. Until September 30, 1965, PKI Affair, that is.[96]

Only after 1965, the second Madiun, during the thirty years of Soeharto's
rule, Helena Lucia says, were there problems. For instance, the husband of
Damaris, their older sister—she was already dead at the time of the interview—
went through "an endless process" of screening because he worked for the
state oil company.[97] So, Helena Lucia says, he switched to Philips.

HELENA LUCIA: Often people did not even know that we were papi's
daughters. . . .
ANDREA: I did not go into politics.
HELENA LUCIA: I went into law, and our elder sister also went into law.[98]

"Mami had been overprotective," recalls Helena Lucia at this moment talking to the journalists: "'You cannot do this! You cannot do that!' she was so anxious. I went to the University of Indonesia. 'How many lectures do you have
today?' 'Two, mami.' 'Until what time?' 'Eleven.' 'I'll send you the car. Wait for
it.' 'Can't I go by bus?' 'No.' . . . After I mentioned that there was a boyfriend, she
would ask: 'Who is he?' 'Batak?' 'No?' 'What is his religion?'—No kidding!"[99]

The interview was published online, and it was accompanied by a photograph. Helena Lucia and Andrea, two elderly women, sit on a sofa side by side,
with their backs against the white wall, facing the camera. High above them,
high as is often in Indonesian households, there is a framed photograph—of
Amir, and above it, almost touching the ceiling, there is a cross.

QUESTION: Are you proud to be the children of *Bung* Amir Sjarifoeddin?
ANDREA: Yes, I am proud.
HELENA LUCIA: Of course, I am proud. People talk, *okey*, big *okey*! It does not bother me. You do not accept him, *no problem* ["no problem" like "okey" is in English]. Who can erase his name? It's like erasing history. Let people talk!
ANDREA: We often say that only papi and God know. When people say papi was a Communist, *it's okey*. . . . I tell my children, "We believe what we saw. Your grandfather, when they exhumed his corpse, was holding the Bible."[100]

According to Pastor Verkuyl, it was Hanns Lilje's prayer book they found next to Amir's body. According to Pastor Pakpahan, who was also present, it was the Bible, and he says that he brought it to the family. Djaenah mentions the Bible, too, and even recalls that there were three dates written by Amir on the end paper:

December 17, 1944: Malang
October 1, 1945
July 20, 1947[101]

In 1979, Bernhard Dahm, a German historian and a biographer of Soekarno, visited Padang Sidempuan, the place in North Sumatra where Amir's ancestral house still stood at the time, and where were his family ancestral graves. Dr. Dahm met an old lady in Padang Sidempuan who (she was changing her story as she talked) was either the oldest daughter or a sister of Baginda Saripada, Amir's father. A daughter would make more sense, a sister of Amir. The lady stated her age as ninety-five and, on a second thought, as eighty-five. She told Dahm a story about what she said she was positive it was the Bible Amir "had on his chest when they shot him." When the Bible was brought to the family, she said, it appeared to be in good condition. But, as the family touched it, "the book turned into ashes."[102]

Chapter 16

The Observers

> It became Kierkegaard's nightmare ... the "aesthetic world" of the mere onlooker.
>
> —Adorno, *Jargon of Authenticity*, 78

Van Mook, Van der Plas, Schermerhorn, Logemann, or Schepper, whatever differences there were between them, along whichever routes they moved, closer or more distant to Indonesia and to Amir Sjarifoeddin, they were all defeated.

The colonial radicals prevailed. In two police actions, the compromises of Linggadjati, Renville, and the Hague, the ideas, and the aspirations of the Dutch neo-ethical, dissidents and sailors, from Van Mook to Schepper, had dissipated, and the men (there were no women among them, at least not prominently) left the Indies/Indonesia during the 1940s never really to return.

They could do it, however disillusioned or despairingly they left, because they owned return tickets, each of them, metaphorically and in reality. If they had not thought so before, now they knew: their homes were elsewhere. They left their posts and built their places of memory at the new elsewhere, observers' memories.

Hubertus van Mook resigned as, now, the acting governor-general, and left Batavia/Djakarta a disappointed man. He traveled around for a while and then was offered and accepted the position of a professor at the University of California in Berkeley. Now, he was an expert on subject Indonesia, and, by extension on subject Soekarno, subject Sjahrir, and subject Amir.

"Among their leading figures," Van Mook wrote in 1950 in his US book, *The Stakes of Democracy in Southeast Asia*, "was Mr. Sutan Sharir [sic], who had been interned before the war by the colonial government—a confirmed socialist with a well-posed, rather philosophical, and strong character." "Mr. Amir Sharifoeddin [sic], belonged to the same category, he had had only a minor brush with the law [during the Indies time], but he was much less stable, though very intelligent."

"On 15 Augustus 1945, as the Japanese capitulated," Van Mook wrote, "Sharir doubted whether the Indonesians were indeed capable of taking the whole responsibility of government."[1] Then, "Sharir" reconsidered and became prime minister. Then, disillusioned, he left the government again. "For a short while it was supposed that the loss of Mr. Sharir's wisdom be made up for, in part at least, by the quick intelligence of Mr. Sharifuddin . . . and by his popularity with the more vehement youth organizations. But although he seemed plausible enough in Batavia, he showed no moderation or strength of character in Jogjakarta. . . . Mr. Sharifuddin . . . played fast and loose. . . . We had to choose between abandoning the country and re-establishing security ourselves."[2]

It was "Sharifuddin's" being "unbalanced and insanely ambitious" that made him "declare himself a communist of old standing . . . which he was not."[3] "Sharifuddin," in contrast to "Sharir," wrote Van Mook, "slipped into Communism."

The revived magazine *Kritiek en Opbouw*, one of the advanced outlets for Dutch intellectuals and dissident officials in the prewar Indies, and one of Amir's prewar, sort of, homes, became a voice of observers, of people about to leave. In the first issue of the *Kritiek en Opbouw*, which came out in the weeks before Madiun, headlines already sounded as if they were from elsewhere and about elsewhere: "Deciding Lightly: Van Mook to the Hague," "The Upward Business Trend in the United States," "The Philippines," "On Freedom." There was a short article on the Indonesian Left taken over from Sjahrir's magazine *Sikap*: "There is a new song," the author of the article wrote, "that Sjarifoeddin's trumpet is playing conducted by Moeso and Stalin. It scares many people." Other articles in the same issue were "The Dollar Help," and "The Communist Threat." "The Communist Threat" was a review of a new book by Jacques de Kadt, a prewar member of the *Kritiek en Opbouw* circle and, at one time close to Amir. "Socialism," the reviewer conveyed what De Kadt had written, "is a many-sided, consequential, and perspectival movement towards the realization of freedom, civilization and welfare . . . nothing more and nothing less." The title of the book was *Verdediging van het Westen*, "Defense of the West."[4]

As one after the other of the Dutch authors of the *Kritiek en Opbouw* circle left, for the West and mostly for the Netherlands, a new tone was introduced in the magazine; nostalgic might be a crude but overall correct description: "Figuren uit de Indische journalistiek," "Figures from the Indies journalism," was a typical new series. The first journalist to be presented was J. H. Ritman, one of those leaving.[5]

In an issue of *Kritiek en Opbouw* published half a year before Madiun, an author signed "K" (almost certainly Jacques de Kadt) reviewed a just-published book by Pastor Verkuyl: "By publisher *Opbouw* ['Construction'] in Batavia, a booklet appeared from the hand of Dr. J. Verkuyl, a well-known pastor in Batavia, *De geest van communisme en kapitalisme en het evangelie van Christus* ['The Specter of Communism, Capitalism, and the Evangelium of Christ']. The writer gives his views of communism and capitalism, and what position the Christians must take in solving the social problems of our time. 'The gospel of Jesus Christ,' author writes, 'is a message of social economic justice.'" The book, the reviewer wrote, firmly rejects both "communism and mammonist capitalism." "The practical solution is the socialist solution. . . . Dr. Verkuyl explains the teaching of Christ as opposing capitalism as well as the (Russian) communism, which he sees as an extension and application of Marx's and Engels' teaching."[6]

Jacques de Kadt, by January 1949 already in the Netherlands, published his own book, with an observer's, a spectator's title, *De Indonesische Tragedie: Het Treurspel der Gemiste Kansen*, "An Indonesian Tragedy: The Tragic Drama of Missed Chances." Amir Sjarifoeddin is mentioned this time, as a minor actor, especially compared with Sjahrir who with his socialism-cum-democracy plays it big. Amir, as "the drama" is being presented, had been "drowned by the Communist influence." "The commune of Madiun," De Kadt also wrote, "was a stillborn act of Moeso's radical communism."[7]

The participants from the countries other than the colonial metropolis had an easier time settling into the characters of observers. Frank Graham was a man about whom it had been whispered in 1948, in Washington as well as in Batavia/Djakarta, that he was too engaged with the Indonesian side. He was said to, and he later confirmed it to be true, read the Bible with Amir on board the USS *Renville*. Frank Graham was succeeded in 1948 by H. Merle Cochran. He left Indonesia and, among friends, he did not, like Van Mook, conceal a deep disappointment at the turn of events.

Graham went on to a distinguished career in US academia and politics. He did not leave memoirs, and, as far as I know, never lectured or wrote on Indonesia and his experience there. He appeared to be an "all too private individual" somewhat like Ernst Bloch describes it: "he puts the cards of the common good . . . on the table and calls it a day." A "petit bourgeois," Bloch says of the type.[8]

Tine Fransz, was Amir's schoolmate at the Law School in Batavia and his friend at least until he was arrested by the Japanese in 1943. She became involved in the affairs of the church after the war and, as a representative of the Indonesian churches, met Frank Graham at a Christian conference in Evanston, Illinois, in 1954, where she got a chance to ask him about Amir. Graham began, Tine Fransz wrote, by telling her the story about Amir Sjarifoeddin and himself, "how the night before the conference on board Renville began, he was walking on the deck of the ship. Amir had a cabin on the deck, too. Graham saw the door of Amir's cabin open and he called in 'good night.' He was invited in and he saw that Amir was reading the Bible. The book, Graham said, had been opened on *I Corinthians* 13, verses about love! 'Someone who reads about love at the night before a conference with an enemy could not be a communist!'" "But what about Madiun?" Tine Fransz asked Graham, and Graham answered: "Perhaps Amir was already tired."[9]

In 1988, General Simatoepang, in Jakarta, related to me how years after Amir's death he spoke to Frank Graham, also at one such conference—he became involved in church affairs, too. He told Graham, "You left Amir up in the air, it was also your doing what happened to him." At which Frank Graham, according to Simatoepang, acknowledged some guilty feeling and that his tactics had failed.[10]

Journalists are engaged observers, and there were some extraordinary examples of this during the Indonesian revolution. Arnold Brackman was well known in the world of journalism already before he arrived in the Indies/Indonesia. He had reported on the trial of Japanese war criminals in Tokyo, at the most politically and ethically charged moment the world could be.[11] Then Brackman was stationed in the Indies/Indonesia throughout the crucial months of the revolution. He was a young American, in his mid-twenties, with broad cultural interests—archeology held for him a special attraction—and with the pronounced views of fascism and democracy at the twilight of the Rooseveltian era and the dawn of the Cold War.

Brackman left Indonesia in 1948. He retired from professional reporting, turned into a historian and professor, and, at last, to his beloved archeology. In the early 1960s, as "the second Madiun" loomed, he came back, kind of, and published an influential history of Indonesian Communism. In it, of course, he also wrote about Amir Sjarifoeddin, whom he came to know when he was in Java.

"Whether Amir, his confession notwithstanding, had been a Communist," Brackman wrote, "has been disputed ever since. Most Indonesians still doubt it." Brackman quoted Hatta: "Amir was too religious to be a Communist." Then, Brackman quoted Sjahrir: "Sjahrir believed that Amir was a frustrated nationalist." Then, Brackman quoted "the Dutch sympathetic to Amir." They "advanced the theory that Amir tried to save the left from Musso's domination and sacrificed himself."[12]

Amir was becoming ranked in retrospective and for the new age. Brilliant, moral, misled, too emotional, too religious to be a Communist, too complicated to be real. Spectacularly so. "The Madiun Affair was a terrible tragedy," wrote Anthony Reid in his history of the Indonesian revolution.[13] Theatre, drama, or tragedy, became observers' tropes. One observes history and expects a curtain. Instead of heroes, there are actors. Slavoj Žižek recalls Marx's "insight that the political struggle is a spectacle" and "the problem of freedom [is] contained ... in liberal discourse."[14]

John Coast was an Englishman seven years older than Arnold Brackman but sharing with him the life-changing experience of the Second World War and of the contest between democracy and fascism. Coast was ten years younger than Amir, and the same age as many of Amir's and Sjahrir's young followers. He served in the British Army, was captured, and spent the rest of the war in the Japanese POW camp on the Burmese–Thai border, on the railway of death. The first months after the war, back in London, he became involved in the campaign of Dorothy Woodman and Benjamin Britten, among others, in support of the struggle for independence of Asian countries, most importantly Burma and Indonesia, of these countries' struggle against fascism, colonialism, and for democracy.

In the Japanese camp, Coast became an admirer of, as he put it, "classical dance of Indonesia."[15] In the camp, he wrote, "Dutchmen, Eurasians and Indonesians," fellow POWs, introduced him to the dance. "A Javanese dancer called Bertling [sic]," Coast recalled, who was said to be originally from Surakarta, "formed an Anglo-Dutch Company that produced in some of its programs some Javanese and some allegedly Balinese dancing."[16]

After liberation, already in London, Coast got to know another Javanese dancer, named Soeripno, who had arrived from the Netherlands on a political mission and was preparing for his return to Java. Soeripno in London, among other activities, had been translating Soetan Sjahrir's manifesto *Perdjoeangan Kita*, "Our Struggle," to be distributed to the United Nations delegations when they would, early in 1946, meet in Westminster Hall.[17]

Coast volunteered to help the Indonesian Republic and became one of the republic's handful of pilots. He decided to do so, he writes in his memoirs, in hopes of finding in the revolutionary Java, what might be "a state of utter youth and complete freedom." Yet, after a few months of working for the republic, mostly between his flying missions staying in Jogjakarta, he found "there was something bizarre in my partisanship."[18]

Coast happened to be in Jogjakarta when, in August 1948, he met Soeripno again. Soeripno just came with Musso from Prague. In recalling the moment, Coast writes of a "shock": "Musso had arrived back under the protection [sic] of my old friend Soeripno. . . . I found to my distress that a little iron curtain had come down between Soeripno and me. . . . I realized that my Socialist friend from the London days had moved far more left."[19]

A few days later—it was already September and everybody knew that something big was going to happen—John Coast writes, "Soeripno made an appointment with Amir Sjarifoeddin at his house, where I had a long talk with him about communism and his FDR [People's Democratic Front]. Amir Sjarifoeddin was a thick set, powerful-looking man of approaching forty [sic], with curly and thick, but carefully done hair, a square face and strong-jaw [sic], and with his shortsighted eyes hidden behind thick, tortoise-shell-rimmed spectacles. A staunch Socialist of many years standing, he had hated Fascism more even than Colonialism, so that after 1940 he had for a while joined the Dutch East Indies government service." Here, as he leaves direct personal observation, Coast evidently begins to rely more on what others told him:

> Extreme left forced him to split the Socialist Party; for although he had performed a miraculous job as Minister of Defense, when he helped to coordinate the youthful and fiery component bit of the Indonesian Army, Sjarifoeddin was not in all way[s] as independent as he looked.
>
> His whole life in fact was a curious compound of opposites. . . . He led a Marxist Party, yet . . . he had been a convert to Christianity, and still carried with him a small pocket Bible.
>
> Bung Amir was too easily influenced. When I saw Soeripno with him, I might have imagined that Soeripno was the veteran, not Sjarifoeddin, and he was also overpowered by boisterous Musso while the cunning, clever Setiadjit, keeping carefully in the background, could also pull him here and there at will.
>
> A good man, he listened to too many people, too trustingly, so that his judgements were not always sound.
>
> Very popular with the people, with a finely developed sense of publicity, his vanity sometimes ran away with him. Soeripno would frequently complain to me that Amir was too nice, too simple, and even that he was quite stupid. . . .
>
> On this occasion . . . of my meeting Sjarifoeddin I had asked him plainly whether he was a Communist. Sjarifoeddin replied that I could write him down as a Left Wing Socialist, for how, he asked, producing his Bible, and holding it up like a conspirer, could I call him a Communist?

A few days after their meeting, John Coast writes, Amir Sjarifoeddin "made the widely publicized statement *or perhaps the Dutch Information Service invented it for him*, declaring that he had been a secret Communist since 1936."[20]

Much of what Coast observed can be explained by the people Coast spoke to and whom he befriended in Jogjakarta. Increasingly, rather than to Soeripno, the group around Sjahrir was in many ways more like him. They hated fascism, believed in democracy, and in socialism, but they did not want to go too far. They also, something of a rarity in Jogjakarta at the time, mostly spoke good English. And English, not Malay-Indonesian and not Dutch, was becoming the language of the observers.

"On the previous day," Coast wrote in his entry on September 20, 1948, after he was back in Jogjakarta again after one of his missions, this time to Bangkok, "communists had staged a coup d'état in Madiun." "From Ali Budiardjo, who was the government liaisons officer with the military, from Sjahrir, *Pa* [Hadji Agoes] Salim [Minister of Foreign Affairs], and the President himself, I was able to piece together the events leading up to the revolt.... Gatot Soebroto was appointed Military Governor of Solo [Surakarta], Madiun, and most of republican East Java. At the time, the excellently disciplined, and incidentally most loyal republican members of the Siliwangi (West Java) Division, were sent to Solo [Surakarta] to carry out cleaning-up operations."[21]

Frank Graham, John Coast, Arnold Brackman, and even Hubertus van Mook, if they tried to prove a point or refresh their memory, might naturally turn to George Kahin's *Nationalism and Revolution in Indonesia,* published by Cornell University Press in 1952. It came to be considered the most authoritative account of the last three years of Dutch colonial rule, as well as the Indonesian nationalism and Indonesian revolution.

This was the US era, at the end of the Second World War, in all ways, in all places, and in scholarship—and of memory refreshed and corrected of Indonesia as well. Kahin's book became a classic and a reference for anyone outside Indonesia interested in Indonesia, in the United States, through the English-reading world, and finally everywhere including Indonesia itself. A photographic montage circulated on the internet a few years ago, of unknown origin, possibly by students, portraits of Indonesian *pahlawan nasional,* "national heroes," civilian and military, politicians and freedom fighters shows George Kahin, with his elbows on an invisible table, as perhaps he is lecturing.[22]

Kahin was born in 1918. He grew up in the US Northwest. He liked archeology, like Brackman, and was equally Rooseveltian, anti-fascist, and democratic. After Pearl Harbor, in his early twenties, he volunteered to assist the American Japanese who, as enemy aliens were interned in the camps. As a college student, he volunteered again, and joined the US military. It so happened that his unit was to take part in the US invasion of the Japanese occupied Indies/Indonesia. Kahin went through basic training at the US military base, learning Malay-Indonesian, GI Indonesian as he later put it, geography, all from the manuals they had.

The US invasion of the Indies/Indonesia did not take place. US forces in the Southwest Pacific area were redirected straight north against Japan proper, touching the Indonesian archipelago at a small area of New Guinea. Kahin was sent to Italy instead, where, he said, he did not see much fighting anymore.

But Indonesia remained with him. Helped by the GI Bill, he set out to finish his studies interrupted by the war. His dissertation supervisor at Johns Hopkins was Rupert Emerson, arguably the most distinguished US scholar in Asian studies. In nearby Washington, Kahin met Claire Holt, a dancer and student of art, then with the OSS (Office of Strategic Services), the future Central Intelligence Agency. She had lived the most intense years of her life, during the 1930s, in Java. She introduced Kahin, among others, to a seventeen-year-old sailor from the Indies stuck in the United States, who gave him some introduction to Malay and to what Indies/Indonesian culture might mean. Sailor's stuff no doubt.

Kahin met some representatives of the newly born Indonesian republic in the United Nations in New York, as well, Sjahrir and Soedjatmoko among them. In 1948, he was awarded a Social Science Research Council scholarship and set out for what was planned to be a year of field research in Java to write a thesis on Indonesian nationalism and revolution.[23]

Kahin sailed to Europe, and from Europe to the Indies/Indonesia on a Dutch ship full of Dutch returning to the former colony.[24] On the ship, Kahin met and befriended Kees van Mook, the son of Hubertus van Mook. George received some language lessons in Malay (that kind of Malay) from Kees, who spent his youth in the Indies before going to study in the United States.[25] Before they landed at Tandjong Priok, Batavia/Djakarta, Kees wrote a letter (in English) to his father:

RMS SS 'Veendam' June 14th, 1948, Holland-America Line

Dear Father:
  This letter is meant to introduce Mr. G. McT. Kahin. . . . I am quite sure this gentleman has adequate introduction to see you anyway, but since he and I have had many an interesting conversation together on board of this respectable old lady, I think it proper to add a personal touch to the introductions.

"George had," Kees wrote:

> a grant . . . to spend year in Indonesia, studying the political situation in as well as outside the republic. . . .
>
> When I first met George a few days ago, I discovered he was studying Malay—and as a matter of courtesy offered him such help as I could give with my limited and unscholarly knowledge of that language. Since then, we have entered into long discussions of politics and policies in Indonesia, which proved to be greatly interesting. Frankly, I am a little amazed at the amount of information that man has . . . particularly when I consider the relative superficial and naive interest that most Americans have for Far Eastern Affairs.
>
> I hope you will find him as interesting to talk to as I did, and that you will find time to discuss our point of view in the matter explicitly.
>
> Good luck,
> Kees[26]

George Kahin and Kees van Mook arrived in Batavia/Djakarta on June 14, 1948. It was after the first Dutch police action, after the Renville compromise, after Sjarifoeddin's cabinet fell, and after Hatta's cabinet had taken over, just a few weeks before Musso and Soeripno arrived from Prague.

Kahin was indeed received by Hubertus van Mook. He was also introduced to one of Van Mook's principal assistants, P. J. Koets. Kahin later recalled the meeting: "Among the republican leaders for whom [Koets] appeared to have a high regard were Vice-President Hatta and former Prime Minister Sjahrir. He did not appear to want to discuss Sukarno, and he was clearly negative in his appraisal of former Prime Minister Amir Sjarifoeddin, who was now leading a left-wing political coalition."[27]

Helped perhaps by Kees van Mook's letter, and certainly by other letters from US academics and representatives of the US Social Science Research Council (now among the Van Mook papers in The Hague),[28] with the help by the Indonesian republican delegates whom he had met in New York, and, of course, helped by his perseverance, Kahin got rare permission to travel from the Dutch- to the Indonesian-controlled territories. He was permitted to cross the Van Mook line, a "no-man's land of about 10–15 km," which cut Java in parts.[29]

Kahin decided to travel his own way. As a veteran GI he managed to buy a second-hand jeep at auction in Batavia/Djakarta for $502. He attached a US flag to the hood of the jeep. On August 24, for the first section of the way he put the jeep on the train car and for the rest of the journey, across the line to Jogjakarta, he drove. "You will be adding to mobility of Republican army, by 5%," he was told. He arrived at the capital of the republic on August 28, 1948, fourteen days after Musso's and Soeripno's arrival.[30]

Helped by Hadji Agoes Salim, whom he also met in New York, the minister of foreign affairs of the republic (in 1928, Salim's daughter accompanied Wage Rudolf Soepratman on piano as he played on violin "Indonesia Raja" for the first time, at Kramat 106, with Amir among those who listened), Kahin was accommodated at a government guesthouse in Terban Taman 8, in Jogjakarta's city center. Another guest in Terban Taman 8, Kahin later wrote in his memoirs, "was *Raden* Soeripno, who had arrived in Yogyakarta shortly before me, escorting Musso from Prague." Kahin added, "My other housemate was John Coast."[31]

The students at the Jogjakarta Gadjah Mada University nicknamed the exotic visitor—who was soon to be seen everywhere—"Hanuman," and Kahin recalls how he "went through a few days of despondency, thinking my new friends were mocking me." He knew so little of Javanese culture, he recalls, of Hindu mythology, of wayang and of Hanuman, the *Ramayana*'s noble hero, "despite what Claire Holt had briefly taught me."[32]

It all happened in a very small place. Abu Hanifah, former Amir's friend at Kramat 106, stayed at the same guesthouse. Usually of a sharp tongue and sometimes harsh in his comments, he recalls Kahin in Jogjakarta during these weeks just before Madiun with unmitigated respect: "I had the opportunity to talk to him several times and gave him some inside information. He was a well-known figure among the leaders of the republic because nearly everybody of some importance had given him some information—about things they superficially knew about. Possibly no other foreigner had such a golden opportunity to see the republic from the inside." Abu Hanifah also recalled another American living in the same guesthouse, "Mr. C."[33]

Kahin mentions the same man and uses his full name and profession: Arturo Campbell, "the first CIA agent to reach the republic." When Soeripno left on his fateful mission in September, Kahin writes, Campbell occupied Soeripno's room. Assuming my "fluency" in Indonesian, writes Kahin, Campbell "wanted me to assist him." Fortunately, so Kahin recalls with clear relief, he was not fluent.[34]

Kahin inevitably met Amir Sjarifoeddin, too. He was urged to meet Amir, as he recalls, by the people of Sjahrir's circle with whom he had a warm connection since meeting Sjahrir and Soedjatmoko in New York. Time was sliding toward Madiun. Evidently, Kahin wrote, Sjahrir's people thought that Amir might still be convinced to "mend his ways." "As late as August 27, one influential non-Communist leader felt that [Amir's] decision was still in balance and urged the writer to see [Amir] on that day in order to try and disabuse him of his belief that the anticolonial forces in the United States and the ideas of Franklin Roosevelt towards colonial peoples were now too weak to influence American policy. Sjarifoeddin expressed keen interest in the probable outcome of the impending American presidential elections." Amir asked Kahin what his estimation was and Kahin answered truthfully that he felt, quite pessimistically, that it would take another election cycle, at least, before some real change to the present policy—meaning a return to FDR's wartime policy of anti-colonialism—might be expected. Amir, writes Kahin, "indicated that this was already his conviction, too, and stated: 'That will be too long.'"[35]

Kahin's meetings with Sjahrir and Soedjamoko in New York before he departed for the Indies/Indonesia, according to Kahin, was "the beginning of friendships with both that lasted until their death."[36] It was Sjahrir's letter to Hadji Agoes Salim that might have been most instrumental in the opening the republican territory to Kahin. In a similar way, wrote Kahin, Sjahrir's "confidence" in him was "passed on to some of his lieutenants in Yogyakarta—especially Ali Boediardjo, Soebadio Sastrosatomo, and Dr. Soedarsono—with all of whom I quickly developed a friendly relationship."[37]

"Ali Boediardjo apparently still felt considerable warmth towards Amir," writes Kahin. Ali and his associates, Kahin was told, "believed [Amir's] bitterness" being to a large extent caused by "what he saw as an 'American betrayal.'" "These young adherents of Sjahrir," Kahin recalled, "were deeply worried." In his *Southeast Asia: A Testament*, published posthumously, Kahin returned to the story of his meeting with Amir, in more detail:

> They seemed to think that having the credentials of a "progressive American" I might be able to convince Amir that belief in the prospect of a more even-handed American policy need not be abandoned. . . . I agreed to try , , . to meet him in his office there.
>
> I'd never before met Sjarifoeddin and was surprised at the warmth of reception he gave me. He was relaxed and friendly I declined the cigar he offered me (no other Indonesian ever offered me one) and on his initiative we immediately began a most intensive discussion about American politics—a subject in which it was evident he was . . . surprisingly knowledgeable. . . . He had been closely following the upcoming American presidential election and . . . he seemed to want me to assess his conclusion.

Kahin recalls Amir's "great admiration for Roosevelt." "He asked me when I thought that the progressive forces . . . could be expected to come back to power. Believing full well this would not be possible before the succeeding election four years hence. I told him that. I vividly remember the drawn look on his face and the helpless gesture he made with his hands."[38]

"Two days later, on 29 August," Kahin says, "Sjarifoeddin made a public pronouncement . . . that he himself had been [a] member of the underground Communist Party since 1935."[39] It would put Kahin, the progressive American yet skeptical, an observer, in the middle of the revolution making, or unmaking; whether he just imagined it, or if it was for real.

Kahin was still in Jogjakarta when the fighting in Surakarta and the Madiun affair broke out, and from the capital he observed what was happening. Observing as if in a hall of mirrors. It was no surprise that he was watched, too. He had been a suspect since he arrived at Tandjong Priok, suspicious to the Dutch and Indonesians both, an observed observer

> *From*: Attorney General of the Supreme Court, Indonesia, February 18, 1949
>
> *Language*: Indonesian
>
> *Short description*: Copy of a report dated September 27, 1948, by the Inspector of the Police 1st class Muharam of the republican state police in Jogjakarta concerning Miss M. Jordan, an ex-member of the secretariat of the US delegation of the U.N. Committee of Good Offices, from which it appears that Miss Jordan is a communist sympathizer. In Jogjakarta she had a contact with George Kahin, student of the "Hopkins" university in America, who stayed with Soeripno. . . .
>
> *Note*: Miss Myra Jordan, left Indonesia and returned to America on October 28, 1948.[40]

Kahin was observed and suspected by the Muso camp, too. "Communist underground press," Kahin recalled, "right after Madiun." "Kahin tears off his mask and exposes self for what he's been—secret agent of the State Department;" and later: "Foreign relations of Republic turned over to U.S. via intermediary of G.K."[41] Attempts might have been done at Kahin to be used. After the Communists were defeated and documents compromising the Communist Party had been discovered by the army in Amir Sjarifoeddin's house, and after suspicion was growing that the documents were an army invention, Kahin was still in Jogjakarta. A US scholar might be useful for providing the documents with an aura of authenticity. Around October, Kahin was briefly allowed to see the documents at the Ministry of Information. He made notes of them and some quotations appeared in his book.

Kahin expressed doubts about the documents, at least about their most scurrilous parts.[42] However, as Ann Swift, US historian of Madiun, of the next generation and a student of Kahin, later wrote, "Regardless of the Kahin documents' authenticity, no one will ever be able to say definitely whether the PKI [Communist Party of Indonesia] was plotting a takeover. . . . Kahin is the only source available for these documents as they have never been published by the Indonesian government."[43]

Kahin was watched and attempts might have been done for him to be used. Early in December 1948, with the Madiun rebellion to all effects defeated, and with Amir Sjarifoeddin and other top leaders either dead, in prison, or in hiding, Roeslan Abdoelgani, the republican minister of information took Kahin on a ministry inspection tour through the area of the recent conflict. Kahin's jeep carried some members of the team. An Indonesian flag had been added to the US flag on the hood of the jeep. They traveled through the area ravaged by the fighting. An awkward report had been produced on Kahin by the minister:

> *Report on the trip to Kedoe, Wonosobo and Bandjermasin, from December 1, 1949, to December 5, 1948,* [by] *Roeslan Abdoelgani. the Minister of Information.*
>
> . . .
>
> *4. Report on drs. George Mct [sic]. Kahin. Delivered personally.*
>
> In an illegal PKI broadcast from the past September, Musso mentioned Kahin as a secret agent of the American State Department with strong connections to our own Ministry of Foreign Affairs.

During the present trip,

> Kahin made attempts to talk with the local leaders between four eyes. But he was rarely successful, and that kind of interviews arose suspicion. . . .
>
> As regards as the Madiun Affair, Kahin expressed himself in warning that, now, when the "extreme left" [English is in the text] had been put down, all should be done so that the "extreme right" [in English] does not rise. . . .
>
> *Jogjakarta, December 12, 1948.*
[signed] *Roeslan Abdoelgani.*[44]

Kahin was still in Jogjakarta on the morning of December 19, when the Dutch expeditionary force entered the city. Dutch paratroopers appeared at the government guesthouse in Terban Taman 8.

John Coast's former room was now occupied by Hamid Algadri, an official of the republican Foreign Ministry and also of Sjahrir's circle. They were captured together, Kahin wrote. "Hamid was ordered to sit on the curb, and the rest of us," Kahin and Campbell evidently, the foreigners, "the whites," "on the porch." Kahin protested and "the Dutch lieutenant finally consented to [Hamid] joining the rest of us on the porch."[45] Hamid mentions the scene in a special chapter of his memoirs called "Jasa George Kahin," "Merits of George Kahin."[46]

Kahin, as a foreigner, was escorted by the Dutch military (still in his jeep) to the Maguwo airport to be deported to Batavia. When they arrived at Maguwo, Kahin saw "Dutch planes of American origin still bearing the US star that the Dutch had not bothered to paint over." "Many trucks" of the invasion force were "still bearing the same US insignia."[47]

After some more adventures, getting back his jeep, returning to Jogjakarta for a few days to collect his baggage, after selling the jeep and using the money to travel for some more months through Indonesia, but not to Jogjakarta, after getting permission to visit the interned republican leaders including Soekarno and Hatta, Kahin had to return home.[48]

Like van Mook, De Kadt or Schepper, Kahin returned home to the West that became West-West. Kahin arrived as the Rooseveltian twilight had grown dense and as the US was moving fast into the Joseph McCarthy era. Kahin's industry and engagement, his contacts and indeed friendships with Soekarno, Hatta, Natsir, Abu Hanifah, Sjahrir, and especially with Soeripno, his meeting with Amir, which has always raised some eyebrows in Washington, now made Kahin-observer into Kahin-suspect.

In 1950, as Kahin was making his dissertation into a book, his request for a visa renewal for a planned follow-up trip to Indonesia was denied.[49] "[B]ecause I had dwelt in the same house," Kahin wrote about himself and Soeripno, "Merle Cochran, then American first ambassador to Indonesia, charged that I had been close to the Indonesian Communists and therefore should be denied a passport for a return trip to Indonesia."[50] "Letters of support," Kahin had asked for, "including a magnificent one from Sukarno," were judged "irrelevant," "as were letters from American academics . . . testifying to my non-Communist views and affiliations."[51]

Kahin traveled to Washington to appeal for the visa personally. He recalled decades later how he visited the passport office and how its chief "Mrs. Shipley" told him: "Mr. Kahin, the line between Communists and non-Communists is very clear, and you're on the wrong side of the line."[52]

The McCarthy moment in the United States was less bloody than the show trials in Eastern Europe or the Madiun affair. US Cold War vigilance, certainly as far as academia was concerned, was "democratic" and liberal. Kahin was permitted to defend his dissertation, he turned it into a book, and the book was published by an Ivy League university press. On the wave of the book's success, Kahin was hired as an assistant professor of government at Cornell.

The Cornell Modern Indonesia Project was established in 1954 and, over the following years, under Kahin's guidance, a collection of books and newspapers on Indonesian modern history became a part of the Cornell Library, the finest modern Indonesian history collection in the world.

A colleague was assigned a task, as Kahin also later recalled, of "ascertaining whether I had any communist proclivities."[53] One year, Kahin noticed two of his students most diligently visiting his lectures and making notes of every word. A member of the Cornell student journal staff made discreet inquiries and found out that they both were paid for their information.[54]

George Kahin did not become Edgar Snow of *Red Star over China*, though their life trajectories might have touched the same points. John K. Fairbank, the man who had been introducing the Snow book to the public at the time of the Cold War, was Kahin's dissertation supervisor.[55] There were similar possibilities.

"I had little to cheer me on my way," Edgar Snow recalled on embarking on *his* "research trip," for *his* "dissertation," on *his* meeting with a revolution. "Nothing, in truth," he wrote, "but a letter of introduction to Mao Tse-Tung, Chairman of the Soviet government. All I had to do was to find him."[56]

Like Kahin, Snow approached the revolution, the Chinese Reds in his case, in 1936, with only a smattering of Chinese; Kahin spoke GI Indonesian. They barely touched the place. Snow spent three months among the Chinese Communists (between June and October), while Kahin was in republican territory between August and December.

Snow found Mao in the north of China. He must have been as exotic to Mao as Kahin was to the Indonesians. He won Mao's confidence, at first in awkward, but then in increasingly open and even compassionate conversations. Above Snow and the Chinese, as above Kahin and the Indonesians, the *possibly* progressive United States hovered, building trust and solidarity in hope. Edgar Snow wrote that "It seem[s] to me that [Mao] found it difficult to understand why, in a country where workers were enfranchised, there was still no worker's government. I was afraid my answers did not satisfy him.... He asked innumerable questions about the New Deal and Roosevelt's foreign policy."[57]

Mao Tse-Tung was forty-three years old when Snow met him in 1936. "Mao described the Long March to the Northwest," writes Snow, and "wrote a classical poem about it for me."[58]

Yet, Kahin did not become Snow, and he did not write a book about Amir. "Instability of character," Kahin wrote about Amir, "and political ambition were certainly of great importance in Sjarifoeddin's decision to cast his lot with the Stalinists."

CHAPTER 16

Kahin came to describe democracy, socialism, and Amir, "as related to the writer"—by those directly engaged. He kept a distance.

> As related by them to the writer . . . the opinion of most responsible non-Communist leaders, including Sukarno, Hatta and Sjahrir, was that Sjarifoeddin had not previously been a member of the PKI, though he did have connections with the "illegal PKI" underground beginning in 1939. . . .
>
> Those who knew him will testify to the instability of his philosophical and religious moorings. None of his connections seemed very solidly based to them [and] when depressed he was especially amenable to the persuasion of others. . . . [T]he belief is widespread that Musso's dramatic arrival must have somewhat panicked Sjarifuddin. They [those who knew him well] believed that he felt it necessary to cooperate with Musso or else become politically isolated. . . . Undoubtedly, both Musso and Sjarifuddin felt that they could use each other.[59]

There was, of course, also, and perhaps most heavily on Kahin's mind, the matter of the US betrayal. This is the word Kahin used. He had written about the US betrayal of Amir Sjarifoeddin already in *Nationalism and Revolution*, and with notably greater openness, and indeed bitterness, in his *Testament*: "Frank Graham had led . . . Amir Sjarifuddin . . . to believe that the U.S. would pressure the Dutch to live up to their end of the Renville Agreement. . . . Amir, *together with political conscious Indonesians in general* saw this [as] an American betrayal. . . . Graham shared Amir's perception. . . . Indeed, when many years later I discussed the matter with him . . . [h]e bitterly complained that there had been a *double* betrayal, of him [and Amir]."[60] Betrayal of Graham, betrayal of Amir, betrayal of Indonesian aspirations—some of them, at least.

In *Testament*, Kahin writes about "one of the great betrayals by American policy makers."[61] It was an "irony," Kahin writes in his last book on Indonesia,

> the rebellion [at Madiun] and the republic's strong response to it constituted the major factor in shifting US backing away from the Netherlands in favor of the republic. For once the government led by Sukarno and Hatta put down the rebellion and shot its leaders, it was no longer possible [to consider the republic] a bridge to an ultimately Communist Indonesia. . . . [S]hift to the right . . . increased the caution that Hatta, Sukarno, and Sjahrir had already manifested before the rebellion broke out. . . . Rightwards tendency in both civilian and military spheres was further exacerbated. . . . [T]he republic became more dependent on American support. . . . [T]the republic's leaders felt they could not risk

alienating the US by embarking on radical socioeconomic revolutionary change or resisting . . . their pressure to reach a compromise.⁶²

It was sometimes in the nineteen-nineties. We had a coffee with Kahin, in Jakarta, in the house of one of his former Cornell students. Kahin came late and he told us that he was delayed at an interview. He talked to a woman, he said, about whom there were whispers that she had known Amir intimately.⁶³ No, he added with a smile, he did not get very far with her in the interview. She only said that she and Amir were holding hands. Yes, Kahin said, he was still after Amir.⁶⁴

Benedict Anderson was born in 1936 in Kunming, China, and, as he liked to say, he could almost hear Mao's army on its real Long March passing by. His father was English, his mother Irish, and he got his secondary education in the United States. Then he went to Eton and Cambridge, where he studied classics. For his graduate study he went to Cornell, where he became a star student of George Kahin.

In 1963, Kahin sent him for two years of field study in Indonesia. The idea was that he would study the Indonesian politics of the 1960s as part of the Cornell Modern Indonesia—in fact Kahin's—Project's series of book-length studies on post-1945 Indonesian history, a series launched by Kahin's *Nationalism and Revolution in Indonesia*. Anderson rebelled and, while in Indonesia, he became deeply engaged in studying Javanese culture, and at the same time the revolutionary years Kahin had written about. Anderson's *Java in the Time of Revolution*, published in 1972, became a study on par with Kahin's, written with equal zeal and soon of equal influence.

Anderson's interest and engaging was of a different era and different focus than those of Kahin. Anderson's younger brother Perry, a historian of the absolutist states of Europe of the eighteenth century, and a British public intellectual, was one of the founders of the *New Left Review*. Since the *New Left Review*'s beginning, Ben was a part of the New-Left circle. In 1982, ten years after *Java in the Time of Revolution*, he published the first edition of *Imagined Communities*, which made him kind of an intellectual celebrity and a world expert on the problems of nationalism. But he never allowed himself to be led completely away from his study of Indonesia, or, more precisely, Java.

John Wolff, who taught Indonesian and Javanese at Cornell for half a century, the author of the best textbook of Indonesian, considered Anderson the most brilliant student of languages he had ever met. Anderson's curiosity about the Indonesian revolution passed through a thick filter of deep affection for culture—wayang shadow puppet theater, gamelan music, language, its accents, jokes as well as body language, Javanese dance—in sum what, in one of his most influential essays he called "the Javanese concept of power."[65]

"Anthropological Place," Marc Augé wrote, manifests that "all the inhabitants have to do is recognize themselves in it when the occasion arises, . . . to defend against external and internal threats to ensure that the language of identity retains a meaning."[66] Friedrich Nietzsche placed the "anthropological place," though he did not call it thus, where most of the Westerners did—in the East: "Will it perhaps be said of us one day," he asked, "that we too steering westward hoped to reach an India—but that it was our fate to be wrecked against infinity? Or, my brothers, Or?—"[67]

A fictional tourist company in Georges Perec's *Life: A User Manual*, "proposed selection of twenty-four strategic sites in twenty-four countries . . . twenty-four hotels. . . . A good hotel they believed was one whom a client can go out if he wants, and not go out if going out is a burden for him . . . to review Old Delft with potters, wavers . . . dressed in traditional costumes working by candlelight . . . rotating features from one site to another . . . Balinese dancers . . . Tyrolean waitresses, bullfighters . . . cattle, banyans, Pyramids."[68]

Anderson told his friends about how his initiation into politics had happened, kind of. His glasses were broken during a demonstration in London, England (was it for nuclear disarmament?). He was still a student at the time and, as he said, still rather a bystander than anything else. It was also about the time, he said, he attended one of the World Youth Festivals. Not the one that Soeripno and Francisca Fanggidaej attended in Prague in 1947; he was too young for that.

As George Kahin belonged to the 1940s, Benedict Anderson belonged to the 1960s. "All the recrimination that replaces revolutionary thought today," wrote Jean Baudrillard, the author of *Simulacra*, of the time, "comes back to incriminate capital for not following the rules of the game."[69] "I was considered to be vaguely 'left-wing'—whatever that means," wrote Hans Magnus Enzensberger, an icon of the European-mainly student-mainly movement of the 1960s.[70]

"Tumult," says Enzensberger. "Just as the Spanish anarchists died in the past," Enzensberger wrote, "just as the members of the Paris Commune shot at the clock towers in order to gain time," so the youth of the 1960s had been marching through the Western cities' streets with "Ho! Ho! Ho Chi Minh!" and "What do we want? A red West Berlin!'"[71] "The spectacle is our essential form," wrote Baudrillard.[72] It was, to use the words of Emmanuel Levinas, a little old by then and a little bitter, it is true: "the red march of the intelligentsia."[73] In a British cartoon, "a man named 'Revolution'" in a caballero costume serenades a sad woman looking from a window: "'What, you again?' says she."[74]

This might also have been "what Francis Fukuyama spoke of as 'good news,' [that] . . . Liberal democracy remains the only coherent political aspiration that spans different regions and cultures around the world."[75] The list Saint Just in the French Revolution already enumerated: "enlightenment, citizenship, republicanism, hygiene and antisepsis, longer life-span for a majority, universal elementary schooling and easy access to the middle and higher schooling, urbanization, easier transport and communication, and so on and on—in sum, the twin peaks of *easier living*, made possible by industrial productivity, and *happiness*—'a new idea of Europe'."[76]

Kahin's *Nationalism and Revolution in Indonesia* concluded on a moment of victory of the revolution: a compromise was achieved, the independent Indonesia was internationally recognized under the leadership of Soekarno and Hatta—the proclamators—as a nation state in the borders of the former Dutch Indies, except for the disputed area of the West New Guinea.

Anderson's *Java in the Time of Revolution* concluded on a moment of the defeat of the revolution. For Anderson the defeat came as a death of a revolutionary—but not Amir Sjarifoeddin. Tan Malaka was the hero, the proponent of *100% Merdeka*, "100% Freedom," never in government, élan, euphoria, chaos, pure flame. His execution, also by the Indonesian military, two months after Amir's, in February 1949, was that moment.

"It is probably safe to say," wrote Robert Musil in the notes for his *The Man without Qualities*, "that in all the revolutions that have ever taken place in this world, it has always been the thinking men who have come off worst. They always begin with the premise of a new civilization, make a clear sweep of every advance hitherto achieved by the human mind as though it were enemy property, and are overtaken by the next upheaval before they can surpass the heights previously attained." The men (and women) of feeling, on the other hand, wrote Musil, have fared better, for a while. "Only God knows," wrote Musil about them (and himself), "why this [revolution] should arouse in [them] such a sensation of passionate tenderness." Perhaps it is, he wrote, "the legendary voluptuousness that overcomes mythic heroes on the point of being devoured by the goddesses they had wooed."[77]

Whatever élan, wisdom, and courage there might have been in Amir, during the time of the colonial Indies, in the time of Japanese occupation, and during the revolution, either Kahin or Anderson saw the motor of history elsewhere. There was Tan Malaka, the man of tumult for Anderson, and there was Soekarno, Hatta, and Sjahrir especially, for Kahin; they knew when to stop.

For Anderson, Amir was "a man even his political adversaries found it difficult to hate. . . . Highly intelligent, energetic, and ambitious, his personal warmth, humor, and emotional romanticism elicited an intense loyalty among his followers that was *largely unaffected by the political line he took any one time.*"[78]

Soe Hok Gie was a friend of Anderson. Born in 1942, Soe was Chinese Indonesian, one of the leaders of the Generation 1965, almost exclusively a student movement. Soe initially supported the military in their suppression of the second Madiun, but, in a matter of months turned against the army when it became clear it was using the Communist coup" as a pretext for suppressing dissent and taking complete power over the state.

Soe Hok Gie died tragically in 1969, at the age of twenty-seven years, when on vacation, was killed by poisonous gas at Mount Semeru, one of East Java's majestic volcanoes. Soe was a student of history at the University of Indonesia and he had just defended his PhD dissertation on the Indonesian revolution with an extensive chapter on Madiun.[79] Under Soeharto military regime, after Soe's death, the thesis could not be published but it circulated clandestinely.

Ben Anderson used five lines from Soe Hok Gie's still unpublished dissertation as a motto for his 1972 book on revolution:

My sympathy is for those
Who have sacrificed everything
For the freedom of the nation, the state,
And the people of Indonesia,
Those on the left side and those on the right—
The late Soe Hok Gie.[80]

Soe Hok Gie's view of the Indonesian revolution, is that of a pure flame, élan, euphoria, and chaos—of *pemoeda*, "youth," aroused by destruction of family and society during the Japanese occupation. The youth stays with us. The youth of the youth and the youth of the nation.

The story lasts, and the nation lasts, as long as the youth's élan, euphoria, and chaos last. Anderson's book, when in its dissertation form, was called "Pemoeda Revolution," "The Youth Revolution." The death of Soe Hok Gie in the mountains gave the image an additional appeal, Sturm und Drang, power of dying young.

"This radicalism," wrote Soe Hok Gie, *"left or right."*[81] "While for the majority of the Indonesian people and the youth," wrote Soe Hok Gie, "revolution and freedom spoke for aspirations towards 'the beautiful,' for a small part of leaders, revolution and freedom were matters of strategy and tactic that had to be carefully calculated."[82] The radicalism of the youth revolution "was like driving in a racing car on a mountainous road which is every moment becoming narrower. Certainly, at one moment, the madly turning wheels will stuck, flames will burst out and everything will burn down."[83]

When Soe Hok Gie's dissertation at last appeared as a book, in 1997, after Soeharto and the military regime were gone, in another moment of hope that with Soeharto's fall a really new era was coming, it became a classic for the Indonesian post-Soeharto generations. It was, in fact, as much a classic as Anderson's *Java in a Time of Revolution*, now translated in Indonesian. In the introduction to Soe's book, Amir is mentioned: "It seems that Amir Sjarifoeddin forgot that, when he was imprisoned by Japan and sentenced to death, it was Hatta with Soekarno who succeeded in liberating him [*sic*]."[84]

"The history of Indonesia after the proclamation," wrote the new introduction to Soe's book, "did not escape blips of ideology. And because of these blips much of the blood of the children of our nation had been shed. Can these moments repeat themselves? No one can answer this. We can only pray."[85] "Madiun," Soe Hok Gie had written, "was planned," and Amir's motivation was "frustration." "At the moment of frustration," Soe Hok Gie wrote, "Musso emerged like the pied piper from the Grimms' story, and Amir, with Setiadjit, Soeripno, Maroeto Daroesman followed him like obedient children."[86]

This seems to be what remains. For one more generation, at least, this became the memory for this youth engendering their kind of élan, euphoria, and chaos, of holding the world, and changing it, in small steps, democratically, not crossing the line—in the words of Hans Magnus Enzensberger, "vaguely 'left-wing' whatever that means." Or, to end on Homer's epos of the (possible) heroes to which Thomas Carlyle refers at the end of his *French Revolution*: "it does not conclude, but merely ceases."[87]

Conclusion

> There is nothing more practical than escape. . . .
> —Adorno, *Minima Moralia*, 202

The nightmare had been at the beginning of this book, its motivation, sort of, and it stayed with me up to the book's conclusion. "Nightmare?" my mother would say when she was still alive. "Rudo" (she called me Rudo), "you read too much." Yet, "More and more fearful as I write," felt Franz Kafka, and I, as I wrote, felt like that, too.[1]

What might have happened is a question a historian may be excused of asking if he asks it as a nightmare. What might have happened if the Madiun leaders, Amir and Musso, against all odds, defeated Siliwangi, and if the revolution proceeded their way? Already at the time some suggested that Musso would become the president after Soekarno, like Beneš, would fade out, and that Amir would become the prime minister. But what would become next?

Since I began to think about writing this book, there was an idea that kept coming back—to write of Amir as part of a twin biography, one life of two possible heroes.

Vladimír Clementis was born in 1902, five years before Amir, in the village of Tisovec, Central Slovakia, later the eastern part of Czechoslovakia, in foothills remarkably like the landscape between Medan and Sibolga. Tisovec and Slovakia, when Clementis was born, were part of the Austro-Hungarian Empire, as tightly and loosely, socially, politically, culturally, and linguistically, part of the Habsburg Empire as was Medan part of the Dutch colonial one.

Clementis's mother tongue was Slovak, but the family had strong and still well-remembered roots in Bohemia to the west, where the Czech language was spoken. Like Amir, Clementis was sent to the best schools there were and as far as the family could afford it, first an elementary school in Tisovec, with Slovak and Hungarian as the languages of instruction, and then a Gymnasium beyond the hills with Hungarian and German. After graduation from the Gymnasium, Clementis went to Prague to study law. It was already the Czechoslovak time. The empire had disintegrated as the result of the First World War and a republic was declared.

Clementis's family was devotedly Protestant and Luther's "Hier stehe ich. Ich kann nicht anders," is often mentioned in Clementis's biography. Like Amir, Clementis "discovered politics" in the Law School. The Czechoslovak Communist Party was founded in 1920, and Clementis became an activist and, in a short time, a member. Like Amir, he was recalled as brilliant, music loving, well read. A practicing lawyer, he spent his professional time defending other party activists, striking workers, and peasants. In 1935 he became a member of the Czechoslovak parliament for the Communist Party.

Unlike Amir, Clementis escaped fascist prison. Like Amir's, his life was absorbed in confronting fascism. He fled to France when Czechoslovakia was occupied by Germany in 1939. When in France, in conversation with a small group of comrades in exile, Clementis expressed his disappointment about the Molotov–Ribbentrop Pact of August 1939. He saw it as a betrayal of the policy of the united front against fascism, and he said it. His remarks were reported to Moscow, but at the moment nothing more happened.

His remarks in France seemed to be forgotten. When France was defeated, in 1940, he escaped to London and President Beneš offered him to take part in the Czechoslovak government in exile. The Communist Party approved.

He was brilliant, charming, to use Anderson's words about Amir, "a man even his political adversaries found it difficult to hate."[2] He became one of the point men in London when an uprising against the Nazis in the closing year of the war, in 1944, broke out in his native Slovakia.

After the German surrender in May 1945, Clementis returned to Prague. Like Amir after the Japanese capitulation, he had risen fast in the Communist Party apparatus as well as in the government. He was a *communiste maudit*, too, and it was good for the moment. He became the general secretary, in the Ministry of Foreign Affairs under Jan Masaryk, a son of the late founding father of the republic and Beneš's predecessor. He became a member of the Executive of the Communist Party Central Committee.

On February 28, 1948, Vladimír Clementis stood on the balcony of the Kinský Palace on the Old Town Square in Prague, as Klement Gottwald, to the gathered mass of people, announced the upcoming Victory of the Czechoslovak Working Class. Under the balcony, almost certainly, Soeripno was standing somewhere in the crowd, listening, applauding, euphoric, and thinking about the world and Indonesian revolution.

There is a story made familiar by Czech writer Milan Kundera. It was a cold February day in Prague and Clementis offered Gottwald his fur cap. On the original photograph from the historical event, Gottwald is wearing Clementis's cap and Clementis stands next to him in Gottwald's hat. On the same photograph, only corrected (the only one I had ever seen in my youth), the fur cap is there, on Gottwald's head, but Clementis is missing.

It is curious that, like about Amir, people were saying about Clementis that he was fluent "in eight languages," not seven, not nine, eight. Like Amir, Clementis traveled to places where most people around him had never been. He liked to sing. He was not easy to rank. Like Amir, Clementis had always been looked at with a little suspicion.

Only weeks after the February Victory of the Czechoslovak Working Class, on March 10, 1948, Clementis's boss at the Ministry of Foreign Affairs, Jan Masaryk, committed suicide (or, as some said, was thrown out of the window by agents from Moscow). Clementis was appointed Masaryk's successor. It is very possible that in this function Clementis met Musso and Soeripno when Musso arrived in Prague.[3]

It was now only months before the show trials in Eastern Europe were to begin. Clementis's transgression from the time of war, when he talked too much in France, filed away in the party memory, resurged. He was brilliant, spoke eight languages, there had been that *maudit*-ness about him. There was increasing talk about a Third World War, and the Communist parties of Eastern Europe were fresh in their victories—glorious and anxious. Clementis happened to be in New York leading the Czechoslovak delegation to the United Nations when he was warned, by a US columnist Joseph Alsop among others, not to go back. But he believed in Gottwald, whom he had known since his early lawyer years in Slovakia, their early Communist years, and Gottwald wrote him a personal letter not to worry.

Clementis returned from New York, was arrested, and assigned the role of one of the principals accused in the trial with the former general secretary of the Communist Party Rudolf Slánský, another *communiste maudit* and, moreover, unlike Clementis, a Jew.[4]

During the interrogation and as they were made ready for the trial—it lasted for more than a year—a once-monthly letter home was allowed to the prisoners. "But the pipes, I still do like," wrote Clementis to his wife in one of the letters from prison, on August 20, 1952: "to the 'new mix' (which I alternate with

'Monopol')—especially when I am lucky to get to an apple to flavor the mix—I got used. Only one of the two pipes that I still have with me, begins to crack—the Lewis one bought during war at the Haymarket. But I guess it will still last. I finish the last pipe and listen."⁵ He was hanged on the same day, December 3, 1952.

D. N. Aidit, Amir Sjarifoeddin's follower and protégé since the late 1930s and, after Amir's death, one of the big four of the rejuvenated Communist Party under the Soekarno pajung, learned many lessons through the revolution. Perhaps the most important was how to keep the apparatus going.

Throughout the early 1950s, in addition to it, Aidit learned from the ways of the other Communist parties how the world was going. Among other lessons learned, he repeatedly mentioned in his public speeches, the way to deal with traitors and spies, very importantly among them, "Rudolf Slánský and his band."⁶ "Aidit's international Road," wrote Arnold Brackman, now turned historian, "unwaveringly followed the Moscow line . . . assailing the 'reactionary imperialist forces whose cowardly acts and crimes became clear when United States imperialist agents like Tito of Yugoslavia, Rajk in Hungary, Slánský in Czechoslovakia, Gomulka in Poland, and Kostov in Bulgaria carried out their dirty tasks.'"⁷

Musso and Amir, were they victorious in Madiun, might have ended up accused at a trial like those with Slánský, or Rajk, or Tito. Musso might have gone first. With his claims, or boasting, that he defended Madrid in the Spanish Civil War in 1936, he might have fit the rest. Artur London and Josef Pavel of Prague, two of the accused, had fought in Spain. Laszlo Rajk of Budapest was a commissar of the Rákossi Battalion and he "'confessed' at his trial in 1949 that he went to Spain on behalf of the police of [the fascist] Admiral Horthy." "I also carried on Trotskyist propaganda in the Rákossi Battalion," Rajk "admitted" on his trial before he was executed on October 15, 1949.⁸

Nothing of this kind happened in Indonesia. Amir and Musso did not win, and they could not be—physically—killed again. Nothing remained to be done in their matter, except, perhaps, the "neutral," still vaguely in the air, as Roland Barthes defined it: "Neutral is desire for . . . suspension [*epoché*] of orders."⁹

"Heroes without heroic deeds," wrote Marx in his *Eighteenth Brumaire*, make "history without events."¹⁰ This might be what we got. Or perhaps not. "What remains irreducible to any deconstruction," wrote Jacques Derrida who made his name by being able to deconstruct practically everything, "[w]hat remains indestructible as the possibility itself of deconstruction is perhaps, a certain experience of the emancipationary promise."¹¹

"For the observer," Kierkegaard wrote about the fall of another possible hero, of another time, he "is like a magnificent pause in the course of history . . . we do not hear him at all; a profound stillness prevails." He, Kierkegaard wrote, "arrived at the idea of the good, the beautiful, the true only as the boundary . . . that it came upon to ideal infinity as possibility." This book tried to argue, and Kierkegaard comes in handy, that a possible hero "as a citizen [is] not a point on the periphery of the state gravitating toward its center but rather tangent continually touching the peripheral complexities of the state."[12] That, whatever modernity might mean, so says Virilio, "avoiding accidents," the world is still "utterly suspended on the threshold." Therefore, he says, the moment "does not stop coming, that we can't stop waiting for."[13]

Among the many questions left unanswered by this book, one to me is the most vexing. Was it the Bible they found in the shoulder bag next to Amir's body when it was exhumed in 1950? Was the notebook some Marxist text, like Lenin's *State and Revolution*, for instance? Did Amir really ask the lieutenant for an hour to pray before they fired? Or did he ask for a moment to sing the "Internationale"? Or both? Against all the testimonies, I hope he asked for twenty minutes, say, to smoke the last pipe, and that he got it.

Notes

Preface

1. Brecht, *Poems 1913–1956*, 277.
2. The term is taken from Virilio's *The Aesthetics of Disappearance*.
3. Benjamin, "One-Way Street," in *Selected Writings*, 1:484.
4. Benjamin, "One-Way Street," in *Selected Writings*, 1:454.
5. Barthes, *The Neutral*, 52.
6. Lacan, *Anxiety*, 115.

1. Sumatra

1. "Cratylus," in *Republic*, 1:161.
2. Marx quoted in Derrida, *Specters of Marx*, 137.
3. Kraemer, "Batak Report," 44–45, 51.
4. According to Jacques Leclerc, based on what he learned from the family, "Since he was little, Amir could speak the area language of Tapanoeli Sipirok, Sidempoean, the language of his family." Leclerc, "Amir Sjarifuddin 75 Tahun," 61.
5. Wellem, "Mr. Amir Sjarifuddin," 51; Harahap, "Amir Sjarifoeddin," in Komunikasi 38, 23. In Leclerc Papers no. 362, there is handwritten genealogical scheme possibly by F. K. N. Harahap, Amir's cousin. Year 1861 of Goenoeng Toea's baptism must be an error by Sjarief Bachroen, Amir's younger brother, who was the informant: "In 1861 when the first German missionaries of the Rheinish Missionary Society arrived, these Bataks were still utter pagans." Kraemer, "Batak Report," 43.
6. Leclerc Papers no. 375.
7. Heidegger quoted in Levinas, *On Escape*, 103n21.
8. The younger siblings were Maslia, Anwar Mahajoedin, Sjarief Bachroen, Arifin Harahap, Fatimah Harahap, and Zainab Harahap. Wellem, "Mr. Amir Sjarifuddin," 50.
9. Leclerc Papers no. 375.
10. Wellem, "Mr. Amir Sjarifuddin," 32.
11. Klinken, *Minorities*, 116. According to Amir's younger brother Sjarief Bachroen the name means *Pembaharu Iman*, "Renewer of Creed." Bachroen to Wellem, in Wellem, "Mr. Amir Sjarifuddin," 50.
12. Leclerc, "Amir Sjarifuddin 75 Tahun," 61.
13. *Deli-Maatschappij*, 17, 44, 78.
14. *Jaarverslag*, 89.
15. *Jaarverslag*, 63.

16. Blanchot, *Writing of the Disaster*, 127.
17. Grossman, *End of the Land*, 403.
18. Proust, *Time Regained*, 242–243.
19. Interview with Pangèran Puger, Yogyakarta, August 5, 1997, in Mrázek, *Certain Age*, 155.
20. Wellem, "Mr. Amir Sjarifuddin," 54.
21. Encyclopedie van Nederlandsch-Indië, The Hague Nijhof, 1919, vol. 3, 941.
22. Van der Wal, *Het onderwijsbeleid in Nederlands-Indië*, 117n1.
23. From interviews with Amir's relatives: "Amir as a son of a senior and well-off official never experienced difficulties when he was a child." Wellem, "Mr. Amir Sjarifuddin," 53.
24. Bos, "Hoe het groeide," 14.
25. Bos, "Hoe het groeide," 16.
26. Hoogeveen, *Handleiding*, 3.
27. The director of education to the governor general, March 16, 1914, in Van der Wal, *Het onderwijsbeleid in Nederlands-Indië*, 248.
28. Wesseling and Dane, "Are 'the Natives' Educable?" 32.
29. Walhout and Dane, "Picturing the East," 185.
30. Rijsen, *Hoofdpersonen*, 1, 26.
31. Wesseling and Dane, "Are 'the Natives' Educable?" 32.
32. Benjamin, "A Glimpse into the World of Children's Books," in *Selected Writings*, 1:435.
33. Wesseling and Dane, "Are 'the Natives' Educable?" 28.
34. Hilgers, *Onze vriendjes op reis*, 14.
35. Hilgers, *Onze vriendjes op reis*, 1.
36. Hilgers, *Onze vriendjes op reis*, 70–71.
37. Benjamin, "Notes for a Study of the Beauty of Colored Illustrations in Children's Books," in *Selected Writings*, 1:264.
38. Hilgers, *Onze vriendjes op reis*, 20.
39. Hilgers, *Onze vriendjes op reis*, 28, 29.
40. *Deli-Maatschappij*, 44.
41. Walhout and Dane, "Picturing the East," 173.
42. Walhout and Dane, "Picturing the East," 176.
43. Walhout and Dane, "Picturing the East," 178–189.
44. Benjamin, "Notes for a Study of the Beauty of Colored Illustrations in Children's Books," in *Selected Writings*, 1:261.
45. Benjamin, "One-Way Street," in *Selected Writings*, 1:468.
46. Nieuwenhuis, *Assaineering van Sibolga*, 3.
47. Nieuwenhuis, *Assaineering van Sibolga*, 5.
48. Nieuwenhuis, *Assaineering van Sibolga*, 11.
49. Kraemer, "Batak Report," 48–49, 45.
50. Augé, *Non-Places*, 87.
51. *Come to Sumatra*, n.p.
52. Musil, *Diaries*, 286, 290.
53. Charles Baudelaire quoted in Virilio, *Aesthetics of Disappearance*, 39.
54. Benjamin, "One-Way Street," in *Selected Writings*, 1:454.

55. Benjamin, "The Lamp," in *Selected Writings*, 2:691.
56. Proust, *Time Regained*, 3.

2. Holland

1. Saripada carefully planned Amir's study in Holland. "To prepare his son, he hired a private teacher of English and French so that Amir is able to speak both languages fluently." Wellem, "Mr. Amir Sjarifuddin," 55.
2. Rabelais, *Gargantua and Pantagruel*, 48.
3. Verkuyl, *Gedenken en verwachten*, 180.
4. "Scheepvaartbericht," *Bataviaasch Nieuwsblad*, July 12, 1921; *Het Nieuws van de dag*, August 6, 1921; "Father, mother, and younger siblings accompanied him to the ship," Wellem, "Mr. Amir Sjarifuddin," 56.
5. Leclerc Papers no. 375.
6. A. P. van de Loosdrecht-Sizoo, "Zendeling van de Loosdrecht," *Alle Volken* (Vlaardingen), January 1, 1918, 2–3. Also see Wellem, "Mr. Amir Sjarifuddin," 57–58.
7. Moelia would come back to the Netherlands to finish his thesis, titled "Het primitieve denken in de moderne wetenschap," "The primitive thinking in modern science," which he defended on November 3, 1933. Leclerc, "Amir Sjarifuddin 75 Tahun," 59.
8. Leclerc Papers no. 267.
9. P. J. Smink to Leclerc, November 26, 1979, in Leclerc Papers no. 267.
10. Smink to Leclerc. Also see Leclerc, "Amir Sjarifuddin 75 Tahun," 58. Wellem confuses Leiden, Amir's first home, and Haarlem, his second. Wellem, "Mr. Amir Sjarifuddin," 56ff.
11. Benjamin, "A Glimpse into the World of Children's Books," in *Selected Writings*, 1:435.
12. W. B. van Haard (City Gymnasium archivist) to Jacques Leclerc, May 4, 1979, in Leclerc Papers no. 243. Amir Sjarifoedin (with one "d") signed himself on the verso side of the school photo of the fourth grade students; photo in Leclerc Papers no. 243.
13. Diotima to Socrates, Plato, *Lysis. Symposium. Phaedrus*, 195, 197.
14. Frijhoff, Baronner, and Pollmann, *Tempel van hovaardij*, 65.
15. Frijhoff, Baronner, and Pollmann, *Tempel van hovaardij*, 60.
16. *Haarlemsche Courant*, July 4, 1924, in Frijhoff, Baronner, and Pollmann, *Tempel van hovaardij*, 105.
17. Lecture by van Duyn, June 26, 1924, in Frijhoff, Baronner, and Pollmann, *Tempel van hovaardij*, 104–105.
18. Frijhoff, Baronner, and Pollmann, *Tempel van hovaardij*, 60, 75.
19. Frijhoff, Baronner, and Pollmann, *Tempel van hovaardij*, 137.
20. Bloch, *Traces*, 66.
21. Loes Spruit to Leclerc, June 20, 1979, in Leclerc Papers no. 271.
22. W. B. van Haard to Leclerc, May 4, 1979, in Leclerc Papers no. 243.
23. Loes Spruit to Leclerc, June 20, 1979, in Leclerc Papers no. 271.
24. Interview with Dr. Johannes Verkuyl, November 10, 1992, in Klinken, *Minorities*, 116. Verkuyl, as mentioned elsewhere, studied at the time in Haarlem as Amir but at another school. He later became Amir's friend and, after Amir's death, kept in touch with several Amir's former classmates in Haarlem.

25. Loes Spruit to Leclerc June 6, 1979, in Leclerc Papers no. 271.
26. Frijhoff, Baronner, and Pollmann, *Tempel van hovaardij*, 141.
27. Frijhoff, Baronner, and Pollmann, *Tempel van hovaardij*, 56.
28. Frijhoff, Baronner, and Pollmann, *Tempel van hovaardij*, 138.
29. The photograph of the board of Amitie with Amir from 1926/1927 is in Frijhoff, Baronner, and Pollmann, *Tempel van hovaardij*, 73.
30. Frijhoff, Baronner, and Pollmann, *Tempel van hovaardij*, 139–140.
31. Loes Spruit to Leclerc, July 7, 1979, in Leclerc Papers no. 271. The school was an important city institution. In *Nieuwe Haarlemsche Courant* of July 17, 1926, for instance, Amir class's advancement from the fifth to sixth grade had been announced, with all the eighteen students named in the paper. Liesbeth Dolk pointed me to the paper.
32. Loes Spruit to Leclerc, June 20, 1979, in Leclerc Papers no. 271.
33. Verkuyl, *Gedenken en verwachten*, 180.
34. F. M. A. Schokeling to Leclerc, December 14, 1979, in Leclerc Papers no. 271.
35. Dr. Wijs to Leclerc, January 1980, in Leclerc Papers no. 271.
36. Loes Spruit to Leclerc, June 20, 1979, in Leclerc Papers no. 271.
37. Loes Spruit to Leclerc, June 20, 1979, in Leclerc Papers no. 271.
38. Homer, *Iliad*, 326.
39. Leclerc Papers no. 243. Announcement is in *De Tijd: godsdienstig-staatkundig Dagblad*, July 11, 1927. Liesbeth Dolk pointed me to the paper.
40. Loes Spruit to Leclerc, July 11, 1979, in Leclerc Papers no. 271.
41. Wellem, "Mr. Amir Sjarifuddin," 61.
42. Homer, *Odyssey*.
43. Berge, *H.J., van Mook*, 84. It is the same thing: "According to a remark by Musset, the 'East Indies' begin at a point beyond the boundary of the boulevards." Benjamin, *Arcades Project*, 438.
44. Loes Spruit to Leclerc, June 20, 1979, in Leclerc Papers no. 271.

3. The Batavia Law School

1. The event is recorded in *Het Nieuws van den dag voor Nederlandsch-Indië*, July 10, 1928.
2. Homer, *Odyssey*, 207.
3. Mrázek, "Coughing Heavily," 155.
4. Resink, "Rechtshoogeschool," 428.
5. Brecht, *Poems, 1913–1956*, 301.
6. Resink, "Rechtshoogeschool," 445; Resink, *Gedenkboek*.
7. B. van Tijn, "Prof. J. van Gelderen," in Resink, *Gedenkboek*, 22.
8. Resink, "Rechtshoogeschool," 429.
9. Leclerc Papers no. 363.
10. Resink, *Gedenkboek*, 7.
11. Schrieke, *De Gang der Communistische Beweging*.
12. "J. Van Kan," in Resink, *Gedenkboek*, 16.
13. "J. Van Kan," in Resink, *Gedenkboek*, 16.
14. "J. Van Kan," in Resink, *Gedenkboek*, 17.

15. Resink, "Rechtshoogeschool," 428–431.
16. Klinken, *Minorities*, 72.
17. Resink, "Rechtshoogeschool," 430.
18. S. C. van Randwijk, telephone interview by Gerry van Klinken, October 9, 1992, in Van Klinken Papers.
19. Th. van den End, personal communication, December 12, 2019. J. M. J. Schepper (1887–1967) "came from the circle of sectarian *Darbistis*. . . . It is not surprising," wrote van Randwijk, "that he always searched for connections between Christian spirit and what is called Christian culture . . . he was always aware of a danger of romantizations of the mission. He was the consul of the missions in 1918–1922 and advised the upcoming missionaries in his lectures 'not to present themselves as just escaping from the jaws of a crocodile.' . . . In 1922, Schepper took a leave from his duties as a consul and traveled to the Netherlands mainly to express his opposition against the mission central board which in his view became too dependent on the Indies big capital (*modal-besar*)." Randwijk, *Oegstgeest*, 620, 630.
20. Th. van den End, personal communication, December 13, 2019. A long review of Schepper's dissertation appeared in 1918, see Scholten, "J.M.J. Schepper's proefschrift," 209–229. The review introduced Schepper's thesis as a part of the *Zurück zu Kant*, "Back-to-Kant," movement.
21. Th. van den End, personal communication, April 14, 2020.
22. *Het Indisch Hooger Onderwijs in het algemeen, Mededeelingen*, no. 68 (1924): 126–127.
23. *Het Indisch Hooger Onderwijs in het algemeen, Mededeelingen*, no. 68 (1924): 126–127.
24. Foucault, "What Is Critique?" 43.
25. Resink, "Rechtshoogeschool," 436.
26. Amir also used to visit Professor Kollewijn's house. Resink, "Rechtshoogeschool," 443.
27. Resink, "Rechtshoogeschool," 446. See also Han Resink, interview by Gerry van Klinken, November 23, 1993, Jakarta, in Van Klinken Papers.
28. Peter van der Veen to Th. van den End, February 1, 2004. Van den End personal communication.
29. Resink, interview. In *Bataviasche studenten almanac*, 1931, p. 138: "Mr. J. M. J. Schepper. . . . office hours, each Tuesday in the building of the RHS or by appointment in his house. Kebon Sirih 34—tel. WI 620." A full-page photo of Schepper appears on the opposite side.
30. Klinken, *Minorities*, 122–123; Resink, interview.
31. Paul Carus, afterword to Kant, *Prolegomena*, 212, 182, 173.
32. Klinken, *Minorities*, 122–123.
33. Klinken, *Minorities*, 123.
34. Axling, *Kagawa*, 73; Klinken, *Minorities*, 122.

4. Kramat 106

1. Adorno, *Minima Moralia*, 65. Kant speaks of "the possibility of experience." Kant, *Prolegomena*, 68.

2. Musil, *Diaries*, 234.
3. Musil, *Diaries*, 476.
4. Kafka, *Letters to Friends*, 290–291.
5. Miharja, *Pemberontakan Madiun (Amir Syarifuddin)*, 7.
6. Miharja, *Pemberontakan Madiun (Amir Syarifuddin)*, 9.
7. Leclerc, "Amir Sjarifuddin 75 Tahun," 59.
8. Luth Dul Arnowo to Jacques Leclerc, January 26, 1983, Surabaya, in Leclerc Papers no. 369.
9. Leclerc, "Amir Sjarifoeddin," 28.
10. Klinken, *Minorities*, 117.
11. Lupitasari, "Cerita Museum," n.p.
12. Wellem, "Mr. Amir Sjarifuddin," 93, writes "7,50 *gulders*."
13. Attorney general to governor general, February 25, 1933, in Kwantes, *De ontwikkeling van de nationalistische beweging*, 3:719n.
14. Amir Sjarifoeddin "Amir Sjarifoeddin," 2.
15. Friedrich Nietzsche quoted in Prideaux, *I Am Dynamite*, 53.
16. Abu Hanifah, *Tales of a Revolution*, 45.
17. Abu Hanifah, *Tales of a Revolution*, 193.
18. Abu Hanifah, *Tales of a Revolution*, 13.
19. Abu Hanifah, *Tales of a Revolution*, 212.
20. Sartre, *Baudelaire*, 159.
21. Sartre, *Baudelaire*, 134, 137.
22. Preface to Goethe's *Faust* quoted in Safranski, *Goethe*, 420.
23. Abu Hanifah, "Amir Sjarifudin," 192.
24. Carlyle, *French Revolution*, 452.
25. Carlyle, *French Revolution*, 405.
26. Carlyle, *French Revolution*, 19–20.
27. Marx, *Eighteenth Brumaire*, 15.
28. Robespierre, "On the Condition of Free Men of Color, May 13, 1791," in Žižek, *Robespierre*, 21.
29. Robespierre, "On the Rights of Societies and Clubs, September 29, 1791," in Žižek, *Robespierre*, 23.
30. Robespierre, "On the Principles of the Political Morality That Should Guide the National Convention in the Domestic Administration of the Republic, February 5, 1794," in Žižek, *Robespierre*, 23, 111.
31. Klinken, *Minorities*, 120. Dr. C. (Kees) van Doorn (1896–1979), originally an agronomy expert, arrived at the Indies in 1922. He was active in the Netherlands Christian Student Movement and he opened a dormitory for the Christian students in Tanah Abang, Batavia, which was then moved to Kebon Sirih 44. Leirissa, "Biografi Dr. J. Leimena," 13.
32. Klinken, *Minorities*, 121.
33. Abu Hanifah, *Tales of a Revolution*, 69.
34. Abu Hanifah, "Amir Sjarifudin," 199.
35. Fransz, "Masa Muda," 19; "Mr. A. L. Tina Fransz was a motor of Kebon Sirih 44," Leirissa, "Biografi Dr. J. Leimena," 13.
36. Fransz, "Masa Muda," 16.

37. The originals of the two handwritten letters are in Leclerc Papers no. 317; also see Verkuyl, *Gedenken en verwachten*, 180.

38. The prayer book of the German Christian students movement by Hanns Lilje. Television interview with Verkuyl, in Leclerc Papers no. 296. G. J. Sizoo, brother of the widow, told Wellem that the book was the Bible and that it was full of Ferdinand Tambubolon's notes at the margins. Wellem, "Mr. Amir Sjarifuddin," 58.

39. Hering, *Soekarno*, 12.

40. Abu Hanifah, *Tales of a Revolution*, 64.

41. Amir Sjarifoeddin, "Amir Sjarifoeddin," 1.

42. Amir Sjarifoeddin is listed as a member of the executive of Jong Sumatra Bond in 1929. Kwantes, *De ontwikkeling van de nationalistische beweging*, 3:926n.

43. Klinken, *Minorities*, 118.

44. Simbolon, *Menjadi Indonesia*, 1:681.

45. Simbolon, *Menjadi Indonesia*, 1:682. There is a photo of all participants; no one can be identified.

46. Resink Papers no. 978.

47. *Empatpuluh-lima tahun Sumpah Pemuda*, 146.

48. Miert, *Een koel hoofd en een warm hart*, 332.

49. Resink, "Rechtshoogeschool," 433, 433n16.

5. Soekarno

1. Abu Hanifah, *Tales of a Revolution*, 79.

2. Abu Hanifah, *Tales of a Revolution*, 81; Abu Hanifah, *Menteng 31*, n.p.

3. Attorney general to governor general, February 25, 1933, in Kwantes, *De Ontwikkeling van de nationalistische beweging*, 3:719n.

4. Sjah to Leclerc, January 22, 1980, in Leclerc Papers no. 290.

5. *Bunga rampai setengah abad Perguruan Rakyat*, 67.

6. Soetan Mohammad Sjah to Leclerc, January 22, 1980, in Leclerc Papers no. 290.

7. Dahm, *Sukarno*, 108.

8. Amir Sjarifoeddin, "Amir Sjarifoeddin," 1.

9. Dahm, *Sukarno*, 104.

10. Dahm, *Sukarno*, 114. "Apart from [one] rally there was hardly ever a murmur of protest of the arrest." Legge, *Sukarno*, 118.

11. Dahm, *Sukarno*, 124. Gatot received two years, Maskoen twenty months, Soepriadinata fifteen months.

12. Abu Hanifah, *Tales of a Revolution*, 45.

13. Adams, *Sukarno*, 18.

14. Dahm, *Sukarno*, 29.

15. Dahm, *Sukarno*, 44; Legge, *Sukarno*, 77.

16. Saleh Efendi interview by author, August 21, 1993, Bandung, in Mrázek, *Certain Age*, 171.

17. Foucault, *Politics of Truth*, 123.

18. Mrázek, "Coughing Heavily."

19. Bondan, *Spanning a Revolution*, 67.

20. Nancy, *Adoration*, 19.

21. Tynianov, "Lexicon of Lenin," 203, 206.
22. Sukarno, "Kongres Kaum Ibu," *Soeloeh Indonesia Moeda*, 1928, reprinted in *Dibawah Bendera Revolusi Indonesia*, 1:107.
23. Sukarno, "Dubbele Les," *Soeloeh Indonesia Moeda*, 1928, reprinted in *Dibawah Bendera Revolusi Indonesia*, 1:49.
24. Dahm, *Sukarno*, 41.
25. Dahm, *Sukarno*, 43.
26. McIntyre, *Indonesian Political Biography*, 294.
27. Dahm, *Sukarno*, 103n146. Soekarno used "perutnja jang krontjong," literally "bellies playing *krontjong*." *Krontjong*—Indonesian street music.
28. *Soeloeh Indonesia Moeda*, no. 1, December 1927, quoted in Dahm, *Sukarno*, 83.
29. Sukarno, "Nasionalisme, Islamisme, Marxisme," originally in *Soeloeh Indonesia Moeda*, 1926, reprinted in *Dibawah Bendera Revolusi Indonesia*, 1:19f.
30. Saleh Efendi interview.
31. Sukarno, "Nasionalisme, Islamisme, Marxisme," originally in *Indonesia Moeda* 1926, reprinted in *Dibawah Bendera Revolusi Indonesia*, 1:6.
32. Augé, *Non-Places*, 44–46.
33. Blanchot, *Writing of the Disaster*, 86.
34. The term is from Kant, *Prolegomena*, 29.
35. Nancy, *Sense of the World*, 99.
36. Amir Sjarifoeddin, "Amir Sjarifoeddin," 1.
37. Klinken, *Minorities*, 119.
38. Bondan, *Spanning a Revolution*, 77.
39. Hering, *Soekarno*, 283.
40. *Politiek-Politioneele Overzichten* 3 (January 1932): 140. In March 1932 in Batavia, Amir Sjarifoeddin was listed as present at the establishment of Partindo. Kwantes,. *De ontwikkeling van de nationalistische beweging*, 3:926.
41. Malik, *Mengabdi Republik*, 1:19.
42. Tynianov, "The Lexicon of Lenin as Polemicist," 203, 206.
43. *Persatoean Indonesia*, March 16–23, 1932.
44. Adviser for native affairs to governor general, May 31, 1932, in Kwantes, *De ontwikkeling van de nationalistische beweging*, 3:635–636; Hering, *Soekarno*, 283.
45. Kwantes, *De ontwikkeling van de nationalistische beweging*, 4:55.
46. Adviser for native affairs to governor general, May 31, 1932; Hering, *Soekarno*, 283.
47. G. F. P. Pijper and Datoek Toemenggung, "Congres Partai Indonesia, May 14–17, 1932 te Batavia. Verslag," in Kwantes, *De ontwikkeling van de nationalistische beweging*, 3:635n; adviser for native affairs to governor general, May 31, 1932.
48. Adviser for native affairs to governor general, September 22, 1932, in Kwantes, *De ontwikkeling van de nationalistische beweging*, 3:666.
49. Dahm, *Sukarno*, 126. Soekamiskin prison was designed in 1921 by Soekarno's professor at Bandoeng Institute of Technology, Wolf Schoemaker. Rumors circulated that Schoemaker had used the help of his favorite student, Soekarno, to design the prison; some said, only the interior of the director's office. All was hardly possible, if only because of the chronology. Soekarno was just beginning his study when Soekamiskin was built. See on the rumors Dullemen, *Tropical Modernity*, 262.

50. Ali Sastroamidjojo. *Milestones on My Journey*, 72.
51. Supardi, "Bung Karno," quoted in in Dahm, *Sukarno*, 134–135.
52. Report on the 2nd Congress of the Partai Indonesia held at Soerrabaja, April 14–19, 1933, in Ingleson, *Road to Exile*, 214.
53. Poeze, *Politiek-Politioneele Overzichten*, 3:277.
54. Legge, *Sukarno*, 129
55. Leclerc Papers no. 375.
56. Ingleson, *Road to Exile*, 212.
57. Poeze, *Overzicht van de inlandsche*, no. 47 (1933), 740, 741.
58. See announcement of the Central Executive of Partindo, November 24, 1933, signed by Sartono and Amir Sjarifoeddin, in Bondan, *Spanning a Revolution*, 95.
59. Dahm, *Sukarno*, 164–165.
60. Four letters sent by Soekarno between August and September 1933 from prison to the attorney general, where he asked for mercy and promised not to engage anymore in political activity, became public much later and after all these histories were over. The letters are in full in Hering, *From Soekamiskin to Endeh*, 54–57.
61. Legge, *Sukarno*, 136.
62. Poeze, *Overzicht van de inlandsche*, no. 47 (1933), 743.
63. *Bintang Timoer*, January 30 and 31, 1934, in Poeze, *Overzicht van de inlandsche*, no. 5 (1934), 72.

6. Sleep, Baby, Sleep I

1. Amir Sjarifoeddin, "Het rassenprobleem in Nederlandsch-Indië," 1.
2. *Cratylus* quoted in Alain Badiou and Barbara Cassin, *Heidegger*, 22.
3. Heidegger, *Being and Time*, 391; *Cratylus* quoted in Badiou and Cassin, *Heidegger*, 22; Heidegger, *On the Way to Language*, 15.
4. Nancy, *Sense of the World*, 121.
5. Benjamin, "The Task of the Translator," in *Selected Writings*, 1:258–259.
6. Prideaux, *I Am Dynamite*, 100.
7. Safranski, *Goethe*, 425, 426.
8. Bishop, "Brecht, Hegel, Lacan," 267.
9. Benjamin, "The Political Groupings of Russian Writers," in *Selected Writings*, 2:9, emphasis mine.
10. Leclerc Papers no. 375.
11. This was Amir's comment on an article with the same title published in a white and arch-colonial magazine on October 15, 1930.
12. Derrida, *Specters of Marx*, 43, quoting Maurice Blanchot.
13. Derrida, *Specters of Marx*, 27.
14. Derrida, *Specters of Marx*, 40, quoting Blanchot.
15. Derrida, *Specters of Marx*, 52, emphasis mine.
16. *New York Times*, February 11, 1933.
17. *Indonesia Raja*, March–April 1933.
18. Poeze, *Overzicht van de inlandsche*, no. 7 (1933), 107.
19. Poeze, *Overzicht van de inlandsche*, no. 7 (1933), 107.
20. Klinken, *Minorities*, 118.

21. *Banteng* 1, no. 4 (February 28, 1933). Amir wrote in his "autobiography" that the article was deemed *haatzaaiend*, "sowing hate." Amir Sjarifoeddin, "Amir Sjarifoeddin," 1.

22. *Banteng* 1, no. 9 (July 15, 1933).

23. Barthes, *Sade, Fourier, Loyola*, 181.

7. Sleep, Baby, Sleep II

1. Van Randwijk to Jacques Leclerc, March 11, 1979, in Leclerc Papers no. 248.

2. By May 24, 1929, Baginda Soripada was forgiven the rest of his sentence and given a (lower-level) job of *commies*, "clerk," in government service in Taroetoeng; Leclerc Papers no. 375.

3. Harahap, "Amir Sjarifoeddin," *Komunikasi*, no. 39: 29.

4. Leclerc, "Amir Sjarifuddin," 29. Leclerc himself writes more carefully: "many people suspected," he writes, a connection between Amir's conversion and Basoenoe's suicide. Leclerc mentions that Basoenoe had been known for a long time to be depressive. Leclerc, "Amir Sjarifuddin 75 Tahun," 59.

5. Fransz, "Masa Muda," in Fransz, *Pelaku wacana*, 17.

6. Schepper, and some of his colleagues, namely Logemann, had been known and kind of respected as outspoken critics of the *exorbitante rechten* (exorbitant laws). A few years before the Schepper "scandal," "the so called 'Schepper Commission' [was] appointed by the Volksraad to review repressive laws against political propaganda." Klinken, *Minorities*, 120n9. See also Professor Logemann's writing in *De Stuw* 1, nos. 2, 3, 4 (1930) also mentioned by Resink. Resink, "Rechtshoogeschool," 448, 448n45.

7. Schepper, *Vonnis in de P.N.I. Zaak*, 3. For commentary see Locher-Scholten, *Ethiek in Fragmenten*, 141–144.

8. Schepper, *Vonnis in de P.N.I. Zaak*, 4–5.

9. Verkuyl interview, in Klinken, *Minorities*, 122.

10. Schepper, *Vonnis in de P.N.I. Zaak*, 7.

11. Schepper, *Vonnis in de P.N.I. Zaak*, 7–8.

12. Schepper, *Vonnis in de P.N.I. Zaak*, 9.

13. Schepper, *Vonnis in de P.N.I. Zaak*, 10–11.

14. Schepper, *Vonnis in de P.N.I. Zaak*, 12–13.

15. Schepper, *Vonnis in de P.N.I. Zaak*, 19.

16. De Jonge, *Herinneringen*, 138–139.

17. Quoted in De Jonge, *Herinneringen*, 139n176.

18. Jacques Rolland, quoted in Levinas, *On Escape*, 85.

19. Attorney general's letter, November 19, 1930, in Van Asbeck Papers no. 140, emphasis mine.

20. Van Asbeck Papers no. 140.

21. Van Asbeck Papers no. 140.

22. Van Asbeck Papers no. 140.

23. Barthes, *Sade Fourier Loyola*, 181.

24. Van Asbeck Papers no. 140.

25. Van Asbeck Papers no. 140.

26. "Attorney general to government spokesman in *Volksraad*, June 28, 1932," in Kwantes, *De ontwikkeling van de nationalistische beweging*, 3:645–646.

27. Ministerie van Koloniën, *Mail Report*, no. 572geheim/35, 1–3. A whole-page report of Amir's interrogation before a judge, declining to name the *Massa Actie* article's author, is in "De Zaak Sjarifoeddin," *De Java Boide*, December 7, 1933.
28. Kwantes, *De ontwikkeling van de nationalistische beweging*, 4:56–57.
29. Ministerie van Koloniën, *Mail Report*, no. 572geheim/35.
30. Ministerie van Koloniën, *Mail Report*, no. 1935 no. 1479; and Kwantes, *De ontwikkeling van de nationalistische beweging*, 4:XXVI.
31. Ministerie van Koloniën, *Mail Report*, no. 572geheim/35.
32. Leclerc Papers no. 363.
33. Klinken, *Minorities*, 127.
34. Wellem, "Mr. Amir Sjarifuddin," 62.
35. It was announced in *Het Nieuws van den dag voor Nederlandsch-Indië*, December 6, 1933.
36. Leclerc Papers no. 375.

8. Julius Martin Johannes Schepper

1. Walraven, *Een maand in het boevenpak*, 101–102.
2. Walraven, *Een maand in het boevenpak*, 103.
3. Walraven, *Een maand in het boevenpak*, 31.
4. Walraven, *Een maand in het boevenpak*, 30–31.
5. Walraven, *Een maand in het boevenpak*, 30,
6. Walraven, *Een maand in het boevenpak*, 92–93.
7. Ministerie van Koloniën, *Mail Report*, no. 572geheim/35.
8. Ministerie van Koloniën, *Mail Report*, no. 572geheim/35.
9. Bloch, *Spirit of Utopia*, 185.
10. Ministerie van Koloniën, *Mail Report*, no. 572geheim/35.
11. Ministerie van Koloniën, *Mail Report*, no. 572geheim/35.
12. Ministerie van Koloniën, *Mail Report*, no. 572geheim/35, emphasis mine.
13. Ministerie van Koloniën, *Mail Report*, no. 572geheim/35.
14. *Kebangoenan*, November 14, 1941; Klinken, *Minorities*, 127n25.
15. "Government spokesman at the Volksraad to the governor general, June 29, 1935," in Kwantes, *De ontwikkeling van de nationalistische Beweging*, 4:318–319.
16. When Amir's cousin Datoek Moelia in the Netherlands befriended Kraemer, Kraemer was a young man of his age who was just preparing for a mission in the Indies. Kraemer arrived in the Indies in 1922.
17. Van Asbeck Papers no. 238.
18. Van Asbeck Papers no. 238. The Theological Seminar, Hogere Theologische School, was founded in 1934 in Buitenzorg (today Bogor). It was to prepare "new leaders" of the church in the Indies. In 1937 the Seminar moved to Batavia. Wellem, "Mr. Amir Sjarifuddin," 177.
19. *Bataviaasch Nieuwsblad*, October 28, 1935.
20. Fransz, "Masa Muda," in Fransz, *Pelaku wacana*, 16, 18.
21. Tine Fransz to John Garrett in 1950, in Garrett, *Visit to Indonesia. Diary*, 2, 2.
22. Djaenah to Leclerc, Jakarta, 1982, in Leclerc Papers no. 367. Djaenah had told Wellem at the same time that before her marriage she "also helped students, how much

she could, like with ironing their clothes and such, and with sometimes taking care of shopping." Wellem, "Mr. Amir Sjarifuddin," 103.

23. Djaenah to Leclerc.
24. Djaenah to Leclerc.
25. *Bangga Jadi Anak Bung Amir*, n.p.
26. Wellem, "Mr. Amir Sjarifuddin," 104.
27. Adorno, *Minima Moralia*, 23.
28. Leclerc Papers no. 375.
29. Wellem, "Mr. Amir Sjarifuddin," 65.
30. Leclerc Papers no. 367.
31. Safranski, *Goethe*, 149.
32. Wellem, "Mr. Amir Sjarifuddin," 106.
33. Sutan Mohammad Sjah to Jacques Leclerc, January 22, 1980, in Leclerc Papers no. 290.
34. Klinken, *Minorities*, 128.
35. Reitsma, *Van Stockum's Travellers' Handbook*, 184.
36. *Bangga Jadi Anak Bung Amir*, n.p.
37. Winoto Danoeasmoro to Jacques Leclerc, March 18, 1981, in Leclerc Papers no. 245.
38. Tjiam Djoe Khiam to Jacques Leclerc, October 21, 1980, in Leclerc Papers no. 289.
39. Leclerc Papers no. 375.
40. Tjiam Djoe Khiam to Jacques Leclerc.
41. Djaenah to Leclerc.
42. Leclerc Papers no. 375. On Musso's presence in Java during 1935 and 1936 in detail, see Poeze, "PKI Muda 1936–1942."
43. Ministerie van Koloniën, *Mail Report*, no. 146 (1938), quoted in Leclerc, "La clandestinité et son double," 234n43.
44. Poeze, *Tan Malaka*, 470.
45. Siti Larang Sosrokardono, interview by Anthon Lucas, December 9, 1982, in Lucas, *Local Opposition*, 89.
46. Klinken, *Minorities*, 128.
47. Ministerie van Koloniën, *Mail Report*, no. 883gehein/37, 714geheim/37.
48. Adviser for native affairs to governor general, September 17, 1937, in Kwantes, *De Ontwikkeling van de nationalistische beweging*, 4:460.
49. *Pemandangan*, July 25, in Poeze, *Overzicht van de inlandsche*, no. 31 (July 30, 1938), 2.
50. *Pemandangan*, July 25, in Poeze, *Overzicht van de inlandsche*, no. 31 (July 30, 1938), 2.
51. Adviser for native affairs to governor general, October 10, 1938, in Kwantes, *De Ontwikkeling van de nationalistische beweging*, 4:541; Poeze, *Overzicht van de inlandsche*, no. 31 (July 30, 1938), 2, 511.
52. Amir Sjarifoeddin, "Amir Sjarifoeddin," 1.
53. Wilopo was listed as president, Amir as the chair of the permanent committee; Leclerc Papers no. 375.
54. Klinken, *Minorities*, 131.

55. *Pelopor Gerindo*, August 1939.
56. Amir Sjarifoeddin, "Gerindo dan Doenia Internasional," *Pelopor Gerindo*, August 1939.
57. Amir Sjarifoeddin, "Gerindo dan Doenia Internasional."
58. *Mirabele Lectu* 1, no. 2 (February 1928): 1.
59. Amir Sjarifoeddin, "Soal Peranakan Indonesia," *Pelopor Gerindo*, August 17, 1939. In November 1941, Amir Sjarifoeddin warned against regional cultures being overemphasized, "like in the time of Father Colijn," the Netherlands' conservative ex-prime minister, at the expense of the things Indonesian and modern. *Kritiek en Opbouw* 4 (November 22, 1941): 327.
60. *Overzicht van de inlandsche en Maleisch-Chineesche pers* 1939, quoted in Pluvier, *Overzicht van de Ontwikkeling der Nationalistisch Beweging*, 112.
61. Wellem, "Mr. Amir Sjarifuddin," 76. "The Gerindo first principle: nationalism is not to be determined by blood or color of the skin." Giok, *Lima jaman: pewijudan integrasi*, 4.
62. Leo Suryadinata, "Peranakan Chinese Politics in Java," quoted in Goto, *Returning to Asia*, 388n56.
63. Leclerc Papers no. 375.
64. Malik, *Mengabdi Republik*, 1:196.
65. *Pelopor Gerindo*, August 1939.
66. *Pelopor Gerindo*, August 1939.
67. Adviser for native affairs to governor general, August 23, 1939, in Kwantes, *De ontwikkeling van de nationalistische beweging*, 4:663.
68. Translator's note in Derrida, *Specters of Marx*, 224n1.
69. Nancy, *Dis-Enclosure*, 1.
70. Leclerc Papers no. 375.
71. Leclerc, "Amir Sjarifuddin," 31.
72. Leclerc Papers no. 375.
73. Amir Sjarifoeddin, "De Sterke man," *Panorama*, January 23, 1937, in Klinken, *Minorities*, 130.
74. Amir Sjarifoeddin, "Tjatatan," *Poedjangga Baroe* 6 (1938): 66–70, in Klinken, *Minorities*, 130. Also Amir Sjarifoeddin, "Pemandangan Internasional," *Toedjoean Rakjat*, December 1938.
75. Leclerc Papers no. 305.
76. Leclerc Papers no. 305.
77. *Indonesia Berdjoeang* 4, no. 1 (January 7, 1936); Leclerc, "La clandestinité et son double," 234.
78. Leclerc Papers no. 379.
79. Barthes, *Neutral*, 6–7, 51–52, 120.
80. *Poedjangga Baroe* 8, nos. 1–2 (July–August 1940): 9.
81. Thomas, *Spanish War*, 356, 889.
82. *Poedjangga Baroe* 8, nos. 1–2 (July–August 1940): 9–11.
83. *Poedjangga Baroe* 4, no. 7 (January 1937): 85–87.
84. *Poedjangga Baroe* 4, no. 12 (June 1937): 170.
85. Sutan Mohammad Sjah to Jacques Leclerc, January 22, 1980, in Leclerc Papers no. 290.

86. *Poedjangga Baroe* 4, no. 12 (June 1937): 170.
87. *Poedjangga Baroe* 4, no. 12 (June 1937): 170.
88. *Poedjangga Baroe* 3, no. 2 (September 1935): 69–73.
89. *Soeara Oemoem* 1, no. 1 (June 24, 1938), in Leclerc Papers nos. 375, 376. In his church, Amir "might have preached in Batak. But he knew it would not be right. He aimed against a possible isolation of HKBP (*Huria Kristen Batak Protestan*), 'Batak Christian Protestant Church,' from the rest of Indonesia. . . . This is why in HKBP he always preached in Indonesian, even when some Bataks might not be happy and might prefer Batak in the church. Was Amir able to preach in Batak? According to the present author [which is Wellem], Amir was." Wellem, "Mr. Amir Sjarifuddin," 130–131.

9. Charles O. van der Plas

1. Fransz, "Masa Muda," in Fransz, *Pelaku wacana*, 17.
2. Han Resink, interview by Gerry van Klinken, November 23, 1993, in Van Klinken Papers. Schepper's brochure on the Soekarno trial was published by the Vereeniging tot Bevordering van de Maatschappelijkee en Staatkundinge Ontwikkeling van Nederlands Indië, the Stuw group. Resink, "Twee Vergeten 'Stuw' Sympathisanten," 582.
3. Brackman, *Indonesian Communism*, 29.
4. Snow, *Red Star over China*, 363.
5. Musil, *Man without Qualities*, 1764.
6. Brackman, *Indonesian Communism*, 29.
7. Legge, *Sukarno*, 143–144.
8. Legge, *Intellectuals and Nationalism*, 39.
9. Legge, *Intellectuals and Nationalism*, 117.
10. Poeze, *Overzicht van de inlandsche*, no. 49 (1937), 796–797. Also *Kebangoenan*, November 29, 1937.
11. Poeze, *Overzicht van de inlandsche*, no. 49 (1937), 798.
12. Governor van der Plas to the governor general, November 16 and 19, 1938, in Klinken, *Minorities*, 133–134.
13. Leclerc Papers no. 375.
14. Leclerc Papers no. 376.
15. Government spokesman at the Volksraad to the governor general, December 7, 1938, in Kwantes, *De ontwikkeling van de nationalistische beweging*, 4:600. GAPI "comprised eight organizations, including Gerindo, PSII and Parindra," Legge, *Sukarno*, 144.
16. Leclerc Papers no. 375.
17. *Tjaja Timoer* and *Pemandangan*, December 27, 1939, in Poeze, *Overzicht van de inlandsche*, no. 52 (1939), 896–897.
18. *Kebangoenan*, July 26–30, 1939, in Leclerc Papers no. 376.
19. "Sedikit tentang Royment Yamin," *Toedjoean Rakjat*, June 1939.
20. Klinken, *Minorities*, 68, 137.
21. Amir Sjarifoeddin, "Kewadjiban kita pada zaman ini," his emphasis.
22. Amir Sjarifoeddin, "Susunan masjarakat dan perang"; also "Kewadjiban kita pada zaman ini."
23. Amir Sjarifoeddin, "Contact antara rakjat dan pemerintah," his emphasis.
24. Amir Sjarifoeddin, "Milisi rakjat," *Kebangoenan*, July 14, 1941, his emphasis.

25. Amir Sjarifoeddin, "Milisi rakjat," *Kebangoenan*, July 19, 1941.
26. Klinken, *Minorities*, 140.
27. Amir Sjarifoeddin, "Di mana tempat pemoeda kita," *Semangat* Baroe, may 24, 1941.
28. Klinken, *Minorities*, 140.
29. Wellem, "Mr. Amir Sjarifuddin," 134; Verkuyl, *Gedenken en verwachten*, 181; Klinken, *Minorities*, 141.
30. Leclerc, "Between the State and the Revolution," 24.
31. Leclerc, "Between the State and the Revolution," 24.
32. Typescript is also in Leclerc Papers no. 246. Gerry van Klinken comments: "Amir brought out a personal political credo . . . stressing the charismatic, prophetic elements in his Christianity and their connection with the nationalist case. . . . [H]e believed there was such a thing as a Christian political ideology. . . . [He] quoted from what sounded like a Social Gospel book from the U.S.: 'Restore the reign of God, do justice, strive for equality of opportunity for all, use the fruits of the earth as true stewards for the benefit of the whole community—that is repentance as the prophets and Christ preached it and as the first Christian community practiced it.'" "'Without that basis,' Amir concluded in the *Kebangoenan* article (which was clearly identical to the speech), 'I would not join the politics.'" Klinken, *Minorities*, 145 quoting from *Kebangoenan* November 22, 1941.
33. Poeze, *Overzicht van de inlandsche*, quoted in van Klinken, *Minorities*, 142–143, 143n48.
34. Klinken, *Minorities*, 143; Natsir, "Siapa dia pemimpin kita," *Pandji Islam*, no. 45 (November 11, 1941): 841–843, in Leclerc Papers no. 364.
35. Wellem, "Mr. Amir Sjarifuddin," 86. For a biography of Natsir, see Kahin, *Islam, Nationalism and Democracy*.
36. Wellem, "Mr. Amir Sjarifuddin," 86.
37. Verkuyl, *Gedenken en verwachten*, 181.
38. Barthes, *Neutral*, 6–7, 51–52, 120.
39. On *Kritiek en Opbouw*, see Locher-Scholten, *Ethiek in Fragmenten*, 150–177.
40. *Kritiek en Opbouw* 1, no. 4 (April 1, 1938): 61–62.
41. *Kritiek en Opbouw* 2, no. 14 (September 1, 1939).
42. Resink, "Rechtshoogeschool," 436.
43. Du Perron to Soetjipto Mangoenkoesoemo, August 1, 1938, in Resink Papers no. 978.
44. Du Perron to Soejitno, March 18, 1939, in Resink Papers no. 978.
45. Du Perron to Soejitno, March 28, 1939, in Resink Papers no. 978.
46. *Kritiek en Opbouw* 5, no. 1 (January 5, 1942): "Permanent collaborators: Soegondo Djojopoespito, Ir. P.de Gruyet, Hadji Agoes Salm, J. de Kadt, Mr. Soejitno Mangoenkoesoemo, R. Nieuwenhuys, Mr. Amir Sjarifoeddin, D. de Vries, Beb Vuyk, W. Walraven."
47. Augé, *In the Metro*, X.
48. Anderson, *Java*, 38.
49. Poeze, *Tan Malaka*, 470.
50. Siauw, *Siauw Giok Tjhan*, 51.
51. Lucas, *Local Opposition*, 7–8.

52. Leclerc, "Between the State and the Revolution," 33.
53. Poeze, *Tan Malaka*, 494n113.
54. Poeze, *Tan Malaka*, 475–476.
55. Soedjono Djojoprajitno, *PKI*, 75.
56. Derrida, *Specters of Marx*, 12; referring to *Hamlet*, Act 1, Scene 1.
57. Soemarsono, *Revolusi Agustus*, 427.
58. Hersri Setiawan, *Negara Madiun?*, 26.
59. Frederick, *Visions and Heat*, 207.
60. Hersri Setiawan, *Negara Madiun?*, 45.
61. *Reuni USI—IVSV—PPPI, 30 Juli 1989 di Hotel Wisata International*, Jakarta, n.p., 1990.
62. According to the *Buku Nyanyian Nostalgie*, which all the reunion's participants took home, the author of the song's lyrics, was M.K., Mang Kuding aka Sjafroeddin Prawiranegara, later an Indonesian Islamic politician and statesman. In the book the song is described as an "original USI song." USI stands for Unitas Studiosorum Indonesiensis, "Indonesian Students' Union."
63. *Reuni USI—IVSV—PPPI*, n.p.
64. Interview with Soedjatmoko and Andi Zainal Abidin in Legge, *Intellectuals and Nationalism*, 118. Soedarpo's biography mentions Amir Sjarifoeddin's "study club for students which Soedarpo and Soedjatmoko also attended." Rosihan Anwar, *Against the Currents*, 78. Also see Soebadio Sastrosatomo, *Masa Muda Saya*, 114; and Mrázek, *Sjahrir*, 226ff.
65. Kierkegaard, *Concept of Irony*, 91, 179.
66. Soedjatmoko, *Choice and Circumstances*, 3.
67. See "Programma Volksuniversiteit, 1941–1942," in Mrázek, *Sjahrir*, 230n102.
68. Leclerc Papers no. 375.
69. Leclerc, "Between the State and the Revolution," 33: "In connection with bulletin *Menara Merah* being discovered at a bus station near Bandung." Leclerc, "Amir Sjarifoeddin 75 Tahun," 69.
70. Poeze, "PKI Muda," 170.
71. Amir Sjarifoeddin, "Amir Sjarifoeddin," 1–2. The appointment was announced in several Indies papers. The title given was "Commerce adviser of the second class at the Office of Commerce of the Department of Economy." See, for example, *Bataviaasch Nieuwsblad*, June 27, 1941.
72. Sipahoetar, "Partij Kristen Baroe?" *Kebangoenan*, November 7, 1941.
73. Sipahoetar, "Kristen-Nasionalis Amir Sjarifoeddin," *Semangat Baroe*, November 13, 1941. Amir's answer is "Censor 'Kristen' A.M. Sipahoetar," *Semangat Baroe*, November 14, 1941.
74. Resink interview, July 25, 1997, Jakarta.
75. Resink, "Rechtshoogeschool," 444. De Stuw was the organ of the Vereeniging tot Bevordering van de Maatschappelijke en staatkundige Ontwikkeling van Nederlandsch-Indië, "Association to Support the Social and Government Development of the Indies." Among the named leadership of the association was Professor ter Haar of the Law School, H. J. van Mook, Logemann and J. M. J. Schepper. Resink, "Rechtshoogeschool," 433–435.
76. Jonge, *Herinneringen*, 205n385.
77. Leclerc, "Between the State and the Revolution," 15.

78. Leclerc Papers no. 375; Leclerc, "Amir Sjarifuddin 75 Tahun," 70.
79. Leclerc Papers no. 376, quoting "Economisch Weekblad voor Nederlands-Indië."
80. Biographical file, October 14, 1947, in NEFIS, "Netherlands East Indies Forces Intelligence Service," quoted in Klinken, *Minorities*, 137.
81. "Testimony van der Plas," *Parlamentaire Enquete*, 1956, 8c, 1353.
82. Amir Sjarifoeddin, "Contact antara rakjat dan pemerintah."
83. Amir Sjarifoeddin, "Kewadjiban kita pada zaman ini."
84. Sutan Mohamad Sjah to Jacques Leclerc, January 22, 1980 in Leclerc Papers no. 290.
85. "Testimony van der Plas." P. J. A. Idenburg told Benedict Anderson after the war that he "in the two months before the capitulation travelled length and breadth of Java looking for 'strong and independent figures.'" "In an interview with the author in August 1964," wrote Anderson, "Dr. Idenburg related that Charles van der Plas, the governor of East Java had obtained money from the Indies government . . . but being little acquainted with nationalist circles in Djakarta, he entrusted some of the money to Idenburg. It was on Idenburg's initiative that Amir was chosen as organizer of the underground." Anderson, *Java in a Time of Revolution*, 37n6.
86. Resink, "Rechtshoogeschool," 506–129. Elsbeth Locher-Scholten lists Van der Plas among thirteen members of the Stuw in the early 1930s, active in the Stuw Batavia section where Van der Plas worked at the office of the government adviser for native affairs. Among the problems they debated was the legitimacy of the "exorbitant rights." Locher-Scholten, *Ethiek in Fragmenten*, 119, 126, 130.
87. Jacques Leclerc, interview with Han Resink, 1979, in Leclerc Papers no. 249.

10. Ships on the Wall

1. Lucas, *Local Opposition*, 13, 95
2. Dahm, *Sukarno*, 185. "Early in 1938, after Sukarno had suffered a severe bout of malaria, it was decided to remove him to a healthier place of exile . . . through Surabaya [he traveled] to Bengkulu in South Sumatra." Legge, *Sukarno*, 149.
3. Abu Hanifah, *Tales of a Revolution*, 87.
4. The Chanafiah's manuscript "Bung Karno dalam pembuangan Benkulu," quoted in Hering, *Soekarno*, 258.
5. Dahm, *Sukarno*, 27.
6. Hatta, *Indonesian Patriot*, 388.
7. Sjahrir, *Out of Exile*, 134–130.
8. Sjahrir, interview by George Kahin, January 6, 1961, in Kahin Papers, box 53, folder 22.
9. Rose, *Indonesia Free*, 89.
10. Sidik Kertapati, *Sekitar Peristiwa 17 Augustus 1945*, 49.
11. *Asia Raja* December 9 and 12, 2042 (1942), quoted in Hering, *Soekarno*, 298.
12. Sjahrir, *Out of Exile*, 241.
13. Hatta, *Indonesian Patriot*, 409–410.
14. *Orang Indonesia jang terkemoeka di Djawa*, 253, 258, 464.
15. Leclerc, "Between the State and the Revolution," 34. "Immediately after the Japanese arrival . . . Dutch missionaries were captured and interned. Many among them

were shot.... For some time German and Swiss had been allowed to work but then they were forbidden too, ... and they returned to their respective countries.... The domination of missions by the West in Indonesia had ended, ... and also the Western financial and spiritual support.... The missionaries were attacked also from the Muslim side. They were suspected to be attached to the Dutch and be their running dogs. Churches were burned or made into army garrisons and warehouses.... Later, priests of the Christian church of Japan arrived." Wellem, "Mr. Amir Sjarifuddin," 148–150.

16. Efimova, *Dari Moskow ke Madiun*, 43.
17. Van den End to Jacques Leclerc, 1983, in Leclerc Papers no. 309.
18. Van den End to Jacques Leclerc, 1983, 1985, in Leclerc Papers no. 309. Benda, *Crescent and the Rising Sun*, 234, 234n27.
19. Leclerc, "Between the State and the Revolution," 34.
20. Van den End to Jacques Leclerc, 1983, 1985, in Leclerc Papers no. 309.
21. Wellem, "Mr. Amir Sjarifuddin," 113.
22. *Asia Raja*, December 26, 2042 (1942), in Klinken, *Minorities*, 189.
23. Interview with T. B. Simatoepang, who evidently was also present, by Wellem, "Mr. Amir Sjarifuddin," 176. Jakarta students and Jakarta's Christian community participated. Interview with J. L. Ch. Abineno, Wellem, "Mr. Amir Sjarifuddin." Wellem says in his dissertation: "This was the first ecumenical Christmas in Indonesia," 176.
24. Verkuyl, *Gedenken en verwachten*, 158–159.
25. Fransz, "Masa Muda," in Fransz, *Pelaku wacana*, 26–27.
26. Amir Sjarifoeddin, "Amir Sjarifoeddin," 2.
27. Interview with Roeslan Abdoelgani, September 28, 1985, by Legge in *Intellectuals and Nationalism*, 55.
28. Ali Sastroamidjojo, *Milestones on My Journey*, 95.
29. Leclerc, "La clandestinité et son double," 344.
30. Lucas, *Local Opposition*, 176–177.
31. Anderson, *Java*, 38–39.
32. Abu Hanifah, *Tales of a Revolution*, 215.
33. Sjahrir, *Out of Exile*, 241.
34. "Testimony van der Plas," *Parlamentaire Enquete*, 1956, 8c, 1353.
35. Frederick, *Visions and Heat*, 121n101.
36. Milovanov and Chernov, "Amir Sharifudin, Indonezija," 247.
37. Djaenah to Jacques Leclerc, 1982, Leclerc Papers no. 367.
38. Verkuyl quoted in Wellem, "Mr. Amir Sjarifuddin," 108.
39. Djaenah to Jacques Leclerc, 1982, Leclerc Papers no. 367.
40. Sidik Kertapati, *Sekitar Peristiwa 17 Augustus 1945*, 20.
41. Milovanov and Chernov, "Amir Sharifudin, Indonezija," 247.
42. Brackman, *Indonesian Communism*, 35. The story of Amir being "crucified head down" was also told by F. K. N. Harahap to Wellem, in Wellem, "Mr. Amir Sjarifuddin," 170.
43. Amir Sjarifoeddin, "Amir Sjarifoeddin," 2.
44. Legge, *Intellectuals and Nationalism*, 177; Kahin, *Nationalism and Revolution*, 112, 112n10.
45. According to Wellem's dissertation, "Dr. Abdul Rasjid, Amir's relative, reported to Hatta about Amir's situation in prison. Rasjid also told Hatta that Amir was sen-

tenced to death. Hatta was shocked to hear the news and attempted to save the life of his courageous comrade in struggle . . . to commute his sentence to imprisonment for life. . . . At the end of 1943, with Soekarno, he went to the Japanese. . . . They told the Japanese that the people would not support Amir's being hanged. . . . Thus, Amir's life was saved." Wellem, "Mr. Amir Sjarifuddin," 164–165.

46. Verkuyl quoted in Wellem, "Mr. Amir Sjarifuddin," 108.
47. Ali Sastroamidjojo, *Milestones on My Journey*, 96.
48. Simatupang, *Laporan dari Banaran*, 78–80.
49. Lucas, *Local Opposition*, 69.
50. Lucas, *Local Opposition*, 69.
51. NEFIS report of December 1945. Van der Wal, *Officiële Bescheiden*, 2:560–561.
52. Soeryana, "Blitar," 273–278.
53. Soeryana, "Blitar," 278. On Gesang, see Mrázek, *A Certain Age*, 113–114.
54. Soeryana, "Blitar," 278.
55. Soeryana, "Blitar," 273–274.
56. Soeryana, "Blitar," 277.
57. Soeryana, "Blitar," 274–275.
58. Soeryana, "Blitar," 288.
59. Leclerc, "La clandestinité et son double," 226.
60. Interview with Zainal Abidin, November 26, 1980, by Legge in *Intellectuals and Nationalism*, 49.
61. Soedjatmoko, July 28, 1980, in Legge, *Intellectuals and Nationalism*, 118.
62. Chairil Anwar, *Complete Poems*, 30.
63. Coast, *Recruit to Revolution*, 9.
64. Legge, *Intellectuals and Nationalism*, 40.
65. Hamid Algadri, *Mengarungi Indonesia*, 45.
66. Soebadio, Aboe Bakar Loebis, Soedarpo, and Sitoroes, interviews by author, 1983–1990, Jakarta.
67. Anderson, *Java*, 206, 208.
68. Legge, *Intellectuals and Nationalism*, 43.
69. Hersri Setiawan, *Negara Madiun?*, 42.
70. Melbourne, June 16, 1944, Van der Plas Collection no. 69.
71. Melbourne, February 19, 1944, Van der Plas Collection no. 69.
72. "Secret: Anti-Japanese Activities in Java," Hollandia, April, 30, 1945, 38, Archief van de Algemene Secretarie, 2de zending no. 2219.
73. Van der Plas Collection no. 33.
74. Van der Plas Collection no. 91.

11. Sjahrir

1. Marx, *Eighteenth Brumaire*, 18–19.
2. Official English translation by the Indonesian Ministry of Foreign Affairs, October 1948.
3. "Of about 80,000 detainees in Java, the great majority were Dutch. The official record says that there were 6,078 POWs, of whom 1,243 were British, 376 Australians, 330 Indians and 61 Americans." Jones, *Storyteller*, 58.

4. Carlyle, *French Revolution*, 169.

5. Archief van de Procureur-Generaal no. 526. An orange rose, a flower in a royal color, had been worn in the Netherlands during the Nazi occupation on jackets, coats, and blouses, as a symbol of defiance.

6. Carlyle, *French Revolution*, 525.

7. Deutscher, *Prophet Outcast*, 1.

8. Djaenah to Jacques Leclerc, 1982, Leclerc Papers no. 367.

9. "On one day, they brought Amir a mattrass and mosquito net. . . . Food became tasty. . . . He became worried that this was a Japanese theater . . . a sign that a next moment he might be shot." Djaenah to Wellem, in Wellem, "Mr. Amir Sjarifuddin," 168.

10. Djaenah to Jacques Leclerc 1982, *Leclerc Papers* no. 367.

11. Rudjito, "Rakjat Membebaskan Bung Amir," unpublished paper, in Leclerc Papers no. 278.

12. Brackman, *Indonesian Communism*, 45n.

13. Resink, "Rechtshoogeschool," 429, 431.

14. Wertheim and Wertheim-Gijse Weenink, *Vier wendingen*, 30.

15. Miharja, *Pemberontakan Madiun (Amir Syarifuddin)*, 30. Verkuyl comments on Amir's appointment: "Soekarno got 'a Trojan horse' in his cabinet." Verkuyl, *De achtergrond*, 37.

16. Adams, *Sukarno*, 182.

17. Anderson, *Java*, 111; Ali Sastroamidjojo, *Milestones on My Journey*, 105.

18. Djaenah to Leclerc.

19. Rudjito, "Rakjat Membebaskan Bung Amir."

20. Rosihan Anwar, *Against the Currents*, 100–101.

21. Amir Sjarifoeddin, "Amir Sjarifoeddin," 2. Andrea was born in Jakarta on March 25, 1940, and she was married as Mrs. Andrea Simanungkalit. Lydia was born in 1941, Kafas was born in 1943 but he died soon after. Wellem, "Mr. Amir Sjarifuddin," 69.

22. Verkuyl, *Gedenken en verwachten*, 182.

23. Personal communication from Nico Schulte-Nordholt, June 18, 2021.

24. University Library Special Collection, Leiden no. 42081.

25. L. M. Sitoroes, interview by Jacques Leclerc, in Leclerc Papers no. 367.

26. Ali Sastroamidjojo. *Milestones on My Journey*, 106.

27. "The building at Kramat 106," at the time, "was used by the youth as a hiding place." Lupitasari, "Cerita Museum Sumpah Pemuda," n.p.

28. Soemarsono, *Revolusi Agustus*, 15.

29. Soemarsono, *Revolusi Agustus*, 17–18, 294.

30. Malik, *Mengabdi Republik*, 2:65.

31. Soemarsono, *Revolusi Agustus*, 17.

32. Rosihan Anwar, *Against the Currents*, 102.

33. Soebadio Sastrosatomo, *Perjuangan revolusi*, 198.

34. Rose, *Indonesia Free*, 126.

35. Mrázek, *Sjahrir*, 23.

36. In his letter from Banda Neira, March 22, 1939, Sjahrir wrote about Amir that he "never met him personally." Letter graciously provided to author by Kees Snoeck.

37. *Berita Indonesia*, October 7, 1945, in Archief van de Procureur-Generaal no. 45–50, 629. The office of the Ministry of Information was simple; "the furniture, chairs,

desks, and cupboards were brought from the former *Volksraad*." Wellem, "Mr. Amir Sjarifuddin," 215.

38. Legge, *Intellectuals and Nationalism*, 102.
39. Weinstein, *Indonesian Foreign Policy*, 60.
40. Derrida, *Specters of Marx*, 110.
41. Kafka, *In the Penal Colony*, 16. The officer in the penal colony shows the traveler a plan of a torture machine.
42. Trotsky quoted in Deutscher, *Prophet Outcast*, 156.
43. Carlyle, *French Revolution*, 608.
44. Soebadio Sastrosatomo, *Masa Muda Saya*, 65; *Maklumat Politik Pemerintah Republik Indonesia*, November 1, 1945, Kementerian Penerangan, Jogjakarta, in Kahin Papers, box 51, folder 36.
45. Rosihan Anwar, *Against the Currents*, 112. As it turned out, Soekarno was in Bogor. Soebadio Sastrosatomo, *Masa Muda Saya*, 101.
46. Reid, *Indonesian National Revolution*, 74.
47. *Merdeka*, November 16, 1945, quoted in Anderson, *Java*, 198.
48. Anderson, *Java*, 198.
49. Leclerc Papers no. 375.
50. *Berita Indonesia*, November 10, 1945, quoted in Anderson, *Java*, 255.
51. Hardjito, *Risalah gerakan pemuda*, 35, quoted in Anderson, *Java*, 255.
52. Francisca C. Fanggidaej was born in 1925 as a "mix-blood Dutch woman" and into a Christian family. She attended Europese Lagere School in Surabaya and medical school in Batavia. When the school was closed by the Japanese, Francisca returned to Soerabaja where she became involved in the resistance underground. Fanggidaej, *Memoar perempuan revolusioner*, 39, 207.
53. Fanggidaej, *Memoar perempuan revolusioner*, 79–81.
54. Carlyle, *French Revolution*, 601.
55. Carlyle, *French Revolution*, 703.
56. Anderson, *Java*, 255.
57. Frederick, *Visions and Heat*, 276n131.
58. Anderson, *Java*, 255.
59. Anderson, *Java*, 126.
60. Reid, *Indonesian National Revolution*, 52.
61. *Merdeka*, November 2, 1945, quoted in Frederick, *Visions and Heat*, 262.
62. Frederick, *Visions and Heat*, 247.
63. Sulistiya Sutomo, *Bung Tomo, suamiku*, 55–56.
64. Reid, *Indonesian National Revolution*, 52.
65. Anderson, *Java*, 176. See *Merdeka*, October 21, 1945, quoted there.
66. The PNI, Soekarno said in the week after the proclamation of independence, would become "the motor of the people's struggle." Speech, August 23, 1945, *Merdeka*, August 25, 1945, quoted in Legge, *Sukarno*, 211.
67. Soedjatmoko, *Choice and Circumstances*, 11–13.
68. Anderson, *Java*, 201.
69. Anderson, *Java*, 201–202. On Parsi and Paras coming to existence see "dossier Soedarsono" in Archief van de Procureur-Generaal no. 5, 342.
70. Anderson, *Java*, 205.

71. Reid, *Indonesian National Revolution*, 87.
72. Netherlands Indies government to the minister of the overseas territories in Van der Wal, *Officiële Bescheiden*, 3:215.
73. Kahin, *Nationalism and Revolution*, 151.
74. Rose, *Indonesia Free*, 119, 132.
75. Wertheim and Wertheim-Gijse Weenink, *Vier wendingen*, 317.
76. Leclerc, "Amir Sjarifoeddin Between the State and the Revolution," 36.
77. Thompson, *Hubbub in Java*, 36.
78. Leclerc, "Amir Sjarifoeddin Between the State and the Revolution," 36.
79. Anderson, *Java*, 259.
80. The program is in *Antara*, December 27, 1945.
81. Brackman, *Indonesian Communism*, 13.
82. Albert Russell, preface to Machiavelli, "Art of War," in Machiavelli, *Essential Writings*, 291.
83. Leclerc, "Amir Sjarifoeddin Between the State and the Revolution," 22.
84. Deutscher, *Prophet Armed*, 397.
85. Simatupang, *Report from Banaran*, 79–80.
86. Simatupang, *Report from Banaran*, 80, 84.
87. Simatupang, *Report from Banaran*, 29.
88. Simatupang, *Report from Banaran*, 87.
89. Soe Hok Gie, *Orang-orang di persimpangan kiri jalan*, 95.
90. Hariandja, "Pokok-pokok tentang Peristiwa Madiun," in Leclerc Papers no. 286.
91. By November 1946, Laurens van der Post became the military attaché to the British Consulate-General in Batavia. He stayed in the Indies/Indonesia until June 1947. Jones, *Storyteller*, 57–59. According to a later testimony by the Dutch admiral Conrad Helfrich, Van der Post was "a dangerous intrigant." Helfrich called him "Lawrence of Java." "Helfrich testimony," in *Parlamentaire Enquete*, 8c, 1094.
92. "Report by Lt. Col. van der Post on His Tour in Sumatra," April 24, 1946, in Archief van de Algemene Secretarie, 2de zending, no. 3091.
93. Carlyle, *French Revolution*, 463, 609.
94. "Report by Lt. Col. van der Post on His Tour in Sumatra."
95. Leclerc Papers no. 375.
96. Simatupang, *Report from Banaran*, 78.
97. Fanggidaej, *Memoar perempuan revolusioner*, 96.
98. Archief van het Ministerie van Buitenlandse Zaken; NEFIS Centrale Militaire Inlichtingendienst 1942–1949, no. 02756.
99. Hariandja, "Pokok-pokok tentang Peristiva Madiun," in Leclerc Papers no. 286.
100. Fanggidaej, *Memoar perempuan revolusioner*, 96.
101. Fanggidaej, *Memoar perempuan revolusioner*, 96.
102. Fanggidaej, *Memoar perempuan revolusioner*, 97–98.
103. Fanggidaej, *Memoar perempuan revolusioner*, 99.
104. Fanggidaej, *Memoar perempuan revolusioner*, 90–91.
105. Fanggidaej, *Memoar perempuan revolusioner*, 94.
106. Yamin, *Tan Malaka*.
107. Reid, *Indonesian National Revolution*, 87.

108. Soebadio Sastrosatomo told Anderson in 1967 that he was one of the couriers and that he delivered the message orally. Anderson, *Java*, 323n35.

109. Rose, *Indonesia Free*, 133. In March 1946, Sajoeti Malik, Tan Malaka, and Chaerul Saleh were arrested. Archief van de Procureur-Generaal, no. 590.

110. *Rakjat*, March 23, 1946. The article was signed "Am," almost certainly initials of Adam Malik. See also Anderson, *Java*, 328. Still, as late as 1957, in his memoirs, Djamaluddin Tamin, a close ally of Tan Malaka,, called Amir "kaki-kaki tangan van Mook-van der Plas," "lackey of van Mook and van der Plas." Djamaluddin Tamin, *Memoir*, n.p.

111. Leclerc, "Between the State and the Revolution," 33; Klinken, *Minorities*, 148.

112. Soemarsono, *Revolusi Agustus*, 294.

113. Sidik, *Sekitar Peristiwa 17 Augustus 1945*, 18. "Widarta was not arrested and he went on building the PKI," Lucas, *Local Opposition*, 332. Pamoedji died in Soerabaja prison in December 1942 as a result of torture. Lucas, *One Soul One Struggle*, 56, 64n8.

114. Lucas, *Local Opposition*, 331.

115. Lucas, *Local Opposition*, 332.

116. Lucas, *Local Opposition*, 174.

117. Hersri, *Negara Madiun?*, 41.

118. Soemarsono, *Revolusi Agustus*, 296.

119. Lucas, *Peristiwa Tiga Daeerah*.

120. Soe Hok Gie, *Orang-orang di persimpangan kiri jalan*, 142.

121. Reid, *Indonesian National Revolution*, 74.

122. Lucas, *Local Opposition*, 77.

123. Lucas, *Local Opposition*, 79–81; Lucas, *One Soul One Struggle*, 281.

124. Leclerc, "Afterword: The Masked Hero," 346. According to Lucas's informants, at the time on Widarta's side, it was Amir Sjarifoeddin, then still the minister of information in the *Buchō* cabinet, who in mid-October 1945 sent Widarta to the region as his personal envoy. Lucas, *One Soul One Struggle*, 192.

125. Amir Sjarifoeddin quoted in *Soeloeh Merdeka* (Medan), April 10, 1946; Reid, *Indonesian National Revolution*, 75.

126. Victor Hugo quoted in Derrida, *Specters of Marx*, 118–119.

127. Van der Plas Collection no. 164.

128. Thompson, *Hubbub in Java*, 24–25.

129. Thomson, *Hubbub in Java*, 52.

130. Thompson, *Hubbub in Java*, 86–88.

131. Anderson, *Java*, 199.

132. Anderson, *Java*, 208.

133. Interview with Soemitro and Soeripno in Soe Hok Gie, *Orang-orang di persimpangan kiri jalan*, 31.

134. Annie van Ommeren-Avenink of the Dutch Communist Party to Jacques Leclerc, April 2, 1981, in Leclerc Papers no. 291. The illegal papers in the Nazi-occupied Netherlands, *Trouw, De Waarheid, Vrij Nederland, Je Maintiendrai, De Geus*, and *De Bevrijding*, all carried the agreement.

135. Smit, *Het dagboek van Schermerhorn*, October 20, 1946, 1:54n2.

136. Leclerc's interviews with Abdoelmadjid and Tamzil quoted in Lucas, *Local Opposition*, 115n31.

137. Soemitro Djojohadikoesoemo, interview, 1986, by Soe Hok Gie, *Orang-orang di persimpangan kiri jalan*, 30.

138. Go Gien Tjwan, interview by author, October 5, 1986, Amsterdam, in Mrázek, *Sjahrir*, 336.

139. Ali Sastroamidjojo, *Milestones on My Journey*, 215n46.

140. Reid, *Indonesian National Revolution*, 83.

141. See, for example, *Kebangoenan*, November 12 and 17, 1937 on the International Conference on the Far East in Brussels and on the new colonial policy of Nazi Germany.

142. Smit, *Het dagboek van Schermerhorn*, October 18, 1946, 1:47.

143. Benedict Anderson's PhD thesis has the title "The Pemoeda Revolution," 308; the quote is from Soe Hok Gie, *Orang-orang di persimpangan kiri jalan*, 33.

144. Van der Wal, *Officiële Bescheiden*, 3:435–436.

145. Archief van het Ministerie van Buitenlandse Zaken; NEFIS Centrale Militaire Inlichtingendienst, 1942–1949, no. 02756.

146. Wertheim and Wertheim-Gijse Weenink, *Vier wendingen*, 316.

147. Abdoelkadir Widjojoatmodjo, November 16, 1945, in Van der Wal, *Officiële Bescheiden*, 2:92.

148. Van der Wal, *Officiële Bescheiden*, 2:112–113.

149. Smit, *Het dagboek van Schermerhorn*, November 8, 1946, 1:92.

150. Smit, *Het dagboek van Schermerhorn*, November 13, 1946, 1:116.

151. "Impressions of Jogja, very secret," Collection Verboekt no. 8.

152. Van Asbeck Collection no. 89.

153. Letter by Peter van der Veen to Van den End, February 1, 2004; Van den End to author, December 14, 2019; see van der Veen and van der Veen, *The Linguist's Family*, 155–156.

154. Personal communication with Van den End, December 14, 2019. In the middle of 1941 Schepper was about to be appointed the professor of philosophy at the planned faculty of literature at the also planned Indies university. Amir wrote a notice about the appointment, enthusiastically welcoming the news. "Today for our youth it is easy to be confused [*kaboer*]," he wrote, "and many of our leaders are not exactly good examples by their way of life and moral[s]. Philosophy professor can teach his students not merely to think, but he also can help them to build their character, honesty, and sincerity." Amir welcomed Schepper's appointment "with joy." "He could accomplish all the above, even when now he might have been thinking about retirement." "He was one of the leaders of the Stuw," Amir wrote, "and he authored a brochure about the PNI case in which he proved also his courage." Amir Sjarifoeddin, "Guru besar ilmu filsafat pada Sekolah Tinggi Kesusasteraan," *Kebangoenan*, June 12, 1941.

155. Anderson, *Java*, 307.

156. Smit, *Het dagboek van Schermerhorn*, October 22, 1946, 1:59.

157. "Speech of Amir Sjarifoeddin," December 6/7, 1946, in Pematangsiantar, *Taman Merdeka*, "Liberty Square," stenographed and translated by a Dutch informant present, Archief van de Algemene Secretarie, 2de zending, no. 4319, secret.

158. "Speech of Amir Sjarifoeddin," December 6/7, 1946, 6.

159. Simatupang, *Report from Banaran*, 81.

160. Lt.-Governor General van Mook to the minister of the overseas territories, December 11, 1946, and Amir Sjarifoeddin's declaration on arrival to Modjokerto, November 29, in Van der Wal, *Officiële Bescheiden*, 6:539.
161. Soedjatmoko, *Choice and Circumstances*, 9, emphasis in original.
162. Badiou, *I Know*, 51.
163. Soedjatmoko, *Choice and Circumstances*, 3.
164. Reid, *Indonesian National Revolution*, 98.
165. Sjahrir, *Pidato Radio*, 2–7.
166. Sjahrir, *Kebangsaan kita hanja Djembatan*, 4–8.
167. Quoted in Deutscher, *Prophet Armed*, 201.
168. Amir Sjarifoeddin, *Pidato Radio*.
169. Hindley, *Communist Party*, 19.
170. Kahin, *Nationalism and Revolution*, 207–208.
171. Anderson, *Java*, 311.
172. Legge, *Intellectuals and Nationalism*, 119.

12. Musso

1. For the initial membership of Amir Sjarifoeddin's cabinet see Kahin, *Nationalism and Revolution*, 210–211.
2. Soemarso, *Mohammad Roem*, 101.
3. Reid, *Indonesian National Revolution*, 127.
4. Minister of foreign affairs to the chief director of police, September 22, 1947, in Van der Wal, *Officiële Bescheiden*, 11:148.
5. Brackman, *Indonesian Communism*, 60.
6. Reid, *Indonesian National Revolution*, 96.
7. Abu Hanifah, *Tales of a Revolution*, 272.
8. Milovanov and Chernov, "Manovar Musso, Indonezija," 218.
9. Reid, *Indonesian National Revolution*, 99.
10. Milovanov and Chernov, "Amir Sharifudin, Indonezija," 340, 344.
11. Wilopo, "Kesadaran Mengabdi Negara," in Latuihamallo et al., *Kewarganegaraan yang bertanggungjawab*, 327.
12. Minutes of the meeting of the Good Offices Committee, October 29, 1947, in Van der Wal, *Officiële Bescheiden*, 11:439.
13. Kahin, *Nationalism and Revolution*, 229.
14. Ashby, *Frank Peter Graham*, 213.
15. Ali Sastroamidjojo, *Milestones on My Journey*, 147.
16. Ali Sastroamidjojo, *Milestones on My Journey*, 145.
17. Jonge, *De Waaier van het Fortuin*, 597. *Het Parool* reported a disappointment among the Dutch military over the actions being stopped before Jogjakarta was burned, "following the example of Indochina." *Het Parool* quoted in *Kritiek en Opbouw* 5, no. 17 (July 15, 1948): 83.
18. Milovanov and Chernov, "Amir Sharifudin, Indonezija," 244. It is on record that Amir at least once before, during the Renville negotiations spoke in Indonesian, so this might be the Soviet reporter trying to make a dramatic effect.

19. Simatupang, *Report from Banaran*, 32.
20. Ashby, *Frank Peter Graham*, 214.
21. Ashby, *Frank Peter Graham*, 216–217.
22. Prime minister to the deputy prime minister, December 31, 1947, in Van der Wal, *Officiële Bescheiden*, 11:366.
23. Simatupang, *Report from Banaran*, 16.
24. Simatupang, *Report from Banaran*, 32, emphasis mine.
25. Verkuyl, *Gedenken en verwachten*, 182.
26. *Berita Indonesia*, January 10, 1948, in Swift, *Road to Madiun*, 18; also, Van der Wal, *Officiële Bescheiden*, 12:463.
27. Soemarsono, *Revolusi Agustus*, 74.
28. Leclerc, "Amir Sjarifoeddin: Entre l'État et la Revolution," in Leclerc Papers no. 403.
29. Soemarsono, *Revolusi Agustus*, 74, 81. Based on an interview George Kahin had with Soedjatmoko in 1949, there was another reason for Amir losing his nerve. "Amir felt himself responsible for Renville," Soedjatmoko told Kahin. Yet, "Sukarno told Sjarifoeddin that he had received letters from some commanders about their very great shortage of ammunition and did not feel that he could call on ill-armed and already exhausted troops to fight more—because it was felt by all, indeed, by Sjahrir, that non-acceptance of [the Renville] Agreement would precipitate another Dutch assault." Kahin Papers, box 52, folder 5.
30. Siauw Giok Tjhan, *Lima jaman*, 132.
31. Leclerc, "Between the State and the Revolution," 38.
32. Soemarsono, *Revolusi Agustus*, 81.
33. *De Volkskrant*, February 2, 1948.
34. Brackman, *Indonesian Communism*, 68–69.
35. It was "kabinet pisau cukur," *Nasional*, February 1, 1948, in Soe Hok Gie, *Orang-orang di persimpangan kiri jalan*, 164.
36. Abu Hanifah, *Tales of a Revolution*, 274.
37. "The Siliwangi division assigned to Amir Sjarifoeddin the rank of colonel, but he seemed never to use it." Bachroen to Wellem, in Wellem, "Mr. Amir Sjarifuddin," 237.
38. Leimena, *Dutch–Indonesian Conflict*, 11.
39. Quoted in Soe Hok Gie, *Orang-orang di persimpangan kiri jalan*, 154.
40. *Berbagai fakta dan kesaksian sekitar*, 17.
41. Leclerc, "Between the State and the Revolution," 17.
42. Soeharto, *My Thoughts, Words and Deeds*, 39.
43. *Siasat*, June 20, 1948, quoted in Soe Hok Gie, *Orang-orang di persimpangan kiri jalan*, 157.
44. *Merdeka*, October 13, 23, 1948, in Anderson, "Military Aspect," 47.
45. Simatupang, *Report from Banaran*, 54.
46. Lucas, *Local Opposition*, 12–13.
47. *Trompet Masjarakat*, October 5, 1948, in Lucas, *Local Opposition*, 95.
48. Alers, *Om een Rode of Groene Merdeka*, 188.
49. Abu Hanifah, *Tales of a Revolution*, 274.
50. Hariandja, "Pokok-pokok tentang Peristiwa Madiun," in Leclerc Papers no. 286.
51. Anderson, "Military Aspect," 22.

52. Rose, *Indonesia Free*, 149.
53. Anderson, "Military Aspect," 1.
54. Soe Hok Gie, *Orang-orang di persimpangan kiri jalan*, 145. For a survey of the social unrest during August–September 1948, see Reid, "Marxist Attitude to Social Revolution," 53.
55. Rose, *Indonesia Free*, 148.
56. Kahin, *Southeast Asia*, 55–56.
57. Soerjono, "On Musso's Return," 69–70.
58. Brown, "Political Trade Union Formation," 83–98.
59. *Merdeka*, October 7, 1948, quoted in Nasution, *Sekitar Perang Kemerdekaan Indonesia*, 8:340.
60. Brackman, *Indonesian Communism*, 70.
61. Interview with Suryono, November 6, 1992, by Klinken in *Minorities*, 195n38.
62. Amir Sjarifoeddin, interview by Arnold Brackman, February 20, 1948, Jogjakarta, in Brackman, 71.
63. Coast, *Recruit to Revolution*, 61.
64. Sjahrir, "Political Conditions in Indonesia," 14, 21; Mrázek, *Sjahrir*, 370–371.
65. Sent to cultural magazine *Gema*, "Echo." Manuscript is in Resink Papers no. 169.
66. Kahin, *Nationalism and Revolution*, 258.
67. "Politieke toestand in Indonesië," Archief van het Ministerie van Buitenlandse Zaken, Indische Archief Serie V, no. 39.
68. Kahin, *Nationalism and Revolution*, 260.
69. Swift, *Road to Madiun*, 23. Kahin noted that especially point 11 was "very possibly a forgery." Swift, *Road to Madiun*, 24n37, 93.
70. "Politieke toestand in Indonesië."
71. Archief van de Procureur-Generaal, no. 956.
72. Smit, *Het dagboek van Schermerhorn*, June 27, 1947, 2:674–675. Three days later Schermerhorn wrote: "My only hope is that Setiadjit's influence will work." Smit, *Het dagboek van Schermerhorn*, July 1, 1947, 2:704.
73. Smit, *Het dagboek van Schermerhorn*, July 19, 1947, 2:766.
74. Smit, *Het dagboek van Schermerhorn*, July 19, 1947, 2:773.
75. Smit, *Het dagboek van Schermerhorn*, July 19, 1947, 2:775.
76. Smit, *Het dagboek van Schermerhorn*, September 13, 1947, 2:849.
77. Coast, *Recruit to Revolution*, 61.
78. Archief van de Procureur-Generaal, no. 956.
79. Consulate general in Singapore to attorney general, June 18, 1948, in Archief van de Algemene Secretarie, 2de zending, no. 4881.
80. Fanggidaej, *Memoar perempuan revolusioner*, 106–107.
81. Fanggidaej, *Memoar perempuan revolusioner*, 108, 111.
82. Fanggidaej, *Memoar perempuan revolusioner*, 116.
83. NEFIS, very secret, March 10, 1948, in Archief van de Procureur-Generaal, no. 549.
84. Dutch ambassador to Prague to attorney general, May 3, 1948, in Archief van de Procureur-Generaal, no. 549.
85. Consulate general in Singapore to attorney general, June 18, 1948, in Archief van de Algemene Secretarie, 2de zending, no. 4881.

86. Fanggidaej, *Memoar perempuan revolusioner*, 118.
87. Centrale Militaire Inlichtingendienst, 1942–1949, Documentatie Afdeeling 5, very secret, received December 26, 1948, in Archief van Strijdkrachten no. 594.
88. *Berbagai fakta dan kesaksian sekitar*, n.p.
89. AVPRF (State Archives of the Russian Federation), quoted in Efimova, *Dari Moskow ke Madiun*, 21.
90. AVPRF quoted in Efimova, *Dari Moskow ke Madiun*, 23.
91. Efimova, *Dari Moskow ke Madiun*, 24.
92. Dutch ambassador to Prague to the minister of foreign affairs, October 11, 1948, in Archief van de Algemene Secretarie, 2de zending, no. 4881.
93. Bulletin of the Information Bureau of the Communist Party of the Soviet Union no. 18 (42) October 1, 1946, quoted in Efimova, *Dari Moskow ke Madiun*, 40.
94. Quoted in Efimova, *Dari Moskow ke Madiun*, 42–44.
95. Efimova, *Dari Moskow ke Madiun*, 44.
96. Centrale Militaire Inlichtingendienst, 1942–1949, Documentatie Afdeeling 5, very secret, received December 26, 1948, in Archief van Strijdkrachten no. 594.
97. Centrale Militaire Inlichtingendienst, 1942–1949, Documentatie Afdeeling 5, very secret, received December 26, 1948, in Archief van Strijdkrachten, no. 594.
98. Archief van de Algemene Secretarie, 2de zending, no. 4881.
99. Archief van de Algemene Secretarie, 2de zending, no. 4881.
100. Batavia, October 16, 1948, Archief van het Ministerie van Buitenlandse Zaken, NEFIS/Centrale Militaire Inlichtingendienst, 1942–1949, no. 02756, emphasis mine.
101. Quoted in Efimova, *Dari Moskow ke Madiun*, 70.
102. Archief van het Ministerie van Buitenlandse Zaken, NEFIS/Centrale Militaire Inlichtingendienst, no. 030756.
103. Soerjono, "On Musso's Return," 78.
104. Soerjono, "On Musso's Return," 78.
105. Derrida, *Specters of Marx*, 224n1.
106. Nancy, *Dis-Enclosure*, 1.
107. Archief van de Procureur-Generaal, no. 549, emphasis mine.
108. Wellem, "Mr. Amir Sjarifuddin," 185.
109. H. B. Jassin to Jacques Leclerc, March 12, 1982, in Leclerc Papers no. 247: "I do not know why, (I forgot), but when Musso met President Soekarno, I was the single one invited to the palace to see."
110. *Revolusioner*, August 19, 194,8 quoted in Poeze, *Madiun 1948*, 28–29.
111. *Revolusioner*, August 19, 1948, quoted in Poeze, *Madiun 1948*, 28–29.
112. Jassin to Leclerc.
113. Archief van het Ministerie van Buitenlandse Zaken, Centrale Militaire Inlichtingendienst, no. 02756.
114. Kahin, *Nationalism and Revolution*, 272.
115. Reid, *Indonesian National Revolution*, 137.
116. Abdulgani-Knapp, *Fading Dream*, 150.
117. Poeze, *Verguisd en vergeten*, 1088–1089.
118. Quoted in Efimova, *Dari Moskow ke Madiun*, 41.
119. Reed, "Ten Days," 216.
120. *Djalan Baru*, quoted in Swift, *Road to Madiun*, 54–56.

121. Brackman, *Indonesian Communism*, 83. Bung Kecil, one of the Soerabaja underground during the war, and a close ally of Widarta recalled: "We were not sure of our strength, we followed every voice. The party was dependent on whom? On the masses! Yet when the masses rose up unafraid in 1945, the party itself became afraid! We dared to take up arms against the Dutch, yet we hesitated about the Dutch trained officials and police and the colossal apparatus that remained." Bung Kecil, interview by Anton Lucas, July 6, 1978, Jakarta, in Lucas, *One Soul One Struggle*, 191.

122. *Antara News Bulletin*, September 1, 1948; Brackman, *Indonesian Communism*, 83. Amir's statement of August 29, 1948, is in *Kedaulatan Rakjat*, August 30, 1948; see also Kahin, *Nationalism and Revolution*, 272–273.

123. Brackman, *Indonesian Communism*, 83–84.

124. Soemarsono, *Revolusi Agustus*, 301.

125. Van der Plas to lieutenant-governor general, September 10, 1948, in Archief van de Algemene Secretarie, 2de zending, no. 274.

126. US ambassador in the Netherlands to secretary of state, September 3, 1948, *Foreign Relations of the United States, 1948*, 6:1237.

127. Kahin, *Nationalism and Revolution*, 276, quoting from *Suara Ibu Kota*, the official newspaper of the PKI, September 1, 1948.

128. Alers, *Om een Rode of Groene Merdeka*, 185.

129. Kahin, *Nationalism and Revolution*, 272; Swift, *Road to Madiun*, 60.

130. Soerjono, "On Musso's Return," 81.

131. Klinken, *Minorities*, 198.

132. *Merdeka*, September 11, 1948, in Swift, *Road to Madiun*, 52, 52n9.

133. Milovanov and Chernov, "Manovar Musso, Indonezija," 214–216.

134. Bloch, *On Karl Marx*, 18.

135. Bloch, *On Karl Marx*, 118.

136. Bloch, *On Karl Marx*, 22, referring to Marx's "Introduction to Critique of the Hegelian Philosophy of Rights."

137. Augé, *Non-Places*, 114–116.

138. Soerjono, "On Musso's Return," 85.

139. Soemarsono, *Revolusi Agustus*, 98–99.

140. Of course, if Beneš would not accept the right-wing ministers' resignation, a general strike was to be called with a strong possibility of civil war. See Kaplan and Kosatík, *Gottwaldovi muži*, 43. The Gottwald plan as a way to a Communist victory was based on illusions, too, as the next few years would show. No completed Communist revolution happened in Czechoslovakia either.

141. Soerjono, "On Musso's Return," 80.

142. Soemarsono, *Revolusi Agustus*, 278.

143. Poeze, *Verguisd en vergeten*, 1100. "Musso openly declared that his strategy was based on the 'Gottwald Plan.'" Kahin, *Nationalism and Revolution*, 275.

144. Soemarsono, *Revolusi Agustus*, 299.

145. Alimin, in the plenary session of the Working Committee of the KNIP (Central Indonesian National Council), spoke about Trotsky's strategy of Brest-Litovsk "neither war nor peace" (not so different from Amir's approach to Linggadjati, it has been suggested). Musso rejected the Brest-Litovsk idea. Soemarsono, *Revolusi Agustus*, 101.

146. Reid, *Indonesian National Revolution*, 139.

147. *Buruh*, September 4, 1948, in Reid, *Indonesian National Revolution*, 139.
148. Soerjono, "On Musso's Return," 62, 71, 85.
149. *Locomotief*, September 2, 1948, in Poeze, *Verguisd en vergeten*, 1126.
150. Poeze, *Verguisd en vergeten*, 1127.
151. Swift, *Road to Madiun*, 59.
152. Soerjono, "On Musso's Return," 74.
153. Soerjono, "On Musso's Return," 61.
154. Quoted in Efimova, *Dari Moskow ke Madiun*, 19.
155. *Berita Indonesia*, June 2, 1948, in Swift, *Road to Madiun*, 38.
156. Abu Hanifah, *Tales of a Revolution*, 276.
157. Brackman, *Indonesian Communism*, 81.
158. Hariandja, "Pokok-pokok tentang Peristiva Madiun."
159. Koets Collection no. 382.
160. Klinken, *Minorities*, 202.
161. Djamaluddin Tamin, *Sedjarah PKI*, 1–2, 83–86.

162. According to comments not friendly to the Communist movement at the time, "*Menara Merah* was a so-called communist periodical[sic] but in fact issued with government subsidies and under the secret editorship of Amir Sjarifoeddin.... In view of some of its receivers it never could have been illegally printed in Indonesia since it looked far too good for it." Adam Malik, interview, August 22, 1980, Roeslan Abdoelgani, interview, November 12, 1980, and Ismail, interview, November 10, 1980, by Poeze in "PKI Muda," 169n49, also quoting Djamaluddin Tamin, *Sedjarah P.K.I.*, 86.

163. "Adam Malik, Sajoeti Malik and Pandoe Kartowigoena were released in May. In late July... Trimoerti [and others were released, and finally]... all the remaining [were let out on the basis of an] amnesty of August 17, 1948. Tan Malaka and Abikoesno [were] released... on September 16, 1948." Swift, *Road to Madiun*, 49n91.

164. Nasution, *Sekitar Perang Kemerdekaan Indonesia*, 8:169.
165. Brackman, *Indonesian Communism*, 84.
166. Amir's speech is in Archief van het Ministerie van Buitenlandse Zaken, NEFIS-Centrale Militaire Inlichtingendienst, no. 06980.
167. Archief van de Procureur-Generaal, no. 590.
168. Archief van de Procureur-Generaal, no. 590.
169. Abu Hanifah, "Amir Sjarifudin," 98.
170. Ali Sastroamidjojo, *Milestones on My Journey*, 162.
171. Poeze, *Madiun 1948*, 66.
172. Gouda, *Dutch Culture Overseas*, 362n42.
173. *Sin Po*, September 16, 1948, in Poeze, *Madiun 1948*, 68.
174. Lilje, *Valley of the Shadow*, 51.
175. Lilje, *Valley of the Shadow*, 55.
176. Lilje, *Valley of the Shadow*, 32.
177. Lilje, *Valley of the Shadow*, 65.
178. Lilje, *Valley of the Shadow*, 61.
179. Lilje, *Valley of the Shadow*, 118–119.

180. J. M. Panggabean, a family friend of Amir, a Christian Batak, too, recalls that Amir preached from I Corinthians 3... on the spirit of unity. Panggabean to Wellem, in Wellem, "Mr. Amir Sjarifuddin," 130. Amir and his family were in church every Sun-

day, witnesses said, and when a scheduled preacher did not show up, Amir took over. Interviews with Djaenah, Sjarief Bachroen, J. M. Panggabean, S. P. Poerbawijaya, and Harahap, in Wellem, "Mr. Amir Sjarifuddin," 308.

181. Personal communication from Nico Schulte-Nordholt, October 2019, Leiden.

182. Ali Sastroamidjojo. *Milestones on My Journey*, 162.

183. Blauw, "Een Zendingsreis," 196–200. Schepper visited Sumatra in April 1948 "with a view to sound the general feeling in the Batak Church towards receiving some Dutch missionaries and others." Pedersen, *Batak Blood and Protestant Soul*, 183.

184. Blauw, "Een Zendingsreis," 196–200.

185. Harahap, "Amir Sjarifoeddin," *Komunikasi*, no. 38: 25.

186. Blauw, "Een Zendingsreis," 202.

187. Blauw, "Een Zendingsreis," 203.

188. "*Prof. Schepper in Jogja. Reunion with Sjarifoeddin*. . . . In the house of the republic's ex-premier and Christian Amir Sjarifoeddin, a reunion took place with Professor Schepper's former students," *Het Parool*, May 5, 1948, 13.

189. Graaf van Randwijk to Jacques Leclerc, March 11, 1979, in Leclerc Papers no. 248.

190. Verkuyl, *Gedenken en verwachten*, 152.

191. Verkuyl, *Gedenken en verwachten*, 177.

192. Verkuyl to Jacques Leclerc, June 8, 1979, in Leclerc Papers no. 269.

193. "Memo by Mgr. de Jonghe d'Ardoy, the apostolic delegate for Indonesia on catholicism in the Netherlands Indies," sent to Van Mook and others, published in *Osservatore Romano*, June 7, 8, 10, 1948, in Archief van de Algemene Secretarie, 2de zending, no. 4479.

194. Harahap, "Amir Sjarifoeddin," *Komunikasi*, no. 39: 27, 31

195. Harahap, "Amir Sjarifoeddin," *Komunikasi*, no. 39: 28.

196. It is a text of Professor ter Haar's lecture he gave as a prisoner in Buchenwald. Resink, *Gedenkboek*, 123–126.

197. Jacquet, *Aflossing van de wacht*, 300–301.

198. *Kritiek en Opbouw* 5, no. 10 (April 1, 1948).

199. *Pembela Rakjat*, June 2, 1947.

200. Abu Hanifah, *Tales of a Revolution*, 269–270.

201. Carlyle, *French Revolution*, 592.

202. Soerjono, "On Musso's Return," 70–71.

203. Soerjono, "On Musso's Return," 71.

204. Harahap, "Amir Sjarifoddin," *Komunikasi*, no. 39: 30. Amir Sjarifoeddin has it, as if in an afterthought, as the last sentence of his autobiography: "Of my brothers and sisters, only I mixed [*mentjampoeri*] in politics." Amir Sjarifoeddin, "Amir Sjarifoeddin," 2.

205. Government commissar for administrative matters of Malang to the government commissar for administrative matters in East Java, August 11, 1948, in Archief van de Algemene Secretarie, 2de zending, no. 3419.

206. Introduction to Lilje, *Valley of the Shadow*, 7.

207. Djaenah to Jacques Leclerc, 1982, Jakarta, in Leclerc Papers no. 367. Wellem must have it from his family: "After Musso arrived from Moscow and lived in Amir Sjarifoeddin's house, Amir visited church less frequently." Wellem, "Mr. Amir Sjarifuddin," 312.

208. *Bangga Jadi Anak Bung Amir*, n.p.

209. Odysseus to Laertes, in Homer, *Odyssey*, book 24, 369.

210. They made also "frequent trips to Tawangmangu, to Kopang and to Kaliurang," resorts in East Java. In Tawangmangu, Amir taught the children to ride horses and to swim. Wellem, "Mr. Amir Sjarifuddin," 309–310. (Did horse riding remind him of when he was in Holland?)

211. Wellem, "Mr. Amir Sjarifuddin," 202.

212. According to what the daughters told Wellem, Soekarno had also been present at that last Christmas in Amir's house, together with "Amir's friends from Tapanuli, and other youth and guests." Wellem, "Mr. Amir Sjarifuddin," 311.

213. *Bangga Jadi Anak Bung Amir*, n.p.

214. Quoted in Efimova, *Dari Moskow ke Madiun*, 73.

215. "Politieke toestand in Indonesië," Archief van het Ministerie van Buitenlandse Zaken, Indiesche Archief, Serie V, no. 39.

216. Archief van het Ministerie van Buitenlandse Zaken, NEFIS/Centrale Militaire Inlichtingendienst, 1942–1949, no. 07031.

217. Archief van het Ministerie van Buitenlandse Zaken, NEFIS/Centrale Militaire Inlichtingendienst, 1942–1949, no. 02756.

218. Poeze, *Madiun 1948*, 69.

219. Van der Wal, *Officiële Bescheiden* 15:11.

220. Van der Wal, *Officiële Bescheiden*, 15:61.

221. Legge, *Intellectuals and Nationalism*, 119–120.

222. Consul general at Batavia to secretary of state, September 7, 1948, in *Foreign Relations of the United States, 1948*, 6:325.

223. *Foreign Relations of the United States, 1948*, 6:327–328.

224. *Foreign Relations of the United States, 1948*, 6:328.

225. *Merdeka*, September 16 and 18, 1948; *Berita Indonesia*, September 18, 1948; Swift, *Road to Madiun*, 86.

226. Foucault quoted by Žižek in Robespierre, *Virtue and Terror*, XXXIII.

227. Robespierre, *Virtue and Terror*, XXXIII–XXXIV.

228. Žižek, *Violence*, 65.

229. Lilje refers to this "beloved" and "incomparable Pascal's meditation upon the story of Gethsemane." Lilje, *Valley of the Shadow*, 78.

230. Letter to Oskar Pollak in Kafka, *Letters to Friends*, 2.

231. Letter to Max Brod in Kafka, *Letters to Friends*, 287.

13. The Long March

1. Rose, *Indonesia Free*, 149.

2. Alers, *Om een Rode of Groene Merdeka*, 187.

3. Anderson, "Military Aspect," 19–20.

4. Reitsma, *Van Stockum's Travellers' Handbook*, 242–242.

5. Fanggidaej, *Memoar perempuan revolusioner*, 87–88.

6. For a day-to-day description of Madiun during the events, see Anderson, "Military Aspect," 25–26.

7. Archief van de Algemene Secretarie, 2de zending, no. 2731.

8. Harahap, "Amir Sjarifoeddin," *Komunikasi*, no. 39: 31.
9. Kahin, *Nationalism and Revolution*, 286–287.
10. Kahin, *Nationalism and Revolution*, 292.
11. Hersri Setiawan, *Negara Madiun?*, 93. In the Kahin Papers at Cornell there is a transcript and translation of "ANTARA photographer on the Madiun Coup," dated "Jogjakarta, October 8, 1948." "The night of the 17th we spent in Purwodadi. There I saw things which I never saw before during the trip. At the public meeting in Purwodadi (approximately 40,000 people attended) I saw many people carrying red banners and hammer-and-sickle flags and as we were leaving this town, Musso's party was for the first time escorted by a heavily armed truck.—After leaving Ngawi it became increasingly evident that the people were expecting something to happen. Some people were carrying bamboo spears, other sharp weapons, and at the head of the group, the leader was armed with firearms.—We arrived at Redjanggu (near Madiun) at midnight of the 18th and spent the night at Sumarsono's house. . . . I also saw there Wikana, Setyadjit and others I didn't know.—Musso, Sjarifoeddin, Wikana and Setyadjit quietly talked in a room. The other people in the house were most of them armed with pistols and seemed to be very busy. Because I was very tired, I fell asleep at one o'clock and what happened I didn't know.—At 8 o'clock next morning I left Soemarsono's house and went to the office of ANTARA. It was not until I arrived there that I knew a coup had taken place.—During a search by authorities, still in Madiun, all my films were confiscated." Kahin Papers, box 54, folder 26.
12. Alers, *Om een Rode of Groene Merdeka*, 190.
13. Oey Hong Le, *War and Diplomacy in Indonesia*, 190.
14. Nasution, *Sekitar Perang Kemerdekaan Indonesia*, 8:239–240.
15. Simatupang, *Report from Banaran*, 81.
16. The speech transcript and translation is in Kahin Papers, box 53, folder 31. The Sultan of Jogjakarta in an interview with Kahin in 1960 said that he, "Halim and Natsir drafted Soekarno's radio speech, except for the section wherein he said that the populace must choose between him and Musso." Interview with Sultan Hamengkubuwono IX, October 31, 1960, in Kahin Papers, box 52, folder 5. It might be one of the speeches like Frank Graham described to George Kahin, recalling it vividly still fourteen years later: he heard Sukarno speak once, to a crowd of about ten thousand people. "I didn't know a word he said, but I understand that those people would enlist under his leadership in a great revolution to the death, the power of that man, that is a magnetism there, the resonance of his voice, flash of the eye, and meaningful gestures, and carrying power, that is now seldom felt or seen in our time." Frank Graham's interview with George Kahin, 1962, transcript of the tape, 11, Kahin Papers, box 58, folder 1.
17. Leclerc, "Between the State and the Revolution," 18.
18. Kahin, *Nationalism and Revolution*, 287. Amir's family recalled, he "packed for the trip reserve clothes only for one week. He planned to be back and visit his father in Sumatra who was seriously ill. . . . He has asked his younger brother, Sjarief Bachroen, to book a seat for him in a plane to Padang. Sjarief Bachroen contacted . . . Vice-President Hatta and asked for the seat, and Hatta arranged for a ticket to be issued for Amir for September 19. Amir promised to his brother to be home before September 19." Wellem, "Mr. Amir Sjarifuddin," 293.

19. Kahin, *Nationalism and Revolution*, 293–294. The speech as published in *Front Nasional* (Madiun), September 20, 1948, is translated in Kahin Papers, box 54, folder 23.
20. Nasution, *Sekitar Perang Kemerdekaan Indonesia*, 8:249.
21. Pinardi, *Peristiwa Madiun*, quoted in Swift, *Road to Madiun*, 76n130.
22. "Sura XC—The Soil, 10," *Koran*, 35.
23. Swift, *Road to Madiun*, 76.
24. *Aneta News* quoted in Archief van de Algemene Secretarie, 2de zending, no. 4889. According to *Nasional*: "In connection with the present situation the Indonesian Socialist Party expresses its disappointment of the deteriorated political relations between the parties. The party further expected that the measures taken by the Government should only be directed towards the rebels but not towards any political ideology. The party is also of the opinion that if the Madiun affair is exactly that as depicted by the Government then the action is really anti-revolutionary and reactionary and is only carried on by Dutch stooges. The party hopes that the Government organs will oppose the rebels (not the people)." *Nasional*, September 21, 1948, in Kahin Papers, box 54, folder 24.
25. Archief van de Algemene Secretarie, 2de zending, no. 2731.
26. Van der Wal, *Officiële Bescheiden*, 15:136.
27. *Foreign Relations of the United States, 1948*, 6:357.
28. *Times of India*, September 22, 1948.
29. *New York Times*, September 17, 1948.
30. Soemarsono, *Revolusi Agustus*, 139.
31. *Front Nasional*, September 21, 1948, in Kahin, *Nationalism and Revolution*, 298.
32. Soe Hok Gie, *Orang-orang di persimpangan kiri jalan*, 227. Djokosoejono's speech is in Kahin Papers, box 52, folder 27.
33. Kahin, *Nationalism and Revolution*, 298.
34. Soemarsono, *Revolusi Agustus*, 428. On "Jogjakarta Regimental Commander Lt. Col. Soeharto" mission see also Nasution, *Sekitar Perang Kemerdekaan Indonesia*, 8:571–572.
35. Soeharto, *My Thoughts, Words and Deeds*, 44. Another, authorized biography of Soeharto describes the encounter in Madiun between Soeharto and Musso (Amir is not mentioned this time): "While on a trip to East Java, Lieutenant Colonel Soeharto met Muso, the rebellious PKI leader. Muso confided [*sic*] that he had never been against the country's freedom. He had disagreed with continuing negotiations with the Dutch which President Soekarno and Bung Hatta had favored. Soon Muso declared Madiun as a separate state." Abdulgani-Knapp, *Soeharto*, 33.
36. Soemarsono, *Revolusi Agustus*, 151. According to Nasution, "Then Radio Madiun, as a 'feeler' [*proefballon*], broadcast that the former prime minister Amir Sjarifoeddin and Setiadjit would leave for Yogyakartya to negotiate with the Indonesian Republic how to end the uprising in order to unite in the resistance against the Dutch. But Radio Yogyakartya immediately announced that there would be no negotiation with the rebels." Nasution, *Sekitar Perang Kemerdekaan Indonesia*, 8:259. Soeharto in his second memoir describes his arrest by Siliwangi as, the first point, happening before the events in Madiun even erupted, and, as the second point, he explains his arrest as an act of mistaken identity. There had been another Soeharto in the army, Communist Soeharto, and of different rank. Soeharto. *My Thoughts, Words and Deeds*, 44.

37. *Front Nasional*, September 24, 1948, in Kahin, *Nationalism and Revolution*, 298; Kahin, Kahin Papers, box 52, folder 27.
38. Nasution, *Sekitar Perang Kemerdekaan Indonesia*, 8:258.
39. George Kahin to the Overseas News Agency in New Delhi, in Archief van het Ministerie van Buitenlandse Zaken, NEFIS/Centrale Militaire Inlichtingendienst, 1942–1949, no. 6688. Some of the dispatches are in Kahin Papers, box 49, folder 11.
40. Van der Plas, Surabaja, December 6, 1948, very secret, in Archief van de Algemene Secretarie, 2de zending, no. 2733.
41. Telegram, September 29, 1948, secret, in Archief van de Algemene Secretarie, 2de zending, no. 2731.
42. Nasution, *Sekitar Perang Kemerdekaan Indonesia*, 8:292.
43. Among others, Poeze, *Madiun 1948*, 140.
44. Poeze, *Madiun 1948*, 226.
45. Van der Wal, *Officiële Bescheiden*, 15:178.
46. Consul general at Batavia to secretary of state, secret, urgent, September 25, 1948, in *Foreign Relations of the United States, 1948*, 6:1426, 1431–1433.
47. Netherlands ambassador to Japan, October 29, 1948, in Archief van de Algemene Secretarie, 2de zending, no. 4881.
48. Archief van de Algemene Secretarie, 2de zending, no. 4881.
49. *Foreign Relations of the United States, 1948*, 6:1441.
50. Quoted from Oey Hong Lee, *War and Diplomacy in Indonesia*, 195, in Rose, *Indonesia Free*, 165n57.
51. From the Dutch delegation to the Commission of Good Offices, October 19, 1948, confidential, in Archief van de Algemene Secretarie, 2de zending, no. 4881.
52. Beus, *Het laatste jaar*, 27.
53. Engelen et al., *Lahirnya satu bangsa dan negara*, 284.
54. Van der Wal, *Officiële Bescheiden*, 15:597; Stikker Report in Poeze, *Verguisd en vergeten*, 1296.
55. Talks of Hatta with Neher, Sassen, and Stikker, November 27, 1948, in Van der Wal, *Officiële Bescheiden*, 15:700.
56. Reitsma, *Van Stockum's Travellers' Handbook*, 244.
57. Poeze, *Madiun 1948*, 242.
58. Poeze, *Madiun 1948*, 338.
59. Poeze, *Madiun 1948*, 84.
60. A copy of the pamphlet is in University Library Special Collection, Leiden. KITLV Archives no. 663. Also see Poeze, *Madiun 1948*, 990, 1001.
61. Quoted in Nasution, *Sekitar Perang Kemerdekaan Indonesia*, 8:266. *Merdeka*, September 25, 1948. See also *Sin Po*, October 25, 1948: "From our correspondent: Amir Sjarifoeddin apologized for taking *f.*- 25,000 from the Dutch. This apology was considered by Musso as inevitable for Amir to restore the confidence of the masses in him. But the republican minister of information Natsir used the apology as a weapon against Amir, arguing that by taking the money Amir became a tool of the Dutch to subvert the Republic," in Archief van de Algemene Secretarie, 2de zending, no. 4881.
62. Nasution, *Sekitar Perang Kemerdekaan Indonesia*, 8:267.
63. Nasution, *Sekitar Perang Kemerdekaan Indonesia*, 8:344.
64. Poeze, *Madiun 1948*, 225.

65. Hariandja in Leclerc Papers no. 286, 5. Only one big cache seems to have been discovered by Siliwangi during the Madiun affair. Swift, *Road to Madiun*, 78, 78n130.
66. Kahin, *Nationalism and Revolution*, 299–300.
67. Carlyle, *French Revolution*, 475.
68. Fanggidaej, *Memoar perempuan revolusioner*, 139.
69. Snow, *Red Star over China*, 147, 190–192.
70. Snow, *Red Star over China*, 206.
71. Machiavelli, "The Prince," in Machiavelli, *Essential Writings*, 17.
72. Soemarsono, *Revolusi Agustus*, 161.
73. Nasution, *Sekitar Perang Kemerdekaan Indonesia*, 8:575.
74. Reitsma, *Van Stockum's Travellers' Handbook*, 241.
75. Augé, *Non-Places*, 118–119; Agamben, *Homo Sacer*.
76. "The whole era pushes its way up inside her." Grossman, *To the End*, 334.
77. Carlyle, *French Revolution*, 541.
78. Quoted in Deutscher, *The Prophet Outcast*, 163.
79. Deutscher, *Prophet Outcast*, 163.
80. Virilio, *Landscape of Events*, X.
81. Archief van het Ministerie van Buitenlandse Zaken NEFIS, Centrale Militaire Inlichtingendienst, 1942–1949, no. 06980.
82. Anderson and Arief Djati, "World of Sergeant-Major Bungkus," 15–16.
83. "In the Indonesian/Javanese parlance *going to Java* means going to the Javanese language speaking areas, i.e., to Central or East Java. Thus, one can *go to Java* from Jakarta or Bandung, though both are located on Java." Rosihan Anwar. *Against the Currents*, 78n4.
84. Marx and Engels, *Communist Manifesto*, 24.
85. In spite of some Musso's early intimations, the closest they came to "solving the problem," as Soerjono was later to complain, was "to issue declarations." Abdoelmadjid had been rather a lonely voice in arguing for abolition of "feudal privileges," like those of the Jogjakarta sultanate. Soerjono, "On Musso's Return," 65.
86. Quoted in Foucault, "What is Critique?," 67.
87. "Decree no. 5" created a regional administration with the central "Secretariat of Regions," comprising sixteen districts. The "Decree no 5," however, was issued only on September 27, hours before all the administrative structures in Madiun collapsed. "Decree no. 5" and a list of district heads to be responsible to the Madiun central administration can be found in a captured document in Van der Plas Collection no. 176.
88. Soerjono, "On Musso's Return," 65.
89. Deutscher, *Prophet Armed*, 129.
90. Grossman, *To the End*, 149.
91. Soebagio, I.N., *K.H. Masjkur. Sebuah Biograpfi*, 80.
92. Miharja, *Pemberontakan Madiun*, 37.
93. Abu Hanifah, *Tales of a Revolution*, 284.
94. Abu Hanifah, *Tales of a Revolution*, 289. According to *Murba*, September 15, 1948, on September 13, Dr. Muwardi was kidnapped from the hospital in Solo by five Pesindo men. Kahin Papers, box 54, folder 24.
95. Reid, *Indonesian National Revolution*, 146, 146n37, referring to Jay, *Religion and Politics*, 28.

96. Kahin, *Nationalism and Revolution*, 300.
97. Homer, *Odyssey*, 171.
98. Swift, *Road to Madiun*, 130.
99. Machiavelli, "The Prince," in Machiavelli, *Essential Writings*, 36.
100. Musil, *Diaries, 1899–1941*, 231.
101. Benjamin, "Critique of Violence," in *Selected Writings*, 1:252.
102. Nasution, *Sekitar Perang Kemerdekaan Indonesia*, 8:361–362.
103. For Stikker report, see Poeze, *Verguisd en vergeten*, 1296.
104. Poeze, *Madiun 1948*, 264.
105. Poeze, *Verguisd en vergeten*, 1297.
106. Harahap, "Amir Sjarifoeddin," in *Komunikasi*, no. 39:29.
107. Musil, *Man without Qualities*, 1722–17233.
108. Quoted in Nancy, *Sense of the World*, 18.
109. Nancy, *Sense of the World*, 17.
110. Fanggidaej, *Memoar perempuan revolusioner*, 133.
111. Fanggidaej, *Memoar perempuan revolusioner*, 136.
112. Snow, *Red Star over China*, 174.
113. Machiavelli, "Art of War," Book 7, 311, in Machiavelli, *Essential Writings*, 291.
114. Fanggidaej, *Memoar perempuan revolusioner*, 138.
115. Fanggidaej, *Memoar perempuan revolusioner*, 138.
116. Fanggidaej, *Memoar perempuan revolusioner*, 172.
117. Hariandja, "Pokok-pokok tentang Peristiwa Madiun," in Leclerc Papers no. 286.
118. Soemarsono, *Revolusi Agustus*, 393–394.
119. Hariandja, "Pokok-pokok tentang Peristiwa Madiun," in Leclerc Papers no. 286.
120. Soemarsono, *Revolusi Agustus*, 395.
121. "The last person who spoke to me . . . was the head of the Barisan Pemberontakan Rakjat ['Corps of Insurrection'] . . . for the residency of Kediri. . . . His name was Nata . . . both of us were from Blitar. . . . After meeting with Musso . . . he came and told me: '. . . Pak Musso['s] idea is that we should move our units and be active in the enemy occupied zones . . . whoever's bravest in fighting the Dutch he'll be the one to be recognized by the people.'" Soerjono, "On Musso's Return," 86.
122. "Three times small detachments had been sent to find the unit of Pak Musso, but each time they failed." Hariandja, "Pokok-pokok tentang Peristiwa Madiun," in Leclerc Papers no. 286.
123. Archief van het Ministerie van Buitenlandse Zaken NEFIS, Centrale Militaire Inlichtingendienst, 1942–1949, no. 02756.
124. Headquarters of the Military Command Region Ponorogo, Archief van het Ministerie van Buitenlandse Zaken, Indische Archief Serie V, no. 39.
125. Archief van het Ministerie van Buitenlandse Zaken NEFIS, Centrale Militaire Inlichtingendienst, 1942–1949, no. 02756, nos. 0698 and 02756.
126. State Police, Blitar, July 13, 1949, in Archief van Strijdkrachten, no. 2105. There are several photos of the dead Musso in the same Indonesian police file, later captured by the Dutch military and sent to the office of Van der Plas in Soerabaja.
127. Fanggidaej, *Memoar perempuan revolusioner*, 139–140.
128. Hariandja, "Pokok-pokok tentang Peristiwa Madiun," in Leclerc Papers no. 286.
129. Letter to Max Brod, in Kafka, *Letters to Friends*, 201.

130. Derrida, *Specters of Marx*, 81.
131. Heidegger, *Being and Time*, 221.
132. Kant, *Prolegomena*, 145.
133. Nancy, *Dis-Enclosure*, 157.
134. Nancy, *Adoration*, 39.
135. Heidegger quoted in Adorno, *Jargon of Authenticity*, 132.
136. Fanggidaej, *Memoar perempuan revolusioner*, 143–144.
137. Paul Carus, afterword to Kant, *Prolegomena*, 183, 202–204.
138. Snow, *Red Star over China*, 189.
139. Quoted in Robespierre, *Virtue and Terror*, XIV.
140. Snow, *Red Star over China*, 173.
141. Quoted in Snow, *Red Star over China*, 288.
142. Fanggidaej, *Memoar perempuan revolusioner*, 144.
143. Virilio, *Landscape of Events*, XI.
144. Kafka to Felice Bauer, June 26, 1914, in Kafka, *Letters to Felice*, 428–429.
145. Soemarsono, *Revolusi Agustus*, 388.
146. Siliwangi communication, November 29, 1948, in Van der Wal, *Officiële Bescheiden*, 15:760n.
147. Pinardi, *Peristiwa Madiun*, 116; Swift, *Road to Madiun*, 80n147. "They were captured in Purwodadi and I," writes Francisca, "in village Kelambu, also in district Purwodadi." Fanggidaej, *Memoar perempuan revolusioner*, 141.
148. Poeze, *Madiun 1948*, 269n635.
149. Television interview by Kemal Idris, Jakarta, quoted in Soe Hok Gie, *Orang-orang di persimpangan kiri jalan*, 261.
150. Benjamin, "One-Way Street," in *Selected Writings*, 1:484.
151. Leclerc Papers no. 375.
152. Nasution, *Sekitar Perang Kemerdekaan Indonesia*, 8:370–371.
153. Nasution, *Sekitar Perang Kemerdekaan Indonesia*, 8:309.
154. Tjempaka, "Interview dengan Bung Amir," *Hidup*, December 18, 1948, 3, transcript and translation in Kahin Papers, box 53, folder 45, original in Kahin Papers, box 54, folder 24.
155. Fanggidaej, *Memoar perempuan revolusioner*, 145.
156. Francisca Fanggidaej, quoted in Soemarsono, *Revolusi Agustus*, 387.
157. Fanggidaej, *Memoar perempuan revolusioner*, 146.
158. Soe Hok Gie, *Orang-orang di persimpangan kiri jalan*, 262.
159. Interview with ex-captain Soeharto, Jakarta 1967, in Soe Hok Gie, *Orang-orang di persimpangan kiri jalan*, 261–262. See also Dutch Protestant *Trouw*, December 6, 1948, "Sjarifoeddin Consoles Himself with Shakespeare. Sjarifoeddin sat in the train, calmly reading Shakespeare."
160. Quoted in Poeze, *Verguisd en vergeten*, 1300.
161. Interview with ex-captain Soeharto, Jakarta 1967, in Soe Hok Gie, *Orang-orang di persimpangan kiri jalan*, 262. "According to republican soldiers who escorted Amir Sjarifoeddin, Amir maintained his 'dignity.'" *De vrije pers*, December 23, 1948.
162. Brackman, *Indonesian Communism*, 99.
163. Poeze, *Madiun 1948*, 294.
164. Leclerc, "Between the State and the Revolution," 4.

165. Quoted in Poeze, *Verguisd en vergeten*, 1300.
166. Leclerc writes, "they were clandestinely transferred." In Leclerc Papers no. 375.
167. Soe Hok Gie, *Orang-orang di persimpangan kiri jalan*, 263.
168. Ali Sastroamidjojo, *Milestones on My Journey*, 166.
169. Report by the director of the Centrale Militaire Inlichtingendienst, "Central Intelligence Service," December 22, 1948, in Van der Wal, *Officiële Bescheiden*, 16:238.
170. Fanggidaej, *Memoar perempuan revolusioner*, 146.
171. Simatupang, *Report from Banaran*, 76.
172. Leclerc, "La clandestinité," 223.
173. Fanggidaej, *Memoar perempuan revolusioner*, 146.
174. Fanggidaej, *Memoar perempuan revolusioner*, 155.
175. Francisca Fanggidaej, quoted in Soemarsono, *Revolusi Agustus*, 388.
176. Harahap, "Amir Sjarifoeddin," *Komunikasi*, no. 38: 26–27.
177. *Sin Po*, December 3, 1948; Poeze, *Madiun 1948*, 295.
178. Djaenah to Jacques Leclerc, 1982, Jakarta, in Leclerc Papers no. 367.
179. Ali Sastroamidjojo, *Milestones on My Journey*, 166.
180. Harahap, "Amir Sjarifoeddin," *Komunikasi*, no. 39: 28. On the cabinet meeting of December 18, 1948, see Wellem, "Mr. Amir Sjarifuddin," 198.
181. Suharti Harjono to Jacques Leclerc, 1993, in Leclerc Papers no. 498.
182. David Anderson, quoted in Rose, *Indonesia Free*, 165n52.
183. Soerjono, "On Musso's Return," 84.
184. Schweitzer, *Out of My Life*, 38.
185. Musil, *Man without Qualities*, 689.
186. Žižek, *Violence*, 59.
187. Bloch, *Spirit of Utopia*, 227.
188. Homer, *Iliad*, Book 17, 326.
189. Nancy, *Adoration*, 23.
190. Phaedo, quoted in Levinas, *Totality and Infinity*, 49.
191. Levinas, *Totality and Infinity*, 50.
192. Nancy, *Dis-Enclosure*, 128.
193. Prideaux, *I Am Dynamite*, 123.
194. Sjarief Bachrun, in Poeze, *Madiun 1948*, 297n696.
195. Leclerc Paper no. 375.
196. Djaenah to Leclerc.

14. The Victors

1. Kahin, *Southeast Asia*, 96.
2. Report by Captain Gulden, December 22, 1948, in Centrale Militaire Inlichtingendienst, 1942–1949; Van der Wal, *Officiële Bescheiden*, 16:277, emphasis in the original. Texts of undelivered speeches by Soekarno, Hatta, and Natsir on late evening December 19 are in Kahin Papers, box 53, folder 44.
3. Archief van het Ministerie van Buitenlandse Zaken, NEFIS Centrale Militaire Inlichtingendienst, 1942–1949; Van der Wal, *Officiële Bescheiden*, 16:278.
4. Archief van het Ministerie van Buitenlandse Zaken, NEFIS Centrale Militaire Inlichtingendienst, 1942–1949; Van der Wal, *Officiële Bescheiden*, 16:278.

5. Archief van de Algemene Secretarie, 2de zending, no. IX-2-1,2. From Jogjakarta, the leaders were flown to Bangka; Soekarno, Sjahrir, and Hadji Agoes Salim were separated from them on January 5, 1949, and moved to Brastagi.

6. Van der Wal, *Officiële Bescheiden*, 16:279.

7. Leimena, *Dutch–Indonesian Conflict*, 19.

8. Kahin, *Nationalism and Revolution*, 285n52. The whole interview is in Kahin Papers, box 53, folder 44.

9. Simatupang, *Report from Banaran*, 31.

10. Simatupang, *Report from Banaran*, 31.

11. Simatupang, *Report from Banaran*, 35.

12. Simatupang, *Laporan dari Banaran*, 78.

13. Simatupang, *Laporan dari Banaran*, 78.

14. Simatupang, *Report from Banaran*, 81.

15. Leimena, *Dutch–Indonesian Conflict*, 19.

16. Anderson and Arief Djati, "World of Sergeant-Major Bungkus," 17.

17. Simatupang, *Report from Banaran*, 12.

18. Simatupang, *Report from Banaran*, 73. For *Panglima Besar* Sudirman's travels between December 19, 1948, and April 1, 1949, as compared (and compatible) with Amir's travels the few months before, see Simatupang, *Report from Banaran*, 154.

19. Simatupang, *Report from Banaran*, 140.

20. Simatupang, *Report from Banaran*, 83.

21. Simatupang, *Report from Banaran*, 40–41. Since December 12, 1949, a sister of Ali Budiardjo had been Simatupang's wife. Simatupang, *Report from Banaran*, 183.

22. Simatupang, *Report from Banaran*, 72–73.

23. Simatupang, *Report from Banaran*, 53.

24. Simatupang, *Report from Banaran*, 56.

25. Simatupang, *Report from Banaran*, 41.

26. Simatupang, *Report from Banaran*, 153.

27. Simatupang, *Report from Banaran*, 48.

28. Simatupang, *Report from Banaran*, 55.

29. Simatupang, *Report from Banaran*, 68.

30. Simatupang, *Report from Banaran*, 141.

31. Simatupang, *Report from Banaran*, 60.

32. Simatupang, *Report from Banaran*, 84.

33. Simatupang, *Report from Banaran*, 58–59.

34. Simatupang, *Report from Banaran*, 75.

35. Simatupang, *Report from Banaran*, 41.

36. Simatupang, *Report from Banaran*, 144.

37. Simatupang, *Report from Banaran*, 145.

38. Simatupang, *Report from Banaran*, 159–160.

39. Simatupang, *Report from Banaran*, 160.

40. Simatupang, *Report from Banaran*, 173.

41. Simatupang, *Report from Banaran*, 174.

42. Simatupang, *Report from Banaran*, 181.

43. Soerjono, "On Musso's Return," 88.

44. Soe Hok Gie, *Orang-orang di persimpangan kiri jalan*, 262–264, quoting "Soeripno Memoirs" indirectly again, from Djamal Marsudi, *Menjingkap tabir fakta-fakta*. For an extensive summary see Kahin Papers, box 53, folder 44.
45. Brackman, *Indonesian Communism*, 101.
46. Soerjono, "On Musso's Return," 88.
47. Soerjono, "On Musso's Return," 88,
48. Nasution, *Sekitar Perang Kemerdekaan Indonesia*, 8:274.
49. *Pedoman*, December 6, 1948; Swift, *Road to Madiun*, 88–89.
50. Nora, *Realms of Memory*.
51. Leclerc, "La clandestinité," 223.
52. Koolhaas, *Delirious New York*, 88, 101.
53. Virilio, *Lost Dimension*, 72, 163.
54. Heidegger, *Being and Time*, 229–230.
55. Translator's note in Derrida, *Specters of Marx*, 231n7.
56. Derrida, *Specters of Marx*, 120.
57. Kierkegaard, *Diary*, 24.
58. Djamal Marsudi, *Menjingkap tabir fakta-fakta*, 21.
59. Djamal Marsudi, *Menjingkap tabir fakta-fakta*.
60. Dolar, *Voice and Nothing Else*, 99.
61. Žižek, *Violence*, 83.
62. Kierkegaard, *Diary*, 25.
63. Anshary, Wibisono, and Usman, *Bahaja Merah di Indonesia*.
64. Notosoetardjo, *Peristiwa Madiun*.
65. Djamal Marsudi, *Menjingkap tabir fakta-fakta*.
66. Soekarno's speech "Pantja Sila," July 1, 1945, see Legge, *Sukarno*, 184.
67. Anderson, "Military Aspect," 53.
68. Anderson, McVey, and Bunnel, *Preliminary Analysis*.
69. Virilio, *Aesthetics of Disappearance*, 60.
70. Augé, *Non-Places*, 103.
71. Poeze, *Madiun 1948*, 357–360.
72. Poeze, *Madiun 1948*, 360.
73. Nancy, *Dis-Enclosure*, 109.
74. Nancy, *Dis-Enclosure*, 107.
75. Pauker, *Rise and Fall*, 15.
76. Abu Hanifah, *Tales of a Revolution*, 273.
77. Kahin, *Southeast Asia*, 52.
78. Anderson, "Military Aspect," 45.
79. Marx, *Eighteenth Brumaire*, 44.
80. Marx, *Eighteenth Brumaire*, 119.
81. Marx, *Eighteenth Brumaire*, 120.
82. Speech by Soedirman, March 9, 1948, in Van der Wal, *Officiële Bescheiden*, 16:668.
83. Poeze, *Madiun 1948*, 305.
84. Poeze, *Madiun 1948*, 337.
85. Soemarsono, *Revolusi Agustus*, 140.
86. Adams, *Sukarno*, 269–270; Adams, *My Friend the Dictator*, 213.

87. Quoted in Poeze, *Verguisd en vergeten*, 1329–1330.
88. Yasni, *Bung Hatta Menjawab*, 16.
89. Hatta, interview by Soe Hok Gie, September 25, 1967, Jakarta, in Soe Hok Gie, *Orang-orang di persimpangan kiri jalan*, 95n40.
90. Yasni, *Bung Hatta Menjawab*, 22–23.
91. Brackman, *Indonesian Communism*, 84.
92. Kahin, *Southeast Asia*, 51. In October 1948, Hatta gave an interview to George Kahin talking about PKI and Amir: "Sjarifoeddin," was Hatta's first sentence, as Kahin noted it down, "[was] the real leader and planner of the Communist revolt." Hatta went on: "Felt that he could use Musso because of his popularity deriving from his role of revolutionary leader in the past." Hatta, interview by George Kahin, October 9, 1948, in Kahin Papers, box 58, folder 40.
93. Rose, *Indonesia Free*, 151.
94. Kahin, *Southeast Asia*, 51.
95. Bloch, *Traces*, 33.
96. Leclerc, "Afterword: The Masked Hero," 331.
97. Leclerc, "Afterword: The Masked Hero," 327.
98. Reid, *Indonesian National Revolution*, 147.
99. Abu Hanifah, "Amir Sjarifudin," 190.
100. Abu Hanifah, *Tales of a Revolution*, 285–286.
101. Brackman, *Indonesian Communism*, 83.
102. For Sjahrir's statement to the Associated Press (Brackman?) quoted in *Nieuwsgier*, September 2, 1948, on Amir being *opgegaan* "wrapped up in, lost in," see Mrázek, *Sjahrir*, 376. On September 30, 1948, Sjahrir told Kahin about Amir Sjarifoeddin as "unstable political and philosophical and religious mooring." In this communication Sjahrir repeated a story about "a Dutch pastor (Schepper) converting Amir to Christianity when Amir was in Dutch prison." According to Sjahrir, Amir "panicked" when Musso came to Java. He had been "pushed into the self-assumed role of a Communist by the dictates of expediency and general political opportunism." Kahin Papers, box 50, folder 2.
103. *Aneta*, September 24, 1945, in Mrázek, *Sjahrir*, 378.
104. Centrale Militaire Inlichtingendienst, 1942–1949, December 27, 1948 based upon information by "X" in Archief van de Algemene Secretarie, 2de zending, no. XIV-5-81.
105. Sjahrir, quoted in *Aneta*, October 3, 1948, in dossier "Sjahrir" in Archief van de Algemene Secretarie, 2de zending, no. 3-262.
106. Sjahrir, interview by Kahin, November 21, 1948, in Kahin Papers, box 49, folder 23.
107. Personal communication with Tom van den End. See also Suharti Harjono to Jacques Leclerc in Leclerc Papers no. 498. Wellem also told Van Klinken that his book was banned because of the foreword written by Pastor Harahap, where the cabinet session at which Soekarno vetoed the proposal for Amir's execution was described. Klinken to Leclerc, in Leclerc Papers no. 317.
108. Suharti Harjono to Jacques Leclerc, in Leclerc Papers no. 498. Leclerc himself spoke about his text for *Prisma* as a "cautious biographical sketch." Leclerc, "Between the State and the Revolution," 2–3.

109. Quoted in Reid, "Remembering and Forgetting," 171.
110. Goenawan Mohamad, *Sidelines*, 202.
111. Personal communication from Goenawan Mohamad, March 17, 2022.
112. Harahap, "Amir Sjarifoeddin," *Komunikasi*, no. 38, 26–27. "During the exhumation, the Bible was found in the pocket of his shirt." Wellem, "Mr. Amir Sjarifoeddin," xxii.
113. Verkuyl, *Gedenken en verwachten*, 174–175.
114. Van Klinken, interview by Verkuyl, November 26, 1992, in Klinken, *Minorities*, 147n52.
115. Transcript of a television interview with Verkuyl, in Leclerc Papers no. 296.
116. Schepper, *Vrijheid van Godsdienst*, 46, 94.
117. Garrett, *Visit to Indonesia*, 1, 7.
118. Garrett, *Visit to Indonesia*, 1, 8.

15. The Defeated

1. Nancy, *Dis-Enclosure*, 92.
2. Nancy, *Noli Me Tangere*, 18.
3. Nancy, *Noli Me Tangere*, 15.
4. Nancy, *Noli Me Tangere*, 55.
5. Benjamin, "On the Concept of History," in *Selected Writings*, 4:390.
6. Schweitzer, *Quest of the Historical Jesus*, 147.
7. Kahin, *Nationalism and Revolution*, 300, quoting *Antara*, December 7, 1948.
8. Poeze, *Madiun 1948*, 303.
9. Poeze, *Verguisd en vergeten*, 1324–1325.
10. Soerjono, "On Musso's Return," 60.
11. Poeze, *Madiun 1948*, 303.
12. Hariandja, "Pokok-pokok tentang Peristiwa Madiun," in Leclerc Papers no. 286.
13. Soemarsono, *Revolusi Agustus*, 225.
14. Sutan Mohammad Sjah to Jacques Leclerc, January 22, 1980, in Leclerc Papers no. 290, emphasis in the original.
15. Leclerc Papers no. 290.
16. Nancy, *Noli Me Tangere*, 30.
17. Tur, *Wawancara dengan Sumarsono*, 91.
18. Dr. Verkuyl to Jacques Leclerc, April 8, 1979, in Leclerc Papers no. 269.
19. Tur, *Wawancara dengan Sumarsono*, 91.
20. Soemarsono, *Revolusi Agustus*, 429.
21. Soerjono, "On Musso's Return," 84.
22. Fanggidaej, *Memoar perempuan revolusioner*, 152–153.
23. Francisca Fanggidaej in Soemarsono, *Revolusi Agustus*, 388. The series of interviews with Francisca had taken place from 1995 through 2006. Mrs. Fanggidaej was in her late seventies and early eighties. Fanggidaej, *Memoar perempuan revolusioner*, 220n1.
24. Falia Nadia, introduction to Fanggidaej, *Memoar perempuan revolusioner*, 8.
25. Fanggidaej, *Memoar perempuan revolusioner*, 96.
26. Fanggidaej, *Memoar perempuan revolusioner*, 133. Hersri Setiawan, an ex-*tapol* himself, was one of the people interviewing Francisca Fanggidaej. According to W. F.

Wertheim, "The word *inkwartiering* refers to the fact that the Indonesia-ruling military were permanently present in the homes and lives of their victims and let them be spied upon by their neighbors." See Wertheim, "'Eiland van Hoop' (Boeroe)," 131–135.

27. Fanggidaej, *Memoar perempuan revolusioner*, 133.
28. Soemarsono, *Revolusi Agustus*, 389.
29. Swift, *Road to Madiun*, 90.
30. Schweitzer, *Quest of the Historical Jesus*, 147.
31. Virilio, *Lost Dimension*, 44.
32. Virilio, *Aesthetics of Disappearance*, 107.
33. Virilio, *Aesthetics of Disappearance*, 47.
34. Geertz, *Religion of Java*, 375–377. "But an age without passion has no value and everything is transformed into representational idea. . . . Let others complain that the age is wicked; my complaint is that it is paltry; for it lacks passion. Men's thoughts are thin and flimsy. . . . If one say[s] of the revolutionary period that it runs wild, one would have to say of the present age that it runs badly. . . . It is a time of self-combustion of the human race. . . . It is, of course, possible that . . . the present age may ultimately be explained in a higher form of existence." Kierkegaard, *Present Age*, 26, 33, 40, 55.
35. Carlyle, *French Revolution*, 632.
36. Carlyle, *French Revolution*, 249
37. *Lesson*, in Ionesco, *Bald Soprano*, 77.
38. Virilio, *Lost Dimension*, 166.
39. Baudrillard, *Simulacra and Simulation*, 146.
40. Barthes, *Neutral*, 91.
41. Dolar, *Voice and Nothing Else*, 101.
42. Barthes, *Neutral*, 33.
43. Adorno, *Minima Moralia*, 200.
44. Kierkegaard, *Diary*, 153.
45. Aidit, "Kaum kerdja dan Parlementarisme," March 5, 1947, quoted in Soe Hok Gie, *Orang-orang di persimpangan kiri jalan*, 152.
46. Soe Hok Gie, *Orang-orang di persimpangan kiri jalan*, 152.
47. Aidit's speech at the Fifth Congress of PKI, March 1954, quoted in and translated by McVey, "Enchantment of the Revolution," 353.
48. Aidit, "Menggugat Peristiwa Madiun," 369–371.
49. Carlyle, *French Revolution*, 712.
50. Aidit, "Menggugat Peristiwa Madiun," 387–389. Widarta, who had crossed the line, was not mentioned. "Because many of Widarta's judges and executioners later became leaders of the PKI after 1948 and because Musso condemned the execution on his return to Indonesia, the PKI for many years kept silent about the underground and Widarta's role . . . leading people to believe that it never existed." Lucas, *One Soul One Struggle*, 281.
51. Aidit, "Menggugat Peristiwa Madiun," 398–399.
52. Aidit, "Menggugat Peristiwa Madiun," 390.
53. Aidit, "Menggugat Peristiwa Madiun," 391–392.
54. Aidit, "Menggugat Peristiwa Madiun," 399.
55. Partai Komunis Indonesia, *Buku putih tentang peristowa Madiun*, 2.

56. Harahap, "Amir Sjarifoeddin," *Komunikasi*, no. 39: 27.
57. Fanggidaej, *Memoar perempuan revolusioner*, 16.
58. Leclerc, "La clandestinité."
59. Resink Papers no. 106.
60. Interview of August 3, 1992, in Klinken, *Minorities*, 136n38.
61. Pinardi, *Peristiwa Madiun*, 106, quoted in Swift, *Road to Madiun*, 78, 78n130. Also Brackman: "The suspicion was that the Communists had cached their arms for further use." Brackman, *Indonesian Communism*, 99.
62. US consul general in Batavia to secretary of state, December 5, 1948, *Foreign Relations of the United States, 1948*, 6:520–521.
63. Report by Van der Plas, January 27, 1949, in Van der Plas Collection no. 143.
64. "Overzicht van de laatste gegevens omtrent de Ontwikkeling van het Communisme in Oost-Java," signed Van der Plas, in Van der Plas Collection no. 154.
65. *Perdamaian*, October 21, 1949. Van der Plas saved the clippings: "The victory of Hatta in the area around Blitar was a victory of the United Nations and still more of the United States made by Cochran. . . . The government of the Republic of Indonesia through the suppression of the communist action (the Madiun and July 3 Affair) made itself into a servant. . . . The *regisseur* was Uncle Sam. . . . It is a new style of colonialism. . . . It is to be regretted that the energy of the proclamation had been kidnapped and destroyed." Van der Plas to the high representative of the crown in Indonesia, Batavia, October 24, 1949, in Van der Plas Collection no. 154.
66. Van der Plas Collection no. 175A.
67. *Pacifik*, October 2, 1948, in Poeze, *Verguisd en vergeten*, 962.
68. Associated Press in *South China Morning Post*, October 19, 1948.
69. *Sin Po*, August 26, 1948, in Poeze, *Madiun 1948*, 299. "Mr. Amir still at freedom. The military governor of Solo has declared that the red units are being signaled at Sarangan and operate under the leadership of the ex-premier *mr. Amir Sjarifoeddin.*" *Nieuwsgier*, November 9, 1948. On November 11, *Nieuwsgier* wrote: "In the Lawoe complex the strength [of the 'red units'] is 1500 men, 15 light machine guns, 5 heavy machine guns and 30 Sten guns." According to *Volkskrant* a week later, "Sjarifoeddin and Djokosoejono Are Marching on Tjepoe." *De Volkskrant*, November 17, 1948, in Poeze, *Madiun 1948*, 299.
70. *Sin Po*, December 24, 1948, in Poeze, *Madiun 1948*, 298.
71. Archief van het Ministerie van Buitenlandse Zaken, NEFIS Centrale Militaire Inlichtingendienst, 1942–1949, no. 02756.
72. Archief van het Ministerie van Buitenlandse Zaken, NEFIS Centrale Militaire Inlichtingendienst, 1942–1949, no. 02756.
73. Archief van de Algemene Secretarie, 2de zending, no. 4881.
74. Levinas, *Totality and Infinity*, 57.
75. Plato, *Euthyphro. Apology. Crito. Phaedo*, I:405.
76. Archief van het Ministerie van Buitenlandse Zaken, NEFIS Centrale Militaire Inlichtingendienst, 1942–1949, no. 02756.
77. Archief van Strijdkrachten, no. 2105.
78. Archief van het Ministerie van Buitenlandse Zaken, NEFIS Centrale Militaire Inlichtingendienst, 1942–1949, no. 02756.
79. Archief van het Ministerie van Buitenlandse Zaken, NEFIS Centrale Militaire Inlichtingendienst, 1942–1949, no. 02756.

80. *Chicago Daily Tribune*, June 26, 1949.
81. *De Waarheid*, December 18, 1949, in Poeze, *Madiun 1948*, 310.
82. Poeze, *Madiun 1948*, 300.
83. *Merdeka*, January 26, 1950, in Poeze, *Madiun 1948*, 300. Some papers mentioned "a mass grave of 2×5 m." For example, *Nieuwe Courant*, September 9, 1950.
84. Aidit, "Menggugat Peristiwa Madiun," 393.
85. *Merdeka*, September 15, 1950; Poeze, *Madiun 1948*, 300.
86. Djaenah to Jacques Leclerc, 1982, Jakarta, Leclerc Papers no. 367.
87. Harahap, "Amir Sjarifoeddin," *Komunikasi*, no. 38: 22. "Mrs. Amir could not be present at the exhumation. . . . She asked Reverend Harahap and Dr. Tambunan to represent the family and to receive Amir's corpse." Wellem, "Mr. Amir Sjarifuddin," 304.
88. Report on the "reburial" is in *Bintang Merah*, December 15, 1950; also, Soe Hok Gie, *Orang-orang di persimpangan kiri jalan*, 265n17. Photos of the event are in *Berbagai Fakta dan Kesaksian*, 137.
89. It seems it was a wound from a traffic accident Amir had in recent months.
90. Wellem, "Mr. Amir Sjarifuddin," 200. Also "Laporan tentang pemakan kembali tokoh PKI," *Bintang Merah*, December 15, 1950.
91. Wellem, "Mr. Amir Sjarifuddin," 201.
92. Poeze, *Verguisd en vergeten*, 1327.
93. Djaenah to Leclerc. See also "Grave of Sjarifoeddin Destroyed," *Algemeen Handlesblad*, October 19, 1967.
94. *Bangga Jadi Anak Bung Amir*, n.p.
95. Djaenah to Leclerc.
96. *Bangga Jadi Anak Bung Amir*, n.p.
97. *Bangga Jadi Anak Bung Amir*, n.p.
98. *Bangga Jadi Anak Bung Amir*, n.p.
99. *Bangga Jadi Anak Bung Amir*, n.p.
100. *Bangga Jadi Anak Bung Amir*, n.p.
101. Djaenah to Leclerc.
102. Bernhard Dahm to Jacques Leclerc, November 10, 1979, in Leclerc Papers no. 260.

16. The Observers

1. Van Mook, *Stakes of Democracy*, 208.
2. Van Mook, *Stakes of Democracy*, 242–243.
3. Van Mook, *Stakes of Democracy*, 287.
4. *Kritiek en Opbouw* 5, no. 22 (October 1, 1948).
5. *Kritiek en Opbouw* 5, no. 22 (October 1, 1948): 127–128.
6. *Kritiek en Opbouw* 5, no. 10 (April 1, 1948): 194–195.
7. De Kadt, *De Indonesische Tragedie*, 153, 155.
8. Bloch, *On Karl Marx*, 17.
9. Fransz, "Masa Muda," in Fransz, *Pelaku wacana*, 18.
10. Simatupang, interview by author, January 4, 1987, Jakarta, in Mrázek *Sjahrir*, 370n606.
11. See Brackman, *Other Nuremberg*, 1987.

12. Brackman, *Indonesian Communism*, 84.
13. Reid, *Indonesian National Revolution*, 146.
14. Robespierre, *Virtue and Terror*, XXII.
15. Coast, *Recruit to Revolution*, 14.
16. Coast, *Recruit to Revolution*, 3.
17. Coast, *Recruit to Revolution*, 19.
18. Coast, *Recruit to Revolution*, 98.
19. John Coast to Jacques Leclerc, January 24, 1978, in Leclerc Papers no. 294.
20. Coast, *Recruit to Revolution*, 161–163, emphasis mine.
21. Coast, *Recruit to Revolution*, 194–195.
22. George Kahin is there, the only non-Indonesian.
23. Kahin, *Southeast Asia*, 14–15.
24. Kahin, *Southeast Asia*, 23.
25. Kahin, *Southeast Asia*, 2.
26. Van Mook Collection no. 297.
27. Kahin, *Southeast Asia*, 28. "Sjarifoeddin," Koets told Kahin at the meeting that "he feels, Amir is primarily interested in himself and in power to advance his own strong ambition." Kahin Papers, box 52, folder 28.
28. Owen Lattimore to the Dutch authorities in Indonesia, June 1948, in Kahin Papers, box 58, folder 41.
29. Kahin, *Southeast Asia*, 30.
30. Kahin, *Southeast Asia*, 30, 35, 54.
31. Kahin, *Southeast Asia*, 41–42.
32. Kahin, *Southeast Asia*, 78.
33. Abu Hanifah, *Tales of a Revolution*, 289.
34. Kahin, *Southeast Asia*, 63.
35. Kahin, *Nationalism and Revolution*, 274.
36. Kahin, *Southeast Asia*, 21.
37. Kahin, *Southeast Asia*, 49.
38. Kahin, *Southeast Asia*, 49–50. In the initial transcript made in the wake of the interview Kahin notes: "I tried to put it as strongly as I could for the prospect of the resurgence of progressive policy in America, saying I regretted the fact that so many Indonesians viewed the U.S. as a set and crystallized political structure that would stay as it is now under Truman and the Republicans. I told him the prospects were certain [sic] that within eight years and probably within four that progressive forces would be in power in the U.S., a government that would much more actively oppose colonialism than the present. That progressive forces in America were only temporarily out of power and would certainly come back. . . . I don't know whether my 'mission to Sjarifoeddin' will do any good or not, but at least I thought it was worth a try. . . . It was perhaps somewhat premature for me to visit him, particularly without making an appointment in advance and not through the channels of an introduction from someone in the gov't here, but I felt the time was critical." Kahin Papers, box 52, folder 5. In his "Memorandum to Passport Division" of summer 1950, Kahin wrote: "Ali Boediardjo urged me to see Sjarifoeddin. We talked for several hours, but evidently my arguments made little impression on him. . . . I never saw him again," in Kahin Papers, box 52, folder 34.

39. Kahin, *Southeast Asia*, 50–51.

40. Archief van het Ministerie van Buitenlandse Zaken, NEFIS Centrale Militaire Inlichtingendienst, 1942–1949, no. 06819.

41. Kahin, "Problems and Impressions."

42. On the document as Kahin got it, in his hand is written: "Very possibly this is a forgery. G.K." Kahin Papers, box 52, folder 27.

43. Swift, *Road to Madiun*, 89, 89n43.

44. Archief van het Ministerie van Buitenlandse Zaken, NEFIS Centrale Militaire Inlichtingendienst, 1942–1949, no. 6688.

45. Kahin, *Southeast Asia*, 92.

46. "On our house I placed an American flag to show that an American lived here. So it was not a surprise that when the [Dutch] army entered, to George Kahin they behaved politely.... But I was ordered to get out from the house even when the bullets were flying through our street. George Kahin protested ... After a week George managed to get back to Yogyakarta as a journalist.... I was in the Wiragunan prison. What George did for my wife, I will never forget. He was bringing milk and food. Adila was then seven months old." Hamid Algadri, *Mengarungi Indonesia*, 60–61, 74–75.

47. Kahin, *Southeast Asia*, 93, 97. On Kahin's evacuation to Semarang and Batavia, see the US consul general to the State Department, December 27, 1948. There is also a long Kahin statement about it. The document was declassified and is included in Kahin Papers, box 58, folder 47.

48. Kahin left Batavia on March 8, 1949, via Singapore and Hong Kong to San Francisco where he arrived in June 1949. Kahin Papers, box 49, folder 11. On his short visit to the exiled republican leaders see Kahin Papers, box 52, folder 27.

49. Kahin, *Southeast Asia*, 126–127.

50. Kahin, *Southeast Asia*, 59. This became quite a sensation in Indonesia and the Netherlands, too. "Kahin wishes to [return to] Indonesia. Has no passport. Reason is "Kahin held close contacts with a Soviet agent." *Pedoman* was quoted in *Nieuwe Courant*, November 29, 1950. "Kahin is non-communist but a serious student," *Java Bode* reported on November 29, 1950, the news is *"shocking,"* "George Kahin is an assistant of Prof. Owen Lattimore, who is also suspected of being a communist." wrote *Bredasche Courant* on December 15, 1950 under a headline: "Student of Lattimore Holds No Passport."

51. Kahin, *Southeast Asia*, 128.

52. Kahin, *Southeast Asia*, 127. Letters by Frank Graham to James Webb, the undersecretary of state (November 8, 1950), and Ali Sastroamidjojo, the Indonesian ambassador to the United States (August 4, 1950), both in Kahin Papers, box 53, folder 34. There is also, in the same folder, Kahin's letter to Mrs. R. S. Shipley (August 17 [sic], 1950) and Kahin's "Memorandum to Passport Division."

53. Kahin, *Southeast Asia*, 136

54. Kahin, *Southeast Asia*, 137.

55. John K. Fairbank, introduction to Snow, *Red Star over China*, 11–13. See also, "I moved over into Far Eastern History where I found myself the first honors applicant of the young and newly arrived Chinese specialist, Assistant Professor John K. Fairbank," in Kahin, *Southeast Asia*, 3.

56. Snow, *Red Star over China*, 39.

57. Snow, *Red Star over China*, 94.
58. Snow, *Red Star over China*, 90.
59. Kahin, *Nationalism and Revolution*, 273, 274–275.
60. Kahin, *Southeast Asia*, 32, emphasis mine. Most extensively, and intensely, Frank Graham talked about Amir Sjarifoeddin to Kahin in a taped interview in 1962: "Sjariufuddin . . . he was so disillusioned and frustrated that he went over to the Communists. . . . You can never make me believe that he was ever a Communist. From my personal observations with him, when he wasn't on guard or on the record he was a Christian, think of a Christian Prime Minister in an Islamic country! I remember I was invited to attend the baptism of his child in this Protestant Christian church . . . may have been a comment as his way of carrying a revolution . . . he thought I would do my best. . . . Of course, [then, when Graham left Indonesia] I was out of the picture back in Chapel Hill [in academia] and all he knew we had let him down. . . . . . I wish I could have talked to him before he was shot." Kahin made a note to the interview on a piece of paper: "At one point, after the tape-recorder had been turned off, Graham spoke of Sjarifuddin having been betrayed, and went on to say that he, too, felt betrayed by 'people in the State Department.' He gave me the impression of feeling guilty because of the assurances given Sjarifuddin regarding American policy—assurances he gave because he had understood the Department backed his position. He didn't want the taped interview to be made public until at least 10 years." Frank Graham, interview by George Kahin, 1962, in Kahin Papers, box 58, folder 1.
61. Kahin, *Southeast Asia*, 124.
62. Kahin, *Southeast Asia*, 62.
63. In correspondence with Jaques Leclerc, as Kahin was asking for some sources on Amir, Leclerc suggested meeting Tine Fransz, Amir's schoolmate at the Batavia Law School and friend since before the war, still alive at the time. "Anyway," Leclerc wrote to Kahin, "speaking of Amir in Indonesia is very touchy even now, and after so many years of brainwashing, old folks have recorded what they felt not forbidden or dangerous, giving birth to surprising stories and reconstructions." Leclerc to Kahin, December 4, 1992, in Kahin Papers, box 58, folder 53. Through another contact Kahin got Tine Fransz's address (Hirami to Kahin via Barbara Harvey, in the same file).
64. In 1996 Kahin found and saved in his papers in the Madiun file. From *Trouw*, March, 28, 1996, "Horrible Pictures Discovered of Execution of Indonesian Communists in 1948. The Hague photographic historian Louis Zweers found unknown horrible photos of the killings near Madioen (Java) of Indonesian Communists after their uprising in 1948 against Soekarno's rule. Twelve black-and-white pictures show phases of an execution by the Indonesian army (TNI)." Kahin Papers, box 54, folder 26.
65. Anderson, "The Idea of Power in Javanese Culture," 1–69.
66. Augé, *Non-Places*, 44–46.
67. Quoted in Prideaux, *I Am Dynamite*, 185.
68. Perec, *Life*, 479–483.
69. Baudrillard, *Simulacra and Simulation*, 15.
70. Enzensberger, *Tumult*, 4.
71. Enzensberger, *Tumult*, 137, 152.
72. Baudrillard, *Simulacra and Simulation*, 132.
73. Levinas, *Of God*, 33.

74. Thomas, *Spanish War*, 334. The image is from *Punch*, July 20, 1936.
75. Francis Fukuyama, quoted in Derrida, *Specters of Marx*, 71–72.
76. Suvin, "In the Shadow," 364.
77. Musil, *Man without Qualities*, 2, 690.
78. Anderson, *Java*, 206, emphasis mine.
79. Ahmad Syafii Maarif, introduction to Soe Hok Gie, *Orang-orang di persimpangan kiri jalan*, IX.
80. Anderson, *Java*, VI.
81. Soe Hok Gie, *Orang-orang di persimpangan kiri jalan*, 153, emphasis mine.
82. Soe Hok Gie, *Orang-orang di persimpangan kiri jalan*, 65.
83. Soe Hok Gie, *Orang-orang di persimpangan kiri jalan*, 273.
84. Maarif, introduction to Soe Hok Gie, *Orang-orang di persimpangan kiri jalan*, XIV.
85. Maarif, introduction to Soe Hok Gie, *Orang-orang di persimpangan kiri jalan*, XVI.
86. Soe Hok Gie, *Orang-orang di persimpangan kiri jalan*, 213.
87. Carlyle, *French Revolution*, 773.

Conclusion

1. Kafka, *Diaries 1914–23*, 232.
2. Anderson, *Java in a Time of Revolution*, 206.
3. A friend of mine, a Czech historian, was lucky, in the 1970s, to be allowed into the Czechoslovak Communist Party archives in Prague. By chance, looking for other things, he found a receipt for $300 signed by Soeparto (Musso) and cosigned by Bedřich Geminder, the head of the Party Foreign Department (and one of the men later hanged with Rudolf Slánský). Professor Jan Kuklík, personal communication to the author, 1978, Prague.
4. "The trial with Rudolf Slánský and his 'center' began November 20, and lasted for a week. An official brochure from the trial had been published *in eight languages*." Kaplan and Kosatík, *Gottwaldovi muži*, 118, 120, emphasis added.
5. Clementis and Clementisová, *Listy z väzenia*, 54, 69.
6. This was the official formulation, and it had been used throughout and also as the title of the published official transcript.
7. "Draft Program, Fifth Party Congress, Part 2, Section 3," in Brackman, *Indonesian Communism*, 210.
8. Thomas, *Spanish War*, 926–927. To have been in Spain became now dangerous not only "behind the Iron Curtain." After 1945, in the United States, "any connection with [the] Spanish cause came to be regarded as subversive. The Abraham Lincoln Battalion itself was declared so in 1946." Thomas, *Spanish War*, 928.
9. Barthes, *Neutral*, 112–113.
10. Marx, *Eighteenth Brumaire*, 43.
11. Derrida, *Specters of Marx*, 74
12. Kierkegaard, *Concept of Irony*, 183, 197–198.
13. Virilio, *Aesthetics of Disappearance*, 69, 103.

Bibliography

Archival Sources

Algemeen Rijskarchief (Nationaal Archief), The Hague
    Archief van de Algemene Secretarie te Batavia, 1ste and 2de zending
    Archief van de Procureur-Generaal bij het Hooggerechtshof van Nederlandsch-Indië, 1945–1949
    Archief van het Ministerie van Buitenlandse Zaken
    Archieven van Strijdkrachten in Ned. Indië, 1941–1957
    Centrale Militaire Inlichtingendienst, 1942–1949
    Netherlands East Indies Forces Intelligence Service (NEFIS)

Private Papers

De Jonge, B. C., National Archives, The Hague
Gobée, E., National Archives, The Hague
Kahin, G. McT., Cornell University Library, Ithaca, NY
Koets, P. J., National Archives, The Hague
Leclerc, J., University Library Special Collection, Leiden
Resink, G. J., University Library Special Collection, Leiden
Van Asbeck, F. M., National Archives, The Hague
Van der Plas, Ch. O., National Archives, The Hague
Van Klinken, G., Brisbane, Australia
Van Mook, H. J., National Archives, The Hague
Verboekt, K. F. J. National Archives, The Hague

Published Primary Sources

Foreign Relations of the United States, 1948. Vol. VI, *Far East and Australasia*. Washington, DC: U.S. Government Printing Office, 1974.
Kwantes, R. C., ed. *De ontwikkeling van de nationalistische beweging in Nederlands-Indië*. Vol. 3, *1928–Aug 1933*. Groningen: Wolters-Noordhoff, 1981.
Kwantes, R. C., ed. *De ontwikkeling van de nationalistische beweging in Nederlands-Indië*. Vol. 4, *1933–Aug 1942*. Groningen: Wolters-Noordhoff, 1982.
Poeze, Harry A., ed. *Overzicht van de inlandsche en Maleisch-Chineesche pers*. 13 vols. Weltevreden: Volkslectuur, 1928–1940.

Poeze, Harry A., ed. *Politiek-Politioneele Overzichten van Nederlandsch Indië*, Vols. I–IV, *1927–1941*. Leiden: Nijhoff and Brill, 1982–1994.

Van der Wal, S. L., ed. *Het onderwijsbeleid in Nederlands-Indië, 1900–1940*. Groningen: Wolters, 1963.

Van der Wal, S. L., ed. *Officiële Bescheiden betreffende de Nederlands-Indonesische Betrekkiingen, 1945–1950*. The Hague: Martinus Nijhoff, 1971.

Secondary Sources

Abdulgani, H. Ruslan. *Seratus Hari Di Surabaya Yang Menggemparkan Indonesia.* Jakarta: Yayasan Idayu, 1980.

Abdulgani-Knapp, Retnowati. *A Fading Dream: The Story of Roeslan Abdulgani and Indonesia.* Singapore: Times Books International, 2003.

Abdulgani-Knapp, Retnowati. *Soeharto: The Life and Legacy of Indonesia's Second President.* Singapore: Marshall Cavendish, 2007.

Abu Hanifah. "Amir Sjarifuddin: Revolusi Memakan Anak Sendiri." *Prisma* 8 (August 1977): 86–100.

Abu Hanifah. *Menteng 31: Membangun Jembatan Dua Angkatan.* Jakarta: Sinar Harapan, 1997.

Abu Hanifah. *Tales of a Revolution: A Leader of the Indonesian Revolution Looks Back.* Sydney: Angus and Robertson, 1972.

Adams, Cindy. *My Friend the Dictator.* New York: Bobbs Merrill, 1967.

Adams, Cindy. *Sukarno: An Autobiography as Told to Cindy Adams.* New York: Bobbs Merrill, 1965.

Adorno, Theodor W. *The Jargon of Authenticity.* Translated by Knut Tarnowski and Frederic Wils. Evanston, IL: Northwestern University Press, 1973.

Adorno, Theodor W. *Minima Moralia: Reflections from Damaged Life.* Translated by E. F. N. Jephcott. London: Verso, 1999.

Agamben, Giorgio. *The Adventure.* Translated by Lorenzo Chiesa. Cambridge, MA: MIT Press, 2018.

Agamben, Giorgio. *Homo Sacer: Sovereign Power and Bare Life.* Translated by Daniel Heller-Roazen. Stanford, CA: Stanford University Press, 1998.

Aidit, Dipa Nusantara. *Indonesian Society and the Indonesian Revolution.* Djakarta: Jajasan Pembaruan, 1958.

Aidit, Dipa Nusantara. "Konfrontasi Peristiwa Madiun (1948)—Peristiwa Sumatra (1956)." In *Pilihan Tulisan*, vol. 2, 123–142. Djakarta: Jajasan Pembaruan, 1960.

Aidit, Dipa Nusantara. "Menggugat Peristiwa Madiun." In *Pilihan Tulisan*, vol. 1, 367–400. Djakarta: Jajasan Pembaruan, 1959.

Alers, Henri J. H. *Om een Rode of Groene Merdeka: 10 jaren binnenlandse politiek Indonesië, 1943–1953.* Eindhoven: Vulkaan, 1956.

Algadri, see Hamid Algadri.

Ali Sastroamidjojo. *Milestones on My Journey: The Memoirs of Ali Sastroamidjojo, Indonesian Patriot and Political Leader.* Translated by C. L. M. Penders. St. Lucia: University of Queensland Press, 1979.

Ali Sastroamidjojo. *Tonggak-tonggak di perjalanku.* Jakarta: Kinta, 1974.

Alimin. *Riwajat hidup.* Djakarta: [Djanah?], 1959.

Amir Sjarifoeddin, *Amir Sjarifoeddin*. In Archief van de Algemene Secretarie 2de zending, no. 398 (October 1945?).
Amir Sjarifoeddin. "Arti perang bagi kita." *Kebangoenan*, December 17, 20, 1941.
Amir Sjarifoeddin. "Beberapa tjatatan tentang perekonomian di desa-desa." *Kebangoenan*, August 21, 1941.
Amir Sjarifoeddin. "Christelijke Studenten Vereniging." *Uitzicht*, April 23, 1947, 4.
Amir Sjarifoeddin. "Contact antara rakjat dan pemerintah." *Kebangoenan*, August 14, 1941.
Amir Sjarifoeddin. "Dagang ketjil di Filipina." *Kebangoenan*, September 12, 1941.
Amir Sjarifoeddin. "De cassava-ruwhandel in de Preanger." *Economisch Weekblad*, October 11, 1941, 1946–1949.
Amir Sjarifoeddin. "De (georganiseerde) arbeid en de oorlog." *Nationale Commentaren*, November 1, 1941, 3929–3931.
Amir Sjarifoeddin. "De Pan-Aziatische Beweging." *Kritiek en Opbouw* 2, no. 14 (September 1, 1939).
Amir Sjarifoeddin. "De Parijsche Koloniale Tentoonstelling." *Indonesia Raja* 3, no. 7 (October 3, 1931).
Amir Sjarifoeddin, "De sterke man." *Panorama*, January 23, 1937.
Amir Sjarifoeddin. "De toekomst der indonesisch-nationale scholen." *Kritiek en Opbouw* 4, no. 21 (November 22, 1941).
Amir Sjarifoeddin. "De Vlaamsche beweging." *Indonesia Raja* 1, no. 17 (1929).
Amir Sjarifoeddin. "De Wilderscholenordonnantie." *Indonesia Raja* 5, nos. 3–4 (March–April 1933).
Amir Sjarifoeddin. "De Zeven Provinciën: de loyaliteitsdemonstratie de Sana Pers." *Indonesia Raja* 5, nos. 3–4 (March–April 1933).
Amir Sjarifoeddin. "Dimana tempat pemoeda kita?" *Semangat Baroe*, May 24, 1941.
Amir Sjarifoeddin. "Doenia Baroe." *Kebangoenan*, August 16, 1941.
Amir Sjarifoeddin. "Gerindo dan doenia internasional." *Pelopor Gerindo*, August 1939.
Amir Sjarifoeddin. "Goeroe besar ilmoe filsafat pada Sekolah Tinggi Kesoesasteraan." *Kebangoenan*, June 12, 1941.
Amir Sjarifoeddin. "Het milieu in Indië en zijne invloed op de Europeesche jeugd." *Indonesia Raja* 2, no. 10 (December 1930).
Amir Sjarifoeddin. "Het rassenprobleem in Nederlandsch-Indië." *Mirabele Lectu* 1, no. 2 (February 1928). In Leclerc Papers no. 222.
Amir Sjarifoeddin. "Indonesië in de wereld." *Kritiek en Opbouw* 2, no. 10 (July 1, 1939).
Amir Sjarifoeddin. "Kawadjiban kita pada zaman ini." *Kebangoenan*, September 13, 1941.
Amir Sjarifoeddin. "Kerakjatan dan Tweede Kamer." *Banteng* 1, nos. 1–2 (1933).
Amir Sjarifoeddin. "Keterangan tentang memorandum GAPI." *Kebangoenan*, May 19–20, 1941.
Amir Sjarifoeddin, "Kewadjiban kita pada zaman ini." *Semangat Baroe*, September 20, 1941.
Amir Sjarifoeddin. "Menjesoeaikan kata dan faham asing kepada Bahasa Indonesia." *Kebangoenan*, June 22, 23, 27, 1938.
Amir Sjarifoeddin. "Milisi rakjat." *Kebangoenan*, July 14, 19, 26, 1941.

Amir Sjarifoeddin. "Nabetrachting." *Panorama*, January 23, 1937.
Amir Sjarifoeddin. "Nieuwe aspecten in de rijstsituatie van Azië." *Economisch Weekblad*, January 31, 1942, 110–114.
Amir Sjarifoeddin, "Pemandangan Internasional." *Toedjoean Rakjat*, December 1938.
Amir Sjarifoeddin. "Pemandangan loear negeri." *Kebangoenan*, June 11, 18, July 3, 1941.
Amir Sjarifoeddin. "Pengalaman saja dalam tahanan Djepang." *Merdeka*, October 7, 1945.
Amir Sjarifoeddin. "Pergoeroean kebangsaan dan kemadjoean." *Semangat Baroe*, November 1, 1941.
Amir Sjarifoeddin. *Pidato Radio P.J.M. Menteri Pertahanan mr. Amir Sjarifoeddin tg. 7 Djoeni 1946*. Djakarta: Kementerian Penerangan, 1946.
Amir Sjarifoeddin. "Pleidooi dalam perkara Indonesia Moeda." *Kebangoenan*, nos. 4, 5, 6, February 1937.
Amir Sjarifoeddin. "Sedikit keterangan." *Kebangoenan*, November 11, 1941.
Amir Sjarifoeddin. "Sikap kita sebagai rakjat Indonesia." *Semangat Baroe*, February 7, 1942.
Amir Sjarifoeddin. "Soal pergerakan Indonesia." *Pelopor Gerindo*, August 1939.
Amir Sjarifoeddin. "Soesoenan masjarakat dan perang." *Kebangoenan*,(June 14, 26, July 10, 12, 1941.
Amir Sjarifoeddin. *Soesoenan Pemerintah dalam keadaan bahaja. Siaran kilas*. Djakarta: Kementeian Penerangan, 1946.
Amir Sjarifoeddin, "Susunan masjarakat dan perang." *Kebangoenan*, June 14, 26, 1941.
Amir Sjarifoeddin. "Twee werelden." *Kritiek en Opbouw* 1, no. 4 (April 1, 1938): 61–62.
Amir Sjarifoeddin. "Van geld en zaken: De binnenlandsche handel in bevolkingskapok." *Indisch Weekblad*, December 19, 26, 1941.
Anderson, Benedict R.O'G. "The Idea of Power in Javanese Culture." In *Culture and Politics in Indonesia*, edited by Clair Holt, 1–69. Ithaca, NY: Cornell University Press, 1972.
Anderson, Benedict R.O'G. *Java in a Time of Revolution: Occupation and Resistance, 1944–1946*. Ithaca, NY: Cornell University Press, 1972.
Anderson, Benedict R.O'G., and Arief Djati. "The World of Sergeant-Major Bungkus: Two Interviews." *Indonesia*, no. 78 (October 2004): 1–60.
Anderson, Benedict R.O'G., and Ruth T. McVey. *A Preliminary Analysis of the October 1, 1965, Coup in Indonesia*. With the assistance of Frederick P. Bunnel. Ithaca, NY: Modern Indonesia Project, 1971.
Anderson, David Charles. "The Military Aspect of the Madiun Affair." *Indonesia*, no. 21 (April 1976): 1–63.
Anshary, Isha, Jusuf Wibisono, and Sjarif Usman. *Bahaja Merah di Indonesia*. Bandung: Front Anti-Komunis, 1955.
Apriansi, Rut. "Biografi perjuangan Amir Sjarifuddin (1927–1948)." Unpublished BA thesis, Universitas Negeri, Medan, 2015.
Ashby, Warren. *Frank Peter Graham: A Southern Liberal*. Winston-Salem, NC: John F. Blair, 1980.

Augé, Marc. *In the Metro*. Translated and introduced by Tom Conley. Minneapolis: University of Minnesota Press, 2002.

Augé, Marc. *Non-Places: Introduction to an Anthropology of Supermodernity*. Translated by John Howe. London: Verso, 2000.

Axling, William. *Kagawa*. London: Student Christian Movement Press, 1932.

Badiou, Alain. *I Know There Are So Many of You*. Translated by Susan Spitzer. Cambridge: Polity, 2019.

Badiou, Alain and Barbara Cassin. *Heidegger: His Life and His Philosophy*. Translated by Susan Spitzer. New York: Columbia University Press, 2010.

Bangga Jadi Anak Bung Amir. Majalah Tetap. Arsip digital, 2010. https://koleksidiskursus.blogspot.com/2017/06/bangga-jadi-anak-bung-amir.html.

Barthes, Roland. *The Neutral: Lecture Course of the Collège de France (1977–1978)*. Translated by Rosalind E. Krauss and Denis Hellier. New York: Columbia University Press, 2005.

Barthes, Roland. *Sade, Fourier, Loyola*. Berkeley: University of California Press, 1989.

Baudrillard, Jean. *Simulacra and Simulation*. Translated by Sheila Faria Glaser. Ann Arbor: University of Michigan Press, 1994.

Benda, Harry J. *The Crescent and the Rising Sun: Indonesian Islam under the Japanese Occupation, 1942–1945*. The Hague: W. van Hoeve, 1958.

Benjamin, Walter. *Arcades Project*. Translated by Howard Eiland and Kevin McLaughlin. Cambridge, MA: Harvard University Press, 1999.

Benjamin, Walter. *Selected Writings*. Vol. 1, *1913–1926*, multiple translators, edited by Marcus Bullock and Michael W. Jennings. Cambridge, MA: Harvard University Press, 1996.

Benjamin, Walter. *Selected Writings*. Vol. 2, *1927–1934*, multiple translators, edited by Michael W. Jennings, Howard Eiland, and Gary Smith. Cambridge, MA: Harvard University Press, 1999.

Benjamin, Walter. *Selected Writings*. Vol. 4, *1939–1940*, multiple translators, edited by Howard Eiland and Michael W. Jennings. Cambridge, MA: Harvard University Press, 2003.

Berbagai fakta dan kesaksian sekitar "Peristiwa Madiun". Jakarta: Pustaka Pena, 1995.

Berge, Tom van den. *H.J. van Mook 1894–1965: Een vrij en gelukkig Indonesië*. Bussum: Thoth, 2014.

Beus, J. G. de. *Het laatste jaar van Nederlands-Indië, van de zwaardhouw der Tweede Politionele Actie tot de handtekening onder de Souvereiniteitsoverdracht*. Rotterdam: Ad. Donker, 1987.

Bishop, Philip E. "Brecht, Hegel, Lacan: Brecht's Theory of Gest and the Problem of the Subject." *Studies in 20th Century Literature* 10, no. 2 (1986): 267.

Blanchot, Maurice. *The Step Not Beyond*. Translated by Lycette Nelson. Albany, NY: State University of New York Press, 1982.

Blanchot, Maurice. *The Writing of the Disaster*. Translated by Ann Smock. Lincoln: University of Nebraska Press, 1995.

Blauw, J. "Een Zendingsreis." *De Heerbaan: Algemeen Zendingstijdschrift* 1, no. 4 (1948): 195–205.

Bloch, Ernst. *On Karl Marx*. Translated by John Maxwell. London: Verso, 2018.

Bloch, Ernst. *The Spirit of Utopia*. Translated by Anthony A. Nassar. Stanford, CA: Stanford University Press, 2000.
Bloch, Ernst. *Traces*. Translated by Anthony A. Nassar. Stanford, CA: Stanford University Press, 2006.
Blumberger, J. Th. Petrus. *Le communisme aux Indes néerlandaises*. Paris: Aux Editions du Monde Nouveau, 1929.
Bondan, Molly. *Spanning a Revolution: The Story of Mohamad Bondan and the Indonesian Nationalist Movement*. Jakarta: Sinar Harapan, 1992.
Bos, R. "Hoe het groeid." *Tropisch Nederland in Zakformaat VIII. Het onderwijs in Nederlandsch-Indië*. Den Haag: Hofstad, 1941, 14–16, 21–23.
Boynik, Sezgin, ed. *Coiled Verbal Spring: Devices of Lenin's Language*. Translated by Thomas Campbell and Mikko Viljanen. Helsinki: Rab-Rab Press, 2018.
Brackman, Arnold C. *Indonesian Communism: A History*. New York: Praeger, 1963.
Brackman, Arnold C. *The Other Nuremberg: The Untold Story of the Tokyo War Crimes Trials*. New York: William Morrow, 1987.
Brecht, Bertolt. *Poems, 1913–1956*. Edited by John Willett and Ralph Manheim. Multiple translators. New York: Routledge, 1987.
Brown, Colin. "The Political Trade Union Formation in the Java Sugar Industry, 1945–1949." *Modern Asian Studies* 28, no. 1 (February 1994): 77–98.
Bunga rampai setengah abad Perguruan Rakyat: 1928–1978. Jakarta: Perguruan Rakjat, 1978.
Carlyle, Thomas. *The French Revolution: A History*. New York: Modern Library, 2002.
Chairil Anwar. *The Complete Poems*. Translated by Liaw Yock Fang with the assistance of H. B. Jasin. Singapore: University Education Press, 1974.
Clementis, Vladimír and Lída Clementisová. *Listy z väzenia*. Bratislava: Tatran, 1968.
Coast, John. *Recruit to Revolution: Adventure and Politics in Indonesia*. London: Christophers, 1952.
Come to Sumatra: Sumatra Isle of Infinite Variety. Batavia: Official Tourist Bureau, n.d.
Dahm, Bernhard. *Sukarno and the Struggle for Indonesian Independence*. Translated by Mary F. Somers Heidhues. Ithaca, NY: Cornell University Press, 1969.
Dane, Jacques. "Een 5 voor vijft." *Toets*, October 2014, 66–67.
De Jonge, see Jonge.
De sociale en geografische herkomst van de westersch opgeleide Inlanders. Hollandsch-Inlandsch Onderwijs Commissie. Weltevreden: Kolff, 1930.
De uitbreiding van het westersch onderwijs in Nederlandsch-Indië sedert 1900. Hollandsch-Inlandsch Onderwijs Commissie. Buitenzorg: Archipel, 1929.
Deli-Maatschappij: gedenkschrift bij gelegenheid van het vijftigjarig bestaan. Medan: De Maatschappij, 1919.
Derrida, Jacques. *Specters of Marx: The State of the Debt, the Work of Mourning and the New International*. Translated by Peggy Kamuf. New York: Praeger, 1994.
Deutscher, Isaac. *The Prophet Armed: Trotsky 1879–1921*. London: Verso, 2003.
Deutscher, Isaac. *The Prophet Outcast: Trotsky 1929–1940*. London: Verso, 2003.
Deutscher, Isaac. *The Prophet Unarmed: Trotsky 1879–1921*. London: Verso, 2003.
Djamal Marsudi. *Menjingkap tabir fakta-fakta pemberontakan PKI dalam peristiwa Madiun*. Djakarta: Merdeka Press, 1965.

Djamaluddin Tamin. "Sedjarak PKI: Memoir." Unpublished manuscript. Marxists Internet Archive. Catatan Sejarah Regimen 10, Historia.id. Collection of the author.
Djamaluddin Tamin. *Sedjarah P.K.I.* Djakarta: n.p., 1957.
Dokumentasi Pemuda: sekitar proklamasi Indonesia merdeka. Jogjakarta: SPBI, 1948.
Dolar, Mladen. *A Voice and Nothing Else*. Cambridge, MA: MIT Press, 2005.
Donker, L. A., J. Schilthuis, and Th. D. J. M. Koersen, eds. *Parlementaire enquete-commissie regeringsbeleid 1940–1945: Militair beleid 1940–45 Terugkeer naar Nederlandsch-Indië*. 's-Gravenhage: Staatsdrukkerij, 1956.
Dullemen, C. J. van. *Tropical Modernity: Life and Work of C.P. Wolff Schoemaker*. Amsterdam: SUN, 2010.
Efimova, Larissa M. *Dari Moskow ke Madiun: Stalin-PKI dan hubungan diplomatik Uni Soviet-Indonesia, 1947–1953*. Yogyakarta: Syarikat, 2010.
Empatpuluh-lima tahun Sumpah Pemuda. Jakarta: Yayasan Gedung-gedung Bersejarah Jakarta, 1974.
Encyclopedie van Nederlandsch-Indië. Vol 3. The Hague: Nijhof, 1919.
Engelen, O. E., Aboe Bakara Loebis, and Jules F. Pattiasina. *Lahirnya satu bangsa dan negara*. Jakarta: Universitas Indonesia, 1997.
Enzensberger, Hans Magnus. *Tumult*. Translated by Mike Mitchell. London: Seagull, 2016.
Fanggidaej, Francisca C.. *Memoar Perempuan revolusioner*. Edited by Hersri Setiawan. Yogyakarta: Galangpress, 2006.
Foucault, Michel. *The Politics of Truth*. Translated by Lysa Hochroth and Catherine Porter. South Pasadena, CA: Semiotext(e), 2007.
Foucault, Michel. "What Is Critique?" In Foucault, *The Politics of Truth*, 41–81.
Foucault, Michel. "What Is Enlightenment?" In Foucault, *The Politics of Truth*, 97–119.
Foucault, Michel. "For an Ethics of Discomfort." In Foucault, *The Politics of Truth*, 121–127.
Fransz, Augustine Leonore. "Masa Muda dan Pendidikan (1907–1933)." In Fransz, *Pelaku wacana*, 13–32.
Fransz, Augustine Leonore, ed. *Pelaku wacana: peringatan asta dasa warsa*. Jakarta: Badan Penelitan dan Pengembangan Persekutuan Gereja-gereja di Indonesia, 1987.
Frederick, William H. *Visions and Heat: The Making of the Indonesian Revolution*. Athens: Ohio University Press, 1989.
Frijhoff, W. T. M., E. Buronner, und J. Pollmann. *Tempel van hovuurdij: Zes Eeuwen Stedelijk Gymnasium Haarlem*. Haarlem: De Vrieseborch, 1990.
Garrett, John, "Visit to Indonesia: Report Submitted by the Rev. John Garrett." Unpublished manuscript of the report and a diary, 1950. Collection of Gerry Van Klinken.
Geertz, Clifford. *The Religion of Java*. Glencoe: Free Press, 1965.
Gerards, W. J. *Teekenatlas van Nederland: Oost Indië voor de lagere school*. Seventh printing. Heerenveen: A. L. Land, 1914.
Giebels, Lambert J. *Soekarno: Nederlandsch onderdaan; een biografie, 1901–1950*. Amsterdam: Bakker, 1999.

Goenawan Mohamad. *Sidelines: Thought Pieces from TEMPO Magazine*. Translated by Jennifer Lindsay. Jakarta: Lontar, 1994.
Goethe, Johann Wolfgang von. *Italian Journey*. Translated by W. H. Auden and Elizabeth Mayer. London: Penguin, 1970.
Goto, Keinichi. *"Returning to Asia": Japan–Indonesia Relations, 1930s–1942*. Tokyo: Ryukei Shyosha, 1997.
Gouda, Frances. *Dutch Culture Overseas: Colonial Practice in the Netherlands Indies, 1900–1942*. Amsterdam: Amsterdam University Press, 1995.
Grossman, David. *A Horse Walks into a Bar*. Translated by Jessica Cohen. New York: Vintage, 2018.
Grossman, David. *To the End of the Land*. Translated by Jessica Cohen. New York: Vintage, 2010.
Hamid Algadri. *Mengarungi Indonesia: Memoar Perintis Kemerdekaan*. Jakarta: Lentera, 1999.
Hanifah, see Abu Hanifah.
Harahap, F. K. N. "Amir Sjarifoeddin." *Komunikasi. Bulletin Partai Protestan Indonesia*, no. 38 (January 25, 1971): 22–27.
Harahap, F. K. N. "Amir Sjarifoeddin." *Komunikasi. Bulletin Partai Protestan Indonesia*, no. 39 (February 2, 1971): 27–31.
Hardjito, ed. *Risalah gerakan pemuda*. Djakarta: Pustaka Antara, 1952.
Hariandja, "Pokok-pokok tentang Peristiwa Madiun." In Leclerc Papers no 286.
Harjono, Anwar, ed. *Pemikiran dan Perjuangan Mohammad Natsir*. Jakarta: Pustaka Firdaus, 1996.
Hatta, Mohammad. *Indonesian Patriot: Memoirs*. Translated by C. L. M. Penders. Singapore: Gunung Agung, 1981.
Heidegger, Martin. *Being and Time*. Translated by Joan Stambaugh. Albany: SUNY Press, 2010.
Heidegger, Martin. *On the Way to Language*. Translated by Peter D. Hertz. New York: Harper and Row, 1971.
Hering, Bob. *From Soekamiskin to Endeh*. North Queensland: James Cook University, 1979.
Hering, Bob. *Soekarno: Founding Father of Indonesia, 1901–1945*. Leiden: KITLV Press, 2002.
Hersri Setiawan, ed. *Negara Madiun? Kesaksian Soemarsono Pelaku Perjuangan*. Yogyakarta: Indonesia Tera, 2008.
Hilgers, Th. J. A. *Onze vriendjes op reis: leesboek voor de indische scholen*. 's Gravenhage: Blankwaard en Schoonhoven, 1910.
Hindley, Donald. *The Communist Party of Indonesia, 1951–1963*. Berkeley: University of California Press, 1966.
Homer. *The Iliad*. Translated by Peter Green. Oakland: California University Press, 2015.
Homer. *The Odyssey*. Translated by Peter Green. Oakland: California University Press, 2018.
Hoogeveen, M. B. *Handleiding voor het aanvankelijk leesonderwijs*. Groningen: J. B. Wolters, 1917.

Ingleson, John. *Road to Exile: The Indonesian Nationalist Movement, 1927–1934*. Singapore: Heinemann, 1979.
Ionesco, Eugène. *The Bald Soprano and Other Plays*. Translated by Donald M. Allen. New York: Grove, 1958.
Jaarverslag: Deli Spoorwegmaatschappij 1916. Amsterdam: De Bussy, 1917.
Jamin, Muhammad. *Tan Malaka: Bapak Republik Indonesia*. Djakarta: Berita Indonesia, 1946.
Jaquet, Louis G. M. *Aflossing van de wacht. Bestuurlijke en politieke ervaringen in de nadagen van Nederlandsch-Indië*. Rotterdam: Ad Donker, 1978.
Jay, Robert R. *Religion and Politics in Rural Central Java*. New Haven, CT: Yale University Southeast Asian Studies, 1963.
Jones, J. D. F. *Storyteller: The Many Lives of Laurens van der Post*. London: John Murray, 2001.
Jong, J. J. J. P. *De Waaier van het Fortuin: De Nederlanders in Azië en de Indonesische Archipel, 1595–1950*. The Hague: Sdu, 2003.
Jonge, B. C. de. *Herinneringen*. Edited by S. L. van de Wal. Groningen: Wolters-Noordhoff, 1968.
Kadt, J. de. "Amir Sjarifoeddin." *De Baanbreker* 2, no. 7 (February 16, 1946).
Kadt, J. de. *De Indonesische Tragedie: Het treurspel der gemiste kansen*. Amsterdam: G. A. van Oorschot, 1949.
Kafka, Franz. *Diaries 1914–23*. Translated by Max Brod. New York: Schocken, 1965.
Kafka, Franz. *In the Penal Colony*. Translated by Michael Hofmann. London: Penguin, 2007.
Kafka, Franz. *Letters to Felice*. Translated by James Stern and Elisabeth Duckworth. New York: Schocken, 1973.
Kafka, Franz. *Letters to Friends, Family, and Editors*. Translated by Richard and Clara Winston. New York: Schocken, 1977.
Kahin, Audrey. *Islam, Nationalism and Democracy: A Political Biography of Mahammad Natsir*. Singapore: National University of Singapore Press, 2012.
Kahin, George McTurnan. *Nationalism and Revolution in Indonesia*. Ithaca, NY: Cornell University Press, 1952.
Kahin, George McTurnan. *Southeast Asia: A Testament*. London: Routledge, 2003.
Kant, Immanuel. *Prolegomena to Any Future Metaphysics That Can Qualify as a Science*. Translated and with an afterword by Paul Carus. La Salle, IL: Open Court, 1989.
Kaplan, Karel and Pavel Kosatík. *Gottwaldovi muži*. Praha: Paseka, 2004.
Kierkegaard, Søren. *The Concept of Irony: With Continual Reference to Socrates*. Translated by Edward V. Hong and Edna H. Hong. Princeton, NJ: Princeton University Press, 1989.
Kierkegaard, Søren. *The Diary*. Translated by Peter P. Rohde. New York: Carol, 1993.
Kierkegaard, Søren. *The Present Age and on the Difference between Genius and an Apostle*. Translated by Alexander Dru. New York: Harper Torch, 1962.
Klinken, Gerry van. *Minorities, Modernity and the Emerging Nation: Christians in Indonesia, a Biographical Approach*. Leiden: KITLV Press, 2003.
Koolhaas, Rem. *Delirious New York: A Retroactive Manifesto for Manhattan*. New York: The Monacelli Press, 1997.

Koran. Translated by J. M. Rodwell. London: Dent, 1953.
Kraemer, Hendrik. "Batak Report." In *From Mission Field to Independent Church: Report on a Decisive Decade in the Growth of Indigenous Churches in Indonesia*. With an introduction by Dr. W. Visser 't Heet. The Hague: Boekencentrum, 1958.
Lacan, Jacques. *Anxiety: The Seminar of Jacques Lacan, Book X*. Edited by Jacues-Alain Miller. Translated by A. R. Price. Cambridge: Polity Press, 2014.
Latuihamallo, P. D., Peter D. Latuihamallo, and T.B. Simatupang. *Kewarganegaraan yang bertanggung jawab: mengenang Dr. J. Leimena*. Jakarta: Gunung Mulia, 1980.
Leclerc, Jacques. "Afterword: The Masked Hero." In Lucas, *Local Opposition*, 325–368.
Leclerc, Jacques. "Amir Sjariufoeddin. Entre l'État et la Révolution." In Leclerc Papers, no. 403.
Leclerc, Jacques. "Amir Sjarifuddin 75 Tahun," *Prisma*, no. 12 (December 1982): 53–76.
Leclerc, Jacques. "Amir Sjarifuddin: Between the State and the Revolution." In *Indonesian Political Biography: In Search of Cross-Cultural Understanding*, edited by Angus McIntyre, 1–41. Clayton, Victoria: Monash Papers on Southeast Asia, 1993.
Leclerc, Jacques, "La clandestinité et son double (à propos des relations d'Amir Sjarifuddin avec le communisme indonesien)." In *Histoire de l'Asie du Sud-Est: Révoltes, réformes, révolutions*, edited by Pierre Brocheux, 213–246. Lille: Presses Universitaires de Lille, 1981.
Legge, John D. *Intellectuals and Nationalism in Indonesia: A Study of the Following Recruited by Sutan Sjahrir in Occupied Jakarta*. Ithaca, NY: Cornell Modern Indonesian Studies, 1988.
Legge, John D. *Sukarno: A Political Biography*. New York: Praeger, 1972.
Leimena, Johannes. *The Dutch–Indonesian Conflict*. Djakarta: Grafica, 1949.
Leirissa, R. Z. "Biografi Dr. J. Leimena." In Latuihamallo et al., *Kewarganegaraan yang bertanggung jawab*, 1–104.
Levinas, Emmanuel. *Of God Who Comes to Mind*. Translated by Bettina Bergo. Stanford, CA: Stanford University Press, 1998.
Levinas, Emmanuel. *On Escape: De L'évasion*. Translated by Bettina Bergo. Stanford, CA: Stanford University Press, 2003.
Levinas, Emmanuel. *Totality and Infinity: An Essay on Exteriority*. Translated by Alphonso Lingis. Pittsburgh: Pennsylvania, Duquesne University Press, 2012.
Lilje, Hanns, *The Valley of the Shadow*. Philadelphia: Fortress, 1950.
Locher-Scholten, Elsbeth. *Ethiek in fragmenten: Vijf studies over koloniaal denken en doen van Nederlanders in de Indonesische archipel, 1877–1942*. Utrecht: HES, 1981.
Loebis, Aboe Bakar. *Kilas balik revolusi, Kenangan, pelaku dan saksi*. Jakarta: University of Indonesia Press, 1992.
Lucas, Anton. *Local Opposition and Underground Resistance to the Japanese in Java, 1942–1945*. Clayton, Victoria: Monash Papers on Southeast Asia, 1986.
Lucas, Anton. *One Soul One Struggle: Region and Revolution in Indonesia*. Sydney: Allen and Unwin, 1991.
Lucas, Anton. *Peristiwa Tiga Daerah: Revolusi dalam Revolusi*. Jakarta: Pustaka Utama Grafiti, 1989.
Lupitasari, Augustina Rizky. "Cerita Museum Sumpah Pemuda, Gedung Kramat Raya 106 milik Sie Kong Liong." *Kompas*, November 24, 2020.

Machiavelli, Niccolò. *The Essential Writings.* Translated by Peter Constantine and with an introduction by Albert Russell Ascoli. New York: Modern Library, 2007.
Malik, Adam. *Mengabdi Republik.* Vol. 1, *Adam dari Andalas.* Jakarta: Sinar Harapan, 2006.
Malik, Adam. *Mengabdi Republik.* Vol. 2, *Angkatan 45.* Jakarta: Sinar Harapan, 2008.
Marx, Karl and Friedrich Engels. *The Communist Manifesto.* Translated by Samuel Moore. Monee, IL: Forward, 2022.
Marx, Karl. *The Civil War in France.* New York: International, 1962.
Marx, Karl. *The Eighteenth Brumaire of Louis Bonaparte.* New York: International, 1969.
McIntyre, Angus, ed.. *Indonesian Political Biography: In Search of Cross-Cultural Understanding.* Clayton, Victoria: Monash Papers on Southeast Asia, 1993.
McVey, Ruth T., "The Enchantment of the Revolution: History and Action in an Indonesian Communist Text." In *Perception of the Past in Southeast Asia,* edited by Anthony Reid and Davin Marr, 340–358. Singapore: Heinemann, 1979.
Miert, J. J. van. *Een koel hoofd en een warm hart: Nationalisme, javanisme en jeugdbeweging in Nederlands-Indië, 1918–1930.* Amsterdam: De Bataafsche Leeuw, 1995.
Miharja, St. *Pemberontakan Madiun (Amir Syarifuddin).* Bandung: Sarana Panca Karya Nusa, 1986.
Milovanov, I. V. and L. N. Chernov, "Amir Sharifudin, Indonezija: Glava narodnovo pravitelstva." In Milovanov and Chernov, *Zizn otdana bor'be,* 229–247.
Milovanov, I. V. and L. N. Chernov, "Manovar Musso, Indonezija: Glas svobody." In Milovanov and Chernov, *Zizn otdana bor'be,* 201–225.
Milovanov, I. V. and L. N. Chernov. *Zizn otdana bor'be.* Moskva: Nauka, 1963.
Montesquieu. *Persian Letters.* Translated by Margaret Mauldon. Oxford: Oxford University Press, 2008.
Mook, H. J. van. *The Stakes of Democracy in South-East Asia.* London: Allen and Unwin, 1950.
Mrázek, Rudolf. *A Certain Age: Colonial Jakarta in the Memories of Its Intellectuals.* Durham, NC: Duke University Press, 2010.
Mrázek, Rudolf. "Coughing Heavily: Two Interviews with Professor Resink at His Home at Gondangdia Lama 48A, Jakarta, on July 17 and July 25, 1997." *Indonesia,* no. 74 (October 2002): 137–164.
Mrázek, Rudolf. *Sjahrir: Politics and Exile in Indonesia.* Ithaca, NY: Cornell Southeast Asia Program, 1994.
Musil, Robert. *Diaries, 1899–1941.* Translated by Philip Payne. New York: Basic Books, 1998.
Musil, Robert. *The Man without Qualities.* Translated by Sophie Wilkins and Burton Pike. New York: Knopf, 1995.
Nancy, Jean-Luc. *Adoration: The Deconstruction of Christianity II.* Translated by John McKean. New York: Fordham University Press, 2013.
Nancy, Jean-Luc. *Dis-Enclosure: The Deconstruction of Christianity.* Translated by Bettina Bergo, Gabriel Malenfant, and Michael B. Smith. New York: Fordham University Press, 2008.
Nancy, Jean-Luc. *Noli Me Tangere: On the Raising of the Body.* Translated by Sarah Cliff. New York: Fordham University Press, 2008.
Nancy, Jean-Luc. *The Sense of the World.* Translated by Jeffrey S. Librett. Minneapolis: University of Minnesota Press, 1997.

Nasution, Abdul Haris. *Sekitar Perang Kemerdekaan Indonesia.* Vol. 8, *Pemberontakan PKI 1948.* Bandung: Angkasa, 1979.
New Oxford Annotated Bible. Revised standard version. Edited by Herbert G. May and Bruce M. Metzger. New York: Oxford University Press, 1973.
Nieuwenhuis, H. G. *Assaineering van Sibolga.* Weltevreden: Albrecht, 1919.
Nora, Pierre, ed. *Realms of Memory: Rethinking the French Past.* Chicago: University of Chicago Press, 1998.
Notosoetardjo, H. A. *Peristiwa Madiun: tragedi nasional.* Djakarta: Endang, 1966.
Oey Hong Lee. *War and Diplomacy in Indonesia, 1945–1950.* Townsville: James Cook University, 1981.
Orang Indonesia jang terkemoeka di Djawa. Gunseikanbu. Yogyakarta: Gajah Mada University Press, 1986. First published in 1944.
Partai Komunis Indonesia. *Buku Putih tentang Peristiwa Madiun.* Djakarta: Departemen Agitprop CC PKI, 1954.
Pauker, Guy J. *The Rise and Fall of the Communist Party of Indonesia.* Santa Monica, CA: RAND, 1969.
Pedersen, Paul B. *Batak Blood and Protestant Soul: The Development of National Batak Churches in North Sumatra.* Grand Rapids, MI.: W. B. Eerdmans, 1970.
Perec, Georges. *Life: A User's Manual.* Translated by David Bellos. New York: Verba Mundi, 2009.
Pinardi. *Peristiwa coup berdarah P.K.I. September 1948 di Madiun.* Djakarta: Inkopak-Hazera, 1967.
Plato. *Euthyphro. Apology. Crito. Phaedo.* Edited and translated by Chris Emlyn-Jones and William Preddy. Cambridge, MA: Harvard University Press, 2017.
Plato. *Lysis. Symposium. Phaedrus.* Edited and translated by Chris Emlyn-Jones and William Preddy. Cambridge, MA: Harvard University Press, 2022.
Plato. *Republic.* Edited and translated by Chris Emlyn-Jones and William Preddy. Cambridge, MA: Harvard University Press, 2017.
Pluvier, J. M. *Overzicht van de ontwikkeling der nationalistische beweging in Indonesië in de jaren 1930 tot 1942.* 's Gravenhage: W. van Hoeve, 1953.
Poeze, Harry A. *Madiun 1948: PKI Bergerak.* Jakarta: KITLV Press, 2011.
Poeze, Harry A. "The PKI Muda 1936–1942," *Kabar Seberang Suling Maphilindo,* nos. 13–14 (December 1984): 157–176.
Poeze, Harry A. *Tan Malaka: Strijder voor Indonesië's vrijheid. Levensloop van 1897 to 1945.* 's Gravenhage: Martinus Nijhoff, 1976.
Poeze, Harry A. *Verguisd en vergeten: Tan Malaka, de linkse beweging en de Indonesische Revolutie, 1945–1959.* 3 vols. Leiden: KITLV Press, 2007.
Prideaux, Sue. *I Am Dynamite: A Life of Nietzsche.* London: Faber and Faber, 2018.
Proust, Marcel. *In Search of Lost Time.* Vol. 6, *Time Regained,* translated by Andreas Mayer and Terence Kilmartin. New York: Modern Library, 1993.
Purba, Yema Siska. *Amir Sjarifoeddin: Nasionalis yang Tersisih.* Yogyakarta: Puspol, 2012.
Rabelais, Francois. *Gargantua and Pantagruel.* London: Penguin, 2006.
Randwijk, S. C. Graaf van. *Oegstgeest: kebijaksanaan "Lembaga-lembaga pekabaran Injil yang bekerjasama" 1897–1942.* Jakarta: Gunung Mulia, 1989.

Reed, John. "Ten Days That Shook the World." In *Writing of John Reed*, 93–290. St. Petersburg, FL: Red and Black, 2011.
Reid, Anthony. *The Indonesian National Revolution, 1945–1950*. Hawthorn, Victoria: Longman, 1974.
Reid, Anthony. "Marxist Attitude to Social Revolution." *RIMA*, no. 1 (January–June 1974).
Reid, Anthony. "Remembering and Forgetting. War and Revolution." In *Beginning to Remember: The Past in the Indonesian Present*, edited by Mary S. Zurbuchen, 168–191. Singapore: Singapore University Press, 2005.
Reitsma, S. A. *Van Stockum's Travellers' Handbook for the Dutch East Indies*. The Hague: W. P. van Stockum, 1930.
Resink, G. J. ed. *Gedenkboek uitgegeven ter gelegenheid van het 25-jarig bestaan van het rechtswetenschappelijk hoger onderwijs in Indonesië op 28 October 1949*. Groningen-Djakarta: J. B. Wolters, 1949.
Resink, G. J. "Rechtshoogeschool, Jongereneed, 'Stuw' en Gestuwden." *Bijdragen tot de Taal-, Land- en Volkenkunde* 136, no. 4 (1974): 428–449.
Resink, G. J. "Twee vergeten 'Stuw' sympathisanten." *Bijdragen tot de Taal-, Land- en Volkenkunde* 150, no. 3 (1994): 582–583.
Rijsen, F. van. *Hoofdpersonen uit de algemene geschiedenis*, vol. 1, 12th ed. Groningen and Batavia: Wolters 1928.
Robespierre, Maximilien. *Virtue and Terror*. Translated by John Howe with an introduction by Slavoj Žižek. London: Verso, 2007.
Roeder, O. G. *The Smiling General: President Soeharto of Indonesia*. Djakarta: Gunung Agung, 1969.
Rose, Mavis. *Indonesia Free: A Political Biography of Mohammad Hatta*. Ithaca, NY: Cornell Modern Indonesia Project, 1987.
Rosihan Anwar. *Against the Currents: A Biography of Soedarpo Sastrosatomo*. Translated by Toenggoel P. Siagian. Jakarta: Sinar Harapan, 2003.
Rudjito. "Rakjat Membebaskan Bung Amir." Unpublished paper. In Leclerc Papers no. 278.
Safranski, Rüdiger. *Goethe: Life as a Work of Art*. Translated by David Dollenmayer. New York: Liveright, 2013.
Sartre, Jean-Paul. *Baudelaire*. Translated by Martin Turnell. New York: New Directions, 1967.
Sartre, Jean-Paul. *The Family Idiot: Gustave Flaubert, 1821–1857*, vol. 1. Translated by Carol Cosman. Chicago: University of Chicago Press, 1981.
Sastroamdjojo, see Ali Sastroamidjojo.
Schepper, Julius Marti Johannes. *Nieuw-kantiaansche rechtsbeschouwing*. Haarlem: H. D. Tjeenk Willink, 1917.
Schepper, Julius Marti Johannes. *Het vonnis in de P.N.I.-zaak*. Batavia: De Unie, 1931.
Schepper, Julius Marti Johannes. *Vrijheid van godsdienst en de verhouding kerk en staat*. 's Gravenhage: Boekencentrum, 1948.
Scholten, Gerbert. "Eene bespreking van Mr. J.M.J. Schepper's proefschrift 'Nieuw-Kantiaansche Rechtsbeschrijving, Leiden 1917.'" *Onze Eeuw* 18, no. 3 (1918), 209–229.

Schrieke, Bertram. *De Gang der Communistische Beweging ter Sumatra's Westkust.* Weltevreden: Landsdrukkerij, 1928.
Schweitzer, Albert. *Out of My Life and Thought: An Autobiography.* Translated by Antje Bultmann Lemke. Baltimore, MD: Johns Hopkins University Press, 1990.
Schweitzer, Albert. *The Quest of the Historical Jesus.* Translated by W. Montgomery. New York: Dover, 2005.
Siauw Giok Tjhan. *Lima jaman: perwujudan integrasi wajar.* Jakarta: Yayasan Teratai, 1981.
Siauw Tiong-djin. *Siauw Giok Tjhan: Bicultural Leader in Emerging Indonesia.* Clayton, Victoria: Monash University Press, 2018.
Sidik Kertapati. *Sekitar Peristiwa 17 Agustus 1945.* Jakarta: Pustaka Pena, 2000.
Simatupang, Tahi Bonar. "Khotbah di Bukit." In Fransz, *Pelaku Wacana*, 81–90.
Simatupang, Tahi Bonar. *Laporan dari Banaran: kisah pengalaman seorang prajurit selama perang kemerdekaan.* Jakarta: Sinar Harapan, 1980.
Simatupang, Tahi Bonar. *Report from Banaran: Experience during the People's War.* Translated by Benedict Anderson and Elizabeth Graves. Ithaca, NY: Cornell Modern Indonesian Project, 1972.
Simbolon, Parakitri T. *Menjadi Indonesia.* Vol. 1, *Akar-akar Kebangsaan Indonesia.* Jakarta: Kompas, 1995.
Sintha Melati, "In the Service of the Underground." In Lucas, *Local Opposition*, 123–265.
Sjahrir, Soetan, *Out of Exile.* Translated by Charles Wolf. New York: John Day, 1949.
Sjahrir, Soetan. *Kebangsaan kita hanja djembatan oentoek mentjapai deradjat kemanoesiaan jang sempoerna: Siaran Kilat.* Djakarta: Kementarian Penerangan, 1946.
Sjahrir, Soetan. *Pidato Radio P.J.M. Soetan Sjahrir, Djakarta 18 Agustus 1946 djam 19:30: Siaran Kilat.* Djakarta: Kementarian Penerangan, 1946.
Sjahrir, Soetan. "Political Conditions in Indonesia." Unpublished typescript, 1948. In Archives of George McT. Kahin.
Sjariffoeddin, see Amir Sjarifoeddin.
Smit, C. ed. *Het dagboek van Schermerhorn: geheim verslag van prof. dr. ir. W. Schermerhorn als voorzitter der Commissie-Generaal voor Nederlands-Indië 20 september 1946–7 oktober 1947.* Vol. 1. Groningen: Wolters-Noordhoff, 1970.
Snow, Edgar. *Red Star over China.* Rev. ed. New York: Grove Press, 1968.
Soe Hok Gie. *Orang-orang di persimpangan kiri jalan: kisah pemberontakan Madiun, September 1948.* Yogyakarta: Bentang Budaya, 1997.
Soebagio, I. N. *K.H. Masjkur: sebuah biografi.* Jakarta: Gunung Agung, 1982.
Soebadio Sastrosatomo. "Masa Muda Saya: Indonesia 1940–1942." Unpublished manuscript, n.d. Collection of the author.
Soebadio Sastrosatomo. *Perjuangan revolusi.* Jakarta: Sinar Harapan, 1987.
Soedjatmoko. *Choice and Circumstances: The Indonesian Revolution 45 Years On: Some Personal Reflection.* Leiden: KITLV Press, 2002.
Soedijono Djojoprajitno. *PKI: Sibar Contra Tan Malaka: pemberontakan 1926 dan 'kambing hitam' Tan Malaka.* Djakarta: Yayasan Masa, 1962.
Soeharto. *My Thoughts, Words and Deeds: An Autobiography as Told to G. Dwipayana and Ramadhan K.H.* Translated by Sumadi. Jakarta: Citra Lamtoro Gung Persada, 1991.

Soemarso, ed. *Mohammad Roem 70 Tahun, pejuang perunding.* Jakarta: Bulan Bintang, 1978.

Soemarsono. *Revolusi Agustus: kesaksian seorang pelaku sejarah.* Jakarta: Hasra Mitra, 2008.

Soeripno, R. M. "De Indonesische mensch." In *Indonesiërs spreken*, edited by M. Ford-van Lennep and W. J. Ford, 13–48. 's Gravenhage: W. van Hoeve, 1947.

Soerjono. "On Musso's Return." *Indonesia*, no. 30 (April 1980): 59–90.

Soerjono, *Surat untuk Ben Anderson: Kisah tentang Kembalinya Musso dan Madiun Affair.* Temanggung: Kendi, 2016.

Soeryana. "Blitar: The Changing of the Guard." In Lucas, *Local Opposition*, 263–325.

Sukarno. *Dibawah Bendera Revolusi*, vol. 1. 3rd ed. Djakarta: Panitia Penerbit, 1964.

Sulistina Sutomo, Titie Said, and Lies Said. *Bung Tomo, suamiku.* Jakarta: Sinar Harapan, 1995.

Supardi, I. *Bung Karno sebagai Kokrosono.* Surabaja: Pustaka Nasional, 1950.

Suvin, Darko. "In the Shadow of Never-Ending Warfare." In Boynik, *Coiled Verbal Spring*, 33–367.

Swift, Ann. *The Road to Madiun: The Indonesian Communist Uprising in 1948.* Ithaca, NY: Cornell Modern Indonesia Project, 1989.

Tan Malaka. *Dari Penjara ke Penjara.* 3 vols. Jakarta: Teplok, 2000.

The Indonesian Problem: Facts and Factors. What Happened since the End of the Pacific War. Batavia: Netherlands Indies Government Information, September 1947.

Thomas, Hugh. *The Spanish War.* Rev. ed. New York: Modern Library, 2012.

Thompson, John. *Hubbub in Java.* Sydney: Currawong, 1946.

Tur, Kusalah Subagyo. "Wawancara dengan Sumarsono, saksi utama 'Peristiwa Madiun.'" Tanggal 3 Januari 1998 di Depok, Jakarta. Unpublished paper. January 2000. Collection of the author.

Tynianov, Yuri. "The Lexicon of Lenin as Polemicist." In Boynik, *Coiled Verbal Spring*, 189–224.

Van Mook, see Mook.

Veen, Peter van der, and Marjolein van der Veen. *The Linguist's Family.* Burnaby BC: EMP, 2023.

Verkuyl, Johannes. *De achtergrond van het indonesische vraagstuk.* 's Gravenhage: D. A. Daamen, 1946.

Verkuyl, Johannes. *De geest van communisme en kapitalisme en het evangelie van Christus.* Batavia: Ophouw Pembangunan, 1948.

Verkuyl, Johannes. *Gedenken en verwachten.* Kampen: Kok, 1983.

Verkuyl, Johannes. "T.B. Simatupang sebagai pemimpin teladan." In *Saya adalah orang yang berhutang: 70 tahun T.B. Simatupang*, edited by Samuel Pardede, 367–374. Jakarta: Sinar Harapan, 1990.

Virilio, Paul. *The Aesthetics of Disappearance.* Translated by Philip Beitchman. Los Angeles: Semiotext(e), 2009.

Virilio, Paul. *A Landscape of Events.* Translated by Julie Rose. Cambridge, MA: Cambridge University Press, 2000.

Virilio, Paul. *Lost Dimension.* Translated by Daniel Moshenberg. Los Angeles: Semiotext(e), 2012.

Walhout, Evelien and Jacques Dane. "Picturing the East: A Visual Analysis of Educational Tools from the Collection of the Dutch National Museum of Education." *Yearbook for Women's History*, no. 39 (2019): 173–203.

Walraven, Willem. *Een maand in het boevenpak*. 's Gravenhage: Thomas en Eras, 1978.

Weinstein, Franklin B. *Indonesian Foreign Policy and the Dilemma of Dependence: From Sukarno to Soeharto*. Ithaca, NY: Cornell University Press, 1976.

Wellem, Frederiek Djara. *Amir Sjarifoeddin: Pergumulan Imamnya dalam Perjuangan Kemerdekaan*. Jakarta: Sinar Harapan, 1984. (Banned.)

Wellem, Frederiek Djara. *Amir Sjarifoeddin: Tempatnya dalam Kekristenan dan Perjuangan Kemerdekaan Indonesia*. Jakarta: Ut Omnes Unum Sint Institute, 2009.

Wellem, Frederiek Djara. "Mr. Amir Sjarifuddin: Tempatnya dalam Kekristenan dan Dalam Perjuangan Kemerdekaan Indonesia." Unpublished MA thesis, Sekolah Tinggi, Jakarta, 1982. Collection of the author.

Wertheim, W. F. "'Eiland van Hoop' (Boeroe): Leven als vogelvrijverklaarden." In *Aangeraakt door Insulinde: de boeken van drieëntwintig lezers*, edited by Peter Boomgaard, 131–135. Leiden: KITLV Uitgerij, 1992.

Wertheim, W. F. and Hetty Wertheim-Gijse Weenink. *Vier wendingen in ons bestaan: Indië verloren—Indonesië geboren*. Breda: De Geus, 1991.

Wesseling, Elisabet and Jacques Dane. "Are 'the Natives' Educable? Dutch Schoolchildren Learn Ethical Colonial Policy (1890–1910)." *Memory and Society* 4, no. 1 (Spring 2018): 28–43.

Wilopo. "Kesadaran Mengabdi Negara." In Latuihamallo et al., *Kewarganegaraan yang bertanggungjawab*, 324–333.

Yamin, Muhammad. *Sumpah Indonesia Raja*. Bukittinggi: Nusantara, 1955. (See also Jamin.)

Yasni, Z., ed. *Bung Hatta Menjawab: Wawancara dengan Dr. Z. Yasni*. Jakarta: Gunung Agung, 2002.

Zanoeddin, Ahmad. "Tjatatan-tjatatan Pondok Modern." Typescript. In Archief van het Ministerie van Buitenlandse Zaken, NEFIS Centrale Militaire Inlichtingendienst, 1942–1949, no. 06980.

Žižek, Slavoj. *Robespierre: Virtue and Terror*. London: Verso, 2017.

Žižek, Slavoj. *Violence: Six Sideways Reflections*. London: Profile, 2009.

Index

Abbas-Manoppo, Ani, 30
Abdoelgani, Roeslan, 201, 315
Abdoelmadjid Djajadiningrat, 169, 177, 226, 285
Abikoesno Tjokrosoejoso, 98, 101, 360n163
Adorno, Theodore, 32, 325
aesthetics of disappearance (Virilio), ix
Afrin, George, 185
Agamben, Giorgio, 32, 237
Aidit, Dipa Nusantara, 146, 203, 289, 291–95, 298, 328
Algadri, Hamid, 130, 315
Alimin, 159, 193, 202, 220, 233, 253, 276, 285, 298–99, 359n145
Alsop, Joseph, 327
Anderson, Benedict, xi, 122, 130, 149, 239, 319, 320, 322
Anderson, David, 273, 274
Angkatan Baroe, 117
anthropological place (Augé), 47–48, 56, 98, 320
Anwar, Chairil, 129
Armstrong, Hamilton F., 102
Augé, Marc, 47, 106, 120, 204, 320

Baars, Adolf, 170
Badiou, Alain, 176, 291
Banda Neira, 105
Banteng (publication), 60, 64, 70, 04
Barisan Banteng, 222–23, 241
Barth, Karl, 31, 214
Barthes, Roland, x, 101–2, 126
Basoenoe boru Siregar, 4–5, 65, 340n4
Batak people, 3–5, 13–14
Baudelaire, Charles, 14, 25, 35
Baudrillard, Jean, 320
Bauer, Otto, 46
Beel, Louis, 183–84
Beneš, Edward, 205, 359n140
Benjamin, Walter, ix, x, 9, 10, 12, 242

Biro Perdjoeangan, 158, 186
Blanchot, Maurice, 6, 47
Blitar prison, 125–28, 160, 187
Bloch, Ernst, ix, 20, 204, 254, 278, 305
blockade, 188–89, 207
Boediardjo, Ali, 104–105, 211, 263, 265, 313, 354, 377n38
Boedisoetjitro, 198
Boeke, H., 26, 28
Bondan, Mohammad, 45
Boven Digoel, 59, 75, 80–82, 86, 105, 110, 127, 131–33, 159–60, 208, 240
Brackman, Arnold, 96, 123, 142, 155, 180, 185, 209, 277, 306, 309, 328
Brecht, Bertolt, ix, 57
Buchó cabinet, 147–49, 156, 164, 353n124

Campbell, Arthur, 231–32, 312, 316
Carlyle, Thomas, 141, 150, 158, 216, 236, 237, 290, 323
Chechetkina, Olga, 201–2
China, 5, 88, 192–93, 236, 245–46, 319
Chinese Red Army, 192–93, 236
Clementis, Vladimír, 325–28
Coast, John, 129, 190, 192, 307–9, 315
Cochran, H. Merle, 228, 260, 305, 316
commissars, 157, 159, 186, 252
Communist International Bureau, 193
Communist International, 85, 96–97, 131, 161, 177, 192, 202, 204, 209
Communist Party of Indonesia, 67, 86, 90, 134, 188–89, 202–6, 268, 279–80, 289–90; of the Netherlands, 169, 170, 196, 219–20, 353n134; of the Soviet Union, 219–20, 231; of Czechoslovakia, 194, 196–97, 326–27
concrete utopia (Bloch), ix, 237
Condition Humaine (Malraux), 103
Constitutional Convention (Paris; 1792), 216–17
Cramer, J. C. W., 111–12

397

INDEX

Dahm, Bernhard, 42, 115, 302
dandies, 35, 39, 40, 42, 47, 58, 64, 108, 114, 156, 216
Darbyites, see Vergadering der Gelovigen
De Groot, Paul, 196, 219
De Jonge, Bonifácius Cornelis, 67–68
De Kadt, Jacques, 108, 304–5
De Vries, Dirk, 109
Dekker, Douwes, E.F.E., 260
Deli Maatschappij, 5–6
Derrida, Jacques, 61, 107, 148, 270
Deutscher, Isaac, 141, 237
Diponegoro (prince), 263–64, 275
Djaetan, 159–160
Djajadiningrat, Hussein, 26
djaksa, 4, 5
Djalan Baroe (program), 202, 206
Djamin *gelar* Baginda Soripada, 4, 12, 23–24
Djojobojo (king), 126, 264
Djojopoespito, Soegondo, 38–40, 73, 106
Djojopoespito, Soewarsih, 103–104
Djokosoejono, 86, 106, 158, 187, 225, 229, 249–51, 262
Du Perron, Charles Edgar "Eddy," 103, 104, 105–6

Effendi, Roestam, 209
Eighteenth Brumaire (Marx), 328
ELS (Europese Lagere School), 7–8, 14, 26, 27, 147, 351n52
Emerson, Rupert, 310
Enzensberger, Hans Magnus, 320, 323
Ephraim *gelar* Soetan Goenoeng Toea, 3–4, 12

Fanggidaej, Francisca, 150, 159–60, 193–94, 243–44, 247, 250–53, 287–88, 294, 351n52
fascism, 88, 95–96, 102–3
FDR (Front Demokrasi Rakjat), 191, 201, 206–7, 240, 250, 274, 308, 313
First Police Action, 181
Fransz, Augustine Leonore "Tine," 36–37, 66, 82, 95, 120, 184, 282, 306, 320, 323, 379n61
Frederick, William, 122, 151
French Revolution, 27, 141, 150, 158, 216, 236, 238, 290, 323
Fukuyama, Francis, 321

G30S (Gerakan Tigapuluh September), 272, 279–81, 287–88, 301, 306, 322
gamelan (music), 46, 47, 125, 275, 320
Gandhi, Mahatma, 31
Gani, Adnan K., 86, 87, 97, 179, 298

GAPI (Gaboengan Politik Indonesia), 98, 101
Garrett, John, 282–83
Gatot Subroto, 156–57, 231, 252–54, 270, 277, 280, 296, 309
Geertz, Clifford, 290
Gerindo (Gerakan Rakjat Indonesia), 86–89, 96–101, 110, 115–16, 153
German Ideology (Marx), 61
GKS (Genees-kundigeschool), Batavia, 33
Glodok prison, 252–53, 281
Goenawan Mohamad, 281
Goethe, Johann Wolfgang von, 15, 57
Gottwald Plan, 206, 359n140
Gottwald, Klement, 196, 205–6, 282, 326–27, 359
GPKK (Gerakan Persatoean Kaoem Kristen), 119
Graham, Frank, 182–84, 228, 305, 309, 318, 379n60
Great Depression, 41, 188, 191
Gymnasium Arnhem, 20
Gymnasium Haarlem, 18–23, 25

Hanifah, Abu, 34, 37–38, 41–43, 115, 185, 210–11, 274, 278–79, 312
Harahap, F. K. N., 65, 213, 253, 281–82
hari raja, 5
Hariandja, 244–47
Harjono, 226, 249–51, 254, 298, 372n107
Harrenstein, W. G., 15, 16
Hatta, Mohammad, 104–5, 116–18, 139–40, 152, 185, 234, 245
HBS (Hoogeburgerschool), 44
Heidegger, Martin, 4, 5, 41, 56, 247, 274
Hiroshima, 139
HKBP (Huria Kristen Batak Protestan), 65, 119–20, 213, 217
Ho Chi Minh, 193
Holland, 15–24, 267
homelessness, 47, 238
Homer, 24, 254, 323
Hoytema, Johan Frederik van, 25

Idenburg, P. J. A., 113, 171, 347n85
Indonesia Raja (publication), 38, 58–63
Ivanovich, Musin Makar, 196, 199, also Musso

Jan Pieterszoon Coen (ship), 15–16
Japanese occupation, 114–36, 172–73, 310, 347n15
JBB (Jong Batak Bond), 38
Jesus, 221, 285, 289, 293, 305

INDEX 399

Jogjakarta Youth Congress (1945), 150–51, 155, 158–59, 194
Jogjakarta, 41, 154, 159, 216, 252, 259, 363n11

Kadt, Jacques de, 109, 304–5
Kafka, Franz, 32, 148, 221, 222, 247, 325
Kagawa, Tolyohiko, 31, 213, 283
Kahin, George, xi, 117, 154, 188–89, 190, 229–30, 241–42, 259–60, 261, 285, 309–23
Kandinsky, Wassily, 25
Kant, Immanuel, 23, 30–31, 66, 127, 162, 214
Kats, J., 26
Kierkegaard, Søren, xii, 100, 270, 272, 291, 303, 329
Kirby, Richard Clarence, 182
KJB (Katholieke Jongelingen Bond), 38–40
Klinken, Gerry van, xi–xii
KNIL (Koninklijke Nederlandsch-Indië Leger), 22, 156–57 172, 181, 185, 262
KNIP (Komite Nasional Indonesia Pusat), 148, 227, 235, 359n145
Koets, P. J., 216, 311
Kollewijin, R. D., 26, 28, 30, 37, 70, 142
Kraemer, Hendrik, 3, 13, 81, 144
Kramat 106 (student dormitory), 32–40, 42, 47, 58, 82–4, 99, 115, 145, 155–6, 160, 278, 312
Kritiek en Opbouw (publication), 102–3, 105, 109, 214, 216, 304–5
Kundera, Milan, 327

Lacan, Jacques, x, 221, 247
Land van Herkomst (Du Perron), 103
Language, Batak, 3, 6; Indonesian, 58–61; Javanese, 45, 56; Malay, 30; Dutch, 19, 45, 56, 58–61; English, 19, 182; German, 61; of Gymnasium, 19–20, 26; of Bolsheviks, 45, 57; of Clementis, 326
Lattimore, Owen, 377n28, 378n70
Leclerc, Jacques, xi
Legge, John, 96–97, 108–9, 129–30, 178, 221
Leiden, 16–20, 26, 81, 294
Leimena, Johannes, 119, 260–61
Lenin, Vladimir, 156, 162, 202, 240, 329
Levinas, Emmanuel, 68
Lilje, Hanns, 31, 37, 144, 211–12, 215, 217–18, 337n38
Linggadjati Agreement, 173–76, 178, 182, 206, 216, 224, 303, 359n145
Logemann, J. H. A., 26, 28, 30, 40, 71, 104, 111, 168, 173, 181, 192, 209, 216, 340n6
Long March, Chinese, 236

Long March, Indonesian, 236, 245–47, 319
Lucas, Anton, 86, 106–7, 114, 121, 125, 163, 164

MacArthur, Douglas, 132, 232–33
Machiavelli, Niccolo, 92–93, 100, 154–55, 236, 242
Madiun Affair, 222–43, 274–77, 279, 285–86, 295
Madiun, 158–160, 165, 188–89, 194, 206–243, 249–255, 260–263
Malik, Adam, 48, 89, 146, 162, 300
Malik, Sajoeti, 125, 209–10, 353n109, 360n163
Malraux, André, 103
Mangoenkoesoemo, Darmawan, 120–21
Mangoenkoesoemo, Soejitno, 104, 116, 120
Mangoenkoesoemo, Tjipto, 104, 120
Mao Tse-Tung, 96, 147, 165, 192–93, 197, 236, 247, 317
Marat, Jean-Paul, 35
Maroeto Daroesman, 169, 189, 249–51
Marshall, George C., 221
martyrdom, 115, 215, 284–285, 293
Marx House (dormitory), 159–61
Marx, Karl, 3, 61, 91, 139, 266, 307, 328
Masaryk, Jan, 326
Masjumi, 30, 149, 154, 179, 180, 184–85, 206, 210, 215, 227, 242, 283, 299
Medan, 5–6, 11–12
Meester Cornelis (now Jatinegara), 33, 144, 244
Menara Merah (publication), 106–7, 114, 208, 360n162
militia, 99–100, 151, 155, 178, 184, 186, 217, 222, 236, 246
Mirabele Lectu (publication), 21, 55, 88, 172, 191
Moelia, Todoeng gelar Soetan Goenoeng, 16–17, 33, 99, 100, 111, 123, 333n7, 341n16
Moewardi, Dr., 222, 241
Molière, 93–94
Molotov-Ribbentrop Pact, 326
Musil, Robert, 14, 32, 96, 243
Musso, 85–86, 90, 158, 106–7, 163, 196–221, 224–36, 240–46, 275–7, 296–7, 328, 367n122, 367n126

Nancy, Jean-Luc, 45, 47, 243, 254, 274, 284, 286
Nasoetion, Abdul Haris, 157, 181, 186–89, 216, 225–26, 229–37, 249, 252, 269–277

400   INDEX

Nasoetion, Ida, 216
Natsir, Mohammad, 101, 260, 299
Nehru, Jawaharlal, 194
New Left Review (publication), 319
New Order, 281–85
Nietzsche, Friedrich, 57, 254, 320
NIZB (Nederlandsch Indische Zending Bond), 100
NSB (Nationaal-Socialistische Beweging), 95

Otto, Rudolf, 30

Pan-Asiatic movement, 103–13
Pane, Armijn, 43
Pane, Sanoesi, 50, 90, 111
Paras (Partai Sosialis), 153, 351n69
Parpindo (Partai Persatoean Indonesia), 99
Parsi (Partai Sosialis Indonesia), 153, 351n69
Partindo (Partai Indonesia), 47–51, 67, 73, 80, 85–7, 116, 119, 122, 127–8, 211, 338n40
Pauker, Guy, 274
Perdjoeangan Kita (Sjahrir), 147–148, 307
Pergoeroean Rakjat, Volksuniversiteit, 38, 42, 59, 82–83, 90, 109, 112, 118
Perhimpoenan Indonesia, 73–74, 104, 168, 169, 177
Persatoean Perdjoeangan, 162
Pesindo (Pemuda Sosialis Indonesia), 99–100, 141, 150–51, 155, 158–61, 178, 180, 186–88, 191, 208, 223, 234, 255, 261
Peta (Pembela Tanah Air), 141, 187
Plato, 10, 15, 254
PNI (Partai Nasional Indonesia), 38, 46–50, 66–67, 122, 127–28, 152, 179–184, 211, 274, 351n66
Poedjangga Baroe (publication), 90, 91–92
Poeze, Harry, xi, 110, 285
Potemkin (ship), 62
PPPI (Perhimpeonan Peladjar-Peladjar Indonesia), 38, 58–59, 70, 74, 116
Prague, ix, xi, 32, 193–99, 202, 205–206, 308, 311–12, 320, 326–328, 380n3
Prisma (publication), 280
Proclamation of Independence, 139–49, 177–78, 233–34, 351n66
prophecies, 43, 126, 128, 132, 134, 175, 264
Prophets, 30, 31, 67, 124, 144, 161, 175, 185, 191, 213, 345n32
Proust, Marcel, 7, 14
PSI (Partai Sosialis Indonesia), 189–90, 227, 279
PSII (Partai Sarekat Islam Indonesia, 101

PTI (Partai Tionghoa Indonesia), 163
PvdA (Partij van de Arbeid, 168

radical evil (Kant), 204, 214
rationalization, 186–89, 225
Reed, John, 202
Reid, Anthony, 149, 152, 154, 164, 241, 278
Renville Agreement, 182–88, 191, 206–207, 211, 216, 318, 356n29
Resink, G. J. "Han," 30, 40, 95, 105, 111
RHS (Rechtshoogeschool), Batavia, 25–31, 58, 70–71
Ritman, J. H., 305
Robespierre, Maximilien, 35–36, 40, 216–17, 221
Roosevelt, Franklin Delano, 313
Rose, Mavis, 188–89
Rudjito, 142, 143

Sajap Kiri, 178, 180, 191, 240
Salim, Dolly, 38
Salim, Hadji Agoes, 312
Sardjono, 203, 248–250, 252, 254–55
Sartono, 48, 49, 50, 51, 87
Sartre, Jean-Paul, 35
Sastroamidjojo, Ali, 121, 124, 182, 211, 213
Sastrosatomo, Soebadio, 108, 109, 130, 145–46, 163, 313, 353n108
Sastrosatomo, Soedarpo, 108–109, 128, 130, 143–46
Schepper, Julius Martin Johannes, 28–29, 36–37, 61, 66–67, 74, 76–95, 99, 172, 213, 335n19
Schermerhorn, Willem, 168–169, 170–173, 181, 192, 209, 303, 357n72
Schleiermacher, Friedrich, 31
Scholte-Nordholt, Nico, 144, 213
Schrieke, Bernard J. O., 27
Schurman, Elink, 233, 296
Schweitzer, Albert, 285
second Madiun, see G30S
Second Police Action, 259–67
Semangat Baroe (publication), 99, 100, 112
Semaoen, 159
Setiadjit Soegono, 169, 177, 182, 189, 192, 197, 202, 209–210, 220, 224–226, 240, 277, 282, 296, 308, 323, 357n72, 364n36
Sia Kong Liong, 33
Siauw Giok Tjhan, 106–107, 163, 185
Silin, Mikhail, 195–96
Siliwangi (division), 185–86, 222–25, 229–232, 235, 237, 239–244, 248–49,

INDEX 401

251–52, 261–62, 269, 287, 309, 325, 356n37, 364n36, 366n65
Simatoepang, Tahi Bonar, 124, 155–58, 176, 181–87, 200, 225, 252, 261–302
Singapore, 6, 91, 105
Sintha Melati, 163
Sitor Situmorang, 213
Sitoroes, L. M., 108, 130, 145–46
Sjafroeddin Prawiranegara, 215, 346n62
Sjah, Soetan Mohammad, 84, 93, 286
Sjahrir, Soetan, xi-xii, 104–5, 109116–17, 122, 129–31, 139–78, 189–90, 279–323
Sjahroezah, Djohan, 106, 121, 131
Sjarief Bachroen, 331n5, 363n18
Sjarifoeddin, Andrea, 218–19, 300–302, 350n21
Sjarifoeddin, Djaenah Zainab Harahap, 82–83, 84, 122, 253, 255
Sjarifoeddin, Lucia, Helena, 218, 300–302
Slánský, Rudolf, 327, 328
Smink (family), 17–18
Sneevliet, Henk, 170
Snow, Edgar, 96, 236, 248, 317
Socrates, 3. 108, 297
Soe Hok Gie, 251, 268, 292, 322–23
Soedirman, 185, 186, 225, 229, 261, 263, 264, 266–67, 274–75
Soedisman, 160–161, 171, 289, 292
Soedjatmoko "Koko," 108–9, 128, 144–48, 152–53, 176, 190, 310, 312
Soeharto, xii, 229, 231, 269–71, 276, 280–81, 285, 300–301, 322–23, 364n35
Soekamiskin prison, 49, 75, 76–82, 90, 93, 99, 102, 110, 126, 172, 212, 338n49
Soekarno, 41–51, 56, 66–68, 115–16, 139–43, 185, 227–28, 254, 274–76, 279, 339n60, 347n2,
Soekiman Wirjosandjojo, 149, 179, 299, 300
Soemarsono, 107–8, 131, 145–46, 151, 158, 163–64, 171, 184–85, 188, 203–208, 223–25, 228–29, 234, 236, 240, 243–45, 248, 255, 262, 276, 285–288
Soempah Pemoeda, 38–39, 41, 42
Soepratman, Rudolf Wage, 38, 40, 278, 312
Soerabaja (Idroes), 216
Soeripno, R. M., 193–200, 207, 261, 268, 293, 307–9, 312
Soerjono, 199, 204–5, 206–7, 216–17, 241, 268, 285, 287, 366n85
Soeryana, 125–28
Soetardjo Kartohadikoesoemo, 97
Soviet Red Army, 155, 160, 207, 220

Spanish Civil War, 90, 91, 96, 102, 204–205, 328, 380n8
Spinoza, Baruch, 243
Spoor, S. H., 157, 182, 183, 227
Spruit, Loes, 20–24
Sumatra, 3–14, 17, 27, 33, 157–58
Surabaya, Battle of 114, 151–52
Swift, Ann, 227, 289, 314–15

Tagore, Rabindranath, 31
Tamboenan, Peter, 65, 82, 214, 216, 253
Tambubolon, Ferdinand, 15–16, 23, 37, 211, 337n38
Tan Malaka, xi, 161–63, 189, 202, 208–9, 295, 321
Teeuw, Andries, 294
Ter Haar, Bernard, 26–28, 216, 346n75, 361n196
textbooks, 9–12, 43, 46, 157, 182, 319
The Art of War (Machiavelli), 154, 155
The Religion of Java (Geertz), 290
theater, 34–35, 51, 93, 135, 174, 244, 350n9
Theosophical Society, 37–38
Thompson, John, 166–67
THS (Technische Hoogeschool), 44 169, 170, 196, 219–20
Tjugito, 299
Toer, Kusalah Subagyo, 286
Toer, Pramoedya Ananta, 286, 294
trade-unions, 89, 91, 178, 180, 189, 191, 196, 206, 209, 212, 223–24, 233, 290, 298
trials, 165, 194, 206, 316, 327–329
Trimurti, S. K., 209–10
Trotsky, Leon, 148, 155, 160–61, 170, 177, 206, 237, 328, 359n145
Tynianov, Yuri, 45

UNCGO (United Nations Commission of Good Offices), 181, 184, 169–70, 196, 219–20, 233, 245, 353n134
USS *Renville* (ship), 182, 201, 305

Van Asbeck, F. M., 26, 28, 30, 40, 68–73, 80–82, 88, 132, 139, 171–72
Van de Loosdrecht-Sizoo, A. P., 16, 37
Van de Vlugt, W., 29
Van der Plas, Charles O., 95–114, 122, 131–36, 162, 165–66, 230, 295–96, 347n86
Van der Post, Laurens, 154, 157–58, 352n91
Van Doorn, C. "Kees," 36, 82, 99, 100, 282, 336n31
Van Kan, A. H. M. J., 27–28
Van Lengering, B., 20, 21

Van Mook, Hubertus J. M., 111, 113, 131, 167–68, 185, 303–4, 309, 311
Van Mook, Kees, 310, 311
Van Randwijk, Henk, 214, 335n19
Van Zeggelen, Marie, 22–23, 27
Vergadering de Gelovigen, 28–29
Verkuyl, Johannes, 99, 100–101, 122–24, 144, 214–15, 282, 302, 305, 333n24
Vietnam, 176, 192, 193
Virilio, Paul, 270, 273, 291
Visser, Louis de, 196
Volksraad, 33, 97–99, 340n6
Vrij Nederland (publication), 134

wall charts, 12–13, 19, 22, 24, 43–44, 78, 91, 111, 124–25, 133, 147, 278
Walraven, Willem, 76–77, 102, 345n46
wayang (shadow-puppet theater), 46, 47, 50, 125, 177, 204, 208, 275, 312, 319
Weinstein, Frank, 147

Wellem, Frederiek Djara, xii, 280, 372n107
Wertheim, W. F., 142, 154, 170, 374n26
Widarta, 107, 163–65, 171, 206, 289, 353n113, 353n124, 359n121, 374n50
Widjaja, Roeslan, 151
Widjojoatmodjo, Raden Abdulkadir, 183
Wikana, 107, 146, 163, 203, 224, 362n11
Wikoto, 84–85
Wittgenstein, Ludwig, 186
World Festival of Youth and Students in Prague, 193–95, 320

Yamin, Muhammad, 35, 39–40, 47–51, 70–74, 84, 99, 161–162, 168, 172

Zainal Abidin, 108, 128
Zaman Baroe (publication), 99
Zhdanov (doctrine), 193
Žižek, Slavoj, 221, 254, 272, 307

www.ingramcontent.com/pod-product-compliance
Lightning Source LLC
Chambersburg PA
CBHW032011300426
44117CB00008B/989